The Formal Semantics of Programming Languages

Foundations of Computing
Michael Garey and Albert Meyer, editors

The Formal Semantics of Programming Languages
An Introduction

Glynn Winskel

The MIT Press
Cambridge, Massachusetts
London, England

This book was printed and bound in the United States of America.

Library of Congress Cataloging-in-Publication Data

Winskel, G. (Glynn)
    The formal semantics of programming languages : an introduction
Glynn Winskel.
            p.   cm. – (Foundations of computing)
    Includes bibliographical references and index.
    ISBN 978-0-262-23169-5 (hc. : alk. paper) — 978-0-262-73103-4 (pb. : alk. paper)
    1. Programming languages (Electronic computers)–Semantics.
I. Title. II. Series.
QA76.7.W555   1993
005.13'1–dc20   92-36718
                                                                  CIP

To Kirsten, Sofie and Stine

Contents

Series foreword

Theoretical computer science has now undergone several decades of development. The "classical" topics of automata theory, formal languages, and computational complexity have become firmly established, and their importance to other theoretical work and to practice is widely recognized. Stimulated by technological advances, theoreticians have been rapidly expanding the areas under study, and the time delay between theoretical progress and its practical impact has been decreasing dramatically. Much publicity has been given recently to breakthroughs in cryptography and linear programming, and steady progress is being made on programming language semantics, computational geometry, and efficient data structures. Newer, more speculative, areas of study include relational databases, VLSI theory, and parallel and distributed computation. As this list of topics continues expanding, it is becoming more and more difficult to stay abreast of the progress that is being made and increasingly important that the most significant work be distilled and communicated in a manner that will facilitate further research and application of this work. By publishing comprehensive books and specialized monographs on the theoretical aspects of computer science, the series on Foundations of Computing provides a forum in which important research topics can be presented in their entirety and placed in perspective for researchers, students, and practitioners alike.

Michael R. Garey
Albert R. Meyer

Preface

In giving a formal semantics to a programming language we are concerned with building a mathematical model. Its purpose is to serve as a basis for understanding and reasoning about how programs behave. Not only is a mathematical model useful for various kinds of analysis and verification, but also, at a more fundamental level, because simply the activity of trying to define the meaning of program constructions precisely can reveal all kinds of subtleties of which it is important to be aware. This book introduces the mathematics, techniques and concepts on which formal semantics rests.

For historical reasons the semantics of programming languages is often viewed as consisting of three strands:

Operational semantics describes the meaning of a programming language by specifying how it executes on an abstract machine. We concentrate on the method advocated by Gordon Plotkin in his lectures at Aarhus on "structural operational semantics" in which evaluation and execution relations are specified by rules in a way directed by the syntax.

Denotational semantics is a technique for defining the meaning of programming languages pioneered by Christopher Strachey and provided with a mathematical foundation by Dana Scott. At one time called "mathematical semantics," it uses the more abstract mathematical concepts of complete partial orders, continuous functions and least fixed points.

Axiomatic semantics tries to fix the meaning of a programming contruct by giving proof rules for it within a program logic. The chief names associated with this approach are that of R.W.Floyd and C.A.R.Hoare. Thus axiomatic semantics emphasises proof of correctness right from the start.

It would however be wrong to view these three styles as in opposition to each other. They each have their uses. A clear operational semantics is very helpful in implementation. Axiomatic semantics for special kinds of languages can give strikingly elegant proof systems, useful in developing as well as verifying programs. Denotational semantics provides the deepest and most widely applicable techniques, underpinned by a rich mathematical theory. Indeed, the different styles of semantics are highly dependent on eachother. For example, showing that the proof rules of an axiomatic semantics are correct relies on an underlying denotational or operational semantics. To show an implementation correct, as judged against a denotational semantics, requires a proof that the operational and denotational semantics agree. And, in arguing about an operational semantics it can be an enormous help to use a denotational semantics, which often has the advantage of abstracting away from unimportant, implementation details, as well as providing higher-level concepts with which to understand computational behaviour. Research of the last few years promises a unification of the different approaches, an approach in which we can hope to see denotational, operational and logics of programs developed hand-in-hand. An aim of this book has been to show how operational and denotational semantics fit together.

The techniques used in semantics lean heavily on mathematical logic. They are not always easily accessible to a student of computer science or mathematics, without a good background in logic. There is an attempt here to present them in a thorough and yet as elementary a way as possible. For instance, a presentation of operational semantics leads to a treatment of inductive definitions, and techniques for reasoning about operational semantics, and this in turn places us in a good position to take the step of abstraction to complete partial orders and continuous functions—the foundation of denotational semantics. It is hoped that this passage from finitary rules of the operational semantics, to continuous operators on sets, to continuous functions is also a help in understanding why continuity is to be expected of computable functions. Various induction principles are treated, including a general version of well-founded recursion, which is important for defining functions on a set with a well-founded relation. In the more advanced work on languages with recursive types the use of information systems not only provides an elementary way of solving recursive domain equations, but also yields techniques for relating operational and denotational semantics.

Book description: This is a book based on lectures given at Cambridge and Aarhus Universities. It is introductory and is primarily addressed to undergraduate and graduate students in Computer Science and Mathematics beginning a study of the methods used to formalise and reason about programming languages. It provides the mathematical background necessary for the reader to invent, formalise and justify rules with which to reason about a variety of programming languages. Although the treatment is elementary, several of the topics covered are drawn from recent research. The book contains many exercises ranging from the simple to mini projects.

Starting with basic set theory, structural operational semantics (as advocated by Plotkin) is introduced as a means to define the meaning of programming languages along with the basic proof techniques to accompany such definitions. Denotational and axiomatic semantics are illustrated on a simple language of while-programs, and full proofs are given of the equivalence of the operational and denotational semantics and soundness and relative completeness of the axiomatic semantics. A proof of Gödel's incompleteness theorem is included. It emphasises the impossibility of ever achieving a fully complete axiomatic semantics. This is backed up by an appendix providing an introduction to the theory of computability based on while programs. After domain theory, the foundations of denotational semantics is presented, and the semantics and methods of proof for sev-

eral functional languages are treated. The simplest language is that of recursion equations
with both call-by-value and call-by-name evaluation. This work is extended to languages
with higher and recursive types, which includes a treatment of the eager and lazy λ-
calculi. Throughout, the relationship between denotational and operational semantics
is stressed, and proofs of the correspondence between the operational and denotational
semantics are provided. The treatment of recursive types—one of the more advanced
parts of the book—relies on the use of information systems to represent domains. The
book concludes with a chapter on parallel programming languages, accompanied by a
discussion of methods for verifying nondeterministic and parallel programs.

How to use this book

The dependencies between the chapters are indicated below. It is hoped that this is a
help in reading, reference and designing lecture courses. For example, an introductory
course on "Logic and computation" could be based on chapters 1 to 7 with additional
use of the Appendix. The Appendix covers computability, on the concepts of which
Chapter 7 depends—it could be bypassed by readers with a prior knowledge of this topic.
Instead, a mini course on "Introductory semantics" might be built on chapters 1 to 5,
perhaps supplemented by 14. The chapters 8, 10 and 12 could form a primer in "Domain
theory"—this would require a very occasional and easy reference to Chapter 5. Chapters
8-13 provide "A mathematical foundation for functional programming." Chapter 14,
a survey of "Nondeterminism and parallelism," is fairly self-contained relying, in the
main, just on Chapter 2; however, its discussion of model checking makes use of the
Knaster-Tarski Theorem, of which a proof can be found in Chapter 5.

Some of the exercises include small implementation tasks. In the course at Aarhus
it was found very helpful to use Prolog, for example to enliven the early treatment of
the operational semantics. The use of Standard ML or Miranda is perhaps even more
appropriate, given the treatment of such languages in the later chapters.

Acknowledgements

Right at the start I should acknowledge the foundational work of Dana Scott and Gordon
Plotkin as having a basic influence on this book. As will be clear from reading the book,
it has been influenced a great deal by Gordon Plotkin's work, especially by his notes for
lectures on complete partial orders and denotational semantics at Edinburgh University.

At Cambridge, comments of Tom Melham, Ken Moody, Larry Paulson and Andy
Pitts have been very helpful (in particular, Andy's lecture notes and comments on Eu-
genio Moggi's work have been incorporated into my presentation of domain theory). At
Aarhus, Mogens Nielsen provided valuable feedback and encouragement from a course

he gave from an early draft. Recommendations of Erik Meineche Schmidt improved the proofs of relative completeness and Gödel's theorem. Numerous students at Aarhus have supplied corrections and suggestions. I especially thank Henrik Reif Andersen, Torben Brauner, Christian Clausen, Allan Cheng, Urban Engberg, Torben Amtoft Hansen, Ole Hougaard and Jakob Seligman. Added thanks are due to Bettina Blaaberg Sørensen for her prompt reading and suggestions at various stages in the preparation of this book. I'm grateful to Douglas Gurr for his conscientious criticism of the chapters on domain theory. Kim Guldstrand Larsen suggested improvements to the chapter on nondeterminism and concurrency.

In the fall of '91, Albert Meyer gave a course based on this book. He, with instructors A.Lent, M.Sheldon, and C.Yoder, very kindly provided a wealth of advice from notification of typos to restructuring of proofs. In addition, Albert kindly provided his notes on computability on which the appendix is based. I thank them and hope they are not disappointed with the outcome.

My thanks go to Karen Møller for help with the typing. Finally, I express my gratitude to MIT Press, especially Terry Ehling, for their patience.

The chapter dependencies:

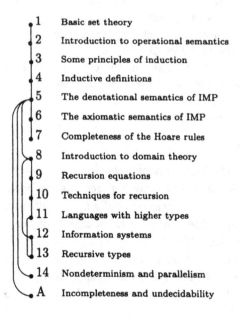

1 Basic set theory

2 Introduction to operational semantics

3 Some principles of induction

4 Inductive definitions

5 The denotational semantics of IMP

6 The axiomatic semantics of IMP

7 Completeness of the Hoare rules

8 Introduction to domain theory

9 Recursion equations

10 Techniques for recursion

11 Languages with higher types

12 Information systems

13 Recursive types

14 Nondeterminism and parallelism

A Incompleteness and undecidability

The Formal Semantics of Programming Languages

1 Basic set theory

This chapter presents the informal, logical and set-theoretic notation and concepts we shall use to write down and reason about our ideas. It simply presents an extension of our everyday language, extended to talk about mathematical objects like sets; it is not to be confused with the formal languages of programming languages or the formal assertions about them that we'll encounter later.

This chapter is meant as a review and for future reference. It is suggested that on a first reading it is read fairly quickly, without attempting to absorb it fully.

1.1 Logical notation

We shall use some informal logical notation in order to stop our mathematical statements getting out of hand. For statements (or assertions) A and B, we shall commonly use abbreviations like:

- A & B for (A and B), the conjunction of A and B,
- $A \Rightarrow B$ for (A implies B), which means (if A then B),
- $A \iff B$ to mean (A iff B), which abbreviates (A if and only if B), and expresses the logical equivalence of A and B.

We shall also make statements by forming disjunctions (A or B), with the self-evident meaning, and negations (not A), sometimes written $\neg A$, which is true iff A is false. There is a tradition to write for instance $7 \not< 5$ instead of $\neg(7 < 5)$, which reflects what we generally say: "7 is not less than 5" rather than "not 7 is less than 5."

The statements may contain variables (or unknowns, or place-holders), as in

$$(x \leq 3) \ \& \ (y \leq 7)$$

which is true when the variables x and y over integers stand for integers less than or equal to 3 and 7 respectively, and false otherwise. A statement like $P(x, y)$, which involves variables x, y, is called a predicate (or property, or relation, or condition) and it only becomes true or false when the pair x, y stand for particular things.

We use logical quantifiers $\exists$, read "there exists", and $\forall$, read " for all". Then you can read assertions like

$$\exists x. \ P(x)$$

as abbreviating "for some x, $P(x)$" or "there exists x such that $P(x)$", and

$$\forall x. \ P(x)$$

as abbreviating " for all x, $P(x)$" or "for any x, $P(x)$". The statement

$$\exists x, y, \cdots, z. \; P(x, y, \cdots, z)$$

abbreviates

$$\exists x \exists y \cdots \exists z. \; P(x, y, \cdots, z),$$

and

$$\forall x, y, \cdots, z. \; P(x, y, \cdots, z)$$

abbreviates

$$\forall x \forall y \cdots \forall z. \; P(x, y, \cdots, z).$$

Later, we often wish to specify a set X over which a quantifier ranges. Then one writes $\forall x \in X. \; P(x)$ instead of $\forall x. \; x \in X \Rightarrow P(x)$, and $\exists x \in X. \; P(x)$ instead of $\exists x. \; x \in X \; \& \; P(x)$.

There is another useful notation associated with quantifiers. Occasionally one wants to say not just that there exists some x satisfying a property $P(x)$ but also that x is the *unique* object satisfying $P(x)$. It is traditional to write

$$\exists! x. \; P(x)$$

as an abbreviation for

$$(\exists x. \; P(x)) \; \& \; (\forall y, z. \; P(y) \; \& \; P(z) \Rightarrow y = z)$$

which means that there is some x satisfying the property P and also that if any y, z both satisfy the property P they are equal. This expresses that there exists a unique x satisfying $P(x)$.

1.2 Sets

Intuitively, a set is an (unordered) collection of objects, called its *elements* or *members*. We write $a \in X$ when a is an element of the set X. Sometimes we write *e.g.* $\{a, b, c, \cdots\}$ for the set of elements $a, b, c, \cdots$.

A set X is said to be a *subset* of a set Y, written $X \subseteq Y$, iff every element of X is an element of Y, *i.e.*

$$X \subseteq Y \iff \forall z \in X. \; z \in Y.$$

A set is determined solely by its elements in the sense that two sets are equal iff they have the same elements. So, sets X and Y are equal, written $X = Y$, iff every element of A is a element of B and *vice versa*. This furnishes a method for showing two sets X and Y are equal and, of course, is equivalent to showing $X \subseteq Y$ and $Y \subseteq X$.

1.2.1   Sets and properties

Sometimes a set is determined by a property, in the sense that the set has as elements precisely those which satisfy the property. Then we write

$$X = \{x \mid P(x)\},$$

meaning the set X has as elements precisely all those x for which $P(x)$ is true.

When set theory was being invented it was thought, first of all, that any property $P(x)$ determined a set

$$\{x \mid P(x)\}.$$

It came as a shock when Bertrand Russell realised that assuming the existence of certain sets described in this way gave rise to contradictions.

Russell's paradox is really the demonstration that a contradiction arises from the liberal way of constructing sets above. It proceeds as follows: consider the property

$$x \notin x$$

a way of writing "x is not an element of x". If we assume that properties determine sets, just as described, we can form the set

$$R = \{x \mid x \notin x\}.$$

Either $R \in R$ or not. If so, *i.e.* $R \in R$, then in order for R to qualify as an element of R, from the definition of R, we deduce $R \notin R$. So we end up asserting both something and is negation—a contradiction. If, on the other hand, $R \notin R$ then from the definition of R we see $R \in R$—a contradiction again. Either $R \in R$ or $R \notin R$ lands us in trouble.

We need to have some way which stops us from considering things like R as a sets. In general terms, the solution is to discipline the way in which sets are constructed, so that starting from certain given sets, new sets can only be formed when they are constructed by using particular, safe ways from old sets. We shall not be formal about it, but state those sets we assume to exist right from the start and methods we allow for constructing new sets. Provided these are followed we avoid trouble like Russell's paradox and at the same time have a rich enough world of sets to support most mathematics.

1.2.2   Some important sets

We take the existence of the empty set for granted, along with certain sets of basic elements.

Write $\emptyset$ for the *null*, or *empty* set, and

ω for the set of natural numbers $0, 1, 2, \cdots$.

We shall also take sets of symbols like

$$\{\text{``}a\text{''}, \text{``}b\text{''}, \text{``}c\text{''}, \text{``}d\text{''}, \text{``}e\text{''}, \cdots, \text{``}z\text{''}\}$$

for granted, although we could, alternatively have represented them as particular numbers, for example. The equality relation on a set of symbols is that given by syntactic identity; two symbols are equal iff they are the same.

1.2.3   Constructions on sets

We shall take for granted certain operations on sets which enable us to construct sets from given sets.

Comprehension: If X is a set and $P(x)$ is a property, we can form the set

$$\{x \in X \mid P(x)\}$$

which is another way of writing

$$\{x \mid x \in X \ \& \ P(x)\}.$$

This is the subset of X consisting of all elements x of X which satisfy $P(x)$.

Sometimes we'll use a further abbreviation. Suppose $e(x_1, \ldots, x_n)$ is some expression which for particular elements $x_1 \in X_1, \cdots x_n \in X_n$ yields a particular element and $P(x_1, \ldots, x_n)$ is a property of such $x_1, \ldots, x_n$. We use

$$\{e(x_1, \ldots, x_n) \mid x_1 \in X_1 \ \& \ \cdots \& \ x_n \in X_n \ \& \ P(x_1, \ldots, x_n)\}$$

to abbreviate

$$\{y \mid \exists x_1 \in X_1, \cdots, x_n \in X_n. \ y = e(x_1, \ldots, x_n) \& \ P(x_1, \ldots, x_n)\}.$$

For example,

$$\{2m + 1 \mid m \in \omega \ \& \ m > 1\}$$

is the set of odd numbers greater than 3.

Powerset: We can form a set consisting of the set of all subsets of a set, the so-called *powerset*:

$$\mathcal{P}ow(X) = \{Y \mid Y \subseteq X\}.$$

Indexed sets: Suppose I is a set and that for any $i \in I$ there is a unique object x_i, maybe a set itself. Then

$$\{x_i \mid i \in I\}$$

is a set. The elements x_i are said to be *indexed* by the elements $i \in I$.

Union: The set consisting of the *union* of two sets has as elements those elements which are either elements of one or the other set. It is written and described by:

$$X \cup Y = \{a \mid a \in X \text{ or } a \in Y\}.$$

Big union: Let X be a set of sets. Their *union*

$$\bigcup X = \{a \mid \exists x \in X. \ a \in x\}$$

is a set. When $X = \{x_i \mid i \in I\}$ for some indexing set I we often write $\bigcup X$ as $\bigcup_{i \in I} x_i$.

Intersection: Elements are in the *intersection* $X \cap Y$, of two sets X and Y, iff they are in both sets, *i.e.*

$$X \cap Y = \{a \mid a \in X \ \& \ a \in Y\}.$$

Big intersection: Let X be a nonempty set of sets. Then

$$\bigcap X = \{a \mid \forall x \in X. \ a \in x\}$$

is a set called its *intersection*. When $X = \{x_i \mid i \in I\}$ for a nonempty indexing set I we often write $\bigcap X$ as $\bigcap_{i \in I} x_i$.

Product: Given two elements a, b we can form a set (a, b) which is their ordered pair. To be definite we can take the ordered pair (a, b) to be the set $\{\{a\}, \{a, b\}\}$—this is one particular way of coding the idea of ordered pair as a *set*. As one would hope, two ordered pairs, represented in this way, are equal iff their first components are equal and their second components are equal too, *i.e.*

$$(a, b) = (a', b') \iff a = a' \ \& \ b = b'.$$

In proving properties of ordered pairs this property should be sufficient irrespective of the way in which we have represented ordered pairs as sets.

Exercise 1.1 Prove the property above holds of the suggested representation of ordered pairs. (Don't expect it to be too easy! Consult [39], page 36, or [47], page 23, in case of difficulty.)   □

For sets X and Y, their *product* is the set

$$X \times Y = \{(a, b) \mid a \in X \ \& \ b \in Y\},$$

the set of ordered pairs of elements with the first from X and the second from Y.

A triple (a, b, c) is the set $(a, (b, c))$, and the product $X \times Y \times Z$ is the set of triples $\{(x, y, z) \mid x \in X \ \& \ y \in Y \ \& \ z \in Z\}$. More generally $X_1 \times X_2 \times \cdots \times X_n$ consists of the set of n-tuples $(x_1, x_2, \ldots, x_n) = (x_1, (x_2, (x_3, \cdots)))$.

Disjoint union: Frequently we want to join sets together but, in a way which, unlike union, does not identify the same element when it comes from different sets. We do this by making copies of the elements so that when they are copies from different sets they are forced to be distinct.

$$X_0 \uplus X_1 \uplus \cdots \uplus X_n = (\{0\} \times X_0) \cup (\{1\} \times X_1) \cup \cdots \cup (\{n\} \times X_n).$$

In particular, for $X \uplus Y$ the copies $(\{0\} \times X)$ and $(\{1\} \times Y)$ have to be disjoint, in the sense that

$$(\{0\} \times X) \cap (\{1\} \times Y) = \emptyset,$$

because any common element would be a pair with first element both equal to 0 and 1, clearly impossible.

Set difference: We can subtract one set Y from another X, an operation which removes all elements from X which are also in Y.

$$X \setminus Y = \{x \mid x \in X \ \& \ x \notin Y\}.$$

1.2.4   The axiom of foundation

A set is built-up starting from basic sets by using the constructions above. We remark that a property of sets, called the axiom of foundation, follows from our informal understanding of sets and how we can construct them. Consider an element b_1 of a set b_0. It is either a basic element, like an integer or a symbol, or a set. If b_1 is a set then it must have been constructed from sets which have themselves been constructed earlier. Intuitively, we expect any chain of memberships

$$\cdots b_n \in \cdots \in b_1 \in b_0$$

to end in some b_n which is some basic element or the empty set. The statement that any such descending chain of memberships must be finite is called the axiom of foundation, and is an assumption generally made in set theory. Notice the axiom implies that no set X can be a member of itself as, if this were so, we'd get the infinite descending chain

$$\cdots X \in \cdots \in X \in X,$$

—a contradiction.

1.3   Relations and functions

A *binary relation* between X and Y is an element of $\mathcal{P}ow(X \times Y)$, and so a subset of pairs in the relation. When R is a relation $R \subseteq X \times Y$ we shall often write xRy for $(x, y) \in R$.

A *partial function* from X to Y is a relation $f \subseteq X \times Y$ for which

$$\forall x, y, y'. \ (x, y) \in f \ \& \ (x, y') \in f \Rightarrow y = y'.$$

We use the notation $f(x) = y$ when there is a y such that $(x, y) \in f$ and then say $f(x)$ is *defined*, and otherwise say $f(x)$ is *undefined*. Sometimes we write $f : x \mapsto y$, or just $x \mapsto y$ when f is understood, for $y = f(x)$. Occasionally we write just fx, without the brackets, for $f(x)$.

A *(total) function* from X to Y is a partial function from X to Y such that for all $x \in X$ there is some $y \in Y$ such that $f(x) = y$. Although total functions are a special kind of partial function it is traditional to understand something described as simply a function to be a total function, so we always say explicitly when a function is partial.

Note that relations and functions are also sets.

To stress the fact that we are thinking of a partial function f from X to Y as taking an element of X and yielding an element of Y we generally write it as $f : X \rightharpoonup Y$. To indicate that a function f from X to Y is total we write $f : X \to Y$.

We write $(X \rightharpoonup Y)$ for the set of all partial functions from X to Y, and $(X \to Y)$ for the set of all total functions.

Exercise 1.2 Why are we justified in calling $(X \rightharpoonup Y)$ and $(X \to Y)$ sets when X, Y are sets? □

1.3.1 Lambda notation

It is sometimes useful to use the lambda notation (or λ-notation) to describe functions. It provides a way of refering to functions without having to name them. Suppose $f : X \to Y$ is a function which for any element x in X gives a value $f(x)$ which is exactly described by expression e, probably involving x. Then we sometime write

$$\lambda x \in X.e$$

for the function f. Thus

$$\lambda x \in X.e = \{(x, e) \mid x \in X\},$$

so $\lambda x \in X.e$ is just an abbreviation for the set of input-output values determined by the expression e. For example, $\lambda x \in \omega.(x + 1)$ is the successor function.

1.3.2 Composing relations and functions

We compose relations, and so partial and total functions, R between X and Y and S between Y and Z by defining their *composition*, a relation between X and Z, by

$$S \circ R =_{def} \{(x, z) \in X \times Z \mid \exists y \in Y. \ (x, y) \in R \ \& \ (y, z) \in S\}.$$

Thus for functions $f : X \to Y$ and $g : Y \to Z$ their composition is the function $g \circ f : X \to Z$. Each set X is associated with an identity function Id_X where $Id_X = \{(x,x) \mid x \in X\}$.

Exercise 1.3 Let $R \subseteq X \times Y$, $S \subseteq Y \times Z$ and $T \subseteq Z \times W$. Convince yourself that $T \circ (S \circ R) = (T \circ S) \circ R$ (*i.e.* composition is associative) and that $R \circ Id_X = Id_Y \circ R = R$ (*i.e.* identity functions act like identities with respect to composition). ☐

A function $f : X \to Y$ has an *inverse* $g : Y \to X$ iff $g(f(x)) = x$ for all $x \in X$, and $f(g(y)) = y$ for all $y \in Y$. Then the sets X and Y are said to be in *1-1 correspondence*. (Note a function with an inverse has to be total.)

Any set in 1-1 correspondence with a subset of natural numbers ω is said to be *countable*.

Exercise 1.4 Let X and Y be sets. Show there is a 1-1 correspondence between the set of functions $(X \to \mathcal{P}ow(Y))$ and the set of relations $\mathcal{P}ow(X \times Y)$. ☐

Cantor's diagonal argument

Late last century, Georg Cantor, one of the pioneers in set theory, invented a method of argument, the gist of which reappears frequently in the theory of computation. Cantor used a *diagonal argument* to show that X and $\mathcal{P}ow(X)$ are never in 1-1 correspondence for any set X. This fact is intuitively clear for finite sets but also holds for infinite sets. He argued by *reductio ad absurdum*, *i.e.*, by showing that supposing otherwise led to a contradiction:

Suppose a set X is in 1-1 correspondence with its powerset $\mathcal{P}ow(X)$. Let $\theta : X \to \mathcal{P}ow(X)$ be the 1-1 correspondence. Form the set

$$Y = \{x \in X \mid x \notin \theta(x)\}$$

which is clearly a subset of X and therefore in correspondence with an element $y \in X$. That is $\theta(y) = Y$. Either $y \in Y$ or $y \notin Y$. But both possibilities are absurd. For, if $y \in Y$ then $y \in \theta(y)$ so $y \notin Y$, while, if $y \notin Y$ then $y \notin \theta(y)$ so $y \in Y$. We conclude that our first supposition must be false, so there is no set in 1-1 correspondence with its powerset.

Cantor's argument is reminiscent of Russell's paradox. But whereas the contradiction in Russell's paradox arises out of a fundamental, mistaken assumption about how to construct sets, the contradiction in Cantor's argument comes from denying the fact one wishes to prove.

To see why it is called a diagonal argument, imagine that the set X, which we suppose is in 1-1 correspondence with $\mathcal{P}ow(X)$, can be enumerated as $x_0, x_1, x_2, \cdots, x_n, \cdots$. Imagine we draw a table to represent the 1-1 correspondence θ along the following lines. In the *i*th row and *j*th column is placed 1 if $x_i \in \theta(x_j)$ and 0 otherwise. The table below, for instance, represents a situation where $x_0 \notin \theta(x_0)$, $x_1 \in \theta(x_0)$ and $x_i \in \theta(x_j)$.

	$\theta(x_0)$	$\theta(x_1)$	$\theta(x_2)$	$\cdots$	$\theta(x_j)$	$\cdots$
x_0	0	1	1	$\cdots$	1	$\cdots$
x_1	1	1	1	$\cdots$	0	$\cdots$
x_2	0	0	1	$\cdots$	0	$\cdots$
$\vdots$	$\vdots$	$\vdots$	$\vdots$	$\vdots$	$\vdots$	
x_i	0	1	0	$\cdots$	1	$\cdots$
$\vdots$	$\vdots$	$\vdots$	$\vdots$	$\vdots$	$\vdots$	

The set Y which plays a key role in Cantor's argument is defined by running down the diagonal of the table interchanging 0's and 1's in the sense that x_n is put in the set iff the *n*th entry along the diagonal is a 0.

Exercise 1.5 Show for any sets X and Y, with Y containing at least two elements, that there cannot be a 1-1 correspondence between X and the set of functions $(X \to Y)$. $\square$

1.3.3 Direct and inverse image of a relation

We extend relations, and thus partial and total functions, $R : X \times Y$ to functions on subsets by taking

$$RA = \{y \in Y \mid \exists x \in A.\ (x,y) \in R\}$$

for $A \subseteq X$. The set RA is called the *direct image* of A under R. We define

$$R^{-1}B = \{x \in X \mid \exists y \in B.\ (x,y) \in R\}$$

for $B \subseteq Y$. The set $R^{-1}B$ is called the *inverse image* of B under R. Of course, the same notions of direct and inverse image also apply in the special case where the relation is a function.

1.3.4 Equivalence relations

An *equivalence relation* is a relation $R \subseteq X \times X$ on a set X which is

- reflexive: $\forall x \in X.\ xRx$,
- symmetric: $\forall x, y \in X.\ xRy \Rightarrow yRx$ and
- transitive: $\forall x, y, z \in X.\ xRy \ \& \ yRz \Rightarrow xRz$.

If R is an equivalence relation on X then the *(R-)equivalence class* of an element $x \in X$ is the subset $\{x\}_R =_{def} \{y \in X \mid yRx\}$.

Exercise 1.6 Let R be an equivalence relation on a set X. Show if $\{x\}_R \cap \{y\}_R \neq \emptyset$ then $\{x\}_R = \{y\}_R$, for any elements $x, y \in X$. $\square$

Exercise 1.7 Let xRy be a relation on a set of sets X which holds iff the sets x and y in X are in 1-1 correspondence. Show that R is an equivalence relation. $\square$

Let R be a relation on a set X. Define $R^0 = Id_X$, the identity relation on the set X, and $R^1 = R$ and, assuming R^n is defined, define

$$R^{n+1} = R \circ R^n.$$

So, R^n is the relation $R \circ \cdots \circ R$, obtained by taking n compositions of R. Define the *transitive closure* of R to be the relation

$$R^+ = \bigcup_{n \in \omega} R^{n+1}.$$

Define the transitive, reflexive closure of a relation R on X to be the relation

$$R^* = \bigcup_{n \in \omega} R^n,$$

so $R^* = Id_X \cup R^+$.

Exercise 1.8 Let R be a relation on a set X. Write R^{op} for the opposite, or converse, relation $R^{op} = \{(y, x) \mid (x, y) \in R\}$. Show $(R \cup R^{op})^*$ is an equivalence relation. Show $R^* \cup (R^{op})^*$ need not be an equivalence relation. $\square$

1.4   Further reading

Our presentation amounts to an informal introduction to the Zermelo-Fraenkel axiomatisation of set theory but with atoms, to avoid thinking of symbols as being coded by sets. If you'd like more material to read I recommend Halmos's "Naive Set Theory"[47] for a very readable introduction to sets. Another good book is Enderton's "Elements of set theory" [39], though this is a much larger work.

2 Introduction to operational semantics

This chapter presents the syntax of a programming language, **IMP**, a small language of while programs. **IMP** is called an "imperative" language because program execution involves carrying out a series of explicit commands to change state. Formally, **IMP**'s behaviour is described by rules which specify how its expressions are evaluated and its commands are executed. The rules provide an operational semantics of **IMP** in that they are close to giving an implementation of the language, for example, in the programming language Prolog. It is also shown how they furnish a basis for simple proofs of equivalence between commands.

2.1 IMP—a simple imperative language

Firstly, we list the syntactic sets associated with **IMP**:

- numbers **N**, consisting of positive and negative integers with zero,
- truth values **T** = {**true**, **false**},
- locations **Loc**,
- arithmetic expressions **Aexp**,
- boolean expressions **Bexp**,
- commands **Com**.

We assume the syntactic structure of numbers and locations is given. For instance, the set **Loc** might consist of non-empty strings of letters or such strings followed by digits, while **N** might be the set of signed decimal numerals for positive and negative whole numbers—indeed these are the representations we use when considering specific examples. (Locations are often called program variables but we reserve that term for another concept.)

For the other syntactic sets we have to say how their elements are built-up. We'll use a variant of BNF (Backus-Naur form) as a way of writing down the rules of formation of the elements of these syntactic sets. The formation rules will express things like:

If a_0 and a_1 are arithmetic expressions then so is $a_0 + a_1$.

It's clear that the symbols a_0 and a_1 are being used to stand for any arithmetic expression. In our informal presentation of syntax we'll use such *metavariables* to range over the syntactic sets—the metavariables a_0, a_1 above are understood to range over the set of arithmetic expressions. In presenting the syntax of **IMP** we'll follow the convention that

- n, m range over numbers $\mathbf{N}$,

- X, Y range over locations $\mathbf{Loc}$,

- a ranges over arithmetic expressions $\mathbf{Aexp}$,

- b ranges over boolean expressions $\mathbf{Bexp}$,

- c ranges over commands $\mathbf{Com}$.

The metavariables we use to range over the syntactic categories can be primed or subscripted. So, *e.g.*, X, X', X_0, X_1, Y'' stand for locations.

We describe the formation rules for arithmetic expressions $\mathbf{Aexp}$ by:

$$a ::= n \mid X \mid a_0 + a_1 \mid a_0 - a_1 \mid a_0 \times a_1.$$

The symbol "::=" should be read as "can be" and the symbol "|" as "or". Thus an arithmetic expression a can be a number n or a location X or $a_0 + a_1$ or $a_0 - a_1$ or $a_0 \times a_1$, built from arithmetic expressions a_0 and a_1.

Notice our notation for the formation rules of arithmetic expressions does not tell us how to parse

$$2 + 3 \times 4 - 5,$$

whether as $2 + ((3 \times 4) - 5)$ or as $(2 + 3) \times (4 - 5)$ *etc.*. The notation gives the so-called *abstract syntax* of arithmetic expressions in that it simply says how to build up new arithmetic expressions. For any arithmetic expression we care to write down it leaves us the task of putting in enough parentheses to ensure it has been built-up in a unique way. It is helpful to think of abstract syntax as specifying the parse trees of a language; it is the job of *concrete syntax* to provide enough information through parentheses or orders of precedence between operation symbols for a string to parse uniquely. Our concerns are with the meaning of programming languages and not with the theory of how to write them down. Abstract syntax suffices for our purposes.

Here are the formation rules for the whole of $\mathbf{IMP}$:

For $\mathbf{Aexp}$:

$$a ::= n \mid X \mid a_0 + a_1 \mid a_0 - a_1 \mid a_0 \times a_1.$$

For $\mathbf{Bexp}$:

$$b ::= \mathbf{true} \mid \mathbf{false} \mid a_0 = a_1 \mid a_0 \leq a_1 \mid \neg b \mid b_0 \wedge b_1 \mid b_0 \vee b_1$$

For $\mathbf{Com}$:

$$c ::= \mathbf{skip} \mid X := a \mid c_0; c_1 \mid \mathbf{if}\ b\ \mathbf{then}\ c_0\ \mathbf{else}\ c_1 \mid \mathbf{while}\ b\ \mathbf{do}\ c$$

From a set-theory point of view this notation provides an *inductive definition* of the syntactic sets of **IMP**, which are the least sets closed under the formation rules, in a sense we'll make clear in the next two chapters. For the moment, this notation should be viewed as simply telling us how to construct elements of the syntactic sets.

We need some notation to express when two elements e_0, e_1 of the same syntactic set are identical, in the sense of having been built-up in exactly the same way according to the abstract syntax or, equivalently, having the same parse tree. We use $e_0 \equiv e_1$ to mean e_0 is identical to e_1. The arithmetic expression $3 + 5$ built up from the numbers 3 and 5 is not syntactically identical to the expression 8 or $5 + 3$, though of course we expect them to evaluate to the same number. Thus we do *not* have $3 + 5 \equiv 5 + 3$. Note we *do* have $(3 + 5) \equiv 3 + 5$!

Exercise 2.1 If you are familiar with the programming language ML (see *e.g.*[101]) or Miranda (see *e.g.*[22]) define the syntactic sets of **IMP** as datatypes. If you are familiar with the programming language Prolog (see *e.g.*[31]) program the formation rules of **IMP** in it. Write a program to check whether or not $e_0 \equiv e_1$ holds of syntactic elements e_0, e_1.   □

So much for the syntax of **IMP**. Let's turn to its semantics, how programs behave when we run them.

2.2 The evaluation of arithmetic expressions

Most probably, the reader has an intuitive model with which to understand the behaviours of programs written in **IMP**. Underlying most models is an idea of state determined by what contents are in the locations. With respect to a state, an arithmetic expression evaluates to an integer and a boolean expression evaluates to a truth value. The resulting values can influence the execution of commands which will lead to changes in state. Our formal description of the behaviour of **IMP** will follow this line. First we define *states* and then the *evaluation* of integer and boolean expressions, and finally the *execution* of commands.

The set of *states* Σ consists of functions $\sigma : \mathbf{Loc} \to \mathbf{N}$ from locations to numbers. Thus $\sigma(X)$ is the value, or contents, of location X in state σ.

Consider the evaluation of an arithmetic expression a in a state σ. We can represent the situation of expression a waiting to be evaluated in state σ by the pair $\langle a, \sigma \rangle$. We shall define an evaluation relation between such pairs and numbers

$$\langle a, \sigma \rangle \to n$$

meaning: expression a in state σ evaluates to n. Call pairs $\langle a, \sigma \rangle$, where a is an arithmetic expression and σ is a state, arithmetic-expression *configurations*.

Consider how we might explain to someone how to evaluate an arithmetic expression $(a_0 + a_1)$. We might say something along the lines of:

1. Evaluate a_0 to get a number n_0 as result and

2. Evaluate a_1 to get a number n_1 as result.

3. Then add n_0 and n_1 to get n, say, as the result of evaluating $a_0 + a_1$.

Although informal we can see that this specifies how to evaluate a sum in terms of how to evaluate its summands; the specification is *syntax-directed*. The formal specification of the evaluation relation is given by rules which follow intuitive and informal descriptions like this rather closely.

We specify the evaluation relation in a syntax-directed way, by the following rules:
Evaluation of numbers:

$$\langle n, \sigma \rangle \to n$$

Thus any number is already evaluated with itself as value.
Evaluation of locations:

$$\langle X, \sigma \rangle \to \sigma(X)$$

Thus a location evaluates to its contents in a state.
Evaluation of sums:

$$\frac{\langle a_0, \sigma \rangle \to n_0 \quad \langle a_1, \sigma \rangle \to n_1}{\langle a_0 + a_1, \sigma \rangle \to n} \qquad \text{where } n \text{ is the sum of } n_0 \text{ and } n_1.$$

Evaluation of subtractions:

$$\frac{\langle a_0, \sigma \rangle \to n_0 \quad \langle a_1, \sigma \rangle \to n_1}{\langle a_0 - a_1, \sigma \rangle \to n} \qquad \text{where } n \text{ is the result of subtracting } n_1 \text{ from } n_0.$$

Evaluation of products:

$$\frac{\langle a_0, \sigma \rangle \to n_0 \quad \langle a_1, \sigma \rangle \to n_1}{\langle a_0 \times a_1, \sigma \rangle \to n} \qquad \text{where } n \text{ is the product of } n_0 \text{ and } n_1.$$

How are we to read such rules? The rule for sums can be read as:
If $\langle a_0, \sigma \rangle \to n_0$ and $\langle a_1, \sigma \rangle \to n_1$ then $\langle a_0 + a_1, \sigma \rangle \to n$, where n is the sum of n_0 and n_1. The rule has a *premise* and a *conclusion* and we have followed the common practice of writing the rule with the premise above and the conclusion below a solid line. The rule will be applied in derivations where the facts below the line are derived from facts above.

Some rules like those for evaluating numbers or locations require no premise. Sometimes they are written with a line, for example, as in

$$\frac{}{\langle n, \sigma \rangle \to n}.$$

Rules with empty premises are called *axioms*. Given any arithmetic expression a, state σ and number n, we take a in σ to evaluate to n, *i.e.* $\langle a, \sigma \rangle \to n$, if it can be derived from the rules starting from the axioms, in a way to be made precise soon.

The rule for sums expresses that the sum of two expressions evaluates to the number which is obtained by summing the two numbers which the summands evaluate to. It leaves unexplained the mechanism by which the sum of two numbers is obtained. I have chosen not to analyse in detail how numerals are constructed and the above rules only express how locations and operations $+, -, \times$ can be eliminated from expressions to give the number they evaluate to. If, on the other hand, we chose to describe a particular numeral system, like decimal or roman, further rules would be required to specify operations like multiplication. Such a level of description can be important when considering devices in hardware, for example. Here we want to avoid such details—we all know how to do simple arithmetic!

The rules for evaluation are written using metavariables n, X, a_0, a_1 ranging over the appropriate syntactic sets as well as σ ranging over states. A *rule instance* is obtained by instantiating these to particular numbers, locations and expressions and states. For example, when σ_0 is the particular state, with 0 in each location, this is a rule instance:

$$\frac{\langle 2, \sigma_0 \rangle \to 2 \quad \langle 3, \sigma_0 \rangle \to 3}{\langle 2 \times 3, \sigma_0 \rangle \to 6}$$

So is this:

$$\frac{\langle 2, \sigma_0 \rangle \to 3 \quad \langle 3, \sigma_0 \rangle \to 4}{\langle 2 \times 3, \sigma_0 \rangle \to 12},$$

though not one in which the premises, or conclusion, can ever be derived.

To see the structure of derivations, consider the evaluation of $a \equiv (\text{Init} + 5) + (7 + 9)$ in state σ_0, where Init is a location with $\sigma_0(\text{Init}) = 0$. Inspecting the rules we see that this requires the evaluation of $(\text{Init} + 5)$ and $(7 + 9)$ and these in turn may depend on other evaluations. In fact the evaluation of $\langle a, \sigma_0 \rangle$ can be seen as depending on a tree of evaluations:

$$\frac{\dfrac{\langle \text{Init}, \sigma_0 \rangle \to 0 \quad \langle 5, \sigma_0 \rangle \to 5}{\langle (\text{Init} + 5), \sigma_0 \rangle \to 5} \quad \dfrac{\langle 7, \sigma_0 \rangle \to 7 \quad \langle 9, \sigma_0 \rangle \to 9}{\langle 7 + 9, \sigma_0 \rangle \to 16}}{\langle (\text{Init} + 5) + (7 + 9), \sigma_0 \rangle \to 21}$$

We call such a structure a *derivation tree* or simply a *derivation*. It is built out of instances of the rules in such a way that all the premises of instances of rules which occur are conclusions of instances of rules immediately above them, so right at the top come the axioms, marked by the lines with no premises above them. The conclusion of the bottom-most rule is called the conclusion of the derivation. Something is said to be *derived* from the rules precisely when there is a derivation with it as conclusion.

In general, we write $\langle a, \sigma \rangle \to n$, and say a in σ evaluates to n, iff it can be derived from the rules for the evaluation of arithmetic expressions. The particular derivation above concludes with

$$\langle (\text{Init} + 5) + (7 + 9), \sigma_0 \rangle \to 21.$$

It follows that $(\text{Init} + 5) + (7 + 9)$ in state σ evaluates to 21—just what we want.

Consider the problem of evaluating an arithmetic expression a in some state σ. This amounts to finding a derivation in which the left part of the conclusion matches $\langle a, \sigma \rangle$. The search for a derivation is best achieved by trying to build a derivation in an upwards fashion: Start by finding a rule with conclusion matching $\langle a, \sigma \rangle$; if this is an axiom the derivation is complete; otherwise try to build derivations up from the premises, and, if successful, fill in the conclusion of the first rule to complete the derivation with conclusion of the form $\langle a, \sigma \rangle \to n$.

Although it doesn't happen for the evaluation of arithmetic expressions, in general, more than one rule has a left part which matches a given configuration. To guarantee finding a derivation tree with conclusion that matches, when one exists, all of the rules with left part matching the configuration must be considered, to see if they can be the conclusions of derivations. All possible derivations with conclusion of the right form must be constructed "in parallel".

In this way the rules provide an algorithm for the evaluation of arithmetic expressions based on the search for a derivation tree. Because it can be implemented fairly directly the rules specify the meaning, or semantics, of arithmetic expressions in an operational way, and the rules are said to give an *operational semantics* of such expressions. There are other ways to give the meaning of expressions in a way that leads fairly directly to an implementation. The way we have chosen is just one—any detailed description of an implementation is also an operational semantics. The style of semantics we have chosen is one which is becoming prevalent however. It is one which is often called *structural operational semantics* because of the syntax-directed way in which the rules are presented. It is also called *natural semantics* because of the way derivations resemble proofs in natural deduction—a method of constructing formal proofs. We shall see more complicated, and perhaps more convincing, examples of operational semantics later.

The evaluation relation determines a natural equivalence relation on expressions. Define

$$a_0 \sim a_1 \text{ iff } (\forall n \in \mathbf{N} \forall \sigma \in \Sigma. \ \langle a_0, \sigma \rangle \to n \iff \langle a_1, \sigma \rangle \to n),$$

which makes two arithmetic expressions equivalent if they evaluate to the same value in all states.

Exercise 2.2 Program the rules for the evaluation of arithmetic expressions in Prolog and/or ML (or another language of your choice). This, of course, requires a representation of the abstract syntax of such expressions in Prolog and/or ML. $\quad\square$

2.3   The evaluation of boolean expressions

We show how to evaluate boolean expressions to truth values (**true**, **false**) with the following rules:

$$\langle \mathbf{true}, \sigma \rangle \to \mathbf{true}$$

$$\langle \mathbf{false}, \sigma \rangle \to \mathbf{false}$$

$$\frac{\langle a_0, \sigma \rangle \to n \quad \langle a_1, \sigma \rangle \to m}{\langle a_0 = a_1, \sigma \rangle \to \mathbf{true}} \quad \text{if } n \text{ and } m \text{ are equal}$$

$$\frac{\langle a_0, \sigma \rangle \to n \quad \langle a_1, \sigma \rangle \to m}{\langle a_0 = a_1, \sigma \rangle \to \mathbf{false}} \quad \text{if } n \text{ and } m \text{ are unequal}$$

$$\frac{\langle a_0, \sigma \rangle \to n \quad \langle a_1, \sigma \rangle \to m}{\langle a_0 \leq a_1, \sigma \rangle \to \mathbf{true}} \quad \text{if } n \text{ is less than or equal to } m$$

$$\frac{\langle a_0, \sigma \rangle \to n \quad \langle a_1, \sigma \rangle \to m}{\langle a_0 \leq a_1, \sigma \rangle \to \mathbf{false}} \quad \text{if } n \text{ is not less than or equal to } m$$

$$\frac{\langle b, \sigma \rangle \to \mathbf{true}}{\langle \neg b, \sigma \rangle \to \mathbf{false}} \qquad \frac{\langle b, \sigma \rangle \to \mathbf{false}}{\langle \neg b, \sigma \rangle \to \mathbf{true}}$$

$$\frac{\langle b_0, \sigma \rangle \rightarrow t_0 \quad \langle b_1, \sigma \rangle \rightarrow t_1}{\langle b_0 \wedge b_1, \sigma \rangle \rightarrow t}$$

where t is **true** if $t_0 \equiv$ **true** and $t_1 \equiv$ **true**, and is **false** otherwise.

$$\frac{\langle b_0, \sigma \rangle \rightarrow t_0 \quad \langle b_1, \sigma \rangle \rightarrow t_1}{\langle b_0 \vee b_1, \sigma \rangle \rightarrow t}$$

where t is **true** if $t_0 \equiv$ **true** or $t_1 \equiv$ **true**, and is **false** otherwise.

This time the rules tell us how to eliminate all boolean operators and connectives and so reduce a boolean expression to a truth value.

Again, there is a natural equivalence relation on boolean expressions. Two expressions are equivalent if they evaluate to the same truth value in all states. Define

$$b_0 \sim b_1 \text{ iff } \forall t \forall \sigma \in \Sigma. \ \langle b_0, \sigma \rangle \rightarrow t \iff \langle b_1, \sigma \rangle \rightarrow t.$$

It may be a concern that our method of evaluating expressions is not the most efficient. For example, according to the present rules, to evaluate a conjunction $b_0 \wedge b_1$ we must evaluate both b_0 and b_1 which is clearly unnecessary if b_0 evaluates to **false** before b_1 is fully evaluated. A more efficient evaluation strategy is to first evaluate b_0 and then only in the case where its evaluation yields **true** to proceed with the evaluation of b_1. We can call this strategy *left-first-sequential* evaluation. Its evaluation rules are:

$$\frac{\langle b_0, \sigma \rangle \rightarrow \text{false}}{\langle b_0 \wedge b_1, \sigma \rangle \rightarrow \text{false}}$$

$$\frac{\langle b_0, \sigma \rangle \rightarrow \text{true} \quad \langle b_1, \sigma \rangle \rightarrow \text{false}}{\langle b_0 \wedge b_1, \sigma \rangle \rightarrow \text{false}}$$

$$\frac{\langle b_0, \sigma \rangle \rightarrow \text{true} \quad \langle b_1, \sigma \rangle \rightarrow \text{true}}{\langle b_0 \wedge b_1, \sigma \rangle \rightarrow \text{true}}$$

Exercise 2.3 Write down rules to evaluate boolean expressions of the form $b_0 \vee b_1$, which take advantage of the fact that there is no need to evaluate b in **true** $\vee b$ as the result will be true independent of the result of evaluating b. The rules written down should describe a method of left-sequential evaluation. Of course, by symmetry, there is a method of right-sequential evaluation.   □

Exercise 2.4 Write down rules which express the "parallel" evaluation of b_0 and b_1 in $b_0 \vee b_1$ so that $b_0 \vee b_1$ evaluates to **true** if either b_0 evaluates to **true**, and b_1 is unevaluated, or b_1 evaluates to **true**, and b_0 is unevaluated.   □

It may have been felt that we side-stepped too many issues by assuming we were given mechanisms to perform addition or conjunction of truth values for example. If so try:

Exercise 2.5 Give a semantics in the same style but for expressions which evaluate to strings (or lists) instead of integers and truth-values. Choose your own basic operations on strings, define expressions based on them, define the evaluation of expressions in the style used above. Can you see how to use your language to implement the expression part of **IMP** by representing integers as strings and operations on integers as operations on strings? (Proving that you have implemented the operations on integers correctly is quite hard.)   □

2.4 The execution of commands

The role of expressions is to evaluate to values in a particular state. The role of a program, and so commands, is to execute to change the state. When we execute an **IMP** program we shall assume that initially the state is such that all locations are set to zero. So the *initial state* σ_0 has the property that $\sigma_0(X) = 0$ for all locations X. As we all know the execution may *terminate* in a final state, or may *diverge* and never yield a final state. A pair $\langle c, \sigma \rangle$ represents the *(command) configuration* from which it remains to execute command c from state σ. We shall define a relation

$$\langle c, \sigma \rangle \to \sigma'$$

which means the (full) execution of command c in state σ terminates in final state σ'. For example,

$$\langle X := 5, \sigma \rangle \to \sigma'$$

where σ' is the state σ updated to have 5 in location X. We shall use this notation:

Notation: Let σ be a state. Let $m \in \mathbf{N}$. Let $X \in \mathbf{Loc}$. We write $\sigma[m/X]$ for the state obtained from σ by replacing its contents in X by m, i.e. define

$$\sigma[m/X](Y) = \begin{cases} m & \text{if } Y = X, \\ \sigma(Y) & \text{if } Y \neq X. \end{cases}$$

Now we can instead write

$$\langle X := 5, \sigma \rangle \to \sigma[5/X].$$

The execution relation for arbitrary commands and states is given by the following rules.

Rules for commands

Atomic commands:

$$\langle \mathbf{skip}, \sigma \rangle \to \sigma$$

$$\frac{\langle a, \sigma \rangle \to m}{\langle X := a, \sigma \rangle \to \sigma[m/X]}$$

Sequencing:

$$\frac{\langle c_0, \sigma \rangle \to \sigma'' \quad \langle c_1, \sigma'' \rangle \to \sigma'}{\langle c_0 ; c_1, \sigma \rangle \to \sigma'}$$

Conditionals:

$$\frac{\langle b, \sigma \rangle \to \mathbf{true} \quad \langle c_0, \sigma \rangle \to \sigma'}{\langle \mathbf{if}\ b\ \mathbf{then}\ c_0\ \mathbf{else}\ c_1, \sigma \rangle \to \sigma'}$$

$$\frac{\langle b, \sigma \rangle \to \mathbf{false} \quad \langle c_1, \sigma \rangle \to \sigma'}{\langle \mathbf{if}\ b\ \mathbf{then}\ c_0\ \mathbf{else}\ c_1, \sigma \rangle \to \sigma'}$$

While-loops:

$$\frac{\langle b, \sigma \rangle \to \mathbf{false}}{\langle \mathbf{while}\ b\ \mathbf{do}\ c, \sigma \rangle \to \sigma}$$

$$\frac{\langle b, \sigma \rangle \to \mathbf{true} \quad \langle c, \sigma \rangle \to \sigma'' \quad \langle \mathbf{while}\ b\ \mathbf{do}\ c, \sigma'' \rangle \to \sigma'}{\langle \mathbf{while}\ b\ \mathbf{do}\ c, \sigma \rangle \to \sigma'}$$

Again there is a natural equivalence relation on commands. Define

$$c_0 \sim c_1 \text{ iff } \forall \sigma, \sigma' \in \Sigma.\ \langle c_0, \sigma \rangle \to \sigma' \iff \langle c_1, \sigma \rangle \to \sigma'.$$

Exercise 2.6 Complete Exercise 2.2 of Section 2.2, by coding the rules for the evaluation of boolean expressions and execution of commands in Prolog and/or ML.   □

Exercise 2.7 Let $w \equiv \mathbf{while\ true\ do\ skip}$. By considering the form of derivations, explain why, for any state σ, there is no state σ' such that $\langle w, \sigma \rangle \to \sigma'$.   □

2.5   A simple proof

The operational semantics of the syntactic sets **Aexp**, **Bexp** and **Com** has been given using the same method. By means of rules we have specified the evaluation relations of both types of expressions and the execution relation of commands. All three relations are examples of the general notion of *transition relations*, or *transition systems*, in which the configurations are thought of as some kind of state and the relations as expressing possible transitions, or changes, between states. For instance, we can consider each of

$$\langle 3, \sigma \rangle \to 3, \quad \langle \textbf{true}, \sigma \rangle \to \textbf{true}, \quad \langle X := 2, \sigma \rangle \to \sigma[2/X].$$

to be transitions.

Because the transition systems for **IMP** are given by rules, we have an elementary, but very useful, proof technique for proving properties of the operational semantics **IMP**.

As an illustration, consider the execution of a while-command $w \equiv \textbf{while } b \textbf{ do } c$, with $b \in \textbf{Bexp}, c \in \textbf{Com}$, in a state σ. We expect that if b evaluates to **true** in σ then w executes as c followed by w again, and otherwise, in the case where b evaluates to **false**, that the execution of w terminates immediately with the state unchanged. This informal explanation of the execution of commands leads us to expect that for all states σ, σ'

$$\langle w, \sigma \rangle \to \sigma' \text{ iff } \langle \textbf{if } b \textbf{ then } c; w \textbf{ else skip}, \sigma \rangle \to \sigma',$$

i.e., that the following proposition holds.

Proposition 2.8 *Let* $w \equiv \textbf{while } b \textbf{ do } c$ *with* $b \in \textbf{Bexp}, c \in \textbf{Com}$. *Then*

$$w \sim \textbf{if } b \textbf{ then } c; w \textbf{ else skip}.$$

Proof: We want to show

$$\langle w, \sigma \rangle \to \sigma' \text{ iff } \langle \textbf{if } b \textbf{ then } c; w \textbf{ else skip}, \sigma \rangle \to \sigma',$$

for all states σ, σ'.

"$\Rightarrow$": Suppose $\langle w, \sigma \rangle \to \sigma'$, for states σ, σ'. Then there must be a derivation of $\langle w, \sigma \rangle \to \sigma'$. Consider the possible forms such a derivation can take. Inspecting the rules for commands we see the final rule of the derivation is either

$$\frac{\langle b, \sigma \rangle \to \textbf{false}}{\langle w, \sigma \rangle \to \sigma} \tag{1 $\Rightarrow$}$$

or

$$\frac{\langle b, \sigma \rangle \to \textbf{true} \quad \langle c, \sigma \rangle \to \sigma'' \quad \langle w, \sigma'' \rangle \to \sigma'}{\langle w, \sigma \rangle \to \sigma'} \tag{2 $\Rightarrow$}$$

In case (1 $\Rightarrow$), the derivation of $\langle w, \sigma \rangle \to \sigma'$ must have the form

$$\frac{\vdots}{\dfrac{\langle b, \sigma \rangle \to \textbf{false}}{\langle w, \sigma \rangle \to \sigma}}$$

which includes a derivation of $\langle b, \sigma \rangle \rightarrow$ **false**. Using this derivation we can build the following derivation of $\langle$ **if** b **then** $c; w$ **else skip**, $\sigma \rangle \rightarrow \sigma$:

$$\frac{\overset{\vdots}{\langle b, \sigma \rangle \rightarrow \text{false}} \quad \langle \text{skip}, \sigma \rangle \rightarrow \sigma}{\langle \text{if } b \text{ then } c; w \text{ else skip}, \sigma \rangle \rightarrow \sigma}$$

In case $(2 \Rightarrow)$, the derivation of $\langle w, \sigma \rangle \rightarrow \sigma'$ must take the form

$$\frac{\overset{\vdots}{\langle b, \sigma \rangle \rightarrow \text{true}} \quad \overset{\vdots}{\langle c, \sigma \rangle \rightarrow \sigma''} \quad \overset{\vdots}{\langle w, \sigma'' \rangle \rightarrow \sigma'}}{\langle w, \sigma \rangle \rightarrow \sigma'}$$

which includes derivations of $\langle b, \sigma \rangle \rightarrow$ **true**, $\langle c, \sigma \rangle \rightarrow \sigma''$ and $\langle w, \sigma'' \rangle \rightarrow \sigma'$. From these we can obtain a derivation of $\langle c; w, \sigma \rangle \rightarrow \sigma'$, *viz.*

$$\frac{\overset{\vdots}{\langle c, \sigma \rangle \rightarrow \sigma''} \quad \overset{\vdots}{\langle w, \sigma'' \rangle \rightarrow \sigma'}}{\langle c; w, \sigma \rangle \rightarrow \sigma'}$$

We can incorporate this into a derivation:

$$\frac{\overset{\vdots}{\langle b, \sigma \rangle \rightarrow \text{true}} \quad \frac{\overset{\vdots}{\langle c, \sigma \rangle \rightarrow \sigma''} \quad \overset{\vdots}{\langle w, \sigma'' \rangle \rightarrow \sigma'}}{\langle c; w, \sigma \rangle \rightarrow \sigma'}}{\langle \text{if } b \text{ then } c; w \text{ else skip}, \sigma \rangle \rightarrow \sigma'}$$

In either case, $(1 \Rightarrow)$ or $(2 \Rightarrow)$, we obtain a derivation of

$$\langle \text{if } b \text{ then } c; w \text{ else skip}, \sigma \rangle \rightarrow \sigma'$$

from a derivation of

$$\langle w, \sigma \rangle \rightarrow \sigma'.$$

Thus

$$\langle w, \sigma \rangle \rightarrow \sigma' \text{ implies } \langle \text{if } b \text{ then } c; w \text{ else skip}, \sigma \rangle \rightarrow \sigma',$$

for any states σ, σ'.

"$\Leftarrow$": We also want to show the converse, that $\langle$ **if** b **then** $c; w$ **else skip**, $\sigma \rangle \rightarrow \sigma'$ implies $\langle w, \sigma \rangle \rightarrow \sigma'$, for all states σ, σ'.

Suppose $\langle \textbf{if } b \textbf{ then } c; w \textbf{ else skip}, \sigma \rangle \rightarrow \sigma'$, for states σ, σ'. Then there is a derivation with one of two possible forms:

$$\frac{\overline{\langle b, \sigma \rangle \rightarrow \textbf{false}} \quad \overline{\langle \textbf{skip}, \sigma \rangle \rightarrow \sigma}}{\langle \textbf{if } b \textbf{ then } c; w \textbf{ else skip}, \sigma \rangle \rightarrow \sigma} \qquad (1 \Leftarrow)$$

$$\frac{\overline{\langle b, \sigma \rangle \rightarrow \textbf{true}} \quad \overline{\langle c; w, \sigma \rangle \rightarrow \sigma'}}{\langle \textbf{if } b \textbf{ then } c; w \textbf{ else skip}, \sigma \rangle \rightarrow \sigma'} \qquad (2 \Leftarrow)$$

where in the first case, we also have $\sigma' = \sigma$, got by noting the fact that

$$\overline{\langle \textbf{skip}, \sigma \rangle \rightarrow \sigma}$$

is the only possible derivation associated with **skip**.

From either derivation, $(1 \Leftarrow)$ or $(2 \Leftarrow)$, we can construct a derivation of $\langle w, \sigma \rangle \rightarrow \sigma'$. The second case, $(2 \Leftarrow)$, is the more complicated. Derivation $(2 \Leftarrow)$ includes a derivation of $\langle c; w, \sigma \rangle \rightarrow \sigma'$ which has to have the form

$$\frac{\overline{\langle c, \sigma \rangle \rightarrow \sigma''} \quad \overline{\langle w, \sigma'' \rangle \rightarrow \sigma'}}{\langle c; w, \sigma \rangle \rightarrow \sigma'}$$

for some state σ''. Using the derivations of $\langle c, \sigma \rangle \rightarrow \sigma''$ and $\langle w, \sigma'' \rangle \rightarrow \sigma'$ with that for $\langle b, \sigma \rangle \rightarrow \textbf{true}$, we can produce the derivation

$$\frac{\overline{\langle b, \sigma \rangle \rightarrow \textbf{true}} \quad \overline{\langle c, \sigma \rangle \rightarrow \sigma''} \quad \overline{\langle w, \sigma'' \rangle \rightarrow \sigma'}}{\langle w, \sigma \rangle \rightarrow \sigma'}$$

More directly, from the derivation $(1 \Leftarrow)$, we can construct a derivation of $\langle w, \sigma \rangle \rightarrow \sigma'$ (How?).

Thus if $\langle \textbf{if } b \textbf{ then } c; w \textbf{ else skip}, \sigma \rangle \rightarrow \sigma'$ then $\langle w, \sigma \rangle \rightarrow \sigma'$ for any states σ, σ'.

We can now conclude that

$$\langle w, \sigma \rangle \rightarrow \sigma' \text{ iff } \langle \textbf{if } b \textbf{ then } c; w \textbf{ else skip}, \sigma \rangle \rightarrow \sigma',$$

for all states σ, σ', and hence

$$w \sim \textbf{if } b \textbf{ then } c; w \textbf{ else skip}$$

as required. $\square$

This simple proof of the equivalence of while-command and its conditional unfolding exhibits an important technique: in order to prove a property of an operational semantics it is helpful to consider the various possible forms of derivations. This idea will be used again and again, though never again in such laborious detail. Later we shall meet other techniques, like "rule induction" which, in principle, can supplant the technique used here. The other techniques are more abstract however, and sometimes more confusing to apply. So keep in mind the technique of considering the forms of derivations when reasoning about operational semantics.

2.6 Alternative semantics

The evaluation relations

$$\langle a, \sigma \rangle \to n \text{ and } \langle b, \sigma \rangle \to t$$

specify the evaluation of expressions in rather large steps; given an expression and a state they yield a value directly. It is possible to give rules for evaluation which capture single steps in the evaluation of expressions. We could instead have defined an evaluation relation between pairs of configurations, taking *e.g.*

$$\langle a, \sigma \rangle \to_1 \langle a', \sigma' \rangle$$

to mean one step in the evaluation of a in state σ yields a' in state σ'. This intended meaning is formalised by taking rules such as the following to specify single steps in the left-to-right evaluation of sum.

$$\frac{\langle a_0, \sigma \rangle \to_1 \langle a_0', \sigma \rangle}{\langle a_0 + a_1, \sigma \rangle \to_1 \langle a_0' + a_1, \sigma \rangle}$$

$$\frac{\langle a_1, \sigma \rangle \to_1 \langle a_1', \sigma \rangle}{\langle n + a_1, \sigma \rangle \to_1 \langle n + a_1', \sigma \rangle}$$

$$\langle n + m, \sigma \rangle \to_1 \langle p, \sigma \rangle$$

where p is the sum of m and n.

Note how the rules formalise the intention to evaluate sums in a left-to-right sequential fashion. To spell out the meaning of the first sum rule above, it says: if one step in the evaluation of a_0 in state σ leads to a_0' in state σ then one step in the evaluation of $a_0 + a_1$ in state σ leads to $a_0' + a_1$ in state σ. So to evaluate a sum first evaluate the component expression of the sum and when this leads to a number evaluate the second component of the sum, and finally add the corresponding numerals (and we assume a mechanism to do this is given).

Exercise 2.9 Complete the task, begun above, of writing down the rules for $\rightarrow_1$, one step in the evaluation of integer and boolean expressions. What evaluation strategy have you adopted (left-to-right sequential or $\cdots$) ?   □

We have chosen to define full execution of commands in particular states through a relation

$$\langle c, \sigma \rangle \rightarrow \sigma'$$

between command configurations. We could instead have based our explanation of the execution of commands on a relation expressing single steps in the execution. A single step relation between two command configurations

$$\langle c, \sigma \rangle \rightarrow_1 \langle c', \sigma' \rangle$$

means the execution of one instruction in c from state σ leads to the configuration in which it remains to execute c' in state σ'. For example,

$$\langle X := 5; Y := 1, \sigma \rangle \rightarrow_1 \langle Y := 1, \sigma[5/X] \rangle.$$

Of course, as this example makes clear, if we consider continuing the execution, we need some way to represent the fact that the command is empty. A configuration with no command left to execute can be represented by a state standing alone. So continuing the execution above we obtain

$$\langle X := 5; Y := 1, \sigma \rangle \rightarrow_1 \langle Y := 1, \sigma[5/X] \rangle \rightarrow_1 \sigma[5/X][1/Y].$$

We leave the detailed presentation of rules for the definition of this one-step execution relation to an exercise. But note there is some choice in what is regarded as a single step. If

$$\langle b, \sigma \rangle \rightarrow_1 \langle \textbf{true}, \sigma \rangle$$

do we wish

$$\langle \textbf{if } b \textbf{ then } c_0 \textbf{ else } c_1, \sigma \rangle \rightarrow_1 \langle c_0, \sigma \rangle$$

or

$$\langle \textbf{if } b \textbf{ then } c_0 \textbf{ else } c_1, \sigma \rangle \rightarrow_1 \langle \textbf{if true then } c_0 \textbf{ else } c_1, \sigma \rangle$$

to be a single step? For the language **IMP** these issues are not critical, but they become so in languages where commands can be executed in parallel; then different choices can effect the final states of execution sequences.

Exercise 2.10 Write down a full set of rules for $\rightarrow_1$ on command configurations, so $\rightarrow_1$ stands for a single step in the execution of a command from a particular state, as discussed above. Use command configurations of the form $\langle c, \sigma \rangle$ and σ when there is no more command left to execute. Point out where you have made a choice in the rules between alternative understandings of what constitutes a single step in the execution. (Showing $\langle c, \sigma \rangle \rightarrow_1^* \sigma'$ iff $\langle c, \sigma \rangle \rightarrow \sigma'$ is hard and requires the application of induction principles introduced in the next two chapters.)   □

Exercise 2.11 In our language, the evaluation of expressions has no side effects—their evaluation does not change the state. If we were to model side-effects it would be natural to consider instead an evaluation relation of the form

$$\langle a, \sigma \rangle \rightarrow \langle n, \sigma' \rangle$$

where σ' is the state that results from the evaluation of a in original state σ. To introduce side effects into the evaluation of arithmetic expressions of **IMP**, extend them by adding a construct

$$c \ \mathbf{resultis} \ a$$

where c is a command and a is an arithmetic expression. To evaluate such an expression, the command c is first executed and then a evaluated in the changed state. Formalise this idea by first giving the full syntax of the language and then giving it an operational semantics.   □

2.7   Further reading

A convincing demonstration of the wide applicability of "structural operational semantics", of which this chapter has given a taste, was first set out by Gordon Plotkin in his lecture notes for a course at Aarhus University, Denmark, in 1981 [81]. A research group under the direction Gilles Kahn at INRIA in Sophia Antipolis, France are currently working on mechanical tools to support semantics in this style; they have focussed on evaluation or execution to a final value or state, so following their lead this particular kind of structural operational semantics is sometimes called "natural semantics" [26, 28, 29]. We shall take up the operational semantics of functional languages, and nondeterminism and parallelism in later chapters, where further references will be presented. More on abstract syntax can be found in Wikström's book [101], Mosses' chapter in [68] and Tennent's book [97].

3 Some principles of induction

Proofs of properties of programs often rely on the application of a proof method, or really a family of proof methods, called induction. The most commonly used forms of induction are mathematical induction and structural induction. These are both special cases of a powerful proof method called well-founded induction.

3.1 Mathematical induction

The natural numbers are built-up by starting from 0 and repeatedly adjoining successors. The natural numbers consist of no more than those elements which are obtained in this way. There is a corresponding proof principle called *mathematical induction*.

Let $P(n)$ be a a property of the natural numbers $n = 0, 1, \cdots$. The principle of mathematical induction says that in order to show $P(n)$ holds for all natural numbers n it is sufficient to show

- $P(0)$ is true
- If $P(m)$ is true then so is $P(m+1)$ for any natural number m.

We can state it more succinctly, using some logical notation, as

$$(P(0) \ \& \ (\forall m \in \omega. \ P(m) \Rightarrow P(m+1))) \Rightarrow \forall n \in \omega. \ P(n).$$

The principle of mathematical induction is intuitively clear: If we know $P(0)$ and we have a method of showing $P(m+1)$ from the assumption $P(m)$ then from $P(0)$ we know $P(1)$, and applying the method again, $P(2)$, and then $P(3)$, and so on. The assertion $P(m)$ is called the *induction hypothesis*, $P(0)$ the *basis* of the induction and $(\forall m \in \omega. \ P(m) \Rightarrow P(m+1))$ the *induction step*.

Mathematical induction shares a feature with all other methods of proof by induction, that the first most obvious choice of induction hypothesis may not work in a proof. Imagine it is required to prove that a property P holds of all the natural numbers. Certainly it is sensible to try to prove this with $P(m)$ as induction hypothesis. But quite often proving the induction step $\forall m \in \omega. \ (P(m) \Rightarrow P(m+1))$ is impossible. The rub can come in proving $P(m+1)$ from the assumption $P(m)$ because the assumption $P(m)$ is not strong enough. The way to tackle this is to strengthen the induction hypothesis to a property $P'(m)$ which implies $P(m)$. There is an art in finding $P'(m)$ however, because in proving the induction step, although we have a stronger assumption $P'(m)$, it is at the cost of having more to prove in $P'(m+1)$ which may be unnecessarily difficult, or impossible.

In showing a property $Q(m)$ holds inductively of all numbers m, it might be that the property's truth at $m+1$ depends not just on its truth at the predecessor m but on its truth at other numbers preceding m as well. It is sensible to strengthen $Q(m)$ to an induction hypothesis $P(m)$ standing for $\forall k < m.\ Q(k)$. Taking $P(m)$ to be this property in the statement of ordinary mathematical induction we obtain

$$\forall k < 0.\ Q(k)$$

for the basis, and

$$\forall m \in \omega.((\forall k < m.\ Q(k)) \Rightarrow (\forall k < m+1.\ Q(k)))$$

for the induction step. However, the basis is vacuously true—there are no natural numbers strictly below 0, and the step is equivalent to

$$\forall m \in \omega.(\forall k < m.\ Q(k)) \Rightarrow Q(m).$$

We have obtained *course-of-values induction* as a special form of mathematical induction:

$$(\forall m \in \omega.(\forall k < m.\ Q(k)) \Rightarrow Q(m)) \Rightarrow \forall n \in \omega.\ Q(n).$$

Exercise 3.1 Prove by mathematical induction that the following property P holds for all natural numbers:
$$P(n) \iff {}_{def} \Sigma_{i=1}^{n}(2i-1) = n^2.$$
(The notation $\Sigma_{i=k}^{l} s_i$ abbreviates $s_k + s_{k+1} + \cdots + s_l$ when k, l are integers with $k < l$.)
□

Exercise 3.2 A string is a sequence of symbols. A string $a_1 a_2 \cdots a_n$ with n positions occupied by symbols is said to have *length* n. A string can be empty in which case it is said to have length 0. Two strings s and t can be concatenated to form the string st. Use mathematical induction to show there is no string u which satisfies $au = ub$ for two distinct symbols a and b.
□

3.2   Structural induction

We would like a technique to prove "obvious" facts like

$$\langle a, \sigma \rangle \rightarrow m\ \&\ \langle a, \sigma \rangle \rightarrow m' \Rightarrow m = m'$$

for all arithmetic expressions a, states σ and numbers m, m'. It says the evaluation of arithmetic expressions in **IMP** is *deterministic*. The standard tool is the principle of *structural induction*. We state it for arithmetic expressions but of course it applies more generally to all the syntactic sets of our language **IMP**.

Let $P(a)$ be a property of arithmetic expressions a. To show $P(a)$ holds for all arithmetic expressions a it is sufficient to show:

- For all numerals m it is the case that $P(m)$ holds.

- For all locations X it is the case that $P(X)$ holds.

- For all arithmetic expressions a_0 and a_1, if $P(a_0)$ and $P(a_1)$ hold then so does $P(a_0 + a_1)$.

- For all arithmetic expressions a_0 and a_1, if $P(a_0)$ and $P(a_1)$ hold then so does $P(a_0 - a_1)$.

- For all arithmetic expressions a_0 and a_1, if $P(a_0)$ and $P(a_1)$ hold then so does $P(a_0 \times a_1)$.

The assertion $P(a)$ is called the *induction hypothesis*. The principle says that in order to show the induction hypothesis is true of all arithmetic expressions it suffices to show that it is true of atomic expressions and is preserved by all the methods of forming arithmetic expressions. Again this principle is intuitively obvious as arithmetic expressions are precisely those built-up according to the cases above. It can be stated more compactly using logical notation:

$$(\forall m \in \mathbf{N}.\ P(m))\ \&\ (\forall X \in \mathbf{Loc}.P(X))\ \&$$
$$(\forall a_0, a_1 \in \mathbf{Aexp}.\ P(a_0)\ \&\ P(a_1) \Rightarrow P(a_0 + a_1))\ \&$$
$$(\forall a_0, a_1 \in \mathbf{Aexp}.\ P(a_0)\ \&\ P(a_1) \Rightarrow P(a_0 - a_1))\ \&$$
$$(\forall a_0, a_1 \in \mathbf{Aexp}.\ P(a_0)\ \&\ P(a_1) \Rightarrow P(a_0 \times a_1))$$
$$\Rightarrow$$
$$\forall a \in \mathbf{Aexp}.\ P(a).$$

In fact, as is clear, the conditions above not only imply $\forall a \in \mathbf{Aexp}.\ P(a)$ but also are equivalent to it.

Sometimes a degenerate form of structural induction is sufficient. An argument by cases on the structure of expressions will do when a property is true of all expressions simply by virtue of the different forms expressions can take, without having to use the fact that the property holds for subexpressions. An argument by cases on arithmetic expressions uses the fact that if

$$(\forall m \in \mathbf{N}.\ P(m))\&$$
$$(\forall X \in \mathbf{Loc}.P(X))\ \&$$
$$(\forall a_0, a_1 \in \mathbf{Aexp}.\ P(a_0 + a_1))\ \&$$
$$(\forall a_0, a_1 \in \mathbf{Aexp}.\ P(a_0 - a_1))\ \&$$
$$(\forall a_0, a_1 \in \mathbf{Aexp}.\ P(a_0 \times a_1))$$

then $\forall a \in \mathbf{Aexp}.\ P(a)$.

As an example of how to do proofs by structural induction we prove that the evaluation of arithmetic expression is deterministic.

Proposition 3.3 *For all arithmetic expressions a, states σ and numbers m, m'*

$$\langle a, \sigma \rangle \to m\ \&\ \langle a, \sigma \rangle \to m' \Rightarrow m = m'.$$

Proof: We proceed by structural induction on arithmetic expressions a using the induction hypothesis $P(a)$ where

$$P(a)\ \text{iff}\ \forall \sigma, m, m'.\ (\langle a, \sigma \rangle \to m\ \&\ \langle a, \sigma \rangle \to m' \Rightarrow m = m').$$

For brevity we shall write $\langle a, \sigma \rangle \to m, m'$ for $\langle a, \sigma \rangle \to m$ and $\langle a, \sigma \rangle \to m'$. Using structural induction the proof splits into cases according to the structure of a:

$a \equiv n$: If $\langle a, \sigma \rangle \to m, m'$ then there is only one rule for the evaluation of numbers so $m = m' = n$.

$a \equiv a_0 + a_1$: If $\langle a, \sigma \rangle \to m, m'$ then considering the form of the single rule for the evaluation of sums there must be m_0, m_1 so

$$\langle a_0, \sigma \rangle \to m_0 \text{ and } \langle a_1, \sigma \rangle \to m_1 \text{ with } m = m_0 + m_1$$

as well as m_0', m_1' so

$$\langle a_0, \sigma \rangle \to m_0' \text{ and } \langle a_1, \sigma \rangle \to m_1' \text{ with } m' = m_0' + m_1'$$

By the induction hypothesis applied to a_0 and a_1 we obtain $m_0 = m_0'$ and $m_1 = m_1'$. Thus $m = m_0 + m_1 = m_0' + m_1' = m'$.

The remaining cases follow in a similar way. We can conclude, by the principle of structural induction, that $P(a)$ holds for all $a \in \mathbf{Aexp}$. $\square$

One can prove the evaluation of expressions always terminates by structural induction, and corresponding facts about boolean expressions.

Exercise 3.4 Prove by structural induction that the evaluation of arithmetic expressions always terminates, *i.e.*, for all arithmetic expression a and states σ there is some m such that $\langle a, \sigma \rangle \to m$. $\square$

Exercise 3.5 Using these facts about arithmetic expressions, by structural induction, prove the evaluation of boolean expressions is firstly deterministic, and secondly total.
$\square$

Exercise 3.6 What goes wrong when you try to prove the execution of commands is deterministic by using structural induction on commands? (Later, in Section 3.4, we shall give a proof using "structural induction" on derivations.) $\square$

3.3 Well-founded induction

Mathematical and structural induction are special cases of a general and powerful proof principle called well-founded induction. In essence structural induction works because breaking down an expression into subexpressions can not go on forever, eventually it must lead to atomic expressions which can not be broken down any further. If a property fails to hold of any expression then it must fail on some minimal expression which when it is broken down yields subexpressions, all of which satisfy the property. This observation justifies the principle of structural induction: to show a property holds of all expressions it is sufficient to show that a property holds of an arbitrary expression if it holds of all its subexpressions. Similarly with the natural numbers, if a property fails to hold of all natural numbers then there has to be a smallest natural number at which it fails. The essential feature shared by both the subexpression relation and the predecessor relation on natural numbers is that do not give rise to infinite descending chains. This is the feature required of a relation if it is to support well-founded induction.

Definition: A *well-founded relation* is a binary relation $\prec$ on a set A such that there are no infinite descending chains $\cdots \prec a_i \prec \cdots \prec a_1 \prec a_0$. When $a \prec b$ we say a is a *predecessor* of b.

Note a well-founded relation is necessarily *irreflexive i.e.*, for no a do we have $a \prec a$, as otherwise there would be the infinite deciding chain $\cdots \prec a \prec \cdots \prec a \prec a$. We shall generally write $\preceq$ for the reflexive closure of the relation $\prec$, *i.e.*

$$a \preceq b \iff a = b \text{ or } a \prec b.$$

Sometimes one sees an alternative definition of well-founded relation, in terms of minimal elements.

Proposition 3.7 *Let $\prec$ be a binary relation on a set A. The relation $\prec$ is well-founded iff any nonempty subset Q of A has a minimal element, i.e. an element m such that*

$$m \in Q \ \& \ \forall b \prec m. \ b \notin Q.$$

Proof:
"if": Suppose every nonempty subset of A has a minimal element. If $\cdots \prec a_i \prec \cdots \prec a_1 \prec a_0$ were an infinite descending chain then the set $Q = \{a_i \mid i \in \omega\}$ would be nonempty without a minimal element, a contradiction. Hence $\prec$ is well-founded.
"only if": To see this, suppose Q is a nonempty subset of A. Construct a chain of elements as follows. Take a_0 to be any element of Q. Inductively, assume a chain of

elements $a_n \prec \cdots \prec a_0$ has been constructed inside Q. Either there is some $b \prec a_n$ such that $b \in Q$ or there is not. If not stop the construction. Otherwise take $a_{n+1} = b$. As $\prec$ is well-founded the chain $\cdots \prec a_i \prec \cdots \prec a_1 \prec a_0$ cannot be infinite. Hence it is finite, of the form $a_n \prec \cdots \prec a_0$ with $\forall b \prec a_n.\ b \notin Q$. Take the required minimal element m to be a_n.   □

Exercise 3.8 Let $\prec$ be a well-founded relation on a set B. Prove

1. its transitive closure $\prec^+$ is also well-founded,
2. its reflexive, transitive closure $\prec^*$ is a partial order.

□

The principle of well-founded induction.

Let $\prec$ be a well founded relation on a set A. Let P be a property. Then $\forall a \in A.\ P(a)$ iff

$$\forall a \in A.\ ([\forall b \prec a.\ P(b)] \Rightarrow P(a)).$$

The principle says that to prove a property holds of all elements of a well-founded set it suffices to show that if the property holds of all predecessors of an arbitrary element a then the property holds of a.

We now prove the principle. The proof rests on the observation that any nonempty subset Q of a set A with a well-founded relation $\prec$ has a minimal element. Clearly if $P(a)$ holds for all elements of A then $\forall a \in A.\ ([\forall b \prec a.\ P(b)] \Rightarrow P(a))$. To show the converse, we assume $\forall a \in A.\ ([\forall b \prec a.\ P(b)] \Rightarrow P(a))$ and produce a contradiction by supposing $\neg P(a)$ for some $a \in A$. Then, as we have observed, there must be a minimal element m of the set $\{a \in A \mid \neg P(a)\}$. But then $\neg P(m)$ and yet $\forall b \prec m.\ P(b)$, which contradicts the assumption.

In mathematics this principle is sometimes called *Noetherian induction* after the algebraist Emmy Noether. Unfortunately, in some computer science texts (*e.g.* [59]) it is misleadingly called "structural induction".

Example: If we take the relation $\prec$ to be the successor relation

$$n \prec m \text{ iff } m = n + 1$$

on the non-negative integers the principle of well-founded induction specialises to mathematical induction.   □

Example: If we take $\prec$ to be the "strictly less than" relation $<$ on the non-negative integers, the principle specialises to course-of-values induction.   □

Example: If we take $\prec$ to be the relation between expressions such that $a \prec b$ holds iff a is an immediate subexpression of b we obtain the principle of structural induction as a special case of well-founded induction.   □

Proposition 3.7 provides an alternative to proofs by well-founded induction. Suppose A is a well-founded set. Instead of using well-founded induction to show every element of A satisfies a property P, we can consider the subset of A for which the property P fails, *i.e.* the subset F of counterexamples. By Proposition 3.7, to show F is $\emptyset$ it is sufficient to show that F cannot have a minimal element. This is done by obtaining a contradiction from the assumption that there is a minimal element in F. (See the proof of Proposition 3.12 for an example of this approach.) Whether to use this approach or the principle of well-founded induction is largely a matter of taste, though sometimes, depending on the problem, one approach can be more direct than the other.

Exercise 3.9 For suitable well-founded relation on strings, use the "no counterexample" approach described above to show there is no string u which satisfies $au = ub$ for two distinct symbols a and b. Compare your proof with another by well-founded induction (and with the proof by mathematical induction asked for in Section 3.1).   □

Proofs can often depend on a judicious choice of well-founded relation. In Chapter 10 we shall give some useful ways of constructing well-founded relations.

As an example of how the operational semantics supports proofs we show that Euclid's algorithm for the gcd (greatest common divisor) of two non-negative numbers terminates. Though such proofs are often less clumsy when based on a denotational semantics. (Later, Exercise 6.16 will show its correctness.) Euclid's algorithm for the greatest common divisor of two positive integers can be written in **IMP** as:

$$\text{Euclid} \equiv \textbf{while } \neg(M = N) \textbf{ do}$$
$$\textbf{if } M \leq N$$
$$\textbf{then } N := N - M$$
$$\textbf{else } M := M - N$$

Theorem 3.10 *For all states* σ

$$\sigma(M) \geq 1 \ \& \ \sigma(N) \geq 1 \Rightarrow \exists \sigma'. \ \langle \text{Euclid}, \sigma \rangle \rightarrow \sigma'.$$

Proof: We wish to show the property

$$P(\sigma) \iff \exists \sigma'. \langle \text{Euclid}, \sigma \rangle \rightarrow \sigma'.$$

holds for all states σ in $S = \{\sigma \in \Sigma \mid \sigma(M) \geq 1 \ \& \ \sigma(N) \geq 1\}$.

We do this by well-founded induction on the relation $\prec$ on S where

$$\sigma' \prec \sigma \text{ iff } (\sigma'(M) \leq \sigma(M) \ \& \ \sigma'(N) \leq \sigma(N)) \ \&$$
$$(\sigma'(M) \neq \sigma(M) \text{ or } \sigma'(N) \neq \sigma(N))$$

for states σ', σ in S. Clearly $\prec$ is well-founded as the values in M and N cannot be decreased indefinitely and remain positive.

Let $\sigma \in S$. Suppose $\forall \sigma' \prec \sigma. \ P(\sigma')$. Abbreviate $\sigma(M) = m$ and $\sigma(N) = n$.

If $m = n$ then $\langle \neg(M = N), \sigma \rangle \to \mathbf{false}$. Using its derivation we construct the derivation

$$\frac{\begin{array}{c} \vdots \\ \overline{\langle \neg(M = N), \sigma \rangle \to \mathbf{false}} \end{array}}{\langle \text{Euclid}, \sigma \rangle \to \sigma}$$

using the rule for while-loops which applies when the boolean condition evaluates to false. In the case where $m = n$, $\langle \text{Euclid}, \sigma \rangle \to \sigma$.

Otherwise $m \neq n$. In this case $\langle \neg(M = N), \sigma \rangle \to \mathbf{true}$. From the rules for the execution of commands we derive

$$\langle \mathbf{if} \ M \leq N \ \mathbf{then} \ N := N - M \ \mathbf{else} \ M := M - N, \ \sigma \rangle \to \sigma''$$

where

$$\sigma'' = \begin{cases} \sigma[n - m/N] & \text{if } m < n \\ \sigma[m - n/M] & \text{if } n < m. \end{cases}$$

In either case $\sigma'' \prec \sigma$. Hence $P(\sigma'')$ so $\langle \text{Euclid}, \sigma'' \rangle \to \sigma'$ for some σ'. Thus applying the other rule for while-loops we obtain

$$\frac{\begin{array}{c} \vdots \\ \overline{\langle \neg(M = N), \sigma \rangle \to \mathbf{true}} \end{array}}{}$$

$$\frac{\begin{array}{cc} \vdots & \vdots \\ \overline{\langle \mathbf{if} \ M \leq N \ \mathbf{then} \ N := N - M \ \mathbf{else} \ M := M - N, \sigma \rangle \to \sigma''} & \overline{\langle \text{Euclid}, \sigma'' \rangle \to \sigma'} \end{array}}{\langle \text{Euclid}, \sigma \rangle \to \sigma'}$$

a derivation of $\langle \text{Euclid}, \sigma \rangle \to \sigma'$. Therefore $P(\sigma)$.

By well-founded induction we conclude $\forall \sigma \in S. \ P(\sigma)$, as required. $\square$

Well-founded induction is the most important principle in proving the termination of programs. Uncertainties about termination arise because of loops or recursions in a program. If it can be shown that execution of a loop or recursion in a program decreases the value in a well-founded set then it must eventually terminate.

3.4   Induction on derivations

Structural induction alone is often inadequate to prove properties of operational semantics. Often it is useful to do induction on the structure of derivations. Putting this on a
firm basis involves formalising some of the ideas met in the last chapter.

Possible derivations are determined by means of rules. Instances of rules have the form

$$\frac{}{x} \quad \text{or} \quad \frac{x_1, \ldots, x_n}{x},$$

where the former is an axiom with an empty set of premises and a conclusion x, while the
latter has $\{x_1, \ldots, x_n\}$ as its set of premises and x as its conclusion. The rules specify
how to construct derivations, and through these define a set. The set defined by the
rules consists precisely of those elements for which there is a derivation. A derivation of
an element x takes the form of a tree which is either an instance of an axiom

$$\frac{}{x}$$

or of the form

$$\frac{\vdots \qquad \vdots}{x_1 \quad , \ldots, \quad x_n}$$
$$x$$

which includes derivations of $x_1, \ldots, x_n$, the premises of a rule instance with conclusion
x. In such a derivation we think of $\frac{\vdots}{x_1}, \cdots, \frac{\vdots}{x_n}$ as subderivations of the larger derivation
of x.

Rule instances are got from rules by substituting actual terms or values for metavariables in them. All the rules we are interested in are *finitary* in that their premises are
finite. Consequently, all rule instances have a finite, possibly empty set of premises and a
conclusion. We start a formalisation of derivations from the idea of a set of rule instances.

A *set of rule instances* R consists of elements which are pairs (X/y) where X is a finite
set and y is an element. Such a pair (X/y) is called a *rule instance* with *premises* X
and *conclusion* y.

We are more used to seeing rule instances (X/y) as

$$\frac{}{y} \quad \text{if } X = \emptyset, \text{ and as} \quad \frac{x_1, \cdots, x_n}{y} \quad \text{if } X = \{x_1, \cdots, x_n\}.$$

Assume a set of rule instances R. An *R-derivation* of y is either a rule instance $(\emptyset/y)$ or
a pair $(\{d_1, \cdots, d_n\}/y)$ where $(\{x_1, \cdots, x_n\}/y)$ is a rule instance and d_1 is an R-derivation

of $x_1, \ldots, d_n$ is an R-derivation of x_n. We write $d \Vdash_R y$ to mean d is an R-derivation of y. Thus

$\quad (\emptyset/y) \Vdash_R y$ if $(\emptyset/y) \in R$, and

$\quad (\{d_1, \cdots, d_n\}/y) \Vdash_R y$ if $(\{x_1, \cdots, x_n\}/y) \in R$ & $d_1 \Vdash_R x_1$ & $\cdots$ & $d_n \Vdash_R x_n$.

We say y is derived from R if there is an R-derivation of y, i.e. $d \Vdash_R y$ for some derivation d. We write $\Vdash_R y$ to mean y is derived from R. When the rules are understood we shall write just $d \Vdash y$ and $\Vdash y$.

In operational semantics the premises and conclusions are tuples. There,

$$\Vdash \langle c, \sigma \rangle \to \sigma',$$

meaning $\langle c, \sigma \rangle \to \sigma'$ is derivable from the operational semantics of commands, is customarily written as just $\langle c, \sigma \rangle \to \sigma'$. It is understood that $\langle c, \sigma \rangle \to \sigma'$ includes, as part of its meaning, that it is derivable. We shall only write $\Vdash \langle c, \sigma \rangle \to \sigma'$ when we wish to emphasise that there is a derivation.

Let d, d' be derivations. Say d' is an *immediate subderivation* of d, written $d' \prec_1 d$, iff d has the form (D/y) with $d' \in D$. Write $\prec$ for the transitive closure of $\prec_1$, i.e. $\prec = \prec_1^+$. We say d' is a proper subderivation of d iff $d' \prec d$.

Because derivations are finite, both relations of being an immediate subderivation $\prec_1$ and that of being a proper subderivation are well-founded. This fact can be used to show the execution of commands is deterministic.

Theorem 3.11 *Let c be a command and σ_0 a state. If $\langle c, \sigma_0 \rangle \to \sigma_1$ and $\langle c, \sigma_0 \rangle \to \sigma$, then $\sigma = \sigma_1$, for all states σ, σ_1.*

Proof: The proof proceeds by well-founded induction on the proper subderivation relation $\prec$ between derivations for the execution of commands. The property we shall show holds of all such derivations d is the following:

$$P(d) \iff \forall c \in \mathbf{Com}, \sigma_0, \sigma, \sigma_1, \in \Sigma.\ d \Vdash \langle c, \sigma_0 \rangle \to \sigma\ \&\ \langle c, \sigma_0 \rangle \to \sigma_1 \Rightarrow \sigma = \sigma_1.$$

By the principle of well-founded induction, it suffices to show $\forall d' \prec d.\ P(d')$ implies $P(d)$.

Let d be a derivation from the operational semantics of commands. Assume $\forall d' \prec d.\ P(d')$. Suppose

$$d \Vdash \langle c, \sigma_0 \rangle \to \sigma \text{ and } \Vdash \langle c, \sigma_0 \rangle \to \sigma_1.$$

Then $d_1 \Vdash \langle c, \sigma_0 \rangle \to \sigma_1$ for some d_1.

Now we show by cases on the structure of c that $\sigma = \sigma_1$.

$c \equiv$ **skip**: In this case

$$d = d_1 = \frac{}{\langle \mathbf{skip}, \sigma_0 \rangle \to \sigma_0}.$$

$c \equiv X := a$: Both derivations have a similar form:

$$d = \frac{\vdots \quad \langle a, \sigma_0 \rangle \to m}{\langle X := a, \sigma_0 \rangle \to \sigma_0[m/X]} \qquad d_1 = \frac{\vdots \quad \langle a, \sigma_0 \rangle \to m_1}{\langle X := a, \sigma_0 \rangle \to \sigma_0[m_1/X]}$$

where $\sigma = \sigma_0[m/X]$ and $\sigma_1 = \sigma_0[m_1/X]$. As the evaluation of arithmetic expressions is deterministic $m = m_1$, so $\sigma = \sigma_1$.

$c \equiv c_0; c_1$: In this case

$$d = \frac{\langle c_0, \sigma_0 \rangle \to \sigma' \quad \langle c_1, \sigma' \rangle \to \sigma}{\langle c_0; c_1, \sigma_0 \rangle \to \sigma} \qquad d_1 = \frac{\langle c_0, \sigma_0 \rangle \to \sigma_1' \quad \langle c_1, \sigma_1' \rangle \to \sigma_1}{\langle c_0; c_1, \sigma_0 \rangle \to \sigma_1}.$$

Let d^0 be the subderivation

$$\frac{\vdots}{\langle c_0, \sigma_0 \rangle \to \sigma'}$$

and d^1 the subderivation

$$\frac{\vdots}{\langle c_1, \sigma' \rangle \to \sigma}$$

in d. Then $d^0 \prec d$ and $d^1 \prec d$, so $P(d^0)$ and $P(d^1)$. It follows that $\sigma' = \sigma_1'$, and $\sigma = \sigma_1$ (why?).

$c \equiv$ **if** b **then** c_0 **else** c_1: The rule for conditionals which applies in this case is determined by how the boolean b evaluates. By the exercises of Section 3.2, its evaluation is deterministic so either $\langle b, \sigma_0 \rangle \to \mathbf{true}$ or $\langle b, \sigma_0 \rangle \to \mathbf{false}$, but not both.

When $\langle b, \sigma_0 \rangle \to \mathbf{true}$ we have:

$$d = \frac{\langle b, \sigma_0 \rangle \to \mathbf{true} \quad \langle c_0, \sigma_0 \rangle \to \sigma}{\langle \mathbf{if}\ b\ \mathbf{then}\ c_0\ \mathbf{else}\ c_1, \sigma_0 \rangle \to \sigma} \qquad d_1 = \frac{\langle b, \sigma_0 \rangle \to \mathbf{true} \quad \langle c_0, \sigma_0 \rangle \to \sigma_1}{\langle \mathbf{if}\ b\ \mathbf{then}\ c_0\ \mathbf{else}\ c_1, \sigma_0 \rangle \to \sigma_1}.$$

Let d' be the subderivation of $\langle c_0, \sigma_0 \rangle \to \sigma$ in d. Then $d' \prec d$. Hence $P(d')$. Thus $\sigma = \sigma_1$. When $\langle b, \sigma_0 \rangle \to$ **false** the argument is similar.

$c \equiv$ **while** b **do** c: The rule for while-loops which applies is again determined by how b evaluates. Either $\langle b, \sigma_0 \rangle \to$ **true** or $\langle b, \sigma \rangle \to$ **false**, but not both.

When $\langle b, \sigma_0 \rangle \to$ **false** we have :

$$d = \frac{\displaystyle \vdots \atop \langle b, \sigma_0 \rangle \to \textbf{false}}{\langle \textbf{while } b \textbf{ do } c, \sigma_0 \rangle \to \sigma_0} \qquad d_1 = \frac{\displaystyle \vdots \atop \langle b, \sigma_0 \rangle \to \textbf{false}}{\langle \textbf{while } b \textbf{ do } c, \sigma_0 \rangle \to \sigma_0}$$

so certainly $\sigma = \sigma_0 = \sigma_1$.

When $\langle b, \sigma_0 \rangle \to$ **true** we have:

$$d = \frac{\begin{array}{ccc} \vdots & \vdots & \vdots \\ \langle b, \sigma_0 \rangle \to \textbf{true} & \langle c, \sigma_0 \rangle \to \sigma' & \langle \textbf{while } b \textbf{ do } c, \sigma' \rangle \to \sigma \end{array}}{\langle \textbf{while } b \textbf{ do } c, \sigma_0 \rangle \to \sigma}$$

$$d_1 = \frac{\begin{array}{ccc} \vdots & \vdots & \vdots \\ \langle b, \sigma_0 \rangle \to \textbf{true} & \langle c, \sigma_0 \rangle \to \sigma_1' & \langle \textbf{while } b \textbf{ do } c, \sigma_1' \rangle \to \sigma_1 \end{array}}{\langle \textbf{while } b \textbf{ do } c, \sigma_0 \rangle \to \sigma_1}$$

Let d' be the subderivation of $\langle c, \sigma_0 \rangle \to \sigma'$ and d'' the subderivation of $\langle \textbf{while } b \textbf{ do } c, \sigma' \rangle \to \sigma$ in d. Then $d' \prec d$ and $d'' \prec d$ so $P(d')$ and $P(d'')$. It follows that $\sigma' = \sigma_1'$, and subsequently that $\sigma = \sigma_1$.

In all cases of c we have shown $d \Vdash \langle c, \sigma_0 \rangle \to \sigma$ and $\langle c, \sigma_0 \rangle \to \sigma_1$ implies $\sigma = \sigma_1$.

By the principle of well-founded induction we conclude that $P(d)$ holds for all derivations d for the execution of commands. This is equivalent to

$$\forall c \in \textbf{Com}, \sigma_0, \sigma, \sigma_1, \in \Sigma.\ \langle c, \sigma_0 \rangle \to \sigma \ \&\ \langle c, \sigma_0 \rangle \to \sigma_1 \Rightarrow \sigma = \sigma_1,$$

which proves the theorem. $\square$

As was remarked, Proposition 3.7 provides an alternative to proofs by well-founded induction. Induction on derivations is a special kind of well-founded induction used to prove a property holds of all derivations. Instead, we can attempt to produce a contradiction from the assumption that there is a minimal derivation for which the property is false. The approach is illustrated below:

Proposition 3.12 *For all states σ, σ',*

$$\langle \text{while true do skip}, \sigma \rangle \not\rightarrow \sigma'.$$

Proof: Abbreviate $w \equiv \textbf{while true do skip}$. Suppose $\langle w, \sigma \rangle \rightarrow \sigma'$ for some states σ, σ'. Then there is a minimal derivation d such that $\exists \sigma, \sigma' \in \Sigma$. $d \Vdash \langle w, \sigma \rangle \rightarrow \sigma'$. Only one rule can be the final rule of d, making d of the form:

$$d = \frac{\overline{\langle \text{true}, \sigma \rangle \rightarrow \text{true}} \quad \langle c, \sigma \rangle \rightarrow \sigma'' \quad \langle \text{while true do } c, \sigma'' \rangle \rightarrow \sigma'}{\langle \text{while true do } c, \sigma \rangle \rightarrow \sigma'}$$

But this contains a proper subderivation $d' \Vdash \langle w, \sigma \rangle \rightarrow \sigma'$, contradicting the minimality of d. $\qquad\qquad\qquad\qquad\qquad\qquad\qquad\qquad\qquad\qquad\qquad\qquad\qquad\qquad\qquad\qquad\square$

3.5 Definitions by induction

Techniques like structural induction are often used to define operations on the set defined. Integers and arithmetic expressions share a common property, that of being built-up in a unique way. An integer is either zero or the successor of a unique integer, while an arithmetic expression is either atomic or a sum, or product *etc.* of a unique pair of expressions. It is by virtue of their being built up in a unique way that we can can make definitions by induction on integers and expressions. For example to define the length of an expression it is natural to define it in terms of the lengths of its components. For arithmetic expressions we can define

$$\text{length}(n) = \text{length}(X) = 1,$$
$$\text{length}(a_0 + a_1) = 1 + \text{length}(a_0) + \text{length}(a_1),$$
$$\dots$$

For future reference we define $\text{loc}_L(c)$, the set of those locations which appear on the left of an assignment in a command. For a command c, the function $\text{loc}_L(c)$ is defined by structural induction by taking

$$\text{loc}_L(\textbf{skip}) = \emptyset, \quad \text{loc}_L(X := a) = \{X\},$$
$$\text{loc}_L(c_0; c_1) = \text{loc}_L(c_0) \cup \text{loc}_L(c_1), \quad \text{loc}_L(\textbf{if } b \textbf{ then } c_0 \textbf{ else } c_1) = \text{loc}_L(c_0) \cup \text{loc}_L(c_1),$$
$$\text{loc}_L(\textbf{while } b \textbf{ do } c) = \text{loc}_L(c).$$

In a similar way one defines operations on the natural numbers by mathematical induction and operations defined on sets given by rules. In fact the proof of Proposition 3.7, that every nonempty subset of a well-founded set has a minimal element, contains an implicit use of definition by induction on the natural numbers to construct a chain with a minimal element in the nonempty set.

Both definition by structural induction and definition by mathematical induction are special cases of definition by well-founded induction, also called *well-founded recursion*. To understand this name, notice that both definition by induction and structural induction allow a form of recursive definition. For example, the length of an arithmetic expression could have been defined in this manner:

$$\text{length}(a) = \begin{cases} 1 & \text{if } a \equiv n, \text{ a number} \\ \text{length}(a_0) + \text{length}(a_1) & \text{if } a \equiv (a_0 + a_1), \\ \vdots \end{cases}$$

How the length function acts on a particular argument, like $(a_0 + a_1)$ is specified in terms of how the length function acts on other arguments, like a_0 and a_1. In this sense the definition of the length function is defined recursively in terms of itself. However this recursion is done in such a way that the value on a particular argument is only specified in terms of strictly smaller arguments. In a similar way we are entitled to define functions on an arbitrary well-founded set. The general principle is more difficult to understand, resting as it does on some relatively sophisticated constructions on sets, and for this reason its full treatment is postponed to Section 10.4. (Although the material won't be needed until then, the curious or impatient reader might care to glance ahead. Despite its late appearance that section does not depend on any additional concepts.)

Exercise 3.13 Give definitions by structural induction of $\text{loc}(a)$, $\text{loc}(b)$ and $\text{loc}_R(c)$, the sets of locations which appear in arithmetic expressions a, boolean expressions b and the right-hand sides of assignments in commands c. □

3.6   Further reading

The techniques and ideas discussed in this chapter are well-known, basic techniques within mathematical logic. As operational semantics follows the lines of natural deduction, it is not surprising that it shares basic techniques with proof theory, as presented in [84] for example—derivations are really a simple kind of proof. For a fairly advanced, though accessible, account of proof theory with a computer science slant see [51, 40], which contains much more on notations for proofs (and so derivations). Further explanation and uses of well-founded induction can be found in [59] and [21], where it is called "structural induction", in [58] and [73]), and here, especially in Chapter 10.

4 Inductive definitions

This chapter is an introduction to the theory of inductively defined sets, of which presentations of syntax and operational semantics are examples. Sets inductively defined by rules are shown to be the least sets closed under the rules. As such, a principle of induction, called rule induction, accompanies the constructions. It specialises to proof rules for reasoning about the operational semantics of **IMP**.

4.1 Rule induction

We defined the syntactic set of arithmetic expressions **Aexp** as the set obtained from the formation rules for arithmetic expressions. We have seen there is a corresponding induction principle, that of structural induction on arithmetic expressions. We have defined the operational semantics of while-programs by defining evaluation and execution relations as relations given by rules which relate evaluation or execution of terms to the evaluation or execution of their components. For example, the evaluation relation on arithmetic expressions was defined by the rules of Section 2.2 as a ternary relation which is the set consisting of triples (a, σ, n) of **Aexp** $\times \Sigma \times \mathbf{N}$ such that $\langle a, \sigma \rangle \rightarrow n$. There is a corresponding induction principle which we can see as a special case of a principle we call rule induction.

We are interested in defining a set by rules. Viewed abstractly, instances of rules have the form $(\emptyset/x)$ or $(\{x_1, \ldots, x_n\}/x)$. Given a set of rule instances R, we write I_R for the set defined by R consisting of precisely of those elements x for which there is a derivation. Put another way

$$I_R = \{x \mid \Vdash_R x\}.$$

The principle of rule induction is useful to show a property is true of all the elements in a set defined by some rules. It is based on the idea that if a property is preserved in moving from the premises to the conclusion of all rule instances in a derivation then the conclusion of the derivation has the property, so the property is true of all elements in the set defined by the rules.

The general principle of rule induction

Let I_R be defined by rule instances R. Let P be a property. Then $\forall x \in I_R.\ P(x)$ iff for all rule instances (X/y) in R for which $X \subseteq I_R$

$$(\forall x \in X.\ P(x)) \Rightarrow P(y).$$

Notice for rule instances of the form (X/y), with $X = \emptyset$, the last condition is equivalent to $P(y)$. Certainly then $\forall x \in X.\ x \in I_R \ \& \ P(x)$ is vacuously true because any x in $\emptyset$

satisfies P—there are none. The statement of rule induction amounts to the following. For rule instances R, we have $\forall y \in I_R. \ P(y)$ iff for all instances of axioms

$$\frac{}{x}$$

$P(x)$ is true, and for all rule instances

$$\frac{x_1, \ldots, x_n}{x}$$

if $x_k \in I_R$ & $P(x_k)$ is true for all the premises, when k ranges from 1 to n, then $P(x)$ is true of the conclusion.

The principle of rule induction is fairly intuitive. It corresponds to a superficially different, but equivalent method more commonly employed in mathematics. (This observation will also lead to a proof of the validity of rule induction.) We say a set Q is *closed* under rule instances R, or simply *R-closed*, iff for all rule instances (X/y)

$$X \subseteq Q \Rightarrow y \in Q.$$

In other words, a set is closed under the rule instances if whenever the premises of any rule instance lie in the set so does its conclusion. In particular, an R-closed set must contain all the instances of axioms. The set I_R is the least set closed under R in this sense:

Proposition 4.1 *With respect to rule instances R*
  (i) *I_R is R-closed, and*
  (ii) *if Q is an R-closed set then $I_R \subseteq Q$.*

Proof:
(i) It is easy to see I_R is closed under R. Suppose (X/y) is an instance of a rule in R and that $X \subseteq I_R$. Then from the definition of I_R there are derivations of each element of X. If X is nonempty these derivations can be combined with the rule instance (X/y) to provide a derivation of y, and, otherwise, $(\emptyset/y)$ provides a derivation immediately. In either case we obtain a derivation of y which must therefore be in I_R too. Hence I_R is closed under R.
(ii) Suppose that Q is R-closed. We want to show $I_R \subseteq Q$. Any element of I_R is the conclusion of some derivation. But any derivation is built out of rule instances (X/y). If the premises X are in Q then so is the conclusion y (in particular, the conclusion of any axiom will be in Q). Hence we can work our way down any derivation, starting at

axioms, to show its conclusion is in Q. More formally, we can do an induction on the proper subderivation relation $\prec$ to show

$$\forall y \in I_R.\ d \Vdash_R y \Rightarrow y \in Q$$

for all R-derivations d. Therefore $I_R \subseteq Q$. $\square$

Exercise 4.2 Do the induction on derivations mentioned in the proof above. $\square$

Suppose we wish to show a property P is true of all elements of I_R, the set defined by rules R. The conditions (i) and (ii) in the proposition above furnish a method. Defining the set

$$Q = \{x \in I_R \mid P(x)\},$$

the property P is true of all elements of I_R iff $I_R \subseteq Q$. By condition (ii), to show $I_R \subseteq Q$ it suffices to show that Q is R-closed. This will follow if for all rule instances (X/y)

$$(\forall x \in X.\ x \in I_R\ \&\ P(x)) \Rightarrow P(y)$$

But this is precisely what is required by rule induction to prove the property P holds for all elements of I_R. The truth of this statement is not just sufficient but also necessary to show the property P of all elements of I_R. Suppose $P(x)$ for all $x \in I_R$. Let (X/y) be a rule instance such that

$$\forall x \in X.\ x \in I_R\ \&\ P(x).$$

By (i), saying I_R is R-closed, we get $y \in I_R$, and so that $P(y)$. And in this way we have derived the principle of rule induction from (i) and (ii), saying that I_R is the least R-closed set.

Exercise 4.3 For rule instances R, show

$$\bigcap \{Q \mid Q \text{ is } R\text{-closed}\}$$

is R-closed. What is this set? $\square$

Exercise 4.4 Let the rules consist of $(\emptyset/0)$ and $(\{n\}/(n+1))$ where n is a natural number. What is the set defined by the rules and what is rule induction in this case? $\square$

In presenting rules we have followed the same style as that used in giving operational semantics. When it comes to defining syntactic sets by rules, BNF is the traditional way though it can be done differently. For instance, what is traditionally written as

$$a ::= \cdots \mid a_0 + a_1 \mid \cdots,$$

saying that if a_0 and a_1 are well-formed expressions arithmetic expressions then so is $a_0 + a_1$, could instead be written as

$$\frac{a_0 : \mathbf{Aexp} \quad a_1 : \mathbf{Aexp}}{a_0 + a_1 : \mathbf{Aexp}}.$$

This way of presenting syntax is becoming more usual.

Exercise 4.5 What is rule induction in the case where the rules are the formation rules for **Aexp**? What about when the rules are those for boolean expressions? (Careful! See the next section.)   □

4.2   Special rule induction

Thinking of the syntactic sets of boolean expressions and commands it is clear that sometimes a syntactic set is given by rules which involve elements from another syntactic set. For example, the formation rules for commands say how commands can be formed from arithmetic and boolean expressions, as well as other commands. The formation rules

$$c ::= \cdots \mid X := a \mid \cdots \mid \mathbf{if}\ b\ \mathbf{then}\ c_0\ \mathbf{else}\ c_1 \mid \cdots,$$

can, for the sake of uniformity, be written as

$$\frac{X : \mathbf{Loc} \quad a : \mathbf{Aexp}}{X := a : \mathbf{Com}} \quad \text{and} \quad \frac{b : \mathbf{Bexp} \quad c_0 : \mathbf{Com} \quad c_1 : \mathbf{Com}}{\mathbf{if}\ b\ \mathbf{then}\ c_0\ \mathbf{else}\ c_1 : \mathbf{Com}}.$$

Rule induction works by showing properties are preserved by the rules. This means that if we are to use rule induction to prove a property of all commands we must make sure that the property covers all arithmetic and boolean expressions as well. As it stands, the principle of rule induction does not instantiate to structural induction on commands, but to a considerably more awkward proof principle, simultaneously combining structural induction on commands with that on arithmetic and boolean expressions. A modified principle of rule induction is required for establishing properties of *subsets* of the set defined by rules.

The special principle of rule induction

Let I_R be defined by rule instances R. Let $A \subseteq I_R$. Let Q be a property. Then $\forall a \in A.\ Q(a)$ iff for all rule instances (X/y) in R, with $X \subseteq I_R$ and $y \in A$,

$$(\forall x \in X \cap A.\ Q(x)) \Rightarrow Q(y).$$

The special principle of rule induction actually follows from the general principle. Let R be a set of rule instances. Let A be a subset of I_R, the set defined by R. Suppose $Q(x)$ is a property we are interested in showing is true of all elements of A. Define a corresponding property $P(x)$ by

$$P(x) \iff (x \in A \Rightarrow Q(x)).$$

Showing $Q(a)$ for all $a \in A$ is equivalent to showing that $P(x)$ is true for all $x \in I_R$. By the general principle of rule induction the latter is equivalent to

$$\forall (X/y) \in R. \quad X \subseteq I_R \ \& \ (\forall x \in X.(x \in A \Rightarrow Q(x))) \Rightarrow (y \in A \Rightarrow Q(y)).$$

But this is logically equivalent to

$$\forall (X/y) \in R. \quad (X \subseteq I_R \ \& \ y \in A \ \& \ (\forall x \in X.(x \in A \Rightarrow Q(x)))) \Rightarrow Q(y).$$

This is equivalent to the condition required by the special principle of rule induction.

Exercise 4.6 Explain how structural induction for commands and booleans follows from the special principle of rule induction.   □

Because the special principle follows from the general, any proof using the special principle can be replaced by one using the principle of general rule induction. But in practice use of the special principle can drastically cut down the number of rules to consider, a welcome feature when it comes to considering rule induction for operational semantics.

4.3 Proof rules for operational semantics

Not surprisingly, rule induction can be a useful tool for proving properties of operational semantics presented by rules, though then it generally takes a superficially different form because the sets defined by the rules are sets of tuples. This section presents the special cases of rule induction which we will use later in reasoning about the operational behaviour of **IMP** programs.

4.3.1 Rule induction for arithmetic expressions

The principle of rule induction for the evaluation of arithmetic expressions is got from the rules for their operational semantics. It is an example of rule induction; a property $P(a, \sigma, n)$ is true of all evaluations $\langle a, \sigma \rangle \to n$ iff it is preserved by the rules for building up the evaluation relation.

$$\forall a \in \mathbf{Aexp}, \sigma \in \Sigma, n \in \mathbf{N}. \quad \langle a, \sigma \rangle \to n \Rightarrow P(a, \sigma, n)$$

iff

$$[\forall n \in \mathbf{N}, \sigma \in \Sigma. \ P(n, \sigma, n)$$

&

$$\forall X \in \mathbf{Loc}, \sigma \in \Sigma. \ P(X, \sigma, \sigma(X))$$

&

$$\forall a_0, a_1 \in \mathbf{Aexp}, \sigma \in \Sigma, n_0, n_1 \in \mathbf{N}.$$
$$\langle a_0, \sigma \rangle \to n_0 \ \& \ P(a_0, \sigma, n_0) \ \& \ \langle a_1, \sigma \rangle \to n_1 \ \& \ P(a_1, \sigma, n_1)$$
$$\Rightarrow P(a_0 + a_1, \sigma, n_0 + n_1)$$

&

$$\forall a_0, a_1 \in \mathbf{Aexp}, \sigma \in \Sigma, n_0, n_1 \in \mathbf{N}.$$
$$\langle a_0, \sigma \rangle \to n_0 \ \& \ P(a_0, \sigma, n_0) \ \& \ \langle a_1, \sigma \rangle \to n_1 \ \& \ P(a_1, \sigma, n_1)$$
$$\Rightarrow P(a_0 - a_1, \sigma, n_0 - n_1)$$

&

$$\forall a_0, a_1 \in \mathbf{Aexp}, \sigma \in \Sigma, n_0, n_1 \in \mathbf{N}.$$
$$\langle a_0, \sigma \rangle \to n_0 \ \& \ P(a_0, \sigma, n_0) \ \& \ \langle a_1, \sigma \rangle \to n_1 \ \& \ P(a_1, \sigma, n_1)$$
$$\Rightarrow P(a_0 \times a_1, \sigma, n_0 \times n_1)].$$

Compare this specific principle with that for general rule induction. Notice how all possible rule instances are covered by considering one evaluation rule at a time.

4.3.2 Rule induction for boolean expressions

The rules for the evaluation of boolean expressions involve those for the evaluation of arithmetic expressions. Together the rules define a subset of

$$(\mathbf{Aexp} \times \Sigma \times \mathbf{N}) \cup (\mathbf{Bexp} \times \Sigma \times \mathbf{T}).$$

A principle useful for reasoning about the operational semantics of boolean expressions is got from the special principle of rule induction for properties $P(b, \sigma, t)$ on the subset $\mathbf{Bexp} \times \Sigma \times \mathbf{T}$.

$\forall b \in \mathbf{Bexp}, \sigma \in \Sigma, t \in \mathbf{T}. \quad \langle b, \sigma \rangle \to t \Rightarrow P(b, \sigma, t)$

iff

$[\forall \sigma \in \Sigma. \; P(\mathbf{false}, \sigma, \mathbf{false}) \; \& \; \forall \sigma \in \Sigma. \; P(\mathbf{true}, \sigma, \mathbf{true})$

&

$\forall a_0, a_1 \in \mathbf{Aexp}, \sigma \in \Sigma, m, n \in \mathbf{N}.$

$\langle a_0, \sigma \rangle \to m \; \& \; \langle a_1, \sigma \rangle \to n \; \& \; m = n \Rightarrow P(a_0 = a_1, \sigma, \mathbf{true})$

&

$\forall a_0, a_1 \in \mathbf{Aexp}, \sigma \in \Sigma, m, n \in \mathbf{N}.$

$\langle a_0, \sigma \rangle \to m \; \& \; \langle a_1, \sigma \rangle \to n \; \& \; m \neq n \Rightarrow P(a_0 = a_1, \sigma, \mathbf{false})$

&

$\forall a_0, a_1 \in \mathbf{Aexp}, \sigma \in \Sigma, m, n \in \mathbf{N}.$

$\langle a_0, \sigma \rangle \to m \; \& \; \langle a_1, \sigma \rangle \to n \; \& \; m \leq n \Rightarrow P(a_0 \leq a_1, \sigma, \mathbf{true})$

&

$\forall a_0, a_1 \in \mathbf{Aexp}, \sigma \in \Sigma, m, n \in \mathbf{N}.$

$\langle a_0, \sigma \rangle \to m \; \& \; \langle a_1, \sigma \rangle \to n \; \& \; m \nleq n \Rightarrow P(a_0 \leq a_1, \sigma, \mathbf{false})$

&

$\forall b \in \mathbf{Bexp}, \sigma \in \Sigma, t \in \mathbf{T}.$

$\langle b, \sigma \rangle \to t \; \& \; P(b, \sigma, t) \Rightarrow P(\neg b, \sigma, \neg t)$

&

$\forall b_0, b_1 \in \mathbf{Bexp}, \sigma \in \Sigma, t_0, t_1 \in \mathbf{T}.$

$\langle b_0, \sigma \rangle \to t_0 \; \& \; P(b_0, \sigma, t_0) \; \& \; \langle b_1, \sigma \rangle \to t_1 \; \& \; P(b_1, \sigma, t_1) \Rightarrow P(b_0 \wedge b_1, \sigma, t_0 \wedge t_1)$

&

$\forall b_0, b_1 \in \mathbf{Bexp}, \sigma \in \Sigma, t_0, t_1 \in \mathbf{T}.$

$\langle b_0, \sigma \rangle \to t_0 \; \& \; P(b_0, \sigma, t_0) \; \& \; \langle b_1, \sigma \rangle \to t_1 \; \& \; P(b_1, \sigma, t_1) \Rightarrow P(b_0 \vee b_1, \sigma, t_0 \vee t_1)].$

4.3.3 Rule induction for commands

The principle of rule induction we use for reasoning about the operational semantics of commands is an instance of the special principle of rule induction. The rules for the execution of commands involve the evaluation of arithmetic and boolean expressions. The rules for the operational semantics of the different syntactic sets taken together define a subset of

$$(\mathbf{Aexp} \times \Sigma \times \mathbf{N}) \cup (\mathbf{Bexp} \times \Sigma \times \mathbf{T}) \cup (\mathbf{Com} \times \Sigma \times \Sigma).$$

We use the special principle for properties $P(c, \sigma, \sigma')$ on the subset $\mathbf{Com} \times \Sigma \times \Sigma$. (Try to write it down and compare your result with the following.)

$\forall c \in \mathbf{Com}, \sigma, \sigma' \in \Sigma. \quad \langle c, \sigma \rangle \to \sigma' \Rightarrow P(c, \sigma, \sigma')$

iff

$[\forall \sigma \in \Sigma. \ P(\mathbf{skip}, \sigma, \sigma)$

&

$\forall X \in \mathbf{Loc}, a \in \mathbf{Aexp}, \sigma \in \Sigma, m \in \mathbf{N}. \ \langle a, \sigma \rangle \to m \Rightarrow P(X := a, \sigma, \sigma[m/X])$

&

$\forall c_0, c_1 \in \mathbf{Com}, \sigma, \sigma', \sigma'' \in \Sigma.$

$\langle c_0, \sigma \rangle \to \sigma'' \ \& \ P(c_0, \sigma, \sigma'') \ \& \ \langle c_1, \sigma'' \rangle \to \sigma' \ \& \ P(c_1, \sigma'', \sigma') \Rightarrow P(c_0; c_1, \sigma, \sigma')$

&

$\forall c_0, c_1 \in \mathbf{Com}, b \in \mathbf{Bexp}, \sigma, \sigma' \in \Sigma.$

$\langle b, \sigma \rangle \to \mathbf{true} \ \& \ \langle c_0, \sigma \rangle \to \sigma' \ \& \ P(c_0, \sigma, \sigma') \Rightarrow P(\mathbf{if} \ b \ \mathbf{then} \ c_0 \ \mathbf{else} \ c_1, \sigma, \sigma')$

&

$\forall c_0, c_1 \in \mathbf{Com}, b \in \mathbf{Bexp}, \sigma, \sigma' \in \Sigma.$

$\langle b, \sigma \rangle \to \mathbf{false} \ \& \ \langle c_1, \sigma \rangle \to \sigma' \ \& \ P(c_1, \sigma, \sigma') \Rightarrow P(\mathbf{if} \ b \ \mathbf{then} \ c_0 \ \mathbf{else} \ c_1, \sigma, \sigma')$

&

$\forall c \in \mathbf{Com}, b \in \mathbf{Bexp}, \sigma \in \Sigma.$

$\langle b, \sigma \rangle \to \mathbf{false} \Rightarrow P(\mathbf{while} \ b \ \mathbf{do} \ c, \sigma, \sigma)$

&

$\forall c \in \mathbf{Com}, b \in \mathbf{Bexp}, \sigma, \sigma', \sigma'' \in \Sigma.$

$\langle b, \sigma \rangle \to \mathbf{true} \ \& \ \langle c, \sigma \rangle \to \sigma'' \ \& \ P(c, \sigma, \sigma'') \ \&$

$\langle \mathbf{while} \ b \ \mathbf{do} \ c, \sigma'' \rangle \to \sigma' \ \& \ P(\mathbf{while} \ b \ \mathbf{do} \ c, \sigma'', \sigma')$

$\Rightarrow P(\mathbf{while} \ b \ \mathbf{do} \ c, \sigma, \sigma')].$

As an example, we apply rule induction to show the intuitively obvious fact that if a location Y does not occur in the left hand side of an assignment in a command c then execution of c cannot affect its value. Recall the definition of the locations $\mathrm{loc}_L(c)$ of a command c given in Section 3.5.

Proposition 4.7 *Let $Y \in \mathbf{Loc}$. For all commands c and states σ, σ',*

$$Y \notin loc_L(c) \ \& \ \langle c, \sigma \rangle \to \sigma' \Rightarrow \sigma(Y) = \sigma'(Y).$$

Proof: Let P be the property given by:

$$P(c, \sigma, \sigma') \iff (Y \notin loc_L(c) \Rightarrow \sigma(Y) = \sigma'(Y)).$$

We use rule induction on commands to show that

$$\forall c \in \mathbf{Com}, \sigma, \sigma' \in \Sigma. \ \langle c, \sigma \rangle \to \sigma' \Rightarrow P(c, \sigma, \sigma').$$

Clearly $P(\mathbf{skip}, \sigma, \sigma)$ for any $\sigma \in \Sigma$.

Let $X \in \mathbf{Loc}, a \in \mathbf{Aexp}, \sigma \in \Sigma, m \in \mathbf{N}$. Assume $\langle a, \sigma \rangle \to m$. If $Y \notin loc_L(X := a)$ then $Y \not\equiv X$, so $\sigma(Y) = \sigma[m/X](Y)$. Hence $P(X := a, \sigma, \sigma[m/X])$.

Let $c_0, c_1 \in \mathbf{Com}, \sigma, \sigma' \in \Sigma$. Assume

$$\langle c_0, \sigma \rangle \to \sigma'' \ \& \ P(c_0, \sigma, \sigma'') \ \& \ \langle c_1, \sigma'' \rangle \to \sigma' \ \& \ P(c_1, \sigma'', \sigma'),$$

i.e., that

$$\langle c_0, \sigma \rangle \to \sigma'' \ \& \ (Y \notin loc_L(c_0) \Rightarrow \sigma(Y) = \sigma''(Y)) \ \&$$
$$\langle c_1, \sigma'' \rangle \to \sigma' \ \& \ (Y \notin loc_L(c_1) \Rightarrow \sigma''(Y) = \sigma'(Y)).$$

Suppose $Y \notin loc_L(c_0; c_1)$. Then, as $loc_L(c_0; c_1) = loc_L(c_0) \cup loc_L(c_1)$, we obtain $Y \notin loc_L(c_0)$ and $Y \notin loc_L(c_1)$. Thus, from the assumption, $\sigma(Y) = \sigma''(Y) = \sigma'(Y)$. Hence $P(c_0; c_1, \sigma, \sigma')$.

We shall only consider one other case of rule instances.

Let $c \in \mathbf{Com}, b \in \mathbf{Bexp}, \sigma, \sigma', \sigma'' \in \Sigma$. Let $w \equiv \mathbf{while} \ b \ \mathbf{do} \ c$. Assume

$$\langle b, \sigma \rangle \to \mathbf{true} \ \& \ \langle c, \sigma \rangle \to \sigma'' \ \& \ P(c, \sigma, \sigma'') \ \&$$
$$\langle w, \sigma'' \rangle \to \sigma' \ \& \ P(w, \sigma'', \sigma')$$

i.e.,

$$\langle b, \sigma \rangle \to \mathbf{true} \ \& \ \langle c, \sigma \rangle \to \sigma'' \ \& \ (Y \notin loc_L(c) \Rightarrow \sigma(Y) = \sigma''(Y)) \ \&$$
$$\langle w, \sigma'' \rangle \to \sigma' \ \& \ (Y \notin loc_L(w) \Rightarrow \sigma''(Y) = \sigma'(Y)).$$

Suppose $Y \notin loc_L(w)$. By the assumption $\sigma''(Y) = \sigma'(Y)$. Also, as $loc_L(w) = loc_L(c)$, we see $Y \notin loc_L(c)$, so by the assumption $\sigma(Y) = \sigma''(Y)$. Thus $\sigma(Y) = \sigma'(Y)$. Hence $P(w, \sigma, \sigma')$.

The other cases are very similar and left as an exercise. $\qquad\qquad\qquad\square$

We shall see many more proofs by rule induction in subsequent chapters. In general they will be smooth and direct arguments. Here are some more difficult exercises on using rule induction. As the first two exercises indicate applications of rule induction can sometimes be tricky.

Exercise 4.8 Let $w \equiv$ **while true do skip**. Prove by special rule induction that

$$\forall \sigma, \sigma'. \ \langle w, \sigma \rangle \not\to \sigma'.$$

(Hint: Apply the special principle of rule induction restricting to the set

$$\{(w, \sigma, \sigma') \mid \sigma, \sigma' \in \Sigma\}$$

and take the property $P(w, \sigma, \sigma')$ to be constantly false.
It is interesting to compare the proof for this exercise with that of Proposition 3.12 in Section 3.4—proofs by rule induction can sometimes be less intuitive than proofs in which the form of derivations is considered.)   □

Although rule induction can be used in place of induction on derivations it is no panacea; exclusive use of rule induction can sometimes make proofs longer and more confusing, as will probably become clear on trying the following exercise:

Exercise 4.9 Take a simplified syntax of arithmetic expressions:

$$a ::= n \mid X \mid a_0 + a_1.$$

The evaluation rules of the simplified expressions are as before:

$$\langle n, \sigma \rangle \to n$$

$$\langle X, \sigma \rangle \to \sigma(X)$$

$$\frac{\langle a_0, \sigma \rangle \to n_0 \quad \langle a_1, \sigma \rangle \to n_1}{\langle a_0 + a_1, \sigma \rangle \to n}$$

where n is the number which is the sum of n_0 and n_1.

By considering the unique form of derivations it is easy to see that $\langle n, \sigma \rangle \to m$ implies $m \equiv n$. Can you see how this follows by special rule induction? Use rule induction on the operational semantics (and not induction on derivations) to show that the evaluation of expressions is deterministic.

(Hint: For the latter, take

$$P(a, \sigma, m) \iff _{def} \forall m' \in \mathbf{N}. \ \langle a, \sigma \rangle \to m' \Rightarrow m = m'$$

as induction hypothesis, and be prepared for a further use of (special) rule induction.) An alternative proof, of Proposition 3.3 in Section 3.2, uses structural induction and considers the forms that derivations could take. How does the proof compare with that of Proposition 3.3?   □

The next, fairly long, exercise proves the equivalence of two operational semantics.

Exercise 4.10 (Long) One operational semantics is that of Chapter 2, based on the relation $\langle c, \sigma \rangle \to \sigma'$. The other is the one-step execution relation $\langle c, \sigma \rangle \to_1 \langle c', \sigma' \rangle$ mentioned previously in Section 2.6, but where, for simplicity, evaluation of expressions is treated in exactly the same way as in Chapter 2. For instance, for the sequencing of two commands there are the rules:

$$\frac{\langle c_0, \sigma \rangle \to_1 \langle c_0', \sigma' \rangle}{\langle c_0; c_1, \sigma \rangle \to_1 \langle c_0'; c_1, \sigma' \rangle} \qquad \frac{\langle c_0, \sigma \rangle \to_1 \sigma'}{\langle c_0; c_1, \sigma \rangle \to_1 \langle c_1, \sigma' \rangle}$$

Start by proving the lemma

$$\langle c_0; c_1, \sigma \rangle \to_1^* \sigma' \text{ iff } \exists \sigma''. \ \langle c_0, \sigma \rangle \to_1^* \sigma'' \ \& \ \langle c_1, \sigma'' \rangle \to_1^* \sigma',$$

for all commands c_0, c_1 and all states σ, σ'. Prove this in two stages. Firstly prove

$$\forall \sigma, \sigma'. \ [\langle c_0; c_1, \sigma \rangle \to_1^n \sigma' \Rightarrow \exists \sigma''. \ \langle c_0, \sigma \rangle \to_1^* \sigma'' \ \& \ \langle c_1, \sigma'' \rangle \to_1^* \sigma']$$

by mathematical induction on n, the length of computation. Secondly prove

$$\forall \sigma, \sigma', \sigma''. \ [\langle c_0, \sigma \rangle \to_1^n \sigma'' \ \& \ \langle c_1, \sigma'' \rangle \to_1^* \sigma' \Rightarrow \langle c_0; c_1, \sigma \rangle \to_1^* \sigma']$$

by mathematical induction on n, this time the length of the execution of c_0 from state σ. Conclude that the lemma holds. Now proceed to the proof of the theorem:

$$\forall \sigma, \sigma'. \ [\langle c, \sigma \rangle \to_1^* \sigma' \text{ iff } \langle c, \sigma \rangle \to \sigma'].$$

The "only if" direction of the proof can be done by structural induction on c, with an induction on the length of the computation in the case where c is a while-loop. The "if" direction of the proof can be done by rule induction (or by induction on derivations). □

4.4   Operators and their least fixed points

There is another way to view a set defined by rules. A set of rule instances R determines an operator $\widehat{R}$ on sets, which given a set B results in a set

$$\widehat{R}(B) = \{y \mid \exists X \subseteq B.\ (X/y) \in R\}.$$

Use of the operator $\widehat{R}$ gives another way of saying a set is R-closed.

Proposition 4.11 *A set B is closed under R iff $\widehat{R}(B) \subseteq B$.*

Proof: The fact follows directly from the definitions. $\square$

   The operator $\widehat{R}$ provides a way of building up the set I_R. The operator $\widehat{R}$ is *monotonic* in the sense that

$$A \subseteq B \Rightarrow \widehat{R}(A) \subseteq \widehat{R}(B).$$

If we repeatedly apply $\widehat{R}$ to the empty set $\emptyset$ we obtain the sequence of sets:

$$A_0 = \widehat{R}^0(\emptyset) = \emptyset,$$
$$A_1 = \widehat{R}^1(\emptyset) = \widehat{R}(\emptyset),$$
$$A_2 = \widehat{R}(\widehat{R}(\emptyset)) = \widehat{R}^2(\emptyset),$$
$$\vdots$$
$$A_n = \widehat{R}^n(\emptyset),$$
$$\vdots$$

The set A_1 consists of all the conclusions of instances of axioms, and in general the set A_{n+1} is all things which immediately follow by rule instances with premises in A_n. Clearly $\emptyset \subseteq \widehat{R}(\emptyset)$, *i.e.* $A_0 \subseteq A_1$. By the monotonicity of $\widehat{R}$ we obtain $\widehat{R}(A_0) \subseteq \widehat{R}(A_1)$, *i.e.* $A_1 \subseteq A_2$. Similarly we obtain $A_2 \subseteq A_3$ *etc.*. Thus the sequence forms a chain

$$A_0 \subseteq A_1 \subseteq \cdots \subseteq A_n \subseteq \cdots.$$

Taking $A = \bigcup_{n \in \omega} A_n$, we have:

Proposition 4.12
   (i) *A is R-closed.*
   (ii) *$\widehat{R}(A) = A$.*
   (iii) *A is the least R-closed set.*

Proof:
(i) Suppose $(X/y) \in R$ with $X \subseteq A$. Recall $A = \bigcup_n A_n$ is the union of an increasing chain of sets. As X is a finite set there is some n such that $X \subseteq A_n$. (The set X is either empty, whence $X \subseteq A_0$, or of the form $\{x_1, \ldots, x_k\}$. In the latter case, we have $x_1 \in A_{n_1}, \cdots, x_k \in A_{n_k}$ for some $n_1, \ldots, n_k$. Taking n bigger than all of $n_1, \ldots, n_k$ we must have $X \subseteq A_n$ as the sequence $A_0, A_1, \ldots, A_n, \ldots$ is increasing.) As $X \subseteq A_n$ we obtain $y \in \widehat{R}(A_n) = A_{n+1}$. Hence $y \in \bigcup_n A_n = A$. Thus A is closed under R.
(ii) By Proposition 4.11 the set A is R-closed, so we already know that $\widehat{R}(A) \subseteq A$. We require the converse inclusion. Suppose $y \in A$. Then $y \in A_n$ for some $n > 0$. Thus $y \in \widehat{R}(A_{n-1})$. This means there is some $(X/y) \in R$ with $X \subseteq A_{n-1}$. But $A_{n-1} \subseteq A$ so $X \subseteq A$ with $(X/y) \in R$, giving $y \in \widehat{R}(A)$. We have established the required converse inclusion, $A \subseteq \widehat{R}(A)$. Hence $\widehat{R}(A) = A$.
(iii) We need to show that if B is another R-closed set then $A \subseteq B$. Suppose B is closed under R. Then $\widehat{R}(B) \subseteq B$. We show by mathematical induction that for all natural numbers $n \in \omega$

$$A_n \subseteq B.$$

The basis of the induction $A_0 \subseteq B$ is obviously true as $A_0 = \emptyset$. To show the induction step, assume $A_n \subseteq B$. Then

$$A_{n+1} = \widehat{R}(A_n) \subseteq \widehat{R}(B) \subseteq B,$$

using the facts that $\widehat{R}$ is monotonic and that B is R-closed. $\qquad\qquad\square$

Notice the essential part played in the proof of (i) by the fact that rule instances are finitary, *i.e.* in a rule instance (X/y), the set of premises X is finite.

It follows from (i) and (iii) that $A = I_R$, the set of elements for which there are R-derivations. Now (ii) says precisely that I_R is a fixed point of $\widehat{R}$. Moreover, (iii) implies that I_R is the *least fixed point* of $\widehat{R}$, *i.e.*

$$\widehat{R}(B) = B \Rightarrow I_R \subseteq B,$$

because if any other set B is a fixed point it is closed under R, so $I_R \subseteq B$ by Proposition 4.1. The set I_R, defined by the rule instances R, is the least fixed point, $fix(\widehat{R})$, obtained by the construction

$$fix(\widehat{R}) =_{def} \bigcup_{n \in \omega} \widehat{R}^n(\emptyset).$$

Least fixed points will play a central role in the next chapter.

Exercise 4.13 Given a set of rules R define a different operator $\overline{R}$ by

$$\overline{R}(A) = A \cup \{y \mid \exists X \subseteq A. \ (X/y) \in R\}.$$

Clearly $\overline{R}$ is monotonic and in addition satisfies the property

$$A \subseteq \overline{R}(A).$$

An operator satisfying such a property is called *increasing*. Exhibit a monotonic operator which is not increasing. Show that given any set A there is a least fixed point of $\overline{R}$ which includes A, and that this property can fail for monotonic operations. □

Exercise 4.14 Let R be a set of rule instances. Show that $\widehat{R}$ is *continuous* in the sense that

$$\bigcup_{n \in \omega} \widehat{R}(B_n) = \widehat{R}(\bigcup_{n \in \omega} B_n)$$

for any increasing chain of sets $B_0 \subseteq \cdots \subseteq B_n \subseteq \cdots$.
(The solution to this exercise is contained in the next chapter.)   □

4.5 Further reading

This chapter has provided an elementary introduction to the mathematical theory of *inductive definitions*. A detailed, though much harder, account can be found in Peter Aczel's handbook chapter [4]—our treatment, with just finitary rules, avoids the use of ordinals. The term "rule induction" originates with the author's Cambridge lecture notes of 1984, and seems be catching on (the principle is well-known and, for instance, is called simply R-induction, for rules R, in [4]). This chapter has refrained from any recommendations about which style of argument to use in reasoning about operational semantics; whether to use rule induction or the often clumsier, but conceptually more straightforward, induction on derivations. In many cases it is a matter of taste.

5 The denotational semantics of IMP

This chapter provides a denotational semantics for **IMP**, and a proof of its equivalence with the previously given operational semantics. The chapter concludes with an introduction to the foundations of denotational semantics (complete partial orders, continuous functions and least fixed points) and the Knaster-Tarski Theorem.

5.1 Motivation

We have described the behaviour of programs in **IMP** in an operational manner by inductively defining transition relations to express evaluation and execution. There was some arbitrariness in the choice of rules, for example, in the size of transition steps we chose. Also note that in the description of the behaviour the syntax was mixed-up in the description. This style of semantics, in which the transitions are built out of the syntax, makes it hard to compare two programs written in different programming languages. Still, the style of semantics was fairly close to an implementation of the language, the description can be turned into an interpreter for **IMP** written for example in Prolog, and it led to firm definitions of equivalence between arithmetic expressions, boolean expressions and commands. For example we defined

$$c_0 \sim c_1 \text{ iff } (\forall \sigma, \sigma'. \ \langle c_0, \sigma \rangle \to \sigma' \iff \langle c_1, \sigma \rangle \to \sigma').$$

Perhaps it has already occurred to the reader that there is a more direct way to capture the semantics of **IMP** if we are only interested in commands to within the equivalence $\sim$. Notice $c_0 \sim c_1$ iff

$$\{(\sigma, \sigma') \mid \langle c_0, \sigma \rangle \to \sigma'\} = \{(\sigma, \sigma') \mid \langle c_1, \sigma \rangle \to \sigma'\}.$$

In other words, $c_0 \sim c_1$ iff c_0 and c_1 determine the same partial function on states. This suggests we should define the meaning, or semantics, of **IMP** at a more abstract level in which we take the *denotation* of a command to be a partial function on states. The style we adopt in giving this new description of the semantics of **IMP** is that from *denotational semantics*. Denotational semantics is much more widely applicable than to simple programming languages like **IMP** —it can handle virtually all programming languages, though the standard framework appears inadequate for parallelism and "fairness" (see Chapter 14 on parallelism). The approach was pioneered by Christopher Strachey, and Dana Scott who supplied the mathematical foundations. Our denotational semantics of **IMP** is really just an introductory example. We shall see more on the applications and foundations of denotational semantics in later chapters.

An arithmetic expression $a \in \textbf{Aexp}$ will denote a function $\mathcal{A}[\![a]\!] : \Sigma \to \textbf{N}$.

A boolean expression $b \in \textbf{Bexp}$ will denote a function $\mathcal{B}[\![b]\!] : \Sigma \to \textbf{T}$, from the set of states to the set of truth values.

A command c will denote a partial function $\mathcal{C}[\![c]\!] : \Sigma \rightharpoonup \Sigma$.

The brackets $[\![\ ]\!]$ are traditional in denotational semantics. You see $\mathcal{A}$ is really a function from arithmetic expressions of the type $\mathbf{Aexp} \to (\Sigma \to \mathbf{N})$, and our first thought in ordinary mathematics, when we see an expression, is to evaluate it. The square brackets $[\![a]\!]$ put the arithmetic expression a in quotes so we don't evaluate a. We could have written $e.g.$ $\mathcal{A}(\text{``}3 + 5\text{''})\sigma = 8$ instead of $\mathcal{A}[\![3 + 5]\!]\sigma = 8$. The quotes tell that it is the piece of syntax "3+5" which is being mapped. The full truth is a little more subtle as we shall sometimes write denotations like $\mathcal{A}[\![a_0 + a_1]\!]$, where a_0 and a_1 are metavariables which stand for arithmetic expressions. It is the syntactic object got by placing the sign "+" between the syntactic objects a_0 and a_1 that is put in quotes. So the brackets $[\![\ ]\!]$ do not represent true and complete quotation. We shall use the brackets $[\![\ ]\!]$ round an argument of a semantic function to show that the argument is a piece of syntax.

5.2 Denotational semantics

We define the semantic functions

$$\mathcal{A} : \mathbf{Aexp} \to (\Sigma \to \mathbf{N})$$
$$\mathcal{B} : \mathbf{Bexp} \to (\Sigma \to \mathbf{T})$$
$$\mathcal{C} : \mathbf{Com} \to (\Sigma \rightharpoonup \Sigma)$$

by structural induction. For example, for commands, for each command c we define the partial function $\mathcal{C}[\![c]\!]$ assuming the previous definition of c' for subcommands c' of c. The command c is said to $denote$ $\mathcal{C}[\![c]\!]$, and $\mathcal{C}[\![c]\!]$ is said to be a $denotation$ of c.

Denotations of Aexp:

Firstly, we define the denotation of an arithmetic expression, by structural induction, as a relation between states and numbers:

$$\mathcal{A}[\![n]\!] = \{(\sigma, n) \mid \sigma \in \Sigma\}$$
$$\mathcal{A}[\![X]\!] = \{(\sigma, \sigma(X)) \mid \sigma \in \Sigma\}$$
$$\mathcal{A}[\![a_0 + a_1]\!] = \{(\sigma, n_0 + n_1) \mid (\sigma, n_0) \in \mathcal{A}[\![a_0]\!] \ \& \ (\sigma, n_1) \in \mathcal{A}[\![a_1]\!]\}$$
$$\mathcal{A}[\![a_0 - a_1]\!] = \{(\sigma, n_0 - n_1) \mid (\sigma, n_0) \in \mathcal{A}[\![a_0]\!] \ \& \ (\sigma, n_1) \in \mathcal{A}[\![a_1]\!]\}$$
$$\mathcal{A}[\![a_0 \times a_1]\!] = \{(\sigma, n_0 \times n_1) \mid (\sigma, n_0) \in \mathcal{A}[\![a_0]\!] \ \& \ (\sigma, n_1) \in \mathcal{A}[\![a_1]\!]\}.$$

An obvious structural induction on arithmetic expressions a shows that each denotation $\mathcal{A}[\![a]\!]$ is in fact a function. Notice that the signs "+", "−", "×" on the left-hand sides represent syntactic signs in **IMP** whereas the signs on the right represent operations on numbers, so *e.g.*, for any state σ,

$$\mathcal{A}[\![3+5]\!]\sigma = \mathcal{A}[\![3]\!]\sigma + \mathcal{A}[\![5]\!]\sigma = 3 + 5 = 8,$$

as is to be expected. Note that using λ-notation we can present the definition of the semantics in the following equivalent way:

$$\mathcal{A}[\![n]\!] = \lambda\sigma \in \Sigma.n$$
$$\mathcal{A}[\![X]\!] = \lambda\sigma \in \Sigma.\sigma(X)$$
$$\mathcal{A}[\![a_0 + a_1]\!] = \lambda\sigma \in \Sigma.(\mathcal{A}[\![a_0]\!]\sigma + \mathcal{A}[\![a_1]\!]\sigma)$$
$$\mathcal{A}[\![a_0 - a_1]\!] = \lambda\sigma \in \Sigma.(\mathcal{A}[\![a_0]\!]\sigma - \mathcal{A}[\![a_1]\!]\sigma)$$
$$\mathcal{A}[\![a_0 \times a_1]\!] = \lambda\sigma \in \Sigma.(\mathcal{A}[\![a_0]\!]\sigma \times \mathcal{A}[\![a_1]\!]\sigma).$$

Denotations of Bexp:

The semantic function for booleans is given in terms of logical operations conjunction $\wedge_T$, disjunction $\vee_T$ and negation $\neg_T$, on the set of truth values **T**. The denotation of a boolean expression is defined by structural induction to be a relation between states and truth values.

$$\mathcal{B}[\![\mathbf{true}]\!] = \{(\sigma, \mathbf{true}) \mid \sigma \in \Sigma\}$$

$$\mathcal{B}[\![\mathbf{false}]\!] = \{(\sigma, \mathbf{false}) \mid \sigma \in \Sigma\}$$

$$\mathcal{B}[\![a_0 = a_1]\!] = \{(\sigma, \mathbf{true}) \mid \sigma \in \Sigma \ \& \ \mathcal{A}[\![a_0]\!]\sigma = \mathcal{A}[\![a_1]\!]\sigma\} \cup$$
$$\{(\sigma, \mathbf{false}) \mid \sigma \in \Sigma \ \& \ \mathcal{A}[\![a_0]\!]\sigma \neq \mathcal{A}[\![a_1]\!]\sigma\},$$

$$\mathcal{B}[\![a_0 \leq a_1]\!] = \{(\sigma, \mathbf{true}) \mid \sigma \in \Sigma \ \& \ \mathcal{A}[\![a_0]\!]\sigma \leq \mathcal{A}[\![a_1]\!]\sigma\} \cup$$
$$\{(\sigma, \mathbf{false}) \mid \sigma \in \Sigma \ \& \ \mathcal{A}[\![a_0]\!]\sigma \not\leq \mathcal{A}[\![a_1]\!]\sigma\},$$

$$\mathcal{B}[\![\neg b]\!] = \{(\sigma, \neg_T t) \mid \sigma \in \Sigma \ \& \ (\sigma, t) \in \mathcal{B}[\![b]\!]\},$$

$$\mathcal{B}[\![b_0 \wedge b_1]\!] = \{(\sigma, t_0 \wedge_T t_1) \mid \sigma \in \Sigma \ \& \ (\sigma, t_0) \in \mathcal{B}[\![b_0]\!] \ \& \ (\sigma, t_1) \in \mathcal{B}[\![b_1]\!]\},$$

$$\mathcal{B}[\![b_0 \vee b_1]\!] = \{(\sigma, t_0 \vee_T t_1) \mid \sigma \in \Sigma \ \& \ (\sigma, t_0) \in \mathcal{B}[\![b_0]\!] \ \& \ (\sigma, t_1) \in \mathcal{B}[\![b_1]\!]\}.$$

A simple structural induction shows that each denotation is a function. For example,

$$\mathcal{B}[\![a_0 \leq a_1]\!]\sigma = \begin{cases} \textbf{true} & \text{if } \mathcal{A}[\![a_0]\!]\sigma \leq \mathcal{A}[\![a_1]\!]\sigma, \\ \textbf{false} & \text{if } \mathcal{A}[\![a_0]\!]\sigma \not\leq \mathcal{A}[\![a_1]\!]\sigma \end{cases}$$

for all $\sigma \in \Sigma$.

Denotations of Com:

The definition of $\mathcal{C}[\![c]\!]$ for commands c is more complicated. We will first give denotations as relations between states; afterwards a straightforward structural induction will show that they are, in fact, partial functions. It is fairly obvious that we should take

$$\mathcal{C}[\![\textbf{skip}]\!] = \{(\sigma, \sigma) \mid \sigma \in \Sigma\}$$

$$\mathcal{C}[\![X := a]\!] = \{(\sigma, \sigma[n/X]) \mid \sigma \in \Sigma \ \& \ n = \mathcal{A}[\![a]\!]\sigma\}$$

$$\mathcal{C}[\![c_0; c_1]\!] = \mathcal{C}[\![c_1]\!] \circ \mathcal{C}[\![c_0]\!], \text{ a composition of relations,}$$

the definition of which explains the order-reversal in c_0 and c_1,

$$\mathcal{C}[\![\textbf{if } b \textbf{ then } c_0 \textbf{ else } c_1]\!] =$$
$$\{(\sigma, \sigma') \mid \mathcal{B}[\![b]\!]\sigma = \textbf{true} \ \& \ (\sigma, \sigma') \in \mathcal{C}[\![c_0]\!]\} \cup \{(\sigma, \sigma') \mid \mathcal{B}[\![b]\!]\sigma = \textbf{false} \ \& \ (\sigma, \sigma') \in \mathcal{C}[\![c_1]\!]\}.$$

But there are difficulties when we consider the denotation of a while-loop. Write

$$w \equiv \textbf{while } b \textbf{ do } c.$$

We have noted the equivalence

$$w \sim \textbf{if } b \textbf{ then } c; w \textbf{ else skip}$$

so the partial function $\mathcal{C}[\![w]\!]$ should equal the partial function $\mathcal{C}[\![\textbf{if } b \textbf{ then } c; w \textbf{ else skip}]\!]$. Thus we should have :

$$\mathcal{C}[\![w]\!] = \{(\sigma, \sigma') \mid \mathcal{B}[\![b]\!]\sigma = \textbf{true} \ \& \ (\sigma, \sigma') \in \mathcal{C}[\![c; w]\!]\} \cup$$
$$\{(\sigma, \sigma) \mid \mathcal{B}[\![b]\!]\sigma = \textbf{false}\}$$
$$= \{(\sigma, \sigma') \mid \mathcal{B}[\![b]\!]\sigma = \textbf{true} \ \& \ (\sigma, \sigma') \in \mathcal{C}[\![w]\!] \circ \mathcal{C}[\![c]\!]\} \cup$$
$$\{(\sigma, \sigma) \mid \mathcal{B}[\![b]\!]\sigma = \textbf{false}\}.$$

Writing φ for $\mathcal{C}[\![w]\!]$, β for $\mathcal{B}[\![b]\!]$ and γ for $\mathcal{C}[\![c]\!]$ we require a partial function φ such that

$$\varphi = \{(\sigma, \sigma') \mid \beta(\sigma) = \textbf{true} \ \& \ (\sigma, \sigma') \in \varphi \circ \gamma\} \cup$$
$$\{(\sigma, \sigma) \mid \beta(\sigma) = \textbf{false}\}.$$

But this involves φ on both sides of the equation. How can we solve it to find φ? We clearly require some technique for solving a recursive equation of this form (it is called "recursive" because the value we wish to know on the left recurs on the right). Looked at in another way we can regard Γ, where

$$
\begin{aligned}
\Gamma(\varphi) =& \{(\sigma, \sigma') \mid \beta(\sigma) = \textbf{true } \& \ (\sigma, \sigma') \in \varphi \circ \gamma\} \cup \\
& \{(\sigma, \sigma) \mid \beta(\sigma) = \textbf{false}\} \\
=& \{(\sigma, \sigma') \mid \exists \sigma''. \ \beta(\sigma) = \textbf{true } \& \ (\sigma, \sigma'') \in \gamma \ \& \ (\sigma'', \sigma') \in \varphi\} \cup \\
& \{(\sigma, \sigma) \mid \beta(\sigma) = \textbf{false}\},
\end{aligned}
$$

as a function which given φ returns $\Gamma(\varphi)$. We want a fixed point φ of Γ in the sense that

$$
\varphi = \Gamma(\varphi).
$$

The last chapter provides the clue to finding such a solution in Section 4.4. It is not hard to check that the function Γ is equal to $\widehat{R}$, where $\widehat{R}$ is the operator on sets determined by the rule instances

$$
\begin{aligned}
R =& \{((\{(\sigma'', \sigma')\}/(\sigma, \sigma')) \mid \beta(\sigma) = \textbf{true } \& \ (\sigma, \sigma'') \in \gamma\} \cup \\
& \{((\emptyset/(\sigma, \sigma)) \mid \beta(\sigma) = \textbf{false}\}.
\end{aligned}
$$

As Section 4.4 shows $\widehat{R}$ has a least fixed point

$$
\varphi = \textit{fix}(\widehat{R})
$$

where φ is a set—in this case a set of pairs—with the property that

$$
\widehat{R}(\theta) = \theta \Rightarrow \varphi \subseteq \theta.
$$

We shall take this least fixed point as the denotation of the while program w. Certainly its denotation should be a fixed point. The full justification for taking it to be the *least* fixed point will be given in the next section where we establish that this choice for the semantics agrees with the operational semantics.

Now we can go ahead and define the denotational semantics of commands in the following way, by structural induction:

$$\mathcal{C}[\![\mathbf{skip}]\!] = \{(\sigma, \sigma) \mid \sigma \in \Sigma\}$$

$$\mathcal{C}[\![X := a]\!] = \{(\sigma, \sigma[n/X]) \mid \sigma \in \Sigma \;\&\; n = \mathcal{A}[\![a]\!]\sigma\}$$

$$\mathcal{C}[\![c_0; c_1]\!] = \mathcal{C}[\![c_1]\!] \circ \mathcal{C}[\![c_0]\!]$$

$$\mathcal{C}[\![\mathbf{if}\ b\ \mathbf{then}\ c_0\ \mathbf{else}\ c_1]\!] =$$
$$\{(\sigma, \sigma') \mid \mathcal{B}[\![b]\!]\sigma = \mathbf{true}\ \&\ (\sigma, \sigma') \in \mathcal{C}[\![c_0]\!]\} \cup$$
$$\{(\sigma, \sigma') \mid \mathcal{B}[\![b]\!]\sigma = \mathbf{false}\ \&\ (\sigma, \sigma') \in \mathcal{C}[\![c_1]\!]\}$$

$$\mathcal{C}[\![\mathbf{while}\ b\ \mathbf{do}\ c]\!] = \mathit{fix}(\Gamma)$$

where
$$\Gamma(\varphi) = \{(\sigma, \sigma') \mid \mathcal{B}[\![b]\!]\sigma = \mathbf{true}\ \&\ (\sigma, \sigma') \in \varphi \circ \mathcal{C}[\![c]\!]\} \cup$$
$$\{(\sigma, \sigma) \mid \mathcal{B}[\![b]\!]\sigma = \mathbf{false}\}.$$

In this way we define a denotation of each command as a relation between states. Notice how the semantic definition is *compositional* in the sense that the denotation of a command is constructed from the denotations of its immediate subcommands, reflected in the fact that the definition is by structural induction. This property is a hallmark of denotational semantics. Notice it is not true of the operational semantics of **IMP** because of the rule for **while**-loops in which the **while**-loop reappears in the premise of the rule.

We have based the definition of the semantic function on while programs by the operational equivalence between while programs and one "unfolding" of them into a conditional. Not surprisingly it is straightforward to check this equivalence holds according to the denotational semantics.

Proposition 5.1 *Write*
$$w \equiv \mathbf{while}\ b\ \mathbf{do}\ c$$

for a command c and boolean expression b. Then

$$\mathcal{C}[\![w]\!] = \mathcal{C}[\![\mathbf{if}\ b\ \mathbf{then}\ c; w\ \mathbf{else}\ \mathbf{skip}]\!].$$

Proof: The denotation of w is a fixed point of Γ, defined above. Hence

$$
\begin{aligned}
\mathcal{C}[\![w]\!] =&\,\Gamma(\mathcal{C}[\![w]\!]) \\
=&\,\{(\sigma, \sigma') \mid \mathcal{B}[\![b]\!]\sigma = \textbf{true} \ \& \ (\sigma, \sigma') \in \mathcal{C}[\![w]\!] \circ \mathcal{C}[\![c]\!]\} \cup \\
&\,\{(\sigma, \sigma) \mid \mathcal{B}[\![b]\!]\sigma = \textbf{false}\} \\
=&\,\{(\sigma, \sigma') \mid \mathcal{B}[\![b]\!]\sigma = \textbf{true} \ \& \ (\sigma, \sigma') \in \mathcal{C}[\![c; w]\!]\} \cup \\
&\,\{(\sigma, \sigma') \mid \mathcal{B}[\![b]\!]\sigma = \textbf{false} \ \& \ (\sigma, \sigma') \in \mathcal{C}[\![\textbf{skip}]\!]\} \\
=&\,\mathcal{C}[\![\textbf{if } b \textbf{ then } c; w \textbf{ else skip}]\!]. \square
\end{aligned}
$$

Exercise 5.2 Show by structural induction on commands that the denotation $\mathcal{C}[\![c]\!]$ is a partial function for all commands c.

(The case for while-loops involves proofs by mathematical induction showing that $\Gamma^n(\emptyset)$ is a partial function between states for all natural numbers n, and that these form an increasing chain, followed by the observation that the union of such a chain of partial functions is itself a partial function.) $\square$

In Section 5.4 we shall introduce a general theory of fixed points, which makes sense when the objects defined recursively are not sets ordered by inclusion.

5.3 Equivalence of the semantics

Although inspired by our understanding of the operational behaviour of **IMP** the denotational semantics has not yet been demonstrated to agree with the operational semantics. We first check the operational and denotational semantics agree on the evaluation of expressions:

Lemma 5.3 *For all $a \in$ **Aexp**,*

$$
\mathcal{A}[\![a]\!] = \{(\sigma, n) \mid \langle a, \sigma \rangle \rightarrow n\}.
$$

Proof: We prove the lemma by structural induction. As induction hypothesis we take

$$
P(a) \iff {}_{def} \mathcal{A}[\![a]\!] = \{(\sigma, n) \mid \langle a, \sigma \rangle \rightarrow n\}.
$$

Following the scheme of structural induction the proof splits into cases according to the structure of an arithmetic expression a.

$a \equiv m$: From the definition of the semantic function, in the case where a is a number m, we have

$$
(\sigma, n) \in \mathcal{A}[\![m]\!] \iff \sigma \in \Sigma \ \& \ n \equiv m.
$$

Clearly, if $(\sigma, n) \in \mathcal{A}[\![m]\!]$ then $n \equiv m$ and $\langle m, \sigma \rangle \to n$. Conversely, if $\langle m, \sigma \rangle \to n$ then the only possible derivation is one in which $n \equiv m$ and hence $(\sigma, n) \in \mathcal{A}[\![m]\!]$.

$a \equiv X$: Similarly, if a is a location X,

$$(\sigma, n) \in \mathcal{A}[\![X]\!] \iff (\sigma \in \Sigma \ \& \ n \equiv \sigma(X))$$
$$\iff \langle X, \sigma \rangle \to n.$$

$a \equiv a_0 + a_1$: Assume $P(a_0)$ and $P(a_1)$ for two arithmetic expressions a_0, a_1. We have

$$(\sigma, n) \in \mathcal{A}[\![a_0 + a_1]\!] \iff \exists n_0, n_1. \ n = n_0 + n_1 \ \& \ (\sigma, n_0) \in \mathcal{A}[\![a_0]\!] \ \& \ (\sigma, n_1) \in \mathcal{A}[\![a_1]\!].$$

Supposing $(\sigma, n) \in \mathcal{A}[\![a_0 + a_1]\!]$, there are n_0, n_1 such that $n = n_0 + n_1$ and $(\sigma, n_0) \in \mathcal{A}[\![a_0]\!]$ and $(\sigma, n_1) \in \mathcal{A}[\![a_1]\!]$. From the assumptions $P(a_0)$ and $P(a_1)$, we obtain

$$\langle a_0, \sigma \rangle \to n_0 \quad \text{and} \quad \langle a_1, \sigma \rangle \to n_1.$$

Thus we can derive $\langle a_0 + a_1, \sigma \rangle \to n$. Conversely, any derivation of $\langle a_0 + a_1, \sigma \rangle \to n$ must have the form

$$\frac{\begin{array}{cc} \vdots & \vdots \\ \langle a_0, \sigma \rangle \to n_0 & \langle a_1, \sigma \rangle \to n_1 \end{array}}{\langle a_0 + a_1, \sigma \rangle \to n}$$

for some n_0, n_1 such that $n = n_0 + n_1$. This time, from the assumptions $P(a_0)$ and $P(a_1)$, we obtain $(\sigma, n_0) \in \mathcal{A}[\![a_0]\!]$ and $(\sigma, n_1) \in \mathcal{A}[\![a_1]\!]$. Hence $(\sigma, n) \in \mathcal{A}[\![a]\!]$.

The proofs of the other cases, for arithmetic expressions of the form $a_0 - a_1$ and $a_0 \times a_1$, follow exactly the same pattern. By structural induction on arithmetic expressions we conclude that

$$\mathcal{A}[\![a]\!] = \{(\sigma, n) \mid \langle a, \sigma \rangle \to n\},$$

for all arithmetic expressions a. $\square$

Lemma 5.4 *For* $b \in$ **Bexp**,

$$\mathcal{B}[\![b]\!] = \{(\sigma, t) \mid \langle b, \sigma \rangle \to t\}.$$

Proof: The proof for boolean expressions is similar to that for arithmetic expressions. It proceeds by structural induction on boolean expressions with induction hypothesis

$$P(b) \iff_{def} \mathcal{B}[\![b]\!] = \{(\sigma, t) \mid \langle b, \sigma \rangle \to t\}$$

for boolean expression b.

We only do two cases of the induction. They are typical, and the remaining cases are left to the reader.

$b \equiv (a_0 = a_1)$: Let a_0, a_1 be arithmetic expressions. By definition, we have

$$\mathcal{B}[\![a_0 = a_1]\!] = \{(\sigma, \mathbf{true}) \mid \sigma \in \Sigma \ \& \ \mathcal{A}[\![a_0]\!]\sigma = \mathcal{A}[\![a_1]\!]\sigma\} \cup$$
$$\{(\sigma, \mathbf{false}) \mid \sigma \in \Sigma \ \& \ \mathcal{A}[\![a_0]\!]\sigma \neq \mathcal{A}[\![a_1]\!]\sigma\}.$$

Thus

$$(\sigma, \mathbf{true}) \in \mathcal{B}[\![a_0 = a_1]\!] \iff \sigma \in \Sigma \ \& \ \mathcal{A}[\![a_0]\!]\sigma = \mathcal{A}[\![a_1]\!]\sigma.$$

If $(\sigma, \mathbf{true}) \in \mathcal{B}[\![a_0 = a_1]\!]$ then $\mathcal{A}[\![a_0]\!]\sigma = \mathcal{A}[\![a_1]\!]\sigma$, so, by the previous lemma,

$$\langle a_0, \sigma \rangle \to n \quad \text{and} \quad \langle a_1, \sigma \rangle \to n,$$

for some number n. Hence from the operational semantics for boolean expressions we obtain

$$\langle a_0 = a_1, \sigma \rangle \to \mathbf{true}.$$

Conversely, supposing $\langle a_0 = a_1, \sigma \rangle \to \mathbf{true}$, it must have a derivation of the form

$$\frac{\vdots \qquad \vdots}{\dfrac{\langle a_0, \sigma \rangle \to n \quad \langle a_1, \sigma \rangle \to n}{\langle a_0 = a_1, \sigma \rangle \to \mathbf{true}}}.$$

But then, by the previous lemma, $\mathcal{A}[\![a_0]\!]\sigma = n = \mathcal{A}[\![a_1]\!]\sigma$. Hence $(\sigma, \mathbf{true}) \in \mathcal{B}[\![a_0 = a_1]\!]$. Therefore

$$(\sigma, \mathbf{true}) \in \mathcal{B}[\![a_0 = a_1]\!] \iff \langle a_0 = a_1, \sigma \rangle \to \mathbf{true}.$$

Similarly,

$$(\sigma, \mathbf{false}) \in \mathcal{B}[\![a_0 = a_1]\!] \iff \langle a_0 = a_1, \sigma \rangle \to \mathbf{false}.$$

It follows that

$$\mathcal{B}[\![a_0 = a_1]\!] = \{(\sigma, t) \mid \langle a_0 = a_1, \sigma \rangle \to t\}.$$

$b \equiv b_0 \wedge b_1$: Let b_0, b_1 be boolean expressions. Assume $P(b_0)$ and $P(b_1)$. By definition, we have

$$(\sigma, t) \in \mathcal{B}[\![b_0 \wedge b_1]\!] \iff \sigma \in \Sigma \ \& \ \exists t_0, t_1. \ t = t_0 \wedge_T t_1 \ \& \ (\sigma, t_0) \in \mathcal{B}[\![b_0]\!] \ \& \ (\sigma, t_1) \in \mathcal{B}[\![b_1]\!].$$

Thus, supposing $(\sigma, t) \in \mathcal{B}[\![b_0 \wedge b_1]\!]$, there are t_0, t_1 such that $(\sigma, t_0) \in \mathcal{B}[\![b_0]\!]$ and $(\sigma, t_1) \in \mathcal{B}[\![b_1]\!]$. From the assumptions $P(b_0)$ and $P(b_1)$ we obtain

$$\langle b_0, \sigma \rangle \to t_0 \quad \text{and} \quad \langle b_1, \sigma \rangle \to t_1.$$

Thus we can derive $\langle b_0 \wedge b_1, \sigma \rangle \to t$ where $t = t_0 \wedge_T t_1$. Conversely, any derivation of $\langle b_0 \wedge b_1, \sigma \rangle \to t$ must have the form

$$\frac{\begin{array}{cc} \vdots & \vdots \\ \overline{\langle b_0, \sigma \rangle \to t_0} & \overline{\langle b_1, \sigma \rangle \to t_1} \end{array}}{\langle b_0 \wedge b_1, \sigma \rangle \to t}$$

for some t_0, t_1 such that $t = t_0 \wedge_T t_1$. From the $P(b_0)$ and $P(b_1)$, we obtain $(\sigma, t_0) \in \mathcal{B}[\![b_0]\!]$ and $(\sigma, t_1) \in \mathcal{B}[\![b_1]\!]$. Hence $(\sigma, t) \in \mathcal{B}[\![b]\!]$.

As remarked the other cases of the induction are similar. $\square$

Exercise 5.5 The proofs above involve considering the form of derivations. Alternative proofs can be obtained by a combination of structural induction and rule induction. For example, show

1. $\{(\sigma, n) \mid \langle a, \sigma \rangle \to n\} \subseteq \mathcal{A}[\![a]\!]$,
2. $\mathcal{A}[\![a]\!] \subseteq \{(\sigma, n) \mid \langle a, \sigma \rangle \to n\}$,

for all arithmetic expressions a by using rule induction on the operational semantics of arithmetic expressions for 1 and structural induction on arithmetic expressions for 2. $\square$

Now we can check that the denotational semantics of commands agrees with their operational semantics:

Lemma 5.6 *For all commands c and states σ, σ',*

$$\langle c, \sigma \rangle \to \sigma' \Rightarrow (\sigma, \sigma') \in \mathcal{C}[\![c]\!].$$

Proof: We use rule-induction on the operational semantics of commands, as stated in Section 4.3.3. For $c \in \mathbf{Com}$ and $\sigma, \sigma' \in \Sigma$, define

$$P(c, \sigma, \sigma') \iff_{def} (\sigma, \sigma') \in \mathcal{C}[\![c]\!].$$

If we can show P is closed under the rules for the execution of commands, in the sense of Section 4.3.3, then

$$\langle c, \sigma \rangle \to \sigma' \Rightarrow P(c, \sigma, \sigma')$$

for any command c and states σ, σ'. We check only one clause in Section 4.3.3, that associated with while-loops in the case in which the condition evaluates to true. Recall it is:

$$\frac{\langle b, \sigma \rangle \to \mathbf{true} \quad \langle c, \sigma \rangle \to \sigma'' \quad \langle w, \sigma'' \rangle \to \sigma'}{\langle w, \sigma \rangle \to \sigma'}$$

where we abbreviate $w \equiv$ **while** b **do** c. Following the scheme of Section 4.3.3, assume

$$\langle b, \sigma \rangle \to \textbf{true} \ \& \ \langle c, \sigma \rangle \to \sigma'' \ \& \ P(c, \sigma, \sigma'') \ \& \ \langle w, \sigma'' \rangle \to \sigma' \ \& \ P(w, \sigma'', \sigma').$$

By Lemma 5.4

$$\mathcal{B}[\![b]\!]\sigma = \textbf{true}.$$

From the meaning of P we obtain directly that

$$\mathcal{C}[\![c]\!]\sigma = \sigma'' \text{ and } \mathcal{C}[\![w]\!]\sigma'' = \sigma'.$$

Now, from the definition of the denotational semantics, we see

$$\mathcal{C}[\![w]\!]\sigma = \mathcal{C}[\![c; w]\!]\sigma = \mathcal{C}[\![w]\!](\mathcal{C}[\![c]\!]\sigma) = \mathcal{C}[\![w]\!]\sigma'' = \sigma'.$$

But $\mathcal{C}[\![w]\!]\sigma = \sigma'$ means $P(w, \sigma, \sigma')$ $i.e.\ P$ holds for the consequence of the rule. Hence P is closed under this rule. By similar arguments, P is closed under the other rules for the execution of commands (Exercise!). Hence by rule induction we have proved the lemma. $\qquad \Box$

The next theorem, showing the equivalence of operational and denotational semantics for commands, is proved by structural induction with a use of mathematical induction inside one case, that for while-loops.

Theorem 5.7 *For all commands c*

$$\mathcal{C}[\![c]\!] = \{(\sigma, \sigma') \mid \langle c, \sigma \rangle \to \sigma'\}.$$

Proof: The theorem can clearly be restated as: for all commands c

$$(\sigma, \sigma') \in \mathcal{C}[\![c]\!] \iff \langle c, \sigma \rangle \to \sigma'.$$

for all states σ, σ'. Notice Lemma 5.6 gives the "$\Leftarrow$" direction of the equivalence.

We proceed by structural induction on commands c, taking

$$\forall \sigma, \sigma' \in \Sigma.(\sigma, \sigma') \in \mathcal{C}[\![c]\!] \iff \langle c, \sigma \rangle \to \sigma'.$$

as induction hypothesis.

$c \equiv \textbf{skip}$: By definition, $\mathcal{C}[\![\textbf{skip}]\!] = \{(\sigma, \sigma) \mid \sigma \in \Sigma\}$. Thus if $(\sigma, \sigma) \in \mathcal{C}[\![c]\!]$ then $\sigma' = \sigma$ so $\langle \textbf{skip}, \sigma \rangle \to \sigma'$ by the rule for **skip**. The induction hypothesis holds in this case.

$c \equiv X := a$: Suppose $(\sigma, \sigma') \in \mathcal{C}[\![X := a]\!]$. Then $\sigma' = \sigma[n/X]$ where $n = \mathcal{A}[\![a]\!]\sigma$. By Lemma 5.3, $\langle a, \sigma \rangle \to n$. Hence $\langle c, \sigma \rangle \to \sigma'$. The induction hypothesis holds in this case.

$c \equiv c_0; c_1$: Assume the induction hypothesis holds for c_0 and c_1. Suppose $(\sigma, \sigma') \in C[\![c]\!]$. Then there is some state σ'' for which $(\sigma, \sigma'') \in C[\![c_0]\!]$ and $(\sigma'', \sigma') \in C[\![c_1]\!]$. By the induction hypothesis for commands c_0 and c_1 we know

$$\langle c_0, \sigma \rangle \to \sigma'' \text{ and } \langle c_1, \sigma'' \rangle \to \sigma'.$$

Hence $\langle c_0; c_1, \sigma \rangle \to \sigma'$ for the rules for the operational semantics of commands. Thus the induction hypothesis holds for c.

$c \equiv \textbf{if } b \textbf{ then } c_0 \textbf{ else } c_1$: Assume the induction hypothesis holds for c_0 and c_1. Recall that

$$C[\![c]\!] = \{(\sigma, \sigma') \mid B[\![b]\!]\sigma = \textbf{true} \ \& \ (\sigma, \sigma') \in C[\![c_0]\!]\} \cup$$
$$\{(\sigma, \sigma') \mid B[\![b]\!]\sigma = \textbf{false} \ \& \ (\sigma, \sigma') \in C[\![c_1]\!]\}.$$

So, if $(\sigma, \sigma') \in C[\![c]\!]$ then either
  (i) $B[\![b]\!]\sigma = \textbf{true}$ and $(\sigma, \sigma') \in C[\![c_0]\!]$, or
  (ii) $B[\![b]\!]\sigma = \textbf{false}$ and $(\sigma, \sigma') \in C[\![c_1]\!]$.
Suppose (i). Then $\langle b, \sigma \rangle \to \textbf{true}$ by Lemma 5.4, and $\langle c_0, \sigma \rangle \to \sigma'$ because the induction hypothesis holds for c_0. From the rules for conditionals in the operational semantics of commands we obtain $\langle c, \sigma \rangle \to \sigma'$. Supposing (ii), we can arrive at the conclusion in essentially the same way. Thus the induction hypothesis holds for c.

$c \equiv \textbf{while } b \textbf{ do } c_0$: Assume the induction hypothesis holds for c_0. Recall that

$$C[\![\textbf{while } b \textbf{ do } c_0]\!] = fix(\Gamma)$$

where

$$\Gamma(\varphi) = \{(\sigma, \sigma') \mid B[\![b]\!]\sigma = \textbf{true} \ \& \ (\sigma, \sigma') \in \varphi \circ C[\![c_0]\!]\} \cup$$
$$\{(\sigma, \sigma) \mid B[\![b]\!]\sigma = \textbf{false}\}.$$

So, writing θ_n for $\Gamma^n(\emptyset)$, we have

$$C[\![c]\!] = \bigcup_{n \in \omega} \theta_n$$

where

$$\theta_0 = \emptyset,$$

$$\theta_{n+1} = \{(\sigma, \sigma') \mid B[\![b]\!]\sigma = \textbf{true} \ \& \ (\sigma, \sigma') \in \theta_n \circ C[\![c_0]\!]\} \cup$$
$$\{(\sigma, \sigma) \mid B[\![b]\!]\sigma = \textbf{false}.\}$$

We shall show by mathematical induction that

$$\forall \sigma, \sigma' \in \Sigma. \ (\sigma, \sigma') \in \theta_n \Rightarrow \langle c, \sigma \rangle \to \sigma' \tag{1}$$

for all $n \in \omega$. It then follows, of course, that $(\sigma, \sigma') \in C[\![c]\!] \iff \langle c, \sigma \rangle \to \sigma'$ for states σ, σ'.

We start the mathematical induction on the induction hypothesis (1).

Base case $n = 0$: When $n = 0$, $\theta_0 = \emptyset$ so that induction hypothesis is vacuously true.

Induction Step: We assume (1) holds for an arbitrary $n \in \omega$ and attempt to prove

$$(\sigma, \sigma') \in \theta_{n+1} \Rightarrow \langle c, \sigma \rangle \to \sigma'$$

for any states σ, σ'.

Assume $(\sigma, \sigma') \in \theta_{n+1}$. Then either

(i) $B[\![b]\!]\sigma = \textbf{true}$ and $(\sigma, \sigma') \in \theta_n \circ C[\![c_0]\!]$, or

(ii) $B[\![b]\!]\sigma = \textbf{false}$ and $\sigma' = \sigma$.

Assume (i). Then $\langle b, \sigma \rangle \to \textbf{true}$ by Lemma 5.4. Also $(\sigma, \sigma'') \in C[\![c_0]\!]$ and $(\sigma'', \sigma') \in \theta_n$ for some state σ''. From the induction hypothesis (1) we obtain $\langle c, \sigma'' \rangle \to \sigma'$. By assumption of the structural induction hypothesis for c_0, we have $\langle c_0, \sigma \rangle \to \sigma''$. By the rule for while-loops we obtain $\langle c, \sigma \rangle \to \sigma'$.

Assume (ii). As $B[\![b]\!] = \textbf{false}$, by Lemma 5.4, we obtain $\langle b, \sigma \rangle \to \textbf{false}$. Also $\sigma' = \sigma$ so $\langle c, \sigma \rangle \to \sigma$. In this case the induction hypothesis holds.

This establishes the induction hypothesis (1) for $n + 1$.

By mathematical induction we conclude (1) holds for all n. Consequently:

$$(\sigma, \sigma') \in C[\![c]\!] \Rightarrow \langle c, \sigma \rangle \to \sigma'$$

for all states σ, σ' in the case where $c \equiv \textbf{while } b \textbf{ do } c_0$.

Finally, by structural induction, we have proved the theorem. $\square$

Exercise 5.8 Let $w \equiv \textbf{while } b \textbf{ do } c$. Prove that

$$C[\![w]\!]\sigma = \sigma' \text{ iff } B[\![b]\!]\sigma = \textbf{false } \& \; \sigma = \sigma'$$

$$\text{or}$$

$$\exists \sigma_0, \cdots, \sigma_n \in \Sigma.$$

$$\sigma = \sigma_0 \; \& \; \sigma' = \sigma_n \; \& \; B[\![b]\!]\sigma_n = \textbf{false } \&$$

$$\forall i (0 \le i < n). \; B[\![b]\!]\sigma_i = \textbf{true } \& \; C[\![c]\!]\sigma_i = \sigma_{i+1}.$$

(The proof from left to right uses induction on the $\Gamma^n(\emptyset)$ used in building up the denotation of w; the proof from right to left uses induction on the length of the chain of states.) $\square$

Exercise 5.9 The syntax of commands of a simple imperative language with a repeat construct is given by

$$c ::= \ X := e \mid c_0; c_1 \mid \textbf{if } b \textbf{ then } c_0 \textbf{ else } c_1 \mid \textbf{repeat } c \textbf{ until } b$$

where X is a location, e is an arithmetic expression, b is a boolean expression and c, c_0, c_1 range over commands. From your understanding of how such commands behave explain how to change the semantics of while programs to that of repeat programs to give:
(i) an operational semantics in the form of rules to generate transitions of the form $\langle c, \sigma \rangle \to \sigma'$ meaning the execution of c from state σ terminates in state σ';
(ii) a denotational semantics for commands in which each command c is denoted by a partial function $\mathcal{C}[\![c]\!]$ from states to states;
(iii) sketch the proof of the equivalence between the operational and denotational semantics, that $\langle c, \sigma \rangle \to \sigma'$ iff $\mathcal{C}[\![c]\!]\sigma = \sigma'$, concentrating on the case where c is a repeat loop.
□

5.4   Complete partial orders and continuous functions

In the last chapter we gave an elementary account of the theory of inductive definitions. We have shown how it can be used to give a denotational semantics for **IMP**. In practice very few recursive definitions can be viewed straightforwardly as least fixed points of operators on sets, and they are best tackled using the more abstract ideas of complete partial orders and continuous functions, the standard tools of denotational semantics. We can approach this framework from that of inductive definitions. In this way it is hoped to make the more abstract ideas of complete partial orders more accessible and show the close tie-up between them and the more concrete notions in operational semantics.

Suppose we have a set of rule instances R of the form (X/y). We saw how R determines an operator $\widehat{R}$ on sets, which given a set B results in a set

$$\widehat{R}(B) = \{y \mid \exists (X/y) \in R.\ X \subseteq B\},$$

and how the operator $\widehat{R}$ has a least fixed point

$$fix(\widehat{R}) =_{def} \bigcup_{n \in \omega} \widehat{R}^n(\emptyset)$$

formed by taking the union of the chain of sets

$$\emptyset \subseteq \widehat{R}(\emptyset) \subseteq \cdots \subseteq \widehat{R}^n(\emptyset) \subseteq \cdots.$$

It is a fixed point in the sense that

$$\widehat{R}(\mathit{fix}(\widehat{R})) = \mathit{fix}(\widehat{R}),$$

and it is the least fixed point because $\mathit{fix}(\widehat{R})$ is included in any fixed point B, *i.e.*

$$\widehat{R}(B) = B \Rightarrow \mathit{fix}(\widehat{R}) \subseteq B.$$

In fact Proposition 4.12 of Section 4.4 shows that $\mathit{fix}(\widehat{R})$ was the least R-closed set, where we can characterise an R-closed set as one B for which

$$\widehat{R}(B) \subseteq B.$$

In this way we can obtain, by choosing appropriate rule instances R, a solution to the recursive equation needed for a denotation of the while-loop. However it pays to be more general, and extract from the example above the essential mathematical properties we used to obtain a least fixed point. This leads to the notions of complete partial order and continuous functions.

The very idea of "least" only made sense because of the inclusion, or subset, relation. In its place we take the more general idea of partial order.

Definition: A *partial order* (p.o.) is a set P on which there is a binary relation $\sqsubseteq$ which is:

(i) relexive: $\forall p \in P.\ p \sqsubseteq p$

(ii) transitive: $\forall p, q, r \in P.\ p \sqsubseteq q\ \&\ q \sqsubseteq r \Rightarrow p \sqsubseteq r$

(iii) antisymmetric: $\forall p, q \in P.\ p \sqsubseteq q\ \&\ q \sqsubseteq p \Rightarrow p = q.$

But not all partial orders support the constructions we did on sets. In constructing the least fixed point we formed the union $\bigcup_{n \in \omega} A_n$ of a ω-chain $A_0 \subseteq A_1 \subseteq \cdots A_n \subseteq \cdots$ which started at $\emptyset$—the least set. Union on sets, ordered by inclusion, generalises to the notion of least upper bound on partial orders—we only require them to exist for such increasing chains indexed by ω. Translating these properties to partial orders, we arrive at the definition of a complete partial order.

Definition: For a partial order $(P, \sqsubseteq)$ and subset $X \subseteq P$ say p is an *upper bound* of X iff

$$\forall q \in X.\ q \sqsubseteq p.$$

Say p is a *least upper bound* (lub) of X iff

(i) p is an upper bound of X, and

(ii) for all upper bounds q of X, $p \sqsubseteq q$.

When a subset X of a partial order has a least upper bound we shall write it as $\bigsqcup X$. We write $\bigsqcup \{d_1, \cdots, d_m\}$ as $d_1 \sqcup \cdots \sqcup d_m$.

Definition: Let $(D, \sqsubseteq_D)$ be a partial order.

An ω-*chain* of the partial order is an increasing chain $d_0 \sqsubseteq_D d_1 \sqsubseteq_D \cdots \sqsubseteq_D d_n \sqsubseteq_D \cdots$ of elements of the partial order.

The partial order $(D, \sqsubseteq_D)$ is a *complete partial order* (abbreviated to cpo) if it has lubs of all ω-chains $d_0 \sqsubseteq_D d_1 \sqsubseteq_D \cdots \sqsubseteq_D d_n \sqsubseteq_D \cdots$, *i.e.* any increasing chain $\{d_n \mid n \in \omega\}$ of elements in D has a least upper bound $\bigsqcup\{d_n \mid n \in \omega\}$ in D, often written as $\bigsqcup_{n \in \omega} d_n$.

We say $(D, \sqsubseteq_D)$ is a cpo *with bottom* if it is a cpo which has a least element $\bot_D$ (called "bottom").[1]

Notation: In future we shall often write the ordering of a cpo $(D, \sqsubseteq_D)$ as simply $\sqsubseteq$, and its bottom element, when it has one, as just $\bot$. The context generally makes clear to which cpo we refer.

Notice that any set ordered by the identity relation forms a cpo, certainly without a bottom element. Such cpo's are called *discrete*, or *flat*.

Exercise 5.10 Show $(\mathcal{P}ow(X), \subseteq)$ is a cpo with bottom, for any set X. Show the set of partial functions $\Sigma \rightharpoonup \Sigma$ ordered by $\subseteq$ forms a cpo with bottom. $\qquad\Box$

The counterpart of an operation on sets is a function $f : D \to D$ from a cpo D back to D. We require such a function to respect the ordering on D in a certain way. To motivate these properties we consider the operator defined from the rule instances R. Suppose

$$B_0 \subseteq B_1 \subseteq \cdots B_n \subseteq \cdots.$$

Then

$$\widehat{R}(B_0) \subseteq \widehat{R}(B_1) \subseteq \cdots \widehat{R}(B_n) \subseteq \cdots$$

is an increasing chain of sets too. This is because $\widehat{R}$ is monotonic in the sense that

$$B \subseteq C \Rightarrow \widehat{R}(B) \subseteq \widehat{R}(C).$$

By monotonicity, as each $B_n \subseteq \bigcup_{n \in \omega} B_n$,

$$\bigcup_{n \in \omega} \widehat{R}(B_n) \subseteq \widehat{R}(\bigcup_{n \in \omega} B_n).$$

In fact, the converse inclusion, and so equality, holds too because of the finitary nature of rule instances. Suppose $y \in \widehat{R}(\bigcup_{n \in \omega} B_n)$. Then $(X/y) \in R$ for some *finite* set

---

[1] The cpo's here are commonly called (bottomless) ω-cpo's, or predomains.

$X \subseteq \bigcup_{n \in \omega} B_n$. Because X is finite, $X \subseteq B_n$ for some n. Hence $y \in \widehat{R}(B_n)$. Thus $y \in \bigcup_{n \in \omega} \widehat{R}(B_n)$. We have proved that $\widehat{R}$ is *continuous* in the sense that

$$\bigcup_{n \in \omega} \widehat{R}(B_n) = \widehat{R}(\bigcup_{n \in \omega} B_n)$$

for any increasing chain $B_0 \subseteq \cdots \subseteq B_n \subseteq \cdots$. This followed because the rules are *finitary* i.e. each rule (X/y) involves only a finite set of premises X.

We can adopt these properties to define the continuous functions between a pair of cpos.

Definition: A function $f : D \to E$ between cpos D and E is *monotonic* iff

$$\forall d, d' \in D. \ d \sqsubseteq d' \Rightarrow f(d) \sqsubseteq f(d').$$

Such a function is *continuous* iff it is monotonic and for all chains $d_0 \sqsubseteq d_1 \sqsubseteq \cdots \sqsubseteq d_n \sqsubseteq \cdots$ in D we have

$$\bigsqcup_{n \in \omega} f(d_n) = f(\bigsqcup_{n \in \omega} d_n).$$

An important consequence of this definition is that any continuous function from a cpo with bottom to itself has a least fixed point, in a way which generalises that of operators on sets in Section 4.4. In fact we can catch the notion of a set closed under rules with the order-theoretic notion of a prefixed point (Recall a set B was closed under rule instances R iff $\widehat{R}(B) \subseteq B$).

Definition: Let $f : D \to D$ be a continuous function on a cpo D. A *fixed point* of f is an element d of D such that $f(d) = d$. A *prefixed point* of f is an element d of D such that $f(d) \sqsubseteq d$.

The following simple, but important, theorem gives an explicit construction $fix(f)$ of the least fixed point of a continuous function f on a cpo D.

Theorem 5.11 *(Fixed-Point Theorem)*
Let $f : D \to D$ be a continuous function on a cpo with bottom D. Define

$$fix(f) = \bigsqcup_{n \in \omega} f^n(\bot).$$

Then $fix(f)$ is a fixed point of f and the least prefixed point of f i.e.
(i) $f(fix(f)) = fix(f)$ and (ii) if $f(d) \sqsubseteq d$ then $fix(f) \sqsubseteq d$. Consequently $fix(f)$ is the least fixed point of f.

Proof:
(i) By continuity

$$f(\mathit{fix}(f)) = f(\bigsqcup_{n \in \omega} f^n(\bot))$$

$$= \bigsqcup_{n \in \omega} f^{n+1}(\bot)$$

$$= (\bigsqcup_{n \in \omega} f^{n+1}(\bot)) \sqcup \{\bot\}$$

$$= \bigsqcup_{n \in \omega} f^n(\bot)$$

$$= \mathit{fix}(f).$$

Thus $\mathit{fix}(f)$ is a fixed point.

(ii) Suppose d is a prefixed point. Certainly $\bot \sqsubseteq d$. By monotonicity $f(\bot) \sqsubseteq f(d)$. But d is prefixed point, *i.e.* $f(d) \sqsubseteq d$, so $f(\bot) \sqsubseteq d$, and by induction $f^n(\bot) \sqsubseteq d$. Thus, $\mathit{fix}(f) = \bigsqcup_{n \in \omega} f^n(\bot) \sqsubseteq d$.

As fixed points are certainly prefixed points, $\mathit{fix}(f)$ is the least fixed point of f. $\square$

We say a little about the intuition behind complete partial orders and continuous functions, an intuition which will be discussed further and pinned down more precisely in later chapters. Complete partial orders correspond to types of data, data that can be used as input or output to a computation. Computable functions are modelled as continuous functions between them. The elements of a cpo are thought of as points of information and the ordering $x \sqsubseteq y$ as meaning x approximates y (or, x is less or the same information as y)—so $\bot$ is the point of least information.

We can recast, into this general framework, the method by which we gave a denotational semantics to **IMP**. We denoted a command by a partial function from states to states Σ. On the face of it this does not square with the idea that the function computed by a command should be continuous. However partial functions on states can be viewed as continuous total functions. We extend the states by a new element $\bot$ to a cpo of results $\Sigma_\bot$ ordered by

$$\bot \sqsubseteq \sigma$$

for all states σ. The cpo $\Sigma_\bot$ includes the extra element $\bot$ representing the undefined state, or more correctly null information about the state, which, as a computation progresses, can grow into the information that a particular final state is determined. It is not hard to see that the partial functions $\Sigma \rightharpoonup \Sigma$ are in 1-1 correspondence with the (total) functions $\Sigma \to \Sigma_\bot$, and that in this case any total function is continuous; the inclusion order between partial functions corresponds to the "pointwise order"

$$f \sqsubseteq g \text{ iff } \forall \sigma \in \Sigma. \ f(\sigma) \sqsubseteq g(\sigma)$$

between functions $\Sigma \to \Sigma_\perp$. Because partial functions form a cpo so does the set of functions $[\Sigma \to \Sigma_\perp]$ ordered pointwise. Consequently, our denotational semantics can equivalently be viewed as denoting commands by elements of the cpo of continuous functions $[\Sigma \to \Sigma_\perp]$. Recall that to give the denotation of a while program we solved a recursive equation by taking the least fixed point of a continuous function on the cpo of partial functions, which now recasts to one on the cpo $[\Sigma \to \Sigma_\perp]$.

For the cpo $[\Sigma \to \Sigma_\perp]$, isomorphic to that of partial functions, more information corresponds to more input/output behaviour of a function and no information at all, $\perp$ in this cpo, corresponds to the empty partial function which contains no input/output pairs. We can think of the functions themselves as data which can be used or produced by a computation. Notice that the information about such functions comes in discrete units, the input/output pairs. Such a discreteness property is shared by a great many of the complete partial orders that arise in modelling computations. As we shall see, that computable functions should be continuous follows from the idea that the appearance of a unit of information in the output of a computable function should only depend on the presence of finitely many units of information in the input. Otherwise a computation of the function would have to make use of infinitely many units of information before yielding that unit of output. We have met this idea before; a set of rule instances determines a continuous operator when the rule instances are finitary, in that they have only finite sets of premises.

Exercise 5.12
(i) Show that the monotonic maps from Σ to $\Sigma_\perp$ are continuous and in 1-1 correspondence with the partial functions $\Sigma \rightharpoonup \Sigma$. Confirm the statement above, that a partial function is included in another iff the corresponding functions $\Sigma \to \Sigma_\perp$ are ordered pointwise.
(ii) Let D and E be cpo's. Suppose D has the property that every ω-chain $d_0 \sqsubseteq d_1 \sqsubseteq \cdots \sqsubseteq d_n \sqsubseteq \cdots$ is stationary, in the sense that there is an n such that $d_m = d_n$ for all $m \geq n$. Show that all monotonic functions from D to E are continuous. $\square$

Exercise 5.13 Show that if we relax the condition that rules be finitary, and so allow rule instances with an infinite number of premises, then the operator induced by a set of rule instances need not be continuous. $\square$

5.5   The Knaster-Tarski Theorem

In this section another abstract characterisation of least fixed points is studied. It results are only used much later, so it can be skipped at a first reading. Looking back to the last chapter, there was another characterisation of the least fixed point of an operator on sets. Recall from Exercise 4.3 of Section 4.1 that, for a set of rule instances R,

$$I_R = \bigcap \{Q \mid Q \text{ is } R\text{-closed}\}.$$

In view of Section 4.4, this can be recast as saying

$$fix(\widehat{R}) = \bigcap \{Q \mid \widehat{R}(Q) \subseteq Q\},$$

expressing that the least fixed point of the operator $\widehat{R}$ can be characterised as the intersection of its prefixed points. This is a special case of the *Knaster-Tarski Theorem*, a general result about the existence of least fixed points. As might be expected its statement involves a generalisation of the operation of intersection on sets to a notion dual to that least upper bound on a partial order.

Definition: For a partial order $(P, \sqsubseteq)$ and subset $X \subseteq P$ say p is an *lower bound* of X iff

$$\forall q \in X.\ p \sqsubseteq q.$$

Say p is a *greatest lower bound* (glb) of X iff
   (i) p is a lower bound of X, and
   (ii) for all lower bounds q of X, we have $q \sqsubseteq p$.
   When a subset X of a partial order has a greatest lower bound we shall write it as $\bigsqcap X$. We write $\bigsqcap \{d_0, d_1\}$ as $d_0 \sqcap d_1$.

Just as sometimes lubs are called *suprema* (or *sups*), glbs are sometimes called *infima* (or *infs*).

Definition: A *complete lattice* is a partial order which has greatest lower bounds of arbitrary subsets.

Although we have chosen to define complete lattices as partial orders which have all greatest lower bounds we could alternatively have defined them as those partial orders with all least upper bounds, a consequence of the following exercise.

Exercise 5.14 Prove a complete lattice must also have least upper bounds of arbitrary subsets. Deduce that if $(L, \sqsubseteq)$ is a complete lattice then so is $(L, \sqsupseteq)$, ordered by the converse relation. $\qquad\square$

Theorem 5.15 *(Knaster-Tarski Theorem for minimum fixed points)*
Let $(L, \sqsubseteq)$ be a complete lattice. Let $f : L \to L$ be a monotonic function, i.e. such that if $x \sqsubseteq y$ then $f(x) \sqsubseteq f(y)$ (but not necessarily continuous). Define

$$m = \bigsqcap \{x \in L \mid f(x) \sqsubseteq x\}.$$

Then m is a fixed point of f and the least prefixed point of f.

Proof: Write $X = \{x \in L \mid f(x) \sqsubseteq x\}$. As above, define $m = \bigsqcap X$. Let $x \in X$. Certainly $m \sqsubseteq x$. Hence $f(m) \sqsubseteq f(x)$ by the monotonicity of f. But $f(x) \sqsubseteq x$ because $x \in X$. So $f(m) \sqsubseteq x$ for any $x \in X$. It follows that $f(m) \sqsubseteq \bigsqcap X = m$. This makes m a prefixed point and, from its definition, it is clearly the least one. As $f(m) \sqsubseteq m$ we obtain $f(f(m)) \sqsubseteq f(m)$ from the monotonicity of f. This ensures $f(m) \in X$ which entails $m \sqsubseteq f(m)$. Thus $f(m) = m$. We conclude that m is indeed a fixed point and is the least prefixed point of f. $\quad\square$

As a corollary we can show that a monotonic function on a complete lattice has a *maximum* fixed point.

Theorem 5.16 *(Knaster-Tarski Theorem for maximum fixed points)*
Let $(L, \sqsubseteq)$ be a complete lattice. Let $f : L \to L$ be a monotonic function. Define

$$M = \bigsqcup \{x \in L \mid x \sqsubseteq f(x)\}.$$

Then M is a fixed point of f and the greatest postfixed point of f. (A postfixed point is an element x such that $x \sqsubseteq f(x)$.)

Proof: This follows from the theorem for the minimum-fixed-point case by noticing that a monotonic function on $(L, \sqsubseteq)$ is also a monotonic function on the complete lattice $(L, \sqsupseteq)$. $\quad\square$

The Knaster-Tarski Theorem is important because it applies to any monotonic function on a complete lattice. However most of the time we will be concerned with least fixed points of continuous functions which we shall construct by the techniques of the previous section, as least upper bounds of ω-chains in a cpo.

5.6 Further reading

This chapter has given an example of a denotational semantics. Later chapters will expand on the range and power of the denotational method. Further elementary material can be found in the books by Bird [21], Loeckx and Sieber [58], Schmidt [88], and Stoy [95] (though the latter bases its treatment on complete lattices instead of complete partial orders). A harder but very thorough book is that by de Bakker [13]. The denotational semantics of **IMP** has come at a price, the more abstract use of least fixed points in place of rules. However there is also a gain. By casting its meaning within the framework of cpo's and continuous functions **IMP** becomes amenable to the techniques there. The book [69] has several examples of applications to the language of while programs.

6 The axiomatic semantics of IMP

In this chapter we turn to the business of systematic verification of programs in **IMP**. The Hoare rules for showing the partial correctness of programs are introduced and shown sound. This involves extending the boolean expressions to a rich language of assertions about program states. The chapter concludes with an example of verification conducted within the framework of Hoare rules.

6.1 The idea

We turn to consider the problem of how to prove that a program we have written in **IMP** does what we require of it.

Let's start with a simple example of a program to compute the sum of the first hundred numbers, the naive way. Here is a program in **IMP** to compute $\sum_{1 \leq m \leq 100} m$ (The notation $\sum_{1 \leq m \leq 100} m$ means $1 + 2 + \cdots + 100$).

$$S := 0;$$
$$N := 1;$$
$$(\textbf{while } \neg(N = 101) \textbf{ do } S := S + N; N := N + 1)$$

How would we prove that this program, when it terminates, is such that the value of S is $\sum_{1 \leq m \leq 100} m$?

Of course one thing we could do would be to run it according to our operational semantics and see what we get. But suppose we change our program a bit, so that instead of "**while** $\neg(N = 101)$ **do** $\cdots$" we put "**while** $\neg(N = P + 1)$ **do** $\cdots$" and imagine making some arbitrary assignment to P before we begin. In this case the resulting value of S after execution should be $\sum_{1 \leq m \leq P} m$, no matter what the value of P. As P can take an infinite set of values we cannot justify this fact simply by running the program for all initial values of P. We need to be a little more clever, and abstract, and use some logic to reason about the program.

We'll end up with a formal proof system for proving properties of **IMP** programs, based on proof rules for each programming construct of **IMP**. Its rules are called Hoare rules or Floyd-Hoare rules. Historically R.W.Floyd invented rules for reasoning about flow charts, and later C.A.R.Hoare modified and extended these to give a treatment of a language like **IMP** but with procedures. Originally their approach was advocated not just for proving properties of programs but also as giving a method for explaining the meaning of program constructs; the meaning of a construct was specified in terms of "axioms" (more accurately rules) saying how to prove properties of it. For this reason, the approach is traditionally called axiomatic semantics.

For now let's not be too formal. Let's look at the program and reason informally about it, for the moment based on our intuitive understanding of how it behaves. Straightaway we see that the commands $S := 0; N := 1$ initialise the values in the locations. So we can annotate our program with a comment:

$$S := 0; N := 1$$
$$\{S = 0 \ \wedge \ N = 1\}$$
$$(\textbf{while } \neg(N = 101) \textbf{ do } S := S + N; N := N + 1)$$

with the understanding that $S = 0$ for example means the location S has value 0, as in the treatment of boolean expressions. We want a method to justify the final comment in:

$$S := 0; N := 1$$
$$\{S = 0 \ \wedge \ N = 1\}$$
$$(\textbf{while } \neg(N = 101) \textbf{ do } S := S + N; N := N + 1)$$
$$\{S = \sum_{1 \le m \le 100} m\}$$

—meaning that if $S = 0 \ \wedge \ N = 1$ before the execution of the while-loop then $S = \sum_{1 \le m \le 100} m$ after its execution.

Looking at the boolean, one fact we know holds after the execution of the while-loop is that we cannot have $N \ne 101$; because if we had $\neg(N = 101)$ then the while-loop would have continued running. So, at the end of its execution we know $N = 101$. But we want to know S!

Of course, with a simple program like this we can look and see what the values of S and N are the first time round the loop, $S = 1, N = 2$. And the second time round the loop $S = 1 + 2, N = 3 \cdots$ and so on, until we see the pattern: after the i th time round the loop $S = 1 + 2 + \cdots + i$ and $N = i + 1$. From which we see, when we exit the loop, that $S = 1 + 2 + \cdots + 100$, because when we exit $N = 101$.

At the beginning and end of each iteration of the while-loop we have

$$S = 1 + 2 + 3 + \cdots + (N - 1) \tag{I}$$

which expresses the key relationship between the value at location S and the value at location N. The assertion I is called an *invariant* of the while-loop because it remains true under each iteration of the loop. So finally when the loop terminates I will hold at the end. We shall say more about invariants later.

For now it appears we can base a proof system on assertions of the form

$$\{A\}c\{B\}$$

where A and B are assertions like those we've already seen in **Bexp** and c is a command. The precise interpretation of such a compound assertion is this:

> for all states σ which satisfy A if the execution c from state σ terminates in state σ' then σ' satisfies B.

Put another way, $\{A\}c\{B\}$ means that any successful (*i.e.*, terminating) execution of c from a state satisfying A ends up in a state satisfying B. The assertion A is called the precondition and B the postcondition of the partial correctness assertion $\{A\}c\{B\}$.

Assertions of the form $\{A\}c\{B\}$ are called *partial correctness assertions* because they say nothing about the command c if it fails to terminate. As an extreme example consider

$$c \equiv \textbf{while true do skip}.$$

The execution of c from any state does not terminate. According to the interpretation we give above the following partial correctness assertion is valid:

$$\{\textbf{true}\}c\{\textbf{false}\}$$

simply because the execution of c does not terminate. More generally, because c loops, any partial correctness assertion $\{A\}c\{B\}$ is valid. Contrast this with another notion, that of total correctness. Sometimes people write

$$[A]c[B]$$

to mean that the execution of c from any state which satisfies A will terminate in a state which satisfies B. In this book we shall not be concerned much with total correctness assertions.

Warning: There are several different notations around for expressing partial and total correctness. When dipping into a book make doubly sure which notation is used there.

We have left several loose ends. For one, what kinds of assertions A and B do we allow in partial correctness assertions $\{A\}c\{B\}$? We say more in a moment, and turn to a more general issue.

The next issue can be regarded pragmatically as one of notation, though it can be viewed more conceptually as the semantics of assertions for partial correctness—see the "optional" Section 7.5 on denotational semantics using predicate transformers. Firstly let's introduce an abbreviation to mean the state σ satisfies assertion A, or equivalently the assertion A is true at state σ. We abbreviate this to:

$$\sigma \models A.$$

Of course, we'll need to define it, though we all have an intuitive idea of what it means. Consider our interpretation of a partial correctness assertion $\{A\}c\{B\}$. As a command c denotes a partial function from initial states to final states, the partial correctness assertion means:

$$\forall\sigma.\ (\sigma \models A\ \&\ \mathcal{C}[\![c]\!]\sigma \text{ is defined}) \Rightarrow \mathcal{C}[\![c]\!]\sigma \models B.$$

It is awkward working so often with the proviso that $\mathcal{C}[\![c]\!]\sigma$ is defined. Recall Chapter 5 on the denotational semantics of **IMP**. There we suggested that we use the symbol $\bot$ to represent an undefined state (or more strictly, null information about the state). For a command c we can write $\mathcal{C}[\![c]\!]\sigma = \bot$ whenever $\mathcal{C}[\![c]\!]\sigma$ is undefined, and, in accord with the composition of partial functions, take $\mathcal{C}[\![c]\!]\bot = \bot$. If we adopt the convention that $\bot$ satisfies any assertion, then our work on partial correctness becomes much simpler notationally. With the understanding that

$$\bot \models A$$

for any assertion A, we can describe the meaning of $\{A\}c\{B\}$ by

$$\forall\sigma \in \Sigma.\ \sigma \models A \Rightarrow \mathcal{C}[\![c]\!]\sigma \models B.$$

Because we are dealing with partial correctness this convention is consistent with our previous interpretation of partial correctness assertions. It's quite intuitive too; diverging computations denote $\bot$ and as we've seen they satisfy any postcondition.

6.2   The assertion language Assn

What kind of assertions do we wish to make about **IMP** programs? Because we want to reason about boolean expressions we'll certainly need to include all the assertions in **Bexp**. Because we want to make assertions using the quantifiers "$\forall i \cdots$" and "$\exists i \cdots$" we will need to work with extensions of **Bexp** and **Aexp** which include integer variables i over which we can quantify. Then, for example, we can say that an integer k is a multiple of another l by writing

$$\exists i.\ k = i \times l.$$

It will be shown in reasonable detail how to introduce integer variables and quantifiers for a particular language of assertions **Assn**. In principle, everything we'll do with assertions can be done in **Assn**—it is expressive enough—but in examples and exercises we will extend **Assn** in various ways, without being terribly strict about it. (For instance, in one example we'll use the notation $n! = n \times (n-1) \times \cdots \times 2 \times 1$ for the factorial function.)

Firstly, we extend **Aexp** to include integer variables i, j, k, *etc.*. This is done simply by extending the BNF description of **Aexp** by the additional rule which makes any integer variable $i, j, k, \cdots$ an integer expression. So the extended syntactic category **Aexpv** of arithmetic expressions is given by:

$$a ::= n \mid X \mid i \mid a_0 + a_1 \mid a_0 - a_1 \mid a_0 \times a_1$$

where

n ranges over numbers, **N**

X ranges over locations, **Loc**

i ranges over integer variables, **Intvar**.

We extend boolean expressions to include these more general arithmetic expressions and quantifiers, as well as implication. The rules are:

$$A ::= \textbf{true} \mid \textbf{false} \mid a_0 = a_1 \mid a_0 \leq a_1 \mid A_0 \wedge A_1 \mid A_0 \vee A_1 \mid \neg A \mid A_0 \Rightarrow A_1 \mid \forall i.A \mid \exists i.A$$

We call the set of extended boolean assertions, **Assn**.

At school we have had experience in manipulating expressions like those above, though in those days we probably wrote mathematics down in a less abbreviated way, not using quantifiers for instance. When we encounter an integer variable i we think of it as standing for some arbitrary integer and do calculations with it like those "unknowns" $x, y, \cdots$ at school. An implication like $A_0 \Rightarrow A_1$ means if A_0 then A_1, and will be true if either A_0 is false or A_1 is true. We have used implication before in our mathematics, and now we have added it to our set of formal assertions **Assn**. We have a "commonsense" understanding of the expressions and assertions (and this should be all that is needed when doing the exercises). However, because we want to reason about proof systems based on assertions, not just examples, we shall be more formal, and give a theory of the meaning of expressions and assertions with integer variables. This is part of the predicate calculus.

6.2.1 Free and bound variables

We say an occurrence of an integer variable i in an assertion is *bound* if it occurs in the scope of an enclosing quantifier $\forall i$ or $\exists i$. If it is not bound we say it is *free*. For example, in

$$\exists i. \ k = i \times l$$

the occurrence of the integer variable i is bound, while those of k and l are free—the variables k and l are understood as standing for particular integers even if we are not precise about which. The same integer variable can have different occurrences in the same assertion one of which is free and another bound. For example, in

$$(i + 100 \leq 77) \wedge (\forall i.\ j + 1 = i + 3)$$

the first occurrence of i is free and the second bound, while the sole occurrence of j is free.

Although this informal explanation will probably suffice, we can give a formal definition using definition by structural induction. Define the set $\mathrm{FV}(a)$ of free variables of arithmetic expressions, extended by integer variables, $a \in \mathbf{Aexpv}$, by structural induction

$$\mathrm{FV}(n) = \mathrm{FV}(X) = \emptyset$$
$$\mathrm{FV}(i) = \{i\}$$
$$\mathrm{FV}(a_0 + a_1) = \mathrm{FV}(a_0 - a_1) = \mathrm{FV}(a_0 \times a_1) = \mathrm{FV}(a_0) \cup \mathrm{FV}(a_1)$$

for all $n \in \mathbf{N}, X \in \mathbf{Loc}, i \in \mathbf{Intvar}$, and $a_0, a_1 \in \mathbf{Aexpv}$. Define the free variables $\mathrm{FV}(A)$ of an assertion A by structural induction to be

$$\mathrm{FV}(\mathbf{true}) = \mathrm{FV}(\mathbf{false}) = \emptyset$$
$$\mathrm{FV}(a_0 = a_1) = \mathrm{FV}(a_0 \leq a_1) = \mathrm{FV}(a_0) \cup \mathrm{FV}(a_1)$$
$$\mathrm{FV}(A_0 \wedge A_1) = \mathrm{FV}(A_0 \vee A_1) = \mathrm{FV}(A_0 \Rightarrow A_1) = \mathrm{FV}(A_0) \cup \mathrm{FV}(A_1)$$
$$\mathrm{FV}(\neg A) = \mathrm{FV}(A)$$
$$\mathrm{FV}(\forall i.A) = \mathrm{FV}(\exists i.A) = \mathrm{FV}(A) \setminus \{i\}$$

for all $a_0, a_1 \in \mathbf{Aexpv}$, integer variables i and assertions A_0, A_1, A. Thus we have made precise the notion of free variable. Any variable which occurs in an assertion A and yet is not free is said to be bound. An assertion with no free variables is *closed*.

6.2.2   Substitution

We can picture an assertion A as

$$---i---i-\!-\!-$$

say, with free occurrences of the integer variable i. Let a be an arithmetic expression, which for simplicity we assume contains no integer variables. Then

$$A[a/i] \equiv ---a---a-\!-\!-$$

is the result of substituting a for i. If a contained integer variables then it might be necessary to rename some bound variables of A in order to avoid the variables in a becoming bound by quantifiers in A—this is how it's done for general substitutions.

We describe substitution more precisely in the simple case. Let i be an integer variable and a be an arithmetic expression without integer variables, and firstly define substitution into arithmetic expressions by the following structural induction:

$$n[a/i] \equiv n \qquad X[a/i] \equiv X$$
$$j[a/i] \equiv j \qquad i[a/i] \equiv a$$
$$(a_0 + a_1)[a/i] \equiv (a_0[a/i] + a_1[a/i])$$
$$(a_0 - a_1)[a/i] \equiv (a_0[a/i] - a_1[a/i])$$
$$(a_0 \times a_1)[a/i] \equiv (a_0[a/i] \times a_1[a/i])$$

where n is a number, X a location, j is an integer variable with $j \not\equiv i$ and $a_0, a_1 \in$ **Aexpv**. Now we define substitution of a for i in assertions by structural induction—remember a does not have any free variables so we need not take any precautions to avoid its variables becoming bound:

$$\textbf{true}[a/i] \equiv \textbf{true} \qquad \textbf{false}[a/i] \equiv \textbf{false}$$
$$(a_0 = a_1)[a/i] \equiv (a_0[a/i] = a_1[a/i]) \qquad (a_0 \le a_1)[a/i] \equiv (a_0[a/i] \le a_1[a/i])$$
$$(A_0 \wedge A_1)[a/i] \equiv (A_0[a/i] \wedge A_1[a/i]) \qquad (A_0 \vee A_1)[a/i] \equiv (A_0[a/i] \vee A_1[a/i])$$
$$(\neg A)[a/i] \equiv \neg(A[a/i]) \qquad (A_0 \Rightarrow A_1)[a/i] \equiv (A_0[a/i] \Rightarrow A_1[a/i])$$
$$(\forall j.A)[a/i] \equiv \forall j.(A[a/i]) \qquad (\forall i.A)[a/i] \equiv \forall i.A$$
$$(\exists j.A)[a/i] \equiv \exists j.(A[a/i]) \qquad (\exists i.A)[a/i] \equiv \exists i.A$$

where $a_0, a_1 \in$ **Aexpv**, A_0, A_1 and A are assertions and j is an integer variable with $j \not\equiv i$.

As was mentioned, defining substitution $A[a/i]$ in the case where a contains free variables is awkward because it involves the renaming of bound variables. Fortunately we don't need this more complicated definition of substitution for the moment.

We use the same notation for substitution in place of a location X, so if an assertion $A \equiv ---X--$ then $A[a/X] = ---a--$, putting a in place of X. This time the (simpler) formal definition is left to the reader.

Exercise 6.1 Write down an assertion $A \in$ **Assn** with one free integer variable i which expresses that i is a prime number, *i.e.* it is required that:

$$\sigma \models^I A \text{ iff } I(i) \text{ is a prime number.}$$

$\square$

Exercise 6.2 Define a formula $LCM \in$ **Assn** with free integer variables i, j and k, which means "i is the least common multiple of j and k," *i.e.* it is required that:

$\sigma \models^I LCM$ iff $I(k)$ is the least common multiple of $I(i)$ and $I(j)$.

(Hint: The least common multiple of two numbers is the smallest non-negative integer divisible by both.)   □

6.3 Semantics of assertions

Because arithmetic expressions have been extended to include integer variables, we cannot adequately describe the value of one of these new expressions using the semantic function $\mathcal{A}$ of earlier. We must first interpret integer variables as particular integers. This is the role of interpretations.

An *interpretation* is a function which assigns an integer to each integer variable *i.e.* a function $I : \textbf{Intvar} \to \textbf{N}$.

The meaning of expressions, Aexpv

Now we can define a semantic function $\mathcal{A}v$ which gives the value associated with an arithmetic expression with integer variables in a particular state in a particular interpretation; the value of an expression $a \in \textbf{Aexpv}$ in a an interpretation I and a state σ is written as $\mathcal{A}v[\![a]\!]I\sigma$ or equivalently as $(\mathcal{A}v[\![a]\!](I))(\sigma)$. Define, by structural induction,

$$\mathcal{A}v[\![n]\!]I\sigma = n$$
$$\mathcal{A}v[\![X]\!]I\sigma = \sigma(X)$$
$$\mathcal{A}v[\![i]\!]I\sigma = I(i)$$
$$\mathcal{A}v[\![a_0 + a_1]\!]I\sigma = \mathcal{A}v[\![a_0]\!]I\sigma + \mathcal{A}v[\![a_1]\!]I\sigma$$
$$\mathcal{A}v[\![a_0 - a_1]\!]I\sigma = \mathcal{A}v[\![a_0]\!]I\sigma - \mathcal{A}v[\![a_1]\!]I\sigma$$
$$\mathcal{A}v[\![a_0 \times a_1]\!]I\sigma = \mathcal{A}v[\![a_0]\!]I\sigma \times \mathcal{A}v[\![a_1]\!]I\sigma$$

The definition of the semantics of arithmetic expressions with integer variables extends the denotational semantics given in Chapter 5 for arithmetic expressions without them.

Proposition 6.3 *For all* $a \in \textbf{Aexp}$ *(without integer variables), for all states* σ *and for all interpretations* I

$$\mathcal{A}[\![a]\!]\sigma = \mathcal{A}v[\![a]\!]I\sigma.$$

Proof: The proof is a simple exercise in structural induction on arithmetic expressions.   □

The meaning of assertions, Assn

Because we include integer variables, the semantic function requires an interpretation function as a further argument. The role of the interpretation function is solely to provide a value in N which is the interpretation of integer variables.

Notation: We use the notation $I[n/i]$ to mean the interpretation got from interpretation I by changing the value for integer-variable i to n *i.e.*

$$I[n/i](j) = \begin{cases} n & \text{if } j \equiv i, \\ I(j) & \text{otherwise.} \end{cases}$$

We could specify the meanings of assertions in **Assn** in the same way we did for expressions with integer variables, but this time taking the semantic function from assertions to functions which, given an interpretation and state as an argument, returned a truth value. We choose an alternative though equivalent course. Given an interpretation I we define directly those states which satisfy an assertion.

In fact, it is convenient to extend the set of states Σ to the set $\Sigma_\perp$ which includes the value $\perp$ associated with a nonterminating computation—so $\Sigma_\perp =_{def} \Sigma \cup \{\perp\}$. For $A \in$ **Assn** we define by structural induction when

$$\sigma \models^I A$$

for a state $\sigma \in \Sigma$, in an interpretation I, and then extend it so $\perp \models^I A$. The relation $\sigma \models^I A$ means state σ *satisfies* A in interpretation I, or equivalently, that assertion A is true at state σ, in interpretation I. By structural induction on assertions, for an interpretation I, we define for all $\sigma \in \Sigma$:

$$\sigma \models^I \textbf{true},$$
$$\sigma \models^I (a_0 = a_1) \text{ if } \mathcal{A}v[\![a_0]\!]I\sigma = \mathcal{A}v[\![a_1]\!]I\sigma,$$
$$\sigma \models^I (a_0 \leq a_1) \text{ if } \mathcal{A}v[\![a_0]\!]I\sigma \leq \mathcal{A}v[\![a_1]\!]I\sigma,$$
$$\sigma \models^I A \wedge B \text{ if } \sigma \models^I A \text{ and } \sigma \models^I B,$$
$$\sigma \models^I A \vee B \text{ if } \sigma \models^I A \text{ or } \sigma \models^I B,$$
$$\sigma \models^I \neg A \text{ if not } \sigma \models^I A,$$
$$\sigma \models^I A \Rightarrow B \text{ if } (\text{not } \sigma \models^I A) \text{ or } \sigma \models^I B,$$
$$\sigma \models^I \forall i.A \text{ if } \sigma \models^{I[n/i]} A \text{ for all } n \in N,$$
$$\sigma \models^I \exists i.A \text{ if } \sigma \models^{I[n/i]} A \text{ for some } n \in N$$
$$\perp \models^I A.$$

Note that, not $\sigma \models^I A$ is generally written as $\sigma \not\models^I A$.

The above tells us formally what it means for an assertion to be true at a state once we decide to interpret integer variables in a particular way fixed by an interpretation. The semantics of boolean expressions provides another way of saying what it means for certain kinds of assertions to be true or false at a state. We had better check that the two ways agree.

Proposition 6.4 *For* $b \in$ **Bexp**, $\sigma \in \Sigma$,

$$\mathcal{B}[\![b]\!]\sigma = \mathbf{true} \;\; \textit{iff} \; \sigma \models^I b, \; \textit{and}$$
$$\mathcal{B}[\![b]\!]\sigma = \mathbf{false} \;\; \textit{iff} \; \sigma \not\models^I b$$

for any interpretation I.

Proof: The proof is by structural induction on boolean expressions, making use of Proposition 6.3. $\square$

Exercise 6.5 Prove the above proposition. $\square$

Exercise 6.6 Prove by structural induction on expressions $a \in$ **Aexpv** that

$$\mathcal{A}v[\![a]\!]I[n/i]\sigma = \mathcal{A}v[\![a[n/i]]\!]I\sigma.$$

(Note that n occurs as an element of $\mathbf{N}$ on the left and as the corresponding number in $\mathbf{N}$ on the right.)

By using the fact above, prove

$$\sigma \models^I \forall i.A \quad \text{iff} \quad \sigma \models^I A[n/i] \text{ for all } n \in \mathbf{N} \quad \text{and}$$
$$\sigma \models^I \exists i.A \quad \text{iff} \quad \sigma \models^I A[n/i] \text{ for some } n \in \mathbf{N}.$$

$\square$

The extension of an assertion

Let I be an interpretation. Often when establishing properties about assertions and partial correctness assertions it is useful to consider the extension of an assertion with respect to I *i.e.* the set of states at which the assertion is true.

Define the extension of A, an assertion, with respect to an interpretation I to be

$$A^I = \{\sigma \in \Sigma_\perp \mid \sigma \models^I A\}.$$

Partial correctness assertions

A partial correctness assertion has the form

$$\{A\}c\{B\}$$

where $A, B \in$ **Assn** and $c \in$ **Com**. Note that partial correctness assertions are not in **Assn**.

Let I be an interpretation. Let $\sigma \in \Sigma_\perp$. We define the satisfaction relation between states and partial correctness assertions, with respect to I, by

$$\sigma \models^I \{A\}c\{B\} \text{ iff } (\sigma \models^I A \Rightarrow C[\![c]\!]\sigma \models^I B).$$

for an interpretation I. In other words, a state σ satisfies a partial correctness assertion $\{A\}c\{B\}$, with respect to an interpretation I, iff any successful computation of c from σ ends up in a state satisfying B.

Validity

Let I be an interpretation. Consider $\{A\}c\{B\}$. We are not so much interested in this partial correctness assertion being true at a particular state so much as whether or not it is true at all states *i.e.*

$$\forall \sigma \in \Sigma_\perp.\ \sigma \models^I \{A\}c\{B\},$$

which we can write as

$$\models^I \{A\}c\{B\},$$

expressing that the partial correctness assertion is valid with respect to the interpretation I, because $\{A\}c\{B\}$ is true regardless of which state we consider. Further, consider *e.g.*

$$\{i < X\}X := X + 1\{i < X\}$$

We are not so much interested in the particular value associated with i by the interpretation I. Rather we are interested in whether or not it is true at all states for all interpretations I. This motivates the notion of *validity*. Define

$$\models \{A\}c\{B\}$$

to mean for all interpretations I and all states σ

$$\sigma \models^I \{A\}c\{B\}.$$

When $\models \{A\}c\{B\}$ we say the partial correctness assertion $\{A\}c\{B\}$ is *valid*.

Similarly for any assertion A, write $\models A$ iff for all interpretations I and states σ, $\sigma \models^I A$. Then say A is *valid*.

Warning: Although closely related, our notion of validity is not the same as the notion of validity generally met in a standard course on predicate calculus or "logic programming." There an assertion is called valid iff for all interpretations for operators like $+, x \cdots$, numerals $0, 1, \cdots$, as well as free variables, the assertion turns out to be true. We are not interested in arbitrary interpretations in this general sense because **IMP** programs operate on states based on locations with the standard notions of integer and integer operations. To distinguish the notion of validity here from the more general notion we could call our notion arithmetic-validity, but we'll omit the "arithmetic."

Example: Suppose $\models (A \Rightarrow B)$. Then for any interpretation I,

$$\forall \sigma \in \Sigma. \; ((\sigma \models^I A) \Rightarrow (\sigma \models^I B))$$

i.e. $A^I \subseteq B^I$. In a picture:

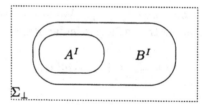

So $\models (A \Rightarrow B)$ iff for all interpretations I, all states which satisfy A also satisfy B.   □

Example: Suppose $\models \{A\}c\{B\}$. Then for any interpretation I,

$$\forall \sigma \in \Sigma. \; ((\sigma \models^I A) \Rightarrow (\mathcal{C}[\![c]\!]\sigma \models^I B)),$$

i.e. the image of A under $\mathcal{C}[\![c]\!]$ is included in B *i.e.*

$$\mathcal{C}[\![c]\!]A^I \subseteq B^I.$$

In a picture:

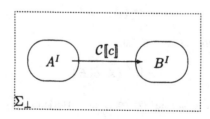

So $\models \{A\}c\{B\}$ iff for all interpretations I, if c is executed from a state which satisfies A then if its execution terminates in a state that state will satisfy B.[1]   □

Exercise 6.7 In an earlier exercise it was asked to write down an assertion $A \in$ **Assn** with one free integer variable i expressing that i was prime. By working through the appropriate cases in the definition of the satisfaction relation $\models^I$ between states and assertions, trace out the argument that $\models^I A$ iff $I(i)$ is indeed a prime number.   □

6.4 Proof rules for partial correctness

We present proof rules which generate the valid partial correctness assertions. The proof rules are syntax-directed; the rules reduce proving a partial correctness assertion of a compound command to proving partial correctness assertions of its immediate subcommands. The proof rules are often called *Hoare rules* and the proof system, consisting of the collection of rules, *Hoare logic*.

Rule for **skip***:*

$$\{A\}\mathbf{skip}\{A\}$$

Rule for assignments:

$$\{B[a/X]\}X := a\{B\}$$

Rule for sequencing:

$$\frac{\{A\}c_0\{C\} \quad \{C\}c_1\{B\}}{\{A\}c_0; c_1\{B\}}$$

Rule for conditionals:

$$\frac{\{A \wedge b\}c_0\{B\} \quad \{A \wedge \neg b\}c_1\{B\}}{\{A\}\mathbf{if}\ b\ \mathbf{then}\ c_0\ \mathbf{else}\ c_1\{B\}}$$

Rule for while loops:

$$\frac{\{A \wedge b\}c\{A\}}{\{A\}\mathbf{while}\ b\ \mathbf{do}\ c\{A \wedge \neg b\}}$$

Rule of consequence:

$$\frac{\models (A \Rightarrow A') \quad \{A'\}c\{B'\} \quad \models (B' \Rightarrow B)}{\{A\}c\{B\}}$$

---

[1]The picture suggests, incorrectly, that the extensions of assertions A^I and B^I are disjoint; they will both always contain $\perp$, and perhaps have other states in common.

Being rules, there is a notion of derivation for the Hoare rules. In this context the Hoare rules are thought of as a proof system, derivations are called *proofs* and any conclusion of a derivation a *theorem*. We shall write $\vdash \{A\}c\{B\}$ when $\{A\}c\{B\}$ is a theorem.

The rules are fairly easy to understand, with the possible exception of the rules for assignments and while-loops. If an assertion is true of the state before the execution of **skip** it is certainly true afterwards as the state is unchanged. This is the content of the rule for **skip**.

For the moment, to convince that the rule for assignments really is the right way round, it can be tried for a particular assertion such as $X = 3$ for the simple assignment like $X := X + 3$.

The rule for sequential compositions expresses that if $\{A\}c_0\{C\}$ and $\{C\}c_1\{B\}$ are valid then so is $\{A\}c_0; c_1\{B\}$: if a successful execution of c_0 from a state satisfying A ends up in one satisfying C and a successful execution of c_1 from a state satisfying C ends up in one satisfying B, then any successful execution of c_0 followed by c_1 from a state satisfying A ends up in one satisfying B.

The two premises in the rule for conditionals cope with two arms of the conditional.

In the rule for while-loops **while** b **do** c, the assertion A is called the *invariant* because the premise, that $\{A \wedge b\}c\{A\}$ is valid, says that the assertion A is preserved by a full execution of the body of the loop, and in a while loop such executions only take place from states satisfying b. From a state satisfying A either the execution of the while-loop diverges or a finite number of executions of the body are performed, each beginning in a state satisfying b. In the latter case, as A is an invariant the final state satisfies A and also $\neg b$ on exiting the loop.

The consequence rule is peculiar because the premises include valid implications. Any instance of the consequence rule has premises including ones of the form $\models (A \Rightarrow A')$ and $\models (B' \Rightarrow B)$ and so producing an instance of the consequence rule with an eye to applying it in a proof depends on first showing assertions $(A \Rightarrow A')$ and $(B' \Rightarrow B)$ are valid. In general this can be a very hard task—such implications can express complicated facts about arithmetic. Fortunately, because programs often do not involve deep mathematical facts, the demonstration of these validities can frequently be done with elementary mathematics.

6.5   Soundness

We consider for the Hoare rules two very general properties of logical systems:

Soundness: Every rule should preserve validity, in the sense that if the assumptions in the rule's premise is valid then so is its conclusion. When this holds of a rule it is called *sound*. When every rule of a proof system is sound, the proof system itself is said to be *sound*. It follows then by rule-induction that every theorem obtained from the proof system of Hoare rules is a valid partial correctness assertion. (The comments which follow the rules are informal arguments for the soundness of some of the rules.)

Completeness: Naturally we would like the proof system to be strong enough so that all valid partial correctness assertions can be obtained as theorems. We would like the proof system to be *complete* in this sense. (There are some subtle issues here which we discuss in the next chapter.)

The proof of soundness of the rules depends on some facts about substitution.

Lemma 6.8 *Let I be an interpretation. Let $a, a_0 \in$ **Aexpv**. Let $X \in$ **Loc**. Then for all interpretations I and states σ*

$$\mathcal{A}v[\![a_0[a/X]]\!]I\sigma = \mathcal{A}v[\![a_0]\!]I\sigma[\mathcal{A}v[\![a]\!]I\sigma/X].$$

Proof: The proof is by structural induction on a_0—exercise!   □

Lemma 6.9 *Let I be an interpretation. Let $B \in$ **Assn**, $X \in$ **Loc** and $a \in$ **Aexp**. For all states $\sigma \in \Sigma$*

$$\sigma \models^I B[a/X] \quad \text{iff} \quad \sigma[\mathcal{A}[\![a]\!]\sigma/X] \models^I B.$$

Proof: The proof is by structural induction on B—exercise!   □

Exercise 6.10 Provide the proofs for the lemmas above.   □

Theorem 6.11 *Let $\{A\}c\{B\}$ be a partial correctness assertion.*
If $\vdash \{A\}c\{B\}$ then $\models \{A\}c\{B\}$.

Proof: Clearly if we can show each rule is sound (*i.e.* preserves validity in the sense that if its premise consists of valid assertions and partial correctness assertions then so is its conclusion) then by rule-induction we can see that every theorem is valid.

The rule for **skip***:* Clearly $\models \{A\}$**skip**$\{A\}$ so the rule for **skip** is sound.

The rule for assignments: Assume $c \equiv (X := a)$. Let I be an interpretation. We have $\sigma \models^I B[a/X]$ iff $\sigma[\mathcal{A}[\![a]\!]\sigma/X] \models^I B$, by Lemma 6.9. Thus

$$\sigma \models^I B[a/X] \Rightarrow \mathcal{C}[\![X := a]\!]\sigma \models^I B,$$

and hence $\models \{B[a/X]\}X := a\{B\}$, showing the soundness of the assignment rule.

The rule for sequencing: Assume $\models \{A\}c\{{}_{}0 C$ and $\models \{C\}c\{{}_{}1 B$. Let I be an interpretation. Suppose $\sigma \models^I A$. Then $\mathcal{C}[\![c_0]\!]\sigma \models^I C$ because $\models^I \{A\}c\{{}_{}0 C$. Also $\mathcal{C}[\![c_1]\!](\mathcal{C}[\![c_0]\!]\sigma) \models_I B$ because $\models^I \{C\}c\{{}_{}1 B$. Hence $\models \{A\}c_0; c_1\{B\}$.

The rule for conditionals: Assume $\models \{A \wedge b\}c_0\{B\}$ and $\models \{A \wedge \neg b\}c_1\{B\}$. Let I be an interpretation. Suppose $\sigma \models_I A$. Either $\sigma \models_I b$ or $\sigma \models_I \neg b$. In the former case $\sigma \models_I A \wedge b$ so $\mathcal{C}[\![c_0]\!]\sigma \models^I B$, as $\models^I \{A \wedge b\}c_0\{B\}$. In the latter case $\sigma \models_I A \wedge \neg b$ so $\mathcal{C}[\![c_1]\!]\sigma \models^I B$, as $\models^I \{A \wedge \neg b\}c_1\{B\}$. This ensures $\models \{A\}$**if** b **then** c_0 **else** $c_1\{B\}$.

The rule for while-loops: Assume $\models \{A \wedge b\}c\{A\}$, *i.e.* A is an invariant of

$$w \equiv \text{\textbf{while} } b \text{ \textbf{do} } c.$$

Let I be an interpretation. Recall that $\mathcal{C}[\![w]\!] = \bigcup_{n \in \omega} \theta_n$ where

$\theta_0 = \emptyset,$

$\theta_{n+1} = \{(\sigma, \sigma') \mid \mathcal{B}[\![b]\!]\sigma = \text{\textbf{true}} \ \& \ (\sigma, \sigma') \in \theta_n \circ \mathcal{C}[\![c]\!]\} \cup \{(\sigma, \sigma) \mid \mathcal{B}[\![b]\!]\sigma = \text{\textbf{false}}.\}$

We shall show by mathematical induction that $P(n)$ holds where

$$P(n) \iff {}_{def} \forall \sigma, \sigma' \in \Sigma. \ (\sigma, \sigma') \in \theta_n \ \&$$
$$\sigma \models^I A \ \Rightarrow \ \sigma' \models^I A \wedge \neg b$$

for all $n \in \omega$. It then follows that

$$\sigma \models^I A \Rightarrow \mathcal{C}[\![w]\!]\sigma \models^I A \wedge \neg b$$

for all states σ, and hence that $\models \{A\}w\{A \wedge \neg b\}$, as required.

Base case $n = 0$: When $n = 0$, $\theta_0 = \emptyset$ so that induction hypothesis $P(0)$ is vacuously true.

Induction Step: We assume the induction hypothesis $P(n)$ holds for $n \geq 0$ and attempt to prove $P(n+1)$. Suppose $(\sigma, \sigma') \in \theta_{n+1}$ and $\sigma \models^I A$. Either

(i) $\mathcal{B}[\![b]\!]\sigma = \text{\textbf{true}}$ and $(\sigma, \sigma') \in \theta_n \circ \mathcal{C}[\![c]\!]$, or

(ii) $\mathcal{B}[\![b]\!]\sigma = \text{\textbf{false}}$ and $\sigma' = \sigma$.

We show in either case that $\sigma' \models^I A \wedge \neg b$.

Assume (i). As $\mathcal{B}[\![b]\!]\sigma = \mathbf{true}$ we have $\sigma \models^I b$ and hence $\sigma \models^I A \wedge b$. Also $(\sigma, \sigma'') \in \mathcal{C}[\![c]\!]$ and $(\sigma'', \sigma') \in \theta_n$ for some state σ''. We obtain $\sigma'' \models^I A$, as $\models \{A \wedge b\}c\{A\}$. From the assumption $P(n)$, we obtain $\sigma' \models^I A \wedge \neg b$.

Assume (ii). As $\mathcal{B}[\![b]\!]\sigma = \mathbf{false}$ we have $\sigma \models^I \neg b$ and hence $\sigma \models^I A \wedge \neg b$. But $\sigma' = \sigma$.

This establishes the induction hypothesis $P(n + 1)$. By mathematical induction we conclude $P(n)$ holds for all n. Hence the rule for while loops is sound.

The consequence rule: Assume $\models (A \Rightarrow A')$ and $\models \{A'\}c\{B'\}$ and $\models (B' \Rightarrow B)$. Let I be an interpretation. Suppose $\sigma \models^I A$. Then $\sigma \models^I A'$, hence $\mathcal{C}[\![c]\!]\sigma \models^I B'$ and hence $\mathcal{C}[\![c]\!]\sigma \models^I B$. Thus $\models \{A\}c\{B\}$. The consequence rule is sound.

By rule-induction, every theorem is valid. $\qquad\qquad\qquad\qquad\qquad\qquad\square$

Exercise 6.12 Prove the above using only the operational semantics, instead of the denotational semantics. What proof method is used for the case of while-loops? $\qquad\square$

6.6 Using the Hoare rules—an example

The Hoare rules determine a notion of formal proof of partial correctness assertions through the idea of derivation. This is useful in the mechanisation of proofs. But in practice, as human beings faced with the task of verifying a program, we need not be so strict and can argue at a more informal level when using the Hoare rules. (Indeed working with the more formal notion of derivation might well distract from getting the proof; the task of producing the formal derivation should be delegated to a proof assistant like LCF or HOL [74], [43].)

As an example we show in detail how to use the Hoare rules to verify that the command

$$w \equiv (\mathbf{while}\ X > 0\ \mathbf{do}\ Y := X \times Y; X := X - 1)$$

does indeed compute the factorial function $n! = n \times (n-1) \times (n-2) \times \cdots \times 2 \times 1$, with $0!$ understood to be 1, given that $X = n$, a nonnegative number, and $Y = 1$ initially. [2]

More precisely, we wish to prove:

$$\{X = n \wedge n \geq 0 \wedge Y = 1\}w\{Y = n!\}.$$

To prove this we must clearly invoke the proof rule for while-loops which requires an invariant. Take

$$I \equiv (Y \times X! = n! \wedge X \geq 0).$$

---

[2]For this example, we imagine our syntax of programs and assertions to be extended to include $>$ and the factorial function which strictly speaking do not appear in the boolean and arithmetic expressions defined earlier.

We show I is indeed an invariant *i.e.*

$$\{I \wedge X > 0\}Y := X \times Y; X := X - 1\{I\}.$$

From the rule for assignment we have

$$\{I[(X-1)/X]\}X := X - 1\{I\}$$

where $I[(X-1)/X] \equiv (Y \times (X-1)! = n! \wedge (X-1) \geq 0)$. Again by the assignment rule:

$$\{X \times Y \times (X-1)! = n! \wedge (X-1) \geq 0\}Y := X \times Y\{I[(X-1)/X]\}.$$

Thus, by the rule for sequencing,

$$\{X \times Y \times (X-1)! = n! \wedge (X-1) \geq 0\}Y := X \times Y; X := (X-1)\{I\}.$$

Clearly

$$I \wedge X > 0 \Rightarrow Y \times X! = n! \wedge X \geq 0 \wedge X > 0$$
$$\Rightarrow Y \times X! = n! \wedge X \geq 1$$
$$\Rightarrow X \times Y \times (X-1)! = n! \wedge (X-1) \geq 0.$$

Thus by the consequence rule

$$\{I \wedge X > 0\}Y := X \times Y; X := (X-1)\{I\}$$

establishing that I is an invariant.

Now applying the rule for while-loops we obtain

$$\{I\}w\{I \wedge X \not> 0\}.$$

Clearly $(X = n) \wedge (n \geq 0) \wedge (Y = 1) \Rightarrow I$, and

$$I \wedge X \not> 0 \Rightarrow Y \times X! = n! \wedge X \geq 0 \wedge X \not> 0 \qquad\qquad (*)$$
$$\Rightarrow Y \times X! = n! \wedge X = 0$$
$$\Rightarrow Y \times 0! = Y = n!$$

Thus by the consequence rule we conclude

$$\{(X = n) \wedge (Y = 1)\}w\{Y = n!\}.$$

There are a couple of points to note about the proof given in the example. Firstly, in dealing with a chain of commands composed in sequence it is generally easier to proceed in a right-to-left manner because the rule for assignment is of this nature. Secondly, our choice of I may seem unduly strong. Why did we include the assertion $X \geq 0$ in the invariant? Notice where it was used, at (∗), and without it we could not have deduced that on exiting the while-loop the value of X is 0. In getting invariants to prove what we want they often must be strengthened. They are like induction hypotheses. One obvious way to strengthen an invariant is to specify the range of the variables and values at the locations as tightly as possible. Undoubtedly, a common difficulty in examples is to get stuck on proving the "exit conditions". In this case, it is a good idea to see how to strengthen the invariant with information about the variables and locations in the boolean expression.

Thus it is fairly involved to show even trivial programs are correct. The same is true, of course, for trivial bits of mathematics, too, if one spells out all the details in a formal proof system. One point of formal proof systems is that proofs of properties of programs can be automated as in *e.g.*[74][41]—see also Section 7.4 on verification conditions in the next chapter. There is another method of application of such formal proof systems which has been advocated by Dijkstra and Gries among others, and that is to use the ideas in the study of program correctness in the design and development of programs. In his book "The Science of Programming" [44], Gries says

> "the study of program correctness proofs has led to the discovery and elucidation of methods for developing programs. Basically, one attempts to develop a program and its proof hand-in-hand, with the proof ideas leading the way!"

See Gries' book for many interesting examples of this approach.

Exercise 6.13 Prove, using the Hoare rules, the correctness of the partial correctness assertion:

$$\{1 \leq N\}$$
$$P := 0;$$
$$C := 1;$$
$$(\textbf{while } C \leq N \textbf{ do } P := P + M; C := C + 1)$$
$$\{P = M \times N\}$$

□

Exercise 6.14 Find an appropriate invariant to use in the while-rule for proving the following partial correctness assertion:

$$\{i = Y\}\textbf{while } \neg(Y = 0) \textbf{ do } Y := Y - 1; X := 2 \times X\{X = 2^i\}$$

□

Exercise 6.15 Using the Hoare rules, prove that for integers n, m,

$$\{X = m \wedge Y = n \wedge Z = 1\}c\{Z = m^n\}$$

where c is the while-program

> **while** $\neg(Y = 0)$ **do**
> $((\textbf{while } even(Y) \textbf{ do } X := X \times X; Y := Y/2);$
> $Z := Z \times X; Y := Y - 1)$

with the understanding that $Y/2$ is the integer resulting from dividing the contents of Y by 2, and $even(Y)$ means the content of Y is an even number.
(Hint: Use $m^n = Z \times X^Y$ as the invariants.)   □

Exercise 6.16
(i) Show that the greatest common divisor, $\gcd(n, m)$ of two positive numbers n, m satisfies:

$$(a)\ n > m \Rightarrow \gcd(n, m) = \gcd(n - m, m)$$
$$(b)\ \gcd(n, m) = \gcd(m, n)$$
$$(c)\ \gcd(n, n) = n.$$

(ii) Using the Hoare rules prove

$$\{N = n \wedge M = m \wedge 1 \le n \wedge 1 \le m\}\text{Euclid}\{X = \gcd(n, m)\}$$

where

> $\text{Euclid} \equiv \textbf{while } \neg(M = N) \textbf{ do}$
> $\qquad \textbf{if } M \le N$
> $\qquad\quad \textbf{then } N := N - M$
> $\qquad\quad \textbf{else } M := M - N.$

□

Exercise 6.17 Provide a Hoare rule for the repeat construct and prove it sound.
(*cf.* Exercise 5.9.)   □

6.7   Further reading

The book [44] by Gries has already been mentioned. Dijkstra's "A discipline of programming" [36] has been very influential. A more elementary book in the same vein is Backhouse's "Program construction and verification" [12]. A recent book which is recommended is Cohen's "Programming in the 1990's" [32]. A good book with many exercises is Alagić and Arbib's "The design of well-structured and correct programs" [5]. An elementary treatment of Hoare logic with a lot of informative discussion can be found in Gordon's recent book [42]. Alternatives to this book's treatment, concentrating more on semantic issues than the other references, can be found in de Bakker's "Mathematical theory of program correctness" [13] and Loeckx and Sieber's "The foundations of program verification" [58].

7 Completeness of the Hoare rules

In this chapter it is discussed what it means for the Hoare rules to be complete. Gödel's Incompleteness Theorem implies there is no complete proof system for establishing precisely the valid assertions. The Hoare rules inherit this incompleteness. However by separating incompleteness of the assertion language from incompleteness due to inadequacies in the axioms and rules for the programming language constructs, we can obtain relative completeness in the sense of Cook. The proof that the Hoare rules are relatively complete relies on the idea of weakest liberal precondition, and leads into a discussion of verification-condition generators.

7.1 Gödel's Incompleteness Theorem

Look again at the proof rules for partial correctness assertions, and in particular at the consequence rule. Knowing we have a rule instance of the consequence rule requires that we determine that certain assertions in **Assn** are valid. Ideally, of course, we would like a proof system of axioms and rules for assertions which enabled us to prove all the assertions of **Assn** which are valid, and none which are invalid. Naturally we would like the proof system to be *effective* in the sense that it is a routine matter to check that something proposed as a rule instance really is one. It should be routine in the sense that there is a computable method in the form of a program which, with input a real rule instance, returns a confirmation that it is, and returns no confirmation on inputs which are not rule instances, without necessarily even terminating. Lacking such a computable method we might well have a proof derivation without knowing it because it uses a step we cannot check is a rule instance. We cannot claim that the proof system of Hoare rules is effective because we do not have a computable method for checking instances of the consequence rule. Having such depends on having a computable method to check that assertions of **Assn** are valid. But here we meet an absolute limit. The great Austrian logician Kurt Gödel showed that it is logically impossible to have an effective proof system in which one can prove precisely the valid assertions of **Assn**. This remarkable result, called Gödel's Incompleteness Theorem[1] is not so hard to prove nowadays, if one goes about it via results from the theory of computability. Indeed a proof of the theorem, stated now, will be given in Section 7.3 based on some results from computability. Any gaps or shortcomings there can be made up for by consulting the Appendix on computability and undecidability based on the language of while programs, **IMP**.

---

[1] The Incompleteness Theorem is not to be confused with Gödel's Completeness Theorem which says that the proof system for predicate calculus generates precisely those assertions which are valid for *all* interpretations.

Theorem 7.1 *Gödel's Incompleteness Theorem (1931):*
There is no effective proof system for **Assn** *such that the theorems coincide with the valid assertions of* **Assn***.*

This theorem means we cannot have an effective proof system for partial correctness assertions. As $\models B$ iff $\models \{\textbf{true}\}\textbf{skip}\{B\}$, if we had an effective proof system for partial correctness it would reduce to an effective proof system for assertions in **Assn**, which is impossible by Gödel's Incompleteness Theorem. In fact we can show there is no effective proof system for partial correctness assertions more directly.

Proposition 7.2 *There is no effective proof system for partial correctness assertions such that its theorems are precisely the valid partial correctness assertions.*

Proof: Observe that $\models \{\textbf{true}\}c\{\textbf{false}\}$ iff the command c diverges on all states. If we had an effective proof system for partial correction assertions it would yield a computable method of confirming that a command c diverges on all states. But this is known to be impossible—see Exercise A.13 of the Appendix.   □

Faced with this unsurmountable fact, we settle for the proof system of Hoare rules in Section 6.4 even though we know it to be not effective because of the nature of the consequence rule; determining that we have an instance of the consequence rule is dependent on certain assertions being valid. Still, we can inquire as to the completeness of this system. That it is complete was established by S. Cook in [33]. If a partial correctness assertion is valid then there is a proof of it using the Hoare rules, *i.e.* for any partial correctness assertion $\{A\}c\{B\}$,

$$\models \{A\}c\{B\} \text{ implies } \vdash \{A\}c\{B\},$$

though the fact that it is a proof can rest on certain assertions in **Assn** being valid. It is as if in building proofs one could consult an oracle at any stage one needs to know if an assertion in **Assn** is valid. For this reason Cook's result is said to establish the *relative completeness* of the Hoare rules for partial correctness—their completeness is relative to being able to draw from the set of valid assertions about arithmetic. In this way one tries to separate concerns about programs and reasoning about them from concerns to do with arithmetic and the incompleteness of any proof system for it.

7.2 Weakest preconditions and expressiveness

The proof of relative completeness relies on another concept. Consider trying to prove

$$\{A\}c_0; c_1\{B\}.$$

In order to use the rule for composition one requires an intermediate assertion C so that

$$\{A\}c_0\{C\} \text{ and } \{C\}c_1\{B\}$$

are provable. How do we know such an intermediate assertion C can be found? A sufficient condition is that for every command c and postconditions B we can express their weakest precondition[2] in **Assn**.

Let $c \in$ **Com** and $B \in$ **Assn**. Let I be an interpretation. The weakest precondition $wp^I[\![c, B]\!]$ of B with respect to c in I is defined by:

$$wp^I[\![c, B]\!] = \{\sigma \in \Sigma_\perp \mid C[\![c]\!]\sigma \models^I B\}.$$

It's all those states from which the execution of c either diverges or ends up in a final state satisfying B. Thus if $\models^I \{A\}c\{B\}$ we know

$$A^I \subseteq wp^I[\![c, B]\!]$$

and *vice versa*. Thus $\models^I \{A\}c\{B\}$ iff $A^I \subseteq wp^I[\![c, B]\!]$.

Suppose there is an assertion A_0 such that in all interpretations I,

$$A_0^I = wp^I[\![c, B]\!].$$

Then

$$\models^I \{A\}c\{B\} \text{ iff } \models^I (A \Rightarrow A_0),$$

for any interpretation I *i.e.*

$$\models \{A\}c\{B\} \text{ iff } \models (A \Rightarrow A_0).$$

So we see why it is called the weakest precondition, it is implied by any precondition which makes the partial correctness assertion valid. However it's not obvious that a particular language of assertions has an assertion A_0 such that $A_0^I = wp^I[\![c, B]\!]$.

Definition: Say **Assn** is *expressive* iff for every command c and assertion B there is an assertion A_0 such that $A_0^I = wp^I[\![c, B]\!]$ for any interpretation I.

In showing expressiveness we will use Gödel's β predicate to encode facts about sequences of states as assertions in **Assn**. The β predicate involves the operation a **mod** b which gives the remainder of a when divided by b. We can express this notion as an assertion in **Assn**. For $x = a$ **mod** b we write

---

[2]What we shall call weakest precondition is generally called weakest liberal precondition, the term weakest precondition referring to a related notion but for total correctness.

$$a \geq 0 \ \wedge \ b \geq 0 \ \wedge$$
$$\exists k.[k \geq 0 \ \wedge \ k \times b \leq a \ \wedge \ (k+1) \times b > a \ \wedge \ x = a - (k \times b)].$$

Lemma 7.3 *Let $\beta(a, b, i, x)$ be the predicate over natural numbers defined by*

$$\beta(a, b, i, x) \Leftrightarrow_{def} x = a \ \mathbf{mod}(1 + (1 + i) \times b).$$

For any sequence $n_0, \ldots, n_k$ of natural numbers there are natural numbers n, m such that for all j, $0 \leq j \leq k$, and all x we have

$$\beta(n, m, j, x) \Leftrightarrow x = n_j.$$

Proof: The proof of this arithmetical fact is left to the reader as a small series of exercises at the end of this section.   □

The β predicate is important because with it we can encode a sequence of k natural numbers $n_0, \cdots, n_k$ as a pair n, m. Given n, m, for any length k, we can extract a sequence, *viz.* that sequence of numbers $n_0, \cdots, n_k$ such that

$$\beta(n, m, j, n_j)$$

for $0 \leq j \leq k$. Notice that the definition of β shows that the list $n_0, \cdots, n_k$ is uniquely determined by the choice of n, m. The lemma above asserts that any sequence $n_0, \cdots, n_k$ can be encoded in this way.

We must now face a slight irritation. Our states and our language of assertions can involve negative as well as positive numbers. We are obliged to extend Gödel's β predicate so as to encode sequences of positive and negative numbers. Fortunately, this is easily done by encoding positive numbers as the even and negative numbers as the odd natural numbers.

Lemma 7.4 *Let $F(x, y)$ be the predicate over natural numbers x and positive and negative numbers y given by*

$$F(x, y) \ \equiv \ x \geq 0 \ \&$$
$$\exists z \geq 0. \qquad [(x = 2 \times z \Rightarrow y = z) \ \&$$
$$(x = 2 \times z + 1 \Rightarrow y = -z)]$$

Define

$$\beta^{\pm}(n, m, j, y) \Leftrightarrow_{def} \exists x.(\beta(n, m, j, x) \wedge F(x, y)).$$

Then for any sequence $n_0, \ldots, n_k$ of positive or negative numbers there are natural numbers n, m such that for all j, $0 \leq j \leq k$, and all x we have

$$\beta^{\pm}(n, m, j, x) \Leftrightarrow x = n_j.$$

Proof: Clearly $F(n, m)$ expresses the 1-1 correspondence between natural numbers $m \in \omega$ and $n \in \mathbf{N}$ in which even m stand for non-negative and odd m for negative numbers. The lemma follows from Lemma 7.3. $\qquad\qquad\qquad\qquad\qquad\qquad\qquad\qquad\qquad\qquad\qquad\square$

The predicate $\beta^{\pm}$ is expressible in **Assn** because β and F are. To avoid introducing a further symbol, let us write $\beta^{\pm}$ for the assertion in **Assn** expressing this predicate. This assertion in **Assn** will have free integer variables, say n, m, j, x, understood in the same way as above, *i.e.* n, m encodes a sequence with jth element x. We will want to use other integer variables besides n, m, j, x, so we write $\beta^{\pm}(n', m', j', x')$ as an abbreviation for $\beta^{\pm}[n'/n, m'/m, j'/j, x'/x]$, got by substituting the the integer variable n' for n, m' for m, and so on. We have not give a formal definition of what it means to substitute integer variables in an assertion. The definition of substitution in Section 6.2.2 only defines substitutions $A[a/i]$ of arithmetic expressions a without integer variables, for an integer variable i in an assertion A. However, as long as the variables n', m', j', x' are "fresh" in the sense of their being distinct and not occurring (free or bound) in $\beta^{\pm}$, the same definition applies equally well to the substitution of integer variables; the assertion $\beta^{\pm}[n'/n, m'/m, j'/j, x'/x]$ is that given by $\beta^{\pm}[n'/n][m'/m][j'/j][x'/x]$ using the definition of Section 6.2.2.[3]

Now we can show:

Theorem 7.5 Assn *is expressive.*

Proof: We show by structural induction on commands c that for all assertions B there is an assertion $w[c, B]$ such that for all interpretations I

$$wp^I[c, B] = w[c, B]^I,$$

for all commands c.

Note that by the definition of weakest precondition that, for I an interpretation, the equality $wp^I[c, B] = w[c, B]^I$ amounts to

$$\sigma \models^I w[c, B] \text{ iff } \mathcal{C}[c]\sigma \models^I B,$$

---

[3]To illustrate the technical problem with substitution of integer variables which are not fresh, consider the assertion $A \equiv (\exists i'.\ 2 \times i' = i)$ which means "i is even." The naive definition of $A[i'/i]$ yields the assertion $(\exists i'.\ 2 \times i' = i')$ which happens to be valid, and so certainly does not mean "i is even."

holding for all states σ, a fact we shall use occasionally in the proof.

$c \equiv \mathbf{skip}$: In this case, take $w[\![\mathbf{skip}, B]\!] \equiv B$. Clearly, for all states σ and interpretations I,

$$\sigma \in wp^I[\![\mathbf{skip}, B]\!] \text{ iff } C[\![\mathbf{skip}]\!]\sigma \models^I B$$
$$\text{iff } \sigma \models^I B$$
$$\text{iff } \sigma \models^I w[\![\mathbf{skip}, B]\!].$$

$c \equiv (X := a)$: In this case, define $w[\![X := a, B]\!] \equiv B[a/X]$. Then

$$\sigma \in wp^I[\![X := a, B]\!] \text{ iff } \sigma[\mathcal{A}[\![a]\!]\sigma/X] \models^I B$$
$$\text{iff } \sigma \models^I B[a/X] \qquad \text{by Lemma 6.9}$$
$$\text{iff } \sigma \models^I w[\![X := a, B]\!].$$

$c \equiv c_0; c_1$: Inductively define $w[\![c_0; c_1, B]\!] \equiv w[\![c_0, w[\![c_1, B]\!]]\!]$. Then, for $\sigma \in \Sigma$ and interpretation I,

$$\sigma \in wp^I[\![c_0; c_1, B]\!] \text{ iff } C[\![c_0; c_1]\!]\sigma \models^I B$$
$$\text{iff } C[\![c_1]\!](C[\![c_0]\!]\sigma) \models^I B$$
$$\text{iff } C[\![c_0]\!]\sigma \models^I w[\![c_1, B]\!], \qquad \text{by induction,}$$
$$\text{iff } \sigma \models^I w[\![c_0, w[\![c_1, B]\!]]\!], \qquad \text{by induction,}$$
$$\text{iff } \sigma \models^I w[\![c_0; c_1, B]\!].$$

$c \equiv \mathbf{if}\ b\ \mathbf{then}\ c_0\ \mathbf{else}\ c_1$: Define

$$w[\![\mathbf{if}\ b\ \mathbf{then}\ c_0\ \mathbf{else}\ c_1, B]\!] \equiv [(b \wedge w[\![c_0, B]\!]) \vee (\neg b \wedge w[\![c_1, B]\!])].$$

Then, for $\sigma \in \Sigma$ and interpretation I,

$$\sigma \in wp^I[\![c, B]\!] \text{ iff } C[\![c]\!]\sigma \models^I B$$
$$\text{iff } ([\mathcal{B}[\![b]\!]\sigma = \mathbf{true} \ \& \ C[\![c_0]\!]\sigma \models^I B] \text{ or}$$
$$[\mathcal{B}[\![b]\!]\sigma = \mathbf{false} \ \& \ C[\![c_1]\!]\sigma \models^I B])$$
$$\text{iff } ([\sigma \models^I b \ \& \ \sigma \models^I w[\![c_0, B]\!]] \text{ or}$$
$$[\sigma \models^I \neg b \ \& \ \sigma \models^I w[\![c_1, B]\!]]), \quad \text{by induction,}$$
$$\text{iff } \sigma \models^I [(b \wedge w[\![c_0, B]\!]) \vee (\neg b \wedge w[\![c_1, B]\!])]$$
$$\text{iff } \sigma \models^I w[\![c, B]\!].$$

$c \equiv$ **while** b **do** c_0: This is the one difficult case. For a state σ and interpretation I, we have (from Exercise 5.8) that $\sigma \in wp^I[\![c, B]\!]$ iff

$$\forall k \; \forall \sigma_0, \ldots, \sigma_k \in \Sigma.$$
$$[\sigma = \sigma_0 \; \&$$

$$\forall i(0 \leq i < k). \; (\; \sigma_i \models^I b \; \&$$

$$\mathcal{C}[\![c_0]\!]\sigma_i = \sigma_{i+1})]$$

$$\Rightarrow (\sigma_k \models^I b \vee B). \tag{1}$$

As it stands the mathematical characterisation of states σ in $wp^I[\![c, B]\!]$ is not an assertion in **Assn**; in particular it refers directly to states $\sigma_0, \cdots, \sigma_k$. However we show how to replace it by an equivalent description which is. The first step is to replace all references to the states $\sigma_0, \ldots, \sigma_k$ by references to the values they contain at the locations mentioned in c and B. Suppose $\bar{X} = X_1, \ldots, X_l$ are the locations mentioned in c and B—the values at the remaining locations are irrelevant to the computation. We make use of the following fact:
Suppose A is an assertion in **Assn** which mentions only locations from $\bar{X} = X_1, \ldots, X_l$. For a state σ, let $s_i = \sigma(X_i)$, for $1 \leq i \leq l$, and write $\bar{s} = s_1, \cdots, s_l$. Then

$$\sigma \models^I A \text{ iff } \models^I A[\bar{s}/\bar{X}] \tag{$*$}$$

for any interpretation I. The assertion $A[\bar{s}/\bar{X}]$ is that obtained by the simultaneous substitution of $\bar{s}$ for $\bar{X}$ in A. This fact can be proved by structural induction (Exercise!).

Using the fact $(*)$ we can convert (1) into an equivalent assertion about sequences. For $i \geq 0$, let $\bar{s}_i$ abbreviate $s_{i1}, \ldots, s_{il}$, a sequence in **N**. We claim: $\sigma \in wp^I[\![c, B]\!]$ iff

$$\forall k \; \forall \bar{s}_0, \ldots, \bar{s}_k \in \mathbf{N}.$$
$$[\sigma \models^I \bar{X} = \bar{s}_0 \; \&$$

$$\forall i \; (0 \leq i < k). \; (\models^I b[\bar{s}_i/\bar{X}] \; \&$$

$$\models^I (w[\![c_0, \bar{X} = \bar{s}_{i+1}]\!] \wedge \neg w[\![c_0, \mathbf{false}]\!])[\bar{s}_i/\bar{X}])$$

$$\Rightarrow \models^I (b \vee B)[\bar{s}_k/\bar{X}] \tag{2}$$

We have used $\bar{X} = \bar{s}_0$ to abbreviate $X_1 = s_{01} \wedge \ldots \wedge X_l = s_{0l}$.

To prove the claim we argue that (1) and (2) are equivalent. Parts of the argument are straightforward. For example, it follows directly from $(*)$ that, assuming state σ_i has values $\bar{s}_i$ at $\bar{X}$,

$$\sigma_i \models^I b \text{ iff } \models^I b[\bar{s}_i/\bar{X}],$$

for an interpretation I. The hard part hinges on showing that assuming σ_i and σ_{i+1} have values $\bar{s}_i$ and $\bar{s}_{i+1}$, respectively, at $\bar{X}$ and agree elsewhere, we have

$$\mathcal{C}[c_0]\sigma_i = \sigma_{i+1} \text{ iff } \models^I (w[c_0, \bar{X} = \bar{s}_{i+1}] \wedge \neg w[c_0, \mathbf{false}])[\bar{s}_i/\bar{X}],$$

for an interpretation I. To see this we first observe that

$$\mathcal{C}[c_0]\sigma_i = \sigma_{i+1} \text{ iff } \sigma_i \in wp^I[c_0, \bar{X} = \bar{s}_{i+1}] \,\&\, \mathcal{C}[c_0]\sigma_i \text{ is defined.}$$

(Why?) From the induction hypothesis we obtain

$$\sigma_i \in wp^I[c_0, \bar{X} = \bar{s}_{i+1}] \quad \text{iff} \quad \sigma_i \models^I (w[c_0, \bar{X} = \bar{s}_{i+1}], \text{ and}$$
$$\mathcal{C}[c_0]\sigma_i \text{ is defined} \quad \text{iff} \quad \sigma_i \models^I \neg w[c_0, \mathbf{false}]$$

—recall that $\sigma_i \in wp^I[c_0, \mathbf{false}]$ iff c_0 diverges on σ_i. Consequently,

$$\mathcal{C}[c_0]\sigma_i = \sigma_{i+1} \text{ iff } \sigma_i \models^I (w[c_0, \bar{X} = \bar{s}_{i+1}] \wedge \neg w[c_0, \mathbf{false}])$$
$$\text{iff } \models^I (w[c_0, \bar{X} = \bar{s}_{i+1}] \wedge \neg w[c_0, \mathbf{false}])[\bar{s}_i/\bar{X}] \qquad \text{by } (*).$$

This covers the difficulties in showing (1) and (2) equivalent.

Finally, notice how (2) can be expressed in **Assn**, using the Gödel predicate $\beta^{\pm}$. For simplicity assume $l = 1$ with $\bar{X} = X$. Then we can rephrase (2) to get: $\sigma \in wp^I[c, B]$ iff

$\sigma \models^I \forall k \, \forall m, n \geq 0.$

$[\beta^{\pm}(n, m, 0, X) \wedge$

$\forall i \,(0 \leq i < k).\,(\forall x.\, \beta^{\pm}(n, m, i, x) \Rightarrow b[x/X]) \wedge$

$\forall x, y.\, (\beta^{\pm}(n, m, i, x) \wedge \beta^{\pm}(n, m, i+1, y) \Rightarrow$
$(w[c_0, X = y] \wedge \neg w[c_0, \mathbf{false}])[x/X])]$

$\Rightarrow (\beta^{\pm}(n, m, k, x) \Rightarrow (b \vee B)[x/X])$

This is the assertion we take as $w[c, B]$ in this case. (In understanding this assertion compare it line-for-line with (2), bearing in mind that $\beta^{\pm}(n, m, i, x)$ means that x is the

ith element of the sequence encoded by the pair n, m.) The form of the assertion in the general case, for arbitrary l, is similar, though more clumsy, and left to the reader.

This completes the proof by structural induction.   □

As **Assn** is expressive for any command c and assertion B there is an assertion $w[\![c, B]\!]$ with the property that

$$w[\![c, B]\!]^I = wp^I[\![c, B]\!]$$

for any interpretation I. Of course, the assertion $w[\![c, B]\!]$ constructed in the proof of expressiveness above, is not the unique assertion with this property (Why not?). However suppose A_0 is another assertion such that $A_0^I = wp^I[\![c, B]\!]$ for all I. Then

$$\models (w[\![c, B]\!] \iff A_0).$$

So the assertion expressing a weakest precondition is unique to within logical equivalence. The useful key fact about such an assertion $w[\![c, B]\!]$ is that, from the definition of weakest precondition, it is characterised by:

$$\sigma \models^I w[\![c, B]\!] \text{ iff } C[\![c]\!]\sigma \models^I B,$$

for all states σ and interpretations I.

From the expressiveness of **Assn** we shall prove relative completeness. First an important lemma.

Lemma 7.6 *For $c \in$ **Com** and $B \in$ **Assn**, let $w[\![c, B]\!]$ be an assertion expressing the weakest precondition i.e. $w[\![c, B]\!]^I = wp^I[\![c, B]\!]$ (the assertion $w[\![c, B]\!]$ need not be necessarily that constructed by Theorem 7.5 above). Then*

$$\vdash \{w[\![c, B]\!]\}c\{B\}.$$

Proof: Let $w[\![c, B]\!]$ be an assertion which expresses the weakest precondition of a command c and postcondition B. We show by structural induction on c that

$$\vdash \{w[\![c, B]\!]\}c\{B\} \quad \text{for all } B \in \textbf{Assn},$$

for all commands c.
(In all but the last case, the proof overlaps with that of Theorem 7.5.)

$c \equiv$ **skip** : In this case $\models w[\![\textbf{skip}, B]\!] \iff B$, so $\vdash \{w[\![\textbf{skip}, B]\!]\}\textbf{skip}\{B\}$ by the consequence rule.

$c \equiv (X := a)$: In this case

$$\sigma \in wp^I[\![c, B]\!] \text{ iff } \sigma[\mathcal{A}[\![a]\!]\sigma/X] \models^I B$$
$$\text{iff } \sigma \models^I B[a/X].$$

Thus $\models (w[\![c, B]\!] \iff B[a/X])$. Hence by the rule for assignment with the consequence rule we see $\vdash \{w[\![c, B]\!]\}c\{B\}$ in this case.

$c \equiv c_0; c_1$: In this case, for $\sigma \in \Sigma$ and interpretation I,

$$\sigma \models^I w[\![c_0; c_1, B]\!] \text{ iff } \mathcal{C}[\![c_0; c_1]\!]\sigma \models^I B$$
$$\text{iff } \mathcal{C}[\![c_1]\!](\mathcal{C}[\![c_0]\!]\sigma) \models^I B$$
$$\text{iff } \mathcal{C}[\![c_0]\!]\sigma \models^I w[\![c_1, B]\!]$$
$$\text{iff } \sigma \models^I w[\![c_0, w[\![c_1, B]\!]]\!].$$

Thus $\models w[\![c_0; c_1, B]\!] \iff w[\![c_0, w[\![c_1, B]\!]]\!]$. By the induction hypothesis

$$\vdash \{w[\![c_0, w[\![c_1, B]\!]]\!]\}c_0\{w[\![c_1, B]\!]\} \quad \text{and}$$
$$\vdash \{w[\![c_1, B]\!]\}c_1\{B\}.$$

Hence, by the rule for sequencing, we deduce

$$\vdash \{w[\![c_0, w[\![c_1, B]\!]]\!]\}c_0; c_1\{B\}$$

By the consequence rule we get

$$\vdash \{w[\![c_0; c_1, B]\!]\}c_0; c_1\{B\}.$$

$c \equiv \textbf{if } b \textbf{ then } c_0 \textbf{ else } c_1$: In this case, for $\sigma \in \Sigma$ and interpretation I,

$$\sigma \models^I w[\![c, B]\!] \text{ iff } \mathcal{C}[\![c]\!]\sigma \models^I B$$
$$\text{iff } ([\mathcal{B}[\![b]\!]\sigma = \textbf{true} \ \& \ \mathcal{C}[\![c_0]\!]\sigma \models^I B] \text{ or}$$
$$[\mathcal{B}[\![b]\!]\sigma = \textbf{false} \ \& \ \mathcal{C}[\![c_1]\!]\sigma \models^I B])$$
$$\text{iff } ([\sigma \models^I b \ \& \ \sigma \models^I w[\![c_0, B]\!]] \text{ or}$$
$$[\sigma \models^I \neg b \ \& \ \sigma \models^I w[\![c_1, B]\!]])$$
$$\text{iff } \sigma \models^I [(b \wedge w[\![c_0, B]\!]) \vee (\neg b \wedge w[\![c_1, B]\!])].$$

Hence

$$\models w[\![c, B]\!] \iff [(b \wedge w[\![c_0, B]\!]) \vee (\neg b \wedge w[\![c_1, B]\!])].$$

Now by the induction hypothesis

$$\vdash \{w[\![c_0, B]\!]\}c_0\{B\} \text{ and } \vdash \{w[\![c_1, B]\!]\}c_1\{B\}.$$

But

$$\models (w[\![c, B]\!] \wedge b) \iff w[\![c_0, B]\!] \text{ and}$$
$$\models (w[\![c, B]\!] \wedge \neg b) \iff w[\![c_1, B]\!].$$

So by the consequence rule

$$\vdash \{w[\![c, B]\!] \wedge b\}c_0\{B\} \text{ and } \vdash \{w[\![c, B]\!] \wedge \neg b\}c_1\{B\}.$$

By the rule for conditionals we obtain $\vdash \{w[\![c, B]\!]\}c\{B\}$ in this case.

Finally we consider the case:
$c \equiv \textbf{while } b \textbf{ do } c_0$: Take $A \equiv w[\![c, B]\!]$. We show

(1) $\models \{A \wedge b\}c_0\{A\}$,
(2) $\models (A \wedge \neg b) \Rightarrow B$.

Then, from (1), by the induction hypothesis we obtain $\vdash \{A \wedge b\}c_0\{A\}$, so that by the while-rule $\vdash \{A\}c\{A \wedge \neg b\}$. Continuing, by (2), using the consequence rule, we obtain $\vdash \{A\}c\{B\}$. Now we prove (1) and (2).

(1) Let $\sigma \models^I A \wedge b$, for an interpretation I. Then $\sigma \models^I w[\![c, B]\!]$ and $\sigma \models^I b$, i.e. $C[\![c]\!]\sigma \models^I B$ and $\sigma \models^I b$. But $C[\![c]\!]$ is defined so

$$C[\![c]\!] = C[\![\textbf{if } b \textbf{ then } c_0; c \textbf{ else skip}]\!],$$

which makes $C[\![c_0; c]\!]\sigma \models^I B$, i.e. $C[\![c]\!](C[\![c_0]\!]\sigma) \models^I B$. Therefore $C[\![c_0]\!]\sigma \models^I w[\![c, B]\!]$, i.e. $C[\![c_0]\!]\sigma \models^I A$. Thus $\models \{A \wedge b\}c_0\{A\}$.

(2) Let $\sigma \models^I A \wedge \neg b$, for an interpretation I. Then $C[\![c]\!]\sigma \models^I B$ and $\sigma \models^I \neg b$. Again note $C[\![c]\!] = C[\![\textbf{if } b \textbf{ then } c_0; c \textbf{ else skip}]\!]$, so $C[\![c]\!]\sigma = \sigma$. Therefore $\sigma \models^I B$. It follows that $\models^I A \wedge \neg b \Rightarrow B$. Thus $\models A \wedge \neg b \Rightarrow B$, proving (2).

This completes all the cases. Hence, by structural induction, the lemma is proved. $\square$

Theorem 7.7 *The proof system for partial correctness is relatively complete, i.e. for any partial correctness assertion $\{A\}c\{B\}$,*

$$\vdash \{A\}c\{B\} \text{ if } \models \{A\}c\{B\}.$$

Proof: Suppose $\models \{A\}c\{B\}$. Then by the above lemma $\vdash \{w[\![c, B]\!]\}c\{B\}$ where $w[\![c, B]\!]^I = wp^I[\![c, B]\!]$ for any interpretation I. Thus as $\models (A \Rightarrow w[\![c, B]\!])$, by the consequence rule, we obtain $\vdash \{A\}c\{B\}$. □

Exercise 7.8 (The Gödel β predicate)

(a) Let $n_0, \ldots, n_k$ be a sequence of natural numbers and let

$$m = (\max \{k, n_0, \ldots, n_k\})!$$

Show that the numbers

$$p_i = 1 + (1 + i) \times m, \text{ for } 0 \le i \le k$$

are coprime (*i.e.*, $\gcd(p_i, p_j) = 1$ for $i \ne j$) and that $n_i < p_i$.

(b) Further, define

$$c_i = p_0 \times \ldots \times p_k / p_i, \text{ for } 0 \le i \le k.$$

Show that for all i, $0 \le i \le k$, there is a unique d_i, $0 \le d_i < p_i$, such that

$$(c_i \times d_i) \bmod p_i = 1$$

(c) In addition, define

$$n = \sum_{i=0}^{k} c_i \times d_i \times n_i.$$

Show that

$$n_i = n \bmod p_i$$

when $0 \le i \le k$.

(d) Finally prove lemma 3.

□

7.3 Proof of Gödel's Theorem

Gödel's Incompleteness Theorem amounts to the fact that the subset of valid assertions in **Assn** is not recursively enumerable (*i.e.*, there is no program which given assertions as input returns a confirmation precisely on the valid assertions—see the Appendix on computability for a precise definition and a more detailed treatment).

Theorem 7.9 *The subset of assertions* $\{A \in \mathbf{Assn} \mid \models A\}$ *is not recursively enumerable.*

Proof: Suppose on the contrary that the set $\{A \in \mathbf{Assn} \mid \models A\}$ is recursively enumerable. Then there is a computable method to confirm that an assertion is valid. This provides a computable method to confirm that a command c diverges on the zero-state σ_0, in which each location X has contents 0:
Construct the assertion $w[\![c, \mathbf{false}]\!]$ as in the proof of Theorem 7.5. Let $\vec{X}$ consist of all the locations mentioned in $w[\![c, \mathbf{false}]\!]$. Let A be the assertion $w[\![c, \mathbf{false}]\!][\vec{0}/\vec{X}]$, obtained by replacing the locations by zeros. Then the divergence of c on the zero-state can be confirmed by checking the validity of A, for which there is assumed to be a computable method.
But it is known that the commands c which diverge on the zero-state do not form a recursively enumerable set—see Theorem A.12 in the Appendix. This contradiction shows $\{A \in \mathbf{Assn} \mid \models A\}$ to not be recursively enumerable. □

As a corollary we obtain Gödel's Incompleteness Theorem:

Theorem 7.10 *(Theorem 7.1 restated) (Gödel's Incompleteness Theorem):*
There is no effective proof system for **Assn** *such that its theorems coincide with the valid assertions of* **Assn**.

Proof: Assume there were an effective proof system such that for an assertion A, we have A is provable iff A is valid. The proof system being effective implies that there is a computable method to confirm precisely when something is a proof. Searching through all proofs systematically till a proof of an assertion A is found provides a computable method of confirming precisely when an assertion A is valid. Thus there cannot be an effective proof system.   □

Although we have stated Gödel's Theorem for assertions **Assn** the presence of locations plays no essential role in the results. Gödel's Theorem is generally stated for the smaller language of assertions without locations—the language of arithmetic. The fact that the valid assertions in this language do not form a recursively enumerable set means that the axiomatisation of arithmetic is never finished—there will always be some fact about arithmetic which remains unprovable. Nor can we hope to have a program which generates an infinite list of axioms and effective proof rules so that all valid assertions about arithmetic follow. If there were such a program there would be an effective proof system for arithmetical assertions, contradicting Gödel's Incompleteness Theorem.

Gödel's result had tremendous historical significance. Gödel did not have the concepts of computability available to him. Rather his result stimulated logicians to research different formulations of what it meant to be computable. The original proof worked by expressing the concept of provability of a formal system for assertions as an assertion itself, and constructing an assertion which was valid iff it was not provable. It should be admitted that we have only considered Gödel's First Incompleteness Theorem; there is also a second which says that a formal system for arithmetic cannot be proved free of contradiction in the system itself. It was clear to Gödel that his proofs of incompleteness hinged on being able to express a certain set of functions on the natural numbers by assertions—the set has come to be called the *primitive recursive functions*. The realisation that a simple extension led to a stable notion of computable function took some years longer, culminating in the Church-Turing thesis. The incompleteness theorem devastated the programme set up by Hilbert. As a reaction to paradoxes like Russell's in mathematical foundations, Hilbert had advocated a study of the finitistic methods employed when reasoning within some formal system, hoping that this would lead to proofs of consistency and completeness of important proof systems, like one for arithmetic. Gödel's Theorem established an absolute limit on the power of finitistic reasoning.

7.4   Verification conditions

In principle, the fact that **Assn** is expressive provides a method to reduce the demonstration that a partial correctness assertion is valid to showing the validity of an assertion in **Assn**; the validity of a partial correctness assertion of the form $\{A\}c\{B\}$ is equivalent to the validity of the assertion $A \Rightarrow w[\![c, B]\!]$, from which the command has been eliminated. In this way, given a theorem prover for predicate calculus we might hope to derive a theorem prover for **IMP** programs. Unfortunately, the method we used to obtain $w[\![c, B]\!]$ was convoluted and inefficient, and definitely not practical.

However, useful automated tools for establishing the validity of partial correctness assertions can be obtained along similar lines once we allow a little human guidance. Let us annotate programs by assertions. Define the syntactic set of annotated commands by:

$$c ::= \textbf{skip} \mid X := a \mid c_0; (X := a) \mid c_0; \{D\}c_1 \mid$$
$$\textbf{if } b \textbf{ then } c_0 \textbf{ else } c_1 \mid \textbf{while } b \textbf{ do } \{D\}c$$

where X is a location, a an arithmetic expression, b is a boolean expression, c, c_0, c_1 are annotated commands and D is an assertion such that in $c_0; \{D\}c_1$, the annotated command c_1, is *not* an assignment. The idea is that an assertion at a point in an annotated command is true whenever flow of control reaches that point. Thus we only annotate a command of the form $c_0; c_1$ at the point where control shifts from c_0 to c_1. It is unnecessary to do this when c_1 is an assignment $X := a$ because in that case an annotation can be derived simply from a postcondition. An annotated while-loop

$$\textbf{while } b \textbf{ do } \{D\}c$$

contains an assertion D which is intended to be an invariant.

An *annotated partial correctness assertion* has the form

$$\{A\}c\{B\}$$

where c is an annotated command. Annotated commands are associated with ordinary commands, got by ignoring the annotations. It is sometimes convenient to treat annotated commands as their associated commands. In this spirit, we say an annotated partial correctness assertion is valid when its associated (unannotated) partial correctness assertion is.

An annotated while-loop

$$\{A\}\textbf{while } b \textbf{ do } \{D\}c\{B\}$$

contains an assertion D, which we hope has been chosen judiciously so D is an invariant. Being an invariant means that

$$\{D \wedge b\}c\{D\}$$

is valid. In order to ensure

$$\{A\} \textbf{ while } b \textbf{ do } \{D\}c\{B\}$$

is valid, once it is known that D is an invariant, it suffices to show that both assertions

$$A \Rightarrow D, \quad D \wedge \neg b \Rightarrow B$$

are valid. A quick way to see this is to notice that we can derive $\{A\}\textbf{while } b \textbf{ do } c\{B\}$ from $\{D \wedge b\}c\{D\}$ using the Hoare rules which we know to be sound. As is clear, not all annotated partial correctness assertions are valid. To be so it is sufficient to establish the validity of certain assertions, called *verification conditions* for which all mention of commands is eliminated. Define the verification conditions (abbreviated to vc) of an annotated partial correctness assertion by structural induction on annotated commands:

$$
\begin{aligned}
vc(\{A\}\textbf{skip}\{B\}) &= \{A \Rightarrow B\} \\
vc(\{A\}X := a\{B\}) &= \{A \Rightarrow B[a/X]\} \\
vc(\{A\}c_0; X := a\{B\}) &= vc(\{A\}c_0\{B[a/X]\}) \\
vc(\{A\}c_0; \{D\}c_1\{B\}) &= vc(\{A\}c_0\{D\}) \cup vc(\{D\}c_1\{B\}) \\
&\qquad \text{where } c_1 \text{ is not an assignment} \\
vc(\{A\}\textbf{if } b \textbf{ then } c_0 \textbf{ else } c_1\{B\}) &= vc(\{A \wedge b\}c_0\{B\}) \cup vc(\{A \wedge \neg b\}c_1\{B\}) \\
vc(\{A\}\textbf{while } b \textbf{ do } \{D\}c\{B\}) &= vc(\{D \wedge b\}c\{D\}) \cup \{A \Rightarrow D\} \\
&\qquad \cup \{D \wedge \neg b \Rightarrow B\}
\end{aligned}
$$

Exercise 7.11 Prove by structural induction on annotated commands that for all annotated partial correctness assertions $\{A\}c\{B\}$ if all assertions in $vc(\{A\}c\{B\})$ are valid then $\{A\}c\{B\}$ is valid. (The proof follows the general line of Lemma 7.6. A proof can be found in [42], Section 3.5.)   □

Thus to show the validity of an annotated partial correctness assertion it is sufficient to show its verification conditions are valid. In this way the task of program verification can be passed to a theorem prover for predicate calculus. Some commercial program-verification systems, like Gypsy [41], work in this way.

Note, that while the validity of its verification conditions is sufficient to guarantee the validity of an annotated partial correctness assertion, it is not necessary. This can occur because the invariant chosen is inappropriate for the pre and post conditions. For example, although

$$\{\text{true}\}\textbf{while false do } \{\text{false}\}\textbf{skip}\{\text{true}\}$$

is certainly valid with **false** as an invariant, its verification conditions contain

$$\text{true} \Rightarrow \text{false},$$

which is certainly not a valid assertion.

We conclude this section by pointing out a peculiarity in our treatment of annotated commands. Two commands, built up as $(c; X := a_1); X := a_2$ and $c; (X := a_1; X := a_2)$, are understood in essentially the same way; indeed in many imperative languages they would both be written as:

$$c;$$
$$X := a_1;$$
$$X := a_2$$

However the two commands support different annotations according to our syntax of annotated commands. The first would only allow possible annotations to appear in c whereas the second would be annotated as $c; \{D\}(X := a_1; X := a_2)$. The rules for annotations do not put annotations before a single assignment but would put an annotation in before any other chain of assignments. This is even though it is still easily possible to derive the annotation from the postcondition, this time through a series of substitutions.

Exercise 7.12 Suggest a way to modify the syntax of annotated commands and the definition of their verification conditions to address this peculiarity, so that any chain of assignments or **skip** is treated in the same way as a single assignment is presently.   □

Exercise 7.13 A larger project is to program a verification-condition generator (*e.g.* in standard ML or prolog) which, given an annotated partial correctness assertion as input, outputs a set, or list, of its verification conditions. (See Gordon's book [42] for a program in lisp.)   □

7.5 Predicate transformers

This section is optional and presents an abstract, rather more mathematical view of assertions and weakest preconditions. Abstractly a command is a function $f : \Sigma \to \Sigma_\perp$ from states to states together with an element $\perp$, standing for undefined; such functions are sometimes called *state transformers*. They form a cpo, isomorphic to that of the partial functions on states, when ordered pointwise. Abstractly, an assertion for partial correctness is a subset of states which contains $\perp$, so we define the set of *partial correctness predicates* to be

$$\text{Pred}(\Sigma) = \{Q \mid Q \subseteq \Sigma_\perp \ \& \ \perp \in Q\}.$$

We can make predicates into a cpo by ordering them by reverse inclusion. The cpo of predicates for partial correctness is

$$(\text{Pred}(\Sigma), \supseteq).$$

Here, more information about the final state delivered by a command configuration corresponds to having bounded it to lie within a smaller set provided its execution halts. In particular the very least information corresponds to the element $\perp_{Pred} = \Sigma \cup \{\perp\}$. We shall use simply $\text{Pred}(\Sigma)$ for the cpo of partial-correctness predicates.

The weakest precondition construction determines a continuous function on the cpo of predicates—a predicate transformer.[4]

Definition: Let $f : \Sigma \to \Sigma_\perp$ be a partial function on states. Define

$$W f : \text{Pred}(\Sigma) \to \text{Pred}(\Sigma);$$
$$(W f)(Q) = (f^{-1}Q) \cup \{\perp\}$$
$$i.e., (W f)(Q) = \{\sigma \in \Sigma_\perp \mid f(\sigma) \in Q\} \cup \{\perp\}.$$

A command c can be taken to denote a state transformer $\mathcal{C}[\![c]\!] : \Sigma \to \Sigma_\perp$ with the convention that undefined is represented by $\perp$. Let B be an assertion. According to this understanding, with respect to an interpretation I,

$$(W(\mathcal{C}[\![c]\!]))(B^I) = wp^I[\![c, B]\!].$$

---

[4]This term is generally used for the corresponding notion when considering total correctness.

Exercise 7.14 Write ST for the cpo of state transformers $[\Sigma_\perp \to_\perp \Sigma_\perp]$ and PT for the cpo of predicate transformers $[\mathrm{Pred}(\Sigma) \to \mathrm{Pred}(\Sigma)]$.
Show $W : ST \to_\perp PT$ and W is continuous (Care! there are lots of things to check here).
Show $W(Id_{\Sigma_\perp}) = Id_{Pred(\Sigma)}$ *i.e.*, W takes the identity function on the cpo of states to the identity function on predicates $\mathrm{Pred}(\Sigma)$.
Show $W(f \circ g) = (Wg) \circ (Wf)$. $\square$

In the context of total correctness Dijkstra has argued that one can specify the meaning of a command as a predicate transformer [36]. He argued that to understand a command amounts to knowing the weakest precondition which ensures a given postcondition. We do this for partial correctness. As we now have a cpo of predicates we also have the cpo

$$[\mathrm{Pred}(\Sigma) \to \mathrm{Pred}(\Sigma)]$$

of predicate transformers. Thus we can give a denotational semantics of commands in **IMP** as predicate transformers, instead of as state transformers. We can define a semantic function

$$\mathcal{Pt} : \mathbf{Com} \to [\mathrm{Pred}(\Sigma) \to \mathrm{Pred}(\Sigma)]$$

from commands to predicate transformers. Although this denotational semantics, in which the denotation of a command is a predicate transformer is clearly a different denotational semantics to that using partial functions, if done correctly it should be equivalent in the sense that two commands denote the same predicate transformer iff they denote the same partial function. You may like to do this as the exercise below.

Exercise 7.15 (Denotations as predicate transformers)

Define a semantic function

$$\mathcal{Pt} : \mathbf{Com} \to PT$$

by

$$\mathcal{Pt}[\![X := a]\!]Q = \{\sigma \in \Sigma_\perp \mid \sigma[\mathcal{A}[\![a]\!]\sigma/X] \in Q\}$$

$$\mathcal{Pt}[\![\mathbf{skip}]\!]Q = Q$$

$$\mathcal{Pt}[\![c_0; c_1]\!]Q = \mathcal{Pt}[\![c_0]\!](\mathcal{Pt}[\![c_1]\!]Q)$$

$$\mathcal{Pt}[\![\mathbf{if}\ b\ \mathbf{then}\ c_0\ \mathbf{else}\ c_1]\!]Q = \mathcal{Pt}[\![c_0]\!](\overline{b} \cap Q) \cup \mathcal{Pt}[\![c_1]\!](\overline{\neg b} \cap Q)$$

$$\text{where } \overline{b} = \{\sigma \mid \sigma = \perp \text{ or } \mathcal{B}[\![b]\!]\sigma = \mathbf{true}\} \text{ for any boolean } b$$

$$\mathcal{Pt}[\![\mathbf{while}\ b\ \mathbf{do}\ c]\!]Q = \mathit{fix}(G)$$

where $G : PT \to PT$ is given by $G(p)(Q) = (\overline{b} \cap \mathcal{Pt}[\![c_0]\!](p(Q)) \cup (\overline{\neg b} \cap Q)$.
Show G is continuous.

Show $W(\mathcal{C}[\![c]\!]\perp) = Pt[\![c]\!]$ for any command c. Observe

$$Wf = Wf' \Rightarrow f = f'$$

for two strict continuous functions f, f' on $\Sigma_\perp$. Deduce

$$\mathcal{C}[\![c]\!] = \mathcal{C}[\![c']\!] \text{ iff } Pt[\![c]\!] = Pt[\![c']\!]$$

for any commands c, c'.

Recall the ordering on predicates. Because it is reverse inclusion:

$$fix(G) = \bigcap_{n \in \omega} G^n(\perp_{Pred}).$$

This suggests that if we were to allow infinite conjunctions in our language of assertions, and did not have quantifiers, we could express weakest preconditions directly. Indeed this is so, and you might like to extend **Bexp** by infinite conjunctions, to form another set of assertions to replace **Assn**, and modify the above semantics to give an assertion, of the new kind, which expresses the weakest precondition for each command. Once we have expressiveness a proof of relative completeness follows for this new kind of assertion, in the same way as earlier in Section 7.2.   □

7.6 Further reading

The book "What is mathematical logic?" by Crossley *et al* [34] has an excellent explanation of Gödel's Incompleteness Theorem, though with the details missing. The logic texts by Kleene [54], Mendelson [61] and Enderton [38] have full treatments. A treatment aimed at Computer Science students is presented in the book [11] by Kfoury, Moll and Arbib. Cook's original proof of relative completeness in [33] used "strongest postconditions" instead of weakest preconditions; the latter are used instead by Clarke in [23] and his earlier work. The paper by Clarke has, in addition, some negative results showing the impossibility of having sound and relatively complete proof systems for programming languages richer than the one here. Apt's paper [8] provides good orientation. Alternative presentations of the material of this chapter can be found in [58], [13]. Gordon's book [42] contains a more elementary and detailed treatment of verification conditions.

8 Introduction to domain theory

Domain theory is the mathematical foundation of denotational semantics. This chapter extends the work on complete partial orders (domains) and continuous functions with constructions on complete partial orders which are important for the mathematical description of programming languages. It provides the mathematical basis for our subsequent work on denotational semantics. A metalanguage to support semantic definitions is introduced; functions defined within it are guaranteed to be continuous.

8.1 Basic definitions

In denotational semantics a programming construct (like a command, or an expression) is given a meaning by assigning to it an element in a "domain" of possible meanings. The programming construct is said to *denote* the element and the element to be a *denotation* of the construct. For example, commands in **IMP** are denoted by elements from the "domain" of partial functions, while numerals in **IMP** can denote elements of **N**. As the denotational semantics of **IMP** in Chapter 5 makes clear it can sometimes be necessary for "domains" to carry enough structure that they enable the solution of recursive equations. Chapter 5 motivated complete partial orders as structures which support recursive definitions, and these are reasonable candidates to take as "domains" of meanings. Of course, the appropriateness of complete partial orders can only be justified by demonstrating their applicability over a range of programming languages and by results expressing their relation with operational semantics. However, experience and results have born out their importance; while it is sometimes necessary to add structure to complete partial orders, it appears they underlie any general theory capable of giving compositional[1] semantic definitions to programming languages. Recall the definition from Chapter 5:

Definition: A partial order $(D, \sqsubseteq)$ is a *complete partial order* (abbreviated to cpo) if it has has a least upper bound $\bigsqcup_{n \in \omega} d_n$ in D of any ω-chain $d_0 \sqsubseteq d_1 \sqsubseteq \cdots \sqsubseteq d_n \sqsubseteq \cdots$ of elements of D.
We say $(D, \sqsubseteq)$ is a cpo *with bottom* if it is a cpo which has a least element $\bot$ (called "bottom").[2]

Occasionally we shall introduce a cpo as $e.g.(D, \sqsubseteq_D)$ and make explicit to which cpo the order $\sqsubseteq_D$ and bottom element $\bot_D$ belong. More often however we will write $\sqsubseteq$ and $\bot$ because the context generally makes clear to which cpo we refer. Often, when it is clear what we mean, we will write $\bigsqcup_n d_n$ instead of $\bigsqcup_{n \in \omega} d_n$.

---

[1] Recall from Chapter 5 that a semantics is compositional if the meaning of a programming expression is explained in terms of the meaning of its immediate subexpressions.

[2] The cpo's here are commonly called (bottomless) ω-cpo's, or predomains.

We have already encountered several examples of cpo's:

Example:
(i) Any set ordered by the identity relation forms a *discrete* cpo.
(ii) A powerset $Pow(X)$ of any set X, ordered by $\subseteq$, or by $\supseteq$, forms a cpo as indeed does any complete lattice (see Section 5.5).
(iii) The two element cpo $\bot \sqsubseteq \top$ is called **O**. Such an order arises as the powerset of a singleton ordered by $\subseteq$.
(iv) The set of partial functions $X \rightharpoonup Y$ ordered by inclusion, between sets X, Y, is a cpo.
(v) Extending the nonnegative integers ω by ∞ and ordering them in a chain

$$0 \sqsubseteq 1 \sqsubseteq \cdots \sqsubseteq n \sqsubseteq \cdots \infty$$

yields a cpo, called Ω. $\square$

Complete partial orders give only half the picture. Only by ensuring that functions between cpo's preserve least upper bounds of ω-chains do we obtain a framework supporting recursive definitions.

Definition: A function $f : D \to E$ between cpo's D and E is *monotonic* iff

$$\forall d, d' \in D.\ d \sqsubseteq d' \Rightarrow f(d) \sqsubseteq f(d').$$

Such a function is *continuous* iff it is monotonic and for all chains $d_0 \sqsubseteq d_1 \sqsubseteq \cdots \sqsubseteq d_n \sqsubseteq \cdots$ in D we have

$$\bigsqcup_{n \in \omega} f(d_n) = f(\bigsqcup_{n \in \omega} d_n).$$

Example:
(i) All functions from discrete cpo's, *i.e.* sets, to cpo's are continuous.
(ii) Let the cpo's Ω and **O** be as in the above example. For $n \in \Omega$, define the function $f_n : \Omega \to$ **O** to be

$$f_n(x) = \begin{cases} \top & \text{if } n \sqsubseteq x, \\ \bot & \text{otherwise.} \end{cases}$$

The continuous functions $\Omega \to$ **O** consist of the constantly $\bot$ function, $\lambda x.\bot$, together with all f_n where $n \in \omega$. Note, however, that the function f_∞ is *not* continuous. (Why not?) $\square$

Proposition 8.1 *The identity function Id_D on a cpo D is continuous. Let $f : D \to E$ and $g : E \to F$ be continuous functions on cpo's D, E, F. Then their composition $g \circ f : D \to F$ is continuous.*

Exercise 8.2 Prove the previous proposition. □

In Section 5.4 we showed a central property of a cpo with ⊥; any continuous function on it has a least fixed point:

Theorem 8.3 *(Fixed-Point Theorem)*
Let $f : D \to D$ *be a continuous function on* D *a cpo with bottom* ⊥. *Define*

$$fix(f) = \bigsqcup_{n \in \omega} f^n(\bot).$$

Then $fix(f)$ *is a fixed point of* f *and the least prefixed point of* f *i.e.*
(i) $f(fix(f)) = fix(f)$ *and (ii) if* $f(d) \sqsubseteq d$ *then* $fix(f) \sqsubseteq d$. *Consequently* $fix(f)$ *is the least fixed point of* f.

8.2 Streams—an example

Complete partial orders and continuous functions have been motivated in Chapter 5 from the viewpoint of inductive definitions associated with finitary rules, by extracting those properties used to obtain least fixed points of operators on sets. Given that an operational semantics can generally be presented as a set of finitary rules, the relevance of continuity to computation is not surprising. However, the significance of continuity can be understood more directly, and for this we will consider computations on sequences, as an example.

As input values we take finite and infinite sequences of 0's and 1's where in addition we allow, but don't insist, that a finite sequence can end with a special symbol "$". The idea is that the sequences represent the possible input, perhaps from another computation or a user; a sequence of 0's or 1's is delivered with the option of explicity notifying by $ that the sequence is now ended. The sequence can grow unboundedly in length over time unless it has been terminated with $. The sequences can remain finite without being terminated; perhaps the inputting device breaks down, or goes into a diverging computation, or, in the case of a user, gets bored, before inputting the next element of the sequence or terminating it with $.

These sequences are sometimes called streams, or lazy lists or "stoppered sequences" ($ is the "stopper"). They admit an intuitive partial order. Say one sequence s is below another s' if s is a prefix of s'. Increasing in the partial order is associated with sequences containing increasing information. With respect to this partial order there is then a least sequence, the empty sequence ϵ. There are maximal sequences which are "stoppered", like

0101$

and infinite sequences, like

$$000 \cdots 00 \cdots$$

which we abbreviate to 0^ω. In fact the sequences form a cpo with bottom element ϵ. Call the cpo S.

Imagine we wish to detect whether or not 1 appears in the input. It seems we would like a function

$$isone : S \rightarrow \{\mathbf{true}, \mathbf{false}\}$$

that given a sequence returned **true** if the sequence contained 1 and **false** if not. But this is naive. What if the sequence at some stage contained no 1's and then at a later time 1 appeared, as could happen through starting at the empty sequence ϵ and becoming 10 say? We would have to update our original output of **false** to **true**? We would prefer that when the *isone* returns **false** on some input it really means that no 1's can appear there. Whereas we require $isone(000\$) = \mathbf{false}$, because 1 certainly can't appear once the sequence is terminated, we want $isone\ (000)$ to be different from **false**, and certainly it can't be **true**. We have two options: either we allow *isone* to be a partial function, or we introduce a "don't know" element standing for undefined in addition to the truth values. It is technically simpler to follow the latter course.

The new "don't know" value can be updated to **false** or **true** as more of the input sequence is revealed. We take the "don't know" value to be $\bot$ below both **true** and **false**, as drawn here:

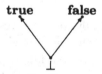

Write $\{\mathbf{true}, \mathbf{false}\}_\bot$ for this simple cpo with least element $\bot$. Now more information about the input is reflected in more information about the output. Put in mathematical terms, *isone* should be a monotonic function from S to $\{\mathbf{true}, \mathbf{false}\}_\bot$.

Deciding that

$$isone : S \longrightarrow \{\mathbf{true}, \mathbf{false}\}_\bot$$

is monotonic does not fully determine it as a function, even when constraining it so

$$
\begin{array}{llll}
isone\ (1s) & = & \mathbf{true}, & \quad isone\ (\$) & = & \mathbf{false}, \\
isone\ (0s) & = & isone\ (s), & \quad isone\ (\epsilon) & = & \bot,
\end{array}
$$

for any sequence s. What about $isone\ (0^\omega)$? The constraints allow either $isone\ (0^\omega) = \mathbf{false}$ or $isone\ (0^\omega) = \bot$. However the former is not computationally feasible; outputting

false involves surveying an infinite sequence and reporting on the absence of 1's. Its computational infeasibility is reflected by the fact that taking *isone* (0^ω) to be **false** yields a function which is not continuous. Any finite subsequence of 0^ω takes the form 0^n consisting of n 0's. The infinite sequence 0^ω is the least upper bound $\bigsqcup_{n\in\omega} 0^n$. We have *isone* $(0^n) = \bot$ and so

$$\bigsqcup_{n\in\omega} isone\,(0^n) = \bot$$

and continuity forces *isone* $(0^\omega) = \bot$.

Exercise 8.4 Cpo's can be viewed as topological spaces and continuous functions as functions which are continuous in the traditional sense of topology (You need no knowledge of topology to do this exercise however). Given a cpo $(D, \sqsubseteq)$ define a topology (called the *Scott topology* after Dana Scott) as follows. Say $U \subseteq D$ is *open* iff

$$\forall d, e \in D.\ d \sqsubseteq e\ \&\ d \in U \Rightarrow e \in U$$

and for all chains $d_0 \sqsubseteq d_1 \sqsubseteq \cdots \sqsubseteq d_n \sqsubseteq \cdots$ in D

$$\bigsqcup_{n\in\omega} d_n \in U \Rightarrow \exists n \in \omega.\ d_n \in U.$$

(i) Show this does indeed determine a topology on a cpo D (*i.e.* that $\emptyset$ and D itself are open and that any finite intersection of open sets is open and that the union of any set of open sets is open.)

(ii) Show that for any element d of a cpo D, the set $\{x \in D \mid x \not\sqsubseteq d\}$ is open.

(iii) Show that $f : D \to E$ is a continuous function between cpo's D, E iff f is topologically-continuous. (Such a function f is topologically-continuous iff for any open set V of E the inverse image $f^{-1}V$ is an open set of D.)

(iv) Show that in general the open sets of a cpo D can be characterised as precisely those sets $f^{-1}\{\top\}$ for a continuous function $f : D \to \mathbf{O}$. Describe the open sets of the particular cpo of streams considered in this section. □

8.3 Constructions on cpo's

Complete partial orders can be formed in a rich variety of ways. This richness is important because it means that cpo's can be taken as the domains of meaning of many different kinds of programming constructs. This section introduces various constructions on cpo's along with particular continuous functions which are associated with the constructions. These will be very useful later in the business of giving denotational semantics to programming languages.

Sometimes in giving the constructions it is a nuisance to specify exactly what sets are built in the constructions; there are many different ways of achieving essentially the same construction. There was a similar awkwardness in the first introductory chapter on basic set theory; there were several ways of defining products of sets depending on how we chose to realise the notion of ordered pair, and, of course in forming disjoint unions we first had to make disjoint copies of sets—we chose one way but there are many others. In this section we will take a more abstract approach to the constructions. For example, in forming a sum of cpo's $D_1 + \cdots + D_k$, intuitively got by juxtaposing disjoint copies of the cpo's $D_1, \ldots, D_k$, we shall simply postulate that there are functions in_i, for $1 \leq i \leq k$, which are 1-1 and ensure the elements $in_l(d_l)$ and $in_m(d_m)$ are distinct whenever $l \neq m$. Of course, it is important that we know such functions exist; in this case they do because one possibility is to realise $in_i(x)$ as (i, x). There is nothing lost by this more abstract approach because the sum construction will be *essentially the same* no matter how we choose to realise the functions in_i provided that they satisfy the distinctness conditions required of them.

The mathematical way of expressing that structures are "essentially the same" is through the concept of *isomorphism* which establishes when structures are *isomorphic*. A continuous function $f : D \to E$ between cpo's D and E is said to be an *isomorphism* if there is a continuous function $g : E \to D$ such that $g \circ f = Id_D$ and $f \circ g = Id_E$—so f and g are mutual inverses. This is actually an instance of a general definition which applies to a class of objects and functions between them (cpo's and continuous functions in this case). It follows from the definition that isomorphic cpo's are essentially the same but for a renaming of elements.

Proposition 8.5 *Let* $(D, \sqsubseteq_D)$ *and* $(E, \sqsubseteq_E)$ *be two cpo's. A function* $f : D \to E$ *is an isomorphism iff* f *is a 1-1 correspondence such that*

$$x \sqsubseteq_D y \text{ iff } f(x) \sqsubseteq_E f(y)$$

for all $x, y \in D$.

8.3.1 Discrete cpo's

The simplest cpo's are simply sets where the partial ordering relation is the identity. An ω-chain has then to be constant. Cpo's in which the partial order is the identity relation are said to be *discrete*. Basic values, like truth values or the integers form discrete cpo's, as do syntactic sets. We remarked that any function from a discrete cpo to a cpo is always continuous (so, in particular, semantic functions from syntactic sets are continuous).

Exercise 8.6 Precisely what kinds of functions are continuous from a cpo with $\perp$ to a discrete cpo?   □

8.3.2   Finite products

Assume that $D_1, \cdots, D_k$ are cpo's. The underlying set of their *product* is

$$D_1 \times \cdots \times D_k,$$

consisting of k-tuples $(d_1, \cdots, d_k)$ for $d_1 \in D_1, \cdots, d_k \in D_k$. The partial order is determined "coordinatewise", i.e.

$$(d_1, \cdots, d_k) \sqsubseteq (d_1', \cdots, d_k') \text{ iff } d_1 \sqsubseteq d_1' \text{ and } \cdots \text{ and } d_k \sqsubseteq d_k'$$

It is easy to check that an ω-chain $(d_{1n}, \cdots, d_{kn})$, for $n \in \omega$, of the product has least upper bound calculated coordinatewise:

$$\bigsqcup_{n \in \omega} (d_{1n}, \cdots, d_{kn}) = (\bigsqcup_{n \in \omega} d_{1n}, \cdots, \bigsqcup_{n \in \omega} d_{kn})$$

Thus the product of cpo's is itself a cpo. Important too are the useful functions associated with a product $D_1 \times \cdots \times D_k$.

The *projection function* $\pi_i : D_1 \times \cdots \times D_k \to D_i$, for $i = 1, \cdots, k$, selects the ith coordinate of a tuple:

$$\pi_i(d_1, \cdots, d_k) = d_i$$

Because least upper bounds of chains are got in a coordinatewise fashion, the projection functions are easily seen to be continuous.

We can extend tupling to functions. Let $f_1 : E \to D_1, \cdots, f_k : E \to D_k$ be continuous functions. Define the function

$$\langle f_1, \cdots, f_k \rangle : E \longrightarrow D_1 \times \cdots \times D_k$$

by taking

$$\langle f_1, \cdots, f_k \rangle(e) = (f_1(e), \cdots, f_n(e)).$$

The function $\langle f_1, \cdots, f_n \rangle$ clearly satisfies the property that

$$\pi_i \circ \langle f_1, \cdots, f_k \rangle = f_i \quad \text{for } i = 1, \cdots, k,$$

and, in fact, $\langle f_1, \cdots, f_n \rangle$ is the unique function $E \longrightarrow D_1 \times \cdots \times D_k$ with this property. This function is easily seen to be monotonic. It is continuous because for any ω-chain $e_0 \sqsubseteq e_1 \sqsubseteq \cdots \sqsubseteq e_n \sqsubseteq \cdots$ in E we have

$$
\begin{aligned}
\langle f_1, \cdots, f_k \rangle(\bigsqcup_{n \in \omega} e_n) &= (f_1(\bigsqcup_{n \in \omega} e_n), \cdots, f_k(\bigsqcup_{n \in \omega} e_n)) && \text{by definition,} \\
&= (\bigsqcup_{n \in \omega} f_1(e_n), \cdots, \bigsqcup_{n \in \omega} f_k(e_n)) && \text{as each } f_i \text{ is continuous,} \\
&= \bigsqcup_{n \in \omega}(f_1(e_n), \cdots, f_k(e_n)) && \text{as lubs of products are} \\
& && \text{formed coord'wise,} \\
&= \bigsqcup_{n \in \omega} \langle f_1, \cdots, f_k \rangle(e_n)
\end{aligned}
$$

We can extend the product construction on cpo's to functions. For $f_1 : D_1 \to E_1, \cdots, f_k : D_k \to E_k$ define

$$f_1 \times \cdots \times f_k : D_1 \times \cdots \times D_k \to E_1 \times \cdots \times E_k$$

by taking

$$f_1 \times \cdots \times f_k(d_1, \cdots, d_k) = (f_1(d_1), \cdots, f_k(d_k)).$$

In other words $f_1 \times \cdots \times f_k = \langle f_1 \circ \pi_1, \cdots, f_k \circ \pi_k \rangle$. Each component $f_i \circ \pi_i$ is continuous, being the composition of continuous functions, and, as we have seen, so is the tuple $\langle f_1 \circ \pi_1, \cdots, f_k \circ \pi_k \rangle$. Hence $f_1 \times \cdots \times f_k$ is a continuous function.

Example: As an example of a product of complete partial orders consider $\mathbf{T}_\perp \times \mathbf{T}_\perp = \mathbf{T}_\perp^2$ which is most conveniently drawn from an "aerial" view:

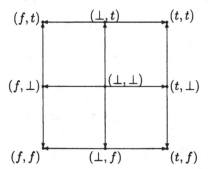

We have used t and f to stand for the truth values **true** and **false**.   □

Exercise 8.7 Draw the products $\mathbf{O}^0$, $\mathbf{O}^1$, $\mathbf{O}^2$, and $\mathbf{O}^3$.   □

There are two easy-to-prove but important properties of products one of which we shall make great use of later. (The first is an instance of a general fact from topology.)

Lemma 8.8 *Let $h : E \to D_1 \times \cdots \times D_k$ be a function from a cpo E to a product of cpo's. It is continuous iff for all $i, 1 \le i \le k$, the functions $\pi_i \circ h : E \to D_i$ are continuous.*

Proof:
"only if": follows as the composition of continuous functions is continuous.
"if": Suppose $\pi_i \circ h$ is continuous for all i with $1 \le i \le k$. Then for any $x \in E$

$$h(x) = (\pi_1(h(x)), \cdots, \pi_k(h(x))) = (\pi_1 \circ h(x), \cdots, \pi_k \circ h(x)) = \langle \pi_1 \circ h, \cdots, \pi_k \circ h \rangle(x)$$

Therefore $h = \langle \pi_1 \circ h, \cdots, \pi_k \circ h \rangle$ which is continuous as each $\pi_i \circ h$ is continuous.   □

The second more useful lemma relies on the order. Its proof uses a little, but important, result about least upper bounds of an "array" of elements of a cpo:

Proposition 8.9 *Suppose $e_{n,m}$ are elements of a cpo E for $n, m \in \omega$ with the property that $e_{n,m} \sqsubseteq e_{n',m'}$ when $n \leq n'$ and $m \leq m'$. Then the set $\{e_{n,m} \mid n, m \in \omega\}$ has a least upper bound*

$$\bigsqcup_{n,m\in\omega} e_{n,m} = \bigsqcup_{n\in\omega}(\bigsqcup_{m\in\omega} e_{n,m}) = \bigsqcup_{m\in\omega}(\bigsqcup_{n\in\omega} e_{n,m}) = \bigsqcup_{n\in\omega} e_{n,n}.$$

Proof: The proposition follows by showing that all of the sets

$$\{e_{n,m} \mid n, m \in \omega\}, \quad \{\bigsqcup_{m\in\omega} e_{n,m} \mid n \in \omega\}, \quad \{\bigsqcup_{n\in\omega} e_{n,m} \mid m \in \omega\}, \quad \{e_{n,n} \mid n \in \omega\}$$

have the same upper bounds, and hence the same least upper bounds. For example, it is easy to see that $\{e_{n,m} \mid n, m \in \omega\}$ and $\{e_{n,n} \mid n \in \omega\}$ have the same upper bounds because any element $e_{n,m}$ can be dominated by one of the form $e_{n,n}$. Certainly the lub of an ω-chain $\bigsqcup_n e_{n,n}$ exists, and hence the lub $\bigsqcup_{n,m} e_{n,m}$ exists and is equal to it. Any upper bound of $\{\bigsqcup_m e_{n,m} \mid n \in \omega\}$ must be an upper bound of $\{e_{n,m} \mid n, m \in \omega\}$, and conversely any upper bound of $\{e_{n,m} \mid n, m \in \omega\}$ dominates any lub $\bigsqcup_m e_{n,m}$ for any $m \in \omega$. Thus we see $\{e_{n,m} \mid n, m \in \omega\}$ and $\{\bigsqcup_{m\in\omega} e_{n,m} \mid n \in \omega\}$ share the same upper bounds, and so have equal lubs. The argument showing $\bigsqcup_m(\bigsqcup_n e_{n,m}) = \bigsqcup_{n,m} e_{n,m}$ is similar.   □

Lemma 8.10 *Let $f : D_1 \times \cdots \times D_k \to E$ be a function. Then f is continuous iff f is "continuous in each argument separately", i.e. for all i with $1 \leq i \leq k$ for any $d_1, \ldots, d_{i-1}, d_{i+1}, \ldots, d_k$ the function $D_i \to E$ given by $d_i \longmapsto f(d_1, \ldots, d_i, \ldots, d_k)$ is continuous.*

Proof:
"$\Rightarrow$" obvious. (Why?)
"$\Leftarrow$" For notational convenience assume $k = 2$ (the proof easily generalises to more arguments). Let $(x_0, y_0) \sqsubseteq \cdots \sqsubseteq (x_n, y_n) \sqsubseteq \cdots$ be a chain in the product $D_1 \times D_2$. Then

$$f(\bigsqcup_n (x_n, y_n)) = f(\bigsqcup_p x_p, \bigsqcup_q y_q) \text{ as lubs are determined coordinatewise,}$$

$$= \bigsqcup_p f(x_p, \bigsqcup_q y_q) \text{ as } f \text{ is continuous in its 1st argument,}$$

$$= \bigsqcup_p \bigsqcup_q f(x_p, y_q) \text{ as } f \text{ is continuous in its 2nd argument,}$$

$$= \bigsqcup_n f(x_n, y_n) \text{ by Proposition 8.9 above.}$$

Hence f is continuous.   □

This last fact is *very* useful; on numerous occasions we will check the continuity of a function from a product by showing it is continuous in each argument separately. [3]

One degenerate case of a finite product is the empty product $\{()\}$ consisting solely of the empty tuple $()$. We shall often use **1** to name the empty product.

8.3.3 Function space

Let D, E be cpo's. It is a very important fact that the set of all continuous functions from D to E can be made into a complete partial order. The *function space* $[D \to E]$ consists of elements

$$\{f \mid f : D \to E \text{ is continuous}\}$$

ordered pointwise by

$$f \sqsubseteq g \text{ iff } \forall d \in D.\ f(d) \sqsubseteq g(d).$$

This makes the function space a complete partial order. Note that, provided E has a bottom element $\perp_E$, such a function space of cpo's has a bottom element, the constantly $\perp_E$ function $\perp_{[D \to E]}$ which acts so

$$\perp_{[D \to E]}(d) = \perp_E, \text{ for all } d \in D.$$

Least upper bounds of chains of functions are given pointwise *i.e.* a chain

$$f_0 \sqsubseteq f_1 \sqsubseteq \cdots \sqsubseteq f_n \sqsubseteq \cdots$$

of functions has lub $\bigsqcup_{n \in \omega} f_n$ which

$$(\bigsqcup_n f_n)(d) = \bigsqcup_n (f_n(d))$$

---

[3] A pro erty corresponding to Lemma 8.10 does *not* hold of functions in analysis of real and complex numbers where a verification of the continuity of a function in several variables can be much more involved. For example:

$$p(x) = \begin{cases} \frac{xy}{x^2 + y^2} & \text{if } (x, y) \neq (0, 0), \\ 0 & \text{if } x = y = 0. \end{cases}$$

for $d \in D$. The fact that this lub exists as a function in $[D \to E]$ requires that we check its continuity.

Suppose $d_0 \sqsubseteq d_1 \sqsubseteq \cdots \sqsubseteq d_m \sqsubseteq \cdots$ is a chain in D. Then

$$
\begin{aligned}
(\bigsqcup_n f_n)(\bigsqcup_m d_m) &= \bigsqcup_n f_n(\bigsqcup_m d_m) && \text{by the definition of lubs of functions,} \\
&= \bigsqcup_n (\bigsqcup_m f_n(d_m)) && \text{as each } f_n \text{ is continuous,} \\
&= \bigsqcup_m (\bigsqcup_n f_n(d_m)) && \text{by Proposition 8.9,} \\
&= \bigsqcup_m ((\bigsqcup_n f_n)(d_m)) && \text{by the definition of lubs of functions.}
\end{aligned}
$$

Special function spaces of the form $[I \to D]$, for I a set and D a cpo, are called *powers* and will often be written as D^I. Elements of the cpo D^I can be thought of as tuples $(d_i)_{i \in I}$ ordered coordinatewise (though these tuples can be infinite if the set is infinite). When I is the finite set $\{1, 2, \cdots, k\}$, the cpo D^I is isomorphic to the product $D \times \cdots \times D$, the product of k cpo's D, generally written D^k.

There are two key operations associated with the function space construction, *application* and *currying*.[4] Define

$$ apply : [D \to E] \times D \to E $$

to act as $apply(f, d) = f(d)$. Then $apply$ is continuous by Lemma 8.10 because it is continuous in each argument separately:

Let $f_0 \sqsubseteq \cdots \sqsubseteq f_n \sqsubseteq \cdots$ be a chain of functions. Then

$$
\begin{aligned}
apply(\bigsqcup_n f_n, d) &= \bigsqcup_n f_n(d) && \text{because lubs are given pointwise,} \\
&= \bigsqcup_n apply(f_n, d) && \text{by the definition of } apply.
\end{aligned}
$$

Let $d_0 \sqsubseteq \cdots \sqsubseteq d_n \sqsubseteq \cdots$ be a chain in D. Then

$$ apply(f, \bigsqcup_n d_n) = f(\bigsqcup_n d_n) = \bigsqcup_n f(d_n) = \bigsqcup_n apply(f, d_n). $$

Assume F is a cpo and that

$$ g : F \times D \to E $$

is continuous. Define

$$ curry(g) : F \to [D \to E] $$

---

[4] The operation of *currying* is named after the American logician Haskell Curry.

to be the function

$$curry(g) = \lambda v \in F \lambda d \in D.g(v,d)$$

So $(curry(g))(v)$ is the function which takes $d \in D$ to $g(v,d)$. So writing h for $curry(g)$ we have

$$(h(v))(d) = g(v,d)$$

for any $v \in F$, $d \in D$. Of course, we need to check that each such $h(v)$ is a continuous function and that $curry(g)$ is itself a continuous function $F \to [D \to E]$:

Firstly assume $v \in F$. We require that $h(v) = \lambda d \in D.g(v,d)$ is continuous. However g is continuous and so continuous in each argument separately making $h(v)$ continuous. Secondly, let

$$v_0 \sqsubseteq v_1 \sqsubseteq \cdots \sqsubseteq v_n \sqsubseteq \cdots$$

be an ω-chain of elements in F. Let $d \in D$. Then

$$
\begin{aligned}
h(\bigsqcup_n v_n)(d) &= g(\bigsqcup_n v_n, d) \quad \text{by the definition of } h, \\
&= \bigsqcup_n g(v_n, d) \quad \text{by the continuity of } g, \\
&= \bigsqcup_n (h(v_n)(d)) \quad \text{by the definition of } h, \\
&= (\bigsqcup_n h(v_n))(d) \quad \text{by the definition of lub of a sequence of functions.}
\end{aligned}
$$

Thus $h(\bigsqcup_n v_n) = \bigsqcup_n h(v_n)$ so h is continuous. In fact, $curry(g)$ is the unique continuous function $h : F \to [D \to E]$ such that

$$apply(h(v), d) = g(v,d), \text{ for all } v \in F, \ d \in D$$

Exercise 8.11 A power is a form of, possibly infinite, product with elements of a cpo D^I, for D a cpo and I a set, being thought of as tuples $(d_i)_{i \in I}$ ordered coordinatewise (these tuples are infinite if the set is infinite). As such, the notion of a function being continuous in a particular argument generalises from Lemma 8.10. Show however that the generalisation of Lemma 8.10 need not hold, *i.e.* a function from a power cpo D^I with the set I infinite need not be continuous even when continuous in each argument separately. (Hint: Consider functions $\mathbf{O}^\omega \to \mathbf{O}$.)   □

8.3.4 Lifting

We have already met situations where we have adjoined an extra element $\bot$ to a set to obtain a cpo with a bottom element (see, for example, Section 5.4 where the set of states was extended by an "undefined state" to get a cpo $\Sigma_\bot$). It is useful to generalise this construction, called *lifting*, to all cpo's. Lifting adjoins a bottom element below a copy of the original cpo.

Let D be a cpo. The lifting construction assumes an element $\bot$ and a function $\lfloor - \rfloor$ with the properties

$$\lfloor d_0 \rfloor = \lfloor d_1 \rfloor \Rightarrow d_0 = d_1, \text{ and}$$

$$\bot \neq \lfloor d \rfloor$$

for all $d, d_0, d_1 \in D$. The *lifted* cpo $D_\bot$ has underlying set

$$D_\bot = \{\lfloor d \rfloor \mid d \in D\} \cup \{\bot\},$$

and partial order

$$d_0' \sqsubseteq d_1' \text{ iff } (d_0' = \bot) \text{ or}$$

$$(\exists d_0, d_1 \in D. d_0' = \lfloor d_0 \rfloor \ \& \ d_1' = \lfloor d_1 \rfloor \ \& \ d_0 \sqsubseteq_D d_1).$$

It follows that $\lfloor d_0 \rfloor \sqsubseteq \lfloor d_1 \rfloor$ in $D_\bot$ iff $d_0 \sqsubseteq d_1$, so $D_\bot$ consists of a copy of the cpo D below which a distinct bottom element $\bot$ is introduced. Clearly the function $\lfloor - \rfloor : D \to D_\bot$ is continuous. Although there are different ways of realising $\lfloor - \rfloor$ and $\bot$ they lead to isomorphic constructions.

We can picture the lifting construction on a cpo D as:

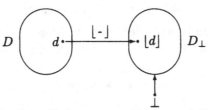

A continuous function $f : D \to E$, from a cpo D to a cpo E with a bottom element, can be extended to a continuous function

$$f^* : D_\bot \to E$$

by defining

$$f^*(d') = \begin{cases} f(d) & \text{if } d' = \lfloor d \rfloor \text{ for some } d \in D, \\ \bot & \text{otherwise.} \end{cases}$$

Suppose the function f is described by a lambda expression $\lambda x.e$. Then we shall write

$$let\ x \Leftarrow d'.\ e$$

for the result

$$(\lambda x.e)^*(d')$$

of applying f^* to an element $d' \in D_\perp$. This notation is suggestive; only if d' is a non-$\perp$ value is this used in determining a result from e, and otherwise the result is $\perp_E$.

The operation $(\text{-})^*$ is continuous: Let d' be an arbitrary element of $D_\perp$ and suppose $f_0 \sqsubseteq \cdots \sqsubseteq f_n \sqsubseteq \cdots$ is an ω-chain of functions in $[D \to E]$. In the case where $d' = \perp$ we directly obtain that both $(\bigsqcup_n f_n)^*(d')$ and $(\bigsqcup_n f_n^*)(d')$ are $\perp_E$. Otherwise $d' = \lfloor d \rfloor$ and we see

$$(\bigsqcup_n f_n)^*(d') = (\bigsqcup_n f_n)(d) \quad \text{by the definition of } (\text{-})^*,$$

$$= \bigsqcup_n (f_n(d)) \quad \text{as lubs are determined pointwise,}$$

$$= \bigsqcup_n ((f_n^*)(d')) \quad \text{by the definition of } (\text{-})^*,$$

$$= (\bigsqcup_n f_n^*)(d') \quad \text{as lubs are determined pointwise.}$$

As d' was arbitrary, we obtain $(\bigsqcup_n f_n)^* = \bigsqcup_n (f_n^*)$, *i.e.* the operation $(\text{-})^*$ is continuous.

We shall abbreviate

$$let\ x_1 \Leftarrow c_1.\ (let\ x_2 \Leftarrow c_2.\ (\cdots\ (let\ x_k \Leftarrow c_k.\ e) \cdots)$$

to

$$let\ x_1 \Leftarrow c_1, \cdots, x_k \Leftarrow c_k.\ e$$

Operations on sets S can be extended to their liftings $S_\perp$ using the *let*-notation. For example the or-function $\vee : \mathbf{T} \times \mathbf{T} \to \mathbf{T}$, on truth values $\mathbf{T} = \{\mathbf{true}, \mathbf{false}\}$, can be extended to

$$\vee_\perp : \mathbf{T}_\perp \times \mathbf{T}_\perp \to \mathbf{T}_\perp$$

by taking

$$x_1 \vee_\perp x_2 =_{def} (let\ t_1 \Leftarrow x_1, t_2 \Leftarrow x_2.\ \lfloor t_1 \vee t_2 \rfloor).$$

This extension is often called *strict* because if either x_1 is $\perp$ or x_2 is $\perp$ then so is $x_1 \vee_\perp x_2$. There are other computable ways of extending $\vee$ so e.g. $\mathbf{true} \vee \perp = \mathbf{true}$ (see the exercise below). Similarly, arithmetic operations on $\mathbf{N}$ can be extended strictly to operations on $\mathbf{N}_\perp$. For example,

$$x_1 +_\perp x_2 =_{def} let\ n_1 \Leftarrow x_1, n_2 \Leftarrow x_2.\ \lfloor n_1 + n_2 \rfloor.$$

Exercise 8.12 Describe in the form of "truth tables" all of the continuous extensions of the usual boolean or-operation $\vee$. □

8.3.5   Sums

It is often useful to form disjoint unions of cpo's, for example to adjoin error values to the usual values of computations. The *sum* construction on cpo's generalises that of disjoint unions on sets. Let $D_1, \cdots, D_k$ be cpo's. A sum $D_1 + \cdots + D_k$ has underlying set

$$\{in_1(d_1) \mid d_1 \in D_1\} \cup \cdots \cup \{in_k(d_k) \mid d_k \in D_k\}$$

and partial order

$$d \sqsubseteq d' \text{ iff } (\exists d_1, d_1' \in D_1.\ d = in_1(d_1) \ \& \ d' = in_1(d_1') \ \& \ d_1 \sqsubseteq d_1') \text{ or}$$

$$\vdots$$

$$(\exists d_k, d_k' \in D_k.\ d = in_k(d_k) \ \& \ d' = in_k(d_k') \ \& \ d_k \sqsubseteq d_k')$$

where all we need assume of the functions in_i is that they are 1-1 such that

$$in_i(d) \neq in_j(d')$$

for all $d \in D_i, d' \in D_j$ where $i \neq j$. It is easy to see that $D_1 + \cdots + D_k$ is a cpo, consisting as it does of disjoint copies of the cpo's $D_1, \ldots, D_k$ and that the *injection* functions $in_i : D_i \to D_1 + \cdots + D_k$, for $i = 1, \cdots k$, are continuous. Although there are different ways of realising the functions in_i they lead to isomorphic constructions.

Suppose $f_1 : D_1 \to E, \cdots, f_k : D_k \to E$ are continuous functions. They can be combined into a single continuous function

$$[f_1, \cdots, f_k] : D_1 + \cdots + D_k \to E$$

given by

$$[f_1, \cdots, f_k](in_i(d_i)) = f_i(d_i), \quad \text{for all } d_i \in D_i,$$

for $i = 1, \cdots, k$. In other terms,

$$[f_1, \cdots, f_k] \circ in_i = f_i,$$

for $i = 1, \cdots, k$, and this property on functions $D_1 + \cdots + D_k \to E$ characterises $[f_1, \cdots, f_k]$ uniquely.

Exercise 8.13 Show the operation yielding $[f_1, \cdots, f_k]$ from $f_1 \in [D_1 \to E], \cdots, f_k \in [D_k \to E]$ is continuous. (Use Lemma 8.10.) □

The truth values $\mathbf{T} = \{\mathbf{true}, \mathbf{false}\}$ can be regarded as the sum of the two singleton cpo's $\{\mathbf{true}\}$ and $\{\mathbf{false}\}$ with injection functions $in_1 : \{\mathbf{true}\} \to \mathbf{T}$ taking $\mathbf{true} \mapsto \mathbf{true}$ and, similarly, $in_2 : \{\mathbf{false}\} \to \mathbf{T}$ taking $\mathbf{false} \mapsto \mathbf{false}$. Let

$$\lambda x_1.e_1 : \{\mathbf{true}\} \to E \text{ and}$$
$$\lambda x_2.e_2 : \{\mathbf{false}\} \to E$$

be two, necessarily continuous, functions to a cpo E. Then it is not hard to see that

$$cond(t, e_1, e_2) =_{def} [\lambda x_1.e_1, \lambda x_2.e_2](t)$$

behaves as a conditional, *i.e.*

$$cond(t, e_1, e_2) = \begin{cases} e_1 & \text{if } t = \mathbf{true}, \\ e_2 & \text{if } t = \mathbf{false} \end{cases}$$

with arguments $t \in \mathbf{T}$ and $e_1, e_2 \in E$. Because the truth value in a conditional will often be the result of a computation we will make more use of a conditional where the test lies in $\mathbf{T}_\perp$. Assume that the cpo E has a bottom element $\perp_E$. The conditional defined as

$$(b \to e_1 \mid e_2) =_{def} \text{let } t \Leftarrow b. \ cond(t, e_1, e_2)$$

acts so

$$(b \to e_1 \mid e_2) = \begin{cases} e_1 & \text{if } b = \lfloor \mathbf{true} \rfloor, \\ e_2 & \text{if } b = \lfloor \mathbf{false} \rfloor, \\ \perp & \text{if } b = \perp \end{cases}$$

where $b \in \mathbf{T}_\perp$ and $e_1, e_2 \in E$. The demonstration that both these conditionals are continuous is postponed to the Section 8.4.

Exercise 8.14 Verify that the operations $cond$ and $(\text{-} \to \text{-} \mid \text{-})$ defined above do indeed behave as the conditionals claimed. $\square$

The sum construction and its associated functions enable us to define a general cases-construction which yields different results according to which component of a sum an element belongs. Assume that E is a cpo. Let $(D_1 + \cdots + D_k)$ be a sum of cpo's with an element d. Suppose

$$\lambda x_i.e_i : D_i \to E$$

are continuous functions for $1 \leq i \leq k$. The intention is that a cases construction

$$case \ d \ of \ in_1(x_1). \ e_1|$$

$$\vdots$$

$$in_k(x_k). \ e_k$$

should yield e_i in the case where $d = in_i(d_i)$ for some $d_i \in D_i$. This is achieved by defining the cases-construction to be

$$[\lambda x_1.e_1, \cdots, \lambda x_k.e_k](d).$$

Exercise 8.15 Why?   □

Finally, we remark that the empty cpo $\emptyset$ is a degenerate case of a finite sum, this time with no components.

8.4 A metalanguage

When defining the semantics of programming languages we shall often require that functions are continuous in order to take their least fixed points. This raises the issue that we don't want always to interrupt definitions in order to check that expressions are well-defined and do indeed represent continuous functions. A great deal of tedious work can be saved by noticing, once and for all, that provided mathematical expressions fit within a certain informal syntax then they will represent continuous functions. Its expressions constitute a metalanguage within which we can describe the denotational semantics of particular programming languages.

We have already encountered an occasional use of lambda notation. In domain theory we shall make frequent use of it. Let e be an expression which represents an element of the cpo E, whenever x is an element of the cpo D. For example, e might be a conditional "$cond(x, 0, 1)$" where D is $\mathbf{T}$, the truth values, and E is ω, the natural numbers. We write

$$\lambda x \in D.\, e$$

for the function $h : D \to E$ such that $h(d) = e[d/x]$ for all $d \in D$. Often we abbreviate it to $\lambda x.e$ when x is understood to range over elements of D. Suppose e is an expression which refers to elements $x \in D_1$ and $y \in D_2$. Instead of writing the somewhat clumsy

$$\lambda z \in D_1 \times D_2.\; e[\pi_1(z)/x, \pi_2(z)/y]$$

we can write

$$\lambda(x, y) \in D_1 \times D_2.\; e.$$

More usually though this function will be written as

$$\lambda x \in D_1, y \in D_2.\, e,$$

or just

$$\lambda x, y.\, e.$$

We would like to use lambda notation as freely as possible and yet still be assured that when we do so we define continuous functions. We shall typically encounter expressions e which represent an element of a cpo E and depend on variables like x in a cpo D. Say such an expression e is *continuous in the variable* $x \in D$ iff the function $\lambda x \in D.\ e : D \to E$ is continuous. Say e is *continuous in its variables* iff e is continuous in all variables. Of course, the expression e will depend on some variables and not on others; if a variable $x \in D$ does not appear in e then the function $\lambda x \in D.e$ is constant, and so certainly continuous.

We can build up expressions for elements of cpo's in the following ways, using the operations we have seen, and be assured by the results of this chapter that the expressions will be continuous in their variables:

Variables: An expression consisting of a single variable x ranging over elements of a cpo E is continuous in its variables because, for $y \in D$ the abstraction $\lambda y.x$ is either the identity function $\lambda x.x$ (if y is the variable x) or a constant function.

Constants: We have met a number of special elements of cpo's, for example, $\perp_D \in D$ a cpo with bottom, truth values **true, false** $\in \mathbf{T}$, projection functions like $\pi_1 \in [D_1 \times D_2 \to D_1]$ associated with a product, $apply \in [[D \to E] \times D \to E]$ with a function space, the function $(\text{-})^*$ associated with lifting, injection functions and the operation $[\,,\ldots,\,]$ with a sum, and several others including $fix \in [[D \to D] \to D]$ (though the justification that fix is a continuous function, and so indeed an element of the cpo claimed, is postponed to the end of this section). Such constant expressions give fixed elements of a cpo and so are continuous in their variables.

Tupling: Given expressions $e_1 \in E_1, \cdots, e_k \in E_k$ of cpo's $E_1, \cdots, E_k$ we can form the tuple $(e_1, \cdots, e_k)$ in the product cpo $E_1 \times \cdots \times E_k$. Such a tuple is continuous in a variable $x \in D$ iff

$$\lambda x.(e_1, \cdots, e_k) \text{ is continuous}$$
$$\iff \pi_i \circ (\lambda x.(e_1, \cdots, e_k)) \text{ is continuous for } 1 \leq i \leq k \text{ (by Lemma 8.8)}$$
$$\iff \lambda x.e_i \text{ is continuous for } 1 \leq i \leq k$$
$$\iff e_i \text{ is continuous in } x \text{ for } 1 \leq i \leq k.$$

Hence tuples are continuous in their variables provided their components are.

Application: Given a fixed continuous function K of the kind discussed above (in "Constants") we can apply it to an appropriate argument expression e. The result $K(e)$

is continuous in x iff

$$\lambda x.\ K(e) \text{ is continuous}$$
$$\Longleftrightarrow K \circ (\lambda x.e) \text{ is continuous}$$
$$\Leftarrow \quad \lambda x.e \text{ is continuous (by Proposition 8.1)}$$
$$\Longleftrightarrow e \text{ is continuous in } x.$$

Hence such applications are continuous in their variables provided their arguments are. In particular, it follows that general applications of the form $e_1(e_2)$ are continuous in variables if e_1, e_2 are; this is because $e_1(e_2) = apply(e_1, e_2)$ the result of applying the constant $apply$ to the tuple (e_1, e_2).

λ-**abstraction:** Suppose $e \in E$ is continuous in its variables. Then choosing a particular variable y ranging over a cpo D we can form the necessarily continuous function $\lambda y.e : D \to E$. We would like that this abstraction is itself continuous in its variables x. Certainly if x happens to be the variable y this is assured, the result being a function which is constantly $\lambda y.e$. Otherwise $\lambda y.e$ is continuous in x iff

$$\lambda x.\ \lambda y.\ e \text{ is continuous}$$
$$\Longleftrightarrow \quad curry(\lambda x, y.\ e) \text{ is continuous}$$
$$\Leftarrow \quad \lambda x, y.\ e \text{ is continuous (as } curry \text{ preserves continuity)}$$
$$\Longleftrightarrow \quad e \text{ is continuous in } x \text{ and } y.$$

Hence abstractions are continuous in their variables provided their bodies are.[5] In particular, we obtain that function composition preserves the property of being continuous in variables because:

$$e_1 \circ e_2 = \lambda x.\ e_1(e_2(x)).$$

Note that more general abstractions like $\lambda x, y \in D_1 \times D_2.\ e$ are also admissible because they equal $\lambda z \in D_1 \times D_2.\ e[\pi_1(z)/x, \pi_2(z)/y]$.

Thus any expression is continuous in its variables when built up from fixed continuous functions or elements in the ways above. It follows that other constructions preserve this property, other important ones being:

let-**construction:** Assume D is a cpo and E is a cpo with bottom. If $e_1 \in D_\perp$ and $e_2 \in E$ are continuous in variables then we can form the expression

$$let\ x \Leftarrow e_1.\ e_2$$

---

[5]This condition is also necessary because the implication "$\Leftarrow$" in the argument can be replaced by an equivalence "$\Longleftrightarrow$," though this has not yet been shown. It follows by Exercise 8.16 ending this section.

also continuous in its variables. This is because

$$(let \ x \Leftarrow e_1. \ e_2) = (\lambda x.e_2)^*(e_1)$$

and the expression on the right can be built up from e_1 and e_2 solely by the methods admitted above.

case-**construction:** Assume that E is a cpo. Let $(D_1 + \cdots + D_k)$ be a sum of cpo's with an element e, an expression assumed continuous in its variables. Suppose expressions $e_i \in E$ are continuous in variables for $1 \leq i \leq k$. Then the cases construction

$$case \ e \ of \ in_1(x_1). \ e_1|$$

$$\vdots$$

$$in_k(x_k). \ e_k$$

is continuous in its variables because it is defined to be

$$[\lambda x_1.e_1, \cdots, \lambda x_k.e_k](e),$$

a form obtainable by the methods above—recall the operation $[-, \ldots, -]$ associated with a sum has been shown to be continuous and is admitted as one of our constants. In particular conditional expressions of the form $cond(t, e_1, e_2)$, introduced in Section 8.3.5, where t is a truth value and e_1, e_2 belong to the same cpo, are continuous in their variables because they equal $[\lambda x_1.e_1, \lambda x_2.e_2](t)$. The variant $b \rightarrow e_1|e_2$, also from Section 8.3.5, defined on cpo's with bottom elements is then continuous in its variables because it is definable as $let \ t \Leftarrow b. \ cond(t, e_1, e_2)$.

Fixed-point operators: Each cpo D with bottom is associated with a fixed-point operator $fix : [D \rightarrow D] \rightarrow D$. In fact the function fix is itself continuous. To see this note

$$fix = \bigsqcup_{n \in \omega} (\lambda f. \ f^n(\bot)),$$

i.e. fix is the least upper bound of the ω-chain of the functions

$$\lambda f.\bot \sqsubseteq \lambda f.f(\bot) \sqsubseteq \lambda f.f(f(\bot)) \sqsubseteq \cdots$$

where each of these is continuous and so an element of the cpo $[[D \rightarrow D] \rightarrow D]$ by the methods above. It follows that their lub fix exists in $[[D \rightarrow D] \rightarrow D]$.

Notation: We shall often use $\mu x.e$ to abbreviate $fix(\lambda x.e)$.

We shall use results like the above to show expressions are well-defined. Although we shall be informal we could formalise the language above, saying precisely what the types are, and what the constant operations are to form a particular typed λ-calculus in whose standard interpretation terms would denote elements of cpo's—the construction rules of the language would ensure that no non-continuous functions could creep in. An approach of this kind led to Dana Scott's LCF (Logic of Computable Functions) which consists of a typed λ-calculus like this with predicates and a proof rule (fixed-point induction, see Chapter 10) for reasoning about least fixed points.

Exercise 8.16 Recall, from 8.3.3, the function $curry = \lambda g \lambda v \lambda d.g(v,d)$ from $A = [F \times D \to E$ to $B = [F \to [D \to E]]$. This exercise shows $curry$ is an *isomorphism* from A to B. Why is $curry$ a *continuous* function $A \to B$? Define a function $uncurry : B \to A$ inverse to $curry$, *i.e.* so $curry \circ uncurry = Id_B$ and $uncurry \circ curry = Id_A$. Show $uncurry$ is continuous and inverse to $curry$.   □

8.5   Further reading

The presentation is mainly based on Gordon Plotkin's lecture notes (both the "Pisa notes" [80] and his later work [83]) though the presentation, while elementary, has been influenced by Eugenio Moggi's work [67] and Andrew Pitts' presentation [75]. The essentials go back to work of Dana Scott in the late '60's. I'd also like to acknowledge learning from Christopher Wadworth's excellent Edinburgh lecture notes which unfortunately never reached print. Larry Paulson's book [74] provides background on the logic LCF and the proof assistant implemented in ML. Alternative introductions to denotational semantics can be found in: [88], [95], [91]. This chapter has in fact introduced the *category* of cpo's and continuous functions and shown that it is *cartesian closed* in that the category has *products* and *function spaces*; it also has *coproducts* given by the sum construction. Elementary accounts of category theory are given in [10], [15].

9 Recursion equations

This chapter explores a simple language **REC** which supports the recursive definition of functions on the integers. The language is applicative in contrast to the imperative language of **IMP**. It can be evaluated in a call-by-value or call-by-name manner. For each mode of evaluation operational and denotational semantics are provided and proved equivalent.

9.1 The language REC

REC is a simple programming language designed to support the recursive definition of functions. It has these syntactic sets:

- numbers $n \in \mathbf{N}$, positive and negative integers,
- variables over numbers $x \in \mathbf{Var}$, and
- function variables $f_1, \ldots, f_k \in \mathbf{Fvar}$.

It is assumed that each function variable $f_i \in \mathbf{Fvar}$ possesses an *arity* $a_i \in \omega$ which is the number of arguments it takes—it is allowed for a_i to be 0 when $f_i()$, consisting of the function f_i of arity 0 applied to the empty tuple, is generally written as just f_i. Terms $t, t_0, t_1, \ldots$ of **REC** have the following syntax:

$$t ::= n \mid x \mid t_1 + t_2 \mid t_1 - t_2 \mid t_1 \times t_2 \mid \text{if } t_0 \text{ then } t_1 \text{ else } t_2 \mid f_i(t_1, \ldots, t_{a_i})$$

For simplicity we shall take boolean expressions to be terms themselves with 0 understood as true and all nonzero numbers as false. (It is then possible to code disjunction as $\times$, negation $\neg b$ as a conditional **if** b **then** 1 **else** 0 and a basic boolean like the equality test $(t_0 = t_1)$ between terms as $(t_0 - t_1)$—see also Exercise 9.1 below.) We say a term is *closed* when it contains no variables from **Var**.

The functions variables f are given meaning by a *declaration*, which consists of equations typically of the form

$$f_1(x_1, \ldots, x_{a_1}) \quad = \quad t_1$$
$$\vdots$$
$$f_k(x_1, \ldots, x_{a_k}) \quad = \quad t_k$$

where the variables of t_i are included in $x_1, \ldots, x_{a_i}$, for $i = 1, \cdots, k$. The equations can be recursive in that the terms t_i may well contain the function variable f_i and indeed other function variables of $f_1, \ldots, f_k$. Reasonably enough, we shall not allow two defining equations for the same function variable.

In a defining equation

$$f_i(x_1, \ldots, x_{a_i}) = t_i$$

we call the term t_i the *definition* of f_i.

What to take as the operational semantics of **REC** is not so clear-cut. Consider a defining equation

$$f_1(x) = f_1(x) + 1.$$

Computational intuition suggests that $f_1(3)$, say, should evaluate to the same value as $f_1(3) + 1$ which should, in turn, evaluate to the same value as $(f_1(3) + 1) + 1$, and so on. The evaluation of $f_1(3)$ should never terminate. Indeed if the evaluation of $f_1(3)$ were to terminate with an integer value n then this would satisfy the contradictory equation $n = n + 1$. Now suppose, in addition, we have the defining equation

$$f_2(x) = 1.$$

In evaluating $f_2(t)$, for a term t, we have two choices: one is to evaluate the argument t first and once an integer value n is obtained to then proceed with the evaluation of $f_2(n)$; another is to pass directly to the definition of f_2, replacing all occurrences of the variable x by the argument t. The two choices have vastly different effects when taking the argument t to be $f_1(3)$; the former diverges while the latter terminates with result 1. The former method of evaluation, which requires that we first obtain values for the arguments before passing them to the definition is called *call-by-value*. The latter method, where the unevaluated terms are passed directly to the definition, is called *call-by-name*. It is clear that if an argument is needed then it is efficient to evaluate it once and for all; otherwise the same term may have to be evaluated several times in the definition. On the other hand, as in the example of $f_2(f_1(3))$, if the argument is never used its divergence can needlessly cause the divergence of the enclosing term.

Exercise 9.1 Based on your informal understanding of how to evaluate terms in **REC** what do you expect the function s in the following declaration to compute?

$$s(x) = \textbf{if } x \textbf{ then } 0 \textbf{ else } f(x, 0 - x)$$
$$f(x, y) = \textbf{if } x \textbf{ then } 1 \textbf{ else } (\textbf{if } y \textbf{ then } -1 \textbf{ else } f(x - 1, y - 1))$$

Define a function $lt(x, y)$ in **REC** which returns 0 if $x < y$, and a nonzero number otherwise.   □

9.2   Operational semantics of call-by-value

Assume a declaration d of

$$f_1(x_1, \ldots, x_{a_1}) \;=\; d_1$$
$$\vdots$$
$$f_k(x_1, \ldots, x_{a_k}) \;=\; d_k$$

The term d_i is the definition of f_i, for $i = 1, \ldots, k$. With respect to these we give rules to specify how closed terms in **REC** evaluate.

We understand $t \to^d_{va} n$ as meaning the closed term t evaluates to integer value n under call-by-value with respect to the declaration d. The rules giving this evaluation relation are as follows:

$$(num) \qquad n \to^d_{va} n$$

$$(op) \qquad \frac{t_1 \to^d_{va} n_1 \quad t_2 \to^d_{va} n_2}{t_1 \; \mathbf{op} \; t_1 \to^d_{va} n_1 \; op \; n_2}$$

$$(condt) \qquad \frac{t_0 \to^d_{va} 0 \quad t_1 \to^d_{va} n_1}{\mathbf{if} \; t_0 \; \mathbf{then} \; t_1 \; \mathbf{else} \; t_2 \to^d_{va} n_1}$$

$$(condf) \qquad \frac{t_0 \to^d_{va} n_0 \quad t_2 \to^d_{va} n_2 \quad n_0 \not\equiv 0}{\mathbf{if} \; t_0 \; \mathbf{then} \; t_1 \; \mathbf{else} \; t_2 \to^d_{va} n_2}$$

$$(fn) \qquad \frac{t_1 \to^d_{va} n_1 \quad \cdots \quad t_{a_i} \to^d_{va} n_{a_i} \quad d_i[n_1/x_1, \ldots, n_{a_i}/x_{a_i}] \to^d_{va} n}{f_i(t_1, \ldots, t_{a_i}) \to^d_{va} n}$$

The rules are straightforward. Notice that we distinguish a syntactic operation **op** from the associated operation on integers op; an instance of the rule (op), in the case of addition, is:

$$\frac{3 \to^d_{va} 3 \quad 4 \to^d_{va} 4}{3 + 4 \to^d_{va} 7}$$

The slightly odd rules for conditionals arise simply from our decision to regard 0 as true and any non-zero value as false. Notice how the rules for the evaluation of functions insist on the evaluation of arguments before the function definition is used.

The evaluation relation is deterministic:

Proposition 9.2 *If $t \rightarrow^d_{va} n_1$ and $t \rightarrow^d_{va} n_2$ then $n_1 \equiv n_2$.*

Proof: By a routine application of rule induction.   □

9.3   Denotational semantics of call-by-value

Terms will be assigned meanings in the presence of environments for the variables and function variables. An *environment* for variables is a function

$$\rho : \mathbf{Var} \rightarrow \mathbf{N}$$

We shall write $\mathbf{Env}_{va} = [\mathbf{Var} \rightarrow \mathbf{N}]$ for the cpo of all such environments.

An environment for the function variables $f_1, \ldots, f_k$ is a tuple $\varphi = (\varphi_1, \ldots, \varphi_k)$ where

$$\varphi_i : \mathbf{N}^{a_i} \rightarrow \mathbf{N}_\perp$$

We write $\mathbf{Fenv}_{va}$ for $[\mathbf{N}^{a_1} \rightarrow \mathbf{N}_\perp] \times \cdots \times [\mathbf{N}^{a_k} \rightarrow \mathbf{N}_\perp]$, the cpo of environments for function variables. As expected, a declaration determines a particular function environment.

Given environments φ, ρ for function variables and variables, a term denotes an element of $\mathbf{N}_\perp$. More precisely, a term t denotes a function

$$[t]_{va} \in [\mathbf{Fenv}_{va} \rightarrow [\mathbf{Env}_{va} \rightarrow \mathbf{N}_\perp]]$$

given by the following structural induction:

$$
\begin{aligned}
[n]_{va} &= \lambda\varphi\lambda\rho.\lfloor n \rfloor \\
[x]_{va} &= \lambda\varphi\lambda\rho.\lfloor \rho(x) \rfloor \\
[t_1 \text{ op } t_2]_{va} &= \lambda\varphi\lambda\rho.\ [t_1]_{va}\varphi\rho \text{ op}_\perp [t_2]_{va}\varphi\rho \\
&\quad \text{for operations } \mathbf{op} \text{ taken as } +, -, \times \\
[\textbf{if } t_0 \textbf{ then } t_1 \textbf{ else } t_2]_{va} &= \lambda\varphi\lambda\rho.\ Cond([t_0]_{va}\varphi\rho,\ [t_1]_{va}\varphi\rho,\ [t_2]_{va}\varphi\rho) \\
[f_i(t_1, \ldots, t_{a_i})]_{va} &= \lambda\varphi\lambda\rho. \\
&\quad (let\ v_1 \Leftarrow [t_1]_{va}\varphi\rho, \ldots, v_{a_i} \Leftarrow [t_{a_i}]_{va}\varphi\rho.\ \varphi_i(v_1, \ldots, v_{a_i}))
\end{aligned}
$$

The definition has used the strict extensions $+_\perp, -_\perp, \times_\perp$ of the usual arithmetic operations on $\mathbf{N}$; recall, for instance, from 8.3.4 that

$$
z_1 +_\perp z_2 = \begin{cases} \lfloor n_1 + n_2 \rfloor \text{ if } & z_1 = \lfloor n_1 \rfloor \text{ and } z_2 = \lfloor n_2 \rfloor \\ & \text{for some } n_1, n_2 \in \mathbf{N}, \\ \perp & \text{otherwise} \end{cases}
$$

for $z_1, z_2 \in \mathbf{N}$. The function

$$Cond : \mathbf{N}_\perp \times \mathbf{N}_\perp \times \mathbf{N}_\perp \to \mathbf{N}_\perp$$

is used in defining the meaning of a conditional. It satisfies

$$Cond(z_0, z_1, z_2) = \begin{cases} z_1 & \text{if} & z_0 = \lfloor 0 \rfloor, \\ z_2 & \text{if} & z_0 = \lfloor n \rfloor \text{ for some } n \in \mathbf{N} \text{ with } n \neq 0, \\ \perp & \text{otherwise} \end{cases}$$

for $z_0, z_1, z_2 \in \mathbf{N}_\perp$. It can be obtained from the conditional introduced earlier in 8.3.5. Let $iszero : \mathbf{N} \to \mathbf{T}$ take the value **true** on argument 0 and **false** elsewhere. The function $iszero$ is continuous being a function between discrete cpo's, so its strict extension

$$iszero_\perp = \lambda z \in \mathbf{N}_\perp. \ let \ n \Leftarrow z. \ \lfloor iszero(n) \rfloor$$

is continuous and acts so

$$iszero_\perp(z) = \begin{cases} \lfloor \textbf{true} \rfloor & \text{if } z = \lfloor 0 \rfloor, \\ \lfloor \textbf{false} \rfloor & \text{if } z = \lfloor n \rfloor \ \& \ n \neq 0, \\ \perp & \text{otherwise.} \end{cases}$$

Now we see

$$Cond(z_0, z_1, z_2) = (iszero_\perp(z_0) \to z_1 | z_2)$$

for $z_0, z_1, z_2 \in \mathbf{N}_\perp$. Thus certainly it is a continuous function by Section 8.4. Indeed, for any term t of **REC**, the semantic function $[\![t]\!]_{va}$ is a continuous function. This follows directly from the following lemma:

Lemma 9.3 *For all terms t of **REC**, the denotation $[\![t]\!]_{va}$ is a continuous function in* $[\mathbf{Fenv}_{va} \to [\mathbf{Env}_{va} \to \mathbf{N}_\perp]]$.

Proof: The proof proceeds by structural induction on terms t using the results from Section 8.4. □

We observe that the intuitively obvious fact that the result of the denotation of a term in an environment does not depend on the assignment of values to variables outside the term:

Lemma 9.4 *For all terms t of **REC**, if environments $\rho, \rho' \in \mathbf{Env}_{va}$ yield the same result on all variables which appear in t then, for any $\varphi \in \mathbf{Fenv}_{va}$,*

$$[\![t]\!]_{va} \varphi \rho = [\![t]\!]_{va} \varphi \rho'.$$

In particular, the denotation $[\![t]\!]_{va} \varphi \rho$ of a closed term t is independent of the environment ρ.

Proof: A straightforward structural induction on terms t. $\square$

The semantics above expresses the meaning of a term with respect to a function environment $\varphi = (\varphi_1, \ldots, \varphi_k)$. The exact function environment is determined by a declaration consisting of defining equations

$$f_1(x_1, \ldots, x_{a_1}) \;=\; d_1$$

$$\vdots$$

$$f_k(x_1, \ldots, x_{a_k}) \;=\; d_k$$

This can be understood as recursive equations in $f_1, \ldots, f_k$ which must be satisfied by the function environment $\delta = (\delta_1, \ldots, \delta_k)$:

$$\delta_1(n_1, \ldots, n_{a_1}) \;=\; [\![d_1]\!]_{va}\delta\rho[n_1/x_1, \ldots, n_{a_1}/x_{a_1}], \text{ for all } n_1, \ldots, n_{a_1} \in \mathbf{N},$$

$$\vdots$$

$$\delta_k(n_1, \ldots, n_{a_k}) \;=\; [\![d_k]\!]_{va}\delta\rho[n_1/x_1, \ldots, n_{a_k}/x_{a_k}], \text{ for all } n_1, \ldots, n_{a_k} \in \mathbf{N}$$

We have used some new notation for updating the environment ρ. Define $\rho[n/x]$, where $x \in \mathbf{Var}$ and $n \in \mathbf{N}$, to be the environment such that

$$(\rho[n/x])(y) = \begin{cases} \rho(y) & \text{if } y \not\equiv x, \\ n & \text{if } y \equiv x. \end{cases}$$

Alternatively we can define the updated environment in the metalanguage of Section 8.4. Notice that the discrete cpo $\mathbf{Var}$ can be regarded as a sum of the singleton $\{x\}$ and $\mathbf{Var} \setminus \{x\}$ in which the injection functions $in_1 : \{x\} \to \mathbf{Var}$ and $in_2 : (\mathbf{Var} \setminus \{x\}) \to \mathbf{Var}$ are the inclusion functions. Now we see that $\rho[n/x]$ is equal to

$$\lambda y \in \mathbf{Var}. \; case \; y \; of \; in_1(x). \; n \; |$$
$$in_2(w). \; \rho(w).$$

We have used terms like $\rho[n_0/x_0, n_1/x_1]$ etc. to abbreviate $(\rho[n_0/x_0])[n_1/x_1]$ etc. (Note that this argument assumes nothing special about the cpo of integers, and in fact similar updating operations can be defined in the metalanguage when variables are bound to elements of other more complicated cpo's.)

The equations will not in general determine a unique solution. However there is a least solution, that obtained as the least fixed point of the continuous function

$$F : \mathbf{Fenv}_{va} \to \mathbf{Fenv}_{va}$$

given by

$$F(\varphi) \;=\; (\lambda n_1, \ldots, n_{a_1} \in \mathbf{N}.\ [\![d_1]\!]_{va}\varphi\rho[n_1/x_1, \ldots, n_{a_1}/x_{a_1}], \ldots,$$
$$\lambda n_1, \ldots, n_{a_k} \in \mathbf{N}.\ [\![d_k]\!]_{va}\varphi\rho[n_1/x_1, \ldots, n_{a_k}/x_{a_k}]).$$

The function F is continuous because it is built up from the functions $[\![d_1]\!]_{va}, \ldots, [\![d_k]\!]_{va}$, known to be continuous by Lemma 9.3, using the methods admitted in Section 8.4.

Now we can define the function environment determined by the declaration d to be the least fixed point

$$\delta = fix(F).$$

A closed term t denotes a result $[\![t]\!]_{va}\delta\rho$ in $\mathbf{N}_\perp$ with respect to this function environment, independent of what environment ρ is used. Of course, we had better check it agrees with the value given by the operational semantics. But this we do in the next section.

We conclude our presentation of the denotational semantics for the call-by-value evaluation of **REC** by considering some examples to illustrate how the semantics captures evaluation.

Example: To see how the denotational semantics captures the call-by-value style of evaluation, consider the declaration:

$$f_1 = f_1 + 1$$
$$f_2(x) = 1$$

(Here f_1 is a function taking no arguments, *i.e.* a constant, defined recursively.)
According to the denotational semantics, the effect of this declaration is that f_1, f_2 are denoted by $\delta = (\delta_1, \delta_2) \in \mathbf{N}_\perp \times [\mathbf{N} \to \mathbf{N}_\perp]$ where

$$(\delta_1, \delta_2) = \mu\varphi.\ ([\![f_1 + 1]\!]_{va}\varphi\rho,\ \lambda m \in \mathbf{N}.\ [\![1]\!]_{va}\varphi\rho[m/x])$$
$$= \mu\varphi.\ (\varphi_1 +_\perp \lfloor 1 \rfloor,\ \lambda m \in \mathbf{N}.\ \lfloor 1 \rfloor)$$

In this case it is easy to see that

$$(\perp, \lambda m \in \mathbf{N}.\ \lfloor 1 \rfloor)$$

is the required least fixed point (it can simply be checked that this pair is a fixed point of $\lambda\varphi.\ (\varphi_1 +_\perp \lfloor 1 \rfloor,\ \lambda m \in \mathbf{N}.\ \lfloor 1 \rfloor)$ and has to be the least). Thus

$$\delta_1 = \perp$$
$$\delta_2 = \lambda m \in \mathbf{N}.\ \lfloor 1 \rfloor$$

from which

$$[\![f_2(f_1)]\!]_{va}\delta\rho = let \; n_1 \Leftarrow \delta_1. \; \delta_2(n_1)$$
$$= \perp.$$

□

Example: This next example involves a more detailed analysis of a least fixed point. Consider the declaration

$$f(x) = \textbf{if } x \textbf{ then } 1 \textbf{ else } x \times f(x-1).$$

In this example we are only interested in f, so for simplicity we take the function environment $\textbf{Fenv}_{va}$ to simply be $[\textbf{N} \rightarrow \textbf{N}_\perp]$. According to the denotational semantics this declares f to be the function δ where, letting t be the definition and ρ an arbitrary environment for variables:

$$
\begin{aligned}
\delta &= \mu\varphi. \; (\lambda m. \; [\![t]\!]_{va}\varphi\rho[m/x]) \\
&= fix(\lambda\varphi. \; (\lambda m. \; [\![t]\!]_{va}\varphi\rho[m/x])) \\
&= \bigsqcup_{r\in\omega} \delta^{(r)}.
\end{aligned}
$$

Above we have taken

$$F(\varphi) = (\lambda m. \; [\![t]\!]_{va}\varphi\rho[m/x]).$$

and defined

$$\delta^{(r)} = F^r(\perp).$$

From the denotational semantics, recalling the definition of *Cond*, we obtain

$$
\begin{aligned}
F(\varphi)(m) &= Cond(\lfloor m \rfloor, \lfloor 1 \rfloor, \lfloor m \rfloor \times_\perp \varphi(m-1)) \\
&= iszero_\perp(\lfloor m \rfloor) \rightarrow \lfloor 1 \rfloor \mid \lfloor m \rfloor \times_\perp \varphi(m-1)
\end{aligned}
$$

for $\varphi \in [\textbf{N} \rightarrow \textbf{N}_\perp]$ and $m \in \textbf{N}$. Now note

$$F(\varphi)(m) = cond(iszero(m), \lfloor 1 \rfloor, \lfloor m \rfloor \times_\perp \varphi(m-1))$$

where we make use of the function $cond : \textbf{T} \times \textbf{N}_\perp \times \textbf{N}_\perp \rightarrow \textbf{N}_\perp$ from Section 8.3.5 on sums of cpo's. For an arbitrary $m \in \textbf{N}$, we calculate:

$$\delta^{(0)}(m) = \perp$$

$$\delta^{(1)}(m) = F(\delta^{(0)})(m) = cond(iszero(m), \lfloor 1 \rfloor, \lfloor m \rfloor \times_\perp \delta^{(0)}(m-1))$$

$$= \begin{cases} \lfloor 1 \rfloor & \text{if } m = 0 \\ \bot & \text{otherwise.} \end{cases}$$

$$\delta^{(2)}(m) = F(\delta^{(1)})(m) = cond(iszero(m), \lfloor 1 \rfloor, \lfloor m \rfloor \times_\bot \delta^{(1)}(m-1))$$
$$= \begin{cases} \lfloor 1 \rfloor & \text{if } m = 0 \text{ or } m = 1 \\ \bot & \text{otherwise.} \end{cases}$$

Generally we have

$$\delta^{(r)}(m) = F(\delta^{(r-1)})(m) = cond(iszero(m), \lfloor 1 \rfloor, \lfloor m \rfloor \times_\bot \delta^{(r-1)}(m-1))$$

and, by mathematical induction, we can obtain

$$\delta^{(r)}(m) = \begin{cases} \lfloor m! \rfloor & \text{if } 0 \leq m < r \\ \bot & \text{otherwise.} \end{cases}$$

As we expect the least upper bound δ is the factorial function on non-negative integers and $\bot$ elsewhere:

$$\delta(m) = \begin{cases} \lfloor m! \rfloor & \text{if } 0 \leq m \\ \bot & \text{otherwise.} \end{cases}$$

(This example is not changed substantially in moving to a call-by-name regime.) $\square$

9.4 Equivalence of semantics for call-by-value

The two semantics, operational and denotational, agree. Let δ be the function environment determined as a least fixed point of F got from the declaration d. The main result of this section shows that for a closed term t, and number n

$$\llbracket t \rrbracket_{va} \delta \rho = \lfloor n \rfloor \quad \text{iff} \quad t \rightarrow^d_{va} n.$$

Because t is closed the environment ρ can be arbitrary—it does not affect the denotation.

The proof factors into two main lemmas, one for each direction of the equivalence. The first's proof rests on a subsidiary fact to do with substitutions.

Lemma 9.5 *(Substitution Lemma)*
Let t be a term and n a number. Let $\varphi \in \mathbf{Fenv}_{va}$, $\rho \in \mathbf{Env}_{va}$. Then

$$\llbracket t \rrbracket_{va} \varphi \rho[n/x] = \llbracket t[n/x] \rrbracket_{va} \varphi \rho.$$

Proof: The proof is a simple structural induction on t. $\square$

Lemma 9.6 *Let t be a closed term and n a number. Let $\rho \in \mathbf{Env}_{va}$. Then*

$$t \rightarrow_{va}^{d} n \;\; \Rightarrow \llbracket t \rrbracket_{va} \delta\rho = \lfloor n \rfloor.$$

Proof: We use rule-induction with the property

$$P(t,n) \quad \text{iff} \quad \llbracket t \rrbracket_{va} \delta\rho = \lfloor n \rfloor,$$

for a term t and number n. (Here ρ can be any environment as t is closed.)

Consider a rule instance $n \rightarrow_{va}^{d} n$, for a number n. Certainly $\llbracket n \rrbracket_{va} \delta\rho = \lfloor n \rfloor$, so $P(n,n)$ holds.

Assume now the property P holds of the premises of the rule (op). Precisely, assume

$$t_1 \rightarrow_{va}^{d} n_1 \text{ and } \llbracket t_1 \rrbracket_{va} \delta\rho = \lfloor n_1 \rfloor, \text{ and}$$
$$t_2 \rightarrow_{va}^{d} n_2 \text{ and } \llbracket t_2 \rrbracket_{va} \delta\rho = \lfloor n_2 \rfloor.$$

It follows that

$$
\begin{aligned}
\llbracket t_1 \mathbf{\ op\ } t_2 \rrbracket_{va} \delta\rho &= \llbracket t_1 \rrbracket_{va} \delta\rho \; op_\perp \; \llbracket t_2 \rrbracket_{va} \delta\rho \text{ by definition,}\\
&= \lfloor n_1 \rfloor op_\perp \lfloor n_2 \rfloor \\
&= \lfloor n_1 \; op \; n_2 \rfloor.
\end{aligned}
$$

Hence $P(t_1 \mathbf{\ op\ } t_2, n_1 \; op \; n_2)$, *i.e.* the property holds of the conclusion of the rule (op). The two cases of rules for conditionals $(condt)$, $(condf)$ are similar, and omitted. Finally, we consider a rule-instance of (fn). Assume

$$t_1 \rightarrow_{va}^{d} n_1 \quad \text{and} \quad \llbracket t_1 \rrbracket_{va} \delta\rho = \lfloor n_1 \rfloor,$$

$$\vdots$$

$$t_{a_i} \rightarrow_{va}^{d} n_{a_i} \quad \text{and} \quad \llbracket t_{a_i} \rrbracket_{va} \delta\rho = \lfloor n_{a_i} \rfloor, \text{ and}$$
$$d_i[n_1/x_1, \ldots, n_{a_i}/x_{a_i}] \rightarrow_{va}^{d} n \quad \text{and} \quad \llbracket d_i[n_1/x_1, \ldots, n_{a_i}/x_{a_i}] \rrbracket_{va} \delta\rho = \lfloor n \rfloor.$$

We see

$$
\begin{aligned}
\llbracket f_i(t_1, \ldots, t_{a_i}) \rrbracket_{va} \delta\rho &= let \; v_1 \Leftarrow \llbracket t_1 \rrbracket_{va} \delta\rho, \ldots, v_{a_i} \Leftarrow \llbracket t_{a_i} \rrbracket_{va} \delta\rho. \; \delta_i(v_1, \ldots, v_{a_i}) \\
&= \delta_i(n_1, \ldots, n_{a_i}) \\
&= \llbracket d_i \rrbracket_{va} \delta\rho[n_1/x_1, \ldots, n_{a_i}/x_{a_i}] \text{ by } \delta\text{'s definition as a fixed point,} \\
&= \llbracket d_i[n_1/x_1, \ldots, n_{a_i}/x_{a_i}] \rrbracket_{va} \delta\rho \text{ by the Substitution Lemma,} \\
&= \lfloor n \rfloor \quad \text{by assumption.}
\end{aligned}
$$

Thus the property P holds of the conclusion of the rule (fn).

We conclude, by rule induction, that $P(t,n)$ holds whenever $t \rightarrow_{va}^{d} n$.   □

Lemma 9.7 *Let t be a closed term. Let $\rho \in \mathbf{Env}_{va}$. For all $n \in \mathbf{N}$,*

$$[\![t]\!]_{va}\delta\rho = \lfloor n \rfloor \Rightarrow t \rightarrow^d_{vo} n.$$

Proof: We first define the functions $\varphi_i : \mathbf{N}^{a_i} \rightarrow \mathbf{N}_\perp$, for $i = 1, \ldots, k$, from the operational semantics by taking

$$\varphi_i(n_1, \ldots, n_{a_i}) = \begin{cases} \lfloor n \rfloor & \text{if } d_i[n_1/x_1, \ldots, n_{a_i}/x_{a_i}] \rightarrow^d_{va} n, \\ \perp & \text{otherwise.} \end{cases}$$

We claim that $\varphi = (\varphi_1, \ldots, \varphi_k)$ is a prefixed point of the function F defined in 9.3, and hence $\delta \sqsubseteq \varphi$. The claim will follow from a more general induction hypothesis.

We show by structural induction on t that provided the variables in t are included in the list $x_1, \ldots, x_l$ of variables then

$$[\![t]\!]_{va}\varphi\rho[n_1/x_1, \ldots, n_l/x_l] = \lfloor n \rfloor \Rightarrow t[n_1/x_1, \ldots, n_l/x_l] \rightarrow^d_{va} n \qquad (1)$$

for all $n, n_1, \ldots, n_l \in \mathbf{N}$. (We allow the list of variables to be empty, which is sufficient when no variables appear in t.)

$t \equiv m$: In this simple case the denotational and operational semantics yield the same value.

$t \equiv x$, a variable: In this case x must be a variable x_j, for $1 \leq j \leq l$, and clearly the implication holds.

$t \equiv t_1 \; \mathbf{op} \; t_2$: Suppose $[\![t_1 \; \mathbf{op} \; t_2]\!]_{va}\varphi\rho[n_1/x_1, \ldots, n_l/x_l] = \lfloor n \rfloor$, with the assumption that all variables of t_1, t_2 appear in $x_1, \ldots, x_l$. Then $n = m_1 \; op \; m_2$ for some m_1, m_2 given by

$$[\![t_1]\!]_{va}\varphi\rho[n_1/x_1, \ldots, n_l/x_l] = \lfloor m_1 \rfloor$$
$$[\![t_2]\!]_{va}\varphi\rho[n_1/x_1, \ldots, n_l/x_l] = \lfloor m_2 \rfloor$$

Inductively,

$$t_1[n_1/x_1, \ldots, n_l/x_l] \rightarrow^d_{va} m_1$$
$$t_2[n_1/x_1, \ldots, n_l/x_l] \rightarrow^d_{va} m_2$$

whence

$$(t_1 \; \mathbf{op} \; t_2)[n_1/x_1, \ldots, n_l/x_l] \rightarrow^d_{va} m_1 \; op \; m_2 \equiv n.$$

$t \equiv \mathbf{if} \; t_0 \; \mathbf{then} \; t_1 \; \mathbf{else} \; t_2$: The case of conditionals is similar to that of operations above.

$t \equiv f_i(t_1, \ldots, t_{a_i})$: Suppose

$$[\![f_i(t_1, \ldots, t_{a_i})]\!]_{va}\varphi\rho[n_1/x_1, \ldots, n_l/x_l] = \lfloor n \rfloor$$

and that all the variables of t are included in $x_1, \ldots, x_l$. Recalling the denotational semantics, we see

$$(let \ v_1 \Leftarrow [\![t_1]\!]_{va}\varphi\rho[n_1/x_1, \ldots, n_l/x_l],$$

$$\vdots$$

$$v_{a_i} \Leftarrow [\![t_{a_i}]\!]_{va}\varphi\rho[n_1/x_1, \ldots, n_l/x_l]. \ \varphi_i(v_1, \ldots, v_{a_i})) = \lfloor n \rfloor.$$

But, then there must be $m_1, \ldots, m_{a_i} \in \mathbf{N}$ such that

$$[\![t_1]\!]_{va}\varphi\rho[n_1/x_1, \ldots, n_l/x_l] = \lfloor m_1 \rfloor$$

$$\vdots$$

$$[\![t_{a_i}]\!]_{va}\varphi\rho[n_1/x_1, \ldots, n_l/x_l] = \lfloor m_{a_i} \rfloor$$

where, furthermore,

$$\varphi_i(m_1, \ldots, m_{a_i}) = \lfloor n \rfloor.$$

Now, by induction, we obtain

$$t_1[n_1/x_1, \ldots, n_l/x_l] \rightarrow^d_{va} m_1$$

$$\vdots$$

$$t_{a_i}[n_1/x_1, \ldots, n_l/x_l] \rightarrow^d_{va} m_{a_i}.$$

Note that $\varphi_i(m_1, \ldots, m_{a_i}) = \lfloor n \rfloor$ means

$$d_i[m_1/x_1, \ldots, m_{a_i}/x_{a_i}] \rightarrow^d_{va} n.$$

Combining the facts about the operational semantics, we deduce

$$f_i(t_1, \ldots, t_{a_i})[n_1/x_1, \ldots, n_l/x_l] \rightarrow^d_{va} n,$$

as was to be proved in this case.

We have established the induction hypothesis (1) for all terms t. As a special case of (1) we obtain, for $i = 1, \ldots, k$, that

$$[\![d_i]\!]_{va}\varphi\rho[n_1/x_1, \ldots, n_{a_i}/x_{a_i}] = \lfloor n \rfloor \quad \Rightarrow \quad d_i[n_1/x_1, \ldots, n_{a_i}/x_{a_i}] \rightarrow^d_{va} n,$$

for all $n, n_1, \cdots, n_{a_i} \in \mathbf{N}$, and thus by the definition of φ that

$$\lambda n_1, \ldots, n_{a_1} \in \mathbf{N}. \ [\![d_1]\!]_{va}\varphi\rho[n_1/x_1, \ldots, n_{a_1}/x_{a_1}] \quad \sqsubseteq \quad \varphi_1$$

$$\vdots$$

$$\lambda n_1, \ldots, n_{a_k} \in \mathbf{N}. \ [\![d_k]\!]_{va}\varphi\rho[n_1/x_1, \ldots, n_{a_k}/x_{a_k}] \quad \sqsubseteq \quad \varphi_k.$$

But this makes φ a prefixed point of F as claimed, thus ensuring $\delta \sqsubseteq \varphi$.

Finally, letting t be a closed term, we obtain

$$[\![t]\!]_{va}\delta\rho = \lfloor n \rfloor \quad \Rightarrow \quad [\![t]\!]_{va}\varphi\rho = \lfloor n \rfloor$$

$$\text{by monotonicity of } [\![t]\!]_{va} \text{ given by Lemma 9.3}$$

$$\Rightarrow \quad t \to_{va}^d n$$

$$\text{from (1) in the special case of an empty list of variables.} \square$$

Theorem 9.8 *For t a closed term, n a number, and ρ an arbitrary environment*

$$[\![t]\!]_{va}\delta\rho = \lfloor n \rfloor \quad \text{iff} \quad t \to_{va}^d n.$$

Proof: Combine the two previous lemmas. $\hfill\square$

9.5 Operational semantics of call-by-name

We give rules to specify the evaluation of closed terms in **REC** under call-by-name. Assume a declaration d consisting of defining equations

$$f_1(x_1, \ldots, x_{a_1}) \quad = \quad d_1$$

$$\vdots$$

$$f_k(x_1, \ldots, x_{a_k}) \quad = \quad d_k$$

The evaluation with call-by-name is formalised by a relation $t \to_{na}^d n$ meaning that the closed term t evaluates under call-by-name to the integer value n. The rules giving this evaluation relation are as follows:

$$n \to_{na}^{d} n$$

$$\frac{t_1 \to_{na}^{d} n_1 \quad t_2 \to_{na}^{d} n_2}{t_1 \text{ op } t_2 \to_{na}^{d} n_1 \text{ op } n_2}$$

$$\frac{t_0 \to_{na}^{d} 0 \quad t_1 \to_{na}^{d} n_1}{\text{if } t_0 \text{ then } t_1 \text{ else } t_2 \to_{na}^{d} n_1}$$

$$\frac{t_0 \to_{na}^{d} n_0 \quad t_2 \to_{na}^{d} n_2 \quad n_0 \not\equiv 0}{\text{if } t_0 \text{ then } t_1 \text{ else } t_2 \to_{na}^{d} n_2}$$

$$\frac{d_i[t_1/x_1, \ldots, t_{a_i}/x_{a_i}] \to_{na}^{d} n}{f_i(t_1, \ldots, t_{a_i}) \to_{na}^{d} n}$$

The only difference with the rules for call-by-value is the last, where it is not necessary to evaluate arguments of a function before applying it. Again, the evaluation relation is deterministic:

Proposition 9.9 *If* $t \to_{na}^{d} n_1$ *and* $t \to_{na}^{d} n_2$ *then* $n_1 \equiv n_2$.

Proof: By a routine application of rule induction.   □

9.6 Denotational semantics of call-by-name

As for call-by-value, a term will be assigned a meaning as a value in $\mathbf{N}_\perp$ with respect to environments for variables and function variables, though the environments take a slightly different form. This stems from the fact that in call-by-name functions do not necessarily need the prior evaluation of their arguments. An environment for variables is now a function

$$\rho : \mathbf{Var} \to \mathbf{N}_\perp$$

and we will write $\mathbf{Env}_{na}$ for the cpo

$$[\mathbf{Var} \to \mathbf{N}_\perp]$$

of such environments. On the other hand, an environment for function variables $f_1, \ldots, f_k$ consists of $\varphi = (\varphi_1, \ldots, \varphi_k)$ where each

$$\varphi_i : \mathbf{N}_\perp^{a_i} \to \mathbf{N}_\perp$$

is a continuous function for $i = 1, \ldots, k$; we write $\mathbf{Fenv}_{na}$ for

$$[\mathbf{N}_\perp^{a_1} \to \mathbf{N}_\perp] \times \cdots \times [\mathbf{N}_\perp^{a_k} \to \mathbf{N}_\perp]$$

the cpo of environments for function variables.

Now, we can go ahead and define $[\![t]\!]_{na} : \mathbf{Fenv}_{na} \to [\mathbf{Env}_{na} \to \mathbf{N}_\perp]$, the denotation of a term t by structural induction:

$$
\begin{aligned}
[\![n]\!]_{na} &= \lambda\varphi\lambda\rho.\ \lfloor n \rfloor \\
[\![x]\!]_{na} &= \lambda\varphi\lambda\rho.\ \rho(x) \\
[\![t_1 \ \mathbf{op}\ t_2]\!]_{na} &= \lambda\varphi\lambda\rho.\ [\![t_1]\!]_{na}\varphi\rho \ op_\perp\ [\![t_2]\!]_{na}\varphi\rho \\
&\qquad \text{where } \mathbf{op} \text{ is } +, -, \text{ or } \times \\
[\![\mathbf{if}\ t_0\ \mathbf{then}\ t_1\ \mathbf{else}\ t_2]\!]_{na} &= \lambda\varphi\lambda\rho.\ Cond([\![t_0]\!]_{na}\varphi\rho, [\![t_1]\!]_{na}\varphi\rho, [\![t_2]\!]_{na}\varphi\rho) \\
[\![f_i(t_1, \ldots, t_{a_i})]\!]_{na} &= \lambda\varphi\lambda\rho.\ \varphi_i([\![t_1]\!]_{na}\varphi\rho, \ldots, [\![t_{a_i}]\!]_{na}\varphi\rho)
\end{aligned}
$$

Again, the semantic function is continuous, and its result in an environment is independent of assignments to variables not in the term:

Lemma 9.10 *Let t be a term of* **REC**. *The denotation $[\![t]\!]_{na}$ is a continuous function* $\mathbf{Fenv}_{na} \to [\mathbf{Env}_{na} \to \mathbf{N}_\perp]$.

Proof: By structural induction using the results of Section 8.4.   □

Lemma 9.11 *For all terms t of* **REC**, *if environments $\rho, \rho' \in \mathbf{Env}_{na}$ yield the same result on all variables which appear in t then, for any $\varphi \in \mathbf{Fenv}_{na}$,*

$$[\![t]\!]_{na}\varphi\rho = [\![t]\!]_{na}\varphi\rho'.$$

In particular, the denotation $[\![t]\!]_{na}\varphi\rho$ of a closed term t is independent of the environment ρ.

Proof: A straightforward structural induction on terms t.   □

A declaration d determines a particular function environment. Let d consist of the defining equations

$$f_1(x_1, \ldots, x_{a_1}) \;=\; d_1$$
$$\vdots$$
$$f_k(x_1, \ldots, x_{a_k}) \;=\; d_k.$$

Define $F : \mathbf{Fenv}_{na} \to \mathbf{Fenv}_{na}$ by taking

$$F(\varphi) \;=\; (\lambda z_1, \ldots, z_{a_1} \in \mathbf{N}_\perp.\; [\![d_1]\!]_{na} \varphi \rho[z_1/x_1, \ldots, z_{a_1}/x_{a_1}],$$
$$\vdots$$
$$\lambda z_1, \ldots, z_{a_k} \in \mathbf{N}_\perp.\; [\![d_k]\!]_{na} \varphi \rho[z_1/x_1, \ldots, z_{a_k}/x_{a_k}]).$$

As in the call-by-value case (see Section 9.4), the operation of updating environments is definable in the metalanguage of Section 8.4. By the general arguments of Section 8.4, F is continuous, and so has a least fixed point $\delta = \mathit{fix}(F)$.

Example: To see how the denotational semantics captures the call-by-name style of evaluation, consider the declaration:

$$f_1 = f_1 + 1$$
$$f_2(x) = 1$$

According to the denotational semantics for call-by-name, the effect of this declaration is that f_1, f_2 are denoted by $\delta = (\delta_1, \delta_2) \in \mathbf{N}_\perp \times [\mathbf{N}_\perp \to \mathbf{N}_\perp]$ where

$$(\delta_1, \delta_2) = \mu\varphi.\; ([\![f_1 + 1]\!]_{na} \varphi \rho,\; \lambda z \in \mathbf{N}_\perp.\; [\![1]\!]_{na} \varphi \rho[z/x])$$
$$= \mu\varphi.\; (\varphi_1 +_\perp \lfloor 1 \rfloor,\; \lambda z \in \mathbf{N}_\perp.\; \lfloor 1 \rfloor)$$
$$= (\perp, \lambda z \in \mathbf{N}_\perp.\; \lfloor 1 \rfloor)$$

It is simple to verify that the latter is the required least fixed point. Thus

$$[\![f_2(f_1)]\!]_{na} \delta \rho = \delta_2(\delta_1) = \lfloor 1 \rfloor.$$

$\square$

We can expect that

$$[\![t]\!]_{na} \delta \rho = \lfloor n \rfloor \quad \text{iff} \quad t \to^d_{na} n$$

whenever t is a closed term. Indeed we do have this equivalence between the denotational and operational semantics.

9.7   Equivalence of semantics for call-by-name

The general strategy for proving equivalence between the operational and denotational
semantics for call-by-name follows the same general outline as that for call-by-value. One
part of the equivalence follows by rule induction, and the other uses reasoning about fixed
points, albeit in a different way. We start with a lemma about substitution.

Lemma 9.12 *(Substitution Lemma) Let t, t' be terms. Let $\varphi \in \mathbf{Fenv}_{na}$ and $\rho \in \mathbf{Env}_{na}$.
Then*

$$[\![t]\!]_{na}\varphi\rho[[\![t']\!]_{na}\varphi\rho/x] = [\![t[t'/x]]\!]_{na}\varphi\rho.$$

Proof: The proof is by a simple induction on t, and is left as an exercise.   □

Lemma 9.13 *Letting t be a closed term, n a number, and ρ an environment for variables*

$$t \rightarrow^d_{na} n \Rightarrow [\![t]\!]_{na}\delta\rho = \lfloor n \rfloor.$$

Proof: Let ρ be an environment for variables. The proof uses rule induction with the
property

$$P(t, n) \Leftrightarrow_{def} [\![t]\!]_{na}\delta\rho = \lfloor n \rfloor$$

over closed terms t and numbers n. The only rule causing any difficulty is

$$\frac{d_i[t_1/x_1, \ldots, t_{a_i}/x_{a_i}] \rightarrow^d_{na} n}{f_i(t_1, \ldots, t_{a_i}) \rightarrow^d_{na} n}$$

Suppose $d_i[t_1/x_1, \ldots, t_{a_i}/x_{a_i}] \rightarrow^d_{na} n$ and, inductively, that $P(d_i[t_1/x_1, \ldots, t_{a_i}/x_{a_i}], n)$,
i.e.

$$[\![d_i[t_1/x_1, \ldots, t_{a_i}/x_{a_i}]]\!]_{na}\delta\rho = \lfloor n \rfloor.$$

We deduce

$$
\begin{aligned}
[\![f_i(t_1, \ldots, t_{a_i})]\!]_{na}\delta\rho &= \delta_i([\![t_1]\!]_{na}\delta\rho, \ldots, [\![t_{a_i}]\!]_{na}\delta\rho) \\
&= [\![d_i]\!]_{na}\delta\rho[[\![t_1]\!]_{na}\delta\rho/x_1, \ldots, [\![t_{a_i}]\!]_{na}\delta\rho/x_{a_i}] \\
&\qquad \text{by the definition of } \delta \text{ as a fixed point,} \\
&= [\![d_i[t_1/x_1, \ldots, t_{a_i}/x_{a_i}]]\!]_{na}\delta\rho \\
&\qquad \text{by several applications of the Substitution Lemma 9.12,} \\
&\qquad \text{as each } t_j \text{ is closed so } [\![t_j]\!]_{na}\delta\rho \text{ is independent of } \rho, \\
&= \lfloor n \rfloor.
\end{aligned}
$$

Thus $P(f_i(t_1, \ldots, t_{a_i}), n)$. Showing the other rules preserve property P is simpler. The
lemma follows by rule induction.   □

The proof of the next lemma uses a mathematical induction based on the approximants to the least fixed point δ. Recall $\delta = fix(F)$ so

$$\delta = \bigsqcup_{r \in \omega} F^r(\perp)$$

where

$$F(\varphi) \;\; = \;\; (\lambda z_1, \ldots, z_{a_1} \in \mathbf{N}_\perp. \; [\![d_1]\!]_{na} \varphi \rho[z_1/x_1, \ldots, z_{a_1}/x_{a_1}],$$

$$\vdots$$

$$\lambda z_1, \ldots, z_{a_k} \in \mathbf{N}_\perp. \; [\![d_k]\!]_{na} \varphi \rho[z_1/x_1, \ldots, z_{a_k}/x_{a_k}]).$$

Write

$$\delta^{(r)} = F^r(\perp)$$

for the r'th approximant. Then $\delta_i^{(0)}(z_1, \ldots, z_{a_i}) = \perp$ for all $z_1, \ldots, z_{a_i} \in \mathbf{N}_\perp$, for $1 \leq i \leq k$. For $r > 0$, $\delta^{(r)} = F(\delta^{(r-1)})$, i.e.

$$\delta_i^{(r)}(z_1, \ldots, z_{a_i}) = [\![d_i]\!]_{na} \delta^{(r-1)} \rho[z_1/x_1, \ldots, z_{a_i}/x_{a_i}], \text{ for } i = 1, \ldots, k,$$

a recurrence relation which will be useful in the proof below.

Lemma 9.14 *Let t be a closed term, n a number and ρ an environment for variables. Then*

$$[\![t]\!]_{na} \delta \rho = \lfloor n \rfloor \Rightarrow t \rightarrow_{na}^d n.$$

Proof: Let ρ be an environment for variables. For a closed term t, define

$$res(t) = \begin{cases} \lfloor n \rfloor & \text{if } t \rightarrow_{na}^d n, \\ \perp & \text{otherwise} \end{cases}$$

(This defines the *result* of t under the operational semantics.)

As above, let $\delta^{(r)}$ be the r'th approximant to the recursively-defined, function environment δ. We show by induction on $r \in \omega$ that

$$[\![t]\!]_{na} \delta^{(r)} \rho[res(u_1)/y_1, \ldots, res(u_s)/y_s] = \lfloor n \rfloor \;\; \Rightarrow \;\; t[u_1/y_1, \ldots, u_s/y_s] \rightarrow_{na}^d n \qquad (1)$$

for all terms t, number n, closed terms $u_1, \ldots, u_s$ and variables $y_1, \ldots, y_s$ with the property that they contain all the variables appearing in t. Notice that condition (1) can be recast as the equivalent:

$$[\![t]\!]_{na} \delta^{(r)} \rho[res(u_1)/y_1, \ldots, res(u_s)/y_s] \sqsubseteq res(t[u_1/y_1, \ldots, u_s/y_s]).$$

Basis, $r = 0$: For the basis of the mathematical induction, we require

$$[\![t]\!]_{na}\bot\rho[res(u_1)/y_1,\ldots,res(u_s)/y_s] = \lfloor n \rfloor \Rightarrow t[u_1/y_1,\ldots,u_s/y_s] \to_{na}^{d} n$$

for numbers n, closed terms $u_1,\ldots,u_s$ and a term t with variables inside $\{y_1,\ldots,y_s\}$. This is proved by structural induction on t. One basic case is when t is a variable, necessarily some y_j, with $1 \leq j \leq s$. But then

$$[\![y_j]\!]_{na}\bot\rho[res(u_1)/y_1,\ldots,res(u_s)/y_s] = res(u_j),$$

and by definition $res(u_j) = \lfloor n \rfloor$ implies $y_j[u_1/y_1,\ldots,u_s/y_s] \equiv u_j \to_{na}^{d} n$. In the case where t is $f_i(t_1,\ldots,t_{a_i})$

$$[\![f_i(t_1,\ldots,t_{a_i})]\!]_{na}\bot\rho[res(u_1)/y_1,\ldots,res(u_s)/y_s] = \bot,$$

not a value $\lfloor n \rfloor$, so the implication holds vacuously. The other cases are simple and left to the reader.

Induction step: Suppose $r > 0$ and that the induction hypothesis holds for $(r-1)$. We require

$$[\![t]\!]_{na}\delta^{(r)}\rho[res(u_1)/y_1,\ldots,res(u_s)/y_s] = \lfloor n \rfloor \Rightarrow t[u_1/y_1,\ldots,u_s/y_s] \to_{na}^{d} n$$

for all numbers n, closed terms $u_1,\ldots,u_s$, and terms t with variables in $\{y_1,\ldots,y_s\}$. This is shown by structural induction on t, in a way similar to that above for $r = 0$, except in one case, that when t has the form $f_i(t_1,\ldots,t_{a_i})$. Let $\rho' = \rho[res(u_1)/y_1,\ldots,res(u_s)/y_s]$. By the definition of $\delta^{(r)}$,

$$
\begin{aligned}
[\![f_i(t_1,\ldots,t_{a_i})]\!]_{na}\delta^{(r)}\rho' &= \delta_i^{(r)}([\![t_1]\!]_{na}\delta^{(r)}\rho',\ldots,[\![t_{a_i}]\!]_{na}\delta^{(r)}\rho') \\
&= [\![d_i]\!]_{na}\delta^{(r-1)}\rho'[[\![t_1]\!]_{na}\delta^{(r)}\rho'/x_1,\ldots,[\![t_{a_i}]\!]_{na}\delta^{(r)}\rho'/x_{a_i}]
\end{aligned}
$$

The variables of t_j, for $1 \leq j \leq a_i$, certainly lie within $\{y_1,\ldots,y_s\}$, so by structural induction,

$$
\begin{aligned}
[\![t_j]\!]_{na}\delta^{(r)}\rho' &= [\![t_j]\!]_{na}\delta^{(r)}\rho[res(u_1)/y_1,\ldots,res(u_s)/y_s] \\
&\sqsubseteq res(t_j[u_1/y_1,\ldots,u_s/y_s]).
\end{aligned}
$$

Hence, by the monotonicity of the denotation $[\![d_i]\!]_{na}$—a consequence of Lemma 9.10, we deduce

$$[\![f_i(t_1,\ldots,t_{a_i})]\!]_{na}\delta^{(r)}\rho' \sqsubseteq [\![d_i]\!]_{na}\delta^{(r-1)}\rho'[res(t_1')/x_1,\ldots,res(t_{a_i}')/x_{a_i}]$$

where we have written t'_j to abbreviate $t_j[u_1/y_1, \ldots, u_s/y_s]$, for $1 \leq j \leq a_i$. But now we observe, by mathematical induction, that

$$\llbracket d_i \rrbracket_{na} \delta^{(r-1)} \rho'[res(t'_1)/x_1, \ldots, res(t'_{a_i})/x_{a_i}] \sqsubseteq res(d_i[t'_1/x_1, \ldots, t'_{a_i}/x_{a_i}])$$

—by our assumption about declarations, the variables of d_i lie within $x_1, \ldots, x_{a_i}$. We note from the operational semantics that

$$res(f_i(t'_1, \ldots, t'_{a_i})) = res(d_i[t'_1/x_1, \ldots, t'_{a_i}/x_{a_i}]).$$

It follows that

$$\llbracket f_i(t_1, \ldots, t_{a_i}) \rrbracket_{na} \delta^{(r)} \rho[res(u_1)/y_1, \ldots, res(u_s)/y_s]$$
$$\sqsubseteq res(f_i(t_1, \ldots, t_{a_i})[u_1/y_1, \ldots, u_s/y_s]).$$

Thus, the induction hypothesis is established in this case.

The result of the mathematical induction permits us to conclude

$$\llbracket t \rrbracket_{na} \delta^{(r)} \rho = \lfloor n \rfloor \Rightarrow t \to^d_{na} n$$

for all $r \in \omega$, for any closed term t. Now

$$\llbracket t \rrbracket_{na} \delta \rho = \llbracket t \rrbracket_{na} \bigsqcup_r \delta^{(r)} \rho$$
$$= \bigsqcup_r \llbracket t \rrbracket_{na} \delta^{(r)} \rho$$

by continuity of the semantic function (Lemma 9.10). Thus $\llbracket t \rrbracket_{na} \delta \rho = \lfloor n \rfloor$ implies $\llbracket t \rrbracket_{na} \delta^{(r)} \rho = \lfloor n \rfloor$ for some $r \in \omega$, and hence that $t \to^d_{na} n$, as required. $\square$

Combining the two lemmas we obtain the equivalence of the operational and denotational semantics for call-by-name.

Theorem 9.15 *Let t be a closed term, and n a number. Then*

$$\llbracket t \rrbracket_{na} \delta \rho = \lfloor n \rfloor \quad \text{iff} \quad t \to^d_{na} n$$

Exercise 9.16 The method used in the proof of Lemma 9.14 above can be used instead of that earlier in the call-by-value case. Give an alternative proof of Lemma 9.7 using mathematical induction on approximants. $\square$

9.8 Local declarations

From the point of view of a programming language **REC** is rather restrictive. In particular a program of **REC** is essentially a pair consisting of a term to be evaluated together with a declaration to determine the meaning of its function variables. Most functional programming languages would instead allow programs in which function variables are defined as they are needed, in other words they would allow local declarations of the form:

$$\textbf{let rec } f(x_1, \cdots, x_{a_1}) = d \textbf{ in } t.$$

This provides a recursive definition of f with respect to which the term t is evaluated. The languages generally support simultaneous recursion of the kind we have seen in declarations and allow more general declarations as in

$$\textbf{let } \quad \textbf{rec} \quad f_1(x_1, \cdots, x_{a_1}) \quad = \quad d_1 \textbf{ and}$$
$$\vdots$$
$$f_k(x_1, \cdots, x_{a_k}) \quad = \quad d_k$$
$$\textbf{in} \quad t$$

This simultaneously defines a tuple of functions $f_1, \cdots, f_k$ recursively.

To understand how one gives a denotational semantics to such a language, consider the denotation of

$$S \equiv \textbf{let rec } A \Leftarrow t \textbf{ and } B \Leftarrow u \textbf{ in } v$$

where A and B are assumed to be distinct function variables of arity 0. For definiteness assume evaluation is call-by-name. The denotation of S in a function environment $\varphi \in \textbf{Fenv}_{na}$ and environment for variables $\rho \in \textbf{Env}_{na}$ can be taken to be

$$[\![S]\!]\varphi\rho = [\![v]\!]\varphi[\alpha_0/A, \beta_0/B]\rho$$

where (α_0, β_0) is the least fixed point of the continuous function

$$(\alpha, \beta) \mapsto ([\![t]\!]\varphi[\alpha/A, \beta/B]\rho, [\![u]\!]\varphi[\alpha/A, \beta/B]\rho).$$

Exercise 9.17 Write down a syntax extending **REC** which supports local declarations. Try to provide a denotational semantics for the extended language under call-by-name. How would you modify your semantics to get a semantics in the call-by-value case?   □

In fact, perhaps surprisingly, the facility of simultaneous recursion does not add any expressive power to a language which supports local declarations of single functions, though it can increase efficiency. For example, the program S above can be replaced by

$$T \quad \equiv \quad \textbf{let rec } B \Leftarrow (\textbf{let rec } A \Leftarrow t \textbf{ in } u)$$
$$\textbf{in}(\textbf{let rec } A \Leftarrow t \textbf{ in } v).$$

where A and B are assumed to be distinct function variables of arity 0. The proof that this is legitimate is the essential content of Bekić's Theorem, which is treated in the next chapter.

9.9   Further reading

Alternative presentations of the language and semantics of recursion equations can be found in [59], [21], [13] and [58](the latter is based on [13]) though these concentrate mainly on the call-by-name case. Zohar Manna's book [59] incorporates some of the thesis work of Jean Vuillemin on recursion equations [99]. This chapter has been influenced by some old lecture notes of Robin Milner, based on earlier notes of Gordon Plotkin, (though the proofs here are different). The proof in the call-by-value case is like that in Andrew Pitts' Cambridge lecture notes [75]. The operational semantics for the language extended by local declarations can become a bit complicated, as, at least for static binding, it is necessary to carry information about the environment at the time of declaration—see [101] for an elementary account.

10 Techniques for recursion

This chapter provides techniques for proving properties of least fixed points of continuous functions. The characterisation of least fixed points as least prefixed points gives one method sometimes called Park induction. It is used to establish Bekic's Theorem, an important result giving different methods for obtaining least fixed points in products of cpo's. The general method of Scott's fixed-point induction is introduced along with the notion of inclusive property on which it depends; methods for the construction of inclusive properties are provided. A section gives examples of the use of well-founded induction extending our earlier work and, in particular, shows how to build-up well-founded relations. A general method called well-founded recursion is presented for defining functions on sets with a well-founded relation. The chapter concludes with a small but nontrivial exercise using several of the techniques to show the equality of two recursive functions on lists.

10.1 Bekić's Theorem

The Fixed-Point Theorem, Theorem 5.11, of Chapter 5 tells us that if D is a cpo with $\perp$ and $F : D \to D$ is continuous then $fix(F)$ is the least prefixed point of F. In other words,

$$F(d) \sqsubseteq d \;\Rightarrow\; fix(F) \sqsubseteq d \tag{fix1}$$

for any $d \in D$. Of course, $fix(F)$ is a fixed point, i.e.

$$F(fix(F)) = fix(F) \tag{fix2}$$

Facts (fix1) and (fix2) characterise $fix(F)$, and are useful in proving properties of fixed points generally.[1] The fact (fix1) states a principle of proof sometimes called Park induction, after David Park. We will use (fix1) and (fix2) to establish an interesting result due to Bekić. Essentially, Bekić's Theorem says how a simultaneous recursive definition can be replaced by recursive definitions of one coordinate at a time.

Theorem 10.1 *(Bekić)*
Let $F : D \times E \to D$ and $G : D \times E \to E$ be continuous functions where D and E are cpo's with bottom. The least fixed point of $\langle F, G \rangle : D \times E \to D \times E$ is the pair with coordinates

$$
\begin{aligned}
\hat{f} &= \mu f.\, F(f, \mu g.\, G(\mu f.\, F(f,g), g)) \\
\hat{g} &= \mu g.\, G(\mu f.\, F(f,g), g)
\end{aligned}
$$

---

[1]In fact, because F is monotonic (fix2) could be replaced by $F(fix(F)) \sqsubseteq fix(F)$. Then by monotonicity, we obtain $F(F(fix(F))) \sqsubseteq F(fix(F))$, *i.e.* $F(fix(F))$ is a prefixed point. Now from (fix1) we get $fix(F) \sqsubseteq F(fix(F))$ which yields (fix2) .

Proof: We first show $(\hat{f}, \hat{g})$ is a fixed point of $\langle F, G \rangle$. By definition

$$\hat{f} = \mu f. \; F(f, \hat{g}).$$

In other words $\hat{f}$ is the least fixed point of $\lambda f. \; F(f, \hat{g})$. Therefore $\hat{f} = F(\hat{f}, \hat{g})$. Also, from the definition of $\hat{g}$,

$$\hat{g} = G(\mu f. \; F(f, \hat{g}), \hat{g}) = G(\hat{f}, \hat{g}).$$

Thus $(\hat{f}, \hat{g}) = \langle F, G \rangle (\hat{f}, \hat{g})$ *i.e.* $(\hat{f}, \hat{g})$ is a fixed point of $\langle F, G \rangle$.

Letting (f_0, g_0) be the least fixed point of $\langle F, G \rangle$ we must have

$$f_0 \sqsubseteq \hat{f} \text{ and } g_0 \sqsubseteq \hat{g}. \tag{1}$$

We require the converse orderings as well. As $f_0 = F(f_0, g_0)$,

$$\mu f. \; F(f, g_0) \sqsubseteq f_0.$$

By the monotonicity of G

$$G(\mu f. \; F(f, g_0), g_0) \sqsubseteq G(f_0, g_0) = g_0.$$

Therefore

$$\hat{g} \sqsubseteq g_0 \tag{2}$$

as $\hat{g}$ is the least prefixed point of $\lambda g. \; G(\mu f. \; F(f, g), g)$.

By the monotonicity of F,

$$F(f_0, \hat{g}) \sqsubseteq F(f_0, g_0) = f_0.$$

Therefore

$$\hat{f} \sqsubseteq f_0 \tag{3}$$

as $\hat{f}$ is the least prefixed point of $\lambda f. \; F(f, \hat{g})$.

Combining (1), (2), (3) we see $(\hat{f}, \hat{g}) = (f_0, g_0)$, as required. $\square$

The proof only relied on monotonicity and the properties of least fixed points expressed by (fix1) and (fix2) above. For this reason the same argument carries over to the situation of least fixed points of monotonic functions on lattices (see 5.5).

Bekić's Theorem gives an asymmetric form for the simultaneous least fixed point. We can deduce a symmetric form as a corollary: the simultaneous least fixed point is a pair

$$\begin{aligned}
\hat{f} &= \mu f. \; F(f, \; \mu g.G(f, g)) \\
\hat{g} &= \mu g. \; G(\mu f.F(f, g), \; g)
\end{aligned}$$

To see this notice that the second equation is a direct consequence of Bekić's Theorem while the first follows by the symmetry there is between f and g.

Example: We refer to Section 9.8 where it is indicated how to extend **REC** to allow local declarations. Consider the term

$$T \ \equiv \ \textbf{let rec } B \Leftarrow (\textbf{let rec } A \Leftarrow t \textbf{ in } u)$$
$$\textbf{in } (\textbf{let rec } A \Leftarrow t \textbf{ in } v).$$

where A and B are assumed to be distinct function variables of arity 0. Let ρ, φ be arbitrary variable and function-variable environments. Abbreviate

$$F(f,g) = [\![t]\!]\varphi[f/A, g/B]\rho$$
$$G(f,g) = [\![u]\!]\varphi[f/A, g/B]\rho$$

From the semantics we see that

$$[\![T]\!]\varphi\rho = [\![v]\!]\varphi[\hat{f}/A, \hat{g}/B]\rho$$

where

$$\begin{aligned}
\hat{g} \ &= \ \mu g. \ [\![\textbf{let rec } A \Leftarrow t \textbf{ in } u]\!]\varphi[g/B]\rho \\
&= \ \mu g. \ [\![u]\!]\varphi[g/B, \mu f. \ [\![t]\!]\varphi[f/A, g/B]\rho/A]\rho \\
&= \ \mu g. \ G(\mu f.F(f,g), \ g).
\end{aligned}$$

and

$$\begin{aligned}
\hat{f} &= \mu f. \ [\![t]\!]\varphi[f/A, \hat{g}/B]\rho \\
&= \mu f. \ F(f, \hat{g}).
\end{aligned}$$

By Bekić's Theorem this means $(\hat{f}, \hat{g})$ is the (simultaneous) least fixed point of $\langle F, G \rangle$. consequently we could have achieved the same effect with a simultaneous declaration; we have

$$[\![T]\!] = [\![\textbf{let rec } A \Leftarrow t \textbf{ and } B \Leftarrow u \textbf{ in } v]\!].$$

The argument is essentially the same for function variables taking arguments by either call-by-name or call-by-value. Clearly Bekić's Theorem is crucial for establishing program equivalences between terms involving simultaneous declarations and others. □

Exercise 10.2 Generalise and state Bekić's Theorem for 3 equations. □

Exercise 10.3 Let D and E be cpo's with bottom. Prove that if $f : D \to E$ and $g : E \to D$ are continuous functions on cpo's D, E then

$$fix(g \circ f) = g(fix(f \circ g)).$$

(Hint: Use facts (fix1) and (fix2) above.) □

10.2   Fixed-point induction

Often a property can be shown to hold of a least fixed point by showing that it holds for
each approximant by mathematical induction. This was the case, for example, in Chapter
5 where, in the proof of Theorem 5.7, stating the equivalence between operational and
denotational semantics, the demonstration that

$$(\sigma, \sigma') \in \mathcal{C}[\![c]\!] \Rightarrow \langle c, \sigma \rangle \to \sigma',$$

for states σ, σ', in the case where the command c was a while-loop, was achieved by
mathematical induction on the approximants of its denotation. In this case it was obvious
that a property holding of all the approximants of a least fixed point implied that it held
of their union, the fixed point itself. This need not be the case for arbitrary properties.

As its name suggests fixed-point induction, a proof principle due to Dana Scott, is
useful for proving properties of least fixed points of continuous functions. Fixed-point
induction is a proof principle which essentially replaces a mathematical induction along
the approximants $F^n(\bot)$ of the least fixed point $\bigsqcup_n F^n(\bot)$ of a continuous function
F. However, it is phrased in such a way as to avoid reasoning about the integers. It
only applies to properties which are inclusive; a property being inclusive ensures that its
holding of all approximants to a least fixed point implies that it holds of the fixed point
itself.

Definition: Let D be a cpo. A subset P of D is *inclusive* iff for all ω-chains $d_0 \sqsubseteq d_1 \sqsubseteq$
$\cdots \sqsubseteq d_n \sqsubseteq \cdots$ in D if $d_n \in P$ for all $n \in \omega$ then $\bigsqcup_{n \in \omega} d_n \in P$.

The significance of inclusive subsets derives from the principle of proof called *fixed-point
induction*. It is given by the following proposition:

Proposition 10.4 *(Fixed-point induction—Scott)*
*Let D be a cpo with bottom $\bot$, and $F : D \to D$ be continuous. Let P be an inclusive
subset of D. If $\bot \in P$ and $\forall x \in D.\ x \in P \Rightarrow F(x) \in P$ then $\mathit{fix}(F) \in P$.*

Proof: We have $\mathit{fix}(F) = \bigsqcup_n F^n(\bot)$. If P is an inclusive subset satisfying the condition
above then $\bot \in P$ hence $F(\bot) \in P$, and inductively $F^n(\bot) \in P$. As we have seen, by
induction, the approximants form an ω-chain

$$\bot \sqsubseteq F(\bot) \sqsubseteq \cdots \sqsubseteq F^n(\bot) \sqsubseteq \cdots$$

whence by the inclusiveness of P, we obtain $\mathit{fix}(F) \in P$. $\square$

Exercise 10.5 What are the inclusive subsets of Ω? Recall Ω is the cpo consisting of:

$$0 \sqsubseteq 1 \sqsubseteq \cdots \sqsubseteq n \sqsubseteq \cdots \infty$$

$\square$

Exercise 10.6 A *Scott-closed* subset of a cpo is the complement of a Scott-open subset (defined in Exercise 8.4). Show a Scott-closed subset is inclusive. Exhibit an inclusive subset of a cpo which is not Scott-closed. $\square$

As a first, rather easy, application of fixed-point induction we show how it implies Park induction, discussed in the last section:

Proposition 10.7 *Let $F : D \to D$ be a continuous function on a cpo D with bottom. Let $d \in D$. If $F(d) \sqsubseteq d$ then $fix(F) \sqsubseteq d$.*

Proof: (via fixed-point induction)
Suppose $d \in D$ and $F(d) \sqsubseteq d$. The subset

$$P = \{x \in D \mid x \sqsubseteq d\}$$

is inclusive—if each element of an ω-chain $d_0 \sqsubseteq \cdots \sqsubseteq d_n \sqsubseteq \cdots$ is below d then certainly so is the least upper bound $\bigsqcup_n d_n$. Clearly $\bot \sqsubseteq d$, so $\bot \in P$. We now show $x \in P \Rightarrow F(x) \in P$. Suppose $x \in P$, *i.e.* $x \sqsubseteq d$. Then, because F is monotonic, $F(x) \sqsubseteq F(d) \sqsubseteq d$. So $F(x) \in P$. By fixed-point induction we conclude $fix(F) \in P$, *i.e.* $fix(F) \sqsubseteq d$, as required. $\square$

Of course, this is a round-about way to show a fact we know from the Fixed-Point Theorem. It does however demonstrate that fixed-point induction is at least as strong as Park induction. In fact fixed-point induction enables us to deduce properties of least fixed points unobtainable solely by applying Park induction.

A predicate $Q(x_1, \ldots, x_k)$ with free variables $x_1, \ldots, x_k$, ranging over a cpo's $D_1, \ldots, D_k$ respectively, determines a subset of $D_1 \times \cdots \times D_k$, *viz.*the set

$$P = \{(x_1, \ldots, x_k) \in D_1 \times \cdots \times D_k \mid Q(x_1, \ldots, x_k)\},$$

and we will say the predicate $Q(x_1, \ldots, x_k)$ is inclusive if its extension as a subset of the cpo $D_1 \times \cdots \times D_k$ is inclusive. As with other induction principles, we shall generally use predicates, rather than their extensions as sets, in carrying out a fixed-point induction. Then fixed-point induction amounts to the following statement:

Let $F : D_1 \times \cdots \times D_k \to D_1 \times \cdots \times D_k$ be a continuous function on a product cpo $D_1 \times \cdots \times D_k$ with bottom element $(\perp_1, \ldots, \perp_k)$. Assuming $Q(x_1, \ldots, x_k)$ is an inclusive predicate on $D_1 \times \cdots \times D_k$,

> if $Q(\perp_1, \ldots, \perp_k)$ and
>
> $\forall x_1 \in D_1, \cdots, x_k \in D_k. \, Q(x_1, \ldots, x_k) \Rightarrow Q(F(x_1, \ldots, x_k))$
>
> then $Q(fix(F))$.

Fortunately we will be able to ensure that a good many sets and predicates are inclusive because they are built-up in a certain way:

Basic relations: Let D be a cpo. The binary relations

$$\{(x, y) \in D \times D \mid x \sqsubseteq y\} \text{ and } \{(x, y) \in D \times D \mid x = y\}$$

are inclusive subsets of $D \times D$ (Why?). It follows that the predicates

$$x \sqsubseteq y, \qquad x = y$$

are inclusive.

Inverse image and substitution: Let $f : D \to E$ be a continuous function between cpo's D and E. Suppose P is an inclusive subset of E. Then the inverse image

$$f^{-1}P = \{x \in D \mid f(x) \in P\}$$

is an inclusive subset of D.

This has the consequence that inclusive predicates are closed under the substitution of terms for their variables, provided the terms substituted are continuous in their variables. Let $Q(y_1, \ldots, y_l)$ be an inclusive predicate of $E_1 \times \cdots \times E_l$. In other words,

$$P =_{def} \{(y_1, \ldots, y_l) \in E_1 \times \cdots \times E_l \mid Q(y_1, \ldots, y_l)\}$$

is an inclusive subset of $E_1 \times \cdots \times E_l$. Suppose $e_1, \ldots, e_l$ are expressions for elements of $E_1, \ldots, E_l$, respectively, continuous in their variables $x_1, \ldots, x_k$ ranging, in order, over $D_1, \ldots, D_k$—taking them to be expressions in our metalanguage of Section 8.4 would ensure this. Then, defining f to be

$$\lambda x_1, \ldots, x_k.(e_1, \ldots, e_l),$$

ensures f is a continuous function. Thus $f^{-1}P$ is an inclusive subset of $D_1 \times \cdots \times D_k$. But this simply means

$$\{(x_1, \ldots, x_k) \in D_1 \times \cdots \times D_k \mid Q(e_1, \ldots, e_l)\}$$

is an inclusive subset, and thus that $Q(e_1, \ldots, e_l)$ is an inclusive predicate of $D_1 \times \cdots \times D_k$.

For instance, taking $f = \lambda x \in D.\,(x, c)$ we see if $R(x, y)$ is an inclusive predicate of $D \times E$ then the predicate $Q(x) \iff_{def} R(x, c)$, obtained by fixing y to a constant c, is an inclusive predicate of D. Fixing one or several arguments of an inclusive predicate yields an inclusive predicate.

Exercise 10.8 Show that if $Q(x)$ is an inclusive predicate of a cpo D then

$$R(x, y) \iff_{def} Q(x)$$

is an inclusive predicate of $D \times E$, where the extra variable y ranges over the cpo E. (Thus we can "pad-out" inclusive predicates with extra variables. Hint: projection function.) □

Logical operations: Let D be a cpo. The subsets D and $\emptyset$ are inclusive. Consequently the predicates "true" and "false", with extensions D and $\emptyset$ respectively, are inclusive. Let $P \subseteq D$ and $Q \subseteq D$ be inclusive subsets of D. Then

$$P \cup Q \text{ and } P \cap Q$$

are inclusive subsets. In terms of predicates, if $P(x_1, \ldots, x_k)$ and $Q(x_1, \ldots, x_k)$ are inclusive predicates then so are

$$P(x_1, \ldots, x_k) \text{ or } Q(x_1, \ldots, x_k), \quad P(x_1, \ldots, x_k) \,\&\, Q(x_1, \ldots, x_k)$$

If P_i, $i \in I$, is an indexed family of inclusive subsets of D then $\bigcap_{i \in I} P_i$ is an inclusive subset of D. Consequently, if $P(x_1, \ldots, x_k)$ is an inclusive predicate of $D_1 \times \cdots \times D_k$ then $\forall x_i \in D_i.\, P(x_1, \ldots, x_k)$, with $1 \leq i \leq k$, is an inclusive predicate of D. This is because the corresponding subset

$$\{(x_1, \ldots, x_{i-1}, x_{i+1}, \ldots, x_k) \in D_1 \times \cdots D_{i-1} \times D_{i+1} \times \cdots \times D_k \mid \forall x_i \in D_i.\, P(x_1, \ldots, x_k)\}$$

equals the intersection,

$$\bigcap_{d \in D_i} \{(x_1, \ldots, x_{i-1}, x_{i+1}, \ldots, x_k) \in D_1 \times \cdots D_{i-1} \times D_{i+1} \times \cdots \times D_k \mid$$

$$P(x_1, \ldots, x_{i-1}, d, x_{i+1}, \ldots, x_k)\}$$

of inclusive subsets—each predicate $P(x_1, \ldots, x_{i-1}, d, x_{i+1}, \ldots, x_k)$, for $d \in D_i$, is inclusive because it is obtained by fixing one argument.

However, note that infinite unions of inclusive subsets need not be inclusive, and accordingly, that inclusive predicates are not generally closed under $\exists$-quantification.

Exercise 10.9

(i)Provide a counter example which justifies the latter claim.

(ii) Show that the direct image fP of an inclusive subset $P \subseteq D$, under a continuous function $f : D \to E$ between cpo's, need not be an inclusive subset of E.

(iii) Also, provide examples of inclusive subsets $P \subseteq D \times E$ and $Q \subseteq E \times F$ such that their relation composition

$$Q \circ P =_{def} \{(d, f) \mid \exists e \in E.\ (d, e) \in P \& (e, f) \in Q\}$$

is not inclusive.

(Hint for (iii): Take D to be the singleton cpo $\{\top\}$, E to be the discrete cpo of nonnegative integers ω and F to be the cpo Ω consisting of an ω-chain together with its least upper bound ∞.) $\square$

Athough the direct image of an inclusive subset under a general continuous function need not be inclusive, direct images under *order-monics* necessarily preserve inclusiveness. Let D, E be cpo's. A continuous function $f : D \to E$ is an *order-monic* iff

$$f(d) \sqsubseteq f(d') \Rightarrow d \sqsubseteq d'$$

for all $d, d' \in D$. Examples of order-monics include the "lifting" function $\lfloor \text{-} \rfloor$ and injections in_i associated with a sum. It is easy to see that if P is an inclusive subset of D then so is its direct image fP when f is an order-monic. This means that if $Q(x)$ is an inclusive predicate of D then

$$\exists x \in D.\ y = f(x)\ \&\ Q(x),$$

with free variable $y \in E$, is an inclusive predicate of E.

Now we can consider inclusive subsets and predicates associated with particular cpo's and constructions on them:

Discrete cpo's: Any subset of a discrete cpo, and so any predicate on a discrete cpo, is inclusive.

Products: Suppose $P_i \subseteq D_i$ are inclusive subsets for $1 \le i \le k$. Then

$$P_1 \times \cdots \times P_k = \{(x_1, \ldots, x_k) \mid x_1 \in P_1\ \&\ \cdots\ \&\ x_k \in P_k\}$$

is an inclusive subset of the product $D_1 \times \cdots \times D_k$. This follows from our earlier results, by noting

$$P_1 \times \cdots \times P_k = \pi_1^{-1} P_1 \cap \cdots \cap \pi_k^{-1} P_k.$$

Each inverse image $\pi_i^{-1}P_i$ is inclusive, for $i = 1, \ldots, k$, and therefore so too is their intersection.

Warning: Let $D_1, \ldots, D_k$ be cpo's. It is tempting to believe that a predicate $P(x_1, \ldots, x_k)$, where $x_1 \in D_1, \cdots, x_k \in D_k$, is an inclusive predicate of the product $D_1 \times \cdots \times D_k$ if it is an inclusive predicate in each argument separately. This is not the case however. More precisely, say $P(x_1, \ldots, x_k)$ is *inclusive in each argument separately*, if for each $i = 1, \ldots, k$, the predicate $P(d_1, \ldots, d_{i-1}, x_i, d_{i+1}, \ldots, d_k)$, got by fixing all but the ith argument, is an inclusive predicate of D_i. Certainly if $P(x_1, \ldots, x_k)$ is inclusive then it is inclusive in each argument separately—we can substitute constants for variables and preserve inclusiveness from the discussion above. The converse does not hold however. The fact that $P(x_1, \ldots, x_k)$ is inclusive in each argument separately does *not* imply that it is an inclusive predicate of $D_1 \times \cdots \times D_k$.

Exercise 10.10 Let Ω be the cpo consisting of ω together with ∞ ordered:

$$0 \sqsubseteq 1 \sqsubseteq \cdots \sqsubseteq n \sqsubseteq \cdots \sqsubseteq \infty$$

By considering the predicate

$$P(x, y) \iff {}_{def} (x = y \ \& \ x \neq \infty)$$

show that a predicate being inclusive in each argument separately does not imply that it is inclusive.   □

Function space: Let D and E be cpo's. Suppose $P \subseteq D$, and $Q \subseteq E$ is an inclusive subset. Then

$$P \to Q =_{def} \{f \in [D \to E] \mid \forall x \in P.\ f(x) \in Q\}$$

is an inclusive subset of the function space $[D \to E]$ (Why?). Consequently, the predicate $\forall x \in D.P(x) \Rightarrow Q(f(x))$, with free variable $f \in [D \to E]$, is inclusive when $P(x)$ is a predicate of D and $Q(y)$ is an inclusive predicate of E.

Lifting: Let P be an inclusive subset of a cpo D. Because the function $\lfloor - \rfloor$ is an order-monic, the direct image $\lfloor P \rfloor = \{\lfloor d \rfloor \mid d \in P\}$ is an inclusive subset of $D_\perp$. If $Q(x)$ is an inclusive predicate of D then

$$\exists x \in D.\ y = \lfloor x \rfloor \ \& \ Q(x),$$

with free variable $y \in D_\perp$, is an inclusive predicate of $D_\perp$.

Sum: Let P_i be an inclusive subset of the cpo D_i for $i = 1, \ldots, k$. Then

$$P_1 + \cdots + P_k = in_1 P_1 \cup \cdots \cup in_k P_k$$

is an inclusive subset of the sum $D_1 + \cdots + D_k$. This follows because each injection is an order-monic so each $in_i P_i$ is inclusive, and the finite union of inclusive sets is inclusive. Expressing the same fact using predicates we obtain that the predicate

$$(\exists x_1 \in D_1.\, y = in_1(x_1)\ \&\ Q_1(x_1))\ \text{or} \cdots \text{or}\ (\exists x_k \in D_k.\, y = in_k(x_k)\ \&\ Q_k(x_k)),$$

with free variable $y \in D_1 + \cdots + D_k$, is an inclusive predicate of the sum if each $Q_i(x_i)$ is an inclusive predicate of the component D_i.

The methods described above form the basis of a a language of inclusive predicates. Provided we build up predicates from basic inclusive predicates using the methods admitted above then they are guaranteed to be inclusive. For example, any predicate built-up as a universal quantification over several variables of conjunctions and disjunctions of basic predicates of the form $e_1 \sqsubseteq e_2$ for terms e_1, e_2 in our metalanguage will be inclusive.

Proposition 10.11 *Any predicate of the form*

$$\forall x_1, \ldots, x_n.\ P$$

is inclusive where $x_1, \ldots, x_n$ are variables ranging over specific cpo's, and P is built up by conjunctions and disjunctions of basic predicates of the form $e_0 \sqsubseteq e_1$ or $e_0 = e_1$, where e_0 and e_1 are expressions in the metalanguage of expressions from Section 8.4.

Unfortunately, such syntactic means fail to generate all the predicates needed in proofs and the manufacture of suitable inclusive predicates can become extremely difficult when reasoning about recursively defined domains.

Example: Let $\mathbf{T}_\perp$ be the usual complete partial order of truth values $\{\mathbf{true}, \mathbf{false}\}_\perp$. Abbreviate $\lfloor \mathbf{true} \rfloor$ to tt and $\lfloor \mathbf{false} \rfloor$ to ff. Let $p : D \to \mathbf{T}_\perp$ and $h : D \to D$ be continuous with h strict (*i.e.* $h(\perp) = \perp$). Let $f : D \times D \to D$ be the least continuous function such that

$$f(x, y) = p(x) \to y \mid h(f(h(x), y))$$

for all $x, y \in D$. We prove

(i) $h(b \to d \mid e) = b \to h(d) \mid h(e)$ for all $b \in \mathbf{T}_\perp$ and $d, e \in D$, and
(ii) $h(f(x, y)) = f(x, h(y))$ for all $x, y \in D$.

Part (i) follows easily by considering the three possible values $\perp, tt, ff$ for $b \in \mathbf{T}_\perp$.

If $b = \perp$	then	$h(b \to d \mid e) = h(\perp) = \perp = b \to h(d) \mid h(e)$
If $b = tt$	then	$h(b \to d \mid e) = h(d) = b \to h(d) \mid h(e)$
If $b = ff$	then	$h(b \to d \mid e) = h(e) = b \to h(d) \mid h(e)$

Hence the required equation holds for all possible values of the boolean b.

Part (ii) follows by fixed-point induction. An appropriate predicate is

$$P(g) \Leftrightarrow_{def} \forall x, y \in D. \ h(g(x,y)) = g(x, h(y))$$

The predicate $P(g)$ is inclusive because it can be built-up by the methods described earlier. Because h is strict we see that $P(\bot)$ is true. To apply fixed-point induction we require further that

$$P(g) \Rightarrow P(F(g))$$

where $F(g) = \lambda x, y. \ p(x) \rightarrow y \mid (h(g(h(x), y))$.

Assume $P(g)$. Let $x, y \in D$. Then

$$
\begin{aligned}
h((F(g))(x,y)) &= h(p(x) \rightarrow y \mid h(g(h(x), y))) \\
&= p(x) \rightarrow h(y) \mid h^2(g(h(x), y)), \quad \text{by (i)} \\
&= p(x) \rightarrow h(y) \mid h(g(h(x), h(y))), \quad \text{by the assumption } P(g) \\
&= (F(g))(x, h(y))
\end{aligned}
$$

Thus $P(F(g))$. Hence $P(g) \Rightarrow p(F(g))$.

By fixed-point induction, we deduce $P(fix(F))$ i.e. $P(f)$ i.e. $\forall x, y \in D. \ h(f(x,y)) = f(x, h(y))$ as required. $\qquad\square$

Exercise 10.12 Define $h : \mathbf{N} \rightarrow \mathbf{N}_\bot$ recursively by

$$h(x) = h(x) +_\bot \lfloor 1 \rfloor$$

Show $h = \bot$, the always-$\bot$ function, using fixed-point induction. $\qquad\square$

Exercise 10.13 Let D be a cpo with bottom. Let $p : D \rightarrow \mathbf{T}_\bot$ be continuous and strict (i.e. $p(\bot) = \bot$) and $h : D \rightarrow D$ be continuous. Let $f : D \rightarrow D$ to be the least continuous function which satisfies

$$f(x) = p(x) \rightarrow x \mid f(f(h(x)))$$

for all $x \in D$. Prove

$$\forall x \in D. \ f(f(x)) = f(x).$$

(Hint:Take as induction hypothesis the predicate

$$P(g) \Longleftrightarrow_{def} \forall x \in D. \ f(g(x)) = g(x).)$$

$\qquad\square$

Exercise 10.14 Let $h, k : D \to D$ be continuous functions on a cpo D with bottom, with h strict. Let $p : D \to \mathbf{T}_\perp$ be a continuous function. Let f, g be the least continuous functions $D \times D \to D$ satisfying

$$f(x, y) = p(x) \to y \mid h(f(k(x), y))$$
$$g(x, y) = p(x) \to y \mid g(k(x), h(y))$$

for all $x, y \in D$. Using fixed-point induction show $f = g$.
(Hint: Regard the solutions as simultaneous fixed points and take the inclusive predicate to be

$$P(f, g) \iff {}_{def} \forall x, y. \, [f(x, y) = g(x, y) \,\&\, g(x, h(y)) = h(g(x, y))].)$$

$\square$

It is probably helpful to conclude this section with a general remark on the use of fixed-point induction. Faced with a problem of proving a property holds of a least fixed point it is often not the case that an inclusive property appropriate to fixed point induction suggests itself readily. Like induction hypotheses, or invariants of programs, spotting a suitable inclusive property frequently requires fairly deep insight. The process of obtaining a suitable inclusive property can often make carrying out the actual proof a routine matter. It can sometimes be helpful to start by exploring the first few approximants to a least fixed point, with the hope of seeing a pattern which can be turned into an induction hypothesis. The proof can then be continued by mathematical induction on approximants (provided the property holding of each approximant implies it holds of the least fixed point), or, often more cleanly, by fixed-point induction (provided the property is inclusive).

10.3 Well-founded induction

Fixed-point induction is inadequate for certain kinds of reasoning. For example, suppose we want to show a recursively defined function on the integers always terminates on integer inputs. We cannot expect to prove this directly using fixed-point induction. To do so would involve there being an inclusive predicate P which expressed termination and yet was true of $\perp$, the completely undefined function. An extra proof principle is needed which can make use of the way data used in a computation is inductively defined. An appropriate principle is that of well-founded induction. Recall from Chapter 3 that a well-founded relation on a set A is a binary relation $\prec$ which does not have any infinite descending chains. Remember the principle of well-founded induction says:

Let $\prec$ be a well founded relation on a set A. Let P be a property. Then $\forall a \in A.\ P(a)$ iff

$$\forall a \in A.\ ([\forall b \prec a.\ P(b)] \Rightarrow P(a)).$$

Applying the principle often depends on a judicious choice of well-founded relation. We have already made use of well-founded relations like that of proper subexpression on syntactic sets, or $<$ on natural numbers. Here some well-known ways to construct further well-founded relations are given. Note that we use $x \preceq y$ to mean $(x \prec y$ or $x = y)$.

Product: If $\prec_1$ is well-founded on A_1 and $\prec_2$ is well-founded on A_2 then taking

$$(a_1, a_2) \preceq (a_1', a_2') \Leftrightarrow_{def} a_1 \preceq_1 a_1' \text{ and } a_2 \preceq_2 a_2'$$

determines a well-founded relation $\prec = (\preceq \setminus 1_{A_1 \times A_2})$ in $A_1 \times A_2$. However product relations are not as generally applicable as those produced by lexicographic orderings.

Lexicographic products: Let $\prec_1$ be well-founded on A_1 and $\prec_2$ be well-founded on A_2. Define

$$(a_1, a_2) \prec_{lex} (a_1', a_2') \text{ iff } a_1 \prec_1 a_1' \text{ or } (a_1 = a_1' \ \& \ a_2 \prec_2 a_2')$$

Inverse image: Let $f : A \to B$ be a function and $\prec_B$ a well-founded relation on B. Then $\prec_A$ is well-founded on A where

$$a \prec_A a' \Leftrightarrow_{def} f(a) \prec_B f(a')$$

for $a, a' \in A$.

Exercise 10.15 Let $\prec$ be a well-founded relation on a set X such that $\preceq$ is a total order. Show it need not necessarily satisfy

$$\{x \in X \mid x \prec y\}$$

is finite for all $y \in X$.
(A total order is a partial order $\leq$ such that $x \leq y$ or $y \leq x$ for all its elements x, y.)
(Hint: Consider the lexicographic product of $<$ and $<$ on $\omega \times \omega$.) $\square$

Exercise 10.16 Show the product, lexicographic product and inverse image constructions do produce well-founded relations from well-founded relations. $\square$

Example: A famous example is Ackermann's function which can be defined in **REC** by the declaration:

$$A(x, y) = \textbf{if } x \textbf{ then } y + 1 \textbf{ else}$$
$$\textbf{if } y \textbf{ then } A(x - 1, 1) \textbf{ else}$$
$$A(x - 1, A(x, y - 1))$$

Under the denotational semantics for call-by-value, this declares A to have denotation the least function a in $[\mathbf{N}^2 \to \mathbf{N}_\perp]$ such that

$$a(m, n) = \begin{cases} \lfloor n + 1 \rfloor & \text{if } m = 0 \\ a(m - 1, 1) & \text{if } m \neq 0, n = 0 \\ let \ l \Leftarrow a(m, n - 1). \ a(m - 1, l) & \text{otherwise} \end{cases}$$

for all $m, n \in \mathbf{N}$. The fact that Ackermann's function $a(m, n)$ terminates on all integers $m, n \geq 0$ is shown by well-founded induction on (m, n) ordered lexicographically. □

Exercise 10.17 Prove Ackermann's function $a(m, n)$ terminates on all integers $m, n \geq 0$ by well-founded induction by taking as induction hypothesis

$$P(m, n) \Leftrightarrow_{def} (a(m, n) \neq \perp \text{ and } a(m, n) \geq 0)$$

for $m, n \geq 0$.   □

Exercise 10.18 The 91 function of McCarthy is defined to be the least function in $[\mathbf{N} \to \mathbf{N}_\perp]$ such that

$$f(x) = cond(x > 100, \lfloor x - 10 \rfloor, \ let \ y \Leftarrow f(x + 11). \ f(y)).$$

(This uses the conditional of 8.3.5)
Show this implies

$$f(x) = cond(x > 100, \lfloor x - 10 \rfloor, \lfloor 91 \rfloor)$$

for all nonnegative integers x. Use well-founded induction on ω with relation

$$n \prec m \Leftrightarrow m < n \leq 101,$$

for $n, m \in \omega$. First show $\prec$ is a well-founded relation.   □

10.4   Well-founded recursion

In Chapter 3 we noticed that both definition by induction and structural induction allow a form of recursive definition, that the length of an arithmetic expression can, for instance, be defined recursively in terms of the lengths of its strict subexpressions; how the length function acts on a particular argument, like $(a_1 + a_2)$ is specified in terms of how the length function acts on strictly smaller arguments, like a_1 and a_2. In a similar way we are entitled to define functions on an arbitrary well-founded set. Suppose B is a set with a well-founded relation $\prec$. Definition by well-founded induction, called well-founded recursion, allows the definition of a function f from B by specifying its value $f(b)$ at an arbitrary b in B in terms of $f(b')$ for $b' \prec b$. We need a little notation to state and justify the general method precisely. Each element b in B has a set of predecessors

$$\prec^{-1}\{b\} = \{b' \in B \mid b' \prec b\}.$$

For any $B' \subseteq B$, a function $f : B \to C$ restricts to a function $f \restriction B' : B' \to C$ by taking

$$f \restriction B' = \{(b, f(b)) \mid b \in B'\}.$$

Definition by well-founded recursion is justified by the following theorem:

Theorem 10.19 *(Well-founded recursion)*
Let $\prec$ be a well-founded relation on a set B. Suppose $F(b, h) \in C$, for all $b \in B$ and functions $h :\prec^{-1}\{b\} \to C$. There is a unique function $f : B \to C$ such that

$$\forall b \in B.\ f(b) = F(b, f \restriction \prec^{-1}\{b\}). \qquad (*)$$

Proof: The proof has two parts. We first show a uniqueness property:

$$\forall y \prec^* x.\ f(y) = F(y, f \restriction \prec^{-1}\{y\})\ \&\ g(y) = F(y, g \restriction \prec^{-1}\{y\})$$
$$\Rightarrow f(x) = g(x),$$

for any $x \in B$. This uniqueness property $P(x)$ is proved to hold for all $x \in B$ by well-founded induction on $\prec$: For $x \in B$, assume $P(z)$ for every $z \prec x$. We require $P(x)$. To this end suppose

$$f(y) = F(y, f \restriction \prec^{-1}\{y\})\ \&\ g(y) = F(y, g \restriction \prec^{-1}\{y\})$$

for all $y \prec^* x$. If $z \prec x$, then as $P(z)$ we obtain

$$f(z) = g(z).$$

Hence

$$f \restriction \prec^{-1}\{x\} = g \restriction \prec^{-1}\{x\}.$$

It now follows that

$$f(x) = F(x, f \restriction \prec^{-1}\{x\}) = F(x, g \restriction \prec^{-1}\{x\}) = g(x).$$

Thus $P(x)$.

It follows that there can be at most one function f satisfying $(*)$. We now show that there exists such a function. We build the function by unioning together a set of functions $f_x : \prec^{*-1}\{x\} \to C$, for $x \in B$. To show suitable functions exist we prove the following property $Q(x)$ holds for all $x \in B$ by well-founded induction on $\prec$:

$$\exists f_x : \prec^{*-1}\{x\} \to C.$$
$$\forall y \prec^* x.\ f_x(y) = F(y, f_x \upharpoonright \prec^{-1}\{y\}).$$

Let $x \in B$. Suppose $\forall z \prec x.\ Q(z)$. Then we claim

$$h = \bigcup \{f_z \mid z \prec x\}$$

is a function. Certainly it is a relation giving at least one value for every argument $z \prec x$. The only difficulty is in checking the functions f_z agree on values assigned to common arguments y. But they must—otherwise we would violate the uniqueness property proved above. Taking

$$f_x = h \cup \{(x, F(x, h))\}$$

gives a function $f_x : \prec^{*-1}\{x\} \to C$ such that

$$\forall y \prec^* x.\ f_x(y) = F(y, f_x \upharpoonright \prec^{-1}\{y\}).$$

This completes the well-founded induction, yielding $\forall x \in B.\ Q(x)$.

Now we take $f = \bigcup_{x \in B} f_x$. By the uniqueness property, this yields $f : B \to C$, and moreover f is the unique function satisfying $(*)$.   □

Well-founded recursion and induction constitute a general method often appropriate when functions are intended to be total. For example, it immediately follows from the recursion theorem that that there is a unique total function on the nonnegative integers such that

$$ack(m, n) = \begin{cases} n + 1 & \text{if } m = 0 \\ ack(m - 1, 1) & \text{if } m \neq 0, n = 0 \\ ack(m - 1, ack(m, n - 1)) & \text{otherwise} \end{cases}$$

for all $m, n \geq 0$; observe that the value of ack at the pair (m, n) is defined in terms of its values at the lexicographically smaller pairs $(m - 1, 1)$ and $(m, n - 1)$. In fact, a great many recursive programs are written so that some measure within a well-founded set decreases as they are evaluated. For such programs often the machinery of least fixed points can be replaced by well-founded recursion and induction.

10.5   An exercise

We round off this chapter with an exercise showing that two recursive functions on lists
are equal. The solution of this single problem brings together many of the techniques
for reasoning about recursive definitions. We have tended to concentrate on arithmetical
and boolean operations. Here we look instead at operations on finite lists of integers. An
integer-list is typically of the form

$$[m_1; m_2; \ldots; m_k]$$

consisting of k elements from $\mathbf{N}$. The *empty list* is also a list which will be written as:

$$[\,]$$

There are two basic operations for constructing lists. One is the constant operation
taking the empty tuple of arguments () to the empty list [ ]. The other is generally called
cons and prefixes an integer m to the front of a list l, the result of which is written as:

$$m :: l$$

Thus, for example,

$$1 :: [2; 3; 4] = [1; 2; 3; 4].$$

The set of integer-lists forms a discrete cpo which we will call *List*. It is built up as
the sum of two discrete cpo's

$$List = in_1\{()\} \cup in_2(\mathbf{N} \times List) = \{()\} + (\mathbf{N} \times List)$$

with respect to the injection functions which act so:

$$in_1() = [\,] \quad \text{and}$$
$$in_2(m, l) = m :: l.$$

That lists can be regarded as a sum in this way reflects the fact that the discrete cpo of
integer-lists is isomorphic to that of all tuples of integers including the ().

The sum is accompanied by a cases construction

$$case\ l\ of\ [\,].\ e_1|$$
$$x :: l'.\ e_2.$$

Its use is illustrated in a recursive definition of a function

$$append : List \times List \to (List)_\perp$$

which performs the operation of appending two lists:

$$append = \mu\alpha.\ \lambda l, ls \in List.$$
$$case\ l\ of\ [\ ].\ \lfloor ls \rfloor |$$
$$x :: l'.\ (let\ r \Leftarrow \alpha(l', ls).\ \lfloor x :: r \rfloor).$$

The function append is the least α function in the cpo $[List \times List \to (List)_\perp]$ which satisfies

$$\alpha([\ ], ls) = \lfloor ls \rfloor$$
$$\alpha(x :: l', ls) = (let\ r \Leftarrow \alpha(l', ls).\ \lfloor x :: r \rfloor).$$

An induction on the size of list in the first argument ensures that *append* is always total. Relating lists by $l' \prec l$ iff the list l' is strictly smaller than the list l, we might instead define a slightly different append operation on lists $@ : List \times List \to List$ by well-founded recursion. By the well-founded recursion, Theorem 10.19, $@$ is the unique (total) function such that

$$l@ls = case\ l\ of\ [\ ].\ ls\ |$$
$$x :: l'.\ x :: (l'@ls)$$

for all $l, ls \in List$. The two functions can be proved to be related by

$$append(l, ls) = \lfloor l@ls \rfloor,$$

for all lists l, ls, by well-founded induction.

Now we can state the problem:

Exercise 10.20 Assume functions on integers $s : \mathbf{N} \times \mathbf{N} \to \mathbf{N}$ and $r : \mathbf{N} \times \mathbf{N} \to List$. Let f be the least function in $[List \times \mathbf{N} \to \mathbf{N}_\perp]$ satisfying

$$f([\ ], y) = \lfloor y \rfloor$$
$$f(x :: xs, y) = f(r(x, y)@xs, s(x, y)).$$

Let g be the least function in $[List \times \mathbf{N} \to \mathbf{N}_\perp]$ satisfying

$$g([\ ], y) = \lfloor y \rfloor$$
$$g(x :: xs, y) = let\ v \Leftarrow g(r(x, y), s(x, y)).\ g(xs, v).$$

Prove $f = g$.
Hints: First show g satisfies

$$g(l@xs, y) = let\ v \Leftarrow g(l, y).\ g(xs, v)$$

by induction on the size of list l. Deduce $f \sqsubseteq g$. Now show f satisfies

$$(let\ u \Leftarrow f(l, y).\ f(xs, u)) \sqsubseteq f(l@xs, y)$$

by fixed-point induction—take as inclusive predicate

$$P(F) \iff _{def} [\forall xs, l, y.\ (let\ u \Leftarrow F(l, y).\ f(xs, u)) \sqsubseteq f(l@xs, y)].$$

Deduce $g \sqsubseteq f$.   □

10.6 Further reading

The presentation of this chapter has been influenced by [80], [59], and [89]. In particular, Manna's book [59] is a rich source of exercises in fixed point and well-founded induction (though unfortunately the latter principle is called "structural induction" there). I am grateful to Larry Paulson for the problem on lists. The reader is warned that the terminology for the concept of "inclusive" property and predicate is not universal. The term "inclusive" here is inherited from Gordon Plotkin's lecture notes [80]. Others use "admissible" but there are other names too. The issue of terminology is complicated by option of developing domain theory around directed sets rather than ω-chains—within the wide class of ω-algebraic cpo's this yields an equivalent notion, although it does lean on the terminology used. Other references are [13], [58] and [21] (though the latter wrongly assumes a predicate on a product cpo is inclusive if inclusive in each argument separately). Enderton's book [39] contains a detailed treatment of well-founded recursion (look up references to "recursion" in the index of [39], and bear in mind his proofs are with respect to a "well ordering," a *transitive* well-founded relation.)

11 Languages with higher types

We explore the operational and denotational semantics of languages with higher types, in the sense that they explicitly allow the construction of types using a function space constructor; functions become "first-class" values and can be supplied as inputs to functions or delivered as outputs. Again, we will be faced with a choice as to whether evaluation should proceed in a call-by-value or call-by-name fashion. The first choice will lead to a language behaving much like the eager language Standard ML, the second to one closely similar in behaviour to lazy languages Miranda[1], Orwell or Haskell. This begins a study of the semantics of functional programming languages such as these. As an application of the semantics it is studied how to express fixed-point operators in the eager and lazy cases. This leads to a discussion of the adequacy of the denotational semantics with respect to the operational semantics and to the concept of full abstraction. The main constructions on types considered are products and function space, though the chapter concludes by indicating how its results can be extended to include sums.

11.1 An eager language

In the context of functional programming, call-by-value evaluation is often called *eager*. For efficiency, call-by-name evaluation is implemented in a call-by-need, or *lazy* way; through careful sharing the implementation arranges that an argument is evaluated at most once. Whether we choose a call-by-value (eager) or call-by-name (lazy) mode of evaluation will influence the syntax of our language a little in the manner in which we permit recursive definitions. We begin by studying call-by-value.

As in the language **REC** we will have terms which evaluate to basic printable values like numbers. Such terms can be built up using numerals, variables, conditionals and arithmetic operations and will yield numbers as values or diverge. However in addition there will be terms which can yield pairs or even functions as values. (We will see shortly how to make sense operationally of a computation yielding a function as a value.)

To take account of the different kinds of values terms can evaluate to, we introduce *types* into our programming language. A term which evaluates to a number provided it does not diverge, will receive the type **int**. A term which evaluates to a pair as value will have a product type of the form $\tau_1 * \tau_2$. A term which evaluates to a function will have a function type of shape $\tau_1 -> \tau_2$. To summarise type expressions τ will have the form

$$\tau ::= \mathbf{int} \mid \tau_1 * \tau_2 \mid \tau_1 -> \tau_2$$

To simplify the language, we will assume that variables $x, y, \ldots$ in **Var** are associated with a unique type, given *e.g.* by **type**(x). (In practice, this could be achieved by building

---

[1]Miranda is a trademark of Research Software Ltd

the type τ into the variable name, so variables x have the form $x : \tau$). The syntax of terms $t, t_0, t_1, \ldots$ is given by

$$t ::= x \mid$$
$$n \mid t_1 + t_2 \mid t_1 - t_2 \mid t_1 \times t_2 \mid \text{if } t_0 \text{ then } t_1 \text{ else } t_2 \mid$$
$$(t_1, t_2) \mid \text{fst}(t) \mid \text{snd}(t) \mid$$
$$\lambda x.t \mid (t_1 \; t_2) \mid$$
$$\text{let } x \Leftarrow t_1 \text{ in } t_2 \mid$$
$$\text{rec } y.(\lambda x.t)$$

The syntax describes how

- to write arithmetical expressions in a manner familiar from the language **REC** of Chapter 9. Like there, the conditional branches according to an arithmetical rather than a boolean term. However, unlike **REC** the branches need not evaluate to numbers.

- to construct pairs (t_1, t_2), and project to first and second components with $\text{fst}(t)$ and $\text{snd}(t)$.

- to define functions using λ-abstraction and apply them—$(t_1 \; t_2)$ stands for the application of a function t_1 to t_2.

- to force the prior evaluation of a term t_1 before its value is used in the evaluation of t_2 with $\text{let } x \Leftarrow t_1 \text{ in } t_2$.

- to define a function y recursively to be $\lambda x.t$ using $\text{rec } y.(\lambda x.t)$—the term t can involve y of course. Note, that in this eager language, any recursive definition has to have a function type, *i.e.* if $\text{rec } y.(\lambda x.t) : \tau$ then $\tau \equiv \tau_1 -> \tau_2$ for types τ_1, τ_2. With this choice of syntax, the treatment remains faithful to Standard ML.

We can write down arithmetical terms of the kind we saw in **REC**. However, it is also possible to write down nonsense: to try to add two functions, or give a function too many, or too few, arguments. The well-formed terms t are those which receive a type τ, written $t : \tau$.

We will say a term t is *typable* when $t : \tau$ for some type τ, according to the following rules:

Typing rules

Variables: $x : \tau$ if $type(x) = \tau$

Operations: $n : \textbf{int}$

$$\frac{t_1 : \textbf{int} \ \ t_2 : \textbf{int}}{t_1 \ \textbf{op} \ t_2 : \textbf{int}} \ \text{where} \ \textbf{op} \ \text{is} \ +, -, \ \text{or} \ \times$$

$$\frac{t_0 : \textbf{int} \ \ t_1 : \tau \ \ t_2 : \tau}{\textbf{if} \ t_0 \ \textbf{then} \ t_1 \ \textbf{else} \ t_2 : \tau}$$

Products: $\dfrac{t_1 : \tau_1 \ \ t_2 : \tau_2}{(t_1, t_2) : \tau_1 * \tau_2} \quad \dfrac{t : \tau_1 * \tau_2}{\textbf{fst}(t) : \tau_1} \quad \dfrac{t : \tau_1 * \tau_2}{\textbf{snd}(t) : \tau_2}$

Functions: $\dfrac{x : \tau_1 \ \ t : \tau_2}{\lambda x.t : \tau_1 -> \tau_2} \quad \dfrac{t_1 : \tau_1 -> \tau_2 \ \ t_2 : \tau_1}{(t_1 \ t_2) : \tau_2}$

let: $\dfrac{x : \tau_1 \ \ t_1 : \tau_1 \ \ t_2 : \tau_2}{\textbf{let} \ x \Leftarrow t_1 \ \textbf{in} \ t_2 : \tau_2}$

rec: $\dfrac{y : \tau \ \ \lambda x.t : \tau}{\textbf{rec} \ y.(\lambda x.t) : \tau}$

Exercise 11.1 Say a term t is *uniquely typed* if

$$t : \tau \ \text{and} \ t : \tau' \ \text{implies} \ \tau, \tau' \ \text{are the same type.}$$

Show this property holds of all terms which are typable. □

The set of free variables $FV(t)$ of a term t can be defined straightforwardly by structural induction on t:

$$
\begin{aligned}
FV(n) &= \emptyset \\
FV(x) &= \{x\} \\
FV(t_1 \ \textbf{op} \ t_1) &= FV(t_1) \cup FV(t_2) \\
FV(\textbf{if} \ t_0 \ \textbf{then} \ t_1 \ \textbf{else} \ t_2) &= FV(t_0) \cup FV(t_1) \cup FV(t_2) \\
FV((t_1, t_2)) &= FV(t_1) \cup FV(t_2) \\
FV(\textbf{fst}(t)) &= FV(\textbf{snd}(t)) = FV(t)
\end{aligned}
$$

$$FV(\lambda x.t) \;=\; FV(t)\backslash\{x\}$$
$$FV((t_1\,t_2)) \;=\; FV(t_1) \cup FV(t_2)$$
$$FV(\text{ let } x \Leftarrow t_1 \text{ in } t_2) \;=\; FV(t_1) \cup (FV(t_2)\backslash\{x\})$$
$$FV(\text{rec }y.(\lambda x.t)) \;=\; FV(\lambda x.t)\backslash\{y\}$$

The clause for the **let**-construction is a little tricky: the variable x in t_2 is bound in the let-construction. A term t is *closed* iff $FV(t) = \emptyset$, *i.e.* a term t is closed when it has no free variables.

The operational semantics will require in some cases that we substitute a closed term s for a free variable x in a term t. We write $t[s/x]$ for such a substitution. The reader will have no difficulty formalising substitution. More generally, we write $t[s_1/x_1, \ldots, s_k/x_k]$ for the simultaneous substitution of closed terms s_1 for $x_1, \ldots, s_k$ for x_k in t—it is assumed that $x_1, \ldots, x_k$ are distinct.

11.2   Eager operational semantics

So far the intended behaviour of the programming language has only been explained informally. We consider a call-by-value, or eager, method of evaluation. Just as in the case for **REC**, this means that to evaluate a function applied to certain arguments we should first evaluate the arguments to obtain values on which the function can then act. But what are values in this more general language? Certainly we expect numerals to be values, but in the case where a function is applied to functions as arguments when do we stop evaluating those argument functions and regard the evaluation as having produced a function value? There is a choice here, but a reasonable decision is to take a term as representing a function value when it is a λ-abstraction. More generally, it can be asked of every type which of its terms represent values. Traditionally, such terms are called *canonical forms*. The judgement $t \in C_\tau^e$ that a term t is a canonical form of type τ is defined by the following structural induction on τ:

Ground type: numerals are canonical forms, *i.e.* $n \in C_{\mathbf{int}}^e$.

Product type: pairs of canonical forms are canonical, *i.e.*
$$(c_1, c_2) \in C_{\tau_1 * \tau_2}^e \text{ if } c_1 \in C_{\tau_1}^e \;\&\; c_2 \in C_{\tau_2}^e.$$

Function type: closed abstractions are canonical forms, *i.e.*
$$\lambda x.t \in C_{\tau_1 -> \tau_2}^e \text{ if } \lambda x.t : \tau_1 -> \tau_2 \text{ and } \lambda x.t \text{ is closed.}$$

Note that canonical forms are special kinds of *closed* terms.

Now we can give the rules for the evaluation relation of the form

$$t \to^e c$$

where t is a typable closed term and c is a canonical form, meaning t evaluates to c.

Evaluation rules

Canonical forms: $c \to^e c$ where $c \in C_\tau^e$

Operations: $\dfrac{t_1 \to^e n_1 \quad t_2 \to^e n_2}{(t_1 \text{ op } t_2) \to^e n_1 \text{ op } n_2}$ where **op** is $+, -,$ or $\times$

$$\frac{t_0 \to^e 0 \quad t_1 \to^e c_1}{\text{if } t_0 \text{ then } t_1 \text{ else } t_2 \to^e c_1} \qquad \frac{t_0 \to^e n \quad t_2 \to^e c_2}{\text{if } t_0 \text{ then } t_1 \text{ else } t_2 \to^e c_2} \ n \not\equiv 0$$

Product: $\dfrac{t_1 \to^e c_1 \quad t_2 \to^e c_2}{(t_1, t_2) \to^e (c_1, c_2)}$

$$\frac{t \to^e (c_1, c_2)}{\mathbf{fst}(t) \to^e c_1} \qquad \frac{t \to^e (c_1, c_2)}{\mathbf{snd}(t) \to^e c_2}$$

Function: $\dfrac{t_1 \to^e \lambda x.t_1' \quad t_2 \to^e c_2 \quad t_1'[c_2/x] \to^e c}{(t_1 \ t_2) \to^e c}$

let: $\dfrac{t_1 \to^e c_1 \quad t_2[c_1/x] \to^e c_2}{\mathbf{let} \ x \Leftarrow t_1 \mathbf{\ in \ } t_2 \to^e c_2}$

rec: $\mathbf{rec}\, y.(\lambda x.t) \to^e \lambda x.(t[\mathbf{rec}\, y.(\lambda x.t)/y])$

The rule for canonical forms expresses, as is to be expected, that canonical forms evaluate to themselves. The rules for arithmetical operations and conditionals are virtually the same as those for **REC** in Chapter 9. In this eager regime to evaluate a pair is to evaluate its components, and the projection function **fst** and **snd** can only act once their arguments are fully evaluated. A key rule is that for the evaluation of applications: the evaluation of an application can only proceed once its function part and argument have been evaluated. Notice how the rule for the evaluation of **let** $x \Leftarrow t_1$ **in** t_2 forces the prior evaluation of t_1. The rule for recursive definitions "unfolds" the recursion $\mathbf{rec}\, y.(\lambda x.t)$ once, leading immediately to an abstraction $\lambda x.(t[\mathbf{rec}\, y.(\lambda x.t)/y])$, and so a canonical form. Note that to be typable, $y : \tau_1 \texttt{->} \tau_2$ with $x : \tau_1$, for types τ_1, τ_2. This ensures that y and x are distinct so that we could just as well write $(\lambda x.t)[\mathbf{rec}\,(\lambda x.t)/y]$ instead of $\lambda x.(t[\mathbf{rec}\, y.(\lambda x.t)/y])$.

It is straightforward to show that the evaluation relation is deterministic and respects types:

Proposition 11.2 *If $t \rightarrow^e c$ and $t \rightarrow^e c'$ then $c \equiv c'$ (i.e. evaluation is deterministic). If $t \rightarrow^e c$ and $t : \tau$ then $c : \tau$ (i.e. evaluation respects types).*

Proof: Both properties follow by simple rule inductions.   □

Exercise 11.3 Let fact $\equiv$ **rec** $f.(\lambda x.\text{if } x \text{ then } 1 \text{ else } x \times f(x-1))$. Derive the evaluation of (fact 2) from the operational semantics.   □

11.3   Eager denotational semantics

The denotational semantics will show, for instance, how to think of terms of type $\tau_1 \rightarrow \tau_2$ as functions, so justifying the informal understanding one has in programming within a functional language. Through interpreting the language in the framework of cpo's and continuous functions, the programming language will become amenable to the proof techniques of Chapter 10.

It should first be decided how to interpret type expressions. A closed term t of type τ can either evaluate to a canonical form of type τ or diverge. It seems reasonable therefore to take t to denote an element of $(V_\tau^e)_\perp$ where V_τ^e is a cpo of *values* of type τ, which should include the denotations of canonical forms. With this guiding idea, by structural induction on type expressions, we define:

$$
\begin{aligned}
V_{\textbf{int}}^e &= \textbf{N} \\
V_{\tau_1 * \tau_2}^e &= V_{\tau_1}^e \times V_{\tau_2}^e \\
V_{\tau_1 \rightarrow \tau_2}^e &= [V_{\tau_1}^e \rightarrow (V_{\tau_2}^e)_\perp]
\end{aligned}
$$

The final clause captures the idea that a function value takes a value as input and delivers a value as output or diverges.

In general, terms contain free variables. Then denotational semantics requires a notion of environment to supply values to the free variables. An environment for this eager language is typically a function

$$\rho : \textbf{Var} \rightarrow \bigcup \{V_\tau^e \mid \tau \text{ a type } \}$$

which respects types in that

$$x : \tau \Rightarrow \rho(x) \in V_\tau^e$$

for any $x \in \mathbf{Var}$ and type τ. Write $\mathbf{Env}^e$ for the cpo of all such environments.

Now we can give the denotational semantics for the eager language; a term t, with typing $t : \tau$, will denote an element $[\![t]\!]^e \rho \in (V_\tau^e)_\bot$ in an environment ρ.

Denotational semantics

The denotation of typable terms t is given by the following structural induction:

$$
\begin{aligned}
[\![x]\!]^e &= \lambda\rho.\lfloor \rho(x) \rfloor \\
[\![n]\!]^e &= \lambda\rho.\lfloor n \rfloor \\
[\![t_1 \ \mathbf{op} \ t_2]\!]^e &= \lambda\rho.([\![t_1]\!]^e\rho \ op_\bot \ [\![t_2]\!]^e\rho) \text{ where } \mathbf{op} \text{ is } +, -, \times \\
[\![\mathbf{if} \ t_0 \ \mathbf{then} \ t_1 \ \mathbf{else} \ t_2]\!]^e &= \lambda\rho.Cond([\![t_0]\!]^e\rho, [\![t_1]\!]^e\rho, [\![t_2]\!]^e\rho) \\
[\![(t_1, t_2)]\!]^e &= \lambda\rho.let \ v_1 \Leftarrow [\![t_1]\!]^e\rho, v_2 \Leftarrow [\![t_2]\!]^e\rho. \ \lfloor (v_1, v_2) \rfloor \\
[\![\mathbf{fst}(t)]\!]^e &= \lambda\rho.let \ v \Leftarrow [\![t]\!]^e\rho. \ \lfloor \pi_1(v) \rfloor \\
[\![\mathbf{snd}(t)]\!]^e &= \lambda\rho.let \ v \Leftarrow [\![t]\!]^e\rho. \ \lfloor \pi_2(v) \rfloor \\
[\![\lambda x.t]\!]^e &= \lambda\rho.\lfloor \lambda v \in V_{\tau_1}^e.[\![t]\!]^e\rho[v/x] \rfloor \\
&\quad\text{where } \lambda x.t : \tau_1 {-}{>} \tau_2 \\
[\![(t_1 \ t_2)]\!]^e &= \lambda\rho.let \ \varphi \Leftarrow [\![t_1]\!]^e\rho, v \Leftarrow [\![t_2]\!]^e\rho. \ \varphi(v). \\
[\![\mathbf{let} \ x \Leftarrow t_1 \ \mathbf{in} \ t_2]\!]^e &= \lambda\rho.let \ v \Leftarrow [\![t_1]\!]^e\rho. \ [\![t_2]\!]^e\rho[v/x] \\
[\![\mathbf{rec} \ y.(\lambda x.t)]\!]^e &= \lambda\rho.\lfloor \mu\varphi.(\lambda v.[\![t]\!]^e\rho[v/x, \varphi/y]) \rfloor
\end{aligned}
$$

We have used a generalisation of the conditional *Cond* of Section 9.3 in the clause giving the denotational semantics of conditionals. For a cpo D with bottom, the function

$$Cond : \mathbf{N}_\bot \times D \times D \to D$$

satisfies

$$
Cond(z_0, z_1, z_2) = \begin{cases} z_1 & \text{if} & z_0 = \lfloor 0 \rfloor, \\ z_2 & \text{if} & z_0 = \lfloor n \rfloor \text{ for some } n \in \mathbf{N} \text{ with } n \neq 0, \\ \bot & \text{otherwise} \cdot \end{cases}
$$

for $z_0 \in \mathbf{N}_\bot, z_1, z_2 \in D$. It can be shown to be continuous, as in Section 9.3. Notice that the semantics is expressible in the metalanguage of Section 8.4 ensuring that it is sensible to take fixed points.

Exercise 11.4 According to the denotational semantics, terms $\mathbf{let} \ x \Leftarrow t_1 \ \mathbf{in} \ t_2$ are definable purely using the other constructions (and not $\mathbf{let}$). How? □

Lemma 11.5 *Let t be a typable term. Let ρ, ρ' be environments which agree on the free variables of t. Then $[\![t]\!]^e\rho = [\![t]\!]^e\rho'$.*

Proof: A simple structural induction left to the reader.   □

Lemma 11.6 *(Substitution Lemma) Let s be a closed term with $s : \tau$ such that $[\![s]\!]^e\rho = \lfloor v \rfloor$. Let x be a variable with $x : \tau$. Assume $t : \tau'$. Then $t[s/x] : \tau'$ and $[\![t[s/x]]\!]^e\rho = [\![t]\!]^e\rho[v/x]$.*

Proof: A tedious structural induction.   □

Exercise 11.7 Perform the induction steps in the proof of the Substitution Lemma where t is an abstraction or a **let** construct.   □

As is to be expected a general term of type τ has a denotation in $(V_\tau^e)_\perp$, while denotations of canonical forms are associated with values:

Lemma 11.8 *(i) If $t : \tau$ then $[\![t]\!]^e\rho \in (V_\tau^e)_\perp$, for any ρ.*
(ii) If $c \in C_\tau^e$ then $[\![c]\!]^e\rho \neq \perp$, the bottom element of $(V_\tau^e)_\perp$, for any ρ.

Proof: The proof of (i) is by a simple structural induction on t. The proof of (ii) is by structural induction on canonical forms c.   □

Exercise 11.9 Prove part (ii) of Lemma 11.8.   □

11.4   Agreement of eager semantics

Do the operational and denotational semantics agree? We shall see that they do, though perhaps not to the extent one might at first expect. Previously the operational and denotational semantics have matched each other rather closely, possibly leading us to expect, *incorrectly*, that

$$t \to^e c \iff [\![t]\!]^e\rho = [\![c]\!]^e\rho,$$

for a closed term t and canonical form c. The "$\Leftarrow$" direction does *not* hold at any type involving function spaces. The reason is essentially because there can be many canonical forms with the same denotation and the evaluation of a term can yield at most one of them (see the exercise below). We can however show the "$\Rightarrow$" direction of this equivalence does hold, no matter what the type of t:

$$t \to^e c \;\Rightarrow\; [\![t]\!]^e\rho = [\![c]\!]^e\rho. \tag{1}$$

In addition, the two styles of semantics, operational and denotational, do agree on whether or not the evaluation of a closed term converges.

Consider a typable closed term t. Operationally, according to the evaluation rules, t can either diverge or yield a canonical form. Define operational convergence of t by

$$t \downarrow^e \text{ iff } \exists c. \ t \to^e c.$$

Denotationally, the computation of t is modelled as an element $[\![t]\!]^e\rho$ of $(V_\tau^e)_\perp$, where τ is the type of t and ρ can be an arbitrary environment because t is closed—the idea being that the denotation of t is $\perp$ if t diverges or $\lfloor v \rfloor$, for some v, if t converges. Define denotational convergence by taking

$$t \Downarrow^e \text{ iff } \exists v \in V_\tau^e. \ [\![t]\!]^e\rho = \lfloor v \rfloor.$$

We can rightly hope that the two notions of convergence coincide, that

$$t \downarrow^e \iff t \Downarrow^e . \tag{2}$$

Indeed the "$\Rightarrow$" direction follows from (1) by using Lemma 11.8(ii), which says that canonical forms converge denotationally.

It follows, from (1) and (2), that if $t : \mathbf{int}$ then

$$t \to^e n \iff [\![t]\!]^e\rho = \lfloor n \rfloor. \tag{3}$$

To see that the last claim (3) is entailed by (1) and (2), notice that the "$\Rightarrow$" direction is just a special case of (1) and that the converse "$\Leftarrow$" direction is entailed by the fact that two canonical forms of type $\mathbf{int}$ which have the same denotation must be identical numerals. It is said that (1) and (2) express the *adequacy* of the denotational semantics with respect to the operational semantics. They justify our being able to reason from the denotational semantics about results of the operational, evaluation relation.

Exercise 11.10 Show that for types in general the converse of (1), *viz.*

$$[\![t]\!]^e\rho = [\![c]\!]^e\rho \Rightarrow t \to^e c,$$

does *not* hold. (Hint: Take $t \equiv \lambda x.x$, $c \equiv \lambda x.x + 0$ where $x = \mathbf{int}$.) $\square$

We now prove (1) of the claims above, that the denotational semantics respects the evaluation relation.

Lemma 11.11 *If $t \to^e c$ then $[\![t]\!]^e\rho = [\![c]\!]^e\rho$, for any environment ρ.*

Proof: The proof proceeds by rule induction on the rules for evaluation. Most rules are seen straightforwardly to preserve the property above. Here we present the more interesting cases.

Consider the rule:

$$\frac{t \to^e (c_1, c_2)}{\textbf{fst}(t) \to^e c_1}$$

Assume $[\![t]\!]^e \rho = [\![(c_1, c_2)]\!]^e \rho$, for an arbitrary ρ. Then

$$\begin{aligned}
[\![t]\!]^e \rho &= [\![(c_1, c_2)]\!]^e \rho \\
&= \textit{let } v_1 \Leftarrow [\![c_1]\!]^e \rho, v_2 \Leftarrow [\![c_2]\!]^e \rho. \ \lfloor (v_1, v_2) \rfloor \\
&= \lfloor (v_1, v_2) \rfloor \text{ where } [\![c_1]\!]^e \rho = \lfloor v_1 \rfloor \text{ and } [\![c_2]\!]^e \rho = \lfloor v_2 \rfloor
\end{aligned}$$

as $(c_1, c_2) \Downarrow^e$ by Lemma 11.8. Hence

$$\begin{aligned}
[\![\textbf{fst}(t)]\!]^e \rho &= \textit{let } v \Leftarrow [\![t]\!]^e \rho. \ \lfloor \pi_1(v) \rfloor \\
&= \lfloor v_1 \rfloor \\
&= [\![c_1]\!]^e \rho.
\end{aligned}$$

Consider the rule

$$\frac{t_1 \to^e \lambda x.t_1' \quad t_2 \to^e c_2 \quad t_1'[c_2/x] \to^e c}{(t_1 \ t_2) \to^e c}.$$

Assume $[\![t_1]\!]^e \rho = [\![\lambda x.t_1']\!]^e \rho, [\![t_2]\!]^e \rho = [\![c_2]\!]^e \rho$ and $[\![t_1'[c_2/x]]\!]^e \rho = [\![c]\!]^e \rho$. Whence

$$\begin{aligned}
[\![t_1 \ t_2]\!]^e \rho &= \textit{let } \varphi \Leftarrow [\![t_1]\!]^e \rho, v \Leftarrow [\![t_2]\!]^e \rho. \ \varphi(v) \\
&= \textit{let } \varphi \Leftarrow [\![\lambda x.t_1']\!]^e \rho, v \Leftarrow [\![c_2]\!]^e \rho. \ \varphi(v) \\
&= \textit{let } \varphi \Leftarrow \lfloor \lambda v.[\![t_1']\!]^e \rho[v/x] \rfloor, v \Leftarrow [\![c_2]\!]^e \rho. \ \varphi(v) \\
&= [\![t_1']\!]^e \rho[v/x] \text{ where } [\![c_2]\!]^e \rho = \lfloor v \rfloor, \text{ using Lemma 11.8} \\
&= [\![t_1'[c_2/x]]\!]^e \rho \text{ by the substitution Lemma 11.6} \\
&= [\![c]\!]^e \rho
\end{aligned}$$

Consider the rule

$$\frac{}{\textbf{rec } y.(\lambda x.t) \to^e \lambda x.(t[\textbf{rec } y.(\lambda x.t)/y])}.$$

By definition $[\![\textbf{rec } y.(\lambda x.t)]\!]^e \rho = \lfloor \varphi \rfloor$ where φ is the least solution of

$$\varphi = \lambda v.[\![t]\!]^e \rho[v/x, \varphi/y].$$

Now by the substitution Lemma 11.6,

$$[\![\lambda x.(t[\mathbf{rec}\, y.(\lambda x.t)/y])]\!]^e\rho = [\![\lambda x.t]\!]^e\rho[\varphi/y], \text{ recalling } y \text{ and } x \text{ are distinct,}$$
$$= \lfloor \lambda v.[\![t]\!]^e\rho[v/x,\varphi/y]\rfloor$$
$$= \lfloor \varphi \rfloor$$
$$= [\![\mathbf{rec}\, y.(\lambda x.t)]\!]^e\rho. \qquad \square$$

From Lemma 11.8 and Lemma 11.11 it follows that

$$t \downarrow^e \quad \text{implies} \quad t \Downarrow^e$$

for any typable closed term t. The proof of the converse uses a new idea, the technique of *logical relations*. We want to prove that

$$t \Downarrow^e \quad \text{implies} \quad t \downarrow^e \qquad\qquad\qquad (*)$$

for any typable closed term t. An obvious strategy is to use structural induction on t. So let's proceed naively, with $(*)$ as induction hypothesis. Consider the critical case where t is an application $(t_1\, t_2)$ and, inductively, assume

$$(t_1 \Downarrow^e \quad \text{implies} \quad t_1 \downarrow^e) \text{ and } (t_2 \Downarrow^e \quad \text{implies} \quad t_2 \downarrow^e).$$

Suppose $t \Downarrow^e$ with the aim of establishing $(*)$ for this case. Because

$$[\![t]\!]^e\rho = \mathit{let}\, \varphi \Leftarrow [\![t_1]\!]^e\rho, v \Leftarrow [\![t_2]\!]^e\rho.\, \varphi(v)$$

this ensures $t_1 \Downarrow^e$ and $t_2 \Downarrow^e$, and so, by induction,

$$t_1 \to^e \lambda x.t_1' \text{ and } t_2 \to^e c_2$$

for appropriate canonical forms. Thus $[\![t]\!]^e\rho = \varphi(v)$ where $\varphi = \lambda u.[\![t_1']\!]^e\rho[u/x]$ and $\lfloor v \rfloor = [\![c_2]\!]^e\rho$. Hence

$$[\![t]\!]^e\rho = [\![t_1']\!]^e\rho[v/x]$$
$$= [\![t_1'[c_2/x]]\!]^e\rho$$

by the Substitution Lemma. Because $t \Downarrow^e$ it follows that $t_1'[c_2/x] \Downarrow^e$. At this point we'd like to conclude that $t_1'[c_2/x] \downarrow^e$ so $t_1'[c_2/x] \to^e c$, and therefore, from the operational semantics, that $t \to^e c$. But we can't yet justify doing this, simply because $t_1'[c_2/x]$ bears no obvious structural relationship to t which would make the application of the structural induction hypothesis legitimate.

The solution to this difficulty is, as usual, to strengthen the induction hypothesis. Instead of trying to show that the denotational convergence of a term implies its operational convergence we show a stronger, more detailed, relation of "approximation" holds between the denotational and operational behaviour of a term. This is expressed through relations $\lesssim_\tau$, for type τ, between elements of the cpo $(V^e_\tau)_\perp$ and closed terms of type τ. The relations are defined by structural induction on the types of terms by a method which is often useful in reasoning about higher types; the technique is called that of *logical relations*. (Of course, we should also take better care of free variables than we did when trying naively to verify $(*)$ by structural induction.)

We will define a relation $\lesssim^\circ_\tau \subseteq V^e_\tau \times C^e_\tau$ on types τ. We extend these principal relations to relations between elements d of $(V^e_\tau)_\perp$ and closed terms t by defining

$$d \lesssim_\tau t \text{ iff}$$
$$\forall v \in V^e_\tau.\ d = \lfloor v \rfloor \Rightarrow \exists c.\ t \to^e c\ \&\ v \lesssim^\circ_\tau c.$$

The principal relations $\lesssim^\circ_\tau$ are defined by structural induction on types τ:

Ground type: $n \lesssim^\circ_{\mathbf{int}} n$, for all numbers n.

Product types: $(v_1, v_2) \lesssim^\circ_{\tau_1 * \tau_2} (c_1, c_2)$ iff $v_1 \lesssim^\circ_{\tau_1} c_1\ \&\ v_2 \lesssim^\circ_{\tau_2} c_2$.

Function types: $\varphi \lesssim^\circ_{\tau_1 \to \tau_2} \lambda x.t$ iff $\forall v \in V^e_{\tau_1}, c \in C^e_{\tau_1}.v \lesssim^\circ_{\tau_1} c \Rightarrow \varphi(v) \lesssim_{\tau_2} t[c/x]$.

The key property is expressed by the final clause which says that two representations of functions (denotational and operational) are related iff they take related arguments to related results. This property makes the family $\lesssim_\tau$, for types τ, an example of a *logical relation*.

It is important for the proof later to note some basic properties of the relations $\lesssim_\tau$; in particular, they are inclusive.

Lemma 11.12 *Let $t : \tau$. Then*

(i) $\perp_{(V^e_\tau)_\perp} \lesssim_\tau t$.

(ii) *If $d \sqsubseteq d'$ and $d' \lesssim_\tau t$ then $d \lesssim_\tau t$.*

(iii) *If $d_0 \sqsubseteq d_1 \sqsubseteq \ldots \sqsubseteq d_n \sqsubseteq \ldots$ is an ω-chain in $(V^e_\tau)_\perp$ such that $d_n \lesssim_\tau t$ for all $n \in \omega$ then $\bigsqcup_{n \in \omega} d_n \lesssim_\tau t$.*

Proof: Property (i) follows directly by definition. Properties (ii) and (iii) are shown to hold for all terms by structural induction on types. Certainly they both hold at the ground type **int**. To illustrate the inductions we prove the induction step in the case of a function type. Suppose $d_0 \sqsubseteq \ldots \sqsubseteq d_n \sqsubseteq \ldots$ is an ω-chain in $(V^e_{\tau_1 -> \tau_2})_\perp$ such that $d_n \lesssim_{\tau_1 -> \tau_2} t$ for all $n \in \omega$. Either $d_n = \perp$ for all $n \in \omega$ or we have $t \to^e \lambda x.t'$ and some n for which whenever $m \geq n$ $d_m = \lfloor \varphi_m \rfloor$ and $\varphi_m \lesssim_{\tau_1 -> \tau_2} \lambda x.t'$. In the former case $\bigsqcup_n d_n = \perp \lesssim_{\tau_1 -> \tau_2} t$. In the latter case, assuming $v \lesssim^\circ_{\tau_1} c$ we obtain $\varphi_m(v) \lesssim_{\tau_2} t'[c/x]$ for $m \geq n$. It follows inductively that $\bigsqcup_m (\varphi_m(v)) \lesssim_{\tau_2} t'[c/x]$, and so $(\bigsqcup_m \varphi_m)(v) \lesssim_{\tau_2} t'[c/x]$ whenever $v \lesssim^\circ_{\tau_1} c$. In other words $(\bigsqcup_m \varphi_m) \lesssim^\circ_{\tau_1 -> \tau_2} \lambda x.t'$ whence $\bigsqcup_m d_m = \lfloor \bigsqcup_m \varphi_m \rfloor \lesssim_{\tau_1 -> \tau_2} t$, as required.   □

Exercise 11.13 Prove the remaining induction steps for (ii) and (iii) in Lemma 11.12.

□

The reader may find it instructive to compare the proof below in the case of application with the naive attempt described above.

Lemma 11.14 *Let t be a typable closed term. Then*

$$t \Downarrow^e \text{ implies } t \downarrow^e .$$

Proof: We shall show by structural induction on terms that for all terms $t : \tau$ with free variables among $x_1 : \tau_1, \ldots, x_k : \tau_k$ that if $\lfloor v_1 \rfloor \lesssim_{\tau_1} s_1, \ldots \lfloor v_k \rfloor \lesssim_{\tau_k} s_k$ then

$$\llbracket t \rrbracket^e \rho[v_1/x_1, \ldots, v_k/x_k] \lesssim_\tau t[s_1/x_1, \ldots, s_k/x_k].$$

Taking t closed, it follows from the definition of $\lesssim_\tau$ that if $t \Downarrow^e$ then $\llbracket t \rrbracket^e \rho = \lfloor v \rfloor$ for some v, and hence that $t \to^e c$ for some canonical form c, *i.e.* $t \downarrow^e$.

First note that by Lemma 11.5, in establishing the induction hypothesis for a term t, it suffices to consider the list of precisely those variables which are free in t.

$t \equiv x$, a variable of type τ: Suppose $\lfloor v \rfloor \lesssim_\tau s$. Then from the semantics, $\llbracket x \rrbracket^e \rho[v/x] = \lfloor v \rfloor \lesssim_\tau s \equiv x[s/x]$, as required.

$t \equiv n$, a number: By definition $n \lesssim^\circ_{\mathbf{int}} n$, so the induction hypothesis holds.

$t \equiv t_1 \mathbf{op} t_2$: Suppose $x_1 : \tau_1, \ldots, x_k : \tau_k$ are all the free variables of t. Suppose $\lfloor v_1 \rfloor \lesssim_{\tau_1} s_1, \ldots, \lfloor v_k \rfloor \lesssim_{\tau_k} s_k$. Assume $\llbracket t_1 \mathbf{op} t_2 \rrbracket^e \rho[v_1/x_1, \ldots, v_k/x_k] = \lfloor n \rfloor$. Then, from the denotational semantics,

$$\llbracket t_1 \rrbracket^e \rho[v_1/x_1, \ldots, v_k/x_k] = \lfloor n_1 \rfloor \text{ and}$$
$$\llbracket t_2 \rrbracket^e \rho[v_1/x_1, \ldots, v_k/x_k] = \lfloor n_2 \rfloor$$

for integers n_1, n_2 with $n = n_1 \ op \ n_2$. By induction,

$$[\![t_1]\!]^e \rho[v_1/x_1, \ldots, v_k/x_k] \lesssim_{\mathbf{int}} t_1[s_1/x_1, \ldots, s_k/x_k], \text{ and}$$
$$[\![t_2]\!]^e \rho[v_1/x_1, \ldots, v_k/x_k] \lesssim_{\mathbf{int}} t_2[s_1/x_1, \ldots, s_k/x_k].$$

From the definition of $\lesssim_{\mathbf{int}}$, we see

$$t_1[s_1/x_1, \ldots, s_k/x_k] \rightarrow^e n_1, \text{ and}$$
$$t_2[s_1/x_1, \ldots, s_k/x_k] \rightarrow^e n_2.$$

Hence from the operational semantics

$$(t_1 \ \mathbf{op} \ t_2)[s_1/x_1, \ldots, s_k/x_k] \rightarrow^e n.$$

Thus

$$[\![t_1 \ \mathbf{op} \ t_2]\!]^e \rho[v_1/x_1, \ldots, v_k/x_k] \lesssim_{\mathbf{int}} (t_1 \ \mathbf{op} \ t_2)[s_1/x_1, \ldots, s_k/x_k].$$

$t \equiv \mathbf{if} \ t_0 \ \mathbf{then} \ t_1 \ \mathbf{else} \ t_2$: This case is similar to that when $t \equiv t_1 \ \mathbf{op} \ t_2$ above.

$t \equiv (t_1, t_2)$: Assume $t_1 : \sigma_1, t_2 : \sigma_2$. Suppose $x_1 : \tau_1, \ldots, x_k : \tau_k$ are all the free variables of t and that $\lfloor v_1 \rfloor \lesssim_\tau s_1, \ldots, \lfloor v_k \rfloor \lesssim_{\tau_k} s_k$. Assume $[\![(t_1, t_2)]\!]^e \rho[v_1/x_1, \ldots, v_k/x_k] = \lfloor u \rfloor$. Then from the denotational semantics, there are u_1, u_2 such that

$$[\![t_1]\!]^e \rho[v_1/x_1, \ldots, v_k/x_k] = \lfloor u_1 \rfloor$$
$$[\![t_2]\!]^e \rho[v_1/x_1, \ldots, v_k/x_k] = \lfloor u_2 \rfloor$$

with $u = (u_1, u_2)$. By induction,

$$\lfloor u_1 \rfloor \lesssim_{\sigma_1} t_1[s_1/x_1, \ldots, s_k/x_k]$$
$$\lfloor u_2 \rfloor \lesssim_{\sigma_2} t_2[s_1/x_1, \ldots, s_k/x_k]$$

and so there are canonical forms c_1, c_2 such that

$$u_1 \lesssim_{\sigma_1}^0 c_1 \ \& \ t_1[s_1/x_1, \ldots, s_k/x_k] \rightarrow^e c_1, \text{ and}$$
$$u_2 \lesssim_{\sigma_2}^0 c_2 \ \& \ t_2[s_1/x_1, \ldots, s_k/x_k] \rightarrow^e c_2.$$

It follows that $(u_1, u_2) \lesssim_{\sigma_1 * \sigma_2}^0 (c_1, c_2)$, and $(t_1, t_2)[s_1/x_1, \ldots, s_k/x_k] \rightarrow^e (c_1, c_2)$ from the operational semantics. Thus $[\![(t_1, t_2)]\!]^e \rho[v_1/x_1, \ldots, v_k/x_k] \lesssim_{\sigma_1 * \sigma_2} (t_1, t_2)[s_1/x_1, \ldots, s_k/x_k]$.

$t \equiv \mathbf{fst}(s)$: We are assuming $\mathbf{fst}(s)$ is typable, so s must have type $\sigma_1 * \sigma_2$. Suppose $x_1 : \tau_1, \ldots, x_k : \tau_k$ are all the free variables of t and that $\lfloor v_1 \rfloor \lesssim_{\tau_1} s_1, \ldots, \lfloor v_k \rfloor \lesssim_{\tau_k} s_k$.

Assume $[\![\mathbf{fst}(s)]\!]^e \rho[v_1/x_1, \ldots, v_k/x_k] = \lfloor u \rfloor$. Then from the denotational semantics, $u = u_1$ where $[\![s]\!]^e \rho[v_1/x_1, \ldots, v_k/x_k] = \lfloor (u_1, u_2) \rfloor$ for some $u_1 \in V^e_{\sigma_1}$, $u_2 \in V^e_{\sigma_2}$. By induction,

$$[\![s]\!]^e \rho[v_1/x_1, \ldots, v_k/x_k] \lesssim_{\sigma_1 * \sigma_2} s[s_1/x_1, \ldots, s_k/x_k].$$

Hence there is a canonical form (c_1, c_2) such that

$$(u_1, u_2) \lesssim^0_{\sigma_1 * \sigma_2} (c_1, c_2) \ \& \ s[s_1/x_1, \ldots, s_k/x_k] \to^e (c_1, c_2).$$

This entails $u_1 \lesssim^0_{\sigma_1} c_1$ and $\mathbf{fst}(s[s_1/x_1, \ldots, s_k/x_k]) \to^e c_1$, whence

$$[\![\mathbf{fst}(s)]\!]^e \rho[v_1/x_1, \ldots, v_k/x_k] \lesssim_{\sigma_1} \mathbf{fst}(s[s_1/x_1, \ldots, s_k/x_k]),$$

as required.

$t \equiv \mathbf{snd}(s)$: Similar to the above.

$t \equiv \lambda x.t_2$: Suppose $x : \sigma_1, t_2 : \sigma_2$. Suppose $x_1 : \tau_1, \ldots, x_k : \tau_k$ are all the free variables of t and that $\lfloor v_1 \rfloor \lesssim_{\tau_1} s_1, \ldots, \lfloor v_k \rfloor \lesssim_{\tau_k} s_k$. Assume $[\![\lambda x.t_2]\!]^e \rho[v_1/x_1, \ldots, v_k/x_k] = \lfloor \varphi \rfloor$. Then $\lambda v \in V^e_{\sigma_1}.[\![t_2]\!]^e \rho[v_1/x_1, \ldots, v_k/x_k, v/x] = \varphi$. We require $\varphi \lesssim^0_{\sigma_1 \to \sigma_2} \lambda x.t_2[s_1/x_1, \ldots, s_k/x_k]$. However supposing $v \lesssim^0_{\sigma_1} c$, we have $\lfloor v \rfloor \lesssim_{\sigma_1} c$, so by induction, we obtain

$$\varphi(v) = [\![t_2]\!]^e \rho[v_1/x_1, \ldots, v_k/x_k, v/x] \lesssim_{\sigma_2} t_2[s_1/x_1, \ldots, s_k/x_k, c/x]$$

which is precisely what is required.

$t \equiv (t_1 \ t_2)$: Suppose $t_1 : \sigma_2 \to \sigma, t_2 : \sigma_2$. Assume t has free variables $x_1 : \tau_1, \ldots, x_k : \tau_k$ and that $\lfloor v_1 \rfloor \lesssim_{\tau_1} s_1, \ldots, \lfloor v_k \rfloor \lesssim_{\tau_k} s_k$. From the denotational semantics, we see

$$[\![t_1 \ t_2]\!]^e \rho[v_1/x_1, \ldots, v_k/x_k] =$$
$$let \ \varphi \Leftarrow [\![t_1]\!]^e \rho[v_1/x_1, \ldots, v_k/x_k], v \Leftarrow [\![t_2]\!]^e \rho[v_1/x_1, \ldots, v_k/x_k]. \ \varphi(v)$$

Assume $[\![t_1 \ t_2]\!]^e \rho[v_1/x_1, \ldots, v_k/x_k] = \lfloor u \rfloor$, for $u \in V^e_\sigma$. Then there are φ, v such that

$$[\![t_1]\!]^e \rho[v_1/x_1, \ldots, v_k/x_k] = \lfloor \varphi \rfloor,$$
$$[\![t_2]\!]^e \rho[v_1/x_1, \ldots, v_k/x_k] = \lfloor v \rfloor$$

with $\varphi(v) = \lfloor u \rfloor$. It follows by induction that

$$[\![t_1]\!]^e \rho[v_1/x_1, \ldots, v_k/x_k] \lesssim_{\sigma_2 \to \sigma} t_1[s_1/x_1, \ldots, s_k/x_k], \text{ and}$$
$$[\![t_2]\!]^e \rho[v_1/x_1, \ldots, v_k/x_k] \lesssim_{\sigma_2} t_2[s_1/x_1, \ldots, s_k/x_k].$$

Recalling the definition of $\lesssim_{\sigma_2 \to \sigma}$ and $\lesssim_{\sigma_2}$ in terms of $\lesssim^\circ_{\sigma_2 \to \sigma}$ and $\lesssim^\circ_{\sigma_2}$ we obtain the existence of canonical forms such that

$$t_1[s_1/x_1, \ldots, s_k/x_k] \to^e \lambda x.t'_1 \ \& \ \varphi \lesssim^\circ_{\sigma_2 \to \sigma} \lambda x.t'_1$$

and

$$t_2[s_1/x_1, \ldots, s_k/x_k] \to^e c_2 \ \& \ v \lesssim^\circ_{\sigma_2} c_2.$$

Now, from the definition of $\lesssim^\circ_{\sigma_2 \to \sigma}$ we obtain

$$\varphi(v) \lesssim_\sigma t'_1[c_2/x].$$

As $\varphi(v) = \lfloor u \rfloor$, there is $c \in C^e_\sigma$ such that

$$t'_1[c_2/x] \to^e c \ \& \ u \lesssim^\circ_\sigma c.$$

We can now meet the premise of the evaluation rule (*Function*), and so deduce $(t_1 \ t_2)[s_1/x_1, \ldots, s_k/x_k] \to^e c$. Now because $u \lesssim^\circ_\sigma c$, we conclude

$$[\![t_1 \ t_2]\!]^e \rho[v_1/x_1, \ldots, v_k/x_k] \lesssim_\sigma (t_1 \ t_2)[s_1/x_1, \ldots, s_k/x_k].$$

$t \equiv$ **let** $x \Leftarrow t_1$ **in** t_2: Assume $t_1 : \sigma_1, t_2 : \sigma_2$. Let $x_1 : \tau_1, \ldots, x_k : \tau_k$ be all the free variables of t and $\lfloor v_1 \rfloor \lesssim_{\tau_1} s_1, \ldots, \lfloor v_k \rfloor \lesssim_{\tau_k} s_k$. From the denotational semantics, we see that if $[\![\textbf{ let } x \Leftarrow t_1 \textbf{ in } t_2]\!]^e \rho[v_1/x_1, \ldots, v_k/x_k] = \lfloor u \rfloor$ then there is $u_1 \in V^e_{\sigma_1}$, with

$$[\![t_1]\!]^e \rho[v_1/x_1, \ldots, v_k/x_k] = \lfloor u_1 \rfloor, \text{ and}$$
$$[\![t_2]\!]^e \rho[v_1/x_1, \ldots, v_k/x_k][u_1/x] = \lfloor u \rfloor.$$

(We need to write $\rho[v_1/x_1, \ldots, v_k/x_k][u_1/x]$ instead of $\rho[v_1/x_1, \ldots, v_k/x_k, u_1/x]$ because x may occur in $x_1, \cdots, x_k$.)
By induction there are canonical forms c_1, c_2 such that

$$u_1 \lesssim^\circ_{\sigma_1} c_1 \ \& \ t_1[s_1/x_1, \ldots, s_k/x_k] \to^e c_1, \text{ and}$$
$$u \lesssim^\circ_{\sigma_2} c_2 \ \& \ t_2[c_1/x][s_1/x_1, \ldots, s_k/x_k] \to^e c_2.$$

(Again, because x may occur in $x_1, \cdots, x_k$, we must be careful with the substitution $t_2[c_1/x][s_1/x_1, \ldots, s_k/x_k]$.)
Thus from the operational semantics,

$$(\textbf{ let } x \Leftarrow t_1 \textbf{ in } t_2)[s_1/x_1, \ldots, s_k/x_k] \to^e c_2.$$

We deduce

$$[\![\text{ let } x \Leftarrow t_1 \text{ in } t_2]\!]^e \rho[v_1/x_1, \ldots, v_k/x_k] \lesssim_{\sigma_2} (\text{ let } x \Leftarrow t_1 \text{ in } t_2)[s_1/x_1, \ldots, s_k/x_k].$$

$t \equiv \text{rec} \, y.(\lambda x.t_1)$: Assume $x : \sigma$ and $t_1 : \sigma_1$. Let $x_1 : \tau_1, \ldots, x_k : \tau_k$ be all the free variables of t and suppose $\lfloor v_1 \rfloor \lesssim_{\tau_1} s_1, \ldots, \lfloor v_k \rfloor \lesssim_{\tau_k} s_k$. Suppose

$$[\![\text{rec} \, y.(\lambda x.t_1)]\!]^e \rho[v_1/x_1, \ldots, v_k/x_k] = \lfloor \varphi \rfloor,$$

for $\varphi \in V^e_{\sigma \to \sigma_1}$. Then from its denotational definition, we see

$$\varphi = \mu \varphi. \, \lambda v. [\![t_1]\!]^e \rho[v_1/x_1, \ldots, v_k/x_k, v/x, \varphi/y].$$

Thus $\varphi = \bigsqcup_{n \in \omega} \varphi^{(n)}$ where each $\varphi^{(n)} \in V^e_{\sigma \to \sigma_1}$ is given inductively by:

$$\varphi^{(0)} = \bot_{V^e_{\sigma \to \sigma_1}}$$
$$\varphi^{(n+1)} = \lambda v. [\![t_1]\!]^e \rho[v_1/x_1, \ldots, v_k/x_k, v/x, \varphi^{(n)}/y].$$

We show by induction that

$$\varphi^{(n)} \lesssim^\circ_{\sigma \to \sigma_1} \lambda x.t_1[s_1/x_1, \ldots, s_k/x_k, t[s_1/x_1, \ldots, s_k/x_k]/y]. \tag{1}$$

By Lemma 11.12 it then follows that

$$\varphi \lesssim^\circ_{\sigma \to \sigma_1} \lambda x.t_1[s_1/x_1, \ldots, s_k/x_k, t[s_1/x_1, \ldots, s_k/x_k]/y].$$

Because

$$t[s_1/x_1, \ldots, s_k/x_k] \to^e \lambda x.t_1[s_1/x_1, \ldots, s_k/x_k, t[s_1/x_1, \ldots, s_k/x_k]/y]$$

we can then conclude that

$$\lfloor \varphi \rfloor \lesssim_{\sigma \to \sigma_1} t[s_1/x_1, \ldots, s_k/x_k],$$

as required. We now prove (1) by induction:
Basis $n = 0$: We require $\varphi^{(0)} \lesssim^\circ_{\sigma \to \sigma_1} \lambda x.t_1[s_1/x_1, \ldots, s_k/x_k, t[s_1/x_1, \ldots, s_k/x_k]/y]$ *i.e.*, $\varphi^0(v) \lesssim_{\sigma_1} t_1[s_1/x_1, \ldots, s_k/x_k, t[s_1/x_1, \ldots, s_k/x_k]/y, c/x]$ whenever $v \lesssim^\circ_\sigma c$. But this certainly holds, by Lemma 11.12(i), as $\varphi^{(0)}(v) = \bot$.
Induction step: Assume inductively that

$$\varphi^{(n)} \lesssim^\circ_{\sigma \to \sigma_1} \lambda x.t_1[s_1/x_1, \ldots, s_k/x_k, t[s_1/x_1, \ldots, s_k/x_k]/y].$$

Then
$$\lfloor \varphi^{(n)} \rfloor \lesssim_{\sigma \to \sigma_1} t[s_1/x_1, \ldots, s_k/x_k]. \tag{2}$$

We require
$$\varphi^{(n+1)} \lesssim^0_{\sigma \to \sigma_1} \lambda x.t_1[s_1/x_1, \ldots, s_k/x_k, t[s_1/x_1, \ldots, s_k/x_k]/y]$$

i.e. for all $v \lesssim^\circ_\sigma c$

$$\varphi^{(n+1)}(v) \lesssim_{\sigma_1} t_1[s_1/x_1, \ldots, s_k/x_k, \ c/x, \ t[s_1/x_1, \ldots, s_k/x_k]/y].$$

To this end, suppose $v \lesssim^\circ_\sigma c$, so
$$\lfloor v \rfloor \lesssim_\sigma c. \tag{3}$$

Recall $\varphi^{(n+1)}(v) = [\![t_1]\!]^e \rho[v_1/x_1, \ldots, v_k/x_k, v/x, \varphi^{(n)}/y]$, so, by the main structural induction hypothesis, using (2) and (3),

$$[\![t_1]\!]^e \rho[v_1/x_1, \ldots, v_k/x_k, v/x, \varphi^{(n)}/y] \lesssim_{\sigma_1} t_1[s_1/x_1, \ldots, s_k/x_k, c/x, t[s_1/x_1, \ldots, s_k/x_k]/y]$$

as was required. This completes the mathematical induction, and so the final case of the main structural induction. $\qquad \square$

As remarked early in this section, it follows that evaluation relation and denotational semantics match identically at the ground type **int**.

Corollary 11.15 *Assume t is a closed term with t : **int**. Then*

$$t \to^e n \ \text{ iff } \ [\![t]\!]^e \rho = \lfloor n \rfloor$$

for any $n \in \mathbf{N}$.

11.5   A lazy language

We now consider a language with higher types which evaluates in a call-by-name, or lazy, way. Again we will give an operational and denotational semantics and establish their agreement. The syntax is almost the same as that for the eager language; the only difference is in the syntax for recursion.

A recursive definition can now take the form

$$\mathbf{rec}\, x.t$$

where, unlike the eager case, we do not insist that the body t is an abstraction. Accompanying this is a slightly modified typing rule

$$\frac{x : \tau \quad t : \tau}{\mathbf{rec}\, x.t \ : \tau}$$

But for this slightly more liberal attitude to recursive definitions the syntax of the lazy language is the same as that for the eager one. Again, we will say a term t is *typable* when there is a type τ for which $t : \tau$ is derivable from the typing rules. The free variables of a term are defined as before but with the clause

$$FV(\mathbf{rec}\, x.t) = FV(t) \setminus \{x\}$$

for recursive definitions. A term with no free variables will be called closed.

11.6   Lazy operational semantics

Typable closed terms will evaluate to canonical forms. In the lazy regime canonical forms of ground and function types will be numerals and abstractions respectively. However, unlike the eager case a canonical form of product type will be any pair of typable closed terms, which are not necessarily canonical forms. The lazy canonical forms C_τ^l are given by induction on types τ:

Ground type: $n \in \mathbf{int}$.

Product type: $(t_1, t_2) \in C_{\tau_1 * \tau_2}^l$ if $t_1 : \tau_1$ & $t_2 : \tau_2$ with t_1 and t_2 closed.

Function type: $\lambda x.t \in C_{\tau_1 -> \tau_2}^l$ if $\lambda x.t : \tau_1 -> \tau_2$ with $\lambda x.t$ closed.

Lazy evaluation will be expressed by a relation

$$t \to^l c$$

between typable closed terms t and canonical forms c.

Evaluation rules

Canonical forms: $c \to^l c$ where $c \in C_\tau^l$

Operations: $\dfrac{t_1 \to^l n_1 \quad t_2 \to^l n_2}{t_1 \text{ op } t_2 \to^l n_1 \text{ op } n_2}$ where **op** is $+, -, \times$

$\dfrac{t_0 \to^l 0 \quad t_1 \to^l c_1}{\text{if } t_0 \text{ then } t_1 \text{ else } t_2 \to^l c_1} \qquad \dfrac{t_0 \to^l n \quad t_2 \to^l c_2 \quad n \not\equiv 0}{\text{if } t_0 \text{ then } t_1 \text{ else } t_2 \to^l c_2}$

Product: $\dfrac{t \to^l (t_1, t_2) \quad t_1 \to c_1}{\mathbf{fst}(t) \to^l c_1} \qquad \dfrac{t \to^l (t_1, t_2) \quad t_2 \to c_2}{\mathbf{snd}(t) \to^l c_2}$

Function: $\dfrac{t_1 \to^l \lambda x.t_1' \quad t_1'[t_2/x] \to^l c}{(t_1\ t_2) \to^l c}$

let: $\dfrac{t_2[t_1/x] \to^l c}{\mathbf{let}\ x \Leftarrow t_1 \mathbf{\ in\ } t_2 \to^l c}$

rec: $\dfrac{t[\mathbf{rec}\ x.t/x] \to^l c}{\mathbf{rec}\ x.t \to^l c}$

A notable difference with eager evaluation occurs in the case of function application; in lazy evaluation it is not first necessary to evaluate the argument to a function—the essence of laziness. Notice too that the rules for product need no longer stipulate how to evaluate pairs—they are already canonical forms and so no further rules are required to formalise their evaluation. As the components of a pair need not be canonical, extraction of the first and second components requires further evaluation. Because it is no longer the case that one unwinding of a recursive definition yields a canonical form the rule for the evaluation of recursive definitions is different from that with eager evaluation. Here in the lazy case we have chosen to interpret the **let** -expression as simply a way to introduce abbreviations.

For future reference we note here that lazy evaluation is deterministic and respects types.

Proposition 11.16 *If* $t \to^l c$ *and* $t \to^l c'$ *then* $c \equiv c'$. *If* $t \to^l c$ *and* $t : \tau$ *then* $c : \tau$.

Proof: By rule induction. $\square$

11.7 Lazy denotational semantics

A typable closed term can evaluate lazily to a canonical form or diverge. Accordingly we will take its denotation to be an element of $(V_\tau^l)_\perp$ where V_τ^l is a cpo of *values*, including the denotations of canonical forms of type τ.

We define V_τ^l by structural induction on the type τ:

$$
\begin{aligned}
V_{\text{int}}^l &= \mathbf{N} \\
V_{\tau_1 * \tau_2}^l &= (V_{\tau_1}^l)_\perp \times (V_{\tau_2}^l)_\perp \\
V_{\tau_1 -> \tau_2}^l &= [(V_{\tau_1}^l)_\perp \to (V_{\tau_2}^l)_\perp]
\end{aligned}
$$

These definitions reflect the ideas that a value of product type is any pair, even with diverging components, and that all that is required of a value of a function type is that it be recognised as a function, and indeed a function which need not evaluate its arguments first.

An environment for the lazy language is a function

$$
\rho : \mathbf{Var} \to \bigcup \{(V_\tau^l)_\perp \mid \tau \text{ a type}\}
$$

which respects types, *i.e.* if $x : \tau$ then $\rho(x) \in (V_\tau^l)_\perp$ for any variable x and type τ. We write $\mathbf{Env}^l$ for the cpo of such lazy environments.

Now we give the denotational semantics of our lazy language. A term t of type τ will be denoted by a function from environments $\mathbf{Env}^l$ to the cpo $(V_\tau^l)_\perp$. The denotation of typable terms t is given by structural induction, again staying within the metalanguage of Section 8.4.

$$
\begin{aligned}
[\![x]\!]^l &= \lambda\rho.\rho(x) \\
[\![n]\!]^l &= \lambda\rho.\lfloor n \rfloor \\
[\![t_1 \text{ op } t_2]\!]^l &= \lambda\rho.([\![t_1]\!]^l\rho \ op_\perp \ [\![t_2]\!]^l\rho) \text{ where } \mathbf{op} \text{ is } +, -, \times \\
[\![\text{if } t_0 \text{ then } t_1 \text{ else } t_2]\!]^l &= \lambda\rho. \ Cond([\![t_0]\!]^l\rho, [\![t_1]\!]^l\rho, [\![t_2]\!]^l\rho) \\
[\![(t_1, t_2)]\!]^l &= \lambda\rho.\lfloor([\![t_1]\!]^l\rho, [\![t_2]\!]^l\rho)\rfloor \\
[\![\mathbf{fst}(t)]\!]^l &= \lambda\rho.let \ v \Leftarrow [\![t]\!]^l\rho.\pi_1(v) \\
[\![\mathbf{snd}(t)]\!]^l &= \lambda\rho.let \ v \Leftarrow [\![t]\!]^l\rho.\pi_2(v) \\
[\![\lambda x.t]\!]^l &= \lambda\rho.\lfloor\lambda d \in (V_{\tau_1}^l)_\perp.[\![t]\!]^l\rho[d/x]\rfloor \\
&\quad\ \ \text{where } \lambda x.t : \tau_1 -> \tau_2 \\
[\![(t_1 \ t_2)]\!]^l &= \lambda\rho.let \ \varphi \Leftarrow [\![t_1]\!]^l\rho.\varphi([\![t_2]\!]^l\rho)
\end{aligned}
$$

$$[\![\text{ let } x \Leftarrow t_1 \text{ in } t_2]\!]^l = \lambda\rho.[\![t_2]\!]^l\rho[[\![t_1]\!]^l\rho/x]$$
$$[\![\text{rec } x.t]\!]^l = \lambda\rho.(\mu d.[\![t]\!]^l\rho[d/x])$$

We note a few facts for later.

Lemma 11.17 *Let t be a typable term. Let ρ, ρ' be environments which agree on* $\mathrm{FV}(t)$. *Then $[\![t]\!]^l\rho = [\![t]\!]^l\rho'$.*

Proof: A simple structural induction.   □

Lemma 11.18 *(Substitution Lemma)*
Let s be a closed term with $s : \tau$. Let x be a variable with $x : \tau$. Assume $t : \tau'$. Then $t[s/x] : \tau'$ and $[\![t[s/x]]\!]^l\rho = [\![t]\!]^l\rho[[\![s]\!]^l\rho/x]$.

Proof: By structural induction.   □

Lemma 11.19
(i) If $t : \tau$ then $[\![t]\!]^l\rho \in (V^l_\tau)_\bot$ for any environment $\rho \in \mathbf{Env}^l$.
(ii) If $c \in C^l_\tau$ then $[\![c]\!]^l\rho \neq \bot$, the bottom element of $(V^l_\tau)_\bot$, for any $\rho \in \mathbf{Env}^l$.

Proof: The proof of (i) is by a simple structural induction on t, and that of (ii) is by structural induction on canonical forms c.   □

11.8 Agreement of lazy semantics

We show that the denotational semantics is adequate with respect to the operational semantics in the sense that it respects the evaluation relation and agrees on when terms converge.

Let t be a typable closed term. Define operational convergence with respect to lazy evaluation by

$$t \downarrow^l \text{ iff } \exists c.t \rightarrow^l c.$$

Define denotational convergence by

$$t \Downarrow^l \text{ iff } \exists v \in V^l_\tau. [\![t]\!]^l\rho = \lfloor v \rfloor$$

where ρ is an arbitrary environment in $\mathbf{Env}^l$.

Suppose $t \downarrow^l$. Then $t \rightarrow^l c$ for some canonical form c. We will show it follows that $[\![t]\!]^l\rho = [\![c]\!]^l\rho$ for an arbitrary environment ρ, and because by Lemma 11.19 $c \Downarrow^l$, this will imply $t \Downarrow^l$. We will also establish the (harder) converse that if $t \Downarrow^l$ then $t \downarrow^l$; if t denotes

$\lfloor v \rfloor$ according to the denotational semantics then its evaluation converges to a canonical form c, necessarily denoting $\lfloor v \rfloor$. The general strategy of the proof follows that in the eager case quite closely.

First we show the denotational semantics respects the evaluation relation:

Lemma 11.20 *If* $t \to^l c$ *then* $[\![t]\!]^l \rho = [\![c]\!]^l \rho$, *for an arbitrary environment* ρ.

Proof: A proof is obtained by rule induction on the lazy evaluation rules. It follows the proof of Lemma 11.11 closely, and is left as an exercise. □

Exercise 11.21 Prove Lemma 11.20 above. □

We turn to the proof of the harder converse that $t \to^l c$, for some canonical form c, if t is closed and $t \Downarrow^l$. As in the eager case, this will be achieved by showing a stronger relationship, expressed by a logical relation, holds between a term and its denotation. We will define logical relations $\lesssim^\circ_\tau \subseteq V^l_\tau \times C^l_\tau$ on types τ. As before we extend these principal relations between values and canonical forms to relations between elements d of $(V^l_\tau)_\perp$ and closed terms t by defining

$$d \lesssim_\tau t \text{ iff}$$
$$\forall v \in V^l_\tau. \; d = \lfloor v \rfloor \Rightarrow \exists c. \; t \to^l c \; \& \; v \lesssim^\circ_\tau c.$$

The principal relations $\lesssim^\circ_\tau$ are defined by structural induction on types τ:

Ground type: $n \lesssim^\circ_{\mathbf{int}} n$, for all numbers n.

Product types: $(d_1, d_2) \lesssim^\circ_{\tau_1 * \tau_2} (t_1, t_2)$ iff $d_1 \lesssim_{\tau_1} t_1 \; \& \; d_2 \lesssim_{\tau_2} t_2$.

Function types: $\varphi \lesssim^\circ_{\tau_1 \to \tau_2} \lambda x.t$ iff $\forall d \in (V^l_{\tau_1})_\perp$, closed $u : \tau_1$. $d \lesssim_{\tau_1} u \Rightarrow \varphi(d) \lesssim_{\tau_2} t[u/x]$.

We observe facts analogous to those of Lemma 11.12:

Lemma 11.22 *Let* $t : \tau$. *Then*

(i) $\perp_{(V^l_\tau)_\perp} \lesssim_\tau t$.
(ii) *If* $d \sqsubseteq d'$ *and* $d' \lesssim_\tau t$ *then* $d \lesssim_\tau t$.
(iii) *If* $d_0 \sqsubseteq d_1 \sqsubseteq \ldots \sqsubseteq d_n \sqsubseteq \ldots$ *is an* ω-*chain in* $(V^l_\tau)_\perp$ *such that* $d_n \lesssim_\tau t$ *for all* $n \in \omega$ *then* $\bigsqcup_{n \in \omega} d_n \lesssim_\tau t$.

Proof: The proof is like that of 11.12. Property (i) follows directly by definition. Properties (ii) and (iii) are shown to hold for all terms by structural induction on types.

$\square$

Lemma 11.23 *Let t be a typable closed term. Then*

$$t \Downarrow^l \text{ implies } t \downarrow^l .$$

Proof: The proof is very similar in outline to that of Lemma 11.14. It can be shown by structural induction on terms that for all terms $t : \tau$ with free variables among $x_1 : \tau_1, \ldots, x_k : \tau_k$ that if $d_1 \lesssim_{\tau_1} s_1, \ldots d_k \lesssim_{\tau_k} s_k$ then

$$[\![t]\!]^l \rho[d_1/x_1, \ldots, d_k/x_k] \lesssim_\tau t[s_1/x_1, \ldots, s_k/x_k].$$

Taking t closed, it follows from the definition of $\lesssim_\tau$ that if $t \Downarrow^l$ then $[\![t]\!]^l \rho = \lfloor v \rfloor$ for some v, and hence that $t \to^l c$ for some canonical form c. Only the cases in the structural induction which are perhaps not straightforward modifications of the proof of Lemma 11.14 for eager evaluation are presented:

$t \equiv \mathbf{fst}(s)$: We are assuming $\mathbf{fst}(s)$ is typable, so s must have type $\sigma_1 * \sigma_2$. Suppose $x_1 : \tau_1, \ldots, x_k : \tau_k$ are all the free variables of t and that $d_1 \lesssim_{\tau_1} s_1, \ldots, d_k \lesssim_{\tau_k} s_k$. Assume $[\![\mathbf{fst}(s)]\!]^l \rho[d_1/x_1, \ldots, d_k/x_k] = \lfloor v_1 \rfloor$. Then from the denotational semantics, $[\![s]\!]^l \rho[d_1/x_1, \ldots, d_k/x_k] = \lfloor u \rfloor$ where $\lfloor v_1 \rfloor = \pi_1(u)$. By induction,

$$[\![s]\!]^l \rho[d_1/x_1, \ldots, d_k/x_k] \lesssim_{\sigma_1 * \sigma_2} s[s_1/x_1, \ldots, s_k/x_k].$$

Thus

$$s[s_1/x_1, \ldots, s_k/x_k] \to^l (t_1, t_2) \text{ where } u \lesssim^\circ_{\sigma_1 * \sigma_2} (t_1, t_2).$$

From the definition of $\lesssim^\circ_{\sigma_1 * \sigma_2}$,

$$\lfloor v_1 \rfloor \lesssim_{\sigma_1} t_1$$

and, further, by the definition of $\lesssim_{\sigma_1}$ we obtain

$$v_1 \lesssim^\circ_{\sigma_1} c_1 \ \& \ t_1 \to^l c_1$$

for some canonical form c_1. From the operational semantics we see

$$\mathbf{fst}(s)[s_1/x_1, \ldots, s_k/x_k] \equiv \mathbf{fst}(s[s_1/x_1, \ldots, s_k/x_k]) \to^l c_1$$

making $[\![\mathbf{fst}(s)]\!]^l \rho[d_1/x_1, \ldots, d_k/x_k] \lesssim_{\sigma_1} \mathbf{fst}(s)[s_1/x_1, \ldots, s_k/x_k]$, as required.

$t \equiv t_1 \; t_2$: Suppose $t_1 : \sigma_2 \!-\!> \sigma$, $t_2 : \sigma_2$. Assume t has free variables $x_1 : \tau_1, \ldots, x_k : \tau_k$ and that $d_1 \lesssim_{\tau_1} s_1, \ldots, d_k \lesssim_{\tau_k} s_k$. Let

$$d = \llbracket t_2 \rrbracket^l \rho[d_1/x_1, \ldots, d_k/x_k].$$

From the denotational semantics, we see

$$\llbracket t_1 \; t_2 \rrbracket^l \rho[d_1/x_1, \ldots, d_k/x_k] =$$
$$let \; \varphi \Leftarrow \llbracket t_1 \rrbracket^l \rho[d_1/x_1, \ldots, d_k/x_k]. \; \varphi(d)$$

Assume $\llbracket t_1 \; t_2 \rrbracket^l \rho[d_1/x_1, \ldots, d_k/x_k] = \lfloor u \rfloor$, for $u \in V_r^l$. Then there is φ such that

$$\llbracket t_1 \rrbracket^l \rho[d_1/x_1, \ldots, d_k/x_k] = \lfloor \varphi \rfloor$$

with

$$\varphi(d) = \lfloor u \rfloor.$$

Noting that by induction we have

$$\llbracket t_1 \rrbracket^l \rho[d_1/x_1, \ldots, d_k/x_k] \lesssim_{\sigma_2 \to \sigma} t_1[s_1/x_1, \ldots, s_k/x_k],$$

we obtain

$$t_1[s_1/x_1, \ldots, s_k/x_k] \to^l \lambda x.t_1' \; \& \; \varphi \lesssim^\circ_{\sigma_2 \to \sigma} \lambda x.t_1'$$

for a canonical form $\lambda x.t_1'$. Also, by induction, as $d = \llbracket t_2 \rrbracket^l \rho[d_1/x_1, \ldots, d_k/x_k]$,

$$d \lesssim_{\sigma_2} t_2[s_1/x_1, \ldots, s_k/x_k].$$

Now, from the definition of $\lesssim^\circ_{\sigma_2 \to \sigma}$, we get

$$\varphi(d) \lesssim_\sigma t_1'[t_2[s_1/x_1, \ldots, s_k/x_k]/x].$$

As $\varphi(d) = \lfloor u \rfloor$, there is $c \in C_\sigma^l$ such that

$$t_1'[t_2[s_1/x_1, \ldots, s_k/x_k]/x] \to^l c \; \& \; u \lesssim^\circ_\sigma c.$$

From the operational semantics we deduce

$$(t_1 \; t_2)[s_1/x_1, \ldots, s_k/x_k] \to^l c$$

and can conclude

$$\llbracket t_1 \; t_2 \rrbracket^l \rho[d_1/x_1, \ldots, d_k/x_k] \lesssim_\sigma (t_1 \; t_2)[s_1/x_1, \ldots, s_k/x_k],$$

as required.

$t \equiv \mathbf{rec}\, y.t_1$: Assume $y : \sigma$ and $t_1 : \sigma$. Let $x_1 : \tau_1, \ldots, x_k : \tau_k$ be all the free variables of t and suppose $d_1 \lesssim_{\tau_1} s_1, \ldots, d_k \lesssim_{\tau_k} s_k$. From the denotational semantics, we see

$$\theta =_{def} [\![\mathbf{rec}\, y.t_1]\!]^l \rho[d_1/x_1, \ldots, d_k/x_k] = \mu\theta.\, [\![t_1]\!]^l \rho[d_1/x_1, \ldots, d_k/x_k, \theta/y].$$

Thus $\theta = \bigsqcup_{n \in \omega} \theta^{(n)}$ where each $\theta^{(n)} \in (V_\sigma^l)_\perp$ is given inductively by:

$$\theta^{(0)} = \perp_{(V_\sigma^l)_\perp}$$
$$\theta^{(n+1)} = [\![t_1]\!]^l \rho[d_1/x_1, \ldots, d_k/x_k, \theta^{(n)}/y].$$

We show by induction that

$$\theta^{(n)} \lesssim_\sigma \mathbf{rec}\, y.t_1[s_1/x_1, \ldots, s_k/x_k]. \tag{1}$$

(Note that all the free variables $x_1, \cdots, x_k$ of $\mathbf{rec}\, y.t_1$ must be distinct from y so which ever way we associate the substitution, as

$$(\mathbf{rec}\, y.t_1)[s_1/x_1, \ldots, s_k/x_k]$$

or as

$$\mathbf{rec}\, y.(t_1[s_1/x_1, \ldots, s_k/x_k])$$

yields the same term.)

By Lemma 11.22 it then follows that

$$\theta \lesssim_\sigma \mathbf{rec}\, y.t_1[s_1/x_1, \ldots, s_k/x_k].$$

We now prove (1) by induction:

Basis $n = 0$: We require $\varphi^{(0)} \lesssim_\sigma \mathbf{rec}\, y.t_1[s_1/x_1, \ldots, s_k/x_k]$. This certainly holds, by Lemma 11.22(i), as $\theta^{(0)} = \perp$.

Induction step: Assume inductively that

$$\theta^{(n)} \lesssim_\sigma \mathbf{rec}\, y.t_1[s_1/x_1, \ldots, s_k/x_k].$$

Now by structural induction

$$\begin{aligned}
\theta^{(n+1)} &= [\![t_1]\!]^l \rho[d_1/x_1, \ldots, d_k/x_k, \theta^{(n)}/y] \\
&\lesssim_\sigma t_1[s_1/x_1, \ldots, s_k/x_k, \mathbf{rec}\, y.t_1[s_1/x_1, \ldots, s_k/x_k]/y] \\
&\equiv t_1[\mathbf{rec}\, y.t_1/y][s_1/x_1, \ldots, s_k/x_k].
\end{aligned}$$

From the operational semantics we see that

$$\mathbf{rec}\, y.t_1[s_1/x_1,\ldots,s_k/x_k] \to^l c \text{ if } t_1[\mathbf{rec}\, y.t_1/y][s_1/x_1,\ldots,s_k/x_k] \to^l c$$

for a canonical form c. Now, from the definition of $\lesssim_\sigma$ we conclude

$$\theta^{(n+1)} \lesssim_\sigma \mathbf{rec}\, y.t_1[s_1/x_1,\ldots,s_k/x_k].$$

This completes the mathematical induction required in this case. $\square$

As a corollary, we deduce that the evaluation relation and denotational semantics match at the ground type **int**.

Corollary 11.24 *Assume t is a closed term with $t :$ **int**. Then*

$$t \to^l n \text{ iff } [\![t]\!]^l\rho = \lfloor n \rfloor$$

for any $n \in \mathbf{N}$.

11.9 Fixed-point operators

The denotational semantics give mathematical models in which to reason about the evaluation of terms in our language with higher types. As an illustration we will study how fixed-point operators can be expressed in both the eager and lazy variants of the language.

At first we assume evaluation is lazy. A fixed-point operator is a closed term Y of type $(\tau\!\!-\!\!>\tau)\!\!-\!\!>\tau$ which when applied to an abstraction F yields a fixed point of F *i.e.*

$$[\![F(YF)]\!]^l\rho = [\![YF]\!]^l\rho$$

Given that Y should satisfy this equation, a reasonable guess of a suitable definition is

$$\mathbf{rec}\, Y.(\lambda f.f(Yf)).$$

Indeed, according to the denotational semantics this does define a fixed-point operator.

To see this we consider the denotation of

$$R \equiv \mathbf{rec}\, Y.(\lambda f.f(Yf))$$

—assumed well-typed so $R : (\tau\!\!-\!\!>\tau)\!\!-\!\!>\tau$. According to the denotational semantics

$$
\begin{aligned}
[\![R]\!]^l\rho &= \mu U.[\![\lambda f.f(Yf)]\!]^l\rho[U/Y] \\
&= \mu U\lfloor\lambda\varphi.\, let\ \varphi' \Leftarrow \varphi.\ \varphi'(let\ U' \Leftarrow U.\ U'(\varphi))\rfloor
\end{aligned}
$$

Before proceeding it is helpful to simplify this expression with the help of continuous functions

$$down_C : C_\perp \longrightarrow C$$

to a cpo C, with bottom $\perp_C$, from its lifting $C_\perp$. Such a function is given by

$$down_C(\varphi) = let\ \varphi' \Leftarrow \varphi.\ \varphi'$$

or, equivalently, as

$$down_C(\varphi) = \begin{cases} \varphi' & \text{if } \varphi = \lfloor\varphi'\rfloor \\ \perp_C & \text{otherwise.} \end{cases}$$

We are concerned with such functions in the special case that C is a function space, say of the form $D \to E$, with E a cpo with bottom. In this case:

Lemma 11.25 *Let C be the cpo $[D \to E]$ where E is a cpo with bottom element $\perp_E$. Then*

$$(down_C(\varphi))(d) = let\ \varphi' \Leftarrow \varphi.\ \varphi'(d)$$

for $\varphi \in C_\perp, d \in D$.

Proof: The equality is clear in the case where φ has the form $\lfloor\varphi'\rfloor$. In the case where $\varphi = \perp$, the right-hand-side is $\perp_E$ which agrees with the left-hand-side which is $(\lambda d \in D.\perp_E)(d) = \perp_E$.   □

Both $V^l_{\tau \to \tau}$ and $V^l_{(\tau \to \tau) \to \tau}$ are cpo's with bottom, of the form required by the lemma. Accordingly, there are functions

$$down : (V^l_{\tau \to \tau})_\perp \to V^l_{\tau \to \tau}\ and$$
$$down : (V^l_{(\tau \to \tau) \to \tau})_\perp \to V^l_{(\tau \to \tau) \to \tau}$$

(where it's hoped the dropped subscripts on the two different "*down*" functions are forgiven).

Using them we can simplify $[\![R]\!]^l\rho$:

$$[\![R]\!]^l\rho = \mu U.\lfloor\lambda\varphi.(down(\varphi))((down(U))(\varphi))\rfloor.$$

From this simplified form of denotation of R we see that

$$\begin{aligned} [\![R]\!]^l\rho &= \bigsqcup_{n\in\omega} U^{(n)} \\ \text{where}\quad U^{(0)} &= \perp \\ U^{(1)} &= \lfloor\lambda\varphi.(down(\varphi))(\perp(\varphi))\rfloor \\ &= \lfloor\lambda\varphi.(down(\varphi))(\perp)\rfloor \end{aligned}$$

and, inductively,

$$U^{(n)} \;=\; \lfloor \lambda\varphi.(down(\varphi))((down(U^{(n-1)}))(\varphi)) \rfloor$$
$$\;=\; \lfloor \lambda\varphi.(down(\varphi))^n(\bot) \rfloor$$

Thus

$$[\![R]\!]^l\rho \;=\; \bigsqcup_{n\in\omega} U^{(n)}$$
$$\;=\; \bigsqcup_{n\in\omega} \lfloor \lambda\varphi.(down(\varphi))^n(\bot) \rfloor$$
$$\;=\; \lfloor \bigsqcup_{n\in\omega} \lambda\varphi.(down(\varphi))^n(\bot) \rfloor \quad \text{by the continuity of } \lfloor\text{-}\rfloor,$$
$$\;=\; \lfloor \lambda\varphi.\bigsqcup_{n\in\omega}(down(\varphi))^n(\bot) \rfloor$$

as lubs of functions are determined pointwise,

$$\;=\; \lfloor \lambda\varphi.\, fix(down(\varphi)) \rfloor \quad \text{by the definition of } fix.$$

From this characterisation, it follows that R is a fixed-point operator. In the case where F is an abstraction of type $\tau \!-\!> \tau$ we have

$$[\![F]\!]^l\rho = \lfloor \varphi' \rfloor$$

for some $\varphi' : (V^l_\tau)_\bot \to (V^l_\tau)_\bot$. Hence

$$[\![F(RF)]\!]^l\rho \;=\; \varphi'([\![RF]\!]^l\rho)$$
$$\;=\; \varphi'(fix(down(\lfloor \varphi' \rfloor)))$$
$$\;=\; \varphi'(fix(\varphi'))$$
$$\;=\; fix(\varphi')$$
$$\;=\; [\![RF]\!]^l\rho$$

Exercise 11.26 Show even if $[\![F]\!]^l\rho = \bot$ for $F : \tau \!-\!> \tau$ it holds that

$$[\![F(RF)]\!]^l\rho = [\![RF]\!]^l\rho.$$

$\square$

The characterisation of $[\![R]\!]^l\rho$ enables us to show that the programs

$$R(\lambda x.t) \qquad\qquad \mathbf{rec}\, x.t$$

are equivalent in the sense of having the same denotation. We simply argue from the denotational semantics that

$$
\begin{aligned}
[\![R(\lambda x.t)]\!]^l \rho &= \mathit{fix}(\lambda d.[\![t]\!]^l \rho[d/x]) \\
&= \mu d.[\![t]\!]^l \rho[d/x] \\
&= [\![\mathbf{rec}\ x.t]\!]^l \rho
\end{aligned}
$$

So the definition of fixed-point operators is reasonably straightforward with lazy evaluation. What about under eager evaluation? The same definition no longer works, as will now be shown. From the denotational semantics of the eager languages we see

$$
\begin{aligned}
[\![R]\!]^e \rho &= \lfloor \mu\, U.(\lambda\varphi.[\![f(Yf)]\!]^e \rho[\varphi/f, U/Y]) \rfloor \\
&= \lfloor \mu\, U.(\lambda\varphi.\ \mathit{let}\ v \Leftarrow U(\varphi).\ \varphi(v)) \rfloor.
\end{aligned}
$$

Now we can argue that

$$
\mu\, U.(\lambda\varphi.\ \mathit{let}\ v \Leftarrow U(\varphi).\varphi(v)) = \lambda\varphi.\bot
$$

by considering its approximants. We know this fixed point is $\bigsqcup_{n \in \omega} U^{(n)}$ where

$$
\begin{aligned}
U^{(0)} &= \lambda\varphi.\ \bot \text{ and, inductively,} \\
U^{(n)} &= \lambda\varphi.(\mathit{let}\ v \Leftarrow U^{(n-1)}(\varphi).\ \varphi(v)) \text{ for } n > 0.
\end{aligned}
$$

From this we see that

$$
\begin{aligned}
U^{(1)} &= \lambda\varphi.(\mathit{let}\ v \Leftarrow \bot.\ \varphi(v)) \\
&= \lambda\varphi.\ \bot
\end{aligned}
$$

and similarly by a simple induction that

$$
\begin{aligned}
U^{(n)} &= \lambda\varphi.(\mathit{let}\ v \Leftarrow U^{n-1}(\varphi).\varphi(v)) \\
&= \lambda\varphi.\bot
\end{aligned}
$$

for all $n > 0$. It follows that

$$
\mu\, U.(\lambda\varphi.\ \mathit{let}\ v \Leftarrow U(\varphi).\ \varphi(v)) = \lambda\varphi.\ \bot
$$

and hence that

$$
[\![R]\!]^e \rho = \lfloor \lambda\varphi.\ \bot \rfloor.
$$

Hence

$$
[\![R(\lambda x.\ t)]\!]^e \rho = \bot.
$$

Instead of delivering a fixed point, an application $R(\lambda x.t)$ yields $\bot$, a diverging computation. Note the key reason why this is so: According to the denotational semantics the definition of $U^{(n)}$ involves the prior evaluation of $U^{(n-1)}(\varphi)$, on arguments φ, and inductively this is always $\bot$.

Exercise 11.27 Argue from the operational semantics that $R(\lambda x.t)$ diverges in the sense that there is no canonical form c such that $R(\lambda x.t) \to^e c$. $\Box$

So how can we define a fixed-point operator under eager evaluation? The key idea is to use abstraction to delay evaluation and in this way mimic the lazy language and its simple expression of fixed-point operators.

Notice an anomaly. Under either eager or lazy evaluation the two terms

$$F(YF), \qquad \lambda x.((F(YF))x)$$

are not evaluated in the same way; the latter is a canonical form and so evaluates directly to itself while the former involves the prior evaluation of F, and also (YF) in the eager case. This is in contrast to mathematics where a mathematical function

$$\varphi : X \to Y$$

is always the same (*i.e.* the same set of ordered pairs) as the function

$$\lambda x \in X.\varphi(x) : X \to Y.$$

We study how this distinction is reflected in the denotational semantics.

Assume τ is a function type of the form $\sigma \text{-}{>} \sigma'$, and that

$$f : \tau \text{-}{>} \tau, \ Y : (\tau \text{-}{>} \tau) \text{-}{>} \tau \text{ and } x : \sigma$$

are variables. We consider the denotations of the terms

$$f(Yf), \qquad \lambda x.((f(Yf))x),$$

both of type τ, in an environment ρ where $\rho(f) = \varphi$ and $\rho(Y) = U$. The simplification of the denotations will make use of the function

$$down : (V_\tau^e)_\bot \to V_\tau^e$$

taking $\lfloor v \rfloor$ to v and $\bot$ to the always $\bot$ function in V_τ^e. As earlier, by Lemma 11.25, we observe that for $\psi \in (V_\tau^e)_\bot$ we have

$$down(\psi) = \lambda w. \ let \ \theta \Leftarrow \psi. \ \theta(w) \qquad (*)$$

a fact which we will make use of shortly. Now, from the denotational semantics, we see on the one hand that

$$[\![f(Yf)]\!]^e\rho = let\ v \Leftarrow U(\varphi).\varphi(v)$$

which may be $\bot \in (V^e_\tau)_\bot$. On the other hand

$$
\begin{aligned}
[\![\lambda x.((f(Yf)x)]\!]^e\rho &= \lfloor \lambda w.\ let\ \theta \Leftarrow [\![f(Yf)]\!]^e\rho.\ \theta(w)\rfloor \\
&= \lfloor \lambda w.\ (down([\![f(Yf)]\!]^e\rho)(w))\rfloor \quad \text{by } (*) \\
&= \lfloor down([\![f(Yf)]\!]^e\rho)\rfloor \\
&\qquad \text{a property of } \textit{mathematical} \text{ functions,} \\
&= \lfloor down(let\ v \Leftarrow U(\varphi).\ \varphi(v))\rfloor
\end{aligned}
$$

which is always a non-$\bot$ element of $(V^e_\tau)_\bot$. This distinction is central to our obtaining a fixed-point operator under eager evaluation.

Redefine R to be

$$\textbf{rec } Y.\ (\lambda f.\ \lambda x.((f(Yf))x)).$$

Then, from the denotational semantics, we obtain

$$[\![R]\!]^e\rho = \lfloor \mu U.\lambda\varphi.[\![\lambda x.(f(Yf))x]\!]^e\rho[\varphi/f, U/Y]\rfloor$$

We have already simplified the denotation of $\lambda x.((f(Yf))x)$, and using this we obtain

$$[\![R]\!]^e\rho = \lfloor \mu U.\lambda\varphi.\lfloor down(let\ v \Leftarrow U(\varphi).\ \varphi(v))\rfloor\rfloor$$

The fixed point

$$\mu U.\lambda\varphi.\lfloor down(let\ v \Leftarrow U(\varphi).\varphi(v))\rfloor$$

is $\bigsqcup_{n\in\omega} U^{(n)}$, the least upper bound of approximants given inductively by:

$$
\begin{aligned}
U^{(0)} &= \lambda\varphi.\bot, \\
U^{(n)} &= \lambda\varphi.\lfloor down(let\ v \Leftarrow U^{(n-1)}(\varphi).\ \varphi(v))\rfloor, \text{ for } n > 0.
\end{aligned}
$$

Thus we obtain that

$$
\begin{aligned}
U^{(1)} &= \lambda\varphi.\lfloor down(\bot)\rfloor = \lambda\varphi.\lfloor\bot\rfloor \\
U^{(2)} &= \lambda\varphi.\lfloor down(\varphi(\bot))\rfloor = \lambda\varphi.\lfloor (down \circ \varphi)(\bot)\rfloor
\end{aligned}
$$

and, by induction, that

$$U^{(n)} = \lambda\varphi.\lfloor (down \circ \varphi)^{(n-1)}(\bot)\rfloor.$$

It follows that

$$\llbracket R \rrbracket^e \rho \;=\; \lfloor \bigsqcup_{n \in \omega} U^{(n)} \rfloor$$

$$=\; \lfloor \bigsqcup_{n \in \omega} (\lambda \varphi.\lfloor (down \circ \varphi)^{(n-1)}(\bot)\rfloor)\rfloor$$

$$=\; \lfloor \lambda \varphi.\lfloor \bigsqcup_{n \in \omega}(down \circ \varphi)^{(n-1)}(\bot)\rfloor\rfloor$$

as lubs of functions are determined pointwise and $\lfloor\,\text{-}\,\rfloor$ is continuous,

$$=\; \lfloor \lambda \varphi.\lfloor fix(down \circ \varphi)\rfloor\rfloor.$$

It now can be shown that:

$$\llbracket R(\lambda y.\lambda x.t) \rrbracket^e \rho = \llbracket \textbf{rec } y.(\lambda x.t) \rrbracket^e \rho$$

Argue from the denotational semantics that

$$\llbracket R(\lambda y.\lambda x.t) \rrbracket^e \rho$$

$$=\; (\lambda \varphi.\lfloor fix(down \circ \varphi)\rfloor)(\lambda \theta.\lfloor \lambda v.\llbracket t \rrbracket^e \rho[v/x, \theta/y]\rfloor)$$

$$=\; \lfloor fix(down \circ (\lambda \theta.\lfloor \lambda v.\llbracket t \rrbracket^e \rho[v/x, \theta/y]\rfloor))\rfloor$$

$$=\; \lfloor fix(\lambda \theta.\lambda v.\llbracket t \rrbracket^e \rho[v/x, \theta/y])\rfloor \text{ by recalling how } down \text{ acts,}$$

$$=\; \lfloor \mu\, \theta.\lambda v.\llbracket t \rrbracket^e \rho[v/x, \theta/y]\rfloor$$

$$=\; \llbracket \textbf{rec } y.(\lambda x.t) \rrbracket^e \rho.$$

11.10   Observations and full abstraction

We have just seen examples of reasoning within the mathematical model provided by denotational semantics to explain the behaviour of programs. According to the denotational semantics certain terms behave as fixed-point operators. Such facts are hard to prove, or even state correctly, solely in terms of the operational semantics. One might wonder why it is we are justified in using the denotational semantics to make conclusions about how programs would run on a machine, assuming of course that the implementation is faithful to our operational semantics. Why are we justified? Because the operational and denotational semantics agree on the "observations of interest." If the denotational semantics says that a closed term of type **int** denotes a particular integer, then it will evaluate to precisely that integer, and conversely. For other types, if a term converges, in the sense of not denoting $\bot$, then its evaluation will converge too, and again conversely. The two semantics, denotational and operational, agree on observations telling whether or not a term converges, and what integer a term of type **int** evaluates to. This agreement is the content of the results expressing the *adequacy* of the denotational with respect to the operational semantics. In fact, we can restrict the observations to just those of convergence. The adequacy with respect to convergence will ensure that the two semantics also agree on how terms of type **int** evaluate. The simple argument is based on enclosing terms in a context

$$\text{if - then } 0 \text{ else Diverge}$$

where Diverge : **int** is a closed term which diverges. For a closed term t : **int** and number n, argue for both the eager and lazy semantics that:

$$t \to n \iff \text{if } (t-n) \text{ then } 0 \text{ else Diverge} \downarrow$$
$$\iff \text{if } (t-n) \text{ then } 0 \text{ else Diverge} \Downarrow \qquad \text{by adequacy,}$$
$$\iff [\![t]\!]\rho = n.$$

Is the evaluation of type **int** and convergence a reasonable choice of observation? Certainly many implementations report back to the user precisely the kind of convergence behaviour we have discussed, only yielding concrete values for concrete datatypes like integers or lists. From that point of view our choice is reasonable. On the other hand, should one broaden one's interest to other properties, such as how long it takes to evaluate a term, one would expect more detailed observations, and, to respect these, more detailed semantics.

It is also possible to restrict the observations, for which a cruder denotational semantics can suffice for a fixed operational semantics. To illustrate this we give an alternative denotational semantics for the lazy language. This one will ignore the convergence behaviour at higher types in general, but still ensure that at ground type **int**

$$t \to^l n \text{ iff } [\![t]\!]\rho = \lfloor n \rfloor$$

for closed term t : **int** and integer n. It is concerned with observations of what printable values ensue from the evaluation of terms of type **int**.

Define D_τ, the cpo of denotations at type τ, by structural induction on τ:

$$
\begin{aligned}
D_{\textbf{int}} &= \mathbf{N}_\perp \\
D_{\tau_1 * \tau_2} &= D_{\tau_1} \times D_{\tau_2} \\
D_{\tau_1 -> \tau_2} &= [D_{\tau_1} \to D_{\tau_2}]
\end{aligned}
$$

An environment for the lazy language is now taken to be a function

$$\rho : \mathbf{Var} \to \bigcup \{ D_\tau \mid \tau \text{ a type} \}$$

such that if $x : \tau$ then $\rho(x) \in D_\tau$ for any variable x and type τ. Write **Env** for the cpo of environments. As earlier, the denotation of typable terms t is an element $[t]$ given by structural induction, staying within the metalanguage of Section 8.4.

$$
\begin{aligned}
[x] &= \lambda\rho.\rho(x) \\
[n] &= \lambda\rho.\lfloor n \rfloor \\
[t_1 \text{ op } t_2] &= \lambda\rho.([t_1]\rho \text{ op}_\perp [t_2]\rho) \text{ where } \mathbf{op} \text{ is } +, -, \times \\
[\text{if } t_0 \text{ then } t_1 \text{ else } t_2] &= \lambda\rho. \ Cond([t_0]\rho, [t_1]\rho, [t_2]\rho) \\
[(t_1, t_2)] &= \lambda\rho.([t_1]\rho, [t_2]\rho) \\
[\mathbf{fst}(t)] &= \lambda\rho.\pi_1([t]\rho) \\
[\mathbf{snd}(t)] &= \lambda\rho.\pi_2([t]\rho) \\
[\lambda x.t] &= \lambda\rho.\lambda d \in D_{\tau_1}.[t]\rho[d/x] \\
&\quad \text{where } \lambda x.t : \tau_1 - > \tau_2 \\
[(t_1 \ t_2)] &= \lambda\rho.[t_1]\rho([t_2]\rho) \\
[\ \text{let } x \Leftarrow t_1 \text{ in } t_2] &= \lambda\rho.[t_2]\rho[[t_1]\rho/x] \\
[\mathbf{rec} \ x.t] &= \lambda\rho.(\mu d.[t]\rho[d/x])
\end{aligned}
$$

Exercise 11.28
(1) Assume variables $x : \mathbf{int}- > \mathbf{int}$, $w : \mathbf{int}- > \mathbf{int}$, and $y : \mathbf{int}$. What are the denotations of $((\lambda x.x) \ \Omega)$ and $((\lambda x.\lambda y.(x \ y))\Omega)$, where $\Omega \equiv \mathbf{rec} \ w.w$?
(2) Show that with respect to the operational semantics of the lazy language

$$
t \rightarrow^l c \Rightarrow [t]\rho = [c]\rho,
$$

for an arbitrary environment ρ. (In the argument, by rule induction, you need only do enough cases to be convincing. You may assume a variant of the Substitution Lemma but state it clearly.)
(3) Show for a closed term $t : \mathbf{int}$ that

$$
t \rightarrow^l n \text{ iff } [t]\rho = \lfloor n \rfloor
$$

for any $n \in \mathbf{N}$. It is suggested that you use logical relations $\precsim_\tau$, between elements of D_τ and closed terms of type τ, given by structural induction on types in the following way:

$$
d \precsim_{\mathbf{int}} t \iff \forall n \in \mathbf{N}. \ d = \lfloor n \rfloor \Rightarrow t \rightarrow^l n,
$$

$$
d \precsim_{\tau_1 * \tau_2} t \iff \pi_1(d) \precsim_{\tau_1} \mathbf{fst}(t) \ \& \ \pi_2(d) \precsim_{\tau_2} \mathbf{snd}(t),
$$

$$
d \precsim_{\tau_1 \rightarrow \tau_2} t \iff \forall e, s. \ e \precsim_{\tau_1} s \Rightarrow d(e) \precsim_{\tau_2} (t \ s).
$$

First show, by structural induction on types τ, that

$$[d \lesssim_\tau t_1 \ \& \ (t_1 \rightarrow^l c \Rightarrow t_2 \rightarrow^l c)] \Rightarrow d \lesssim_\tau t_2.$$

□

Results expressing the adequacy of a denotational semantics with respect to an operational semantics, for a choice of observations, are vital to justify the use of the more mathematically tractible model of denotational semantics to predict and reason about program behaviour. There is another important criterion for a denotational semantics to fit well with a choice of observations. This is that the semantics be *fully abstract*. Full abstraction is often a much more difficult property for a denotational semantics to fulfil than adequacy, and fortunately it is less vital. But it is a useful property to have and is significant, in part, because attempts at obtaining fully abstract semantics have sparked off important lines of research. This is because achieving full abstraction for languages like those of this chapter, involves formalising key operational ideas like sequentiality within the mathematics of domain theory.

To define full abstraction with respect to a particular choice of observations we first show how such a choice induces an equivalence on terms. This requires the notion of a context. Intuitively a context is a term $C[\ ]$ with a "hole" $[\ ]$ into which we can plug typable term t to obtain a typable term $C[t]$; formally, it can be defined to be a term with a distinguished free variable, which can be substituted for. With respect to some choice of observations, for terms t_1, t_2 of the same type, write $t_1 \sim t_2$ iff for all contexts $C[\ ]$ for which $C[t_1]$ and $C[t_2]$ are closed, typable terms, the observations on $C[t_1]$ and $C[t_2]$ agree. For example, if the observations of interest concern just the convergence behaviour of terms, we would have

$$t_1 \sim t_2 \text{ iff } (C[t_1] \downarrow \Longleftrightarrow C[t_2] \downarrow),$$

for all contexts $C[\ ]$ for which $C[t_1]$ and $C[t_2]$ are closed and typable. Note, that although the equivalence relation $\sim$ has been defined via the operational semantics, it could equally well have been defined from a denotational semantics, provided it is adequate. Say a denotational semantics is *fully abstract*, with respect to the observations, iff

$$[\![t_1]\!] = [\![t_2]\!] \text{ iff } t_1 \sim t_2.$$

In fact, the "only if" direction of the equivalence follows provided the denotational semantics is adequate (why?), so the extra difficulty is in obtaining the converse "if" direction.

So, in a sense, a fully abstract semantics is one which makes only those distinctions which are forced by differences in the observations. Unfortunately, full abstraction can be hard to achieve and, in particular, it does not hold of either our eager or lazy denotational semantics with respect to observations of convergence (or of the denotational semantics addressing just observations of evaluation at type **int**, considered in the exercise above).

We sketch why the quest for full abstraction for languages with higher types has motivated a study of sequentiality at higher types. The difficulty in obtaining full abstraction comes about because there are terms, t_1, t_2 say, which cannot be distinguished by contexts definable in the programming language and yet which have different denotations. How is this? It arises because in our cpo's of denotations there are elements like "parallel or"[2] which cannot be defined by terms, and t_1, t_2 act differently on these. The terms have a sequential character not shared by these "parasitic" elements. So, a method suggests itself: to achieve full abstraction redefine the constructions on cpo's to stop these undefinable elements from appearing, and in particular, instead of taking all continuous functions in the function space restrict to "sequential" functions. This has proved very hard to do, at least in a syntax-independent way, without resorting to some form of encoding of the operational semantics in the cpo constructions. The quest for full abstraction has spurred on the search for a general definition of sequentiality. It should be born in mind that the success of this search, measured perhaps against some convincing operational analysis of sequentiality, might not lead automatically to a solution of the full abstraction problem.

11.11 Sums

We consider how to extend our language to include a sum on types. We include a construction $\tau_1 + \tau_2$ between types τ_1, τ_2. Accordingly, the language of terms is extended to include injections of terms, **inl** (t), **inr** (t), into the left and right of a sum. Functions from a sum can be described with a case construction

$$\textbf{case } t \textbf{ of inl}(x_1).\, t_1,\ \textbf{inr}(x_2).\, t_2.$$

Free occurrences of x_1 in t_1, and x_2 in t_2, are bound in this new construct which has free variables

$$\text{FV}(\textbf{case } t \textbf{ of inl}(x_1).\, t_1,\ \textbf{inr}(x_2).\, t_2) = \text{FV}(t) \cup (\text{FV}(t_1) \setminus \{x_1\}) \cup (\text{FV}(t_2) \setminus \{x_2\}).$$

---

[2] "Parallel or" is a continuous function por on $\mathbf{T}_\perp$ extending the usual disjunction on truth values but with the property that $por(\textbf{true}, \perp) = por(\perp, \textbf{true}) = \textbf{true}$; it is as if the the function inspects each argument in parallel, and not sequentially, returning **true** if either argument is **true**.

Informally, such a case construction examines the form of t, and evaluates according to whether it lies in the left or right of a sum. There are these additional typing rules to ensure the well-formedness of terms:

$$\frac{t : \tau_1}{\mathbf{inl}(t) : \tau_1 + \tau_2} \qquad \frac{t : \tau_2}{\mathbf{inr}(t) : \tau_1 + \tau_2}$$

$$\frac{t : \tau_1 + \tau_2 \quad x_1 : \tau_1 \quad x_2 : \tau_2 \quad t_1 : \tau \quad t_2 : \tau}{\mathbf{case} \; t \; \mathbf{of} \; \mathbf{inl} \; (x_1).t_1, \mathbf{inr} \; (x_2).t_2 : \tau}$$

Notice that because of the typing rules for injections, a term can now have more than one type, for example

$$\mathbf{inl}(5) : \mathbf{int} + \mathbf{int} \quad \text{and} \quad \mathbf{inl}(5) : \mathbf{int} + (\mathbf{int} \to \mathbf{int}).$$

How terms involving sums are evaluated depends on whether evaluation is eager or lazy. In the operational semantics of the eager case we can say an injection like $\mathbf{inl}(t)$ is a canonical form iff t is itself in canonical form. We define canonical forms of sum types under eager evaluation by the clauses:

$$\mathbf{inl}(c) \in C^e_{\tau_1+\tau_2} \text{ if } c \in C^e_{\tau_1}, \qquad \mathbf{inr}(c) \in C^e_{\tau_1+\tau_2} \text{ if } c \in C^e_{\tau_2}.$$

Again, such canonical forms evaluate to themselves. The rules for the operational semantics are extended by:

$$\frac{t \to^e \mathbf{inl} \; (c_1) \quad t_1[c_1/x_1] \to^e c}{(\mathbf{case} \; t \; \mathbf{of} \; \mathbf{inl}(x_1).t_1, \mathbf{inr}(x_2).t_2) \to^e c} \qquad \frac{t \to^e \mathbf{inr} \; (c_2) \quad t_2[c_2/x_2] \to^e c}{(\mathbf{case} \; t \; \mathbf{of} \; \mathbf{inl} \; (x_1).t_1, \mathbf{inr} \; (x_2).t_2) \to^e c}$$

For the denotational semantics with eager evaluation, the cpo of values of a sum type is just the sum of the cpo's of values of the components; *i.e.*

$$V^e_{\tau_1+\tau_2} = V^e_{\tau_1} + V^e_{\tau_2}.$$

As before, a term t in an environment ρ is denoted by an element of $(V^e_\tau)_\perp$. However, the extension to sums has meant that t need not have a unique type and, because injection functions might be represented differently as the components of the sum vary, the denotation of a term t is given for some typing $t : \tau$:

$$[\![t : \tau]\!]^e \rho \in (V^e_\tau)_\perp$$

In a lazy regime, a canonical form can be an injection of a closed term which has not itself been evaluated. Following this idea, the canonical forms for the lazy language include canonical forms for sums given by adding the clauses

$$\mathbf{inl}(t) \in C^l_{\tau_1+\tau_2} \text{ if } t : \tau_1 \text{ and } t \text{ is closed,}$$
$$\mathbf{inr}(t) \in C^l_{\tau_1+\tau_2} \text{ if } t : \tau_2 \text{ and } t \text{ is closed.}$$

The lazy evaluation of the cases construction is described by the rules

$$\frac{t \to^l \mathbf{inl}\ (t') \quad t_1[t'/x_1] \to^l c}{(\mathbf{case}\ t\ \mathbf{of}\ \mathbf{inl}(x_1).t_1, \mathbf{inr}(x_2).t_2) \to^l c} \qquad \frac{t \to^l \mathbf{inr}\ (t') \quad t_2[t'/x_2] \to^l c}{(\mathbf{case}\ t\ \mathbf{of}\ \mathbf{inl}\ (x_1).t_1, \mathbf{inr}\ (x_2).t_2) \to^l c}$$

Because the values of a sum type do not need the prior evaluation of the components, the extended denotational semantics is based on the choice of values so

$$V^l_{\tau_1 + \tau_2} = (V^l_{\tau_1})_\perp + (V^l_{\tau_2})_\perp.$$

Again the semantics of a typed term $t : \tau$, in an environment ρ, is described by an element

$$[\![t : \tau]\!]^l \rho \in (V^l_\tau)_\perp.$$

It is not hard to extend the results of this chapter to the language with sums.

Exercise 11.29 Write down the clauses for the denotational semantics of the injection and case construction with respect to the typing

$$\mathbf{inl}(t) : \tau_1 + \tau_2$$

$$(\mathbf{case}\ t\ \mathbf{of inl}(x_1).t_1, \mathbf{inr}(x_2).t_2) : \tau$$

for both eager and lazy evaluation. As a check that your denotational semantics is correct, show by rule induction (you need only consider the new cases) that

$$t \to^e c \Rightarrow [\![t : \tau]\!]^e \rho = [\![c : \tau]\!]^e \rho \text{ and}$$

$$t \to^l c \Rightarrow [\![t : \tau]\!]^l \rho = [\![c : \tau]\!]^l \rho$$

for closed terms t and canonical forms c of type τ_1, and any environment ρ.   □

11.12 Further reading

Three good books on functional programming: (eager) Standard ML [101] and [73]; (lazy) [22]. A good survey on logical relations, their history and use can be found in [65]. The two classic papers on full abstraction are Plotkin's [78] and Milner's [62]. These are both concerned with full abstraction restricted to observations of the evaluation of terms at the ground types integers and booleans. Plotkin shows that full abstraction can be obtained, not just by cutting away the undefinable elements, but also by expanding the language, so that a form of parallel conditional is included. The state of the art in the full abstraction problem for languages like those considered here is conveyed in [94], [16]—the latter was written around 10 years ago but is still a good survey. A recent paper which is reasonably accessible is [27]. Languages like those here, and their relationship to intuitionistic and linear logic, are discussed in [3].

12 Information systems

Information systems provide a representation of an important class of cpo's called Scott domains. This chapter introduces information systems and shows how they can be used to find least solutions to recursive domain equations, important for an understanding of recursive types. The method is based on the substructure relation between information systems. This essentially makes information systems into a complete partial order with bottom. Useful constructions like product, sum and (lifted) function space can be made continuous on this cpo so the solution of recursive domain equations reduces to the familiar construction of forming the least fixed point of a continuous function. There are further technical advantages to working with information systems rather than directly with domains. Properties of cpo's can be derived rather than postulated and the representation makes them more amenable mathematically. In particular we obtain elementary methods for showing such properties as the correspondence between operational and denotational semantics with recursive types, presented in the next chapter.

12.1 Recursive types

To begin with let's remark on a familiar cpo satisfying a recursive domain equation. The equation

$$X = 1 + X$$

is to be understood as specifying those cpo's (or domains) X which are equal to themselves summed with the one-element cpo 1. This is a recursive equation for X. One solution, though not the only one, is a copy of the discrete cpo of natural numbers ω. Many programming languages allow the definition of recursive types (the next chapter treats such a language). Even if they don't it can often be that their semantics is most straightforwardly described through the use of recursively defined cpo's. Programming features like-dynamic binding are also conveniently modelled with help of recursively defined types. In fact, Dana Scott made a fundamental breakthrough with the discovery of a model of the λ-calculus in the form of a nontrivial (*i.e.* non singleton) solution to the recursive type definition

$$D \cong [D \to D].$$

This is not strictly speaking an equation; rather the two cpo's D and $[D \to D]$ are in isomorphism with each other. It highlights the fact that we don't necessarily need solutions to within equality—the more tolerant relation of isomorphism will do.

How are we to define types recursively? We have some of the machinery at hand in the form of inductive definitions, as can be seen through a simple example. Finite lists of integers (discussed in Section 10.5) can be identified with a set L satisfying

$$L = \{()\} + (\mathbf{N} \times L). \tag{$*$}$$

The empty tuple represents the null list while the operation of "*consing*" an integer n to the beginning of a list l is represented by the operation (n, l) of pairing. Finite lists are not the only solution to (*). If L were taken to consists of finite and infinite lists of integers then this too would be a solution. However, taking L to just have finite lists of integers as elements yields the least set satisfying (*). To see this recognise that the definition of finite lists fits the pattern of inductive definitions discussed in Chapter 4. For L to be a solution of (*) requires precisely that L contains () and is closed under *cons*ing with an integer, *i.e.* L is closed under the rules

$$\emptyset/(), \quad \{l\}/(n, l),$$

where $n \in \mathbf{N}$. The set of finite lists is the least set closed under such rules. Alternatively, we can regard the set of finite lists as $fix(\psi)$ where ψ is the monotonic and continuous operator on sets acting so

$$\psi(X) = \{()\} + (\mathbf{N} \times X).$$

Quite a few recursive types can be built up in a similar way using inductive definitions.

Exercise 12.1 Describe how to define the type of binary trees with integer leaves as an inductive definition.   □

Exercise 12.2 Describe a set which is a solution to the domain equation $X = 1 + X$ and is not isomorphic to the natural numbers ω.   □

There are, however, other recursive types which are not directly amenable to the same technique. For example, how are we to define the type of streams, or "stoppered sequences", of Section 8.2 which can be infinite? A reasonable guess would be that streams are the least solution to

$$L = (\{\$\} + \mathbf{N} \times L)_\perp$$

an equation between complete partial orders. Although tentative, we can argue that any complete partial order L satisfying this equation must first contain $\perp$, a copy $\lfloor \$ \rfloor$ of the "stopper", and consequently also sequences like $\lfloor (n, \perp) \rfloor$ and $\lfloor (n, \lfloor \$ \rfloor) \rfloor$, where $n \in \mathbf{N}$. Continuing we can argue that L also contains sequences of the form

$$\lfloor (n_1, \lfloor (n_2 \cdots, \lfloor \$ \rfloor) \cdots) \rfloor) \rfloor \quad \text{and} \quad \lfloor (n_1, \lfloor (n_2 \cdots, \perp) \cdots) \rfloor,$$

where $n_1, n_2, \cdots$ are integers. In other words, L contains all finite "stoppered" or "unstoppered" sequences. But neither this style of argument, nor an inductive definition, can ever yield infinite sequences such as:

$$(n_1, \lfloor (n_2, \lfloor (n_3 \cdots) \cdots)$$

This limitation holds a clue as to how to define such recursive types: use the method of inductive definitions to construct the finite elements and then derive the infinite elements by some form of completion process, an infinite element being built up out of its finite approximations.

An *information system* expresses how to build a cpo out of a notation for its finite elements. Because they only deal explicitly with the finite elements they are amenable to the technique of inductive definitions and so can be defined recursively. An information system can be viewed as a prescription saying how to build a cpo. In more detail, an information system can be thought of as consisting of assertions, or propositions, that might be made about a computation, which are related by entailment and consistency relations. An information system determines a cpo with elements those sets of tokens which are consistent and closed with respect to the entailment relation; the ordering is just set inclusion. The elements of the cpo can be thought of as the set of truths about a possible computation and, as such, should be logically closed and consistent sets of assertions. Although not all cpo's can be represented by information systems, they do represent a rich class, the Scott domains.

We should note now that we cannot expect to solve all domain equations because our cpo's do not necessarily have bottom elements. In particular, by Cantor's argument, we cannot hope to have a solution to the domain equation

$$X \cong [X \to 2]$$

where 2 is the discrete cpo with two elements. We get around this by only allowing a "lifted function space" construction in domain equations; for two cpo's D, E their lifted function space is $[D \to E_\perp]$. The techniques of this chapter will yield least solutions to any domain equation

$$X \cong F(X)$$

where F is built up from the unit domain 1 (with just one element) and empty domain $\emptyset$ using product, lifted function space, lifting and sum.

12.2   Information systems

An information system consists of a set of tokens, to be thought of as assertions, or propositions, one might make about a computation, which are related by consistency and entailment relations. The consistency relation picks out those finite subsets of tokens which can together be true of a computation. For example, the computation of an integer cannot simultaneously be 3 and 5, so tokens asserting these two outputs would not be consistent. It can be that the truth of a finite set of tokens entails the truth of another. For instance, two tokens will entail a third if this stands for their conjunction.

Notation: To signify that X is finite subset of a set A we shall write $X \subseteq^{fin} A$. We write $Fin(A)$ for the set consisting of all finite subsets of A, *i.e.* $Fin(A) = \{X \mid X \subseteq^{fin} A\}$.

Definition: An *information system* is defined to be a structure $\mathcal{A} = (A, \mathrm{Con}, \vdash)$, where A is a countable set (the *tokens*), Con (the *consistent* sets) is a non-empty subset of $Fin(A)$ and $\vdash$ (the *entailment relation*) is a subset of $(\mathrm{Con} \setminus \{\emptyset\}) \times A$ which satisfy the axioms:

1. $X \subseteq Y \in \mathrm{Con} \Rightarrow X \in \mathrm{Con}$
2. $a \in A \Rightarrow \{a\} \in \mathrm{Con}$
3. $X \vdash a \Rightarrow X \cup \{a\} \in \mathrm{Con}$
4. $X \in \mathrm{Con} \ \& \ a \in X \Rightarrow X \vdash a$
5. $(X, Y \in \mathrm{Con} \ \& \ \forall b \in Y.\ X \vdash b \ \& \ Y \vdash c) \Rightarrow X \vdash c$.

The condition that $\vdash \subseteq (\mathrm{Con} \setminus \{\emptyset\}) \times A$ is equivalent to saying that $\emptyset \vdash a$ *never* holds, that nothing is entailed by the empty set. This has a much more specific character than the axioms 1-5 which are reasonable assumptions about a fairly general class of logical systems. Its assumption does however simplify constructions such as the sum, and helps smooth some of the work later. As usually presented in the literature information systems give rise to cpo's with bottom elements. Here the usual definition is modified slightly so as to represent cpo's which do not necessarily have bottoms.

An information system determines a family of subsets of tokens, called its *elements*. Think of the tokens as assertions about computations—assume that a token which is once true of a computation remains true of it. Intuitively an element of an information system is the set of tokens that can be truthfully asserted about a computation. This set of tokens can be viewed as the information content of the computation. As such the tokens should not contradict each other—they should be consistent—and should be closed under entailment. In order to represent cpo's which do not necessarily have a bottom element we insist that that elements also have to be non-empty—in this way the empty set is ruled out.

Definition: The *elements*, $|\mathcal{A}|$, of an information system $\mathcal{A} = (A, \mathrm{Con}, \vdash)$ are those subsets x of A which are

1. *non-empty:* $x \neq \emptyset$
2. *consistent:* $X \subseteq^{fin} x \Rightarrow X \in \mathrm{Con}$
3. *$\vdash$-closed:* $X \subseteq x \ \& \ X \vdash a \Rightarrow a \in x$.

Thus an information system determines a family of sets. Such families have a simple characterisation as can be seen in the next section. These families form cpo's when ordered by inclusion. Notice that the empty set $\emptyset$ is consistent and $\vdash$-closed and so would be the least element but for failing to be non-empty. Because the empty set is removed the cpo's will not necessarily possess a bottom element.

Proposition 12.3 *The elements of an information system ordered by inclusion form a cpo.*

Proof: Let $\mathcal{A} = (A, \text{Con}, \vdash)$ be an information system. We show $|\mathcal{A}|$ is a cpo. Suppose $x_0 \subseteq \cdots \subseteq x_n \subseteq \cdots$ is an ω-chain in $|\mathcal{A}|$. We show $\bigcup_n x_n \in |\mathcal{A}|$. Firstly $\bigcup_n x_n$ is non-empty as any one of its elements is. Secondly $\bigcup_n x_n$ is consistent. Suppose $X \subseteq^{fin} \bigcup_n x_n$. Then, because X is finite, $X \subseteq x_n$ for some $n \in \omega$. Therefore $X \in \text{Con}$. Thirdly $\bigcup_n x_n$ is $\vdash$-closed. Suppose $X \in \text{Con}$, $X \vdash a$ and $X \subseteq \bigcup_n x_n$. Then, as X is finite, $X \subseteq x_n$ for some n. However $x_n \in |\mathcal{A}|$ so $a \in x_n$. Thus $a \in \bigcup_n x_n$. Hence $|\mathcal{A}|$ has unions of ω-chains and is a cpo. $\qquad\square$

So, an information system determines a cpo. The subtle idea of information introduced by Scott in his theory of domains now has an intuitive interpretation. By representing a cpo as an information system we see the information associated with a computation as the set of tokens that are true of it and an increase in information as the addition of true tokens to this set.

Not all cpo's can be generated as elements of an information system, though those cpo's which can be obtained from information systems form a rich and important subclass. Their structure is examined in the next section where elements arising as closures under entailment of finite, but non-empty, consistent sets will play a special role.

Lemma 12.4 *Let $\mathcal{A} = (A, \text{Con}, \vdash)$ be an information system. Suppose $\emptyset \neq X \in \text{Con}$ and let Y be a finite subset of A.*

  1. *If $X \vdash b$ for every $b \in Y$ then $X \cup Y \in \text{Con}$ and $Y \in \text{Con}$.*
  2. *The set $\overline{X} = \{a \in A \mid X \vdash a\}$ is an element of $\mathcal{A}$.*

Proof:
(1) Suppose $X \vdash b$ for every $b \in Y$. We show $X \cup Y \in \text{Con}$ and $Y \in \text{Con}$ by a simple induction on the size of Y. Clearly it holds when Y is empty. Suppose Y is non-empty, containing a token b', and $X \vdash b$ for all $b \in Y$. Then $X \vdash b$ for all $b \in Y \setminus \{b'\}$ so by induction $X \cup (Y \setminus \{b'\}) \in \text{Con}$. By axioms 4 and 5 on an information system, $X \cup (Y \setminus \{b'\}) \vdash b'$. By axiom 3, $X \cup Y \in \text{Con}$. By axiom 1, $Y \in \text{Con}$ too.

(2) It follows from (1) that $\overline{X} = \{a \mid X \vdash a\}$ is consistent. It is $\vdash$-closed because if $Y \subseteq \{a \mid X \vdash a\}$ and $Y \vdash a'$ then $X \vdash a'$ by axiom 5 in the definition of information systems.   □

Notation: The entailment relation, between consistent sets and tokens, extends in an obvious way to a relation between consistent sets. Let $\mathcal{A} = (A, \mathrm{Con}, \vdash)$ be an information system. Let X and Y be in Con_A. We write $X \vdash^* Y$ as an abbreviation for $\forall a \in Y.\ X \vdash a$. Using this notation we see that

$$\emptyset \vdash^* Y \iff Y = \emptyset,$$

a consequence of the original entailment $\vdash$ being a subset of $(\mathrm{Con} \setminus \{\emptyset\}) \times A$. Directly from the definition of $\vdash^*$, we obtain

$$X \vdash^* Y \ \&\ X \vdash^* Y' \Rightarrow X \vdash^* (Y \cup Y'),$$

while we can rewrite axiom 5 on information systems as

$$X \vdash^* Y \ \&\ Y \vdash^* Z \Rightarrow X \vdash^* Z,$$

which makes it clear that axiom 5 expresses the transitivity of entailment.

For X any subset of the tokens of an information system write

$$\overline{X} =_{def} \{a \mid \exists Z \subseteq X.\ Z \vdash a\}.$$

Notice that $\overline{\emptyset} = \emptyset$ because $X \vdash b$ only holds for non-empty X.

12.3   Closed families and Scott predomains

This section characterises those cpo's which arise from the elements of an information system. It is not essential to the remainder of the book, and so might be omitted. However, it does introduce the important and widely current notion of a *Scott domain*. As a beginning we characterise precisely those families of subsets which can arise as elements of an information system.

Definition: A *closed family* of sets is a set $\mathcal{F}$ of subsets of a countable set which satisfies

1. If $x \in \mathcal{F}$ then $x \neq \emptyset$,
2. If $x_0 \subseteq x_1 \subseteq \cdots \subseteq x_n \subseteq \cdots$ is is a ω-chain in $\mathcal{F}$ then $\bigcup_{n \in \omega} x_n \in \mathcal{F}$ and
3. If U is a non-empty subset of $\mathcal{F}$ with $\bigcap U \neq \emptyset$ then $\bigcap U \in \mathcal{F}$.

As we now see there is a 1-1 correspondence between information systems and closed families.

Theorem 12.5
(i) Let $\mathcal{A}$ be an information system. Then $|\mathcal{A}|$ is a closed family of sets.
(ii) Let $\mathcal{F}$ be a closed family of sets. Define

$$A_{\mathcal{F}} = \bigcup \mathcal{F},$$

$$X \in \mathrm{Con}_{\mathcal{F}} \iff X = \emptyset \text{ or } (\exists x \in \mathcal{F}. \; X \subseteq^{fin} x),$$

$$X \vdash_{\mathcal{F}} a \iff \emptyset \neq X \in \mathrm{Con}_{\mathcal{F}} \; \& \; a \in A_{\mathcal{F}} \; \& \; (\forall x \in \mathcal{F}. \; X \subseteq x \Rightarrow a \in x).$$

Then $\mathcal{I}(\mathcal{F}) = (A_{\mathcal{F}}, \mathrm{Con}_{\mathcal{F}}, \vdash_{\mathcal{F}})$ is an information system.
(iii) The maps $\mathcal{A} \mapsto |\mathcal{A}|$ and $\mathcal{F} \mapsto \mathcal{I}(\mathcal{F})$ are mutual inverses giving a 1-1 correspondence between information systems and closed families: if $\mathcal{A}$ is an information system then $\mathcal{I}(|\mathcal{A}|) = \mathcal{A}$; if $\mathcal{F}$ is a closed family then $|\mathcal{I}(\mathcal{F})| = \mathcal{F}$.

Proof:
(i) Let $\mathcal{A} = (A, \mathrm{Con}, \vdash)$ be an information system. We show $|\mathcal{A}|$ is a closed family. Proposition 12.3 establishes 2 above. Suppose $\emptyset \neq U \subseteq |\mathcal{A}|$ with $\bigcap U$ not empty. We show $\bigcap U \in |\mathcal{A}|$. Take $u \in U$. We see $\bigcap U$ is consistent as $\bigcap U \subseteq u$. Suppose $X \subseteq \bigcap U$ and $X \vdash a$. Then $X \subseteq u$ for all $u \in U$. Each $u \in U$ is $\vdash$-closed so $a \in u$. Thus $a \in \bigcap U$. Therefore $\bigcap U$ is non-empty, consistent and $\vdash$-closed, so $\bigcap U \in |\mathcal{A}|$. This proves $|\mathcal{A}|$ is a closed family.
(ii) Let $\mathcal{F}$ be a closed family. The check that $\mathcal{I}(\mathcal{F})$ is an information system is left to the reader.
(iii) Let $\mathcal{A} = (A, \mathrm{Con}, \vdash)$ be an information system. To show $\mathcal{I}(|\mathcal{A}|) = \mathcal{A}$ we need

$$A = \bigcup |\mathcal{A}|,$$

$$X \in \mathrm{Con} \iff X = \emptyset \text{ or } (\exists x \in |\mathcal{A}|. \; X \subseteq^{fin} x),$$

$$X \vdash a \iff \emptyset \neq X \in \mathrm{Con} \; \& \; a \in A \; \& \; (\forall x \in |\mathcal{A}|. \; X \subseteq x \Rightarrow a \in x).$$

Obviously $A = \bigcup |\mathcal{A}|$ by axiom 2 on information systems.
Let $X \subseteq^{fin} A$. If $X \in \mathrm{Con}$ then either $X = \emptyset$ or $X \subseteq \overline{X} = \{a \mid X \vdash a\} \in |\mathcal{A}|$. Conversely, if $X = \emptyset$ or $X \subseteq^{fin} x$, where $x \in |\mathcal{A}|$, then by the definition of such elements x we must have $X \in \mathrm{Con}$.
Suppose $X \in \mathrm{Con}$ and $a \in A$. Clearly if $X \vdash a$ then from the definition of elements of $\mathcal{A}$ we must have $X \subseteq x \Rightarrow a \in x$ for any $x \in |\mathcal{A}|$. Suppose $(\forall x \in |\mathcal{A}|. \; X \subseteq x \Rightarrow a \in x)$. Then $\overline{X} = \{b \mid X \vdash b\} \in |\mathcal{A}|$ so $X \vdash a$. Therefore $\mathcal{I}(|\mathcal{A}|) = \mathcal{A}$.

Let $\mathcal{F}$ be a closed family. We show $|\mathcal{I}(\mathcal{F})| = \mathcal{F}$. If $x \in \mathcal{F}$ then $x \in |\mathcal{I}(\mathcal{F})|$, directly from the definition of consistency and entailment in $\mathcal{I}(\mathcal{F})$. Thus $\mathcal{F} \subseteq |\mathcal{I}(\mathcal{F})|$. Now we show the converse inclusion $|\mathcal{I}(\mathcal{F})| \subseteq \mathcal{F}$. Write $\mathcal{I}(\mathcal{F}) = (A_{\mathcal{F}}, \mathrm{Con}_{\mathcal{F}}, \vdash_{\mathcal{F}})$ as above. Suppose $\emptyset \neq X \in \mathrm{Con}_{\mathcal{F}}$. Then $U = \{y \in \mathcal{F} \mid X \subseteq y\}$ is a non-empty subset of $\mathcal{F}$ from the definition of $\mathrm{Con}_{\mathcal{F}}$ and $\overline{X} = \bigcap U$ from the definition $\vdash_{\mathcal{F}}$. As $\mathcal{F}$ is a closed family and $\bigcap U$ is non-empty, $\overline{X} \in \mathcal{F}$. To complete the argument, let $x \in |\mathcal{I}(\mathcal{F})|$. Assume a particular countable enumeration

$$e_0, e_1, \cdots, e_n, \cdots$$

of the elements of the set x—possible as $\bigcup \mathcal{F}$ and so x are countable sets. Now x_n, for $n \in \omega$, forms an ω-chain in $\mathcal{F}$, where we define $x_n = \overline{X}_n$ in which

$$X_0 = \{e_0\},$$
$$X_{n+1} = X_n \cup \{e_{n+1}\}.$$

As $\mathcal{F}$ is a closed family $\bigcup_n x_n \in \mathcal{F}$ and clearly $\bigcup_n x_n = x$. Thus $|\mathcal{I}(\mathcal{F})| \subseteq \mathcal{F}$. The two inclusions give $|\mathcal{I}(\mathcal{F})| = \mathcal{F}$.

The facts, $\mathcal{I}(|\mathcal{A}|) = \mathcal{A}$ for all information systems $\mathcal{A}$ and $|\mathcal{I}(\mathcal{F})| = \mathcal{F}$ for all closed families $\mathcal{F}$, provide a 1-1 correspondence between information systems and closed families.

□

Exercise 12.6 Do the proof of (ii) above.   □

We turn now to consider the kinds of cpo's which can be represented by information systems. In fact, the cpo's with bottom which can be presented this way are exactly a well-known class of cpo's called *Scott domains* (after Dana Scott).

Definition: An element x of a cpo D is said to be *finite* iff, for every ω-chain $d_0 \sqsubseteq \cdots \sqsubseteq d_n \cdots$ such that $x \sqsubseteq \bigsqcup_{n \in \omega} d_n$, there is $n \in \omega$ for which $x \sqsubseteq d_n$. We will let D^0 denote the set of finite elements of D.

A cpo D is ω-*algebraic* iff the set of finite elements D^0 is countable and, for every $x \in D$, there is an ω-chain of finite elements $e_0 \sqsubseteq \cdots \sqsubseteq e_n \cdots$ such that $x = \bigsqcup_{n \in \omega} e_n$.

A subset X of a cpo D is said to be *bounded* if there is an upper bound of X in D. A cpo D is *bounded complete* if every non-empty, bounded subset of D has a least upper bound.

In the case where a cpo has a bottom element, is a bounded complete and ω-algebraic it is often called a *Scott domain*. In general, when it need not have a bottom, we shall call a bounded complete, ω-algebraic cpo a *Scott predomain*.

Exercise 12.7 Show that in a Scott predomain least upper bounds of finite sets of finite elements are finite, when they exist.   □

Proposition 12.8 *Let $\mathcal{A} = (A, \mathrm{Con}, \vdash)$ be an information system. Its elements, $|\mathcal{A}|$, ordered by inclusion form a Scott predomain. Its finite elements are of the form $\overline{X} = \{a \in A \mid X \vdash a\}$, where $\emptyset \neq X \in \mathrm{Con}$.*

Proof: Let $\mathcal{A} = (A, \mathrm{Con}, \vdash)$ be an information system with elements $|\mathcal{A}|$. As $|\mathcal{A}|$ is a closed family it is a cpo ordered by inclusion.

We require that $|\mathcal{A}|$ is bounded complete *i.e.* if $\forall x \in V.\ x \subseteq y$, for non-empty $V \subseteq |\mathcal{A}|$ and $y \in |\mathcal{A}|$, then there is a least upper bound of V in $|\mathcal{A}|$. However if $\forall x \in V.x \subseteq y$ then $U = \{y \mid \forall x \in V.x \subseteq y\}$ is a non-empty subset of the closed family $|\mathcal{A}|$. As V is non-empty it contains an element v, necessarily non-empty, of $|\mathcal{A}|$. As $v \subseteq \bigcap U$ this ensures that $\bigcap U$ is non-empty. Hence by property 3 in the definition of closed family we have $\bigcap U \in |\mathcal{A}|$, and $\bigcap U$ is clearly a least upper bound of V.

We now show $|\mathcal{A}|$ ordered by inclusion is an algebraic cpo. Firstly we observe a fact about all elements of $|\mathcal{A}|$. Let $x \in |\mathcal{A}|$. Take a countable enumeration $a_0, a_1, \ldots, a_n, \ldots$ of x—possible as A is assumed countable. Define, as above, $x_n = \overline{X}_n$ where

$$X_0 = \{a_0\},$$
$$X_{n+1} = X_n \cup \{a_{n+1}\}.$$

Then $x = \bigcup_n x_n$. We now go on to show that the finite elements of the cpo $|\mathcal{A}|$ are precisely those of the form $\overline{X}$, for $X \in \mathrm{Con}$. Hence it will follow that every element is the least upper bound of an ω-chain of finite elements.

Suppose in particular that $x \in |\mathcal{A}|$ is finite. We have $x = \bigcup_n x_n$, as above, which implies $x = x_n$ for some n. Thus $x = \overline{X}_n$ for some $X_n \subseteq^{fin} x$, which is necessarily in Con. Conversely, assume x is an element of the form $\overline{X}$ for some $X \in \mathrm{Con}$. Suppose $x \subseteq \bigcup x_n$ for some chain $x_0 \subseteq \cdots \subseteq x_n \subseteq \cdots$ of the cpo $|\mathcal{A}|$. Then $X \subseteq x_n$ for some n, making $x \subseteq x_n$ too. This argument shows the finite elements of the cpo $|\mathcal{A}|$ are precisely those elements of the form $\overline{X}$ for $\emptyset \neq X \in \mathrm{Con}$.

We conclude that $(|\mathcal{A}|, \subseteq)$ is a bounded complete ω-algebraic cpo and so a Scott predomain.   □

An arbitrary Scott predomain is associated naturally with an information system. The intuition is that a finite element is a piece of information that a computation realises—uses or produces—in finite time, so it is natural to take tokens to be finite elements. Then the consistency and entailment relations are induced by the original domain. A finite set of finite elements X is consistent if it is bounded and entails an element if its least upper bound dominates the element.

Definition: Let $(D, \sqsubseteq)$ be a Scott predomain. Define $IS(D) = (D^0, \mathrm{Con}, \vdash)$ where D^0 is the set of finite elements of D and Con and $\vdash$ are defined as follows:

$$X \in \mathrm{Con} \iff X \subseteq^{fin} D^0 \ \& \ (X = \emptyset \ \text{or} \ X \text{ is bounded}),$$
$$X \vdash e \iff \emptyset \neq X \in \mathrm{Con} \ \& \ e \sqsubseteq \bigsqcup X.$$

Proposition 12.9 *Let D be a Scott predomain. Then $IS(D)$ is an information system with a cpo of elements, ordered by inclusion, isomorphic to D. The isomorphism pair is*

$$\theta : D \to |IS(D)| \ \text{given by} \ \theta : d \mapsto \{e \in D^0 \mid e \sqsubseteq d\},$$
$$\varphi : |IS(D)| \to D \ \text{given by} \ \varphi : x \mapsto \bigsqcup x.$$

Exercise 12.10 Prove the proposition above. $\qquad\qquad\qquad\qquad\qquad\qquad\qquad\qquad$ □

Thus an information system determines a Scott predomain of elements and, vice versa, a predomain determines an information system with an isomorphic cpo of elements. We are justified in saying information systems represent Scott predomains. Notice that they would represent Scott domains if we were to allow the empty element, which would then always sit at the bottom of the cpo of elements.

The following exercise shows an important negative result: the function space of arbitrary Scott predomains is not a Scott predomain and therefore cannot be represented as an information system. (We will, however, be able to define a lifted-function-space construction $\mathcal{A} \to \mathcal{B}_\perp$ between information systems $\mathcal{A}, \mathcal{B}$, with cpo of elements isomorphic to $[|\mathcal{A}| \to |\mathcal{B}|_\perp]$.)

Exercise 12.11 Let **N** and **T** be the (discrete) Scott predomains of numbers and truth values. Show that their function space, the cpo $[\mathbf{N} \to \mathbf{T}]$ is not a Scott predomain and therefore not representable as an information system.
(Hint: What are its finite elements? Do they form a *countable* set?) $\qquad\qquad$ □

Exercise 12.12 Cpo's are sometimes presented using the concept of directed sets instead of ω-chains. A directed set of a partial order D is a non-empty subset S of D for which, if $s, t \in S$ then there is $u \in S$ with $s, t \sqsubseteq u$. Sometimes a complete partial order is taken to be a partial order which has least upper bounds of all directed sets. In this framework a finite element of a cpo is taken to be an element e such that if $e \sqsubseteq \bigsqcup S$, for S a directed set, then there is $s \in S$ with $e \sqsubseteq s$. An ω-algebraic cpo is then said to be a cpo D for which, given any $x \in D$, the set $S = \{e \sqsubseteq x \mid e \text{ is finite}\}$ is directed with least upper bound x; it is said to be ω-algebraic if the set of finite elements is countable. Show the cpo's which are ω-algebraic in this sense are the same as those which are ω-algebraic in the sense we have taken outside this exercise. Show too that if in the definition of a closed family we replace condition 2 by

$$\text{If } S \text{ is a directed subset of } (\mathcal{F}, \subseteq) \text{ then } \bigcup S \in \mathcal{F}$$

then the same class of families of sets are defined.   □

12.4   A cpo of information systems

Because we work with a concrete representation of cpo's, it turns out that we can solve recursive domain equations by a fixed-point construction on a complete partial order of information systems. The order on information systems, $\trianglelefteq$, captures an intuitive notion, that of one information system being a subsystem, or substructure, of another.

Definition: Let $\mathcal{A} = (A, \text{Con}_A, \vdash_A)$ and $\mathcal{B} = (B, \text{Con}_B, \vdash_B)$ be information systems. Define $\mathcal{A} \trianglelefteq \mathcal{B}$ iff

1. $A \subseteq B$
2. $X \in \text{Con}_A \iff X \subseteq A \ \& \ X \in \text{Con}_B$
3. $X \vdash_A a \iff X \subseteq A \ \& \ a \in A \ \& \ X \vdash_B a$

When $\mathcal{A} \trianglelefteq \mathcal{B}$, for two information systems $\mathcal{A}$ and $\mathcal{B}$, we say $\mathcal{A}$ is a *subsystem* of $\mathcal{B}$.

Thus one information system $\mathcal{A}$ is a subsystem of another $\mathcal{B}$ if the tokens of $\mathcal{A}$ are included those of $\mathcal{B}$ and the relations of consistency and entailment of $\mathcal{A}$ are simply restrictions of those in the larger information system $\mathcal{B}$. Observe that:

Proposition 12.13 *Let* $\mathcal{A} = (A, \text{Con}_A, \vdash_A)$ *and* $\mathcal{B} = (B, \text{Con}_B, \vdash_B)$ *be information systems. If their token-sets are equal, i.e.* $A = B$, *and* $\mathcal{A} \trianglelefteq \mathcal{B}$ *then* $\mathcal{A} = \mathcal{B}$.

Proof: Obvious from the definition of $\trianglelefteq$.   □

This definition of subsystem almost gives a cpo of information systems with a bottom element. There is a least information system, the unique one with the empty set as tokens. Each ω-chain of information systems increasing with respect to $\trianglelefteq$ has a least upper bound, with tokens, consistency and entailment relations the union of those in the chain. But information systems do not form a set and for this reason alone they do not quite form a cpo. We could say they form a *large cpo*. This is all we need.

Theorem 12.14 *The relation $\trianglelefteq$ is a partial order with $0 =_{def} (\emptyset, \{\emptyset\}, \emptyset)$ as least element. Moreover if $\mathcal{A}_0 \trianglelefteq \mathcal{A}_1 \trianglelefteq \dots \trianglelefteq \mathcal{A}_i \trianglelefteq \dots$ is an ω-chain of information systems $\mathcal{A}_i = (A_i, \mathrm{Con}_i, \vdash_i)$ then there exists a least upper bound given by*

$$\bigcup_i \mathcal{A}_i = (\bigcup_i A_i, \bigcup_i \mathrm{Con}_i, \bigcup_i \vdash_i).$$

(Here and henceforth we use the union sign to denote the least upper bound of information systems.)

Proof: That $\trianglelefteq$ is reflexive and transitive is clear from the definition. Antisymmetry of $\trianglelefteq$ follows from the Proposition 12.13 above. Thus $\trianglelefteq$ is a partial order and 0 is easily seen to be the $\trianglelefteq$-least information structure.

Let $\mathcal{A}_0 \trianglelefteq \mathcal{A}_1 \trianglelefteq \dots \trianglelefteq \mathcal{A}_i \trianglelefteq \dots$ be an increasing ω-chain of information systems $\mathcal{A}_i = (A_i, \mathrm{Con}_i, \vdash_i)$. Write $\mathcal{A} = (A, \mathrm{Con}, \vdash) = (\bigcup_i A_i, \bigcup_i \mathrm{Con}_i, \bigcup_i \vdash_i)$. It is routine to check that $\mathcal{A}$ is an information system.

It is an upper bound of the chain: Obviously each A_i is a subset of the tokens A; obviously $\mathrm{Con}_i \subseteq \mathrm{Con}$ while conversely, if $X \subseteq A_i$ and $X \in \mathrm{Con}$ then $X \in \mathrm{Con}_j$ for some $j \geq i$ but then $X \in \mathrm{Con}_i$ as $\mathcal{A}_i \trianglelefteq \mathcal{A}_j$; obviously $\vdash_i \subseteq \vdash$ while conversely if $X \subseteq A_i$, $a \in A_i$ and $X \vdash a$ then $X \vdash_j a$ for some $j \geq i$ but then $X \vdash_i a$ as $\mathcal{A}_i \trianglelefteq \mathcal{A}_j$.

It is a least upper bound of the chain: Assume $\mathcal{B} = (B, \mathrm{Con}_B, \vdash_B)$ is an upper bound of the chain. Clearly then $A = \bigcup_i A_i \subseteq B$. Clearly $\mathrm{Con} = \bigcup_i \mathrm{Con}_i \subseteq \mathrm{Con}_B$. Also if $X \subseteq A$ and $X \in \mathrm{Con}_B$ then as X is finite, $X \subseteq A_i$ for some i. So $X \in \mathrm{Con}_i \subseteq \mathrm{Con}$ as $\mathcal{A}_i \trianglelefteq \mathcal{B}$. Thus $X \in \mathrm{Con} \iff X \subseteq A \,\&\, X \in \mathrm{Con}_B$. Similarly $X \vdash a \iff X \subseteq A \,\&\, a \in A \,\&\, X \vdash_B a$. Thus $\mathcal{A} \trianglelefteq \mathcal{B}$ making $\mathcal{A}$ the least upper bound of the chain. $\square$

We shall be concerned with continuous operations on information systems and using them to define information systems recursively. We proceed just as before—the arguments are unaffected by the fact that information systems do not form a set. An operation F on information systems is said to be *monotonic* (with respect to $\trianglelefteq$) iff

$$\mathcal{A} \trianglelefteq \mathcal{B} \Rightarrow F(\mathcal{A}) \trianglelefteq F(\mathcal{B})$$

for all information systems $\mathcal{A}, \mathcal{B}$. The operation F is said to be *continuous* (with respect to $\trianglelefteq$) iff it is monotonic and for any increasing ω-chain of information systems

$$\mathcal{A}_0 \trianglelefteq \mathcal{A}_1 \trianglelefteq \dots \trianglelefteq \mathcal{A}_i \trianglelefteq \dots$$

we have that

$$\bigcup_i F(\mathcal{A}_i) = F(\bigcup_i \mathcal{A}_i).$$

(Since F is monotonic $\bigcup_i F(\mathcal{A}_i)$ exists.) Using the same arguments as before for least fixed points for cpo's we know that any continuous operation, F, on information systems has a least fixed point $\mathit{fix}(F)$ given by the least upper bound, $\bigcup_i F^i(\mathbf{0})$, of the increasing ω-chain $\mathbf{0} \trianglelefteq F(\mathbf{0}) \trianglelefteq F^2(\mathbf{0}) \trianglelefteq \cdots \trianglelefteq F^n(\mathbf{0}) \trianglelefteq \cdots$.

The next lemma will be a great help in proving operations continuous. Generally it is very easy to show that a unary operation is monotonic with respect to $\trianglelefteq$ and continuous on the token sets, a notion we now make precise.

Definition: Say a unary operation $\mathcal{F}$ on information systems is *continuous on token sets* iff for any ω-chain, $\mathcal{A}_0 \trianglelefteq \mathcal{A}_1 \trianglelefteq \cdots \trianglelefteq \mathcal{A}_i \trianglelefteq \cdots$, each token of $F(\bigcup_i \mathcal{A}_i)$ is a token of $\bigcup_i F(\mathcal{A}_i)$.

Lemma 12.15 *Let F be a unary operation on information systems. Then F is continuous iff F is monotonic with respect to $\trianglelefteq$ and continuous on token sets.*

Proof:
"only if": obvious.
"if": Let $\mathcal{A}_0 \trianglelefteq \mathcal{A}_1 \trianglelefteq \cdots \trianglelefteq \mathcal{A}_i \trianglelefteq \cdots$ be an ω-chain of information systems. Clearly $\bigcup_i F(\mathcal{A}_i) \trianglelefteq F(\bigcup_i \mathcal{A}_i)$ since F is assumed monotonic. Thus from the assumption the tokens of $\bigcup_i F(\mathcal{A}_i)$ are the same as the tokens of $F(\bigcup_i \mathcal{A}_i)$. Therefore they are the same information system by Proposition 12.13. $\qquad\square$

In general, operations on information systems can take a tuple of information systems as argument and deliver a tuple of information systems as result. But again, just as before for ordinary cpo's, in reasoning about the monotonicity and continuity of an operation we need only consider one input and one output coordinate at a time. Lemma 8.8 and Lemma 8.10 generalise straightforwardly. This means that such a general operation on information systems is continuous with respect to $\trianglelefteq$ iff it is continuous in each argument separately (*i.e.*, considered as a function in any one of its argument, holding the others fixed). Similarly it is continuous iff it is continuous considered as a function to each output coordinate. Thus the verification that an operation is continuous boils down to showing certain unary operations are continuous with respect to the subsystem relation $\trianglelefteq$.

The order $\trianglelefteq$ is perhaps not the first that comes to mind. Why not base the cpo of information systems on the simpler inclusion order

$$(A, \mathrm{Con}_A, \vdash_A) \subseteq (B, \mathrm{Con}_B, \vdash_B) \text{ iff } A \subseteq B \;\&\; \mathrm{Con}_A \subseteq \mathrm{Con}_B \;\&\; \vdash_A \subseteq \vdash_B?$$

We do not do so because the lifted-function-space construction on information systems, introduced in the next section, is not even monotonic in its left argument (see Exercise 12.34).

Exercise 12.16 This exercise relates the subsystem relation on information systems to corresponding relations on families of sets and cpo's. Let $\mathcal{A} = (A, \mathrm{Con}_A, \vdash_A)$ and $\mathcal{B} = (B, \mathrm{Con}_B, \vdash_B)$ be information systems.

(i) Assume $\mathcal{A} \trianglelefteq \mathcal{B}$. Show the maps $\theta : |\mathcal{A}| \to |\mathcal{B}|$ and $\varphi : |\mathcal{B}| \to |\mathcal{A}| \cup \{\emptyset\}$, where

$$\theta(x) = \{b \in B \mid \exists X \subseteq x. \ X \vdash_B b\} \text{ and}$$
$$\varphi(y) = y \cap A,$$

are continuous with respect to inclusion and satisfy

$$\varphi \circ \theta(x) = x \quad \text{and} \quad \theta \circ \varphi(y) \subseteq y$$

for all $x \in |\mathcal{A}|$ and $y \in |\mathcal{B}|$.

(ii) For information systems $\mathcal{A}$ and $\mathcal{B}$, show

$$\mathcal{A} \trianglelefteq \mathcal{B} \iff |\mathcal{A}| = \{y \cap A \mid y \in |\mathcal{B}| \ \& \ y \cap A \neq \emptyset\}.$$

(This indicates another approach to solving recursive domain equations using inverse limits of embedding-projection pairs of continuous functions $\theta : D \to E$ and $\varphi : E \to D_\perp$ between cpo's with the property that

$$\varphi \circ \theta(d) = \lfloor d \rfloor \quad \text{and} \quad \theta_\perp \varphi^*(e') \sqsubseteq e'$$

for all $d \in D, e' \in E_\perp$. Recall, from 8.3.4, that $\varphi^* : E_\perp \to D_\perp$ satisfies $\varphi^*(e') = \mathit{let}\ e \Leftarrow e'.\varphi(e)$, while $\theta_\perp : D_\perp \to E_\perp$ is defined so that $\theta_\perp(d') = \mathit{let}\ d \Leftarrow d'.\lfloor \theta(d) \rfloor$.)   □

In the next section we shall see many examples of operations on information systems and how we can use cpo of the subsystem relation to obtain solutions to recursively defined information systems. Because the machinery works for operations taking more than one information system as argument it can be used to define several information systems simultaneously.

12.5   Constructions

In this section we give constructions of *product, lifted-function space, lifting* and *sum* information systems. They induce the corresponding constructions on cpo's. We choose them with a little care so that they are also continuous with respect to $\trianglelefteq$. In this way we will be able to produce solutions to recursive equations for information systems, and so for cpo's, written in terms of these constructions. In fact, lifting $D_\perp$ of domains D can be obtained to within isomorphism from other constructions, *viz.* $[\mathbf{1} \to D_\perp]$ where we have used the lifted function space and the empty product $\mathbf{1}$ which we can define on information systems. However, some work becomes a little smoother with the more direct definition given here.

12.5.1   Lifting

Our aim is to define lifting on information systems which reflects lifting on cpo's.

Definition: Define *lifting* on information systems $\mathcal{A} = (A, \mathrm{Con}, \vdash)$ by taking $\mathcal{A}_\perp = (A', \mathrm{Con}', \vdash')$ where:

1. $A' = \mathrm{Con}$,
2. $X \in \mathrm{Con}' \iff X \subseteq \mathrm{Con}$ & $\bigcup X \in \mathrm{Con}$,
3. $X \vdash' b \iff \emptyset \neq X \in \mathrm{Con}'$ & $\bigcup X \vdash^* b$.

Intuitively, lifting extends the original set of tokens to include a token, the empty set in the above construction, true even in the absence of an original value as output. Lifting, as hoped, prefixes the family by an element, in fact an element consisting of the single extra token $\emptyset$.

Definition: Define $\mathbf{1} = \mathbf{0}_\perp$.

The information system $\mathbf{1}$ has one token $\emptyset$, consistent sets $\emptyset$ and $\{\emptyset\}$, and entailment relation $\{\emptyset\} \vdash \emptyset$. Its only element is $\{\emptyset\}$.

Proposition 12.17 *Let $\mathcal{A}$ be an information system. Then $\mathcal{A}_\perp$ is an information system with*

$$y \in |\mathcal{A}_\perp| \iff y = \{\emptyset\} \text{ or } \exists x \in |\mathcal{A}|. \ y = \{b \mid b \subseteq^{fin} x\}.$$

Proof: Let $\mathcal{A} = (A, \mathrm{Con}, \vdash)$ be an information system.

It is routine to check that $\mathcal{A}_\perp = (A', \mathrm{Con}', \vdash')$ is an information system. Of the axioms, here we shall only verify that axiom 5 holds. Assume $X \vdash' b$ for all $b \in Y$ and $Y \vdash' c$. Note first that $X \neq \emptyset$ because if it were empty so would Y be, making $Y \vdash' c$ impossible. Now observe $\bigcup X \vdash^* b$ for all $b \in Y$. Therefore $\bigcup X \vdash^* \bigcup Y$. As $Y \vdash' c$ we obtain $\bigcup Y \vdash^* c$. Hence as axiom 5 holds for $\mathcal{A}$ we deduce $\bigcup X \vdash^* c$. Recalling $X \neq \emptyset$ we conclude $X \vdash' c$.

Now we show

$$y \in |\mathcal{A}_\perp| \iff y = \{\emptyset\} \text{ or } \exists x \in |\mathcal{A}|. \ y = \{b \mid b \subseteq^{fin} x\}.$$

"$\Leftarrow$": It is easily checked that $\{\emptyset\}$ is consistent and $\vdash'$-closed; hence if $y = \{\emptyset\}$ then $y \in |\mathcal{A}_\perp|$. Now suppose $y = \{b \mid b \subseteq^{fin} x\}$ for $x \in |\mathcal{A}|$. Certainly $\emptyset \in y$ so $y \neq \emptyset$. Suppose $X \subseteq^{fin} y$. Clearly $\bigcup X \subseteq^{fin} x$. Then $X \subseteq \mathrm{Con}$ and $\bigcup X \in \mathrm{Con}$ and hence $X \in \mathrm{Con}'$. Suppose $X \subseteq y$ and $X \vdash' b$. Then $\bigcup X \vdash^* b$ and $\bigcup X \subseteq x$. Hence $b \subseteq^{fin} x$. Therefore $b \in y$. We have thus shown that $y \in |\mathcal{A}_\perp|$.

"$\Rightarrow$": Suppose $y \in |\mathcal{A}_\perp|$ and $y \neq \{\emptyset\}$. Take $x = \bigcup y$. We must check $x \in |\mathcal{A}|$ and $y = \{b \mid b \subseteq^{fin} x\}$.

First observe that $x \neq \emptyset$ as y is neither empty nor $\{\emptyset\}$. Note if $Z \subseteq^{fin} x$ then $Z \subseteq \bigcup X$ for some $X \subseteq^{fin} y$. It follows that if $Z \subseteq^{fin} x$ then $Z \in \text{Con}$. Assume $Z \subseteq x$ and $Z \vdash a$—so $Z \neq \emptyset$. Then again $Z \subseteq \bigcup X$ for some $X \subseteq^{fin} y$ where, as $Z \neq \emptyset$, we also have $X \neq \emptyset$. Therefore $X \vdash' \{a\}$. Hence we must have $\{a\} \in y$ so $a \in x$. We have checked that $x \in |\mathcal{A}|$.

Clearly $y \subseteq \{b \mid b \subseteq^{fin} x\}$. We require the converse inclusion too. As $y \neq \emptyset$ there is some $b \in y$. By definition $\{b\} \vdash' \emptyset$. Hence $\emptyset \in y$. Suppose $\emptyset \neq b \subseteq^{fin} x$. Then $b \subseteq \bigcup X$ for some $X \subseteq^{fin} y$. As $b \neq \emptyset$ so must $X \neq \emptyset$. Clearly $\bigcup X \vdash^* b$. Thus $X \vdash' b$ so $b \in y$. This establishes the converse inclusion, and we can conclude that $y = \{b \mid b \subseteq^{fin} x\}$. $\square$

It follows that lifting on information systems induces lifting on the the cpo of its elements:

Corollary 12.18 *Let $\mathcal{A}$ be an information system. Then there is an isomorphism of cpo's*

$$|\mathcal{A}_\perp| \cong |\mathcal{A}|_\perp$$

given by

$$x \mapsto \begin{cases} \perp & \text{if } x = \{\emptyset\}, \\ \lfloor \bigcup x \rfloor & \text{otherwise.} \end{cases}$$

Theorem 12.19 *The operation $\mathcal{A} \mapsto \mathcal{A}_\perp$ is a continuous operation on information systems ordered by $\trianglelefteq$.*

Proof: We use Lemma 12.15. We first show lifting is monotonic. Assume $\mathcal{A} \trianglelefteq \mathcal{B}$ for two information systems $\mathcal{A} = (A, \text{Con}_A, \vdash_A)$ and $\mathcal{B} = (B, \text{Con}_B, \vdash_B)$. Write $\mathcal{A}_\perp = (A', \text{Con}_A', \vdash_A')$ and $\mathcal{B}_\perp = (B', \text{Con}_B', \vdash_B')$. Let us check $\mathcal{A}_\perp \trianglelefteq \mathcal{B}_\perp$:

Obviously $A' = \text{Con}_A \subseteq \text{Con}_B = B'$. We argue:

$$X \in \text{Con}_A' \iff X \subseteq \text{Con}_A \ \& \ \bigcup X \in \text{Con}_A$$
$$\iff X \subseteq \text{Con}_A \ \& \ \bigcup X \in \text{Con}_B$$
$$\iff X \subseteq A' \ \& \ X \in \text{Con}_B'.$$

Similarly,

$$X \vdash_A' c \iff X \subseteq A' \ \& \ X \neq \emptyset \ \& \ c \in A' \ \& \ \bigcup X \vdash_A^* c$$
$$\iff X \subseteq A' \ \& \ X \neq \emptyset \ \& \ c \in A' \ \& \ \bigcup X \vdash_B^* c$$
$$\iff X \subseteq A' \ \& \ c \in A' \ \& \ X \vdash_B' c.$$

Thus $\mathcal{A}_\perp \trianglelefteq \mathcal{B}_\perp$. Therefore $(-)_\perp$ is monotonic. It remains to show that it acts continuously on token-sets. Let $\mathcal{A}_0 \trianglelefteq \mathcal{A}_1 \trianglelefteq \cdots \trianglelefteq \mathcal{A}_i \trianglelefteq \cdots$ be an ω-chain of information systems $\mathcal{A}_i = (A_i, \mathrm{Con}_i, \vdash_i)$. However, the set of tokens of $(\bigcup_i \mathcal{A}_i)_\perp$ and $\bigcup_i (\mathcal{A}_{i\perp})$ are both clearly equal to $\bigcup_i \mathrm{Con}_i$. Thus by Lemma 12.15 we know lifting is a continuous operation on information systems ordered by $\trianglelefteq$.   □

Exercise 12.20 Draw the domains of elements of $\mathbf{1}_{\perp\perp}$ and $\mathbf{1}_{\perp\perp\perp}$.   □

Exercise 12.21 Because lifting is continuous with respect to $\trianglelefteq$ it has a least fixed point $\Omega = \Omega_\perp$. Work out the set of tokens and show that its cpo of elements $|\Omega|$ is isomorphic to the cpo (seen previously with the same name) consisting of an ω-chain with an additional "infinity" element as least upper bound.   □

Exercise 12.22 Let $\mathcal{A}$ be an information system. Let X be a consistent set of $\mathcal{A}_\perp$ and b a token of $\mathcal{A}$. Show

$$b \in \bigcup \overline{X} \iff \bigcup U \vdash_A b.$$

□

12.5.2   Sums

We have already seen a special case of sum construction, that of the empty sum **0**. In general, we can reflect sums of Scott predomains by *sums* of information systems which are formed by juxtaposing disjoint copies of the two information systems. The tokens then correspond to assertions about one component or the other.

The construction will rely on these simple operations.

Notation: For two sets A and B, let $A \uplus B$ be the disjoint union of A and B, given by $A \uplus B = (\{1\} \times A) \cup (\{2\} \times B)$. Write $inj_1 : A \to A \uplus B$ and $inj_2 : B \to A \uplus B$ be the injections taking $inj_1 : a \mapsto (1, a)$ for $a \in A$ and $inj_2 : b \mapsto (2, b)$ for $b \in B$.

Definition: Let $\mathcal{A} = (A, \mathrm{Con}_A, \vdash_A)$ and $\mathcal{B} = (B, \mathrm{Con}_B, \vdash_B)$ be information systems. Define their *sum*, $\mathcal{A}_1 + \mathcal{A}_2$, to be $\mathcal{C} = (C, \mathrm{Con}, \vdash)$ where:

1. $C = A \uplus B$
2. $X \in \mathrm{Con} \iff \exists Y \in \mathrm{Con}_A.X = inj_1 Y$ or $\exists Y \in \mathrm{Con}_B.X = inj_2 Y$,
3. $X \vdash c \iff$

$\qquad (\exists Y, a.\ X = inj_1 Y \ \& \ c = inj_1(a) \ \& Y \vdash_A a)$ or

$\qquad (\exists Y, b.\ X = inj_2 Y \ \& \ c = inj_2(b) \ \& \ Y \vdash_B b)$.

Example: Let T be the sum $1 + 1$. Then $|T|$ is isomorphic to the discrete cpo of truth values; its tokens are $(1, \emptyset)$ and $(2, \emptyset)$ with elements consisting of precisely the singletons $\{(1, \emptyset)\}$ and $\{(2, \emptyset)\}$.   □

Proposition 12.23 *Let A and B be information systems. Then their sum $A + B$ is an information system such that*

$$x \in |A + B| \iff (\exists y \in |A|.\ x = inj_1 y) \text{ or } (\exists y \in |B|.\ x = inj_2 y).$$

Proof: It is necessary to verify that if A and B are information systems then so is their sum $A + B$. That $A + B$ satisfies the properties 1 to 5 follows, property for property, from the fact that A and B satisfy 1 to 5. It is a routine matter to check that the elements of $A + B$ consist of disjoint copies of elements of A and B (exercise!).   □

It follows that the cpo of elements of a sum of information systems is the same to within isomorphism as the sum of the cpo's of elements:

Corollary 12.24 *Let A and B be information systems. There is an isomorphism of cpo's*

$$|A + B| \cong |A| + |B|$$

given by

$$x \mapsto \begin{cases} in_1(y) & \text{if } x = inj_1 y, \\ in_2(y) & \text{if } x = inj_2 y. \end{cases}$$

Theorem 12.25 *The operation $+$ is a continuous operation on information systems ordered by $\trianglelefteq$.*

Proof: We show that $+$ is continuous with respect to $\trianglelefteq$. By definition of continuity we must show that $+$ is continuous in each argument. We prove $+$ continuous in its first argument. Then, by symmetry, it is easy to see that $+$ will be continuous in its second argument too.

First we show $+$ is monotonic in its first argument. Let $A = (A, \text{Con}_A, \vdash_A)$, $A' = (A', \text{Con}_{A'}, \vdash_{A'})$ and $B = (B, \text{Con}_B, \vdash_B)$ be information systems with $A \trianglelefteq A'$. Write $C = (C, \text{Con}, \vdash) = A + B$ and $C' = (C', \text{Con}', \vdash') = A' + B$. We require $C \trianglelefteq C'$ i.e.

1. $C \subseteq C'$
2. $X \in \text{Con} \iff X \subseteq C\ \&\ X \in \text{Con}'$
3. $X \vdash a \iff X \subseteq C\ \&\ a \in C\ \&\ X \vdash' a$

1. From the definition of $+$ and the assumption $\mathcal{A} \trianglelefteq \mathcal{A}'$ we get $C \subseteq C'$.

2. "$\Rightarrow$". Let $X \in \mathrm{Con}$. Then $X = \{1\} \times X_1$ for some $X_1 \in \mathrm{Con}_A$ or $X = \{2\} \times X_2$ for some $X_2 \in \mathrm{Con}_B$. Assume $X = \{1\} \times X_1$. Then clearly $X \subseteq C$ and $X_1 \in \mathrm{Con}_{A'}$ since $\mathcal{A} \trianglelefteq \mathcal{A}'$. Therefore by the definition of $+$, $X \in \mathrm{Con}'$. Now assume $X = \{2\} \times X_2$ where $X_2 \in \mathrm{Con}_B$. Then directly from the definition of $+$ we have $X \in \mathrm{Con}'$.

2. "$\Leftarrow$". Suppose $X \in \mathrm{Con}'$ and $X \subseteq C$. Then either $X = \{1\} \times X_1$ for some $X_1 \in \mathrm{Con}_{A'}$ or $X = \{1\} \times X_2$ for some $X_2 \in \mathrm{Con}_B$. In the former case $X_1 \subseteq A$ so, as $\mathcal{A} \trianglelefteq \mathcal{A}'$, we obtain $X_1 \in \mathrm{Con}_A$. In the latter case $X \in \mathrm{Con}$ trivially.

3. is very similar to 2.

This shows $+$ monotonic in its first argument. It remains to show that $+$ acts continuously on the token-sets. Let $\mathcal{A}_0 \trianglelefteq \mathcal{A}_1 \trianglelefteq \cdots \trianglelefteq \mathcal{A}_i \trianglelefteq \cdots$ be an ω-chain of information systems $\mathcal{A}_i = (A_i, \mathrm{Con}_i, \vdash_i)$. The set of tokens of $(\bigcup_i \mathcal{A}_i) + \mathcal{B}$ is $((\bigcup_{i \in \omega} A_i) \uplus B$ which is equal to $\bigcup_{i \in \omega} (A_i \uplus B)$ the set of tokens of $\bigcup_i (\mathcal{A}_i + \mathcal{B})$.

Thus $+$ is continuous in its first and, symmetrically, in its second argument, and is therefore continuous. $\square$

Example: Because $+$ is continuous we can construct the least information system $\mathcal{N}$ such that $\mathcal{N} = 1 + \mathcal{N}$. Its elements form a discrete cpo isomorphic to the integers, with tokens:

$$(1, \{\emptyset\}), \ (2, (1, \{\emptyset\})), \ \cdots, \ (2, (2, \cdots (2, (1, \{\emptyset\})) \cdots)), \ \cdots$$

$\square$

12.5.3 Product

The product construction on cpo's is the coordinatewise order on pairs of their elements. The desired effect is obtained on information systems by forming the product of the token sets and taking finite sets to be consistent if their projections are consistent and a consistent set to entail a token if its projections entail the appropriate component.

The construction will rely on these simple operations.

Notation: We use the product $A \times B$ of sets, A and B, consisting of pairs, together with projections $proj_1 : A \times B \to A$ and $proj_2 : A \times B \to B$ acting so $proj_1(a, b) = a$ and $proj_2(a, b) = b$.

Definition: Let $\mathcal{A} = (A, \mathrm{Con}_A, \vdash_A)$ and $\mathcal{B} = (B, \mathrm{Con}_B, \vdash_B)$ be information systems. Define their *product*, $A \times B$, to be the information system $\mathcal{C} = (C, \mathrm{Con}, \vdash)$ where:

1. $C = A \times B$
2. $X \in \mathrm{Con} \iff proj_1 X \in \mathrm{Con}_A \ \& \ proj_2 X \in \mathrm{Con}_B$

3. $X \vdash a \iff proj_1 X \vdash_A proj_1(a) \ \& \ proj_2 X \vdash_B proj_2(a)$.

As intended the elements of the product of two information systems have two components each corresponding to an element from each information system. Intuitively a token of the product $A_1 \times A_2$ is a pair of assertions about the two respective components.

Proposition 12.26 *Let A and B be information systems. Then $A \times B$ is an information system and*

$$x \in |A \times B| \iff \exists x_1 \in |A|, x_2 \in |B|. \ x = x_1 \times x_2.$$

Proof: It is routine to check that the product of two information systems is an information system.

It remains to show

$$x \in |A \times B| \iff x = x_1 \times x_2$$

for some $x_1 \in |A|, x_2 \in |B|$.

"$\Leftarrow$": If $x_1 \in |A|$ and $x_2 \in |B|$ it follows straightforwardly that their product $x_1 \times x_2 \in |A \times B|$.

"$\Rightarrow$": Suppose $x \in |A \times B|$. Define $x_1 = proj_1 x$ and $x_2 = proj_2 x$. It is easy to check that $x_1 \in |A|$ and $x_2 \in |B|$. Clearly $x \subseteq x_1 \times x_2$. To show the converse inclusion assume $(a, b) \in x_1 \times x_2$. Then there must be a', b' such that $(a, b'), (a', b) \in x$. By the definition of entailment in the product we see $\{(a, b'), (a', b)\} \vdash (a, b)$ from which it follows that $(a, b) \in x$. Thus $x = x_1 \times x_2$.   □

Consequently the cpo of elements of the product of information systems is isomorphic to the product of their cpo's of elements:

Corollary 12.27 *Let A and B be information systems. There is an isomorphism of cpo's*

$$|A \times B| \cong |A| \times |B|$$

given by $x \mapsto (proj_1 x, proj_2 x)$ with mutual inverse $(x_1, x_2) \mapsto x_1 \times x_2$.

Theorem 12.28 *The operation $\times$ is a continuous operation on information systems ordered by $\trianglelefteq$.*

Proof: We show that the product operation is monotonic and continuous on token-sets. Then by Lemma 12.15 we know it is continuous with respect to $\trianglelefteq$.

Monotonic: Let $A \trianglelefteq A'$ and B be information systems. The tokens of $A \times B$ obviously form a subset of the tokens of $A' \times B$. Suppose X is a subset of the tokens of $A \times B$. Then X is consistent in $A \times B$ iff $proj_1 X$ and $proj_2 X$ are both consistent in A and B

respectively. Because $\mathcal{A} \unlhd \mathcal{A}'$ this is equivalent to X being consistent in $\mathcal{A}' \times \mathcal{B}$. Suppose X is a finite set of tokens of $\mathcal{A} \times \mathcal{B}$ and c is a token of $\mathcal{A} \times \mathcal{B}$. Then $X \vdash c$ in $\mathcal{A} \times \mathcal{B}$ iff $c = (a_1, a_2)$ and $proj_1 X \vdash_A a_1$ and $proj_2 X \vdash_B a_2$. Because $\mathcal{A} \unlhd \mathcal{A}'$ this is equivalent to $X \vdash c$ in $\mathcal{A}' \times \mathcal{B}$. Thus $\mathcal{A} \times \mathcal{B} \unlhd \mathcal{A}' \times \mathcal{B}$. Thus $\times$ is monotonic in its first argument.

Continuous on token-sets: Now let $\mathcal{A}_0 \unlhd \mathcal{A}_1 \unlhd \cdots \unlhd \mathcal{A}_i \unlhd \cdots$ be an ω-chain of information systems. A token of $(\bigcup_i \mathcal{A}_i) \times \mathcal{B}$ is clearly a token in $\mathcal{A}_i \times \mathcal{B}$ for some $i \in \omega$, and so a token of $\bigcup_i (\mathcal{A}_i \times \mathcal{B})$.

Thus by Lemma 12.15, $\times$ is continuous in its first argument. Similarly it is continuous in its second argument. Thus $\times$ is a continuous operation on information systems with respect to $\unlhd$. $\Box$

The information system **1**, representing a singleton domain, can be taken to be the empty product of information systems, a special case of the product construction.

12.5.4 Lifted function space

Let $\mathcal{A}$ and $\mathcal{B}$ be information systems. It is not possible to represent the space of continuous functions $|\mathcal{A}| \to |\mathcal{B}|$ for arbitrary $\mathcal{B}$ (see Exercise 12.11 above). Nor can we hope to solve domain equations such as

$$X \cong [X \to 2]$$

where **2** is the two element discrete cpo. However, the function spaces which arise in denotational semantics most often have the form $D \to E_\perp$ where the range is lifted. This operation can be mimicked on arbitrary information systems:

Definition: Let $\mathcal{A} = (A, \mathrm{Con}_A, \vdash_A)$ and $\mathcal{B} = (B, \mathrm{Con}_B, \vdash_B)$ be information systems. Their *lifted function space*, $\mathcal{A} \to \mathcal{B}_\perp$, is the information system $(C, \mathrm{Con}, \vdash)$ given by:

1. $C = ((\mathrm{Con}_A \setminus \{\emptyset\}) \times \mathrm{Con}_B) \cup \{(\emptyset, \emptyset)\}$
2. $\{(X_1, Y_1), \ldots, (X_n, Y_n)\} \in \mathrm{Con} \iff$
   $\forall I \subseteq \{1, \ldots, n\}. \bigcup \{X_i \mid i \in I\} \in \mathrm{Con}_A \Rightarrow \bigcup \{Y_i \mid i \in I\} \in \mathrm{Con}_B$
3. $\{(X_1, Y_1), \ldots, (X_n, Y_n)\} \vdash (X, Y) \iff$
   $\{(X_1, Y_1), \ldots, (X_n, Y_n)\} \neq \emptyset \ \& \ \bigcup \{Y_i \mid X \vdash_A^* X_i\} \vdash_B^* Y.$

The intention is that tokens (X, Y) of the function space assert of a function that if its input satisfies X then its output satisfies Y. We check that this construction does indeed give an information system and give an alternative characterisation of the elements of the function space of information systems.

Lemma 12.29 *Let $\mathcal{A} = (A, \mathrm{Con}_A, \vdash_A)$ and $\mathcal{B} = (B, \mathrm{Con}_B, \vdash_B)$ be information systems. Then $\mathcal{A} \to \mathcal{B}_\perp$ is an information system.*

We have $r \in |\mathcal{A} \to \mathcal{B}_\perp|$ iff $r \subseteq \mathrm{Con}_A \times \mathrm{Con}_B$, so r is a relation, which we write in an infix way, which satisfies

(a) $\emptyset r Y \iff Y = \emptyset$,

(b) $XrY \ \& \ XrY' \Rightarrow Xr(Y \cup Y')$

(c) $X' \vdash_A^* X \ \& \ XrY \ \& \ Y \vdash_B^* Y' \Rightarrow X'rY'$

for all $X, X' \in \mathrm{Con}_A$, $Y, Y' \in \mathrm{Con}_B$.

Proof: Let $\mathcal{A}$ and $\mathcal{B}$ be information systems. We should first check that $\mathcal{A} \to \mathcal{B}_\perp$ is an information system. The more difficult conditions are axioms 3 and 5 in the definition of information system, which we verify, leaving the others to the reader:

Axiom 3. Suppose $\{(X_1, Y_1), \ldots, (X_n, Y_n)\} \vdash (X, Y)$. We require

$$\{(X_1, Y_1), \ldots, (X_n, Y_n), (X, Y)\} \in \mathrm{Con}.$$

Thus we require that if $J \subseteq \{1, \ldots, n\}$ and $\bigcup\{X_j \mid j \in J\} \cup X \in \mathrm{Con}_A$ then

$$\bigcup\{Y_j \mid j \in J\} \cup Y \in \mathrm{Con}_B.$$

Assume $\bigcup\{X_j \mid j \in J\} \cup X \in \mathrm{Con}_A$. Then

$$\bigcup\{X_j \mid j \in J\} \cup \bigcup\{X_i \mid X \vdash_A^* X_i\} \in \mathrm{Con}_A.$$

Now as $\{(X_1, Y_1), \ldots, (X_n, Y_n)\} \in \mathrm{Con}$ this makes

$$\bigcup\{Y_j \mid j \in J\} \cup \bigcup\{Y_i \mid X \vdash_A^* X_i\} \in \mathrm{Con}_B.$$

But $\bigcup\{Y_i \mid X \vdash_A^* X_i\} \vdash_B^* Y$, because $\{(X_1, Y_1), \ldots, (X_n, Y_n)\} \vdash (X, Y)$. Consequently

$$\bigcup\{Y_j \mid j \in J\} \cup \bigcup\{Y_i \mid X \vdash_A^* X_i\} \vdash_B^* Y$$

so $\bigcup\{Y_j \mid j \in J\} \cup Y \in \mathrm{Con}_B$, as required to verify 3.

Axiom 5. Suppose

$$\{(X_1, Y_1), \ldots, (X_n, Y_n)\} \vdash^* \{(Z_1, V_1), \ldots, (Z_{m-1}, V_{m-1})\} \vdash (U, W).$$

We require $\{(X_1, Y_1), \ldots, (X_n, Y_n)\} \vdash (U, W)$ *i.e.*

$$\bigcup\{Y_i \mid U \vdash_A^* X_i\} \vdash_B^* W.$$

Suppose $U \vdash_A^* Z_j$. Then because $\bigcup \{Y_i \mid Z_j \vdash_A^* X_i\} \vdash_B^* V_j$ we have $\bigcup \{Y_i \mid U \vdash_A^* X_i\} \vdash_B^*$ V_j. Therefore

$$\bigcup \{Y_i \mid U \vdash_A^* X_i\} \vdash_B^* \bigcup \{V_j \mid U \vdash_A^* Z_j\} \vdash_B^* W.$$

By the transitivity of $\vdash_B^*$ we obtain the required result, and have verified 5.

It remains to verify the characterisation of the elements of $\mathcal{A} \to \mathcal{B}_\perp$ as those relations satisfying (a), (b) and (c) above:

"only if": Suppose r is an element of $\mathcal{A} \to \mathcal{B}_\perp$. Then r is nonempty and so contains some (X, Y). By 3 in the definition of entailment of $\mathcal{A} \to \mathcal{B}_\perp$ we obtain that $(\emptyset, \emptyset) \in r$. This establishes (a)"$\Leftarrow$." The converse, (a)"$\Rightarrow$", holds as the only token of form $(\emptyset, Y)$ in the lifted function space is $(\emptyset, \emptyset)$. The properties (b) and (c) follow fairly directly from 2 and 3 in the definition of $\mathcal{A} \to \mathcal{B}_\perp$.

"if": Assume $r \subseteq \text{Con}_A \times \text{Con}_B$ satisfies (a), (b) and (c). Then certainly r is a nonempty subset of $(\text{Con}_A \setminus \{\emptyset\}) \times \text{Con}_B \cup \{(\emptyset, \emptyset)\}$. In order that $r \in |\mathcal{A} \to \mathcal{B}_\perp|$, we also require that r is consistent and $\vdash$-closed.

Suppose $\{(X_1, Y_1), \ldots, (X_n, Y_n)\} \subseteq r$. Assume $I \subseteq \{1, \cdots, n\}$ and that $X =_{def}$ $\bigcup \{X_i \mid i \in I\} \in \text{Con}_A$. Then for all $i \in I$ we have $X \vdash_A^* X_i$ which with $(X_i, Y_i) \in r$ ensures $(X, Y_i) \in r$ by (c). Using (b), we see $\bigcup \{Y_i \mid i \in I\}) \in \text{Con}_B$. Hence r is consistent.

Now we show r is closed under $\vdash$. Suppose

$$\{(X_1, Y_1), \ldots, (X_n, Y_n)\} \subseteq r \text{ and } \{(X_1, Y_1), \ldots, (X_n, Y_n)\} \vdash (X, Y).$$

We require that $(X, Y) \in r$. By (c), if $X \vdash_A^* X_i$ then $(X, Y_i) \in r$, as $(X_i, Y_i) \in r$. It follows by several applications of (b) that $(X, Y') \in r$ where $Y' =_{def} \bigcup \{Y_i \mid X \vdash_A^* X_i\}$. But now by the definition of $\vdash$ we see $Y' \vdash_B^* Y$. Hence, by (c), we obtain $(X, Y) \in r$. $\square$

Scott calls relations like those above *approximable mappings*. Intuitively, an approximable mapping expresses how information in one information system entails information in another. For an approximable mapping $r \in |\mathcal{A} \to \mathcal{B}_\perp|$, the situation that XrY can be read as saying information X in $\mathcal{A}$ entails Y in $\mathcal{B}$. In particular the relation r might be induced by a computation which given input from $\mathcal{A}$ delivers output values in $\mathcal{B}$. In fact such approximable mappings, which coincide with the elements of

$$|\mathcal{A} \to \mathcal{B}_\perp|$$

are in 1-1 correspondence with continuous functions

$$[|\mathcal{A}| \to |\mathcal{B}|_\perp];$$

the correspondence determines an order isomorphism between the elements $|\mathcal{A} \to \mathcal{B}_\perp|$ ordered by inclusion and the continuous functions $[|\mathcal{A}| \to |\mathcal{B}|_\perp]$ ordered pointwise.

The correspondence is most easily shown for a particular way of representing lifting on cpo's of elements of information systems. Recall from Section 8.3.4 that the lifting construction $D_\perp$ on a cpo D assumes an element $\perp$ and a 1-1 function $\lfloor - \rfloor$ with the property that

$$\perp \neq \lfloor x \rfloor$$

for all $x \in D$. The lifted cpo $D_\perp$ is then a copy of D, consisting of elements $\lfloor x \rfloor$, for $x \in D$, below which the element $\perp$ is adjoined. When lifting a cpo $|\mathcal{A}|$, formed from elements of an information system, we can take advantage of the fact that the elements of $\mathcal{A}$ are always nonempty, and choose $\perp = \emptyset$ and $\lfloor x \rfloor = x$. The following proposition assumes this particular choice of interpretation for lifting. The choice simplifies the associated operation $(-)^*$, introduced in Section 8.3.4. Suppose $f : |\mathcal{A}| \to |\mathcal{B}|_\perp$ is a continuous function between cpo's of elements of information systems $\mathcal{A}$ and $\mathcal{B}$. The function f extends to a function

$$f^* : |\mathcal{A}|_\perp \to |\mathcal{B}|_\perp,$$

which with our choice of $\perp$ and $\lfloor - \rfloor$, is given by

$$f^*(z) = \begin{cases} \emptyset & \text{if } z = \emptyset, \\ f(z) & \text{otherwise.} \end{cases}$$

Theorem 12.30 *Let $\mathcal{A}$ and $\mathcal{B}$ be information systems. Define*

$$|\text{-}| : |\mathcal{A} \to \mathcal{B}_\perp| \to [|\mathcal{A}| \to |\mathcal{B}|_\perp],$$
$$\text{'-'} : [|\mathcal{A}| \to |\mathcal{B}|_\perp] \to |\mathcal{A} \to \mathcal{B}_\perp|,$$

by taking

$$|r| = \lambda x \in |\mathcal{A}|. \bigcup \{Y \mid \exists X \subseteq x.\ (X, Y) \in r\},$$
$$\text{'}f\text{'} = \{(X, Y) \in \text{Con}_A \times \text{Con}_B \mid Y \subseteq f^*(\overline{X})\}.$$

Then $|\text{-}|$, '-' are mutual inverses, giving an isomorphism $|\mathcal{A} \to \mathcal{B}_\perp| \cong [|\mathcal{A}| \to |\mathcal{B}|_\perp]$. The function '-' satisfies:

$$\text{'}f\text{'} = \{(X, Y) \mid \emptyset \neq X \in \text{Con}_A\ \&\ Y \subseteq^{fin} f(\overline{X})\} \cup \{(\emptyset, \emptyset)\}.$$

Proof: It is easy to check that $|\text{-}|$ is well-defined—that $|\text{-}|$ gives values which are continuous functions. Showing that '-' yields elements of $\mathcal{A} \to \mathcal{B}_\perp$ is left as an instructive exercise (see Exercise 12.31). It is clear from their definitions that both $|\text{-}|$ and '-' are monotonic.

We claim

$$(X, Y) \in r \iff Y \subseteq |r|^*(\overline{X})$$

for $r \in |\mathcal{A} \to \mathcal{B}_\perp|$, $X \in \mathrm{Con}_A$ and $Y \in \mathrm{Con}_B$. The direction "$\Rightarrow$" follows directly from the definition of $|\text{-}|$. The direction "$\Leftarrow$" follows from Lemma 12.29 above, using properties (b) and (c) of r:

Assume $Y \subseteq |r|^*(\overline{X})$ for $X \in \mathrm{Con}_A$, $Y \in \mathrm{Con}_B$. By the definition of $|r|$ there must be

$$(X_1, Y_1), \cdots, (X_n, Y_n) \in r$$

such that

$$X_1, \cdots, X_n \subseteq \overline{X}, \quad i.e., \quad X \vdash^* X_1 \cup \cdots \cup X_n \tag{1}$$

with

$$Y \subseteq Y_1 \cup \cdots \cup Y_n, \quad \text{so } Y_1 \cup \cdots \cup Y_n \vdash^* Y. \tag{2}$$

Because $X_1 \cup \cdots \cup X_n \vdash^* X_i$ and $X_i r Y_i$ we obtain by (c) that $(X_1 \cup \cdots \cup X_n) r Y_i$, whenever $1 \le i \le n$. Hence by repeated use of (b),

$$(X_1 \cup \cdots \cup X_n) \, r \, (Y_1 \cup \cdots \cup Y_n).$$

But now by (c), from (1) and (2) we get $X r Y$, as required to prove the claim.

Now we have justified the claim, we can show $|\text{-}|$ and '-' give a 1-1 correspondence. We see, for $r \in |\mathcal{A} \to \mathcal{B}_\perp|$, $X \in \mathrm{Con}_A$ and $Y \in \mathrm{Con}_B$, that

$$(X, Y) \in r \iff Y \subseteq |r|^*(\overline{X})$$
$$\iff (X, Y) \in \text{'}|r|\text{'}$$

directly from the definition of '-'. Therefore $r = \text{'}|r|\text{'}$. We also see, for $f \in [|\mathcal{A}| \to |\mathcal{B}|_\perp]$, $X \in \mathrm{Con}_A$ and $Y \in \mathrm{Con}_B$,

$$Y \subseteq f^*(\overline{X}) \iff (X, Y) \in \text{'}f\text{'} \iff Y \subseteq |\text{'}f\text{'}|^*(\overline{X});$$

this follows immediately from the definition of '-' and the claim above. A continuous function is determined uniquely by the values it gives on finite elements in $|\mathcal{A}|$ of the form $\overline{X}$, for $X \in \mathrm{Con}_A$: any element x is a least upper bound of an ω-chain $\overline{X}_0 \subseteq \overline{X}_1 \subseteq \cdots$ and by continuity $f(x) = \bigcup_n f(\overline{X}_n)$. Therefore $f = |\text{'}f\text{'}|$.

We conclude that $|\text{-}|$ and '-' determine an isomorphism.

The alternative characterisation of '-' follows directly from the particular way the extension f^*, of $f : |\mathcal{A}| \to |\mathcal{B}|_\perp$, is defined. $\qquad\qquad\square$

Exercise 12.31 Show that the '-' of Theorem 12.30 above is well-defined as a function, *i.e.*, that given a continuous function

$$f : |\mathcal{A}| \to |\mathcal{B}|_\perp$$

then

$$`f' = \{(X, Y) \in \text{Con}_A \times \text{Con}_B \mid Y \subseteq f^*(\overline{X})\}$$

is an element of $A \to B_\perp$. □

Exercise 12.32 Describe the tokens in the bottom element of $A \to B_\perp$, for information systems A and B. □

Theorem 12.33 *The operation of lifted function space is a continuous operation on information systems ordered by $\trianglelefteq$.*

Proof: We show that lifted function space is a continuous operation on information systems in each argument separately with respect to $\trianglelefteq$. We use Lemma 12.15.

First we show the construction is monotonic in its first argument. Suppose $A \trianglelefteq A'$ and B are information systems. Write $C = (C, \text{Con}, \vdash) = A \to B_\perp$ and $C' = (C', \text{Con}', \vdash') = A' \to B_\perp$. We require $C \trianglelefteq C'$ so we check conditions 1, 2, 3 in the definition of $\trianglelefteq$ hold:

1. Clearly the tokens of C are included in those of C'.

2. Let $(X_1, Y_1), \ldots, (X_n, Y_n)$ be tokens of C. Because $A \trianglelefteq A'$ we have $\bigcup_{i \in I} X_i \in \text{Con}_A$ iff $\bigcup_{i \in I} X_i \in \text{Con}_{A'}$, for any subset $I \subseteq \{1, \ldots, n\}$. So inspecting the definition of the consistency predicate for the lifted function space we see that

$$\{(X_1, Y_1), \ldots (X_n, Y_n)\} \in \text{Con iff } \{(X_1, Y_1), \ldots (X_n, Y_n)\} \in \text{Con}'.$$

3. Suppose $(X_1, Y_1), \ldots (X_n, Y_n)$ and (X, Y) are tokens of C. Because $A \trianglelefteq A'$ we have $X \vdash_A^* X_i$ iff $X \vdash_{A'}^* X_i$. So inspecting the definition of the entailment relation for the lifted function space we see that

$$\{(X_1, Y_1), \ldots (X_n, Y_n)\} \vdash (X, Y) \text{ iff } \{(X_1, Y_1), \ldots (X_n, Y_n)\} \vdash' (X, Y).$$

Thus $C \trianglelefteq C'$ so lifted function space is monotonic in its first argument.

Now we show it is continuous on token-sets in its first argument. Let $A_0 \trianglelefteq A_1 \trianglelefteq \cdots \trianglelefteq A_i \trianglelefteq \cdots$ be an ω-chain of information systems $A_i = (A_i, \text{Con}_i, \vdash_i)$. Let (X, Y) be a token of $(\bigcup_i A_i) \to B_\perp$. Then X is a consistent set of $\bigcup_i A_i$. But then $X \in \text{Con}_i$, for some i, so (X, Y) is a token of $A_i \to B_\perp$. Thus as required (X, Y) is a token of $\bigcup_i (A_i \to B_{i\perp})$.

By Lemma 12.15 we deduce that lifted function space is continuous in its first argument. A similar but even simpler argument shows that it is continuous in its second argument too, and therefore continuous. □

We can now give definitions of information systems by composing the operations lifting, sum, product, and lifted function space, starting from the information system **0**. Because these operations are all continuous with respect to $\trianglelefteq$ the definitions can be recursive. These constructions can be used to give a semantics to a language with recursive types.

Example: The operation $X \mapsto (X \to X_\perp)$ is a continuous operation on information systems. It has a least fixed point $\mathcal{L} = (\mathcal{L} \to \mathcal{L}_\perp)$. This information system, has a cpo of elements $D = |\mathcal{L}|$ such that the following chain of isomorphisms hold:

$$D = |\mathcal{L}| = |\mathcal{L} \to \mathcal{L}_\perp| \cong [|\mathcal{L}| \to |\mathcal{L}|_\perp] = [D \to D_\perp],$$

These follow from the fact that the information-system construction of lifted function space achieve the same effect as the corresponding cpo constructions to within isomorphism. Thus $D \cong [D \to D_\perp]$. □

Exercise 12.34 Why do we build a large cpo from the relation $\trianglelefteq$ rather than the simpler relation based on coordinatewise inclusion of one information in another? This is a partial order and does indeed give another large cpo. Verify that it suffers a major drawback; the lifted-function-space construction on information systems, while being continuous in its right argument, is not even monotonic in its left argument with respect to this inclusion order. □

12.6 Further reading

Informations systems were introduced by Dana Scott in [90] which is recommended reading, though the presentation here has been more closely based on [103]. Note that usually information systems are used to represent Scott domains *with* a bottom element. The recent book [87] on domain theory, for undergraduate mathematicians, is based on information systems and is quite accessible. Lecture notes of Gordon Plotkin use a variant of information systems to represent predomains (not necessarily with bottoms) as does [19]. Information systems can be regarded as special kinds of *locales* for "pointless topology" (see [53, 98]) in which neighbourhoods rather than points are taken as primary. This view has uses in both topology and logic. Information systems can be given an even more logical character by taking the tokens to be propositions built up syntactically. Such a development coupled to the duality between spaces and their presentation via neighbourhoods led Samson Abramsky to a "logic of domains" [2]. To handle the Plotkin powerdomain requires a generalisation so that a wider class of domains (SFP objects) can be represented. Suitable generalisations can be found in [2] and [108]. In the late '70's Gérard Berry discovered an alternative "stable" domain theory which gives another foundation for much of denotational semantics. Here the cpo's are restricted to special Scott domains called dI-domains and functions are stable as well as continuous. This alternative domain theory has its own special representation in which the role of tokens of an information system is replaced that of "events"; the work here on information systems can be paralleled on "event structures" (see [104, 105]).

13 Recursive types

The functional languages of Chapter 11, their syntax, operational and denotational semantics, are extended to include recursive types. The denotational semantics makes use of information systems to denote such types. Recursive types of natural numbers, lists, and types forming models of λ-calculi are considered for the eager and lazy languages. The use of information systems has an an extra pay-off. It yields relatively simple proofs of adequacy, and characterisations of fixed-point operators in the eager and lazy λ-calculi. The treatment provides a mathematical basis from which to reason about eager functional languages like Standard ML, and lazy functional languages like Miranda, [1] Orwell or Haskell.

13.1 An eager language

In the last chapter we saw a way to understand recursively-defined types. With this in mind we introduce the facility to define types recursively into the language of Chapter 11. Type expressions τ will have the form:

$$\tau ::= 1 \mid \tau_1 * \tau_2 \mid \tau_1 -> \tau_2 \mid \tau_1 + \tau_2 \mid X \mid \mu X.\tau$$

where X ranges over an infinite set of *type variables*, and $\mu X.\tau$ is a recursively-defined type. There are the familiar type constructors of product, function space and sum. There is only one basic type **1**, to be thought of as consisting of a single value, the empty tuple (). Other types like numbers and lists and their operations will be definable. The free and bound variables of a type expression are defined in the standard way and, as usual, we will say a type expression is closed when all its variables are bound.

The raw (untyped) syntax of terms is given by

$$
\begin{aligned}
t ::= \quad & () \mid (t_1, t_2) \mid \mathbf{fst}(t) \mid \mathbf{snd}(t) \mid \\
& x \mid \lambda x.t \mid (t_1\ t_2) \mid \\
& \mathbf{inl}(t) \mid \mathbf{inr}(t) \mid \mathbf{case}\ t\ \mathbf{of}\ \mathbf{inl}(x_1).t_1,\ \mathbf{inr}(x_2).t_2. \mid \\
& \mathbf{abs}(t) \mid \mathbf{rep}(t) \mid \\
& \mathbf{rec}\ f.(\lambda x.t)
\end{aligned}
$$

where x, x_1, x_2, f are variables in **Var**. The syntax includes operations familiar from Chapter 11. The two new operations of **abs** and **rep** accompany recursively defined types and will be explained shortly. The syntax does not include a construction

$$\mathbf{let}\ x \Leftarrow t_1\ \mathbf{in}\ t_2.$$

---

[1] Miranda is a trademark of Research Software Ltd

But this can be defined to stand for $((\lambda x.t_2)\, t_1)$.

We assume each variable x has as unique *closed* type, $type(x)$. So as not to run out of variables we will assume

$$\{x \in \mathbf{Var} \mid type(x) = \tau\}$$

is infinite for each closed type τ.

The assignment of types to variables is extended to a general typing judgement $t : \tau$ where t is a term and τ is a closed type, by the following rules:

Typing rules

Variables:
$$\frac{}{x : \tau} \quad \text{if } type(x) = \tau$$

Products:
$$\frac{}{() : \mathbf{1}}$$

$$\frac{t_1 : \tau_1 \quad t_2 : \tau_2}{(t_1, t_2) : \tau_1 * \tau_2}$$

$$\frac{t : \tau_1 * \tau_2}{\mathbf{fst}(t) : \tau_1} \quad \frac{t : \tau_1 * \tau_2}{\mathbf{snd}(t) : \tau_2}$$

Function types:
$$\frac{x : \tau_1 \quad t : \tau_2}{\lambda x.t : \tau_1 \mathbin{->} \tau_2} \quad \frac{t_1 : \tau_1 \mathbin{->} \tau_2 \quad t_2 : \tau_1}{(t_1\, t_2) : \tau_2}$$

Sums:
$$\frac{t : \tau_1}{\mathbf{inl}(t) : \tau_1 + \tau_2} \quad \frac{t : \tau_2}{\mathbf{inr}(t) : \tau_1 + \tau_2}$$

$$\frac{t : \tau_1 + \tau_2 \quad x_1 : \tau_1 \quad x_2 : \tau_2 \quad t_1 : \tau \quad t_2 : \tau}{\mathbf{case}\ t\ \mathbf{of}\ \mathbf{inl}(x_1).t_1,\ \mathbf{inr}(x_2).t_2 : \tau}$$

Recursive types:
$$\frac{t : \tau[\mu X.\tau/X]}{\mathbf{abs}(t) : \mu X.\tau} \quad \frac{t : \mu X.\tau}{\mathbf{rep}(t) : \tau[\mu X.\tau/X]}$$

rec:
$$\frac{f : \tau \quad \lambda x.t : \tau}{\mathbf{rec}\, f.(\lambda x.t) : \tau}$$

As before, a term t is said to be *typable* when $t : \tau$ for some type τ. The free variables $FV(t)$ of a typable term t are defined exactly as in Chapter 11 (see Section 11.1). Henceforth we will restrict attention to typable terms.

The language allows the definition of recursive types like the natural numbers

$$N \equiv_{def} \mu X.(\mathbf{1} + X),$$

or lists of them

$$L \equiv_{def} \mu Y.(\mathbf{1} + N * Y),$$

or more bizarre types such as

$$\Lambda \equiv_{def} \mu Z.(Z\text{->} Z),$$

which as we will see is a model of an (eager) λ-calculus. The term constructors **abs** and **rep** serve as names of the isomorphisms between a type $\mu X.\tau$ and its unfolding $\tau[\mu X.\tau/X]$. They play an important role in defining useful operations on recursive types. The constructor **rep** takes an element $t : \mu X.\tau$ to its representing element $\mathbf{rep}(t) : \tau[\mu X.\tau/X]$. The constructor **abs** takes such a representation $u : \tau[\mu X.\tau/X]$ to its abstract counterpart $\mathbf{abs}(u) : \mu X.\tau$. To understand the use of **abs** and **rep** we look at two simple types, natural numbers and lists, and how to define functions involving them.

Example: Natural numbers
The type of natural numbers can be defined by

$$N \equiv_{def} \mu X.(\mathbf{1} + X).$$

For this type **rep** can be thought of as a map

$$N \ \xrightarrow{\ \mathbf{rep}\ } \ \mathbf{1} + N$$

and **abs** as a map

$$N \ \xleftarrow{\ \mathbf{abs}\ } \ \mathbf{1} + N.$$

The constant $Zero$ can be defined as:

$$Zero \equiv_{def} \mathbf{abs}(\mathbf{inl}())$$

The successor operation can be defined by taking

$$Succ(t) \equiv_{def} \mathbf{abs}(\mathbf{inr}(t))$$

for any term $t : N$. The successor function is then given as the term

$$\lambda x.\ Succ(x) : N\text{->} N$$

where x is a variable of type N. These operations allow us to build up "numbers" of type N as

$$Zero,$$
$$Succ(Zero),$$
$$Succ(Succ(Zero)),$$

$$\vdots$$

We also want to define functions on natural numbers, most often with the help of a cases construction

$$\textbf{Case } x \textbf{ of } Zero.\ t_1,$$
$$Succ(z).\ t_2.$$

yielding t_1 in the case where x is $Zero$ and t_2, generally depending on z, in the case where x is a successor $Succ(z)$. This too can be defined; regard it as an abbreviation for

$$\textbf{case rep}(x) \textbf{ of inr}(w).t_1,$$
$$\textbf{inl}(z).t_2.$$

Now, for example, addition is definable by:

$$add \equiv_{def} \textbf{rec } f.\ (\lambda x.\lambda y.\ \textbf{Case } x \textbf{ of } Zero.\ y,$$
$$Succ(z).\ Succ((fz)\ y),$$

a term of type $(N \mathbin{-\!>} (N \mathbin{-\!>} N))$. $\square$

Example: Lists

A type of lists over natural numbers N is defined by

$$L \equiv_{def} \mu Y.(\mathbf{1} + N * Y).$$

We can realise the usual list-constructions. The empty list is defined by:

$$Nil \equiv_{def} \textbf{abs}(\textbf{inl}())$$

The *cons*ing operation is defined by taking

$$Cons(p) \equiv_{def} \textbf{abs}(\textbf{inr}(p))$$

for any $p : N * L$. The operation $Cons$ acts on a pair $(n, l) : N * L$, consisting of terms $n : N$ and $l : L$, to produce the list $Cons(n, l)$ with "head" n and "tail" l. It is associated with the function term

$$\lambda x.\ Cons(x) : N * L \mathbin{-\!>} L$$

where x is a variable of type $N * L$. Functions on lists are conveniently defined with the help of a cases construction. The usual cases construction on lists

$$\textbf{Case } l \textbf{ of } Nil. \ t_1,$$

$$Cons(x, l'). \ t_2$$

yields t_1 in the case where the list l is empty and t_2 in the case where it is $Cons(x, l')$. It is definable by

$$\textbf{case rep } (l) \textbf{ of inl}(w). \ t_1,$$

$$\textbf{inr}(z). \ t_2[\textbf{fst}(z)/x, \textbf{snd}(z)/l'].$$

□

13.2   Eager operational semantics

As before, eager evaluation will be expressed by a relation

$$t \to c$$

between typable closed terms t and canonical forms c. The *canonical forms* of type τ, written C_τ, are closed terms given by the following rules:

$$\overline{() \in C_1}$$

$$\frac{c_1 \in C_{\tau_1} \quad c_2 \in C_{\tau_2}}{(c_1, c_2) \in C_{\tau_1 * \tau_2}}$$

$$\frac{\lambda x.t : \tau_1 \mathbin{-\!\!>} \tau_2 \quad \lambda x.t \text{ closed}}{\lambda x.t \in C_{\tau_1 \to \tau_2}}$$

$$\frac{c \in C_{\tau_1}}{\textbf{inl}(c) \in C_{\tau_1 + \tau_2}} \qquad \frac{c \in C_{\tau_2}}{\textbf{inr}(c) \in C_{\tau_1 + \tau_2}}$$

$$\frac{c \in C_{\tau[\mu X.\tau/X]}}{\textbf{abs}(c) \in C_{\mu X.\tau}}$$

The only rule producing canonical forms of recursive types is the last, expressing that the canonical forms of type $\mu X.\tau$ are copies $\textbf{abs}(c)$ of canonical forms of $\tau[\mu X.\tau/X]$. Because $\tau[\mu X.\tau/X]$ is generally not smaller than $\mu X.\tau$, the canonical forms cannot be defined by structural induction on types—the reason they have an inductive definition.

Example: Natural numbers

The type $N \equiv \mu X.(1 + X)$ of natural numbers has canonical forms associated with the two components of the sum. There is a single canonical form

$$Zero \equiv_{def} \mathbf{abs}(\mathbf{inl}())$$

associated with the left-hand-side. Associated with the right-hand-side are canonical forms

$$\mathbf{abs}(\mathbf{inr}(c))$$

where c is a canonical form of N. With the abbreviation

$$Succ(t) \equiv \mathbf{abs}\ inr(t)$$

we obtain these canonical forms for N: $Succ(Zero),\ Succ(Succ(Zero)),\ \cdots$

The canonical forms, which serve as numerals, are built-up from $Zero$ by repeatedly applying the successor operation. In the denotational semantics N will denote the information system with elements isomorphic to the discrete cpo of natural numbers. $\square$

Example: Lists

The type of lists over natural numbers, defined by $L \equiv \mu Y.(1 + N * Y)$, has canonical forms

$$Nil \equiv \mathbf{abs}(\mathbf{inl}()) : L$$
$$Cons(n, l) \equiv \mathbf{abs}(\mathbf{inr}(n, l))$$

for canonical forms $n : N$ and $l : L$. In other words, a canonical forms of type L is either the empty list or a finite list of natural numbers $[n_1, n_2, \cdots]$ built up as

$$Cons(n_1, Cons(n_2, Cons(\cdots)\cdots)).$$

$\square$

The eager evaluation relation between typable closed terms t and canonical forms c is defined by the following rules:

Evaluation rules

$$\frac{}{c \to c} \quad \text{if } c \text{ is canonical}$$

$$\frac{t_1 \to c_1 \quad t_2 \to c_2}{(t_1, t_2) \to (c_1, c_2)}$$

$$\frac{t \to (c_1, c_2)}{\mathbf{fst}(t) \to c_1} \qquad \frac{t \to (c_1, c_2)}{\mathbf{snd}(t) \to c_2}$$

$$\frac{t_1 \to \lambda x.t_1' \quad t_2 \to c_2 \quad t_1'[c_2/x] \to c}{(t_1\, t_2) \to c}$$

$$\frac{t \to \mathbf{inl}(c_1) \quad t_1[c_1/x_1] \to c}{\mathbf{case}\ t\ \mathbf{of}\ \mathbf{inl}(x_1).t_1,\ \mathbf{inr}(x_2).t_2 \to c} \qquad \frac{t \to \mathbf{inr}(c_2) \quad t_2[c_2/x_2] \to c}{\mathbf{case}\ t\ \mathbf{of}\ \mathbf{inr}(x_1).t_1,\ \mathbf{inr}(x_2).t_2 \to c}$$

$$\frac{t \to c}{\mathbf{abs}(t) \to \mathbf{abs}(c)} \qquad \frac{t \to \mathbf{abs}(c)}{\mathbf{rep}(t) \to c}$$

$$\frac{}{\mathbf{rec}\ f.(\lambda x.t) \to \lambda x.t[\mathbf{rec}\ f.(\lambda x.t)/f]}$$

Evaluation is deterministic and respects types:

Proposition 13.1 *Let t be a typable, closed term and c, c_1 and c_2 canonical forms. Then*

(i) $t \to c$ & $t : \tau \Rightarrow c : \tau$,
(ii) $t \to c_1$ & $t \to c_2 \Rightarrow c_1 \equiv c_2$.

Proof: By rule induction.   □

13.3   Eager denotational semantics

A typable, closed term can evaluate to a canonical form or diverge. Accordingly we will take its denotation to be an element of $(V_\tau)_\perp$ where V_τ is a cpo of values, including those for canonical forms, of the type τ. This time the language allows types to be defined recursively. We use the machinery of the last chapter to define an information system of values for each type.

A *type environment* χ is a function from type variables to information systems. By structural induction on type expressions, define

$$
\begin{aligned}
\mathcal{V}[\![1]\!]\chi &= (\emptyset, \{\emptyset\}, \emptyset)_\perp && \text{(also called 1)}\\
\mathcal{V}[\![\tau_1 * \tau_2]\!]\chi &= (\mathcal{V}[\![\tau_1]\!]\chi) \times (\mathcal{V}[\![\tau_2]\!]\chi)\\
\mathcal{V}[\![\tau_1 {-}{>} \tau_2]\!]\chi &= (\mathcal{V}[\![\tau_1]\!]\chi) \to (\mathcal{V}[\![\tau_2]\!]\chi)_\perp\\
\mathcal{V}[\![\tau_1 + \tau_2]\!]\chi &= (\mathcal{V}[\![\tau_1]\!]\chi) + (\mathcal{V}[\![\tau_2]\!]\chi)\\
\mathcal{V}[\![X]\!]\chi &= \chi(X)\\
\mathcal{V}[\![\mu X.\tau]\!]\chi &= \mu I.\mathcal{V}[\![\tau]\!]\chi[I/X]
\end{aligned}
$$

All the operations on the right of the clauses of the semantic definition are operations on information systems. The type expression $\mu X.\tau$, in an environment χ, is denoted by the $\trianglelefteq$-least fixed point of

$$I \mapsto \mathcal{V}[\![\tau]\!]\chi[I/X]$$

in the cpo of information systems.

A closed type τ is thus associated with an information system

$$\mathcal{V}[\![\tau]\!]\chi = (\mathrm{Tok}_\tau, \mathrm{Con}_\tau, \vdash_\tau)$$

whose elements form a cpo of *values*

$$V_\tau =_{def} |\mathcal{V}[\![\tau]\!]\chi|,$$

where the type environment χ does not affect the resulting denotation and can be arbitrary. With respect to an environment for its free variables a term of type τ will denote an element of $(V_\tau)_\perp$. For simplicity we choose the following interpretation of $\perp$ and the lifting function $\lfloor\,\text{-}\,\rfloor : V_\tau \to (V_\tau)_\perp$. Because the elements of an information system are always non-empty, the conditions required of $\lfloor\,\text{-}\,\rfloor$ and $\perp$ are met if we take

$$\perp = \emptyset, \text{ the emptyset, and } \lfloor x \rfloor = x, \text{ for all } x \in V_\tau.$$

The cpo of environments **Env** consists of

$$\rho : Var \to \bigcup \{V_\tau \mid \tau \text{ a closed type expression}\}$$

such that $\rho(x) \in V_{type(x)}$, ordered pointwise.

In presenting the denotational semantics it helps if we make certain identifications. Instead of regarding the sum construction on cpo's of elements of information systems as merely isomorphic to the cpo of elements of the sum of information systems, as expressed by Corollary 12.24, we will actually assume that the two cpo's are equal. That is, for information systems $\mathcal{A}$ and $\mathcal{B}$ we will take

$$|\mathcal{A}| + |\mathcal{B}| = |\mathcal{A} + \mathcal{B}|$$

with the injection functions $in_1 : |\mathcal{A}| \to |\mathcal{A}| + |\mathcal{B}|$, $in_2 : |\mathcal{B}| \to |\mathcal{A}| + |\mathcal{B}|$ given by

$$in_1(x) =_{def} inj_1 x = \{(1, a) \mid a \in x\},$$
$$in_2(x) =_{def} inj_2 x = \{(2, b) \mid b \in x\}.$$

More noteworthy is a similar identification for product. The product $|\mathcal{A}| \times |\mathcal{B}|$, of cpo's of information systems $|\mathcal{A}|$ and $|\mathcal{B}|$, will be taken to *equal* the cpo $|\mathcal{A} \times \mathcal{B}|$. For emphasis:

$$|\mathcal{A}| \times |\mathcal{B}| = |\mathcal{A} \times \mathcal{B}|$$

Recall from Corollary 12.27 that a pair of elements $x \in |\mathcal{A}|, y \in |\mathcal{B}|$ is represented as the element $x \times y \in |\mathcal{A} \times \mathcal{B}|$. So the identification of $|\mathcal{A}| \times |\mathcal{B}|$ with $|\mathcal{A} \times \mathcal{B}|$ means that the operation of pairing in $|\mathcal{A}| \times |\mathcal{B}|$ is represented as the product of sets

$$(x, y) = x \times y$$

for elements $x \in |\mathcal{A}|$ and $y \in |\mathcal{B}|$. The projection functions $\pi_1 : |\mathcal{A}| \times |\mathcal{B}| \to |\mathcal{A}|$ and $\pi_2 : |\mathcal{A}| \times |\mathcal{B}| \to |\mathcal{B}|$ are given by[2]

$$\pi_1(z) =_{def} proj_1 z = \{a \mid \exists b.\ (a, b) \in z\}$$
$$\pi_2(z) =_{def} proj_2 z = \{b \mid \exists a.\ (a, b) \in z\}.$$

With these identifications we avoid the clutter of explicitly mentioning isomorphisms in the semantic definitions associated with sum and product types. We won't however identify continuous functions with their representation as approximable mappings because this might be too confusing. We will use the isomorphisms

$$|\text{-}| : |\mathcal{A} \to \mathcal{B}_\perp| \to [|\mathcal{A}| \to |\mathcal{B}|_\perp],$$
$$'\text{-}' : [|\mathcal{A}| \to |\mathcal{B}|_\perp] \to |\mathcal{A} \to \mathcal{B}_\perp|,$$

of Theorem 12.30, for information systems $\mathcal{A}$ and $\mathcal{B}$. Recall, the functions are given by:

$$|r| = \lambda x \in |\mathcal{A}|.\ \bigcup \{Y \mid \exists X \subseteq x.\ (X, Y) \in r\},$$
$$'f' = \{(X, Y) \mid \emptyset \neq X \in \mathrm{Con}_A\ \&\ Y \subseteq^{fin} f(\overline{X})\} \cup \{(\emptyset, \emptyset)\}.$$

---

[2]Our convention only holds in representing pairs (x, y) in a product of cpo's of information systems as $x \times y$; in particular the convention does *not* extend to pairs of tokens like (a, b) seen here, which is an example of the usual pairing operation of set theory.

As is to be expected, the denotational semantics on terms of nonrecursive types is essentially the same as that of the eager language of Chapter 11 (Section 11.3). There are occasional, superficial differences due to the fact that the elements associated with function types are not functions but instead approximable mappings representing them. So, sometimes the isomorphisms associated with this representation intrude into the semantic definition. The fact that we use information systems means that the clauses of the semantic definitions can be presented in an alternative, more concrete way. These are indicated alongside the semantic definitions. Comments and explanations follow the semantics.

Denotational semantics

$$[\![\,(\,)\,]\!] \quad =_{def} \quad \lambda\rho.\, \lfloor\{\emptyset\}\rfloor$$
$$\qquad\qquad = \quad \lambda\rho.\, \{\emptyset\}$$

$$[\![(t_1, t_2)]\!] \quad =_{def} \quad \lambda\rho.\, let\ v_1 \Leftarrow [\![t_1]\!]\rho, v_2 \Leftarrow [\![t_2]\!]\rho.\lfloor(v_1, v_2)\rfloor$$
$$\qquad\qquad = \quad \lambda\rho.\, [\![t_1]\!]\rho \times [\![t_2]\!]\rho \qquad\qquad\qquad\qquad\qquad (1)$$

$$[\![\mathbf{fst}(t)]\!] \quad =_{def} \quad \lambda\rho.\, let\ v \Leftarrow [\![t]\!]\rho.\ \pi_1(v)$$
$$\qquad\qquad = \quad \lambda\rho.\, proj_1\, [\![t]\!]\rho \qquad\qquad\qquad\qquad\qquad (2)$$

$$[\![\mathbf{snd}(t)]\!] \quad =_{def} \quad \lambda\rho.\, let\ v \Leftarrow [\![t]\!]\rho.\ \pi_2(v)$$
$$\qquad\qquad = \quad \lambda\rho.\, proj_2\, [\![t]\!]\rho$$

$$[\![x]\!] \quad =_{def} \quad \lambda\rho.\, \lfloor\rho(x)\rfloor$$
$$\qquad\qquad = \quad \lambda\rho.\, \rho(x)$$

$$[\![\lambda x.t]\!] \quad =_{def} \quad \lambda\rho.\, \lfloor `(\lambda\, v \in V_{type(x)}.\ [\![t]\!]\rho[v/x])'\rfloor$$
$$\qquad\qquad = \quad \lambda\rho.\, \{(U, V) \mid \emptyset \neq U \in \mathrm{Con}_{type(x)}\ \&\ V \subseteq^{fin} [\![t]\!]\rho\,[\overline{U}/x]\} \cup$$
$$\qquad\qquad\qquad \{(\emptyset, \emptyset)\} \qquad\qquad\qquad\qquad\qquad (3)$$

$$[\![t_1\, t_2]\!] \quad =_{def} \quad \lambda\rho.\, let\ r \Leftarrow [\![t_1]\!]\rho, v \Leftarrow [\![t_2]\!]\rho.\ |r|(v)$$
$$\qquad\qquad = \quad \lambda\rho.\, \bigcup\{V \mid \exists U \subseteq [\![t_2]\!]\rho.\ (U, V) \in [\![t_1]\!]\rho\} \qquad\qquad (4)$$

$$[\![\mathbf{inl}(t)]\!] \quad =_{def} \quad \lambda\rho.\, let\ v \Leftarrow [\![t]\!]\rho.\ \lfloor in_1(v)\rfloor$$
$$\qquad\qquad = \quad \lambda\rho.\, inj_1 [\![t]\!]\rho \qquad\qquad\qquad\qquad\qquad (5)$$

$$[\![\mathbf{inr}(t)]\!] \quad =_{def} \quad \lambda\rho.\, let\ v \Leftarrow [\![t]\!]\rho.\ \lfloor in_2\,(v)\rfloor$$
$$\qquad\qquad = \quad \lambda\rho.\, inj_2\, [\![t]\!]\rho$$

$$[\![\mathbf{case}\ t\ \mathbf{of}\ \mathbf{inl}(x_1).t_1,\ \mathbf{inr}(x_2).t_2]\!]$$
$$\qquad\qquad =_{def} \quad \lambda\rho.\, let\ v \Leftarrow [\![t]\!]\rho.$$
$$\qquad\qquad\qquad case\ v\ of\ in_1(v_1).[\![t_1]\!]\rho[v_1/x_1] \mid in_2(v_2).[\![t_2]\!]\rho[v_2/x_2]$$

$$\llbracket \mathbf{abs}(t) \rrbracket \qquad =_{def} \quad \llbracket t \rrbracket \tag{6}$$

$$\llbracket \mathbf{rep}(t) \rrbracket \qquad =_{def} \quad \llbracket t \rrbracket$$

$$\llbracket \mathbf{rec}\ f.(\lambda x.t) \rrbracket \quad =_{def} \quad \lambda \rho.\ \lfloor \mu r.`(\lambda v.\llbracket t \rrbracket \rho[v/x, r/f])' \rfloor$$
$$= \qquad \lambda \rho.\ \mu r.\llbracket \lambda x.t \rrbracket \rho[r/f] \tag{7}$$

Explanation

(1) Recall that pairing of elements v_1, v_2 in the product of information systems is represented by the product of sets $v_1 \times v_2$. Thus, with our understanding of lifting,

$$\llbracket (t_1, t_2) \rrbracket \rho = let\ v_1 \Leftarrow \llbracket t_1 \rrbracket \rho, v_2 \Leftarrow \llbracket t_2 \rrbracket \rho.\ v_1 \times v_2.$$

This returns the bottom element $\emptyset$ in the case where either $\llbracket t_1 \rrbracket \rho$ or $\llbracket t_2 \rrbracket \rho$ is $\emptyset$, and hence equals

$$\llbracket t_1 \rrbracket \rho \times \llbracket t_2 \rrbracket \rho.$$

(2) With our understanding of the form of products $|\mathcal{A}| \times |\mathcal{B}|$, for information systems $\mathcal{A}$ and $\mathcal{B}$, we see

$$\llbracket \mathbf{fst}\ (t) \rrbracket \rho \quad = \quad let\ v \Leftarrow \llbracket t \rrbracket \rho.\ proj_1\ v$$
$$= \quad proj_1\ \llbracket t \rrbracket \rho$$

because the projection, under $proj_1$, of $\emptyset$ is $\emptyset$.

(3) Recall the isomorphism between approximable mappings and continuous functions

$$|\mathcal{A} \to \mathcal{B}_\perp| \cong [|\mathcal{A}| \to |\mathcal{B}|_\perp]$$

given by the two functions $|\text{-}|$ and '-' in Theorem 12.30. We see that

$$\llbracket \lambda x.t \rrbracket \rho \quad = \quad \lfloor `(\lambda v.\llbracket t \rrbracket \rho[v/x])' \rfloor \quad \text{by definition,}$$

$$= \quad `(\lambda v.\llbracket t \rrbracket \rho[v/x])' \quad \text{from our understanding of lifting,}$$

$$= \quad \{(U, V) \mid \emptyset \neq U \in \text{Con}_{type(x)}\ \&\ V \subseteq^{fin} \llbracket t \rrbracket \rho[\overline{U}/x]\} \cup \{(\emptyset, \emptyset)\}.$$

(4) Suppose $t_1 : \sigma \to \tau$, $t_2 : \sigma$. In the case where $\llbracket t_1 \rrbracket \rho = \lfloor r \rfloor$ and $\llbracket t_2 \rrbracket \rho = \lfloor v \rfloor$, by Theorem 12.30, we see

$$\llbracket t_1\ t_2 \rrbracket \rho \quad = \quad |r|(v)$$

$$= \quad \bigcup \{V \mid \exists U \subseteq v.\ (U, V) \in r\}$$

Thus in this case, the two expressions in (4) agree. Morever they also coincide, yielding $\emptyset$, in the other case, where $\llbracket t_1 \rrbracket \rho$ or $\llbracket t_2 \rrbracket \rho$ is empty.

(5) In the light of the discussion of Section 11.11, we might expect to have to specify the type $\tau_1 + \tau_2$ of $\mathbf{inl}(t)$—the component τ_2 is left unspecified by the type of t_1, and could conceivably affect the denotation of $\mathbf{inl}(t)$. However, because of our particular representation of injections of a sum $|\mathcal{A}| + |\mathcal{B}|$, for information systems $\mathcal{A}$ and $\mathcal{B}$, we can get away without specifying the component τ_2; whatever it is, the denotation of $\mathbf{inl}(t)$ will be the same. Again, the definition simplifies:

$$
\begin{aligned}
[\![\mathbf{inl}(t)]\!]\rho &= \text{let } v \Leftarrow [\![t]\!]\rho. \ \lfloor in_1(v)\rfloor \\
&= \text{let } v \Leftarrow [\![t]\!]\rho. \ inj_1 v \\
&= inj_1 [\![t]\!]\rho.
\end{aligned}
$$

(6) The two halves of the isomorphism between information systems denoted by $\mu X.\tau$ and $\tau[\mu X.\tau/x]$, expressed by **abs** and **rep** are equalities.

(7) From our choice of operations associated with lifting, we simplify:

$$
\begin{aligned}
[\![\mathbf{rec} \ f.(\lambda x.t)]\!]\rho \ =_{def} \ & \lfloor \mu r.{}^{\backprime}(\lambda v.[\![t]\!]\rho \ [v/x, r/f])'\rfloor \\
= \ & \mu r.\lfloor {}^{\backprime}(\lambda v.[\![t]\!]\rho \ [v/x, r/f])'\rfloor \\
= \ & \mu r.[\![\lambda x.t]\!]\rho[r/f].
\end{aligned}
$$

The denotational semantics satisfies the expected properties.
Denotations depend only on the free variables of a term:

Lemma 13.2 *If ρ, ρ' agree on the free variables of t then $[\![t]\!]\rho = [\![t]\!]\rho'$.*

Proof: By structural induction. $\qquad\qquad\qquad\qquad\qquad\qquad\qquad\qquad\qquad\qquad\square$

Canonical forms denote values:

Lemma 13.3 *If $c \in C_\tau$ then $[\![c]\!]\rho \neq \emptyset$, any ρ.*

Proof: By structural induction on c. $\qquad\qquad\qquad\qquad\qquad\qquad\qquad\qquad\qquad\square$

13.4 Adequacy of eager semantics

Both the operational and denotational semantics agree on whether or not the evaluation of a term converges. For a typable, closed term t, define

$$
\begin{aligned}
t \downarrow &\ \text{iff}\ \exists c. \ t \to c \\
t \Downarrow &\ \text{iff}\ [\![t]\!]\rho \neq \emptyset,
\end{aligned}
$$

for an arbitrary environment ρ. So, $t \downarrow$ means the evaluation of the closed term t terminates in a canonical form, while $t \Downarrow$ means its denotation is not bottom.

The proof that the denotational semantics respects evaluation proceeds routinely on the lines of Section 11.4, with the help of a Substitution Lemma:

Lemma 13.4 *(Substitution Lemma)*
Let s be a typable, closed term such that $[\![s]\!]\rho \neq \emptyset$. Then

$$[\![t[s/x]]\!]\rho = [\![t]\!]\rho[[\![s]\!]\rho/x]$$

Proof: By structural induction.   □

Lemma 13.5 *If $t \to c$ then $[\![t]\!]\rho = [\![c]\!]\rho$ for any typable, closed term t and canonical form c, and arbitrary environment ρ.*

Proof: By rule induction.   □

Exercise 13.6 Establish the cases of the above rule induction for the rules for sum and recursive types.   □

By Lemma 13.3, canonical forms denote values. So, it follows that

$$\text{if } t \downarrow \text{ then } t \Downarrow,$$

for any typable, closed term t.

As usual, the converse is harder to prove and is done by means of a logical relation in a manner similar to that followed in Chapter 11. However, this time we have the extra complication of recursive types. In Chapter 11, we could define the logical relations $\lesssim_\tau$ by structural induction on the types τ. We can no longer do this when types can be defined recursively; the definition of $\lesssim_{\mu X.\tau}$ cannot be given straightforwardly in terms of $\lesssim_{\tau[\mu X.\tau/X]}$ as such a definition would not be well-founded. Fortunately we can still give a simple definition of the relations $\lesssim_\tau$ by taking advantage of the information-systems representation. Suitable relations

$$a \; \varepsilon_\tau \; c$$

for a token $a \in \text{Tok}_\tau$, type τ and canonical form $c \in C_\tau$ are definable by well-founded recursion (see Section 10.4). For $d \in (V_\tau)_\perp$ and $t : \tau$, we then take

$$d \lesssim_\tau t \text{ iff } \forall a \in d \exists c \in C_\tau. \; t \to c \; \& \; a\varepsilon_\tau c.$$

The definition of the relation ε makes use the *size* of tokens:

Definition: For sets built up inductively from the empty set by forming finite subsets, pairing with 1 and 2, and pairing define:

$$
\begin{aligned}
size(\emptyset) \quad &= \quad 1 \\
size(X) \quad &= \quad 1 + \Sigma_{a \in X}\, size(a) \qquad \text{(where X is a finite, nonempty subset)} \\
size((a,b)) \quad &= \quad 1 + size(a) + size(b) \\
size((1,a)) \quad &= \quad 1 + size(a) \\
size((2,b)) \quad &= \quad 1 + size(b)
\end{aligned}
$$

Lemma 13.7 *For each closed type τ there is a relation ε_τ between tokens of V_τ and canonical forms C_τ with the following properties:*

- $\emptyset \, \varepsilon_{\mathbf{1}}\,()$
- $(a,b) \, \varepsilon_{\tau_1 * \tau_2}(c_1,c_2)$ *iff* $a \, \varepsilon_{\tau_1} c_1$ *&* $b \, \varepsilon_{\tau_2} c_2$
- $(U,V) \, \varepsilon_{\tau_1 \to \tau_2} \lambda x.t$ *iff* $\forall c \in C_{\tau_1}.\ U \lesssim_{\tau_1}\ c \Rightarrow V \lesssim_{\tau_2} t[c/x]$.
- $(1,a) \, \varepsilon_{\tau_1 + \tau_2} \mathbf{inl}(c)$ *iff* $a \, \varepsilon_{\tau_1} c$
  $(2,b) \, \varepsilon_{\tau_1 + \tau_2} \mathbf{inr}(c)$ *iff* $b \, \varepsilon_{\tau_2} c$.
- $a \, \varepsilon_{\mu X.\tau} \mathbf{abs}(c)$ *iff* $a \, \varepsilon_{\tau[\mu X.\tau / X]}\ c$

where we write

$$
U \lesssim_\tau\ s,
$$

for U a subset of tokens of V_τ and $s : \tau$ a closed term, iff

$$
\forall b \in U\ \exists c \in C_\tau.(b \, \varepsilon_\tau\ c\ \&\ s \to c).
$$

Proof: The relation ε exists by well-founded recursion on the size of tokens and canonical forms combined lexicographically. More precisely, defining

$$
\begin{aligned}
(a,c) < (a',c') \text{ iff } &size(a) < size(a') \text{ or} \\
&(size(a) = size(a')\ \&\ c \text{ is a proper subterm of } c'),
\end{aligned}
$$

for tokens a, a' and canonical forms c, c', produces a well-founded set. On a typical member (a,c) we can define by well-founded recursion those types τ for which $a \, \varepsilon_\tau c$ holds. $\square$

Lemma 13.8 *Assume t is a closed term of type τ, and that $U, V \in Con_\tau$. Then*

$$
U \vdash^*_\tau V\ \&\ U \lesssim_\tau t \Rightarrow V \lesssim_\tau t.
$$

Proof: A necessary and sufficent condition is that

$$U \vdash_\tau a \ \& \ (\forall b \in U. \ b \, \varepsilon_\tau \, c) \Rightarrow a \, \varepsilon_\tau \, c,$$

for any $U \in \text{Con}_\tau, a \in \text{Tok}_\tau$ and $c \in C_\tau$. This is shown by well-founded induction on $size(U \cup \{a\})$, and the structure of c ordered lexicographically. The proof proceeds according to the form of τ.

For example, suppose $\tau \equiv \tau_1 \text{--}> \tau_2$. In this case, assume

$$\{(X_1, Y_1), \cdots (X_n, Y_n)\} \vdash_{\tau_1 \to \tau_2} (X, Y) \tag{1}$$

and

$$(X_i, Y_i) \, \varepsilon_{\tau_1 \to \tau_2} \, \lambda z.t, \text{ for } 1 \le i \le n. \tag{2}$$

To maintain the induction hypothesis, we require $(X, Y) \, \varepsilon_{\tau \to \tau_2} \, \lambda z.t$, *i.e.*

$$\forall c_1 \in C_{\tau_1}. X \lesssim_{\tau_1} c_1 \Rightarrow Y \lesssim_{\tau_2} t[c_1/z].$$

Suppose $X \lesssim_{\tau_1} c_1$ with $c_1 \in C_{\tau_1}$. If $X \vdash_{\tau_1}^* X_i$ then, by well-founded induction, $X_i \lesssim c_1$. Hence by (2) it follows that $Y_i \lesssim_{\tau_2} t[c_1/z]$. Thus

$$\bigcup \{Y_i \mid X \vdash_{\tau_1}^* X_i\} \lesssim_{\tau_2} t[c_1/z].$$

Now by (1),

$$\bigcup \{Y_i \mid X \vdash_{\tau_1}^* X_i\} \vdash_{\tau_2}^* Y.$$

By well-founded induction,

$$Y \lesssim_{\tau_2} t[c_1/z],$$

as required.

The proof for the other cases of τ proceeds more simply; when $\tau \equiv \mu X.\sigma$ the well-founded induction relies on a decrease in the second component of the lexicographic order. $\qquad \square$

Theorem 13.9 *For any typable, closed term t,*

$$if \ t \Downarrow \quad then \ t \downarrow.$$

Proof: It is shown by structural induction on terms t that:

If t has type τ and free variables $x_1 : \tau_1, \cdots, x_k : \tau_k$ and

$$v_1 \lesssim_{\tau_1} s_1, \cdots, v_k \lesssim_{\tau_k} s_k,$$

for $v_1 \in V_{\tau_1}, \cdots, v_k \in V_{\tau_k}$, and closed terms $s_1, \cdots, s_k$, then

$$[\![t]\!]\rho[v_1/x_1, \cdots, v_k/x_k] \lesssim_\tau t[s_1/x_1, \cdots, s_k/x_k].$$

We consider two cases of the structural induction, leaving the remainder to the reader.

Case $(t_1 \ t_2)$: Inductively suppose the property above holds of $t_1 : \sigma -> \tau$ and $t_2 : \sigma$. Assume $(t_1 \ t_2)$ has free variables amongst $x_1 : \tau_1, \cdots, x_k : \tau_k$ matched by $v_1 \lesssim_{\tau_1} s_1, \cdots, v_k \lesssim_k s_k$, for $v_1 \in V_{\tau_1}, \cdots, v_k \in V_{\tau_k}$ and closed terms $s_1, \cdots, s_k$.

Suppose $b \in [\![t_1 \ t_2]\!]\rho[v_1/x_1, \cdots]$. We require the existence of a canonical form c such that $b \ \varepsilon_\tau \ c$ and $(t_1 \ t_2)[s_1/x_1, \cdots] \to c$. From the denotation of $[\![t_1 \ t_2]\!]$,

$$U \subseteq [\![t_2]\!]\rho[v_1/x_1, \cdots] \ \& \ (U, V) \in [\![t_1]\!]\rho[v_1/x_1, \cdots]$$

for some U, V with $b \in V$. By induction,

$$U \lesssim_\sigma t_2[s_1/x_1, \cdots]$$

and

$$\{(U, V)\} \lesssim_{\sigma \to \tau} t_1[s_1/x_1, \cdots].$$

By the property of approximable mappings, V being non-empty ensures U non-empty. Thus there are canonical forms c_2 and $\lambda y.t_1$ such that

$$U \lesssim_\sigma c_2 \ \& \ t_2[s_1/x_1, \cdots] \to c_2, \text{and}$$

$$(U, V) \ \varepsilon_{\sigma \to \tau} \ \lambda y.t_1' \ \& \ t_1[s_1/x_1, \cdots] \to \lambda y.t_1'.$$

Now, by definition of $\varepsilon_{\sigma \to \tau}$,

$$V \lesssim_\tau t_1'[c_2/y].$$

In particular,

$$\{b\} \lesssim_\tau t_1'[c_2/y].$$

Thus

$$b \ \varepsilon_\tau \ c \ \& \ t_1'[c_2/y] \to c$$

for some canonical form c. Combining the various facts about the evaluation relation, from the rule for evaluation of applications, we see that

$$(t_1 \ t_2)[s_1/x_1, \cdots] \to c.$$

Case $\lambda y.t$: Let $y : \sigma$ and $t : \tau$ in a typable abstraction $\lambda y.t$. Assume $\lambda y.t$ has free variables amongst $x_1 : \tau_1, \cdots, x_k : \tau_k$ matched by

$$v_1 \lesssim_{\tau_1} s_1, \cdots, v_k \lesssim_{\tau_k} s_k$$

for $v_1 \in V_{\tau_1}, \cdots, v_k \in V_{\tau_k}$ and closed terms $s_1, \cdots, s_k$. We require that any token in $[\![\lambda y.t]\!]\rho[v_1/x_1, \cdots]$, necessarily of the form (U, V), satisfies

$$(U, V) \ \varepsilon_{\sigma \to \tau} \ (\lambda y.t)[s_1/x_1, \cdots].$$

Suppose $(U, V) \in [\![\lambda y.t]\!]\rho[v_1/x_1, \cdots]$. If $U = \emptyset$ then so is $V = \emptyset$ which ensures $(U, V) \ \varepsilon_{\sigma \to \tau} \ \lambda y.t[s_1/x_1, \cdots]$. Assume otherwise, that $U \ne \emptyset$. Recalling the definition of $\varepsilon_{\sigma \to \tau}$, we require

$$\forall c \in C_\sigma. \ U \lesssim_\tau c \Rightarrow V \lesssim_\tau t[c/y][s_1/x_1, \cdots]$$

Let $U \lesssim_\tau c$, for $c \in C_\sigma$. Then by Lemma 13.8, $\overline{U} \lesssim_\sigma c$. From the denotation of $\lambda y.t$,

$$V \subseteq^{fin} [\![t]\!]\rho[v_1/x_1, \cdots][\overline{U}/y].$$

But from the induction hypothesis,

$$[\![t]\!]\rho[v_1/x_1, \cdots][\overline{U}/y] \lesssim_\tau t[c/y][s_1/x_1, \cdots]$$

which implies

$$V \lesssim_\tau t[c/y][s_1/x_1, \cdots].$$

Hence,

$$(U, V) \ \varepsilon_{\sigma \to \tau} \ (\lambda y.t)[s_1/x_1, \cdots]$$

also in the case where $U \ne \emptyset$. $\square$

Exercise 13.10 Carry through the case of the structural induction of the proof above for terms of the form **rec** $x.t$. $\square$

Corollary 13.11 *For any typable, closed term* t,

$$t \downarrow \quad \textit{iff} \quad t \Downarrow.$$

13.5 The eager λ-calculus

In the eager language we can define the recursive type

$$\Lambda \equiv \mu X.(X \text{--> } X).$$

This type denotes the $\trianglelefteq$-least information system $\mathcal{L}$ such that

$$\mathcal{L} = \mathcal{L} \to \mathcal{L}_\perp$$

—an information system equal to its own lifted function space. The terms built solely out of those of type Λ without **rec** can be described quite simply. They are those terms given by:

$$t ::= x \mid t_1.t_2 \mid \lambda x.t$$

where x ranges over variables of type Λ, and we use the abbreviations

$$t_1.t_2 \equiv (\mathbf{rep}(t_1)\ t_2)$$
$$\lambda x.t \equiv \mathbf{abs}(\lambda x.t)$$

—it is easy to check from the typing rules that if t, t_1, t_2 are terms of type Λ then so are *applications* $t_1.t_2$ and *abstractions* $\lambda x.t$. This is the syntax of a λ-calculus in which we can do paradoxical things like apply functions to themselves and, as we shall see, even define a fixed-point operator.

The only canonical forms amongst the terms are those closed abstractions $\lambda x.t$. Their evaluation to themselves is captured in the rule

$$\frac{}{\lambda x.t \to \lambda x.t} \tag{1}$$

which is, of course, derivable from the operational semantics. It remains to see how applications $(t_1.t_2)$ evaluate. From the operational semantics we obtain the derivation:

$$\frac{\dfrac{t_1 \to \mathbf{abs}(\lambda x.t_1') \equiv \lambda x.t_1'}{\mathbf{rep}(t_1) \to \lambda x.t_1'} \quad t_2 \to c_2 \quad t_1'[c_2/x] \to c}{(t_1.t_2) \equiv (\mathbf{rep}(t_1)\ t_2) \to c}$$

This condenses to the derived rule:

$$\frac{t_1 \to \lambda x.t_1' \quad t_2 \to c_2 \quad t_1'[c_2/x] \to c}{(t_1.t_2) \to c} \tag{2}$$

It is not hard to see that all derivations in the operational semantics determining evaluations of terms in the λ-calculus can be built up out of these derived rules. The second derived rule expresses that applications $(t_1.t_2)$ evaluate in an eager way. The terms form an *eager* λ-calculus.

The eager λ-calculus inherits a denotational semantics from that of the larger language. Simply by restricting the denotational semantics to its terms we obtain:

$$[\![x]\!]\rho = \rho(x)$$

$$[\![t_1.t_2]\!]\rho = [\![t_1]\!]\rho.[\![t_2]\!]\rho$$

where the *application* $\varphi.d$ of $\varphi \in |\mathcal{L}|_\perp$ to $d \in |\mathcal{L}|_\perp$ is defined by

$$\varphi.d =_{def} \bigcup\{V \mid \exists\, U \subseteq d.\ (U,V) \in \varphi\},$$

$$[\![\lambda x.t]\!]\rho = \{(U,V) \mid \emptyset \neq U \in \mathrm{Con}_\Lambda\ \&\ V \subseteq^{fin} [\![t]\!]\rho\,[\overline{U}/x]\} \cup \{(\emptyset,\emptyset)\}$$

We could have proceeded differently, and defined the syntax, operational and denotational semantics of the eager λ-calculus from scratch, simply by taking (1) and (2) as the evaluation rules, and the denotational semantics above as a definition (though then environments would not involve variables other than those of type Λ). The adequacy result for the full language restricts to an adequacy result for the eager λ-calculus: a closed term of the eager λ-calculus denotes a non-bottom (*i.e.* nonempty element) iff it converges with respect to an operational semantics given by the rules (1) and (2) above.

13.5.1   Equational theory

In general we can regard two terms of the same type as equivalent iff they have the same denotation, *i.e.* for t_1, t_2 of the same type, define

$$t_1 = t_2 \text{ iff } [\![t_1]\!] = [\![t_2]\!],$$

i.e., terms t_1, t_2 are equivalent iff $[\![t_1]\!]\rho = [\![t_2]\!]\rho$, for all environments ρ. Similarly, we can define

$$t\!\downarrow \text{ iff } \forall\rho.[\![t]\!]\rho \neq \emptyset,$$

which holds of a typable term t iff it converges in every environment.

Let us examine what rules hold of two relations $=$ and $\downarrow$ but, for brevity, just on terms of the eager λ-calculus. Firstly, the relation $=$ is an equivalence relation—it is reflexive, symmetric and transitive. The relation $=$ is also substitutive: if two terms have the same denotation then replacing one by the other in any context will yield the same denotation. To state such a property in generality, we need to address the issues involved in the substitution of terms which are not closed.

Substitution: An occurrence of a variable x in a term t of the λ-calculus is *bound* if it is inside some subterm of t of the form $\lambda x.t'$; otherwise it is *free*. We use $t[u/x]$ to mean the term obtained from t by substituting u for every free occurrence of x in t. However care must be taken as the following example shows. The two functions denoted by $\lambda y.x$ and $\lambda w.x$ are the same constant function in any environment; we have

$$\lambda y.x = \lambda w.x.$$

However, substituting y for the free occurrence of x we obtain

$$(\lambda y.x)[y/x] \equiv \lambda y.y,$$

denoting the identity function in one case, and

$$(\lambda w.x)[y/x] \equiv \lambda w.y,$$

the constant function we would hope for, in the other. Certainly it is *not* true that

$$\lambda y.y = \lambda w.y.$$

The difficulty is due to the substitution leading to the free variable y becoming bound in the first case. Substitutions $t[u/x]$ only respect the semantics provided no free variable of u becomes bound in t.

We now state the rules for equality, taking care with the substitutions:
Equality rules:

$$(\text{refl}) \ \frac{}{t = t} \qquad\qquad (\text{sym}) \ \frac{t_1 = t_2}{t_2 = t_1} \quad (\text{tran}) \ \frac{t_1 = t_2 \quad t_2 = t_3}{t_1 = t_3}$$

$$(\text{eq1}) \ \frac{t_1 = t_2}{t[t_1/x] = t[t_2/x]} \qquad\qquad (\text{eq2}) \ \frac{t_1 = t_2 \quad t_1\!\downarrow}{t_2\!\downarrow}$$

provided no free variables of t_1 and t_2 become bound by the substitutions into t. The last rule says if t_1 always converges and t_1 has the same denotation as t_2 then t_2 always converges.

Variables and abstractions of type Λ are convergent:

Convergence rules:

$$\frac{}{x\!\downarrow} \ \text{ if } x \text{ is a variable of type } \Lambda, \qquad\qquad\qquad \frac{}{\lambda x.t\!\downarrow}$$

Recall the denotation of a variable in an environment ρ is the *value* $\rho(x)$, which is necessarily convergent. This explains why variables are always regarded as convergent.

The remaining rules are slight variants of the conversion rules from the classical λ-calculus, adjusted to take account of eager evaluation.

Conversion rules:

(α) $$\overline{\lambda x.t = \lambda y.(t[y/x])}$$ provided y does not occur (free or bound) in t.

(β) $$\frac{u\!\downarrow}{(\lambda x.t)u = t[u/x]}$$ provided no free variable of u becomes bound in t.

(η) $$\frac{t\!\downarrow}{t = \lambda x.(t.x)}$$ provided x is not a free variable of t.

The first rule (α) says we can always rename bound variables provided this doesn't make unwelcome identifications. The second rule (β) expresses the essence of eagerness, that an application needs the prior evaluation of the argument. The soundness of the final rule (η) becomes apparent on examining the denotational semantics.

Exercise 13.12 Prove the soundness of the rule (η) from the denotational semantics.
□

Exercise 13.13 Show the following two rules are also sound:

$$\frac{t_1 = t_2 \quad s\!\downarrow}{t_1[s/x] = t_2[s/x]} \qquad \frac{t\!\downarrow \quad s\!\downarrow}{t[s/x]\!\downarrow}$$

provided no free variables of s become bound in t_1, t_2 or t. Explain why anything derived using these rules in addition to the system of rules listed could also have been derived in the original system.
□

Exercise 13.14 Show the soundness of the following two "strictness" rules:

$$\frac{t.u\!\downarrow}{t\!\downarrow} \qquad \frac{t.u\!\downarrow}{u\!\downarrow}$$

Explain why anything derived using these rules in addition to the system of rules listed could also have been derived in the original system.
□

Exercise 13.15 Give rules for $=$ and $\downarrow$ for the full eager language (not just the eager λ-calculus).
□

13.5.2   A fixed-point operator

Like its ancestor the λ-calculus, the eager λ-calculus is amazingly expressive. As there it is possible to encode, for example, the natural numbers and computable operations on them as terms within it. In particular it has a term $\mathcal{Y}$ which behaves like a fixed-point operator. Here it is:

$$\mathcal{Y} \equiv \lambda f.(\lambda x.\lambda y.(f.(x.x).y)).(\lambda x.\lambda y.(f.(x.x).y))$$

(In writing this term we have adopted the convention that $f.g.h$ means $(f.g).h$.) Imagine we apply $\mathcal{Y}$ to a term $F \equiv \lambda g.(\lambda z.h)$—so F is a function which given a function g returns the function $(\lambda z.h)$ possibly involving g. Using the equational laws of the last section, we derive:

$$
\begin{aligned}
\mathcal{Y}.F \quad &= \quad (\lambda x.\lambda y.F.(x.x).y).(\lambda x.\lambda y.F.(x.x).y) \qquad \text{by } (\beta) \text{ as } F{\Downarrow}, \qquad (1)\\
&= \quad \lambda y.(F.((\lambda x.\lambda y.F.(x.x).y)(\lambda x.\lambda y.F.(x.x).y)).y)\\
&\qquad \text{by } (\beta) \text{ as } \lambda x.\lambda y.(F.(x.x).y){\Downarrow},\\
&= \quad \lambda y.(F.(\mathcal{Y}.F).y) \qquad \text{by } (eq1) \text{ using } (1).
\end{aligned}
$$

In particular, it follows that $\mathcal{Y}.F{\Downarrow}$ by $(eq2)$. Hence, by (β),

$$F.(\mathcal{Y}.F) = (\lambda z.h)[\mathcal{Y}.F/g]$$

where because it is an abstraction $(\lambda z.h)[\mathcal{Y}.F/g]{\Downarrow}$. So $F.(\mathcal{Y}.F){\Downarrow}$ by $(eq2)$. Thus, by (η),

$$\lambda y.(F.(\mathcal{Y}.F).y) = F.(\mathcal{Y}.F)$$

and we conclude

$$\mathcal{Y}.F = F.(\mathcal{Y}.F).$$

In other words, $\mathcal{Y}.F$ is a fixed-point of F.

Exercise 13.16

(i) Show from the operational semantics that $\mathcal{Y}_1.F$ diverges for any closed term F of the eager λ-calculus where

$$\mathcal{Y}_1 \equiv \lambda f.(\lambda x.f.(x.x)).(\lambda x.f.(x.x)).$$

(ii) Suppose F is a term $\lambda g.\lambda z.h$ of of the eager λ-calculus. Let

$$\mathcal{Y}' \equiv \lambda f.(\lambda x.f.(\lambda y.x.x.y)).(\lambda x.f.(\lambda y.x.x.y)).$$

Show $\mathcal{Y}'.F = F.(\mathcal{Y}'.F)$. $\square$

To see how $\mathcal{Y}$ is related to the least-fixed-point operator fix, we try to imagine what the denotation of $\mathcal{Y}.f$ is, for a variable $f : \Lambda$, assigned value φ in an environment ρ. Certainly, $\rho(f) = \varphi \in |\mathcal{L}|$. Automatically, from $\mathcal{L}$'s definition, $\varphi \in |\mathcal{L} \to \mathcal{L}_\perp|$. Hence $|\varphi| : |\mathcal{L}| \to |\mathcal{L}|_\perp$. We cannot take the least fixed point of φ as it stands. However, note that $|\mathcal{L}|$ has a bottom element $\perp_{|\mathcal{L}|}$, given by

$$\perp_{|\mathcal{L}|} = \{(X, \emptyset) \mid X \in \mathrm{Con}_\Lambda\}.$$

Thus we can define a continuous function

$$down : |\mathcal{L}|_\perp \to |\mathcal{L}|$$

acting so

$$down(d) = \begin{cases} d & \text{if} \quad d \in |\mathcal{L}|, \\ \perp_{|\mathcal{L}|} & \text{if} \quad d = \emptyset. \end{cases}$$

Or, equivalently, $down$ can be described as acting so that

$$down(d) = d \cup \perp_{|\mathcal{L}|},$$

for any $d \in |\mathcal{L}|_\perp$. The function

$$down \circ |\varphi| : |\mathcal{L}| \to |\mathcal{L}|$$

has a least fixed point. This is the denotation of $[\![\mathcal{Y}.f]\!]\rho$ in an environment ρ with $\rho(f) = \varphi$. We claim:

$$[\![\mathcal{Y}.f]\!]\rho = fix(down \circ |\rho(f)|).$$

We begin the proof of this claim by studying the properties of application of the eager λ-calculus in the model $|\mathcal{L}|_\perp$. Recall, that application in the model $|\mathcal{L}|_\perp$ is defined by

$$\varphi.d = \bigcup \{V \mid \exists\, U \subseteq d.\ (U, V) \in \varphi\},$$

for $\varphi, d \in |\mathcal{L}|_\perp$.

Lemma 13.17 *For $\varphi, d \in |\mathcal{L}|_\perp$, b a token and V a subset of tokens,*

$$V \subseteq^{fin} \varphi.d \Leftrightarrow (V = \emptyset \text{ or } \exists U \subseteq d.\ (U, V) \in \varphi).$$

Proof: In the proof we refer to the properties of an approximable mapping stated in Lemma 12.29. From the definition of $\varphi.d$,

$$V \subseteq^{fin} \varphi.d \Leftrightarrow \quad V = \emptyset \text{ or}$$
$$V \subseteq V_1 \cup \cdots \cup V_k \text{ for some } U_1, \cdots, U_k \subseteq d$$
$$\text{such that } (U_1, V_1), \cdots, (U_k, V_k) \in \varphi.$$

In the latter case, taking $U = U_1 \cup \cdots \cup U_k$, we obtain $(U, V) \in \varphi$ because φ is an approximable mapping. $\qquad\square$

The function *down* is associated with protecting a term from evaluation by enclosing it in an abstraction:

Lemma 13.18 *Let t be a term of the eager λ-calculus which does not contain y as a free variable. Then,*

$$[\![\lambda y.(t.y)]\!]\rho = down([\![t]\!]\rho).$$

Proof: The desired equation follows immediately from the definition of *down*, once we have shown that, for a token b and arbitrary environment ρ,

$$b \in [\![\lambda y.(t.y)]\!]\rho \Leftrightarrow (\exists U \in \mathrm{Con}_\Lambda.\ b = (U, \emptyset)) \text{ or } b \in [\![t]\!]\rho. \qquad (\dagger)$$

To show this, recall from the semantics, that

$$(U, V) \in [\![\lambda y.(t.y)]\!]\rho \Leftrightarrow U = V = \emptyset \text{ or}$$
$$\emptyset \neq U \in \mathrm{Con}_\Lambda\ \&\ V \subseteq^{fin} [\![t.y]\!]\rho[\overline{U}/y].$$

This can be simplified to $(\dagger)$ by the equivalences:

$$V \subseteq^{fin} [\![t.y]\!]\rho[\overline{U}/y] \quad \Leftrightarrow \quad V \subseteq^{fin} [\![t]\!]\rho.\overline{U}$$
$$\text{as } y \text{ is not free in } t\text{---see Lemma 13.2}$$

$$\Leftrightarrow \quad V = \emptyset \text{ or}$$
$$\exists U' \subseteq \overline{U}.\ (U', V) \in [\![t]\!]\rho \quad \text{by Lemma 13.17,}$$

$$\Leftrightarrow \quad V = \emptyset \text{ or}$$
$$\exists U'.\ U \vdash^* U'\ \&\ (U', V) \in [\![t]\!]\rho$$

$$\Leftrightarrow \quad V = \emptyset \text{ or } (U, V) \in [\![t]\!]\rho$$
$$\text{by the properties of an approximable mapping. } \square$$

Let f be a variable of type Λ. By equational reasoning, just like that above, we derive

$$\mathcal{Y}.f = \lambda y.f.(\mathcal{Y}.f).y \quad \text{and} \quad \mathcal{Y}.f\!\downarrow$$

from which we obtain directly that

$$[\![\mathcal{Y}.f]\!]\rho = [\![\lambda y.f.(\mathcal{Y}.f).y]\!]\rho \neq \emptyset$$

for any environment ρ. Whence, by Lemma 13.18, we see that

$$[\mathcal{Y}.f]\rho = down([f.(\mathcal{Y}.f)]\rho)$$
$$= down \circ |\rho(f)|([\mathcal{Y}.f]\rho)$$

from the denotational semantics. Thus $[\mathcal{Y}.f]\rho$ is a fixed point of $down \circ |\rho(f)|$. It follows that

$$fix(down \circ |\rho(f)|) \subseteq [\mathcal{Y}.f]\rho$$

As claimed, the converse inclusion holds too.

Theorem 13.19 *Let*

$$\mathcal{Y} \equiv \lambda f.(\lambda x.\lambda y.f.(x.x).y)(\lambda x.\lambda y.f.(x.x).y).$$

Then, for an arbitrary environment ρ,

$$[\mathcal{Y}.f]\rho = fix(down \circ |\rho(f)|).$$

Proof: In presenting the proof a particular environment ρ will be assumed. With respect to ρ, we will identify a term with its denotation, writing, for example,

$$b \in t \text{ for } b \in [t]\rho.$$

We will write $Fixf$ for $fix(down \circ |\rho(f)|)$. Note, that $Fixf$ has an inductive characterisation as the least set d such that

$$d = \bigcup \{V \mid \exists U \subseteq d. \ (U,V) \in f\} \cup \perp_{|\mathcal{L}|}.$$

From the preceding discussion, it is clear that it remains to prove $\mathcal{Y}.f \subseteq Fixf$. The (β) rule yields

$$\mathcal{Y}.f = (\lambda x.\lambda y.f.(x.x).y).(\lambda x.\lambda y.f.(x.x).y).$$

Consequently,

$$V \subseteq^{fin} \mathcal{Y}.f \quad \Leftrightarrow \quad V \subseteq^{fin} (\lambda x.\lambda y.f.(x.x).y).(\lambda x.\lambda y.f.(x.x).y)$$

$$\Leftrightarrow \quad V = \emptyset \text{ or }$$
$$\exists U \subseteq (\lambda x.\lambda y.f.(x.x).y). \ (U,V) \in (\lambda x.\lambda y.f.(x.x).y).$$

To establish $\mathcal{Y}.f \subseteq Fixf$ it is thus sufficient to show that the property $P(U)$ holds of all $U \in Con_\Lambda$ where

$$P(U) \iff_{def}$$
$$\forall V. \ [U \subseteq (\lambda x.\lambda y.f.(x.x).y) \ \& \ (U,V) \in (\lambda x.\lambda y.f.(x.x).y)] \Rightarrow V \subseteq Fixf.$$

This is shown by induction on the size of U.

Let $U \in \mathrm{Con}_\Lambda$. Suppose the induction hypothesis $P(U')$ holds for all $U' \in \mathrm{Con}_\Lambda$ for which $size(U') < size(U)$. We require

$$[U \subseteq (\lambda x.\lambda y.f.(x.x).y) \ \& \ (U,V) \in (\lambda x.\lambda y.f.(x.x).y)] \Rightarrow V \subseteq Fixf,$$

for any V. This holds trivially when V is empty. In fact, by the following argument, it also suffices to show this not just for nonempty V but also only for the case where $V \cap \perp_{|\mathcal{L}|} = \emptyset$. Of course, in general, $V = V_0 \cup V_1$ where $V_0 \cap \perp_{|\mathcal{L}|} = \emptyset$ and $V_1 \subseteq \perp_{|\mathcal{L}|}$. It is then clear that $V_1 \subseteq Fixf$, while $(U, V_0) \in (\lambda x.\lambda y.f.(x.x).y)$, from the properties of approximable mappings. The original problem reduces to showing

$$[U \subseteq (\lambda x.\lambda y.f.(x.x).y) \ \& \ (U,V_0) \in (\lambda x.\lambda y.f.(x.x).y)] \Rightarrow V_0 \subseteq Fixf,$$

where $V_0 \cap \perp_{|\mathcal{L}|} = \emptyset$.

Suppose

$$U \subseteq (\lambda x.\lambda y.f.(x.x).y) \ \& \ (U,V) \in (\lambda x.\lambda y.f.(x.x).y)$$

where we assume V is nonempty and $V \cap \perp_{|\mathcal{L}|} = \emptyset$, i.e., $V \cap \{(X, \emptyset) \mid X \in \mathrm{Con}_\Lambda\} = \emptyset$. Under these assumptions,

$$
\begin{aligned}
(U,V) \in (\lambda x.\lambda y.f.(x.x).y) &\Leftrightarrow V \subseteq [\![\lambda y.f.(x.x).y]\!]\rho[\overline{U}/x] \quad \text{from the semantics,} \\
&\Leftrightarrow V \subseteq down([\![f.(x.x)]\!]\rho[\overline{U}/x]) \quad \text{by Lemma 13.18,} \\
&\Leftrightarrow V \subseteq [\![f.(x.x)]\!]\rho[\overline{U}/x] \cup \perp_{|\mathcal{L}|} \\
&\Leftrightarrow V \subseteq [\![f.(x.x)]\!]\rho[\overline{U}/x] \quad \text{as } V \cap \perp_{|\mathcal{L}|} = \emptyset, \\
&\Leftrightarrow V \subseteq \rho(f).(\overline{U}.\overline{U}) \quad \text{from the semantics,} \\
&\Leftrightarrow \exists W \subseteq (\overline{U}.\overline{U}). \ (W,V) \in f \quad \text{by Lemma 13.17 as } V \neq \emptyset.
\end{aligned}
$$

Thus we have deduced the existence of $W \in \mathrm{Con}_\Lambda$ such that

$$W \subseteq (\overline{U}.\overline{U}) \ \& \ (W,V) \in f.$$

Because V is nonempty and (W,V) is a token, W is nonempty too. From $W \subseteq (\overline{U}.\overline{U})$ we obtain

$$\exists X \subseteq \overline{U}. \ (X, W) \in \overline{U},$$

$$\textit{i.e. } \exists X. U \vdash_\Lambda^* X \ \& \ U \vdash_\Lambda (X, W).$$

But this simplifies to

$$U \vdash_\Lambda (U, W),$$

by the properties of entailment in $\mathcal{L} = \mathcal{L} \to \mathcal{L}_\perp$. However this is defined to mean precisely that

$$\bigcup \{Y \mid \exists Z.\ U \vdash^*_\Lambda Z\ \&\ (Z,Y) \in U\} \vdash^*_\Lambda W.$$

Consider arbitrary Z, Y for which

$$U \vdash^*_\Lambda Z\ \&\ (Z,Y) \in U.$$

Then $size(Z) < size(U)$, and hence $P(Z)$ by the induction hypothesis. By assumption

$$U \subseteq (\lambda x.\lambda y.f.(x.x).y).$$

Thus

$$(Z,Y) \in (\lambda x.\lambda y.f.(x.x).y),\ \text{ and also } Z \subseteq (\lambda x.\lambda y.f.(x.x).y),$$

as denotations are $\vdash_\Lambda$-closed. By $P(Z)$ we obtain $Y \subseteq Fixf$. Because Y, Z were arbitrary,

$$Fixf \supseteq \bigcup \{Y \mid \exists Z.\ U \vdash^*_\Lambda Z\ \&\ (Z,Y) \in U\} \vdash^*_\Lambda W.$$

Hence, as $Fixf$ is $\vdash_\Lambda$-closed, $W \subseteq Fixf$.

Recall the inductive characterisation of $Fixf$. Because

$$W \subseteq Fixf \text{ and } (W,V) \in f$$

we finally get $V \subseteq Fixf$. This concludes the proof by induction on the size of U.   □

Exercise 13.20 Let

$$\Omega \equiv (\lambda x.x.x).(\lambda x.x.x),$$

a term of the eager λ-calculus. Show

$$[\![\Omega]\!]\rho = \emptyset$$

i.e., Ω denotes the bottom element of $|\mathcal{L}|_\perp$, with respect to an arbitrary environment ρ. (Hint: Adopting the same conventions as used in the proof of Theorem 13.19, first remark that the denotation of Ω is nonempty, so we have nonempty $V \subseteq^{fin} \Omega$, iff

$$U \subseteq (\lambda x.x.x)\ \&\ (U,V) \in (\lambda x.x.x), \tag{$\dagger$}$$

for some $U \in Con_\Lambda$. Secondly, show

$$(U,V) \in (\lambda x.x.x) \Rightarrow U \vdash_\Lambda (U,V).$$

Finally, obtain a contradiction to there being a smallest U with property ($\dagger$), for some V, by examining the definition of $\vdash_\Lambda$.)   □

13.6   A lazy language

In moving over to a language with lazy evaluation it's appropriate to modify the syntax of Section 13.1 slightly. The types are the same as the eager case but for one small change: in the lazy case the smallest type is **0** (and not **1**). The type **0** will have no values; all the terms of type **0** will diverge. The types are:

$$\tau ::= \mathbf{0} \mid \tau_1 * \tau_2 \mid \tau_1 \!-\!> \tau_2 \mid \tau_1 + \tau_2 \mid X \mid \mu X.\tau$$

where X ranges over an infinite set of *type variables*, and $\mu X.\tau$ is a recursively-defined type. The role of () in the eager case will now be taken over by a term $\bullet$ of type **0** which is to denote the diverging computation—it will not be a canonical form. The precise syntax of untyped terms in the lazy case is:

$$
\begin{aligned}
t ::= \quad & \bullet \mid (t_1, t_2) \mid \mathbf{fst}(t) \mid \mathbf{snd}(t) \mid \\
& x \mid \lambda x.t \mid (t_1\ t_2) \mid \\
& \mathbf{inl}(t) \mid \mathbf{inr}(t) \mid \mathbf{case}\ t\ \mathbf{of}\ \mathbf{inl}(x_1).t_1,\ \mathbf{inr}(x_2).t_2. \mid \\
& \mathbf{abs}(t) \mid \mathbf{rep}(t) \mid \\
& \mathbf{rec}\ x.t
\end{aligned}
$$

where x, x_1, x_2 are variables in **Var**. The only differences with the eager case are the replacement of () by $\bullet$ and a more general form of recursive definition. Just as in Chapter 11, a recursive definition in the lazy case can now take the form **rec** $x.t$ where, unlike the eager case, we do not insist that the body t is an abstraction.

Again, any closed type is associated with infinitely many term variables of that type. Accompanying the changes in syntax are the typing rules

$$\frac{}{\bullet : \mathbf{0}} \qquad\qquad \frac{x : \tau \quad t : \tau}{\mathbf{rec}\ x.t\ : \tau}$$

—the other term constructions are typed as in the eager case. The definition of the free variables of a term and the notion of closed term are defined as usual.

13.7   Lazy operational semantics

The canonical forms C_τ of type τ given by the rules:[3]

---

[3]Here, as in the remainder of this chapter, we use the same notation in the lazy case as we used for the corresponding eager concepts. The two treatments are kept separate so this should not cause confusion.

$$\frac{t_1 : \tau_1 \quad t_2 : \tau_2 \quad t_1 \text{ and } t_2 \text{ closed}}{(t_1, t_2) \in C_{\tau_1 * \tau_2}}$$

$$\frac{\lambda x.t : \tau_1 -> \tau_2 \quad \lambda x.t \text{ closed}}{\lambda x.t \in C_{\tau_1 \to \tau_2}}$$

$$\frac{t_1 : \tau_1 \quad t_1 \text{ closed}}{\mathbf{inl}(t_1) \in C_{\tau_1 + \tau_2}} \qquad \frac{t_2 : \tau_2 \quad t_2 \text{ closed}}{\mathbf{inr}(t_2) \in C_{\tau_1 + \tau_2}}$$

$$\frac{c \in C_{\tau[\mu X.\tau/X]}}{\mathbf{abs}(c) \in C_{\mu X.\tau}}$$

The canonical forms can have unevaluated components. Apart from the last, these rules have already appeared in Chapter 11. Canonical forms of recursive types are handled as in the eager case.

Example: The lazy natural numbers
Consider the type

$$nat \equiv_{def} \mu X.(\mathbf{0} + X).$$

in the lazy language. It has canonical forms associated with the left and right components of the sum.

Associated with the left summand are the canonical forms

$$\mathbf{abs}(\mathbf{inl}(t_1))$$

where t_1 is a closed term of type $\mathbf{0}$. There are in fact infinitely many closed terms $t_1 : \mathbf{0}$ (Why?); though, of course, they all denote the same element of $\mid \mathbf{0}_\perp \mid$, namely bottom—there are no others. In particular, $\bullet : \mathbf{0}$ denotes bottom. With it we define

$$Zero \equiv \mathbf{abs}(\mathbf{inl}(\bullet)).$$

Then $Zero : nat$ is a canonical form. Canonical forms associated with the right-hand-side of the sum in $nat \equiv \mu X.(\mathbf{0} + X)$ have the form

$$\mathbf{abs}(\mathbf{inr}(t_2))$$

where t_2 is a closed term of type nat. If we abbreviate $\mathbf{abs}(\mathbf{inr}(t_2))$ to $Succ(t_2)$ we can generate canonical forms:

$$Zero, \; Succ(Zero), \; Succ(Succ(Zero)), \; \cdots$$

These canonical forms are obtained, starting from $Zero$ by repeatedly applying the "successor function"

$$\lambda x.Succ(x) : nat-> nat.$$

Such canonical forms correspond to natural numbers. There are many other canonical forms however: one given by $Succ(\textbf{rec } x.Succ(x))$ corresponds to an "infinite" number, while others like $Succ(Succ(\textbf{rec } x.x))$, where $x : nat$, correspond to partial natural numbers, as we will discuss further following the denotational semantics.   □

We define the evaluation relation between closed terms and canonical forms by the rules:

Evaluation rules

$$\frac{}{c \to c} \quad \text{if } c \text{ is a canonical form}$$

$$\frac{t \to (t_1, t_2) \quad t_1 \to c}{\textbf{fst}(t) \to c} \qquad \frac{t \to (t_1, t_2) \quad t_2 \to c}{\textbf{snd}(t) \to c}$$

$$\frac{t_1 \to \lambda x.t_1' \quad t_1'[t_2/x] \to c}{(t_1 \ t_2) \to c}$$

$$\frac{t \to \textbf{inl}(t') \quad t_1[t'/x_1] \to c}{\textbf{case } t \textbf{ of inl}(x_1).t_1, \textbf{inr}(x_2).t_2 \to c} \qquad \frac{t \to \textbf{inr}(t') \quad t_2[t'/x_2] \to c}{\textbf{case } t \textbf{ of inl}(x_1).t_1, \textbf{inr}(x_2).t_2 \to c}$$

$$\frac{t \to c}{\textbf{abs}(t) \to \textbf{abs}(c)} \qquad \frac{t \to \textbf{abs}(c)}{\textbf{rep}(t) \to c}$$

$$\frac{t[\textbf{rec } x.t/x] \to c}{\textbf{rec } x.t \to c}$$

Evaluation is deterministic and preserves types:

Proposition 13.21 *Let t be a closed term and c, c_1 and c_2 canonical forms. Then*

(i) $t \to c$ & $t : \tau$ implies $c : \tau$,
(ii) $t \to c_1$ & $t \to c_2$ implies $c_1 \equiv c_2$.

Proof: By rule induction.   □

13.8   Lazy denotational semantics

To each type τ we associate an information system with elements the values at type τ. The type τ may contain free type variables, so we need a type environment χ which to each of these assigns an information system. We define the information system denoted by τ by structural induction:

$$
\begin{aligned}
\mathcal{V}[\![0]\!]\chi &= (\emptyset, \{\emptyset\}, \emptyset) \qquad \text{(also called } \mathbf{0}) \\
\mathcal{V}[\![\tau_1 * \tau_2]\!]\chi &= (\mathcal{V}[\![\tau_1]\!]\chi)_\perp \times (\mathcal{V}[\![\tau_2]\!]\chi)_\perp \\
\mathcal{V}[\![\tau_1 \!-\!> \tau_2]\!]\chi &= (\mathcal{V}[\![\tau_1]\!]\chi)_\perp \to (\mathcal{V}[\![\tau_2]\!]\chi)_\perp \\
\mathcal{V}[\![\tau_1 + \tau_2]\!]\chi &= (\mathcal{V}[\![\tau_1]\!]\chi)_\perp + (\mathcal{V}[\![\tau_2]\!]\chi)_\perp \\
\mathcal{V}[\![X]\!]\chi &= \chi(X) \\
\mathcal{V}[\![\mu X.\tau]\!]\chi &= \mu I.\mathcal{V}[\![\tau]\!]\chi[I/X]
\end{aligned}
$$

All the operations on the right hand sides are operations on information systems. Again a recursive type expression $\mu X.\tau$ denotes, in an environment χ, the $\trianglelefteq$-least fixed point of

$$
I \mapsto \mathcal{V}[\![\tau]\!]\chi[I/X]
$$

in the cpo of information systems.

A closed type τ has an information system of *values*

$$
\mathcal{V}_\tau =_{def} \mathcal{V}[\![\tau]\!]\chi,
$$

for some arbitrary type environment χ, which we will write as

$$
\mathcal{V}_\tau = (\mathrm{Tok}_\tau, \mathrm{Con}_\tau, \vdash_\tau).
$$

The corresponding cpo of values is $|\mathcal{V}_\tau|$. With respect to an environment for its free variables, a term will denote an element of the lifted cpo of values. This time, it turns out to be simpler to represent this cpo at type τ as an information system, and define

$$
\mathcal{V}_{\tau_\perp} = (\mathcal{V}_\tau)_\perp
$$

which we will write as

$$
\mathcal{V}_{\tau_\perp} = (\mathrm{Tok}_{\tau_\perp}, \mathrm{Con}_{\tau_\perp}, \vdash_{\tau_\perp}).
$$

A term t of type τ is to denote an element

$$
[\![t]\!]\rho \in |\mathcal{V}_{\tau_\perp}|
$$

with respect to an environment $\rho : \mathbf{Var} \to |\mathcal{V}_{\tau_\perp}|$. We choose the following interpretation of $\perp$ and the lifting function $\lfloor - \rfloor : |\mathcal{V}_\tau| \to |\mathcal{V}_{\tau_\perp}|$: the conditions required by the lifting construction on cpo's in Section 8.3.4 are met if we take

$$\perp = \{\emptyset\},$$

the singleton consisting of the empty set, and

$$\lfloor x \rfloor = Fin(x),$$

consisting of all the finite subsets of x, for all $x \in \mathcal{V}_\tau$. Lifting is associated with the operation $f \mapsto f^*$ extending a continuous function $f : |\mathcal{A}| \to |\mathcal{B}|$ to $f^* : |\mathcal{A}_\perp| \to |\mathcal{B}|$ when the elements $|\mathcal{B}|$ have a bottom element $\perp_\mathcal{B}$. Our choice of lifting construction leads to the following characterisation of f^* and the closely-coupled *let*-notation.

Proposition 13.22 *Let $\mathcal{A}, \mathcal{B}$ be information systems. Assume $|\mathcal{B}|$ has a bottom element $\perp_\mathcal{B}$. Let $f : |\mathcal{A}| \to |\mathcal{B}|$ be a continuous function. Its extension*

$$f^* : |\mathcal{A}_\perp| \to |\mathcal{B}|$$

is given by

$$f^*(x) = \begin{cases} f(\bigcup x) & \text{if } x \neq \{\emptyset\}, \\ \perp_\mathcal{B} & \text{if } x = \{\emptyset\}, \end{cases}$$

for $x \in |\mathcal{A}_\perp|$. Consequently,

$$(let \; v \Leftarrow x. \; f(v)) = \begin{cases} f(\bigcup x) & \text{if } x \neq \{\emptyset\}, \\ \perp_\mathcal{B} & \text{if } x = \{\emptyset\}. \end{cases}$$

Proof: The extension f^* is defined to act on $x \in |\mathcal{A}_\perp|$ so

$$f^*(x) = \begin{cases} f(v) & \text{if } x = \lfloor v \rfloor, \\ \perp_\mathcal{B} & \text{if } x = \{\emptyset\}. \end{cases}$$

However, $x = \lfloor v \rfloor$ is equivalent to $x = Fin(v)$, which implies $v = \bigcup x$. With the remark that the case where $x = \lfloor v \rfloor$, for some v, coincides with that where $x \neq \{\emptyset\}$, we obtain the characterisation claimed in the proposition. Finally, note that, by definition,

$$(let \; v \Leftarrow x. \; f(v)) = f^*(x).$$

$\square$

Remark: The extension of the function $f^* : |\mathcal{A}_\perp| \to |\mathcal{B}|$ of $f : |\mathcal{A}| \to |\mathcal{B}|$ will be used most often in situations where f is described as a set-theoretic operation for which $f(\emptyset) = \emptyset$. In these situations $f^*(x) = f(\bigcup x) \cup \perp_B$.

In presenting the denotational semantics we shall again identify a sum of cpo's $|\mathcal{A}| + |\mathcal{B}|$ with $|\mathcal{A} + \mathcal{B}|$, and a product $|\mathcal{A}| \times |\mathcal{B}|$ with $|\mathcal{A} \times \mathcal{B}|$, for information systems $\mathcal{A}$ and $\mathcal{B}$. The treatment of the the lazy-function-space type will use the following isomorphisms between elements of information systems and continuous functions:

Proposition 13.23 *Let $\mathcal{A}$ and $\mathcal{B}$ be information systems. Define*

$$\| \text{-} \| : |\mathcal{A}_\perp \to \mathcal{B}_\perp| \to [|\mathcal{A}_\perp| \to |\mathcal{B}_\perp|],$$
$$\text{``-''} : [|\mathcal{A}_\perp| \to |\mathcal{B}_\perp|] \to |\mathcal{A}_\perp \to \mathcal{B}_\perp|,$$

by taking

$$\|r\| = \lambda x \in |\mathcal{A}_\perp|. \ \{Y \mid \exists X \subseteq x. \ (X, Y) \in r\},$$
$$\text{``}f\text{''} = \{(X, Y) \mid \emptyset \neq X \in \mathrm{Con}_{A_\perp} \ \& \ Y \in f(\overline{X})\} \cup \{(\emptyset, \emptyset)\}.$$

Then $\| \text{-} \|$ and "-" are mutual inverses, giving an isomorphism

$$|\mathcal{A}_\perp \to \mathcal{B}_\perp| \cong [|\mathcal{A}_\perp| \to |\mathcal{B}_\perp|].$$

Proof: By Theorem 12.30, we have the mutual inverses

$$| \text{-} | : |\mathcal{A}_\perp \to \mathcal{B}_\perp| \to [|\mathcal{A}_\perp| \to |\mathcal{B}|_\perp],$$
$$\text{`-'} : [|\mathcal{A}_\perp| \to |\mathcal{B}|_\perp] \to |\mathcal{A}_\perp \to \mathcal{B}_\perp|,$$

given by:

$$|r| = \lambda x \in |\mathcal{A}_\perp|. \ \bigcup \{Y \mid \exists X \subseteq x. \ (X, Y) \in r\},$$
$$\text{`}f\text{'} = \{(X, Y) \mid \emptyset \neq X \in \mathrm{Con}_{A_\perp} \ \& \ Y \subseteq^{fin} f(\overline{X})\} \cup \{(\emptyset, \emptyset)\}.$$

There is, in addition, an isomorphism between $|\mathcal{B}|_\perp$ and $|\mathcal{B}_\perp|$ given by the mutual inverses $Fin : |\mathcal{B}|_\perp \to |\mathcal{B}_\perp|$ and $\bigcup : |\mathcal{B}_\perp| \to |\mathcal{B}|_\perp$. Thus defining $\|r\| = Fin \circ |r|$ and $\text{``}f\text{''} = \text{`} \bigcup \circ f\text{'}$ yields an isomorphism pair "-", $\| \text{-} \|$ between $|\mathcal{A}_\perp \to \mathcal{B}_\perp|$ and $[|\mathcal{A}_\perp| \to |\mathcal{B}_\perp|]$. From the definition of $| \text{-} |$, we see:

$$\|r\|(x) = Fin(|r|(x))$$
$$= Fin(\bigcup \{Y \mid \exists X \subseteq x. \ (X, Y) \in r\}),$$
$$= \{Y \mid \exists X \subseteq x. \ (X, Y) \in r\}.$$

From the definition of '-', we obtain:

$$"f" =‘\bigcup \circ f’$$
$$=\{(X,Y) \mid \emptyset \neq X \in \mathrm{Con}_{A_\perp} \ \& \ Y \subseteq^{fin} \bigcup f(\overline{X})\} \cup \{(\emptyset,\emptyset)\}$$
$$=\{(X,Y) \mid \emptyset \neq X \in \mathrm{Con}_{A_\perp} \ \& \ Y \in f(\overline{X})\} \cup \{(\emptyset,\emptyset)\}.$$

□

Stated precisely, the cpo of environments consists of

$$\rho : \mathbf{Var} \to \bigcup \{|\mathcal{V}_{\tau_\perp}| \mid \tau \ \text{a closed type}\},$$

such that $\rho(x) \in |V_{type(x)_\perp}|$, ordered pointwise. The denotational semantics extends to recursive types that of Chapter 11 (Section 11.7). We accompany the semantic definitions by alternatives expressed using the information-system representation.

Denotational semantics

$\llbracket \bullet \rrbracket$	$=_{def}$	$\lambda\rho.\ \{\emptyset\}$

(1)

$\llbracket (t_1,t_2) \rrbracket$	$=_{def}$	$\lambda\rho.\ \lfloor(\llbracket t_1 \rrbracket\rho,\ \llbracket t_2 \rrbracket\rho)\rfloor$
	$=$	$\lambda\rho.\ \lfloor\llbracket t_1 \rrbracket\rho \times \llbracket t_2 \rrbracket\rho\rfloor$

(2)

$\llbracket \mathbf{fst}(t) \rrbracket$	$=_{def}$	$\lambda\rho.\ let\ v \Leftarrow \llbracket t \rrbracket\rho.\ \pi_1(v)$
	$=$	$\lambda\rho.\ (proj_1 \bigcup \llbracket t \rrbracket\rho) \cup \{\emptyset\}$

(3)

$\llbracket \mathbf{snd}(t) \rrbracket$	$=_{def}$	$\lambda\rho.\ let\ v \Leftarrow \llbracket t \rrbracket\rho.\ \pi_2(v)$
	$=$	$\lambda\rho.\ (proj_2 \bigcup \llbracket t \rrbracket\rho) \cup \{\emptyset\}$

$\llbracket x \rrbracket$	$=_{def}$	$\lambda\rho.\ \rho(x)$

$\llbracket \lambda x.t \rrbracket$	$=_{def}$	$\lambda\rho.\ \lfloor"(\lambda\ d \in |\mathcal{V}_{type(x)_\perp}|.\ \llbracket t \rrbracket\rho[d/x])"\rfloor$
	$=$	$\lambda\rho.\ \lfloor\{(U,V) \mid \emptyset \neq U \in \mathrm{Con}_{type(x)_\perp} \ \& \ V \in \llbracket t \rrbracket\rho[\overline{U}/x]\} \cup$ $\{(\emptyset,\emptyset)\}\rfloor$

(4)

$\llbracket t_1\ t_2 \rrbracket$	$=_{def}$	$\lambda\rho.\ let\ r \Leftarrow \llbracket t_1 \rrbracket\rho.\ \|r\|(\llbracket t_2 \rrbracket\rho)$
	$=$	$\lambda\rho.\ \{V \mid \exists U \subseteq \llbracket t_2 \rrbracket\rho.\ (U,V) \in \bigcup\llbracket t_1 \rrbracket\rho\} \cup \{\emptyset\}$

(5)

$\llbracket \mathbf{inl}(t) \rrbracket$	$=_{def}$	$\lambda\rho.\ \lfloor in_1(\llbracket t \rrbracket\rho)\rfloor$
	$=$	$\lambda\rho.\ \lfloor inj_1 \llbracket t \rrbracket\rho\rfloor$

(6)

$\llbracket \mathbf{inr}(t) \rrbracket$	$=_{def}$	$\lambda\rho.\ \lfloor in_2(\llbracket t \rrbracket\rho)\rfloor$
	$=$	$\lambda\rho.\ \lfloor inj_2 \llbracket t \rrbracket\rho\rfloor$

$[\![\mathbf{case}\ t\ \mathbf{of}\ \mathbf{inl}(x_1).t_1,\ \mathbf{inr}(x_2).t_2]\!]$

$\qquad =_{def}\ \lambda\rho.\ case\ [\![t]\!]\rho\ of\ in_1(d_1).[\![t_1]\!]\rho[d_1/x_1]\ |\ in_2(d_2).[\![t_2]\!]\rho[d_2/x_2].$

$[\![\mathbf{abs}(t)]\!]\ \ =_{def}\ \ [\![t]\!]$ (7)

$[\![\mathbf{rep}(t)]\!]\ \ =_{def}\ \ [\![t]\!]$

$[\![\mathbf{rec}\ x.t]\!]\ \ =_{def}\ \ \lambda\rho.\ \mu d.[\![t]\!]\rho[d/x]$

Explanation

(1) The term $\bullet$ denotes the bottom and only element of $|\mathbf{0}_\perp|$, *viz.* $\{\emptyset\}$.

(2) We identify the pair $([\![t_1]\!]\rho, [\![t_2]\!]\rho)$ with $[\![t_1]\!]\rho \times [\![t_2]\!]\rho$.

(3) The characterisation of the denotation $[\![\mathbf{fst}(t)]\!]\rho$ depends on Proposition 13.22. From the proposition

$$let\ v \Leftarrow [\![t]\!]\rho.\ \pi_1(v) = \begin{cases} \pi_1(\bigcup[\![t]\!]\rho) & \text{if } [\![t]\!]\rho \neq \{\emptyset\}, \\ \{\emptyset\} & \text{if } [\![t]\!]\rho = \{\emptyset\} \end{cases}$$

$$= \begin{cases} proj_1\bigcup[\![t]\!]\rho & \text{if } [\![t]\!]\rho \neq \{\emptyset\}, \\ \{\emptyset\} & \text{if } [\![t]\!]\rho = \{\emptyset\} \end{cases}$$

$$= (proj_1\bigcup[\![t]\!]\rho) \cup \{\emptyset\}$$

where the final step follows from the fact that $proj_1\emptyset = \emptyset$.

(4) This equality follows by Proposition 13.23.

(5) The characterisation of the *let*-construction in Proposition 13.22 yields

$$let\ r \Leftarrow [\![t_1]\!]\rho.\ \|r\|([\![t_2]\!]\rho) = \begin{cases} \|\bigcup[\![t_1]\!]\rho\|([\![t_2]\!]\rho) & \text{if } [\![t_1]\!]\rho \neq \{\emptyset\}, \\ \{\emptyset\} & \text{if } [\![t_1]\!]\rho = \{\emptyset\} \end{cases}$$

$$= \begin{cases} \{V \mid \exists U \subseteq [\![t_2]\!]\rho.\ (U,V) \in \bigcup[\![t_1]\!]\rho\} & \text{if } [\![t_1]\!]\rho \neq \{\emptyset\}, \\ \{\emptyset\} & \text{if } [\![t_1]\!]\rho = \{\emptyset\} \end{cases}$$

$$= \{V \mid \exists U \subseteq [\![t_2]\!]\rho.\ (U,V) \in \bigcup[\![t_1]\!]\rho\} \cup \{\emptyset\}$$

because the first component gives $\emptyset$ when $[\![t_1]\!]\rho = \{\emptyset\}$.

(6) We identify injections $in_1(d_1), in_2(d_2)$ of a sum with the image $inj_1 d_1$ and $inj_2 d_2$.

(7) The two halves of the isomorphism between information systems denoted by $\mu X.\tau$ and $\tau[\mu X.\tau/x]$, expressed by **abs** and **rep** are equalities.

Example: The lazy natural numbers

The information system denoted by the lazy natural numbers

$$nat \equiv \mu X.(0 + X)$$

will be the $\trianglelefteq$-least solution to

$$\mathcal{L} = 0_\perp + \mathcal{L}_\perp.$$

Terms of type nat will denote elements of $\mathcal{L}_\perp$ where

$$\mathcal{L}_\perp = (0_\perp + \mathcal{L}_\perp)_\perp,$$

with cpo of elements

$$|\mathcal{L}_\perp| \cong (|0|_\perp + |\mathcal{L}_\perp|)_\perp.$$

We can picture its cpo of elements as:

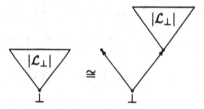

Indeed the cpo $|\mathcal{L}_\perp|$ has the form:

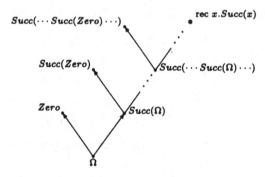

Above, the denotations of various terms of type nat are indicated. We have written Ω for the term $\mathbf{rec}\,x.x$, with $x : nat$. The elements

$$Zero,\ Succ(Zero),\ Succ(Succ(Zero)),\cdots$$

denote numbers while the maximal element, denoted by $\mathbf{rec}\,x.Succ(x)$, can be thought of as the "infinite" number

$$Succ(Succ(\cdots Succ\cdots)).$$

It is the least upper bound of the "partial" numbers:

$$\Omega,\ Succ(\Omega),\ Succ(Succ(\Omega)),\cdots$$

In fact, all but the bottom element are denoted by canonical forms—the "infinite number" is the denotation of the canonical form $Succ(\mathbf{rec}\,x.Succ(x))$. The operation of addition on the lazy natural numbers can be defined as a term just as in the eager case.   □

Exercise 13.24 Explain why it is not possible to define the cpo $\mathbf{N}_\perp$ of lifted natural numbers as a cpo of values or denotations associated with a type of the lazy language. (Lazy languages generally take this type as primitive.)   □

Example: Lazy lists
Let α be some closed type expression—for example α could be the type of lazy natural numbers. The type of lazy lists over α is given by the type term

$$L \equiv \mu Y.(0 + \alpha * Y).$$

Assume $\mathcal{A}$ is the information system denoted by α. This type term denotes the $\trianglelefteq$-least information system satisfying:

$$\mathcal{L} = 0_\perp + \mathcal{A}_\perp \times \mathcal{L}_\perp.$$

Terms of type L will denote members of $D = |\mathcal{L}_\perp|$, the domain of lazy lists over $|\mathcal{A}|_\perp$, where

$$D \cong (|0|_\perp + |\mathcal{A}|_\perp \times D)_\perp.$$

The lazy programming language provides the constant Nil as the canonical form

$$Nil \equiv_{def} \mathbf{abs}(\mathbf{inl}(\bullet)) : L$$

and the list constructor $Cons$ as

$$Cons \equiv_{def} \lambda x.\,\mathbf{abs}(\mathbf{inr}(x)) : \alpha * L \text{--}> L,$$

where x is a variable of type L. In the lazy language we can also define infinite lists. For example, the term

$$\mathbf{rec}\,l.\,Cons(a,l),$$

defines an infinite list in which each component is $a : \alpha$.   □

Exercise 13.25 Classify the different kinds of canonical forms of type lazy lists over a type α, indicating the form of their denotations.   □

13.9 Adequacy of lazy semantics

Let $t : \tau$ be a closed term. We say its evaluation converges with respect to the operational semantics iff it evaluates to some canonical form, *i.e.*

$$t \downarrow \quad \text{iff} \quad \exists c.\, t \to c.$$

As expected, we take t to converge if its denotation is not bottom in the cpo $|V_{\tau_\perp}|$. Recalling that the bottom element of $|V_{\tau_\perp}|$ is $\{\emptyset\}$, this amounts to:

$$t \Downarrow \quad \text{iff} \quad \bigcup \llbracket t \rrbracket \rho \neq \emptyset \text{ for an arbitrary environment } \rho.$$

It is straightforward to show that $t \downarrow$ implies $t \Downarrow$, for typable, closed terms t. The appropriate lemmas are listed here:

Lemma 13.26 *If ρ and ρ' agree on the free variables of t, then $\llbracket t \rrbracket \rho = \llbracket t \rrbracket \rho'$.*

Proof: By structural induction on t. $\square$

Lemma 13.27 *If $c \in C_\tau$ then $c \Downarrow$.*

Proof: By rule induction. $\square$

Lemma 13.28 *(Substitution Lemma)*
Let s be a closed term with $s : \sigma$. Let x be a variable with $x : \sigma$. Assume $t : \tau$. Then $t[s/x] : \tau$ and $\llbracket t[s/x] \rrbracket = \llbracket t \rrbracket [\llbracket s \rrbracket / x]$.

Proof: By structural induction on t. $\square$

Lemma 13.29 *If $t \to c$ then $\llbracket t \rrbracket \rho = \llbracket c \rrbracket \rho$ for any closed term t, canonical form c and arbitrary environment ρ.*

Proof: By rule induction. $\square$

Showing the converse, that $t \Downarrow$ implies $t \downarrow$, for typable, closed terms t, uses a logical relation $\lesssim_\tau$ between subsets of tokens V_τ and canonical forms C_τ. It is derivable from the relation ε_τ constructed in the following lemma:

Lemma 13.30 *For each closed type τ there exists a relation ε_τ between tokens Tok_τ and canonical forms C_τ with the following properties:*

- $(a, b)\ \varepsilon_{\tau_1 * \tau_2}\ (t_1, t_2)$ *iff* $a \lesssim_{\tau_1} t_1\ \&\ b \lesssim_{\tau_2} t_2$

- $(U, V) \; \varepsilon_{\tau_1 \to \tau_2} \; \lambda x.t$ *iff* $(\bigcup U \lesssim_{\tau_1} s \Rightarrow V \lesssim_{\tau_2} t[s/x]$ *for any closed* $s : \tau_1)$
- $(1, a) \; \varepsilon_{\tau_1 + \tau_2} \; \mathbf{inl}(t)$ *iff* $a \lesssim_{\tau_1} t$
- $(2, b) \; \varepsilon_{\tau_1 + \tau_2} \; \mathbf{inr}(t)$ *iff* $b \lesssim_{\tau_2} t$
- $a \; \varepsilon_{\mu X.\tau} \; \mathbf{abs}(c)$ *iff* $a \; \varepsilon_{\tau[\mu X.\tau/x]} \; c$

where we write

$$U \lesssim_\tau t$$

iff

$$\forall b \in U \exists c \in C_\tau. \; (b \; \varepsilon_\tau \; c \; \& \; t \to c),$$

for U a subset of tokens of V_τ and t a closed term.

Proof: The relation exists by well-founded recursion on the size of tokens and the structure of canonical forms ordered lexicographically.   □

Lemma 13.31 *For $U \in \mathrm{Con}_{\tau_\perp}$ and $t : \tau$ a closed term*

$$\bigcup U \lesssim_\tau t \Rightarrow \bigcup \overline{U} \lesssim_\tau t.$$

Proof: The lemma follows from

$$\bigcup U \lesssim_\tau c \; \& \; U \vdash_{\tau_\perp} a \Rightarrow a \lesssim_\tau c$$

for $U \in \mathrm{Con}_{\tau_\perp}$, $a \in \mathrm{Tok}_{\tau_\perp}$ and $c \in C_\tau$. This is shown by well-founded induction on $size(U \cup \{a\})$, and the structure of c ordered lexicographically. The proof proceeds according to the form of τ.   □

Lemma 13.32 *For each typable, closed term t, if $t \Downarrow$ then $t \downarrow$.*

Proof: The proof proceeds by structural induction on terms to show that for all terms $t : \tau$ with free variables among $z_1 : \sigma_1, \ldots, z_k : \sigma_k$ that if $\bigcup d_1 \lesssim_{\sigma_1} s_1, \cdots, \bigcup d_k \lesssim_{\sigma_k} s_k$ for $d_i \in |V_{\sigma_i \perp}|$ and s_i closed terms then

$$\bigcup [\![t]\!]\rho[d_1/z_1, \ldots, d_k/z_k] \lesssim_\tau t[s_1/z_1, \ldots, s_k/z_k].$$

The case where t is an abstraction makes recourse to Lemma 13.31.

Taking t closed, it then follows from the definition of $\lesssim_\tau$ that if $t \Downarrow$, i.e., $\bigcup [\![t]\!]\rho \neq \emptyset$, then $t \to c$ for some canonical form c.   □

13.10   The lazy λ-calculus

In the lazy language we can define the recursive type

$$\Lambda \equiv \mu X.(X\!-\!>X).$$

This type denotes the $\trianglelefteq$-least information system $\mathcal{L}$ such that

$$\mathcal{L} = \mathcal{L}_\perp \to \mathcal{L}_\perp$$

an information system equal to its own lazy function space. This implies that the denotations of terms at type Λ lie in the cpo $D = |\mathcal{L}_\perp|$, satisfying

$$D \cong [D \to D]_\perp.$$

Just as in the eager case, the type Λ has terms which form a λ-calculus:

$$t ::= x \mid t_1.t_2 \mid \lambda x.t$$

where x ranges over variables of type Λ, where again we use the abbreviations

$$t_1.t_2 \equiv ((\mathbf{rep}(t_1)\ t_2)$$
$$\lambda x.t \equiv \mathbf{abs}(\lambda x.t).$$

We inherit an operational and denotational semantics from the full language. The only canonical forms amongst them are those terms which are closed abstractions $\lambda x.t$. From the operational semantics we derive the rules:

$$\frac{}{\lambda x.t \to \lambda x.t} \qquad \frac{t_1 \to \lambda x.t_1'\ \ t_1'[t_2/x] \to c}{(t_1.t_2) \to c}$$

The two rules are sufficient to derive any instance of the evaluation relation $t \to c$ where t is a closed term of the λ-calculus. Because of the way applications are evaluated, the terms under such evaluation form a *lazy* λ-calculus.

By restricting the denotational semantics to terms of the λ-calculus we obtain:

$$[\![x]\!]\rho = \rho(x)$$

$$[\![t_1.t_2]\!]\rho = [\![t_1]\!]\rho.[\![t_2]\!]\rho$$

where the *application* $\varphi.d$ of $\varphi \in |\mathcal{L}_\perp|$ to $d \in |\mathcal{L}_\perp|$ is defined by

$$\varphi.d =_{def} \{V \mid \exists\, U \subseteq d.\ (U,V) \in \bigcup \varphi\} \cup \{\emptyset\},$$

$$[\![\lambda x.t]\!]\rho = \lfloor \{(U,V) \mid \emptyset \neq U \in \mathrm{Con}_{\Lambda_\perp}\ \&\ V \in [\![t]\!]\rho\, [\overline{U}/x]\} \ \cup\ \{(\emptyset,\emptyset)\}\rfloor$$

As far as the lazy λ-calculus is concerned, the only relevant part of an environment ρ is how it takes variables $x : \Lambda$ to elements $|\mathcal{L}_\perp|$.

13.10.1   Equational theory

We regard two terms of the lazy λ-calculus as equivalent iff they have the same denotation, i.e. for t_1, t_2 of the same type, define

$$t_1 = t_2 \text{ iff } [\![t_1]\!] = [\![t_2]\!].$$

We can define

$$t{\downarrow} \text{ iff } \forall \rho. \; \bigcup [\![t_1]\!]\rho \neq \emptyset.$$

We list rules which hold of two relations $=$ and $\downarrow$. They differ from those in the eager λ-calculus in that variables do not converge (because they need not in the lazy case denote only values) and (β) conversion holds irrespective of convergence of the argument. *Equality rules:*

$$\text{(refl) } \frac{}{t = t} \qquad\qquad \text{(sym) } \frac{t_1 = t_2}{t_2 = t_1} \qquad\qquad \text{(tran) } \frac{t_1 = t_2 \quad t_2 = t_3}{t_1 = t_3}$$

$$\text{(eq1) } \frac{t_1 = t_2}{t[t_1/x] = t[t_2/x]} \qquad\qquad\qquad \text{(eq2) } \frac{t_1 = t_2 \quad t_1{\downarrow}}{t_2{\downarrow}}$$

provided no free variables of t_1 and t_2 become bound by the substitutions into t.

Convergence rule: $\qquad\qquad \dfrac{}{\lambda x.t{\downarrow}}$

Conversion rules:

$$(\alpha) \quad \frac{}{\lambda x.t = \lambda y.(t[y/x])} \qquad \text{provided } y \text{ does not occur (free or bound) in } t.$$

$$(\beta) \quad \frac{}{(\lambda x.t)u = t[u/x]} \qquad \text{provided no free variable of } u \text{ becomes bound in } t.$$

$$(\eta) \quad \frac{t{\downarrow}}{t = \lambda x.(t.x)} \qquad \text{provided } x \text{ is not a free variable of } t.$$

Exercise 13.33 Prove the soundness of the rules from the denotational semantics.   □

Exercise 13.34 Show the soundness of the "strictness" rule:

$$\frac{t.u{\Downarrow}}{t{\Downarrow}}.$$

□

Exercise 13.35 Propose rules for $=$ and $\Downarrow$ for the full lazy language.   □

13.10.2   A fixed-point operator

The lazy λ-calculus has a simpler fixed-point operator than that for the eager calculus—it is no longer necessary to protect arguments from evaluation with an abstraction. Define

$$\mathcal{Y} \equiv \lambda f.(\lambda x.f.(x.x)).(\lambda x.f.(x.x)).$$

By equational reasoning, we see that

$$\begin{aligned}
\mathcal{Y}.f &= (\lambda x.f.(x.x)).(\lambda x.f.(x.x)) && \text{by } (\beta), && (1)\\
&= f.((\lambda x.f.(x.x)).(\lambda x.f.(x.x))) && \text{by } (\beta),\\
&= f.(\mathcal{Y}.f) && \text{by } (eq1) \text{ using } (1).
\end{aligned}$$

To understand the denotation of $\mathcal{Y}$ we introduce a function $down : |\mathcal{L}_\perp| \to |\mathcal{L}|$, defined using the bottom element of $|\mathcal{L}|$. Because

$$\mathcal{L} = \mathcal{L}_\perp \to \mathcal{L}_\perp$$

and, by convention,

$$\mathcal{L}_\perp = (\text{Tok}_{\Lambda_\perp}, \text{Con}_{\Lambda_\perp}, \vdash_{\Lambda_\perp})$$

the bottom element of $\mathcal{L}$ is

$$\perp_{|\mathcal{L}|} = \{(U, \emptyset) \mid U \in \text{Con}_{\Lambda_\perp}\}.$$

Define $down : |\mathcal{L}_\perp| \to |\mathcal{L}|$ by taking

$$down(d) = (\bigcup d) \cup \perp_{|\mathcal{L}|}.$$

Lemma 13.36 *Let* $\varphi, d \in |\mathcal{L}_\perp|$. *Then*

$$\varphi.d = \|down(\varphi)\|(d).$$

Proof: Let $\varphi, d \in |\mathcal{L}_\perp|$. By the definition of $\|\text{-}\|$, we obtain

$$\|down(\varphi)\|(d) = \{V \mid \exists U \subseteq d. \ (U, V) \in down(\varphi)\}.$$

By definition, $down(\varphi) = (\bigcup \varphi) \cup \{(U, \emptyset) \mid U \in \text{Con}_{\Lambda_\perp}\}$. Hence

$$\|down(\varphi)\|(d) = \{V \mid \exists U \subseteq d. \ (U, V) \in \bigcup \varphi\} \cup \{\emptyset\} = \varphi.d. \ \square$$

Now, by Lemma 13.36, from the fact that $\mathcal{Y}.f = f.(\mathcal{Y}.f)$, we obtain

$$[\mathcal{Y}.f]\rho = \rho(f).[\mathcal{Y}.f]\rho = \|down(\rho(f))\|([\mathcal{Y}.f]\rho).$$

Thus $[\mathcal{Y}.f]\rho$ is a fixed point of the function $\|down(\rho(f))\| : |\mathcal{L}_\perp| \to |\mathcal{L}_\perp|$. Hence

$$fix(\|down(\rho(f))\|) \subseteq [\mathcal{Y}.f]\rho.$$

As we will now show, the converse inclusion holds too, yielding equality.

Theorem 13.37 *Let*

$$\mathcal{Y} \equiv \lambda f.(\lambda x.f.(x.x)).(\lambda x.f.(x.x)).$$

Then, for an arbitrary environment ρ

$$[\mathcal{Y}.f]\rho = fix(\|down(\rho(f))\|).$$

Proof: The proof of the required converse inclusion is very similar to that of Theorem 13.19, and we will adopt similar abbreviations. A particular environment ρ will be assumed throughout the proof. We write $Fixf$ for $fix(\|down(\rho(f))\|)$. With respect to ρ we will identify a term with its denotation, writing

$$b \in t \text{ for } b \in [t]\rho,$$

and even

$$b \in \bigcup t \text{ for } b \in \bigcup [t]\rho.$$

Before embarking on the proof, we note that $Fixf$ can be characterised as the least $d \in |\mathcal{L}_\perp|$ such that $d = \rho(f).d$, *i.e.*

$$d = \{V \mid \exists U \subseteq d. \ (U, V) \in \bigcup f\} \cup \{\emptyset\}.$$

The (β) rule yields

$$\mathcal{Y}.f = (\lambda x.f.(x.x)).(\lambda x.f.(x.x)).$$

So, we see

$$V \in \mathcal{Y}.f \quad \Leftrightarrow \quad V \in (\lambda x.f.(x.x)).(\lambda x.f.(x.x))$$

$$\Leftrightarrow \quad V = \emptyset \text{ or } \exists U \subseteq (\lambda x.f.(x.x)).\ (U, V) \in \bigcup(\lambda x.f.(x.x)).$$

If $V = \emptyset$ it is clear that $V \in Fixf$ so it is sufficient to show that for all $U \in \text{Con}_{\Lambda_\perp}$, the property $P(U)$ holds, where

$$P(U) \iff_{def}$$

$$\forall V.[U \subseteq (\lambda x.f.(x.x)) \ \& \ (U, V) \in \bigcup(\lambda x.f.(x.x))] \Rightarrow V \in Fixf.$$

This is proved by induction on the size of U.

Let $U \in \text{Con}_{\Lambda_\perp}$. Suppose the induction hypothesis $P(U')$ holds for all $U' \in \text{Con}_{\Lambda_\perp}$ for which $size(U') < size(U)$. Assume

$$U \subseteq (\lambda x.f.(x.x)) \ \& \ (U, V) \in \bigcup(\lambda x.f.(x.x)).$$

If $V = \emptyset$ it is clear that $V \in Fixf$. Suppose otherwise, that $V \neq \emptyset$. Because (U, V) is a token, it follows that $U \neq \emptyset$. Under this supposition, we argue

$$(U, V) \in \bigcup(\lambda x.f.(x.x)) \Leftrightarrow V \in [\![f.(x.x)]\!]\rho[\overline{U}/x]$$

$$\text{from the denotational semantics of 13.10,}$$

$$\Leftrightarrow V \in \rho(f).(\overline{U}.\overline{U}) \quad \text{again from the semantics,}$$

$$\Leftrightarrow \exists W \subseteq (\overline{U}.\overline{U}).\ (W, V) \in \bigcup f.$$

Thus from the assumption that $(U, V) \in \bigcup(\lambda x.f.(x.x))$ we have deduced the existence of $W \in \text{Con}_{\Lambda_\perp}$ such that

$$(W, V) \in \bigcup f \ \text{ and } \ \forall C \in W.\ C \in (\overline{U}.\overline{U}).$$

We show that consequently $W \subseteq Fixf$, from which it follows that $V \in Fixf$.

With the aim of showing $W \subseteq Fixf$, let $C \in W$. If $C = \emptyset$ then clearly $C \in Fixf$. So, suppose otherwise, that $C \neq \emptyset$. Directly from the fact that $C \in (\overline{U}.\overline{U})$ we see

$$\exists Z \subseteq \overline{U}.\ (Z, C) \in \bigcup \overline{U}.$$

But

$$(Z, C) \in \bigcup \overline{U} \Leftrightarrow \bigcup U \vdash_\Lambda (Z, C)$$

—an instance of a general property of the lifting construction on information systems (*cf.* Exercise 12.22). Hence

$$\exists Z.\ U \vdash^*_{\Lambda_\perp} Z \ \& \ \bigcup U \vdash_\Lambda (Z, C)$$

and thus

$$\bigcup U \vdash_\Lambda (U, C).$$

Recall Λ denotes $\mathcal{L} = \mathcal{L}_\perp \to \mathcal{L}_\perp$, a lifted function space of information systems. By the definition of its entailment relation:

$$\bigcup \{Y \mid \exists Z.\ U \vdash^*_{\Lambda_\perp} Z\ \&\ (Z, Y) \in \bigcup U\} \vdash^*_\Lambda C.$$

Consider arbitrary Z, Y for which

$$U \vdash^*_{\Lambda_\perp} Z\ \&\ (Z, Y) \in \bigcup U.$$

Then $size(Z) < size(U)$, and hence $P(Z)$ by the induction hypothesis. By assumption

$$U \subseteq (\lambda x.f.(x.x)).$$

Thus

$$Z \subseteq (\lambda x.f.(x.x)),$$

as the denotation of $(\lambda x.f.(x.x))$ is closed under entailment, and also

$$(Z, Y) \in \bigcup (\lambda x.f.(x.x)).$$

By $P(Z)$ we obtain $Y \in Fix f$. Thus as Z, Y were arbitrary

$$Fix f \supseteq \{Y \mid \exists Z.\ U \vdash^*_{\Lambda_\perp} Z\ \&\ (Z, Y) \in \bigcup U\} \vdash_{\Lambda_\perp} C.$$

Hence $C \in Fix f$, because $Fix f$ is closed under entailment. But C was an arbitrary member of W, so we deduce $W \subseteq Fix f$.

From the characterisation of $Fix f$, we now finally get $V \in Fix f$. This concludes the proof by induction on the size of U. $\qquad\qquad\qquad\qquad\qquad\qquad\qquad\qquad\qquad\qquad\square$

13.11   Further reading

The books [101] by Wikström on the eager language of Standard ML and [22] by Bird and Wadler on a lazy functional language, give clear, elementary explanations of the uses of recursive types. The technique used in proving adequacy follows closely that in Gordon Plotkin's lecture notes—similar methods of proof have been used by Per Martin-Löf in his domain interpretation of type theory (1983), and by Samson Abramsky [1]. The same method of proof also works to prove adequacy for an extension of the language to include polymorphic types as in the student project [17]. Plotkin was early to study different modes of evaluating the λ-calculus in [77]. The rules of for the eager λ-calculus in Section 13.5.1 are essentially those of Eugenio Moggi's λ_p-calculus [66]. The lazy λ-calculus is studied by Abramsky in [1] and the rules of the lazy λ-calculus in Section 13.10.1 correspond to Chih-Hao Ong's rules in [71]. Lazy λ-calculus is also treated in [87], which contains another proof of Theorem 13.37. A recent advance on the methods for proving properties of recursive domains is described in Andrew Pitts' article [76]. The classic book on the classical λ-calculus is Barendregt's [14]. See also Hindley and Seldin's [45]. See Gordon's book [42] for an elementary exposition of the λ-calculus.

14 Nondeterminism and parallelism

This chapter is an introduction to nondeterministic and parallel (or concurrent) programs and systems, their semantics and logic. Starting with communication via shared variables it leads through Dijkstra's language of guarded commands to a language closely related to Occam and Hoare's CSP, and thence to Milner's CCS. In the latter languages communication is solely through the synchronised exchange of values. A specification language consisting of a simple modal logic with recursion is motivated. An algorithm is derived for checking whether or not a finite-state process satisfies a specification. This begins a study of tools for the verification of parallel systems of the kind supported by the Edinburgh-Sussex Concurrency Workbench and the Aalborg TAV system. The chapter concludes with an indication of other approaches and some current research issues in the semantics and logic of parallel processes.

14.1 Introduction

A simple way to introduce some basic issues in parallel programming languages is to extend the simple imperative language **IMP** of Chapter 2 by an operation of parallel composition. For commands c_0, c_1 their parallel composition $c_0 \parallel c_1$ executes like c_0 and c_1 together, with no particular preference being given to either one. What happens, if, for instance, both c_0 and c_1 are in a position to assign to the same variable? One (and by that it is meant either one) will carry out its assignment, possibly followed by the other. It's plain that the assignment carried out by one can affect the state acted on later by the other. This means we cannot hope to accurately model the execution of commands in parallel using a relation between command configurations and final states. We must instead use a relation representing single uninterruptible steps in the execution relation and so allow for one command affecting the state of another with which it is set in parallel.

Earlier, in Chapter 2, we saw there was a choice as to what is regarded as a single uninterruptible step. This is determined by the rules written down for the execution of commands and, in turn, on the evaluation of expressions. But assuming these have been done we can explain the execution of the parallel composition of commands by their rules:

$$\frac{\langle c_0, \sigma \rangle \to_1 \sigma'}{\langle c_0 \parallel c_1, \sigma \rangle \to_1 \langle c_1, \sigma' \rangle} \qquad \frac{\langle c_0, \sigma \rangle \to_1 \langle c_0', \sigma' \rangle}{\langle c_0 \parallel c_1, \sigma \rangle \to_1 \langle c_0' \parallel c_1, \sigma' \rangle}$$

$$\frac{\langle c_1, \sigma \rangle \to_1 \sigma'}{\langle c_0 \parallel c_1, \sigma \rangle \to_1 \langle c_0, \sigma' \rangle} \qquad \frac{\langle c_1, \sigma \rangle \to_1 \langle c_1', \sigma' \rangle}{\langle c_0 \parallel c_1, \sigma \rangle \to_1 \langle c_0 \parallel c_1', \sigma' \rangle}$$

Look at the first two rules. They show how a single step in the execution of a command

c_0 gives rise to a single step in the execution of $c_0 \parallel c_1$—these are two rules corresponding to the single step in the execution of c_0 completing the execution of c_0 or not. There are symmetric rules for the right-hand-side component of a parallel composition. If the two component commands c_0 and c_1 of a parallel composition have locations in common they are likely to influence each others execution. They can be thought of as communicating by shared locations. Our parallel composition gives an example of what is often called *communication by shared variables.*

The symmetry in the rules for parallel composition introduces an unpredictability into the behaviour of commands. Consider for example the execution of the program $(X := 0 \parallel X := 1)$ from the initial state. This will terminate but with what value at X? More generally a program of the form

$$(X := 0 \parallel X := 1); \textbf{ if } X = 0 \textbf{ then } c_0 \textbf{ else } c_1$$

will execute either as c_0 or c_1, and we don't know which.

This unpredictability is called *nondeterminism.* The programs we have used to illustrate nondeterminism are artificial, perhaps giving the impression that it can be avoided. However it is a fact of life. People and computer systems do work in parallel leading to examples of nondeterministic behaviour, not so far removed from the silly programs we've just seen. We note that an understanding of parallelism requires an understanding of nondeterminism.

14.2   Guarded commands

Paradoxically a disciplined use of nondeterminism can lead to a more straightforward presentation of algorithms. This is because the achievement of a goal may not depend on which of several tasks is performed. In everyday life we might instruct someone to either do this or that and not care which. Dijkstra's language of guarded commands uses a nondeterministic construction to help free the programmer from overspecifying a method of solution. Dijkstra's language has arithmetic and boolean expressions $a \in \textbf{Aexp}$ and $b \in \textbf{Bexp}$ which we can take to be the same as those for **IMP** as well as two new syntactic sets that of commands (ranged over by c) and guarded commands (ranged over by gc). Their abstract syntax is given by these rules:

$$c ::= \textbf{skip} \mid \textbf{abort} \mid X := a \mid c_0; c_1 \mid \textbf{if } gc \textbf{ fi} \mid \textbf{ do } gc \textbf{ od}$$

$$gc ::= b \rightarrow c \mid gc_0 [\!] gc_1$$

The constructor used to form guarded commands $gc_0 [\![gc_1$ is called *alternative* (or "fatbar"). The guarded command typically has the form

$$(b_1 \to c_1) [\![\ldots [\![(b_n \to c_n).$$

In this context the boolean expressions are called *guards* – the execution of the command body c_i depends on the corresponding guard b_i evaluating to true. If no guard evaluates to true at a state the guarded command is said to *fail*, in which case the guarded command does not yield a final state. Otherwise the guarded command executes nondeterministically as one of the commands c_i whose associated guard b_i evaluates to true. We have already met **skip**, assignment and sequential composition in our treatment of **IMP**. The new command **abort** does not yield a final state from any initial state. The command **if** gc **fi** executes as the guarded command gc, if gc does not fail, and otherwise acts like **abort**. The command **do** gc **od** executes repeatedly as the guarded command gc, while gc continues not to fail, and terminates when gc fails; it acts like **skip** if the guarded command fails initially.

We now capture these informal explanations in rules for the execution of commands and guarded commands. We inherit the evaluation relations for **Aexp** and **Bexp** from **IMP** in Chapter 2. With an eye to the future section on an extension of the language to handle parallelism we describe one step in the execution of commands and guarded commands. A command configuration has the form $\langle c, \sigma \rangle$ or σ for commands c and states σ.

Initial configurations for guarded commands are pairs $\langle gc, \sigma \rangle$, for guarded commands gc and states σ, as is to be expected, but one step in their execution can lead to a command configuration or to a new kind of configuration called **fail**. Here are the rules for execution:

Rules for commands:

$$\langle \mathbf{skip}, \sigma \rangle \to \sigma$$

$$\frac{\langle a, \sigma \rangle \to n}{\langle X := a, \sigma \rangle \to \sigma[n/X]}$$

$$\frac{\langle c_0, \sigma \rangle \to \sigma'}{\langle c_0; c_1, \sigma \rangle \to \langle c_1, \sigma' \rangle} \qquad \frac{\langle c_0, \sigma \rangle \to \langle c_0', \sigma' \rangle}{\langle c_0; c_1, \sigma \rangle \to \langle c_0'; c_1, \sigma' \rangle}$$

$$\frac{\langle gc, \sigma \rangle \to \langle c, \sigma' \rangle}{\langle \mathbf{if}\ gc\ \mathbf{fi}, \sigma \rangle \to \langle c, \sigma' \rangle}$$

$$\frac{\langle gc, \sigma \rangle \to \mathbf{fail}}{\langle\ \mathbf{do}\ gc\ \mathbf{od}, \sigma \rangle \to \sigma} \qquad \frac{\langle gc, \sigma \rangle \to \langle c, \sigma' \rangle}{\langle\ \mathbf{do}\ gc\ \mathbf{od}, \sigma \rangle \to \langle c;\ \mathbf{do}\ gc\ \mathbf{od}, \sigma' \rangle}$$

Rules for guarded commands:

$$\frac{\langle b, \sigma \rangle \to \mathbf{true}}{\langle b \to c, \sigma \rangle \to \langle c, \sigma \rangle}$$

$$\frac{\langle gc_0, \sigma \rangle \to \langle c, \sigma' \rangle}{\langle gc_0 \| gc_1, \sigma \rangle \to \langle c, \sigma' \rangle} \qquad \frac{\langle gc_1, \sigma \rangle \to \langle c, \sigma' \rangle}{\langle gc_0 \| gc_1, \sigma \rangle \to \langle c, \sigma' \rangle}$$

$$\frac{\langle b, \sigma \rangle \to \mathbf{false}}{\langle b \to c, \sigma \rangle \to \mathbf{fail}} \qquad \frac{\langle gc_0, \sigma \rangle \to \mathbf{fail}\ \langle gc_1, \sigma \rangle \to \mathbf{fail}}{\langle gc_0 \| gc_1, \sigma \rangle \to \mathbf{fail}}$$

The rule for alternatives $gc_0 \| gc_1$ introduces nondeterminism—such a guarded command can execute like gc_0 or like gc_1. Notice the absence of rules for **abort** and for commands **if** gc **fi** in the case where the guarded command gc fails. In such situations the commands do not execute to produce a final state. Another possibility, not straying too far from Dijkstra's intentions in [36], would be to introduce a new command configuration **abortion** to make this improper termination explicit.[1]

As an example, here is a command which assigns the maximum value of two locations X and Y to a location MAX:

$$\mathbf{if}$$
$$X \geq Y \to MAX := X$$
$$\|$$
$$Y \geq X \to MAX := Y$$
$$\mathbf{fi}$$

---

[1]The reader may find one thing curious. As the syntax stands there is an unnecessary generality in the rules. From the rules for guarded commands it can be seen that in transitions $\langle gc, \sigma \rangle \to \langle c, \sigma' \rangle$ which can be derived the state is unchanged, *i.e.* $\sigma = \sigma'$. And thus in all rules whose premises are a transition $\langle gc, \sigma \rangle \to \langle c, \sigma' \rangle$ we could replace σ' by σ. Of course we lose nothing by this generality, but more importantly, the extra generality will be needed when later we extend the set of guards to allow them to have side effects.

The symmetry between X and Y would be lost in a more traditional **IMP** program.

Euclid's algorithm for the greatest common divisor of two numbers is particularly striking in the language of guarded commands:

$$\textbf{do}$$
$$X > Y \rightarrow X := X - Y$$
$$\|$$
$$Y > X \rightarrow Y := Y - X$$
$$\textbf{od}$$

Compare this with its more clumsy program in **IMP** in Section 3.3, a clumsiness which is due to the asymmetry between the two branches of a conditional. See Dijkstra's book [36] for more examples of programs in his language of guarded commands.

Exercise 14.1 Give an operational semantics for the language of guarded commands but where the rules determine transitions of the form $\langle c, \sigma \rangle \rightarrow \sigma'$ and $\langle gc, \sigma \rangle \rightarrow \sigma'$ between configurations and final states.   □

Exercise 14.2 Explain why this program terminates:

$$\textbf{do} \ (2|X \rightarrow X := (3 \times X)/2) \| (3|X \rightarrow X := (5 \times X)/3) \ \textbf{od}$$

where *e.g.* $3|X$ means 3 divides X, and $(5 \times X)/3$ means $5 \times X$ divided by 3.   □

Exercise 14.3 A partial correctness assertion $\{A\}c\{B\}$, where c is a command or guarded command and A and B are assertions about states, is said to be valid if for any state at which A is true the execution of c, if it terminates, does so in a final state at which B is true. Write down sound proof rules for the partial correctness assertions of Dijktra's language. In what sense do you expect the proof rules to be complete? As a test of their completeness, try to use them to prove the partial correctness of Euclid's algorithm, (*cf.* Exercise 6.16). How would you prove its termination under the assumption that initially the locations hold positive numbers?   □

Exercise 14.4 Let the syntax of regular commands c be given as follows:

$$c := \textbf{skip} \mid X := e \mid b? \mid c;c \mid c+c \mid c^*$$

where X ranges over a set of locations, e is an integer expression and b is a boolean expression. States σ are taken to be functions from the set of locations to integers. It is assumed that the meaning of integer and boolean expressions are specified by semantic functions so $I[e]\sigma$ is the integer which integer expression e evaluates to in state σ and $B[b]\sigma$ is the boolean value given by b in state σ. The meaning of a regular command c is given by a relation of the form

$$\langle c, \sigma \rangle \to \sigma'$$

which expresses that the execution of c in state σ can lead to final state σ'. The relation is determined by the following rules:

$$\langle \mathbf{skip}, \sigma \rangle \to \sigma \qquad \frac{I[e]\sigma = n}{\langle X := e, \sigma \rangle \to \sigma[n/X]}$$

$$\frac{B[b]\sigma = true}{\langle b?, \sigma \rangle \to \sigma} \qquad \frac{\langle c_0, \sigma \rangle \to \sigma'' \quad \langle c_1, \sigma'' \rangle \to \sigma'}{\langle c_0; c_1, \sigma \rangle \to \sigma'}$$

$$\frac{\langle c_0, \sigma \rangle \to \sigma'}{\langle c_0 + c_1, \sigma \rangle \to \sigma'} \qquad \frac{\langle c_1, \sigma \rangle \to \sigma'}{\langle c_0 + c_1, \sigma \rangle \to \sigma'}$$

$$\langle c^*, \sigma \rangle \to \sigma \qquad \frac{\langle c, \sigma \rangle \to \sigma'' \quad \langle c^*, \sigma'' \rangle \to \sigma'}{\langle c^*, \sigma \rangle \to \sigma'}$$

(i) Write down a regular command which has the same effect as the while loop

$$\textbf{while } b \textbf{ do } c,$$

where b is a boolean expression and c is a regular command. Your command C should have the same effect as the while loop in the sense that

$$\langle C, \sigma \rangle \to \sigma' \text{ iff } \langle \textbf{while } b \textbf{ do } c, \sigma \rangle \to \sigma'.$$

(This assumes the obvious rules for while loops.)

(ii) For two regular commands c_0 and c_1 write $c_0 = c_1$ when $\langle c_0, \sigma \rangle \to \sigma'$ iff $\langle c_1, \sigma \rangle \to \sigma'$ for all states σ and σ'. Prove from the rules that

$$c^* = skip + c; c^*$$

for any regular command c.

(iii) Write down a denotational semantics of regular commands; the denotation of a regular command c should equal the relation

$$\{(\sigma, \sigma') | \langle c, \sigma \rangle \to \sigma'\}.$$

Describe briefly the strategy you would use to prove that this is indeed true of your semantics.

(iv) Suggest proof rules for partial correctness assertions of regular commands of the form $b?$, $c_0 + c_1$ and c^*. □

14.3 Communicating processes

In the latter half of the seventies Hoare and Milner independently suggested the same novel communication primitive. It was clear that systems of processors, each with its own store, would become increasingly important. A communication primitive was sought which was independent of the medium used to communicate, the idea being that the medium, whether it be shared locations or something else, could itself be modelled as a process. Hoare and Milner settled on atomic actions of synchronisation, with the possible exchange of values, as the central primitive of communication.

Their formulations are slightly different. Here we will assume that a process communicates with other processes via channels. We will allow channels to be hidden so that communication along a particular channel can be made local to two or more processes. A process may be prepared to input or output at a channel. However it can only succeed in doing so if there is a companion process in its environment which performs the complementary action of output or input. There is no automatic buffering; an input or output communication is delayed until the other process is ready with the corresponding output or input. When successful the value output is then copied from the outputting to the inputting process.

We now present the syntax of a language of communicating processes. In addition to a set of locations $X \in \mathbf{Loc}$, boolean expressions $b \in \mathbf{Bexp}$ and arithmetic expressions $a \in \mathbf{Aexp}$, we assume:

Channel names $\quad\quad \alpha, \beta, \gamma, \ldots \in \mathbf{Chan}$
Input expressions $\quad\; \alpha?X \quad\quad$ where $X \in \mathbf{Loc}$
Output expressions $\quad \alpha!a \quad\quad$ where $a \in \mathbf{Aexp}$

Commands:

$$c \quad ::= \quad \mathbf{skip} \mid \mathbf{abort} \mid X := a \mid \alpha?X \mid \alpha!a \mid c_0; c_1 \mid \mathbf{if}\ gc\ \mathbf{fi} \mid \mathbf{do}\ gc\ \mathbf{od} \mid c_0 \parallel c_1 \mid c \setminus \alpha$$

Guarded commands:

$$gc \quad ::= \quad b \to c \mid b \wedge \alpha?X \to c \mid b \wedge \alpha!a \to c \mid gc_0 \| gc_1$$

Not all commands and guarded commands are well-formed. A *parallel composition* $c_0 \parallel c_1$ is only well-formed in case the commands c_0 and c_1 do not contain a common location. In general a command is well-formed if all its subcommands of the form $c_0 \parallel c_1$ are well-formed. A *restriction* $c \setminus \alpha$ hides the channel α, so that only communications internal to c can occur on it.

How are we to formalise the intended behaviour of this language of communicating processes? As earlier, states will be functions from locations to the values they contain, and a command configuration will have the form $\langle c, \sigma \rangle$ or σ for a command c and state σ. We will try to formalise the idea of one step in the execution. Consider a particular command configuration of the form

$$\langle \alpha?X; c, \sigma \rangle.$$

This represents a command which is first prepared to receive a synchronised communication of a value for X along the channel α. Whether it does or not is, of course, contingent on whether or not the command is in parallel with another prepared to do a complementary action of outputting a value to the channel α. Its semantics should express this contingency on the environment. This we do in a way familiar from automata theory. We label the transitions. For the set of labels we take

$$\{\alpha?n \mid \alpha \in \textbf{Chan} \ \& \ n \in \textbf{N}\} \cup \{\alpha!n \mid \alpha \in \textbf{Chan} \ \& \ n \in \textbf{N}\}$$

Now, in particular, we expect our semantics to yield the labelled transition

$$\langle \alpha?X; c_0, \sigma \rangle \xrightarrow{\alpha?n} \langle c_0, \sigma[n/X] \rangle.$$

This expresses the fact that the command $\alpha?X; c_0$ can receive a value n at the channel α and store it in location X, and so modify the state. The labels of the form $\alpha!n$ represent the ability to output a value n at channel α. We expect the transition

$$\langle \alpha!e; c_1, \sigma \rangle \xrightarrow{\alpha!n} \langle c_1, \sigma \rangle$$

provided $\langle e, \sigma \rangle \to n$. Once we have these we would expect a possibility of communication when the two commands are set in parallel:

$$\langle (\alpha?X; c_0) \parallel (\alpha!e; c_1), \sigma \rangle \to \langle c_0 \parallel c_1, \sigma[n/X] \rangle$$

This time we don't label the transition because the communication capability of the two commands has been used up through an internal communication, with no contingency on the environment. We expect other transitions too. Afterall, there may be other processes in the environment prepared to send and receive values via the channel α. So as to not exclude those possibilities we had better also include transitions

$$\langle (\alpha?X; c_0) \parallel (\alpha!e; c_1), \sigma \rangle \xrightarrow{\alpha?n} \langle c_0 \parallel (\alpha!e; c_1), \sigma[n/X] \rangle$$

and

$$\langle (\alpha?X; c_0) \parallel (\alpha!e; c_1), \sigma \rangle \xrightarrow{\alpha!n} \langle (\alpha?X; c_0) \parallel c_1, \sigma[n/X] \rangle.$$

The former captures the possibility that the first component receives a value from the environment and not from the second component. In the latter the second component sends a value received by the environment, not by the first component.

Now we present the full semantics systematically using rules. We assume that arithmetic and boolean expressions have the same form as earlier from **IMP** and inherit the evaluation rules from there.

Guarded commands will be treated in a similar way to before, but allowing for communication in the guards. As earlier guarded commands can sometimes fail at a state.

To control the number of rules we shall adopt some conventions. To treat both labelled and unlabelled transitions in a uniform manner we shall use λ to range over labels like $\alpha?n$ and $\alpha!n$ as well as the empty label. The other convention aims to treat both kinds of command configurations $\langle c, \sigma \rangle$ and σ in the same way. We regard the configuration σ as configuration $\langle *, \sigma \rangle$ where $*$ is thought of as the *empty command*. As such $*$ satisfies the laws

$$*; c \equiv c; * \equiv * \parallel c \equiv c \parallel * \equiv c \quad \text{and} \quad *; * \equiv * \parallel * \equiv (* \setminus \alpha) \equiv *$$

which express, for instance, that $* \parallel c$ stands for the piece of syntax c.

Rules for commands

$$\langle \mathbf{skip}, \sigma \rangle \to \sigma \qquad \frac{\langle a, \sigma \rangle \to n}{\langle X := a, \sigma \rangle \to \sigma[n/X]}$$

$$\langle \alpha?X, \sigma \rangle \xrightarrow{\alpha?n} \sigma[n/X] \qquad \frac{\langle a, \sigma \rangle \to n}{\langle \alpha!a, \sigma \rangle \xrightarrow{\alpha!n} \sigma}$$

$$\frac{\langle c_0, \sigma \rangle \xrightarrow{\lambda} \langle c_0', \sigma' \rangle}{\langle c_0; c_1, \sigma \rangle \xrightarrow{\lambda} \langle c_0'; c_1, \sigma' \rangle}$$

$$\frac{\langle gc, \sigma \rangle \xrightarrow{\lambda} \langle c, \sigma' \rangle}{\langle \mathbf{if} \ gc \ \mathbf{fi}, \sigma \rangle \xrightarrow{\lambda} \langle c, \sigma' \rangle}$$

$$\frac{\langle gc, \sigma \rangle \xrightarrow{\lambda} \langle c, \sigma' \rangle}{\langle\, \mathbf{do}\ gc\ \mathbf{od}, \sigma \rangle \xrightarrow{\lambda} \langle c;\ \mathbf{do}\ gc\ \mathbf{od}, \sigma' \rangle} \qquad \frac{\langle gc, \sigma \rangle \to \mathbf{fail}}{\langle\, \mathbf{do}\ gc\ \mathbf{od}, \sigma \rangle \to \sigma}$$

$$\frac{\langle c_0, \sigma \rangle \xrightarrow{\lambda} \langle c_0', \sigma' \rangle}{\langle c_0 \parallel c_1, \sigma \rangle \xrightarrow{\lambda} \langle c_0' \parallel c_1, \sigma' \rangle} \qquad \frac{\langle c_1, \sigma \rangle \xrightarrow{\lambda} \langle c_1', \sigma' \rangle}{\langle c_0 \parallel c_1, \sigma \rangle \xrightarrow{\lambda} \langle c_0 \parallel c_1', \sigma' \rangle}$$

$$\frac{\langle c_0, \sigma \rangle \xrightarrow{\alpha?n} \langle c_0', \sigma' \rangle \ \langle c_1, \sigma \rangle \xrightarrow{\alpha!n} \langle c_1', \sigma \rangle}{\langle c_0 \parallel c_1, \sigma \rangle \to \langle c_0' \parallel c_1', \sigma' \rangle} \qquad \frac{\langle c_0, \sigma \rangle \xrightarrow{\alpha!n} \langle c_0', \sigma \rangle \ \langle c_1, \sigma \rangle \xrightarrow{\alpha?n} \langle c_1', \sigma' \rangle}{\langle c_0 \parallel c_1, \sigma \rangle \to \langle c_0' \parallel c_1', \sigma' \rangle}$$

$$\frac{\langle c, \sigma \rangle \xrightarrow{\lambda} \langle c', \sigma' \rangle}{\langle c \setminus \alpha, \sigma \rangle \xrightarrow{\lambda} \langle c' \setminus \alpha, \sigma' \rangle} \quad \text{provided neither } \lambda \equiv \alpha?n \text{ nor } \lambda \equiv \alpha!n$$

Rules for guarded commands

$$\frac{\langle b, \sigma \rangle \to \mathbf{true}}{\langle b \to c, \sigma \rangle \to \langle c, \sigma \rangle} \qquad \frac{\langle b, \sigma \rangle \to \mathbf{false}}{\langle b \to c, \sigma \rangle \to \mathbf{fail}}$$

$$\frac{\langle b, \sigma \rangle \to \mathbf{false}}{\langle b \wedge \alpha?X \to c, \sigma \rangle \to \mathbf{fail}} \qquad \frac{\langle b, \sigma \rangle \to \mathbf{false}}{\langle b \wedge \alpha!a \to c, \sigma \rangle \to \mathbf{fail}}$$

$$\frac{\langle gc_0, \sigma \rangle \to \mathbf{fail} \ \langle gc_1, \sigma \rangle \to \mathbf{fail}}{\langle gc_0 \| gc_1, \sigma \rangle \to \mathbf{fail}}$$

$$\frac{\langle b, \sigma \rangle \to \mathbf{true}}{\langle b \wedge \alpha?X \to c, \sigma \rangle \xrightarrow{\alpha?n} \langle c, \sigma[n/X] \rangle} \qquad \frac{\langle b, \sigma \rangle \to \mathbf{true} \ \langle a, \sigma \rangle \to n}{\langle b \wedge \alpha!a \to c, \sigma \rangle \xrightarrow{\alpha!n} \langle c, \sigma \rangle}$$

$$\frac{\langle gc_0, \sigma \rangle \xrightarrow{\lambda} \langle c, \sigma' \rangle}{\langle gc_0 \| gc_1, \sigma \rangle \xrightarrow{\lambda} \langle c, \sigma' \rangle} \qquad \frac{\langle gc_1, \sigma \rangle \xrightarrow{\lambda} \langle c, \sigma' \rangle}{\langle gc_0 \| gc_1, \sigma \rangle \xrightarrow{\lambda} \langle c, \sigma' \rangle}$$

Example: The following illustrate various features of the language and the processes it can describe (several more can be found in Hoare's paper [49]):

A process which repeatedly receives a value from the α channel and transmits it on channel β:

$$\mathbf{do}\ (\mathbf{true} \wedge \alpha?X \to \beta!X)\ \mathbf{od}$$

A buffer with capacity 2 receiving on α and transmitting on γ:

$$(\ \mathbf{do}\ (\mathbf{true} \wedge \alpha?X \to \beta!X)\ \mathbf{od}\ \|\ \mathbf{do}\ (\mathbf{true} \wedge \beta?Y \to \gamma!Y)\ \mathbf{od}) \setminus \beta$$

Notice the use of restriction to make the β channel hidden so that all communications along it have to be internal.

One use of the alternative construction is to allow a process to "listen" to two channels simultaneously and read from one should a process in the environment wish to output there; in the case where it can receive values at either channel a nondeterministic choice is made between them:

$$\mathbf{if}\ (\mathbf{true} \wedge \alpha?X \to c_0) \| (\mathbf{true} \wedge \beta?Y \to c_1)\ \mathbf{fi}$$

Imagine this process in an environment offering values at the channels. Then it will not deadlock (*i.e.*, reach a state of improper termination) if neither c_0 nor c_1 can. On the other hand, the following process can deadlock:

$$\mathbf{if}\ (\mathbf{true} \to (\alpha?X; c_0)) \| (\mathbf{true} \to (\beta?Y; c_1))\ \mathbf{fi}$$

It autonomously chooses between being prepared to receive at the α or β channel. If, for example, it elects the right-hand branch and its environment is only able to output on the α channel there is deadlock. Deadlock can however arise in more subtle ways. The point of Dijkstra's example of the so-called "dining philosophers" is that deadlock can be caused by a complicated chain of circumstances often difficult to forsee (see *e.g.* [49]).

□

The programming language we have just considered is closely related to Occam, the programming language of the transputer. It does not include all the features of Occam however, and for instance does not include the prialt operator which behaves like the alternative construction $\|$ except for giving priority to the execution of the guarded command on the left. On the other hand, it also allows outputs $\alpha!e$ in guards not allowed in Occam for efficiency reasons. Our language is also but a step away from Hoare's language of Communicating Sequential Processes (CSP) [49]. Essentially the only difference is that in CSP process names are used in place of names for channels; in CSP, $P?X$ is an instruction to receive a value from process P and put it in location X, while $P!5$ means output value 5 to process P.

14.4 Milner's CCS

Robin Milner's work on a Calculus of Communicating Systems (CCS) has had an impact
on the foundations of the study of parallelism. It is almost true that the language for his
calculus, generally called CCS, can be derived by removing the imperative features from
the language of the last section, the use of parameterised processes obviating the use of
states. In fact, locations can be represented themselves as CCS processes.

A CCS process communicates with its environment via channels connected to its *ports*,
in the same manner as we have seen. A process p which is prepared to input at the α
and β channels and output at the channels α and γ can be visualised as

with its ports labelled appropriately. The parallel composition of p with a process q, a
process able to input at α and output at β and δ can itself be thought of as a process
$p \parallel q$ with ports $\alpha?, \alpha!, \beta?, \beta!, \gamma!, \delta!$.

The operation of restriction hides a specified set of ports. For example restricting
away the ports specified by the set of labels $\{\alpha, \gamma\}$ from the process p results in a process
$p \backslash \{\alpha, \gamma\}$ only capable of performing inputs from the channel β; it looks like:

Often it is useful to generate several copies of the same process but for a renaming of
channels. A relabelling function is a function on channel names. After relabelling by the
function f with $f(\alpha) = \gamma$, $f(\beta) = \delta$ and $f(\gamma) = \gamma$ the process p becomes $p[f]$ with this
interface with its environment:

In addition to communications $\alpha?n, \alpha!n$ at channels α we have an extra action τ
which can do the duty of the earlier **skip**, as well as standing for actions of internal
communication. Because we remove general assignments we will not need the states σ
of earlier and can use variables $x, y, \ldots$ in place of locations. To name processes we have
process identifiers $P, Q, \ldots$ in our syntax, in particular so we can define their behaviour

recursively. Assume a syntax for arithmetic expressions a and boolean expressions b, with variables instead of locations. The syntax of processes p, $p_0, p_1, \ldots$ is:

$$p \quad ::= \quad \textbf{nil} \mid$$
$$(\tau \to p) \mid (\alpha!a \to p) \mid (\alpha?x \to p) \mid (b \to p)$$
$$p_0 + p_1 \mid p_0 \parallel p_1 \mid$$
$$p \backslash L \mid p[f] \mid$$
$$P(a_1, \cdots, a_k)$$

where a and b range over arithmetic and boolean expressions respectively, x is a variable over values, L is a subset of channel names, f is a relabelling function, and P stands for a process with parameters $a_1, \cdots, a_k$—we write simply P when the list of parameters is empty.

Formally at least, $\alpha?x \to p$ is like a lambda abstraction on x, and any occurrences of the variable x in p will be bound by the $\alpha?x$ provided they are not present in subterms of the form $\beta?x \to q$. Variables which are not so bound will be said to be *free*. Process identifiers P are associated with definitions, written as

$$P(x_1, \cdots, x_k) \stackrel{\text{def}}{=} p$$

where all the free variables of p appear in the list $x_1, \cdots, x_k$ of distinct variables. The behaviour of a process will be defined with respect to such definitions for all the process identifiers it contains. Notice that definitions can be recursive in that p may mention P. Indeed there can be simultaneous recursive definitions, for example if

$$P(x_1, \cdots, x_k) \stackrel{\text{def}}{=} p$$
$$Q(y_1, \cdots, y_l) \stackrel{\text{def}}{=} q$$

where p and q mention both P and Q.

In giving the operational semantics we shall only specify the transitions associated with processes which have no free variables. By making this assumption, we can dispense with the use of environments for variables in the operational semantics, and describe the evaluation of expressions without variables by relations $a \to n$ and $b \to t$. Beyond this, the operational semantics contains few surprises. We use λ to range over actions $\alpha?n$, $\alpha!n$, and τ.

nil process: has no rules.

Guarded processes:

$$(\tau \to p) \xrightarrow{\tau} p$$

$$\frac{a \to n}{(\alpha!a \to p) \xrightarrow{\alpha!n} p} \qquad \frac{}{(\alpha?x \to p) \xrightarrow{\alpha?n} p[n/x]}$$

$$\frac{b \to \mathbf{true} \quad p \xrightarrow{\lambda} p'}{(b \to p) \xrightarrow{\lambda} p'}$$

(By $p[n/x]$ we mean p with n substituted for the variable x. A more general substitution $p[a_1/x_1, \cdots, a_k/x_k]$, stands for a process term p in which arithmetic expressions a_i have replaced variables x_i.)

Sum:

$$\frac{p_0 \xrightarrow{\lambda} p_0'}{p_0 + p_1 \xrightarrow{\lambda} p_0'} \qquad \frac{p_1 \xrightarrow{\lambda} p_1'}{p_0 + p_1 \xrightarrow{\lambda} p_1'}$$

Composition:

$$\frac{p_0 \xrightarrow{\lambda} p_0'}{p_0 \parallel p_1 \xrightarrow{\lambda} p_0' \parallel p_1} \qquad \frac{p_0 \xrightarrow{\alpha?n} p_0' \quad p_1 \xrightarrow{\alpha!n} p_1'}{p_0 \parallel p_1 \xrightarrow{\tau} p_0' \parallel p_1'}$$

$$\frac{p_1 \xrightarrow{\lambda} p_1'}{p_0 \parallel p_1 \xrightarrow{\lambda} p_0 \parallel p_1'} \qquad \frac{p_0 \xrightarrow{\alpha!n} p_0' \quad p_1 \xrightarrow{\alpha?n} p_1'}{p_0 \parallel p_1 \xrightarrow{\tau} p_0' \parallel p_1'}$$

Restriction:

$$\frac{p \xrightarrow{\lambda} p'}{p \backslash L \xrightarrow{\lambda} p' \backslash L},$$

where if $\lambda \equiv \alpha?n$ or $\lambda \equiv \alpha!n$ then $\alpha \notin L$

Relabelling:

$$\frac{p \xrightarrow{\lambda} p'}{p[f] \xrightarrow{f(\lambda)} p'[f]}$$

Identifiers:

$$\frac{p[a_1/x_1, \cdots, a_k/x_k] \xrightarrow{\lambda} p'}{P(a_1, \cdots, a_k) \xrightarrow{\lambda} p'}$$

where $P(x_1, \cdots, x_k) \stackrel{\text{def}}{=} p$.

We expand on our claim that it is sufficient to consider processes without free variables and so dispense with environments in the operational semantics. Consider the process

$$(\alpha?x \to (\alpha!x \to \textbf{nil})).$$

It receives a value n and outputs it at the channel α, as can be derived from the rules. From the rules we obtain directly that

$$(\alpha?x \to (\alpha!x \to \textbf{nil})) \stackrel{\alpha?n}{\longrightarrow} (\alpha!x \to \textbf{nil})[n/x]$$

which is

$$(\alpha?x \to (\alpha!x \to \textbf{nil})) \stackrel{\alpha?n}{\longrightarrow} (\alpha!n \to \textbf{nil}).$$

Then

$$(\alpha!n \to \textbf{nil}) \stackrel{\alpha!n}{\longrightarrow} \textbf{nil}.$$

As can be seen here, when it comes to deriving the transitions of the subprocesses $(\alpha!x \to \textbf{nil})$ the free variable x has previously been bound to a particular number n.

14.5 Pure CCS

Underlying Milner's work is a more basic calculus, which we will call *pure* CCS. Roughly it comes about by eliminating variables from CCS.

We have assumed that the values communicated during synchronisations are numbers. We could, of course, instead have chosen expressions which denote values of some other type. But for the need to modify expressions, the development would have been the same. Suppose, for the moment, that the values lie in a finite set

$$V = \{v_1, \ldots, v_k\}.$$

Extend CCS to allow input actions $\alpha?n$ where α is a channel and $v \in V$. A process

$$(\alpha?n \to p)$$

first inputs the specific value v from channel α and then proceeds as process p; its behaviour can be described by the rule:

$$\frac{}{(\alpha?n \to p) \stackrel{\alpha?n}{\longrightarrow} p}$$

It is not hard to see that under these assumptions the transitions of $\alpha?x \rightarrow p$ are the same as those of

$$(\alpha?n_1 \rightarrow p[v_1/x]) + \ldots + (\alpha?n_k \rightarrow p[v_k/x]).$$

The two processes behave in the same way. In this fashion we can eliminate variables from process terms. Numbers however form an infinite set and when the set of values is infinite, we cannot replace a term $\alpha?x \rightarrow p$ by a finite summation. However, this problem is quickly remedied by introducing arbitrary sums into the syntax of processes. For a set of process terms $\{p_i \mid i \in I\}$ indexed by a set I, assume we can form a term

$$\sum_{i \in I} p_i.$$

Then even when the values lie in the infinite set of numbers we can write

$$\sum_{m \in \mathbf{N}} (\alpha?m \rightarrow p[m/x])$$

instead of $(\alpha?x \rightarrow p)$.

With the presence of variables x, there has existed a distinction between input and output of values. Once we eliminate variables the distinction is purely formal; input actions are written $\alpha?n$ as compared with $\alpha!n$ for output actions. Indeed in pure CCS the role of values can be subsumed under that of port names. It will be, for example, as if input of value v at port α described by $\alpha?n$ is regarded as a pure synchronisation, without the exchange of any value, at a "port" $\alpha?n$.

In pure CCS actions can carry three kinds of name. There are actions ℓ (corresponding to actions $\alpha?n$ or $\alpha!n$), complementary actions $\bar{\ell}$ (corresponding to $\alpha?n$ being complementary to $\alpha!n$, and *vice versa*) and internal actions τ. With our understanding of complementary actions it is natural to take $\bar{\bar{\ell}}$ to be the same as ℓ, which highlights the symmetry we will now have between input and output.

In the syntax of pure CCS we let λ range over actions of the form ℓ, $\bar{\ell}$ and τ where ℓ belongs to a given set of action labels. Terms for processes $p, p_0, p_1, p_i, \ldots$ of pure CCS take this form:

$$p ::= \mathbf{nil} \mid \lambda.p \mid \sum_{i \in I} p_i \mid (p_0 \parallel p_1) \mid p \backslash L \mid p[f] \mid P$$

The term $\lambda.p$ is simply a more convenient way of writing the guarded process $(\lambda \rightarrow p)$. The new general sum $\sum_{i \in I} p_i$ of indexed processes $\{p_i \mid i \in I\}$ has been introduced. We will write $p_0 + p_1$ in the case where $I = \{0, 1\}$. Above, L is to range over subsets of labels. We extend the complementation operation to such a set, taking $\bar{L} =_{\mathrm{def}} \{\bar{\ell} \mid \ell \in L\}$. The symbol f stands for a *relabelling function* on actions. A relabelling function should obey the conditions that $f(\bar{\ell}) = \overline{f(\ell)}$ and $f(\tau) = \tau$. Again, P ranges over identifiers for processes. These are accompanied by definitions, typically of the form

$$P \stackrel{\text{def}}{=} p.$$

As before, they can support recursive and simultaneous recursive definitions.

The rules for the operational semantics of CCS are strikingly simple:

nil has no rules.

Guarded processes:

$$\lambda.p \stackrel{\lambda}{\longrightarrow} p$$

Sums:

$$\frac{p_j \stackrel{\lambda}{\longrightarrow} q}{\sum_{i \in I} p_i \stackrel{\lambda}{\longrightarrow} q} \, j \in I$$

Composition:

$$\frac{p_0 \stackrel{\lambda}{\longrightarrow} p_0'}{p_0 \parallel p_1 \stackrel{\lambda}{\longrightarrow} p_0' \parallel p_1} \qquad \frac{p_1 \stackrel{\lambda}{\longrightarrow} p_1'}{p_0 \parallel p_1 \stackrel{\lambda}{\longrightarrow} p_0 \parallel p_1'}$$

$$\frac{p_0 \stackrel{l}{\longrightarrow} p_0' \quad p_1 \stackrel{\bar{l}}{\longrightarrow} p_1'}{p_0 \parallel p_1 \stackrel{\tau}{\longrightarrow} p_0' \parallel p_1'}$$

Restriction:

$$\frac{p \stackrel{\lambda}{\longrightarrow} q}{p \backslash L \stackrel{\lambda}{\longrightarrow} q \backslash L} \, \lambda \notin L \cup \bar{L}$$

Relabelling:

$$\frac{p \stackrel{\lambda}{\longrightarrow} q}{p[f] \stackrel{f(\lambda)}{\longrightarrow} q[f]}$$

Identifiers:

$$\frac{p \stackrel{\lambda}{\longrightarrow} q}{P \stackrel{\lambda}{\longrightarrow} q} \text{ where } P \stackrel{\text{def}}{=} p.$$

We have motivated pure CCS as a basic language for processes into which the other languages we have seen can be translated. We now show, in the form of a table, how closed terms t of CCS can be translated to terms $\hat{t}$ of pure CCS in a way which preserves their behaviour.

$(\tau \to p)$	$\tau.\widehat{p}$
$(\alpha!a \to p)$	$\overline{\alpha m}.\widehat{p}$ where a denotes the value m
$(\alpha?x \to p)$	$\sum_{m \in \mathbf{N}}(\alpha m.p[\widehat{m/x}])$
$(b \to p)$	$\widehat{p}$ if b denotes **true** **nil** if b denotes $false$
$p_0 + p_1$	$\widehat{p_0} + \widehat{p_1}$
$p_0 \parallel p_1$	$\widehat{p_0} \parallel \widehat{p_1}$
$p \backslash L$	$\widehat{p} \backslash \{\alpha m \mid \alpha \in L \ \& \ m \in \mathbf{N}\}$
$P(a_1, \cdots, a_k)$	$P_{m_1, \cdots, m_k}$ where $a_1, \cdots, a_k$ denote the values $m_1, \cdots, m_k$.

To accompany a definition $P(x_1, \cdots, x_k) \stackrel{\text{def}}{=} p$ in CCS, where p has free variables $x_1, \ldots, x_k$, we have a collection of definitions in the pure calculus

$$P_{m_1, \ldots, m_k} \stackrel{\text{def}}{=} p[m_1/x_1, \widehat{\ldots,} m_k/x_k]$$

indexed by $m_1, \ldots, m_k \in \mathbf{N}$.

Exercise 14.5 Justify the table above by showing that

$$p \stackrel{\lambda}{\to} q \text{ iff } \widehat{p} \stackrel{\widehat{\lambda}}{\to} \widehat{q}$$

for closed process terms p, q, where

$$\widehat{\alpha?n} = \alpha n, \ \widehat{\alpha!n} = \overline{\alpha n}.$$

$\square$

Recursive definition: In applications it is useful to use process identifiers and defining equations. However sometimes in the study of CCS it is more convenient to replace the use of defining equations by the explicit recursive definition of processes. Instead of defining equations such as $P \overset{\text{def}}{=} p$, we then use recursive definitions like

$$\text{rec}(P = p).$$

The transitions of these additional terms are given by the rule:

$$\frac{p[\text{rec}(P = p)/P] \overset{\lambda}{\longrightarrow} q}{\text{rec}(P = p) \overset{\lambda}{\longrightarrow} q}$$

Exercise 14.6 Use the operational semantics to derive the transition system reachable from the process term $\text{rec}(P = a.b.P)$.   □

Exercise 14.7 Let another language for processes have the following syntax:

$$p := 0 \mid a \mid p;p \mid p+p \mid p \times p \mid P \mid \text{rec}(P = p)$$

where a is an action symbol drawn from a set Σ and P ranges over process variables used in recursively defined processes $\text{rec}(P = p)$. Processes perform sequences of actions, precisely which being specified by an execution relation $p \to s$ between closed process terms and finite sequences $s \in \Sigma^*$; when $p \to s$ the process p can perform the sequence of actions s in a complete execution. Note the sequence s may be the empty sequence ϵ and we use st to represent the concatenation of strings s and t. The execution relation is given by the rules:

$$0 \to \epsilon \qquad a \to a \qquad \frac{p \to s \quad q \to t}{p;q \to st}$$

$$\frac{p \to s}{p+q \to s} \qquad \frac{q \to s}{p+q \to s}$$

$$\frac{p \to s \quad q \to s}{p \times q \to s} \qquad \frac{p[\text{rec}(P = p)/P] \to s}{\text{rec}(P = p) \to s}$$

The notation $p[q/P]$ is used to mean the term resulting from substituting q for all free occurrences of P in p.

Alternatively, we can give a denotational semantics to processes. Taking environments ρ to be functions from variables Var to subsets of sequences $P(\Sigma^*)$ ordered by inclusion, we define:

$$[\![0]\!]\rho = \{\epsilon\} \qquad [\![a]\!]\rho = \{a\}$$
$$[\![p; q]\!]\rho = \{st \mid s \in [\![p]\!]\rho \text{ and } t \in [\![q]\!]\rho\}$$
$$[\![p + q]\!]\rho = [\![p]\!]\rho \cup [\![q]\!]\rho \qquad [\![p \times q]\!]\rho = [\![p]\!]\rho \cap [\![q]\!]\rho$$
$$[\![X]\!]\rho = \rho(X)$$
$$[\![\text{rec}(P = p)]\!]\rho = \text{the least solution } S \text{ of } S = [\![p]\!]\rho[S/P]$$

The notation $\rho[S/P]$ represents the environment ρ updated to take value S on P.

(i) Assuming a and b are action symbols, write down a closed process term with denotation the language $\{a, b\}^*$ in any environment.

(ii) Prove by structural induction that

$$[\![p[q/P]]\!]\rho = [\![p]\!]\rho[[\![q]\!]\rho/P]$$

for all process terms p and q, with q closed, and environments ρ.

(iii) Hence prove if $p \to s$ then $s \in [\![p]\!]\rho$, where p is a closed process term, $s \in \Sigma^*$ and ρ is any environment. Indicate clearly any induction principles you use. $\square$

14.6 A specification language

We turn to methods of reasoning about parallel processes. Historically, the earliest methods followed the line of Hoare logics. Instead Milner's development of CCS has been based on a notion of equivalence between processes with respect to which there are equational laws. These laws are sound in the sense that if any two processes are proved equal using the laws then, indeed, they are equivalent. They are also complete for finite-state processes. This means that if any two finite-state processes are equivalent then they can be proved so using the laws. The equational laws can be seen as constituting an algebra of processes. Different languages for processes and different equivalences lead to different process algebras. Pointers to other notable approaches are given in the concluding section of this chapter.

Milner's equivalence is based on a notion of bisimulation between processes. Early on, in exploring the properties of bisimulation, Milner and Hennessy discovered a logical characterisation of this central equivalence. Two processes are bisimilar iff they satisfy precisely the same assertions in a little modal logic, that has come to be called *Hennessy-Milner logic*. The finitary version of this logic has a simple, if perhaps odd-looking syntax:

$$A ::= T \mid F \mid A_0 \wedge A_1 \mid A_0 \vee A_1 \mid \neg A \mid \langle \lambda \rangle A$$

The final assertion $\langle\lambda\rangle A$ is a *modal* assertion (pronounced "diamond λ A") which involves an action name λ. It will be satisfied by any process which can do a λ action to become a process satisfying A. To be specific, we will allow λ to be any action of pure CCS. The other ways of forming assertions are more usual. We use T for true, F for false and build more complicated assertions using conjunctions ($\wedge$), disjunctions ($\vee$) and negations ($\neg$). Thus $(\neg\langle a\rangle T) \wedge (\neg\langle b\rangle T)$ is satisfied by any process which can do neither an a nor a b action. We can define a dual modality in the logic. Take

$$[\lambda]A,$$

(pronounced "box λ A"), to abbreviate $\neg\langle\lambda\rangle\neg A$. Such an assertion is satisfied by any process which cannot do a λ action to become one failing to satisfy A. In other words, $[\lambda]A$ is satisfied by a process which whenever it does a λ action becomes one satisfying A. In particular, this assertion is satisfied by any process which cannot do any λ action at all. Notice $[c]F$ is satisfied by those processes which refuse to do a c action. In writing assertions we will assume that the modal operators $\langle a\rangle$ and $[a]$ bind more strongly than the boolean operations, so *e.g.* $([c]F \wedge [d]F)$ is the same assertion as $(([c]F) \wedge ([d]F))$. As another example,

$$\langle a\rangle\langle b\rangle([c]F \wedge [d]F)$$

is satisfied by any process which can do an a action followed by a b to become one which refuses to do either a c or a d action.

While Hennessy-Milner logic does serve to give a characterisation of bisimulation equivalence (see the exercise ending this section), central to Milner's approach, the finitary language above has obvious shortcomings as a language for writing down specifications of processes; a single assertion can only specify the behaviour of a process to a finite depth, and cannot express, for example, that a process can always perform an action throughout its possibly infinite course of behaviour. To draw out the improvements we can make we consider how one might express particular properties, of undeniable importance in analysing the behaviour of parallel processes.

Let us try to write down an assertion which is true precisely of those processes which can *deadlock*. A process might be said to be capable of deadlock if it can reach a state of improper termination. There are several possible interpretations of what this means, for example, depending on whether "improper termination" refers to the whole or part of the process. For simplicity let's assume the former and make the notion of "improper termination" precise. Assume we can describe those processes which are properly terminated with an assertion *terminal*. A reasonable definition of the characteristic function of this property would be the following, by structural induction on the presentation of pure CCS with explicit recursion:

$$terminal(\mathbf{nil}) = \mathbf{true}$$

$$terminal(\lambda.p) = \mathbf{false}$$

$$terminal(\sum_{i \in I} p_i) = \begin{cases} \mathbf{true} & \text{if } terminal(p_i) = \mathbf{true} \text{ for all } i \in I, \\ \mathbf{false} & \text{otherwise} \end{cases}$$

$$terminal(p_0 \parallel p_1) = terminal(p_0) \wedge_T terminal(p_1)$$

$$terminal(p \backslash L) = terminal(p)$$

$$terminal(p[f]) = terminal(p)$$

$$terminal(P) = \mathbf{false}$$

$$terminal(\mathrm{rec}(P = p)) = terminal(p)$$

This already highlights one way in which it is sensible to extend our logic, *viz.* by adding *constant* assertions to pick out special processes like the properly terminated ones. Now, reasonably, we can say a process represents an improper termination iff it is not properly terminated and moreover cannot do any actions. How are we to express this as an assertion? Certainly, for the particular action a, the assertion $[a]F$ is true precisely of those processes which cannot do a. Similarly, the assertion

$$[a_1]F \wedge \cdots \wedge [a_k]F$$

is satisfied by those which cannot do any action from the set $\{a_1, \cdots, a_k\}$. But without restricting ourselves to processes whose actions lie within a known finite set, we cannot write down an assertion true just of those processes which can (or cannot) do an arbitrary action. This prompts another extension to the assertions. A new assertion of the form

$$\langle . \rangle A$$

is true of precisely those processes which can do any action to become a process satisfying A. Dually we define the assertion

$$[.]A \equiv_{def} \neg \langle . \rangle \neg A$$

which is true precisely of those processes which become processes satifying A whenever they perform an action. The assertion $[.]F$ is satisfied by the processes which cannot do any action. Now the property of *immediate deadlock* can be written as

$$Dead \equiv_{def} ([.]F \wedge \neg terminal).$$

The assertion *Dead* captures the notion of improper termination. A process can deadlock if by performing a sequence of actions it can reach a process satisfying *Dead*. It's tempting to express the possibility of deadlock as an *infinite* disjunction:

$$Dead \vee \langle.\rangle Dead \vee \langle.\rangle\langle.\rangle Dead \vee \langle.\rangle\langle.\rangle\langle.\rangle Dead \vee \cdots \vee (\langle.\rangle \cdots \langle.\rangle Dead) \vee \cdots$$

But, of course, this is not really an assertion because in forming assertions only finite disjunctions are permitted. Because there are processes which deadlock after arbitrarily many steps we cannot hope to reduce this to a finite disjunction, and so a real assertion. We want assertions which we can write down!

We need another primitive in our language of assertions. Rather than introducing extra primitives on an *ad hoc* basis as we encounter further properties we'd like to express, we choose one strong new method of defining assertions powerful enough to define the possibility of deadlock and many other properties. The infinite disjunction is reminiscient of the least upper bounds of chains one sees in characterising least fixed points of continuous functions, and indeed our extension to the language of assertions will be to allow the recursive definition of properties. The possibility of deadlock will be expressed by the least fixed point

$$\mu X.(Dead \vee \langle.\rangle X)$$

which intuitively unwinds to the infinite "assertion"

$$Dead \vee \langle.\rangle(Dead \vee \langle.\rangle(Dead \vee \langle.\rangle(\cdots$$

A little more generally, we can write

$$possibly(B) \equiv_{def} \mu X.(B \vee \langle.\rangle X)$$

true of those processes which can reach a process satisfying B through performing a sequence of actions. Other constructions on properties can be expressed too. We might well be interested in whether or not a process eventually becomes one satisfying assertion B no matter what sequence of actions it performs. This can be expressed by

$$eventually(B) \equiv_{def} \mu X.(B \vee (\langle.\rangle T \wedge [.]X)).$$

As this example indicates, it is not always clear how to capture properties as assertions. Even when we provide the mathematical justification for recursively defined properties in the next section, it will often be a nontrivial task to show that a particular assertion with recursion expresses a desired property. However this can be done once and for all for a batch of useful properties. Because they are all defined using the same recursive mechanism, it is here that the effort in establishing proof methods and tools can be focussed.

In fact, maximum (rather than minimum) fixed points will play the more dominant role in our subsequent work. With negation, one is definable in terms of the other. An assertion defined using maximum fixed points can be thought of as an infinite conjunction. The maximum fixed point $\nu X.(B \wedge [.]X)$ unwinds to

$$B \wedge [.](B \wedge [.](B \wedge [.](B \wedge \cdots$$

and is satisfied by those processes which, no matter what actions they perform, always satisfy B. In a similar way we can express that an assertion B is satisfied all the way along an infinite sequence of computation from a process:

$$\nu X.(B \wedge \langle . \rangle X).$$

Exercise 14.8 What is expressed by the following assertions?

(i) $\mu X.(\langle a \rangle T \vee [.]X)$
(ii) $\nu Y.(\langle a \rangle T \vee (\langle . \rangle T \wedge [.]Y))$

(Argue informally, by unwinding definitions. Later, Exercise 14.13 will indicate how to prove that an assertion expresses a property, at least for finite-state processes.)   □

Exercise 14.9 In [63], Milner defines a *strong bisimulation* to be a binary relation R between CCS processes with the following property: If pRq then

$$\text{(i)}\forall a, p'. \ p \xrightarrow{a} p' \Rightarrow \exists q'.q \xrightarrow{a} q' \text{ and}$$
$$\text{(ii)}\forall a, q'. \ q \xrightarrow{a} q' \Rightarrow \exists p'.p \xrightarrow{a} p'$$

Then *strong bisimulation equivalence* $\sim$ is defined by

$$\sim = \bigcup \{R \mid R \text{ is a strong bisimulation}\}.$$

An alternative equivalence is induced by Hennessy-Milner logic, including a possibly infinite conjunction, where assertions A are given by

$$A ::= \bigwedge_{i \in I} A_i \mid \neg A \mid \langle a \rangle A$$

where I is a set, possibly empty, indexing a collection of asertions A_i, and a ranges over actions. The notion of a process p satisfying an assertion A is formalised in the relation

$p \models A$ defined by structural induction on A:

$$p \models \bigwedge_{i \in I} A_i \text{ iff } p \models A_i \text{ for all } i \in I,$$

$$p \models \neg A \text{ iff not } p \models A,$$

$$p \models \langle a \rangle A \text{ iff } p \xrightarrow{a} q \ \& \ q \models A \text{ for some } q.$$

(An empty conjunction fulfils the role of **true** as it holds vacuously of all processes.)
Now we define $p \asymp q$ iff $(p \models A) \Leftrightarrow (q \models A)$ for all assertions A of Hennessy-Milner logic.
This exercise shows $\asymp$ coincides with strong bisimulation, *i.e.* $\asymp = \sim$:

(i) By structural induction on A show that

$$\forall p, q. \ p \sim q \Rightarrow (p \models A \Leftrightarrow q \models A).$$

(This shows $\asymp \supseteq \sim$.)
(ii) Show $\asymp$ is a strong bisimulation.

(From the definition of $\sim$ it will then follow that $\asymp \subseteq \sim$. Hint: this part is best proved
by assuming that $\asymp$ is not a bisimulation, and deriving a contradiction.)   □

14.7   The modal ν–calculus

We now provide the formal treatment of the specification language motivated in the
previous Section 14.6.

Let $\mathcal{P}$ denote the set of processes in pure CCS. Assertions determine properties of
processes. A property is either true or false of a process and so can be identified with
the subset of processes $\mathcal{P}$ which satisfy it. In fact, we will understand assertions simply
as a notation for describing subsets of processes. Assertions are built up using:

- *constants*: Any subset of processes $S \subseteq \mathcal{P}$ is regarded as a constant assertion taken
  to be true of a process it contains and false otherwise. (We can also use finite
  descriptions of them like *terminal* and *Dead* earlier. In our treatment we will
  identify such descriptions with the subset of processes satisfying them.)

- *logical connectives*: The special constants T, F stand for true and false respectively.
  If A and B are assertions then so are $\neg A$ ("not A"), $A \wedge B$ ("A and B"), $A \vee B$
  ("A or B")

- *modalities*: If a is an action symbol and A is an assertion then $\langle a \rangle A$ is an assertion. If A is an assertion then so is $\langle . \rangle A$. (The box modalities $[a]A$ and $[.]A$ are
  abbreviations for $\neg \langle a \rangle \neg A$ and $\neg \langle . \rangle \neg A$, respectively.)

- *maximum fixed points*: If A is an assertion in which the variable X occurs positively (*i.e.* under an even number of negation symbols for every ocurrence) then $\nu X.A$ (the maximum fixed point of A) is an assertion. (The minimum fixed point $\mu X.A$ can be understood as an abbreviation for $\neg \nu X.\neg A[\neg X/X]$.)

In reasoning about assertion we shall often make use of their *size*. Precisely, the size of an assertion is defined by structural induction:

$$size(S) = size(T) = size(F) = 0 \quad \text{where } S \text{ is a constant}$$
$$size(\neg A) = size(\langle a \rangle A) = size(\nu X.A) = 1 + size(A)$$
$$size(A \wedge B) = size(A \vee B) = 1 + size(A) + size(B).$$

Assertions are a notation for describing subsets of processes. So for example, $A \wedge B$ should be satisfied by precisely those processes which satisfy A and satisfy B, and thus can be taken to be the intersection $A \cap B$. Let's say what subsets of processes all the assertions stand for. In the following, an assertion on the left stands for the set on the right:

$$
\begin{aligned}
S &= S \quad \text{where } S \subseteq \mathcal{P} \\
T &= \mathcal{P} \\
F &= \emptyset \\
A \wedge B &= A \cap B \\
A \vee B &= A \cup B \\
\neg A &= \mathcal{P} \setminus A \\
\langle a \rangle A &= \{p \in \mathcal{P} \mid \exists q.p \xrightarrow{a} q \text{ and } q \in A\} \\
\langle . \rangle A &= \{p \in \mathcal{P} \mid \exists a, q.p \xrightarrow{a} q \text{ and } q \in A\} \\
\nu X.A &= \bigcup \{S \subseteq \mathcal{P} \mid S \subseteq A[S/X]\}
\end{aligned}
$$

Note, this is a good definition because the set associated with an assertion is defined in terms of sets associated with assertions of strictly smaller size. Most clauses of the definition are obvious; for example, $\neg A$ should be satisfied by all processes which do not satisfy A, explaining why it is taken to be the complement of A; the modality $\langle a \rangle A$ is satisfied by any process p capable of performing an a–transition leading to a process satisfying A. If X occurs only positively in A, it follows that the function

$$S \longmapsto A[S/X].$$

is monotonic on subsets of $\mathcal{P}$ ordered by $\subseteq$. The Knaster-Tarski Theorem (see Section 5.5) characterises the maximum fixed point of this function as

$$\bigcup \{S \subseteq \mathcal{P} \mid S \subseteq A[S/X]\}$$

is the union of all postfixed points of the function $S \mapsto A[S/X]$. Above we see the use of an assertion $A[S/X]$ which has a form similar to A but with each occurrence of X replaced by the subset S of processes.

Exercise 14.10 Prove the minimum fixed point $\mu X.A$, where

$$\mu X.A = \bigcap \{S \subseteq \mathcal{P} \mid A[S/X] \subseteq S\},$$

is equal to $\neg \nu X.\neg A[\neg X/X]$.

(Hint: Show that the operation of negation provides a 1-1 correspondence between prefixed points of the function $S \mapsto A[S/X]$ and postfixed points of the function $S \mapsto \neg A[\neg S/X]$.) $\qquad\qquad\square$

Exercise 14.11 Show $[a]A = \{p \in \mathcal{P} \mid \forall q \in \mathcal{P}. \ p \xrightarrow{a} q \Rightarrow q \in A\}$. By considering e.g. a process $\Sigma_{n \in \omega} a.p_n$ where the p_n, $n \in \omega$, are distinct, show that the function $S \mapsto [a]S$ is not continuous with respect to inclusion (it is monotonic). $\qquad\qquad\square$

We can now specify what it means for a process p to satisfy an assertion A. We define the *satisfaction assertion* $p \models A$ to be **true** if $p \in A$, and **false** otherwise.

It is possible to check automatically whether or not a finite-state process p satisfies an assertion A. (One of the Concurrency-Workbench/TAV commands checks whether or not a process p satisfies an assertion A; it will not necessarily terminate for infinite-state processes though in principle, given enough time and space, it will for finite-state processes.) To see why this is feasible let p be a *finite-state* process. This means that the set of processes reachable from it

$$\mathcal{P}_p =_{def} \{q \in \mathcal{P} \mid p \rightarrow^* q\}$$

is finite, where we use $p \rightarrow q$ to mean $p \xrightarrow{a} q$ for some action a. In deciding whether or not p satisfies an assertion we need only consider properties of the reachable processes $\mathcal{P}_p$. We imitate what we did before but using $\mathcal{P}_p$ instead of $\mathcal{P}$. Again, the definition is by induction on the size of assertions. Define:

$$
\begin{aligned}
S \mid_p &= S \cap \mathcal{P}_p \quad \text{where } S \subseteq \mathcal{P} \\
T \mid_p &= \mathcal{P}_p \\
F \mid_p &= \emptyset \\
A \wedge B \mid_p &= A \mid_p \cap B \mid_p \\
A \vee B \mid_p &= A \mid_p \cup A \mid_p \\
\neg A \mid_p &= \mathcal{P}_p \setminus (A \mid_p) \\
\langle a \rangle A \mid_p &= \{r \in \mathcal{P}_p \mid \exists q \in \mathcal{P}_p. r \xrightarrow{a} q \text{ and } q \in A \mid_p\} \\
\langle . \rangle A \mid_p &= \{r \in \mathcal{P}_p \mid \exists a, q \in \mathcal{P}_p. r \xrightarrow{a} q \text{ and } q \in A \mid_p\} \\
\nu X.A \mid_p &= \bigcup \{S \subseteq \mathcal{P}_p \mid S \subseteq A[S/X] \mid_p\}
\end{aligned}
$$

Fortunately there is a simple relationship between the "global" and "local" meanings of assertions, expressed in the following lemma.

Lemma 14.12 *For all assertions A and processes p,*

$$A \mid_p = A \cap \mathcal{P}_p.$$

Proof: We first observe that:

$$A[S/X]\mid_p = A[S \cap \mathcal{P}_p/X]\mid_p.$$

This observation is easily shown by induction on the size of assertions A.

A further induction on the size of assertions yields the result. We consider the one slightly awkward case, that of maximum fixed points. We would like to show

$$\nu X.A\mid_p = (\nu X.A) \cap \mathcal{P}_p$$

assuming the property expressed by the lemma holds inductively for assertion A. Recall

$$\nu X.A = \bigcup \{S \subseteq \mathcal{P} \mid S \subseteq A[S/X]\} \quad \text{and}$$
$$\nu X.A\mid_p = \bigcup \{S' \subseteq \mathcal{P}_p \mid S' \subseteq A[S'/X]\mid_p\}.$$

Suppose $S \subseteq \mathcal{P}$ and $S \subseteq A[S/X]$. Then

$$
\begin{aligned}
S \cap \mathcal{P}_p &\subseteq A[S/X] \cap \mathcal{P}_p \\
&= A[S/X]\mid_p \quad \text{by induction} \\
&= A[S \cap \mathcal{P}_p/X]\mid_p \quad \text{by the observation.}
\end{aligned}
$$

Thus $S \cap \mathcal{P}_p$ is a postfixed point of $S' \mapsto A[S'/X]\mid_p$, so $S \cap \mathcal{P}_p \subseteq \nu X.A\mid_p$. Hence $\nu X.A \cap \mathcal{P}_p \subseteq \nu X.A\mid_p$.

To show the converse, suppose $S' \subseteq \mathcal{P}_p$ and $S' \subseteq A[S'/X]\mid_p$. Then, by induction, $S' \subseteq A[S'/X] \cap \mathcal{P}_p$. Thus certainly $S' \subseteq A[S'/X]$, making S' a postfixed point of $S \mapsto A[S/X]$ which ensures $S' \subseteq \nu X.A$. It follows that $\nu X.A\mid_p \subseteq \nu X.A$.

Whence we conclude $\nu X.A\mid_p = (\nu X.A) \cap \mathcal{P}_p$, as was required.   □

One advantage in restricting to $\mathcal{P}_p$ is that, being a finite set of size n say, we know

$$\nu X.A \mid_p = \bigcap_{0 \le i \le n} A^i[T/X] \mid_p$$

$$= A^n[T/X] \cap \mathcal{P}_p$$

where $A^\circ = T$, $A^{i+1} = A[A^i/X]$. This follows from our earlier work characterising the least fixed point of a continuous function on complete partial order with a bottom element: The function $S \mapsto A[S/X]\|_p$ is monotonic and so continuous on the the *finite* cpo $(\mathcal{P}ow(\mathcal{P}_p), \supseteq)$—the least fixed point with respect to this cpo is of course the maximum fixed point with respect to the converse order $\subseteq$.

In this way maximum fixed points can be eliminated from an assertion A for which we wish to check $p \models A$. Supposing the result had the form $\langle a \rangle B$ we would then check if there was a process q with $p \xrightarrow{a} q$ and $q \models B$. If, on the other hand, it had the form of a conjunction $B \wedge C$ we would check $p \models B$ and $p \models C$. And no matter what the shape of the assertion, once maximum fixed points have been eliminated, we can reduce checking a process satisfies an assertion to checking processes satisfy strictly smaller assertions until ultimately we must settle whether or not processes satisfy constant assertions. Provided the constant assertions represent decidable properties, in this way we will eventually obtain an answer to our original question, whether or not $p \models A$. It is a costly method however; the elimination of maximum fixed points is only afforded through a possible blow-up in the size of the assertion. Nevertheless a similar idea, with clever optimisations, can form the basis of an efficient model-checking method, investigated by Emerson and Lei in [37].

However, we seek another method, called "local model checking" by Stirling and Walker, which is more sensitive to the structure of the assertion being considered, and does not always involve finding the full, maximum-fixed-point set $\nu X.A \mid_p$. It is the method underlying the algorithms in the Concurrency Workbench and TAV system.

Exercise 14.13 (i) Let $\mathcal{S}$ be a finite set of size k and $\Phi : \mathcal{P}ow(\mathcal{S}) \to \mathcal{P}ow(\mathcal{S})$ a monotonic operator. Prove

$$\mu X.\Phi(X) = \bigcup_{n \in w} \Phi^n(\emptyset) = \Phi^k(\emptyset)$$
$$\nu X.\Phi(X) = \bigcap_{n \in w} \Phi^n(\mathcal{S}) = \Phi^k(\mathcal{S})$$

(ii) Let p be a finite-state process. Prove p satisfies $\nu X.(\langle a \rangle X)$ iff p can perform an infinite chain of a-transitions.

What does $\mu X.(\langle a \rangle X)$ mean? Prove it.

In the remainder of this exercise assume the processes under consideration are finite-state (so that (i) is applicable). Recall a process p is finite-state iff the set $\mathcal{P}_p$ is finite, *i.e.* only finitely many processes are reachable from p.

(iii) Prove the assertion $\nu X.(A \wedge [.]X)$ is satisfied by those processes p which always satisfy an assertion A, *i.e.* q satisfies A, for all $q \in \mathcal{P}_p$.

(iv) How would you express in the modal ν-calculus the property true of precisely those processes which eventually arrive at a state satisfying an assertion A? Prove your claim.

(See the earlier text or Exercise 14.15 for a hint.)

□

In the remaining exercises of this section assume the processes are finite-state.

Exercise 14.14

(i) A complex modal operator, often found in temporal logic, is the so-called until operator. Formulated in terms of transition systems for processes the until operator will have the following interpretation:

A process p satisfies A until B (where A and B are assertions) iff for all sequences of transitions

$$p = p_0 \to p_1 \to \ldots \to p_n$$

it holds that

$$\forall i (0 \leq i \leq n).\ p_i \models A$$
$$\text{or } \exists i (0 \leq i \leq n).\ (p_i \models B\ \&\ \forall j (0 \leq j \leq i).\ p_j \models A).$$

Formulate the until operator as a maximum-fixpoint assertion.
(See Exercise 14.15 for a hint.)

(ii) What does the following assertion (expressing so-called "strong-until") mean?

$$\mu X.(B \vee (A \wedge \langle.\rangle T \wedge [.]X))$$

□

Exercise 14.15 What do the following assertions mean? They involve assertions A and B.

(i) $inv(A) \equiv \nu X.(A \wedge [.]X)$
(ii) $ev(A) \equiv \mu X.(A \vee (\langle.\rangle T \wedge [.]X))$
(iii) $un(A, B) \equiv \nu X.(B \vee (A \wedge [.]X))$

□

Exercise 14.16 A process p is said to be *unfair* with respect to an action a iff there is an infinite chain of transitions

$$p = p_0 \xrightarrow{a_0} p_1 \xrightarrow{a_1} \cdots \xrightarrow{a_{n-1}} p_n \xrightarrow{a_n} \cdots$$

such that

(a) $\exists q.\ p_i \xrightarrow{a} q$, for all $i \geq 0$, and

(b) $a_i \neq a$, for all $i \geq 0$.

Informally, there is an infinite chain of transitions in which a can always occur but never does.

(i) Express the property of a process being unfair as an assertion in the modal ν-calculus, and prove that any finite-state process p satisfies this assertion iff p is unfair with respect to a.

(ii) A process p is said to be *weakly unfair* with respect to an action a iff there is an infinite chain of transitions in which a can occur infinitely often but never does. Write down an assertion in the modal ν-calculus to express this property.

$\square$

14.8 Local model checking

We are interested in whether or not a finite-state process p satisfies a recursive modal assertion A, *i.e* in deciding the truth or falsity of $p \models A$. We shall give an algorithm for reducing such a satisfaction assertion to **true** or **false**. A key lemma, the Reduction Lemma, follows from the Knaster-Tarski Theorem of Section 5.5.

Lemma 14.17 *(Reduction Lemma)*
Let φ be a monotonic function on a powerset $\mathcal{P}ow(S)$. For $S \subseteq S$

$$S \subseteq \nu X.\varphi(X) \quad \Leftrightarrow \quad S \subseteq \varphi(\nu X.(S \cup \varphi(X))).$$

Proof:
"$\Rightarrow$" Assume $S \subseteq \nu X.\varphi(X)$. Then

$$S \cup \varphi(\nu X.\varphi(X)) = S \cup \nu X.\varphi(X) = \nu X.\varphi(X).$$

Therefore $\nu X.\varphi(X)$ is a postfixed point of $X \mapsto S \cup \varphi(X)$. As $\nu X.(S \cup \varphi(X))$ is the greatest such postfixed point,

$$\nu X.\varphi(X) \subseteq \nu X.(S \cup \varphi(X)).$$

By monotonicity,

$$\nu X.\varphi(X) = \varphi(\nu X.\varphi(X) \subseteq \varphi(\nu X.(S \cup \varphi(X))).$$

But $S \subseteq \nu X.\varphi(X)$ so $S \subseteq \varphi(\nu X(S \cup \varphi(X)))$, as required.

"$\Leftarrow$" Assume $S \subseteq \varphi(\nu X.(S \cup \varphi(X))$. As $\nu X.(S \cup \varphi(X))$ is a fixed point of $X \mapsto S \cup \varphi(X)$,

$$\nu X.(S \cup \varphi(X)) = S \cup \varphi(\nu X.(S \cup \varphi(X))).$$

Hence, by the assumption

$$\nu X.(S \cup \varphi(X)) = \varphi(\nu X.(S \cup \varphi(X))),$$

i.e. $\nu X.(S \cup \varphi(X))$ is a fixed point, and so a postfixed point of φ. Therefore

$$\nu X.(S \cup \varphi(X)) \subseteq \nu X.\varphi(X)$$

as $\nu X.\varphi(X)$ is the greatest postfixed point. Clearly $S \subseteq \nu X.(S \cup \varphi(X))$ so $S \subseteq \nu X.\varphi(X)$, as required.   □

We are especially concerned with this lemma in the case where S is a singleton set $\{p\}$. In this case the lemma specialises to

$$p \in \nu X.\varphi(X) \Leftrightarrow p \in \varphi(\nu X.(\{p\} \cup \varphi(X))).$$

The equivalence says a process p satisfies a recursively defined property iff the process satisfies a certain kind of unfolding of the recursively defined property. The unfolding is unusual because into the body of the recursion we substitute not just the original recursive definition but instead a recursive definition in which the body is enlarged to contain p. As we shall see, there is a precise sense in which this small modification, $p \in \varphi(\nu X.(\{p\} \cup \varphi(X)))$, is easier to establish than $p \in \nu X.\varphi(X)$, thus providing a method for deciding the truth of recursively defined assertions at a process.

We allow processes to appear in assertions by extending their syntax to include a more general form of recursive assertion, ones in which finite sets of processes can tag binding occurrences of variables:

If A is an assertion in which the variable X occurs positively and $p_1, \cdots, p_n$ are processes, then $\nu X\{p_1, \cdots, p_n\}A$ is an assertion; it is to be understood as denoting the same property as $\nu X.(\{p_1, \cdots, p_n\} \vee A)$.

(The latter assertion is sensible because assertions can contain sets of processes as constants.)

We allow the set of processes $\{p_1, \cdots, p_n\}$ to be empty; in this case $\nu X\{\ \}A$ amounts simply to $\nu X.A$. In fact, from now on, when we write $\nu X.A$ it is to be understood as an abbreviation for $\nu X\{\ \}A$.

Exercise 14.18 Show $(p \models \nu X \{p_1, \cdots, p_n\} A) = $ **true** if $p \in \{p_1, \cdots, p_n\}$. □

With the help of these additional assertions we can present an algorithm for establishing whether a judgement $p \models A$ is **true** or **false**. We assume there are the usual boolean operations on truth values. Write $\neg_T$ for the operation of negation on truth values; thus $\neg_T$ (true) = false and $\neg_T$ (false) = true. Write $\wedge_T$ for the operation of binary conjunction on T; thus $t_0 \wedge_T t_1$ is true if both t_0 and t_1 are true and false otherwise. Write $\vee_T$ for the operation of binary disjunction; thus $t_0 \vee_T t_1$ is true if either t_0 or t_1 is true and false otherwise. More generally, we will use

$$t_1 \vee_T t_2 \vee_T \cdots \vee_T t_n$$

for the disjunction of the n truth values $t_1, \cdots, t_n$; this is true if one or more of the truth values is true, and false otherwise. An empty disjunction will be understood as false.

With the help of the Reduction Lemma we can see that the following equations hold:

$$
\begin{aligned}
(p \models S) &= \textbf{true} \quad \text{if } p \in S \\
(p \models S) &= \textbf{false} \quad \text{if } p \notin S \\
(p \models T) &= \textbf{true} \\
(p \models F) &= \textbf{false} \\
(p \models \neg B) &= \neg_T (p \models B) \\
(p \models A_0 \wedge A_1) &= (p \models A_0) \wedge_T (p \models A_1) \\
(p \models A_0 \vee A_1) &= (p \models A_0) \vee_T (p \models A_1) \\
(p \models \langle a \rangle B) &= (q_1 \models B) \vee_T \cdots \vee_T (q_n \models B) \\
\text{where } \{q_1, \cdots, q_n\} &= \{q | p \xrightarrow{a} q\} \\
(p \models \langle . \rangle B) &= (q_1 \models B) \vee_T \cdots \vee_T (q_n \models B) \\
\text{where } \{q_1, \cdots, q_n\} &= \{q | \exists a.p \xrightarrow{a} q\} \\
(p \models \nu X \{\vec{r}\} B) &= \textbf{true} \quad \text{if } p \in \{\vec{r}\} \\
(p \models \nu X \{\vec{r}\} B) &= (p \models B[\nu X \{p, \vec{r}\} B / X]) \quad \text{if } p \notin \{\vec{r}\}
\end{aligned}
$$

(In the cases where p has no derivatives, the disjunctions indexed by its derivatives are taken to be **false**.)

All but possibly the last two equations are obvious. The last equation is a special case of the Reduction Lemma, whereas the last but one follows by recalling the meaning of a "tagged" maximum fixed point (its proof is required by the exercise above).

The equations suggest reduction rules in which the left-hand-sides are replaced by the corresponding right-hand-sides, though at present we have no guarantee that this reduction does not go on forever. More precisely, the reduction rules should operate on boolean expressions built up using the boolean operations $\wedge, \vee, \neg$ from basic satisfaction expressions, the syntax of which has the form $p \vdash A$, for a process term p and an assertion A. The boolean expressions take the form:

$$b ::= p \vdash A \mid \mathbf{true} \mid \mathbf{false} \mid b_0 \wedge b_1 \mid b_0 \vee b_1 \mid \neg b$$

The syntax $p \vdash A$ is to be distinguished from the truth value $p \models A$.

To make the reduction precise we need to specify how to evaluate the boolean operations that can appear between satisfaction expressions as the reduction proceeds. Rather than commit ourselves to one particular method, to cover the range of different methods of evaluation of such boolean expressions we merely stipulate that the rules have the following properties:

For negations:

$$(b \to^* t \Leftrightarrow \neg b \to^* \neg_T t), \text{ for any truth value } t.$$

For conjunctions:
If $b_0 \to^* t_0$ and $b_1 \to^* t_1$ and $t_0, t_1 \in T$ then

$$(b_0 \wedge b_1) \to^* t \Leftrightarrow (t_0 \wedge_T t_1) = t, \text{ for any truth value } t.$$

For disjunctions:
If $b_0 \to^* t_0$ and $b_1 \to^* t_1$ and $t_0, t_1 \in T$ then

$$(b_0 \vee b_1) \to^* t \Leftrightarrow (t_0 \vee_T t_1) = t, \text{ for any truth value } t.$$

More generally, a disjunction $b_1 \vee b_2 \vee \cdots \vee b_n$ should reduce to **true** if, when all of $b_1, \cdots, b_n$ reduce to values, one of them is **true** and **false** if all of the values are **false**. As mentioned, an empty disjunction is understood as false.

Certainly, any sensible rules for the evaluation of boolean expressions will have the properties above, whether the evaluation proceeds in a left-to-right, right-to-left or parallel fashion. With the method of evaluation of boolean expressions assumed, the heart of the algorithm can now be presented in the form of reduction rules:

$$
\begin{array}{lll}
(p \vdash S) & \to & \mathbf{true} \quad \text{if } p \in S \\
(p \vdash S) & \to & \mathbf{false} \quad \text{if } p \notin S \\
(p \vdash T) & \to & \mathbf{true} \\
(p \vdash F) & \to & \mathbf{false}
\end{array}
$$

$$(p \vdash \neg B) \quad \rightarrow \quad \neg(p \vdash B)$$

$$(p \vdash A_0 \wedge A_1) \quad \rightarrow \quad (p \vdash A_0) \wedge (p \vdash A_1)$$

$$(p \vdash A_0 \vee A_1) \quad \rightarrow \quad (p \vdash A_0) \vee (p \vdash A_1)$$

$$(p \vdash \langle a \rangle B) \quad \rightarrow \quad (q_1 \vdash B) \vee \cdots \vee (q_n \vdash B)$$

$$\text{where } \{q_1, \cdots, q_n\} \;=\; \{q | p \xrightarrow{a} q\}$$

$$(p \vdash \langle . \rangle B) \quad \rightarrow \quad (q_1 \vdash B) \vee \cdots \vee (q_n \vdash B)$$

$$\text{where } \{q_1, \cdots, q_n\} \;=\; \{q | \exists a.p \xrightarrow{a} q\}$$

$$(p \vdash \nu X\{\vec{r}\}B) \quad \rightarrow \quad \mathbf{true} \quad \text{if } p \in \{\vec{r}\}$$

$$(p \vdash \nu X\{\vec{r}\}B) \quad \rightarrow \quad (p \vdash B[\nu X\{p, \vec{r}\}B/X]) \quad \text{if } p \notin \{\vec{r}\}$$

(Again, in the cases where p has no derivatives, the disjunctions indexed by its derivatives are taken to be **false**.)

The idea is that finding the truth value of the satisfaction assertion on the left is reduced to finding that of the expression on the right. In all rules but the last, it is clear that some progress is being made in passing from the left- to the right-hand-side; for these rules either the right-hand-side is a truth value, or concerns the satisfaction of strictly smaller assertions than that on the left. On the other hand, the last rule makes it at least thinkable that reduction may not terminate. In fact, we will prove it does terminate, with the correct answer. Roughly, the reason is that we are checking the satisfaction of assertions by finite-state processes which will mean that we cannot go on extending the sets tagging the recursions forever.

Under the assumptions to do with the evaluation of boolean expressions the reduction rules are sound and complete in the sense of the theorem below. (Notice that the theorem implies the reduction terminates.)

Theorem 14.19 *Let $p \in \mathcal{P}$ be a finite-state process and A be a closed assertion. For any truth value $t \in T$,*

$$(p \vdash A) \rightarrow^* t \;\; \text{iff} \;\; (p \models A) = t.$$

Proof: Assume that p is a finite-state process. Say an assertion is a *p-assertion* if for all the recursive assertions $\nu X\{r_1, \cdots, r_k\}B$ within it $r_1, \cdots, r_k \in \mathcal{P}_p$, *i.e.* all the processes mentioned in the assertion are reachable by transitions from p. The proof proceeds by well-founded induction on p-assertions with the relation

$$A' \prec A \text{ iff } A' \text{ is a proper subassertion of } A$$

$$\text{or } A, A' \text{ have the form}$$

$$A \equiv \nu X\{\vec{r}\}B \text{ and } A' \equiv \nu X\{p, \vec{r}\}B \text{ with } p \notin \{\vec{r}\}$$

As $\mathcal{P}_p$ is a finite set, the relation $\prec$ is well-founded.

We are interested in showing the property

$$Q(A) \Leftrightarrow_{def} \forall q \in \mathcal{P}_p \ \forall t \in T. \ [(q \vdash A) \rightarrow^* t \Leftrightarrow (q \models A) = t]$$

holds for all closed p-assertions A. The proof however requires us to extend the property Q to p-assertions A with free variables $FV(A)$, which we do in the following way: For p-assertions A, define

$$Q^+(A) \Leftrightarrow_{def} \forall \theta, \text{ a substitution from } FV(A) \text{ to closed } p\text{-assertions.}$$
$$[(\forall X \in FV(A). \ Q(\theta(X))) \Rightarrow Q(A[\theta])].$$

Notice that when A is closed $Q^+(A)$ is logically equivalent to $Q(A)$. Here θ abbreviates a substitution like $B_1/X_1, \cdots, B_k/X_k$ and an expression such as $\theta(X_j)$ the corresponding assertion B_j.

We show $Q^+(A)$ holds for all p-assertions A by well-founded induction on $\prec$. To this end, let A be an p-assertion such that $Q^+(A')$ for all p-assertions $A' \prec A$. We are required to show it follows that $Q^+(A)$. So letting θ be a substitution from $FV(A)$ to closed p-assertions with $\forall X \in FV(A). \ Q(\theta(X))$, we are required to show $Q(A[\theta])$ for all the possible forms of A. We select a few cases:

$A \equiv A_0 \wedge A_1$: In this case $A[\theta] \equiv A_0[\theta] \wedge A_1[\theta]$. Let $q \in \mathcal{P}_p$. Let $(q \models A_0[\theta]) = t_0$ and $(q \models A_1[\theta]) = t_1$. As $A_0 \prec A$ and $A_1 \prec A$ we have $Q^+(A_0)$ and $Q^+(A_1)$. Thus $Q(A_0[\theta])$ and $Q(A_1[\theta])$, so $(q \vdash A_0[\theta]) \rightarrow^* t_0$ and $(q \vdash A_1[\theta]) \rightarrow^* t_1$. Now, for $t \in T$,

$$
\begin{aligned}
(q \vdash A_0[\theta] \wedge A_1[\theta]) \rightarrow^* t \quad &\Leftrightarrow \quad ((q \vdash A_0[\theta]) \wedge (q \vdash A_1[\theta])) \rightarrow^* t \\
&\Leftrightarrow \quad t_0 \wedge_T t_1 = t \\
&\qquad \text{by the property assumed for the evaluation of conjunctions} \\
&\Leftrightarrow \quad (q \models A_0[\theta]) \wedge_T (q \models A_1[\theta]) = t \\
&\Leftrightarrow \quad (q \models A_0[\theta] \wedge A_1[\theta]) = t
\end{aligned}
$$

Hence $Q(A[\theta])$ in this case.

$A \equiv X$: In this case, when A is a variable, $Q(A[\theta])$ holds trivially by the assumption on θ.

$A \equiv \nu X\{\vec{r}\}B$: In this case $A[\theta] \equiv \nu X\{\vec{r}\}(B[\theta])$—recall θ is not defined on X because it is not a free variable of A. Let $q \in \mathcal{P}_p$. Either $q \in \{\vec{r}\}$ or not. If $q \in \{\vec{r}\}$ then it is easy to see

$$(q \vdash \nu X\{\vec{r}\}(B[\theta])) \rightarrow^* t \Leftrightarrow t = \mathbf{true}, \text{ for any } t \in T,$$

and that $(q \models \nu X\{\vec{r}\}(B[\theta])) = \mathbf{true}$. Hence $Q(A[\theta])$ when $q \in \{\vec{r}\}$ in this case. Otherwise $q \notin \{\vec{r}\}$. Then $\nu X\{q, \vec{r}\}B \prec A$, so $Q(\nu X\{q, \vec{r}\}(B[\theta]))$. Define a substitution θ'

from $Y \in FV(B)$ to closed p-assertions by taking

$$\theta'(Y) = \begin{cases} \theta(Y) & \text{if } Y \not\equiv X \\ \nu X\{q, \vec{r}\}(B[\theta]) & \text{if } Y \equiv X \end{cases}$$

Certainly $Q(\theta'(Y))$, for all $Y \in FV(B)$. As $B \prec A$ we have $Q^+(B)$. Hence $Q(B[\theta'])$. But $B[\theta'] \equiv (B[\theta])[\nu X\{q, \vec{r}\}(B[\theta])/X]$. Thus from the reduction rules,

$$\begin{aligned} (q \vdash \nu X\{\vec{r}\}(B[\theta])) \to^* t \;\; &\Leftrightarrow\;\; (q \vdash (B[\theta])[\nu X\{q, \vec{r}\}(B[\theta])/X]) \to^* t \\ &\Leftrightarrow\;\; (q \vdash B[\theta']) \to^* t \\ &\Leftrightarrow\;\; (q \models B[\theta']) = t \quad \text{as } Q(B[\theta']) \\ &\Leftrightarrow\;\; (q \models (B[\theta])[\nu X\{q, \vec{r}\}(B[\theta])/X]) = t \\ &\Leftrightarrow\;\; (q \models \nu X\{\vec{r}\}(B[\theta])) = t \quad \text{by the Reduction Lemma.} \end{aligned}$$

Hence, whether $q \in \{\vec{r}\}$ or not, $Q(A[\theta])$ in this case.

For all the other possible forms of A it can be shown (Exercise!) that $Q(A[\theta])$. Using well-founded induction we conclude $Q^+(A)$ for all p-assertions A. In particular $Q(A)$ for all closed assertions A, which establishes the theorem. □

Example: Consider the two element transition system given in CCS by

$$P \stackrel{def}{=} a.Q$$
$$Q \stackrel{def}{=} a.P$$

—it consists of two transitions $P \stackrel{a}{\to} Q$ and $Q \stackrel{a}{\to} P$. We show how the rewriting algorithm establishes the obviously true fact that P is able to do arbitrarily many a's, formally that $P \models \nu X.\langle a \rangle X$. Recalling that $\nu X.\langle a \rangle X$ stands for $\nu X\{\ \}\langle a \rangle X$, following the reductions of the model-checking algorithm we obtain:

$$\begin{aligned} P \vdash \nu X\{\ \}\langle a \rangle X \;&\to\; P \vdash \langle a \rangle X[\nu X\{P\}\langle a \rangle X/X] \\ &i.e.\, P \vdash \langle a \rangle \nu X\{P\}\langle a \rangle X \\ &\to\; Q \vdash \nu X\{P\}\langle a \rangle X \\ &\to\; Q \vdash \langle a \rangle X[\nu X\{Q, P\}\langle a \rangle X/X] \\ &i.e.\, Q \vdash \langle a \rangle \nu X\{Q, P\}\langle a \rangle X \\ &\to\; P \vdash \nu X\{Q, P\}\langle a \rangle X \\ &\to\; \textbf{true}. \end{aligned}$$

□

Hence provided the constants of the assertion language are restricted to decidable properties the reduction rules give a method for deciding whether or not a process satisfies an assertion. We have concentrated on the correctness rather than the efficiency of an algorithm for local model checking. As it stands the algorithm can be very inefficient in the worst case because it does not exploit the potential for sharing data sufficiently (the same is true of several current implementations). The next section contains references to more careful and efficient algorithms.

Exercise 14.20
(i) For the CCS process P defined by

$$P \stackrel{def}{=} a.P$$

show $p \vdash \nu X.\langle a \rangle T \wedge [a]X$ reduces to **true** under the algorithm above.
(ii) For the CCS definition

$$P \stackrel{def}{=} a.Q$$

$$Q \stackrel{def}{=} a.P + a.\textbf{nil}$$

show $P \vdash \mu X.[a]F \vee \langle a \rangle X$ reduces to **true**.   □

Exercise 14.21 (A project) Program a method to extract a transition system table for a finite-state process from the operational semantics in *e.g.* SML or Prolog. Program the model checking algorithm. Use it to investigate the following simple protocol.   □

Exercise 14.22 A simple communication protocol (from [72]) is described in CCS by:

Sender	=	$a.$Sender'
Sender'	=	$\bar{b}.(d.$Sender $+ c.$Sender'$)$
Medium	=	$b.(\bar{c}.$Medium $+ \bar{e}.$Medium$)$
Receiver	=	$e.f.\bar{d}.$Receiver
Protocol	=	(Sender $\parallel$ Medium $\parallel$ Receiver)$\backslash$ $\{b, c, d, e\}$

Use the tool developed in Exercise 14.21 (or the Concurrency Workbench or TAV system) to show the following:
The process Protocol does *not* satisfy $Inv([a](ev\langle f \rangle T))$.

Protocol does satisfy $Inv([f](ev\langle a\rangle T))$.

(Here $Inv(A) \equiv \nu X.(A \wedge [.]X)$ and $ev(A) \equiv \mu X.(A \vee (\langle.\rangle T \wedge [.]X))$, with $Inv(A)$ satisfied by precisely those processes which always satisfy A, and $ev(A)$ satisfied by precisely those processes which eventually satisfy A.)   □

Exercise 14.23 (Bisimulation testing) Strong bisimulation can be expressed as a maximum fixed point (see Exercise 14.9). The testing of bisimulation between two finite-state processes can be automated along the same lines as local model checking. Suggest how, and write a program, in *e.g.* SML or Prolog, to do it? (The method indicated is close to that of the TAV system, though not that of the Concurrency Workbench.)   □

14.9 Further reading

The mathematical theory of how to model and reason about parallel systems is alive, and unsettled. The brief account of this chapter is necessarily incomplete.

We have focussed on Dijkstra's language of guarded commands from [36], its extension by Hoare to communicating sequential processes (CSP) [49], and Milner's approach to a calculus of communicating systems (CCS). Milner's book on CCS [63] is highly suitable as an undergraduate text. Milner's handbook chapter [64] gives a quick run through the more theoretical contents of his book. Hoare's book [50] concentrates on another equivalence ("failures" equivalence) and represents another influential branch of work. A more mathematical treatment of closely related matters is given in Hennessy's book [48]. The programming language Occam [70] is based on the ideas of CCS and CSP. The logic, the modal ν-calculus, follows that presented by Kozen in [55]. To date (1992) this contains the best result that's known on completeness of axiomatisations of the logic— the question of a complete axiomatisation for the full logic is still open! The logic is more traditionally called the (modal) μ-calculus. The emphasis in our treatment on maximum rather than minimum fixed points led to the slight change of name for our treatment.

Class work on CCS is best supplemented by work with tools such as the Edinburgh-Sussex Concurrency Workbench [30] and the Aalborg TAV system [46].[2] Walker's paper

---

[2]The Concurrency Workbench is available from Edinburgh University or North Carolina State University:

George Cleland, LFCS, Dept. of Computer Science, University of Edinburgh, The King's Buildings, Edinburgh EH9 3JZ, Scotland. E-mail: lfcs@ed.ac.uk,

Anonymous FTP: ftp.dcs.ed.ac.uk (Internet no. 129.215.160.150).

Rance Cleaveland, Department of Computer Science, N.C. State University, Raleigh, NC 27695-8206, USA. E-mail: rance@adm.csc.ncsu.edu,

Anonymous FTP: science.csc.ncsu.edu (IP address: 152.1.61.34).

The TAV system is available from Kim G.Larsen or Arne Skou, Institute for Electronic Systems, Department of Mathematics and Computer Science, Aalborg University Centre, Fredrik Bajersvej 7, 9200 Aalborg Ø, Denmark. E-mail: kgl@iesd.auc.dk

[100] gives a good account of the Concurrency Workbench in action in investigating parallel algorithms. The Concurrency Workbench is extended to handle priorities of the kind found in Occam in [52]; the paper [18] in addition provides an equational proof system with respect to a suitably generalised bisimulation. The theoretical basis to the Concurrency Workbench is found in [93, 25] following from that of [57] (the model-checking section of this chapter is based on [106]). Model checking itself has evolved into a flourishing area in recent years. At the time of writing (1992), the Edinburgh-Sussex Concurrency Workbench can take exponential time in both the size of the formula and the size of the transition system (even with only one fixed-point operator). The algorithm described here suffers the same defect. They do not reuse information obtained during a computation as much as possible. For a particular "alternation depth"—a measure of how intertwined the minimum and maximum fixed-points of an assertion are—the TAV system is polynomial in the size of assertion and transition system. To date, the most efficient algorithms for local model checking up to alternation depth 2 are described in [6, 7]. There are many other ways to perform model checking ([37] has already been mentioned) often on logics rather different from that treated here (see *e.g.*, [24] for an accessible paper).

Throughout the book, except in this chapter, we have presented both operational and denotational semantics of programming languages. We have not given a denotational semantics to process languages because within domain theory this involves "powerdomains", not dealt with in this book. Powerdomains are cpo analogues of powersets enabling denotations to represent sets of possible outcomes. They were invented by Plotkin in [79] which also gives a good indication of their use (though the articles [92] and [102] are perhaps less intimidating).

The recent book by Apt and Olderog [9] is concerned with extensions of Hoare logic to parallel programs. Temporal logic has been strongly advocated as a medium for reasoning about parallel processes (see *e.g.*[60, 56]).

The presentation of parallelism here has, in effect, treated parallel composition by regarding it as a shorthand for nondeterministic interleaving of atomic actions of the components. There are other models like Petri nets and event structures which represent parallelism explicitly as a form of independence between actions, and so make a distinction between purely nondeterministic processes and those with parallelism. An introductory book on Petri nets is [85]. There has recently been success in trying to achieve the expressive power of Petri nets within more mathematically amenable frameworks such as structural operational semantics. The forthcoming handbook chapter [107] provides a survey of a range of different models for parallel processes.

A Incompleteness and undecidability

This appendix furnishes a brief introduction to the theory of computability.[1] The basic notions of computable (partial recursive) function, recursively enumerable and decidable set are introduced. The "halting-problem" is shown undecidable and through it that the valid assertions of **Assn** are not recursively enumerable. In particular, it fleshes out the proof in Section 7.3 of Gödel's Incompleteness Theorem. A discussion of a "universal **IMP** program" leads to an alternative proof. The chapter concludes with a closer examination of what it is about **Assn**'s which makes their truth (and falsehood) not recursively enumerable.

A.1 Computability

A command c of **IMP** can be associated with a partial function on $\mathbf{N}$. Throughout we assume locations are listed $X_1, X_2, X_3, \cdots$. Let σ_0 be the state in which each location is assigned 0. For $n \in \mathbf{N}$, define

$$\{c\}(n) = \begin{cases} \sigma(X_1) & \text{if } \sigma = \mathcal{C}[\![c]\!]\sigma_0[n/X_1] \\ \text{undefined} & \text{if } \mathcal{C}[\![c]\!]\sigma_0[n/X_1] \text{ is undefined.} \end{cases}$$

Any partial function $\mathbf{N} \rightharpoonup \mathbf{N}$ which acts as $n \mapsto \{c\}(n)$, on $n \in \mathbf{N}$, for some command c, is called **IMP**-*computable*. Such functions are also called "partial recursive", and "recursive" when they are total. More generally, we can associate a command with a partial function taking k arguments, so defining **IMP**-computable functions from $\mathbf{N}^k$ to $\mathbf{N}$. For $n_1, \cdots, n_k \in \mathbf{N}$, define

$$\{c\}(n_1, \cdots, n_k) = \begin{cases} \sigma(X_1) & \text{if } \sigma = \mathcal{C}[\![c]\!]\sigma_0[n_1/X_1, \cdots, n_k/X_k] \\ \text{undefined} & \text{if } \mathcal{C}[\![c]\!]\sigma_0[n_1/X_1, \cdots, n_k/X_k] \text{ is undefined.} \end{cases}$$

To show that **IMP**-computable functions compose to give an **IMP**-computable function we introduce the idea of a *tidy* command, one which sets all its non X_1 locations to 0 when it terminates.

Definition: Say an **IMP** command c is *tidy* iff for all states σ and numbers n

$$\mathcal{C}[\![c]\!]\sigma_0[n/X_1] = \sigma \Rightarrow \sigma[0/X_1] = \sigma_0.$$

Exercise A.1 Show that if f is **IMP**-computable then there is a tidy **IMP** command c such that $f(n) = m$ iff $\{c\}(n) = m$, for all m, n. □

It is now easy to see that the following holds:

---

[1] The Appendix is based on notes of Albert Meyer which were used to supplement Chapters 1-7 in an undergraduate course at MIT. I'm very grateful to Albert for permission to use his notes freely.

Proposition A.2 *Let c_0 and c_1 be commands. Assume c_0 is tidy. For any $n, m \in \mathbf{N}$,*

$$\{c_1\}(\{c_0\}(n)) = m \quad \textit{iff} \quad \{c_0; c_1\}(n) = m.$$

Notation: For a partial function f and argument n we write $f(n) \downarrow$ to mean $\exists m.\ f(n) = m$, *i.e.* the result is defined, and $f(n)\updownarrow$ to signify the result is undefined.

Note that $\{c\}(n) \downarrow$ coincides with termination of the command c starting from the state $\sigma_0[n/X_1]$. A subset M of $\mathbf{N}$ is **IMP**-*checkable* iff there is an **IMP** command c such that

$$n \in M \quad \text{iff} \quad \{c\}(n) \downarrow.$$

That is, given input n in location X_1, with all other locations initially zero, command c "checks" whether n is in M and stops when its checking procedure succeeds. The command will continue checking forever (and so never succeed) if n is not in M. Checkable sets are usually referred to as "recursively enumerable" (r.e.) sets.

Closely related is the concept of an **IMP**-*decidable* set. A subset $M \subseteq \mathbf{N}$ is **IMP**-*decidable* iff there is an **IMP** command c such that

$$n \in M \quad \text{implies} \quad \{c\}(n) = 1,$$

and

$$n \notin M \quad \text{implies} \quad \{c\}(n) = 0.$$

That is, given input n, command c tests whether $n \in M$, returning output 1 in location X_1 if so, and returning output 0 otherwise. It terminates with such an output for *all* inputs. Decidable sets are sometimes called "recursive" sets.

If c is a "decider" for M, then

$$c;\ \textbf{if } X_1 = 1 \textbf{ then skip else } \text{Diverge}$$

is a "checker" for M, where $\text{Diverge} \equiv \textbf{while true do skip}$. Thus:

Lemma A.3 *If M is decidable, then M is checkable.*

Exercise A.4 Show that if M is decidable, so is the complement $\bar{M} = \mathbf{N} \setminus M$.   □

Exercise A.5 Show that if M is checkable, then there is a checker c for M such that $\{c\}(n) \downarrow$ implies $\mathcal{C}[\![c]\!]\sigma_0[n/X_1] = \sigma_0$ for all $n \in \mathbf{N}$. In other words, c only halts after it has "cleaned up all its locations." (*cf.* Exercise A.1.)   □

Conversely, if c_1 is a checker for M, and c_2 is a checker for $\bar{M}$, then by constructing a command c which "time-shares" or "dovetails" c_1 and c_2, one gets a decider for M.

In a little more detail, here is how c might be written: Let T, F, S be "fresh" locations not in $\mathbf{Loc}(c_1) \cup \mathbf{Loc}(c_2)$. Let "Clear$_i$" abbreviate a sequence of assignments setting $\mathbf{Loc}(c_i) \setminus \{X_1\}$ to 0. Then c might be:

$T := X_1;$	% save X_1 in T
$F := 0;$	% F is a flag
$S := 1;$	% how many steps to try

[while $F = 0$ do

    Clear$_1$; $X_1 := T$;

    "do c_1 for S steps or until c_1 halts";

    if "c_1 has halted in $\leq S$ steps" then

$F := 1;$	% all done
$X_1 := 1;$	% T is in M
else $S := S + 1;$	% increase the step counter

    if $F = 1$ then skip else

        Clear$_2$; $X_1 := T$;

        "do c_2 for S steps or until c_2 halts";

        if "c_2 has halted in $\leq S$ steps" then

$F := 1;$	% all done
$X_1 := 0;$	% T is not in M
else $S := S + 1$];	% increase the step counter

    Clear$_1$; Clear$_2$; $T := 0$; $F := 0$; $S := 0$ % clean up except for X_1

Exercise A.6 Describe how to transform a command c_1 into one which meets the description "do c_1 for S steps or until c_1 halts (whichever happens first)."   □

So we have

Theorem A.7 *A set M is decidable iff M and $\bar{M}$ are checkable.*

A.2 Undecidability

By encoding commands as numbers we can supply them as inputs to other commands. To do this we encode commands c as numbers $\#c$ in the following way. Let mkpair be a pairing function for pairs of integers. For example,

$$\mathrm{mkpair}(n, m) = 2^{\mathrm{sg}(n)} \cdot 3^{|n|} \cdot 5^{\mathrm{sg}(m)} \cdot 7^{|m|}$$

will serve, where

$$sg(n) = \begin{cases} 1 & \text{if } n \geq 0, \\ 0 & \text{if } n < 0. \end{cases}$$

The details of the pairing function don't matter; the important point is that there are functions "left" and "right" such that

$$\text{left}\,(\text{mkpair}(n,m)) \;\; = \;\; n,$$
$$\text{right}\,(\text{mkpair}(n,m)) \;\; = \;\; m,$$

and *moreover* there are **IMP** commands which act like assignment statements of each of the forms

$$X \;\; := \;\; \text{mkpair}(Y, Z),$$
$$X \;\; := \;\; \text{left}(Y), \text{ and}$$
$$X \;\; := \;\; \text{right}(Y).$$

Exercise A.8

(i) Produce **IMP**-commands Mkpair, Left, Right realising the functions above, *i.e.* so

$$\{\text{Mkpair}\}(n, m) = \text{mkpair}(n, m)$$
$$\{\text{Left}\}(n) = \text{left}(n)$$
$$\{\text{Right}\}(n) = \text{right}(n)$$

for all $n, m \in \mathbf{N}$.

(ii) Let c be a text which is of the form of an **IMP** command, except that c contains assignment statements of the form "$X := \text{left}(Y)$." Describe how to construct an authentic **IMP** command $\hat{c}$ which simulates c up to temporary locations.

(iii) Suppose that the definition of **Aexp**, and hence of **IMP**, was modified to allow **Aexp**'s of the form "mkpair(a_1, a_2)," "left(a)" and "right(a)" for a, a_1, a_2 themselves modified **Aexp**'s. Call the resulting language **IMP'**. Explain how to translate every $c' \in \mathbf{Com'}$ into a $c \in \mathbf{Com}$ such that c simulates c'. $\square$

To encode commands as numbers, we make use of the numbering of the set of locations **Loc** as $X_1, X_2, \ldots$. We use 0 as the "location-tag" and define

$$\#(X_i) = \text{mkloc}(i) = \text{mkpair}(0, i).$$

We also encode numerals, using 1 as the "number-tag":

$$\#(n) = \text{mknum}(n) = \text{mkpair}(1, n).$$

We proceed to encode **Aexp**'s by using 2, 3, 4 as tags for sums, differences, and products, for example:

$$\#(a_1 + a_2) = \mathrm{mksum}(\#a_1, \#a_2) = \mathrm{mkpair}\,(2, \mathrm{mkpair}(\#a_1, \#a_2))\,.$$

We encode **Bexp**'s using tags 5, 6, 7, 8, 9 for $\leq$, $=$, $\wedge$, $\vee$, $\neg$, for example:

$$\#(a_1 \leq a_2) = \mathrm{mkleq}(\#a_1, \#a_2) = \mathrm{mkpair}\,(5, \mathrm{mkpair}(\#a_1, \#a_2))\,,$$

$$\#(b_1 \vee b_2) = \mathrm{mkor}(\#b_1, \#b_2) = \mathrm{mkpair}\,(8, \mathrm{mkpair}(\#b_1, \#b_2))\,.$$

Finally, encode **Com** using tags 10–14 for :=, **skip**, **if** , *sequencing*, **while** , *e.g.*,

$$
\begin{aligned}
\#(\textbf{if } b \textbf{ then } c_0 \textbf{ else } c_1) \;&=\; \mathrm{mkif}(\#b, \#c_0, \#c_1) \\
&=\; \mathrm{mkpair}\,(12, \mathrm{mkpair}\,(\#b, \mathrm{mkpair}(\#c_0, \#c_1)))\,.
\end{aligned}
$$

This method of numbering syntactic or finitely structured objects was first used by Kurt Gödel in the 1930's, and $\#(c)$ is called the *Gödel number* of c.

Now that commands are numbered, it makes sense to talk about supplying a command as an input to another command, namely, supply its number. We shall say a subset S of commands is checkable (respectively decidable) if their set of codes

$$\{\#c \mid c \in S\}$$

is checkable (respectively decidable).

Exercise A.9 Describe how to write an **IMP** command which decides whether or not a number encodes a well-formed **IMP** command. Deduce that the set $\{c \mid c \in \textbf{Com}\}$ is decidable. □

Let H be the "self-halting" subset of commands:

$$H = \{\, c \mid \{c\}(\#c) \downarrow \,\}.$$

Write

$$\bar{H} =_{def} \{c \in \textbf{Com} \mid c \notin H\}$$

Theorem A.10 $\bar{H}$ *is not* **IMP**-*checkable.*

Proof: Suppose C was an **IMP**-command which checked $\bar{H}$. That is, for all commands c,

$$c \in \bar{H} \quad \text{iff} \quad \{C\}(\#c) \text{ is defined.}$$

Now C is itself a command, so in particular, recalling the definition of $\bar{H}$,

$$\{C\}(\#C)\updownarrow \quad \text{iff} \quad \{C\}(\#C)\downarrow,$$

a contradiction. Hence, $\bar{H}$ cannot be checkable. $\square$

Corollary A.11 (Halting problem) *The set H is undecidable.*

The undecidability of other properties follows from that of the undecidability of the halting problem. Define

$$H_0 = \{\, c \in \mathbf{Com} \mid \mathcal{C}[\![c]\!]\sigma_0 \neq \bot \,\}.$$

Note that

$$H_0 = \{\, c \in \mathbf{Com} \mid \{c\}(0)\downarrow \,\}.$$

It follows from the fact that $\bar{H}$ is not checkable that neither is $\bar{H}_0 = \{c \in \mathbf{Com} \mid c \notin H_0\}$:

Theorem A.12 (Zero-state halting problem) *The set $\bar{H}_0$ is not checkable.*

Proof: The proof makes use of a command realising the function g such that, for any command c,

$$g(\#c) = \#(X_1 := \#c;\ c).$$

Such a function is obtained by defining

$$g(n) = \mathrm{mkseq}\,(\mathrm{mkassign}\,(\mathrm{mkloc}(1), \mathrm{mknum}(n))\,, n)\,,$$

for $n \in \mathbf{N}$. However, by Exercise A.8, there is a command G such that

$$\{G\}(n) = g(n).$$

By Exercise A.1 we can assume the command G is tidy.

With the aim of obtaining a contradiction, assume $\bar{H}_0$ were checkable, *i.e.* that there is a command C such that

$$c \in \bar{H}_0 \quad \text{iff} \quad \{C\}(\#c)\downarrow$$

for any command c. Then

$$
\begin{aligned}
c \in \bar{H} \quad &\text{iff} \quad \{c\}(\#c)\updownarrow \\
&\text{iff} \quad \{X_1 := \#c;\ c\}(0)\updownarrow \\
&\text{iff} \quad (X_1 := \#c;\ c) \in \bar{H}_0 \\
&\text{iff} \quad \{C\}(\#(X_1 := \#c;\ c))\downarrow \\
&\text{iff} \quad \{C\}(g(\#c))\downarrow \\
&\text{iff} \quad \{C\}(\{G\}(\#c))\downarrow \\
&\text{iff} \quad \{G;C\}(\#c)\downarrow\,.
\end{aligned}
$$

The final step is justified by Proposition A.2. But this makes the command $G; C$ a checker for $\bar{H}$, a contradiction. Hence $\bar{H}_0$ is not checkable.   □

Exercise A.13
(i) Describe an **IMP** command C which given the Gödel number $\#c$ of a command c outputs the maximum k for locations X_k in c. Hence show there is an **IMP** computable function which for input $\#c$ outputs the Gödel number of the command

$$X_1 := 0; \ X_2 := 0; \ \cdots; \ X_k := 0$$

clearing all locations up to the last occurring in c.
(ii) Let
$$D = \{c \in \mathbf{Com} \mid \forall \sigma. \ C[\![c]\!]\sigma = \bot\}.$$

Using part (i), argue from the fact that $\bar{H}_0$ is not checkable that D is not checkable either.   □

A.3 Gödel's incompleteness theorem

If there were a theorem-proving system which was powerful enough to prove *all* (and of course, *only*) the valid assertions in **Assn**, then we would expect to be able to write a program which given input (a code of) an assertion A, searched exhaustively for a proof of A, and halted iff it found such a proof. Such a program would thus be a validity checker.

In more detail, imagine we encode assertions A by Gödel numbers $\#A$ in a way similar to that used for expressions and commands. Any system which could reasonably be called a "theorem-prover" would provide a method for how to *decide* if some structured finite object—commonly a finite sequence of **Assn**'s—was a "proof" of a given assertion. A provability checker would work by exhaustively searching through the structured finite objects to find a proof object. Thus, in order to be worthy of the name "theorem-prover," we insist that the set

$$\mathbf{Provable} = \{A \in \mathbf{Assn} \mid \vdash A\}$$

be **IMP**-checkable. As before, with commands, we say a subset of assertions is checkable iff its corresponding set of Gödel numbers is. Let the valid assertions form the set

$$\mathbf{Valid} = \{A \in \mathbf{Assn} \mid \models A\}.$$

A theorem prover for validity would make this set checkable. However:

Theorem A.14 **Valid** *is not checkable.*

Proof: The proof makes use of a command W which realises the function h such that, for any command c,

$$h(\#c) = \#(w[\![c, \mathbf{false}]\!][\vec{0}/\mathbf{Loc}(c)]).$$

(The hopefully self-evident notation above means substitute 0 for each location of c, and hence every location, which appears in the assertion.)

The existence of such a command follows from constructive nature of the proof of Theorem 7.5; it describes how to construct an assertion $w[\![c, A]\!]$, expressing the weakest precondition, for a command c and assertion A, so that in principle we could write an **IMP** command to achieve this on the Gödel numbers. The remaining proof will rest on there being a command W such that

$$\{W\}(\#c) = \#(w[\![c, \mathbf{false}]\!][\vec{0}/\mathbf{Loc}(c)]).$$

We won't give the detailed construction of W. We will assume W is a tidy command.

Assume that **Valid** were checkable, *i.e.* that there is a command C such that, for any assertion A,

$$A \in \mathbf{Valid} \quad \text{iff} \quad \{C\}(\#A) \downarrow.$$

Let $A \equiv w[\![c, \mathbf{false}]\!][\vec{0}/\mathbf{Loc}(c)]$. Then

$$
\begin{aligned}
c \in \bar{H}_0 \quad &\text{iff} \quad A \in \mathbf{Valid} \\
&\text{iff} \quad \{C\}(\#A) \downarrow \\
&\text{iff} \quad \{C\}(\{W\}(\#c)) \downarrow \\
&\text{iff} \quad \{W; C\}(\#c) \downarrow \text{ by Proposition A.2.}
\end{aligned}
$$

This makes $\bar{H}_0$ checkable by the command $W; C$, a contradiction. Hence **Valid** is not checkable.   □

The proof above can be carried through equally well for that special subset of valid assertions which are closed and location-free in the sense that they do not mention any locations. Such assertions are either true or false independent of the state and interpretation. We let

$$\mathbf{Truth} = \{A \in Assn \mid A \text{ closed } \& \text{ location-free } \& \models A\}.$$

Notice that the assertions "$w[\![c, \mathbf{false}]\!][\vec{0}/\mathbf{Loc}(c)]$" in the proof above are closed and location-free, so that the same argument would carry through to show that **Truth** is *not* **IMP**-checkable. Therefore, for all theorem-provers, **Provable** $\neq$ **Truth**. At best, because we want a sound proof system, **Provable** $\subsetneq$ **Truth**, and so, for any theorem-prover whose provable assertions are indeed true, there must be some true assertion which is not provable. So the theorem-prover cannot *completely* prove the true assertions. This is *Gödel's* (first) *Incompleteness Theorem*. In abstract form, it is simply:

Theorem A.15 Truth *is not checkable.*

The proof of Gödel's Incompleteness Theorem has been based on the construction of an assertion expressing the weakest proecondition. In the next section there is another proof, this time based on the existence of a "universal program."

A.4 A universal program

It is nowadays a commonplace idea (although it was a strikingly imaginative one in the 1930's) that one can write a "simulator" for **IMP** commands; in fact, the simulator itself could be programmed in **IMP**. That is, we want a command *SIM* which, given as input a pair $(\#c, n)$, will give the same output as c running on input n. The precise specification is

$$\{SIM\}(\#c, n) = m \quad \text{iff} \quad \{c\}(n) = m$$

for any command c and $n, m \in \mathbf{N}$.
(Note that we can exclude numbers not encoding commands by Exercise A.9.)

Theorem A.16 (Universal Program Theorem) *There is an* **IMP** *command, SIM, meeting the above specification.*

Proof: A long programming exercise to construct *SIM*, and a longer, challenging exercise to prove it works correctly.   □

Corollary A.17 *The self-halting set H is* **IMP**-*checkable.*

Proof: The command "$X_2 := X_1$; *SIM*" describes an **IMP**-checker for H.   □

A set $M \subseteq \mathbf{N}$ is *expressible* iff there is an $A \in \mathbf{Assn}$ with no locations and only one free integer variable i such that

$$\models A[n/i] \quad \text{iff} \quad n \in M.$$

In other words, the meaning of A is "i is in M." Once i is instantiated with a number, say 7, the resulting assertion $A[7/i]$ is true or false (depending on whether $7 \in M$) independent of the state σ or interpretation I used to determine its truth value.

Theorem A.18 *Every* **IMP**-*checkable set* $M \subseteq \mathbf{N}$ *is expressible.*

Proof: Let $c \in$ **Com** be an M checker. Let $w[c, \textbf{false}] \in$ **Assn** mean the weakest precondition of **false** under c. Then

$$(\neg w[c, \textbf{false}]) \, [i/X_1][\vec{0}/\textbf{Loc}(c)]$$

expresses M. □

Once we assign Gödel numbers to **Assn** just as we did for **Com**, we obtain a numbering which has the following important property: for any assertion A with no locations and a single free integer variable i, let $f(n) = \#(A[n/i])$; then we claim there is an **IMP** command S which realises f, *i.e.*

$$\{S\}(n) = f(n)$$

for any $n \in \textbf{N}$.

One way to see this is to assume that A is of the form

$$\exists j. \, j = i \wedge A'$$

where A' has no free occurrences of i. There is essentially no loss of generality in this assumption, since any $A \in$ **Assn** is equivalent to an assertion of the form above. Now we see that

$$f(n) = \text{mkexistential}(\#(j), \text{mkand}\,(\text{mkeq}\,(\#(j), \text{mknum}(n)), \#(A'))),$$

so $f(n)$ is definable by an **Aexp** extended with a "mkpair" operator, and therefore by the Exercise A.8 above we know there is an **IMP** command S such that $\{S\}(n) = f(n)$, for all n. By Exercise A.1 we can assume S is tidy.

This property is the only fact about the numbering of closed assertions which we need to use in the following alternative proof of the Incompleteness Theorem, as we now show.

Another proof of the Incompleteness Theorem:

Suppose $C \in$ **Com** was a **Truth** checker. Since the self-halting set H is checkable, there is an assertion B such that, for all commands c,

$$c \in H \quad \text{iff} \quad \models B[\#c/i].$$

Letting A be $\neg B$, we have

$$
\begin{aligned}
c \in \bar{H} \quad &\text{iff} \quad \models A[\#c/i] \\
&\text{iff} \quad A[\#c/i] \in \textbf{Truth} \\
&\text{iff} \quad \{C\}(\#(A[\#c/i])) \downarrow \\
&\text{iff} \quad \{C\}(\{S\}(\#c)) \downarrow \\
&\text{iff} \quad \{S; C\}(\#c) \downarrow
\end{aligned}
$$

where S is the tidy command achieving substitution into A.

But then "$S; C$" describes an $\bar{H}$ checker, a contradiction.   □

Exercise A.19 Show that **Truth** is not checkable either.   □

Exercise A.20 Prove or give counter-examples to the claims that decidable (checkable, expressible) sets are closed under complement (union, intersection). Note, this asks nine questions, not three.   □

Exercise A.21 Show that $H_0 = \{\, c \in \mathbf{Com} \mid \mathcal{C}[\![c]\!]\sigma_0 \neq \perp \,\}$ is checkable.   □

A.5 Matijasevic's Theorem

We now examine more closely what it is about **Assn**'s which makes their truth (and falsehood) not even checkable, let alone decidable. It might seem that the source of the problem was the quantifiers "$\forall$" and "$\exists$" whose checking seems to require an infinite search in order to complete a check. However, this is a case where naive intuition is misleading. The "hard part" of **Assn**'s has more to do with the interaction between additive and multiplicative properties of numbers than with quantifiers. In particular, if we let *PlusAssn*'s be assertions which do *not* contain the symbol for multiplication and likewise *TimesAssn* be assertions which do not contain the symbols for addition or subtraction, then validity for *PlusAssn*'s and also for *TimesAssn*'s is actually decidable, and there are logical systems of a familiar kind for proving all the valid *PlusAssn*'s and likewise for *TimesAssn*'s. These facts are not at all obvious, and the long, ingenious proofs won't be given here.

On the other hand, when we narrow ourselves to **Assn**'s without quantifiers, that is **Bexp**'s, it turns out that validity is *still* not checkable. This is an immediate consequence of the undecidability of "Hilbert's 10th Problem," which is to decide, given $a \in \mathbf{Aexp}$, whether a has an integer-vector root. More precisely, let

$$H_{10} = \{\, a \in \mathbf{Aexp} \mid \sigma \models a = 0 \text{ for some } \sigma \in \Sigma \,\}.$$

Remember this is understood to mean that the set

$$\{\, \#a \mid a \in \mathbf{Aexp} \text{ and } \sigma \models a = 0 \text{ for some } \sigma \in \Sigma \,\}.$$

is not a decidable subset of $\mathbf{N}$.

Theorem A.22 (Matijasevic, 1970) H_{10} *is not decidable.*

This is one of the great results of 20th century Mathematics and Logic. Matijasevic, a Russian, building on earlier work of Americans Davis, Putnam and Robinson, learned how to "program" with polynomials over the integers and so obtained this theorem. The proof uses only elementary number theory, but would take several weeks to present in a series of lectures.

Exercise A.23 Explain why H_{10} is checkable, and so $\bar{H}_{10} = \textbf{Aexp}\backslash H_{10}$ is not checkable. □

Matijasevic actually proved the following general result:

Theorem A.24 (Polynomial Programming) *Let M be an r.e. set of nonnegative integers. Then there is an $a \in \textbf{Aexp}$ such that M is the set of nonnegative integers in the range of a.*

Remember that an $a \in \textbf{Aexp}$ can be thought of as describing a polynomial function on the integers. In particular, the *range* of a is $\text{Rge}(a) =_{def} \{ \mathcal{A}[\![a]\!]\sigma \mid \sigma \in \Sigma \}$.

Exercise A.25
(i) Show that it follows from the Polynomial Programming Theorem that

$$\{a \in \textbf{Aexp} \mid \#a \in \text{Rge}(a)\}$$

is not checkable.
(ii) Explain why the undecidability of Hilbert's 10th Problem follows from the Polynomial Programming Theorem. □

We now can conclude that the validity problem for **Assn**'s of the simple form "$\neg(a = 0)$" is not checkable. Let

$$\textbf{ValidNonEq} = \{ \neg(a = 0) \mid a \in \textbf{Aexp} \text{ and } \models \neg(a = 0) \}.$$

Corollary A.26 ValidNonEq *is not checkable.*

Proof: We have $a \in \bar{H}_{10}$ iff $\neg(a = 0) \in \textbf{ValidNonEq}$. So

$$X_1 := \text{mkneg}\,(\text{mkeq}\,(X_1, \text{mknum}(0)))\,;\ c$$

would describe an $\bar{H}_{10}$ checker if c were a **ValidNonEq** checker. □

On the other hand, an easy, informative example which is both decidable and even nicely axiomatizable are the valid *equations*, *i.e.*, **Assn**'s of the form "$a_1 = a_2$."

We begin by giving the inductive definition of the "provable" equations. We write $\vdash e$ to indicate that an equation e is provable.

$$\vdash a = a \qquad \text{(reflexivity)}$$

$$\frac{\vdash a_1 = a_2}{\vdash a_2 = a_1} \qquad \text{(symmetry)}$$

$$\frac{\vdash a_1 = a_2 \quad \vdash a_2 = a_3}{\vdash a_1 = a_3} \qquad \text{(transitivity)}$$

$$\frac{\vdash a_1 = a_2}{\vdash a_1 \textbf{ op } a = a_2 \textbf{ op } a} \qquad \text{(right congruence)}$$

$$\frac{\vdash a_1 = a_2}{\vdash a \textbf{ op } a_1 = a \textbf{ op } a_2} \qquad \text{(left congruence)}$$

$$\text{where } \textbf{op} \in \{+, -, \times\}$$

$$\vdash (a_1 \textbf{ op }' a_2) \textbf{ op }' a_3 = a_1 \textbf{ op }' (a_2 \textbf{ op }' a_3) \qquad \text{(associativity)}$$

$$\vdash a_1 \textbf{ op }' a_2 = a_2 \textbf{ op }' a_1 \qquad \text{(commutativity)}$$

$$\text{where } \textbf{op}' \in \{+, \times\}$$

$$\vdash a + 0 = a \qquad \text{(+-identity)}$$

$$\vdash a \times 1 = a \qquad \text{($\times$-identity)}$$

$$\vdash a - a = 0 \qquad \text{(additive inverse)}$$

$$\vdash a - b = a + ((-1) \times b) \qquad \text{(minus-one)}$$

$$\vdash a_1 \times (a_2 + a_3) = (a_1 \times a_2) + (a_1 \times a_3) \qquad \text{(distributivity)}$$

$$\vdash (-n) = (-1) \times n \qquad \text{(negative numeral)}$$

$$\vdash 1 + 1 = 2, \ \vdash 2 + 1 = 3, \ \vdash 3 + 1 = 4, \ \ldots \qquad \text{(successor)}$$

Theorem A.27 $\vdash a_1 = a_2$ *iff* $\models a_1 = a_2$.

Proof: ($\Rightarrow$) This direction of the "iff" is called *soundness* of the proof system. It follows immediately from the inductive definition of "$\vdash$," once we note the familiar facts that all the rules (including the axioms regarded as rules with no antecedents) preserve validity.

($\Leftarrow$) This direction is called *completeness* of the proof system. The axioms and rules were selected to be sufficient to reduce every expression a to a "canonical form" $\hat{a}$ with the property that

$$\models a_1 = a_2 \quad \text{iff} \quad \hat{a_1} \equiv \hat{a_2}.$$

A canonical form is either "0" or a sum-of-distinct-monomials representation, with each monomial (product of locations) having its locations occurring in increasing order of subscript, and parenthesized to the left. Moreover, each monomial has a "coefficient" of the form "n" where n is a nonzero numeral, and these monomials-with-coefficients are added in decreasing order of degree (*i.e.*, length), in alphabetical order of the monomials for monomials of the same degree, with the sum associated to the left also. $\square$

For example, let a be the **Aexp** corresponding to

$$2 - \left((X_3)^2 - \left((X_2)^2\left((X_3 + 2X_4)X_2\right) + X_3X_4(X_3)^2\right)\right).$$

Then $\hat{a}$ would be described as

$$(X_2)^3 X_3 + 3(X_2)^3 X_4 - (X_3)^2 + 2.$$

We have described a and $\hat{a}$ using the usual mathematical abbreviations in which parentheses and multiplication symbols are omitted, exponents indicate repeated products, etc. The canonical form $\hat{a} \in$ **Assn** would be written formally as follows:

$$(((1 \times (((X_2 \times X_2) \times X_2) \times X_3)) + (3 \times (((X_2 \times X_2) \times X_2) \times X_4)))$$
$$+ ((-1) \times (X_3 \times X_3))) + (2 \times 1).$$

Note that we regard "1" as a monomial of degree zero.

The idea is that, first, subtractions can be eliminated using the (minus-one) axiom. Then distributivity can be applied repeatedly to remove occurrences of products over sums. The result is an expression consisting of sums of products of locations and numbers. The products can be internally sorted using associativity and commutativity, as can the order of the products in the sum. Coefficients of identical monomials can then be combined by distributivity. The monomials will have a sum of numerical products for their coefficients, and these can be simplified in turn to a sum of ones and then a single number using the numerical and identity axioms with associativity, commutativity and distributivity. Enough said; we thus have:

Lemma A.28 *For every* $a \in$ **Aexp**, *there is a canonical form* $\hat{a} \in$ **Aexp** *such that* $\vdash a = \hat{a}$.

We now state the following fact about polynomial functions on the integers.

Fact If $\widehat{a_1}$ and $\widehat{a_2}$ are syntactically distinct canonical forms, then $\mathcal{A}[\![\widehat{a_1}]\!] \neq \mathcal{A}[\![\widehat{a_2}]\!]$.

Exercise A.29 Prove the Fact.   □

Proof: (Completeness) We now can prove completeness. Suppose $\models a_1 = a_2$, *i.e.*, $\mathcal{A}[\![a_1]\!] = \mathcal{A}[\![a_2]\!]$. By the Lemma, $\vdash a_i = \widehat{a_i}$, so by soundness, $\models a_i = \widehat{a_i}$ for $i = 1, 2$. So $\mathcal{A}[\![\widehat{a_1}]\!] = \mathcal{A}[\![a_1]\!] = \mathcal{A}[\![a_2]\!] = \mathcal{A}[\![\widehat{a_2}]\!]$. Then by the Fact above, $\widehat{a_1}$ is actually syntactically identical to $\widehat{a_2}$, so we have

$$\vdash a_1 = \widehat{a_1} \quad \text{and} \quad \vdash a_2 = \widehat{a_1}$$

and by symmetry and transitivity, we conclude $\vdash a_1 = a_2$.   □

A.6   Further reading

The treatment here is based on lecture notes of Albert Meyer, with some modifications by the author. A proof of Matijasevic theorem can be found in [35]. The books by Crossley [34], Kleene [54], Mendelson [61] and Enderton [38] have already been mentioned in Chapter 7, as has [11] by Kfoury, Moll and Arbib which gives a treatment close to that here. A nice book with a more traditional mathematical presentation is Cutland's [20] which might be a warm-up to the encyclopaedic book of Rogers [86].

Bibliography

[1] Abramsky, S., "The lazy lambda calculus." In Research Topics in Functional Programming (ed. Turner,D.A.), The UT Year of Programming Series, Addison-Wesley, 1990.

[2] Abramsky, S., "Domain theory in logical form." In IEEE Proc. of Symposium on Logic in Computer Science, 1987. Revised version in Annals of pure and Applied Logic, 51, 1991.

[3] Abramsky, S., "A computational interpretation of linear logic." To appear in Theoretical Computer Science.

[4] Aczel, P., "An introduction to inductive definitions." A chapter in the **Handbook of Mathematical Logic**, Barwise, J., (ed), North Holland, 1983.

[5] Alagić, S., and Arbib, M., "The design of well-structured and correct programs." Springer-Verlag, 1978.

[6] Andersen, H.R., "Model checking and boolean graphs." Proc. of ESOP 92, Springer-Verlag Lecture Notes in Computer Science vol.582, 1992.

[7] Andersen, H.R., "Local computation of alternating fixed-points." Tehnical Report No. 260, Computer Laboratory, University of Cambridge, 1992.

[8] Apt, K.R., "Ten years of Hoare's Logic: a survey." TOPLAS, 3, pp. 431-483, 1981.

[9] Apt, K.R, and Olderog, E-R., "**Verification of Sequential and Concurrent Programs,**" Springer-Verlag, 1991.

[10] Arbib, M., and Manes, E., "**Arrows, structures and functors.**" Academic Press, 1975.

[11] Kfoury, A.J., Moll, R.N. & Arbib, M.A., "**A programming approach to computability.**" Springer-Verlag, 1982.

[12] Backhouse, R., "**Program construction and verification.**" Prentice Hall, 1986.

[13] de Bakker, J., "**Mathematical theory of program correctness.**" Prentice-Hall, 1980.

[14] Barendregt, H., "**The lambda calculus, its syntax and semantics.**" North Holland, 1984.

[15] Barr, M., and Wells, C., "**Category theory for computer science.**" Prentice-Hall, 1990.

[16] Berry, G., Curien, P-L., and Lévy, J-J., "Full abstraction for sequential languages: the state of the art. In Nivat, M., and Reynolds, J., (ed), Algebraic Methods in Semantics, Cambridge University Press, 1985.

[17] Sørensen, B.B., and Clausen, C., "Adequacy results for a lazy functional language with recursive and polymophic types." DAIMI Report, University of Aarhus, submitted to Theoretical Computer Science.

[18] Camilleri, J.A., and Winskel, G., "CCS with priority choice." Proc. of Symposium on Logic in Computer Science, Amsterdam, IEEE, 1991. Extended version to appear in Information and Computation.

[19] Crole, R., "Programming metalogics with a fixpoint type." University of Cambridge Computer Laboratory Technical Report No. 247, 1992.

[20] Cutland, N.J., "Computability: an introduction to recursive function theory." Cambridge University Press, 1983.

[21] Bird, R., "**Programs and machines.**" John Wiley, 1976.

[22] Bird, R., and Wadler, P., "**Introduction to functional programming.**" Prentice-Hall, 1988.

[23] Clarke, E.M. Jr., "The characterisation problem for Hoare Logics" in Hoare, C.A.R. and Shepherdson, J.C. (eds.), " Mathematical logic and programming languages." Prentice-Hall, 1985.

[24] Clarke, E.M., Emerson, E.A., and Sistla, A.P., "Automatic verification of finite state concurrent sytems using temporal logic." Proc. of 10th Annual ACM Symposium on Principles of Programming Languages, Austin, Texas, 1983.

[25] Cleaveland, R., "Tableau-based model checking in the propositional mu-calculus." Acta Informatica, 27, 1990.

[26] Clément, J., Despeyroux, J., Despeyroux, T., and Kahn, G., "A simple applicative language: mini-ML." Proc. of the 1986 ACM Conference on Lisp and Functional Programming, 1986.

[27] Cosmadakis, S.S., Meyer, A.R., and Riecke, J.G., "Completeness for typed lazy languages (Preliminary report)." Proc. of Symposium on Logic in Computer Science, Philadelphia, USA, IEEE, 1990.

[28] Despeyroux, J., "Proof of translation in natural semantics." Proc. of Symposium on Logic in Computer Science, Cambridge, Massachusetts, USA, IEEE, 1986.

[29] Despeyroux, T., "Typol: a formalism to implement natural semantics." INRIA Research Report 94, Roquencourt, France, 1988.

[30] Cleaveland, R., Parrow, J. and Steffen, B., "The Concurrency Workbench." Report of LFCS, Edinburgh University, 1988.

[31] Clocksin, W.F., and Mellish, C., "**Programming in PROLOG**." Springer-Verlag, 1981.

[32] Cohen, "**Programming for the 1990's**". Springer-Verlag, 1991.

[33] Cook, S.A., "Soundness and completeness of an axiom system for program verification." SIAM J. Comput. 7, pp. 70-90, 1978.

[34] Crossley, J.N., "**What is mathematical logic?.**" Oxford University Press, 1972.

[35] Davis, M., "Hilbert's tenth problem is unsolvable." Am.Math.Monthly 80, 1973.

[36] Dijkstra, E.W., "**A discipline of programming**." Prentice-Hall, 1976.

[37] Emerson, A. and Lei, C., "Efficient model checking in fragments of the propositional mu-calculus." Proc. of Symposium on Logic in Computer Science, 1986.

[38] Enderton, H.B., "**A mathematical introduction to logic**." Academic Press, 1972.

[39] Enderton, H.B., "**Elements of set theory**." Academic Press, 1977.

[40] Girard, J-Y., Lafont, Y., and Taylor, P., "**Proofs and types**." Cambridge University Press, 1989.

[41] Good, D.I., "Mechanical proofs about computer programs." in Hoare, C.A.R., and Shepherdson, J.C. (eds.), "**Mathematical Logic and Programming Languages**." Prentice-Hall, 1985.

[42] Gordon, M.J.C., "**Programming language theory and its implementation**." Prentice-Hall, 1988.

[43] Gordon, M.J.C., HOL: A proof generating system for higher-order logic, in **VLSI Specification, Verification and Synthesis**, (ed. Birtwistle, G., and Subrahmanyam, P.A.) Kluwer, 1988.

[44] Gries, D., "**The science of programming**." Springer Texts and Monographs in Computer Science, 1981.

[45] Hindley, R., and Seldin, J.P, "**Introduction to combinators and lambda-calculus**." Cambridge University Press, 1986.

[46] Godskesen, J.C., and Larsen, K.G., and Zeeberg, M., "TAV (Tools for Automatic Verification) users manual." Technical Report R 89-19, Department of Mathematics and Computer Science, Aalborg University, 1989. Presented at the workshop on Automated Methods for Finite State Systems, Grenoble, France, June 1989.

[47] Halmos, P.R., "**Naive set theory**." Litton Ed Publ. Inc., 1960.

[48] Hennessy, M.C, "**Algebraic theory of processes**." MIT Press, 1988.

[49] Hoare, C.A.R., "Communicating sequential processes." CACM, vol.21, No.8, 1978.

[50] Hoare, C.A.R., "**Communicating sequential processes**." Prentice-Hall, 1985.

[51] Huet, G., "A uniform approach to type theory." In **Logical Foundations of Functional Programming** (ed. Huet,G.), The UT Year of Programming Series, Addison-Wesley, 1990.

[52] Jensen, C.T., "The Concurrency Workbench with priorities." To appear in the proceedings of Computer Aided Verification, Aalborg, 1991, Springer-Verlag Lecture Notes in Computer Science.

[53] Johnstone, P.T., "**Stone spaces**." Cambridge University Press, 1982.

[54] Kleene, S.C., "**Mathematical logic**." John Wiley, 1967.

[55] Kozen, D., "Results on the propositional mu-calculus," Theoretical Computer Science 27, 1983.

[56] Lamport, L., "The temporal logic of actions." Technical Report 79, Digital Equipment Corporation, Systems Research Center, 1991.

[57] Larsen, K.G., "Proof systems for Hennessy-Milner logic." Proc. CAAP, 1988.

[58] Loeckx, J. and Sieber, K. "**The foundations of program verification**." John Wiley, 1984.

[59] Manna, Z., "**Mathematical theory of computation**." McGraw-Hill, 1974.

[60] Manna, Z., and Pnueli, A., "How to cook a temporal proof system for your pet language." Proc. of 10th Annual ACM Symposium on Principles of Programming Languages, Austin, Texas, 1983.

[61] Mendelson, E., "**Introduction to mathematical logic**." Van Nostrand, 1979.

[62] Milner, A.J.R.G., "Fully abstract models of typed lambda-calculi." Theoretical Computer Science 4, 1977.

[63] Milner, A.J.R.G., "**Communication and concurrency**." Prentice Hall, 1989.

[64] Milner, A.J.R.G., "Operational and algebraic semantics of concurrent processes." A chapter in **Handbook of Theoretical Computer Science**, North Holland, 1990.

[65] Mitchell, J.C., "Type systems for programming languages." A chapter in **Handbook of Theoretical Computer Science**, North Holland, 1990.

[66] Moggi, E., "Categories of partial morphisms and the lambda$_p$-calculus." In proceedings of Category Theory and Computer Programming, Springer-Verlag Lecture Notes in Computer Science vol.240, 1986.

[67] Moggi, E., "Computational lambda-calculus and monads." Proc. of Symposium on Logic in Computer Science, Pacific Grove, California, USA, IEEE, 1989.

[68] Mosses, P.D., "Denotational semantics." A chapter in **Handbook of Theoretical Computer Science**, North Holland, 1990.

[69] Nielson. H.R., and Nielson, F., **"Semantics with applications: a formal introduction."** John Wiley, 1992.

[70] inmos, **"Occam programming manual."** Prentice Hall, 1984.

[71] Ong, C-H.L., "The lazy lambda calculus: an investigation into the foundations of functional programming." PhD thesis, Imperial College, University of London, 1988.

[72] Parrow, J., "Fairness properties in process algebra." PhD thesis, Uppsala University, Sweden, 1985.

[73] Paulson,L.C., **"ML for the working programmer."** Cambridge University Press, 1991.

[74] Paulson, L.C., **"Logic and computation: interactive proof with Cambridge LCF."** Cambridge University Press, 1987.

[75] Pitts, A., "Semantics of programming languages." Lecture notes, Computer Laboratory, University of Cambridge, 1989.

[76] Pitts, A., "A co-induction principle for recursively defined domains." University of Cambridge Computer Laboratory Technical Report No.252, 1992.

[77] Plotkin, G.D., "Call-by-name, call-by-value and the lambda calculus." Theoretical Computer Science 1, 1975.

[78] Plotkin, G.D., "LCF considered as programming language." Theoretical Computer Science 5, 1977.

[79] Plotkin, G.D., "A powerdomain construction." SIAM J. Comput.5, 1976.

[80] Plotkin, G.D., "The Pisa lecture notes." Notes for lectures at the University of Edinburgh, extending lecture notes for the Pisa Summerschool, 1978.

[81] Plotkin, G.D., "Structural operational semantics." Lecture Notes, DAIMI FN-19, Aarhus University, Denmark, 1981 (reprinted 1991).

[82] Plotkin, G.D., "An operational semantics for CSP." In Formal Description of Programming Concepts II, Proc. of TC-2 Work. Conf. (ed. Bjørner, D.), North-Holland, 1982.

[83] Plotkin, G.D., "Types and partial functions." Notes of lectures at CSLI, Stanford University, 1985.

[84] Prawitz, D., **"Natural deduction, a proof-theoretical study."** Almqvist & Wiksell, Stockholm, 1965.

[85] Reisig, W., **"Petri nets: an introduction."** EATCS Monographs on Theoretical Computer Science, Springer-Verlag, 1985.

[86] Rogers, H., **"Theory of recursive functions and effective computability."** McGraw-Hill, 1967.

[87] Roscoe,A.W., and Reed,G.M., **"Domains for denotational semantics."** Prentice Hall, 1992.

[88] schmidt, D., **"Denotational semantics: a methodology for language development."** Allyn & Bacon, 1986.

[89] Scott, D.S., "Lectures on a mathematical theory of computation." PRG Report 19, Programming Research Group, Univ. of Oxford, 1980.

[90] Scott, D.S., "Domains for denotational semantics." In proceedings of ICALP '82, Springer-Verlag Lecture Notes in Computer Science vol.140, 1982.

[91] Scott, D.S., and Gunter, C., "Semantic domains." A chapter in **Handbook of Theoretical Computer Science**, North Holland, 1990.

[92] Smyth, M., "Powerdomains." JCSS 16(1), 1978.

[93] Stirling, C. and Walker D., "Local model checking the modal mu-calculus." Proc.of TAPSOFT, 1989.

[94] Stoughton, A., **"Fully abstract models of programming languages."** Pitman, 1988.

[95] Stoy, J., **"Denotational semantics: the Scott-Strachey approach to programming language theory."** MIT Press, 1977.

[96] Tarski, A., "A lattice-theoretical fixpoint theorem and its applications." Pacific Journal of Mathematics, 5, 1955.

[97] Tennent, R.D., **"Principles of programming languages."** Prentice-Hall, 1981.

[98] Vickers, S., "**Topology via logic**." Cambridge University Press, 1989.

[99] Vuillemin, J.E., "Proof techniques for recursive programs." PhD Thesis, Stanford Artificial Intelligence Laboratory, Memo AIM-218, 1973.

[100] Walker, D., "Automated analysis of mutual exclusion algorithms using CCS." Formal Aspects of Computing 1, 1989.

[101] Wikström, Å. "**Functional programming using Standard ML**." Prentice-Hall, 1987.

[102] Winskel, G., "On powerdomains and modality." Theoretical Computer Science 36, 1985.

[103] Winskel, G. and Larsen, K., "Using information systems to solve recursive domain equations effectively." In the proceedings of the conference on Abstract Datatypes, Sophia-Antipolis, France, Springer-Verlag Lecture Notes in Computer Science vol.173, 1984.

[104] Winskel, G., "Event structures." Lecture notes for the Advanced Course on Petri nets, September 1986, Springer-Verlag Lecture Notes in Computer Science, vol.255, 1987.

[105] Winskel, G., "An introduction to event structures." Lecture notes for the REX summerschool in temporal logic, May 88, Springer-Verlag Lecture Notes in Computer Science, vol.354, 1989.

[106] Winskel, G., "A note on model checking the modal nu-calculus." Theoretical Computer Science 83, 1991.

[107] Winskel, G., and Nielsen, M., "Models for concurrency." To appear as a chapter in the **Handbook of Logic and the Foundations of Computer Science**, Oxford University Press.

[108] Zhang, G-Q., "**Logic of domains**." Birkhäuser, 1991.

Index

The MIT Press, with Peter Denning as general consulting editor, publishes computer science books in the following series:

ACL-MIT Press Series in Natural Language Processing
Aravind K. Joshi, Karen Sparck Jones, and Mark Y. Liberman, editors

ACM Doctoral Dissertation Award and Distinguished Dissertation Series

Artificial Intelligence
Patrick Winston, founding editor
J. Michael Brady, Daniel G. Bobrow, and Randall Davis, editors

Charles Babbage Institute Reprint Series for the History of Computing
Martin Campbell-Kelly, editor

Computer Systems
Herb Schwetman, editor

Explorations with Logo
E. Paul Goldenberg, editor

Foundations of Computing
Michael Garey and Albert Meyer, editors

History of Computing
I. Bernard Cohen and William Aspray, editors

Logic Programming
Ehud Shapiro, editor; Fernando Pereira, Koichi Furukawa, Jean-Louis Lassez, and David H. D. Warren, associate editors

The MIT Press Electrical Engineering and Computer Science Series

Research Monographs in Parallel and Distributed Processing
Christopher Jesshope and David Klappholz, editors

Scientific and Engineering Computation
Janusz Kowalik, editor

Technical Communication and Information Systems
Edward Barrett, editor

Printed in the United States
by Baker & Taylor Publisher Services